MAKING A LIVING IN THE MIDDLE AGES

Christopher Dyer is Director of the Centre for English Local History in the University of Leicester. Among his recent publications are *An Age of Transition?: Economy and Society in England in the Later Middle Ages* (2005), and *The Self-Contained Village*, edited with Harold Fox and Nigel Goose (2007). He has been president of the Society for Medieval Archaeology and of the British Agricultural History Society. He was awarded the CBE in 2008.

D0701596

THE NEW ECONOMIC HISTORY OF BRITAIN

Making a Living in the Middle Ages

THE PEOPLE OF BRITAIN 850–1520

CHRISTOPHER DYER

YALE UNIVERSITY PRESS

NEW HAVEN AND LONDON

The New Economic History of Britain
General Editor: David Cannadine

For information about this and other Yale University Press publications, please contact:
U.S. Office: sales.press@yale.edu www.yale.edu/yup
Europe Office: sales@yaleup.co.uk www.yaleup.co.uk

Set in Sabon MT by Best-set Typesetter Ltd., Hong Kong
Printed in Great Britain by TJ International Ltd, Padstow, Cornwall

Library of Congress Cataloging-in-Publication Data

Dyer, Christopher, 1944–
    Making a living in the middle ages : the people of Britain 850–1520/Christopher Dyer.
        p. cm. – (The new economic history of Britain)
    Includes bibliographical references and index.
    ISBN 0–300–09060–9 (cloth: alk. paper)
    1. Great Britain – Economic conditions. 2. Great Britain – Social conditions. 3. Great Britain – History – Medieval period, 1066–1485. 4. England – Economic conditions – 1066–1485. 5. Scotland – Economic conditions. 6. Wales – Economic conditions. 7. Industries – Great Britain – History – To 1500. 8. Working class – Great Britain – History – To 1500. 9. Social classes – Great Britain – History – To 1500. 10. Social change – Great Britain – History – to 1500. 11. Cities and towns – Great Britain – History – To 1500. 12. Great Britain – Population – History – To 1500. 13. Middle Ages. I. Title. II. Series.
    HC 254.D93 2002
    330.941'03 – dc21   2001046865

A catalogue record for this book is available from the British Library.

ISBN 978–0–300–10191–1 (pbk)

10 9 8 7 6 5 4 3 2 1

Contents

Illustrations

Maps

Figures

Preface

This book surveys the society and economy of medieval Britain. It covers the seven centuries from the Vikings to the Reformation, and it aims to deal with Britain, that is England, Scotland and Wales. I have approached the subject by seeking to understand the perspective of those who lived at the time. Changes in the society and economy came about because men and women, as individuals or in groups, made decisions and acted accordingly. We can therefore appreciate why they behaved and acted as they did if we can reconstruct their thinking in the light of their circumstances. Such an exercise requires some imagination, as one of the purposes of this book is to explore the economic contribution of the working population, who are not very fully documented. This is difficult, but is intended to add to the interest of the book, and in the same spirit while scholarly debates and controversies are reflected in these pages, they will be presented without lengthy accounts of the views of contending schools of historians. The writing consciously avoids jargon and technicalities and the more specialized terms will be explained when they are first mentioned.

A book dealing with a long period and many themes is inevitably the product of many years of research, reading, listening and conversation. I could not possibly name the dozens of people who have helped me in various ways, and I hope that they will understand and forgive the omission. The only exception must be Rodney Hilton, whose early tuition and later advice has been an influence and inspiration. To focus on those who helped specifically with the production of this book, David Cannadine suggested that I write it, and commented helpfully on a first draft. I was advised and encouraged by the editors for Penguin and Yale, Simon Winder and Robert Baldock. Chapters were read and improved by Dawn Hadley, Keith Stringer, Phillipp Schofield and two anonymous readers.

The final version of the typescript was prepared by Sue Bowen and Nancy Moore. Jenny Dyer read drafts and helped in other ways. John and Geraldine Brown gave me hospitality when I worked in Edinburgh. Help with preparing illustrations came from Duncan Brown, Bob Croft, Geoff Egan and Andy Isham. Candida Brazil of Yale University Press gave care and encouragement. The University of Birmingham and the Arts and Humanities Research Board allowed me a generous period of study leave.

Christopher Dyer
Birmingham, April 2001

Note on the text. Places are identified here with reference to the counties before the reorganization of local government in the 1970s. Money, length, distance, area, volume and weight are given in measures prevailing before metrication. There were 240d (pence) in a pound (£1), and 12d (pence) made a shilling (1s). To gain a sense of the value of money, a cow could be bought for about 24d (2s) or 36d (3s) before 1200, and between 6s and 11s after that date. A foot is equivalent to 0.3 metre, a yard to 0.9 metre, and a mile to 1.6 kilometres. An acre is 0.4 hectare. Grain was measured in bushels (36 litres) and wine in gallons (4.5 litres). Wool and tin were weighed in pounds (0.45 kilogramme).

Introduction

Approaching the economic history of medieval Britain

We should explore the economic history of medieval Britain for many reasons. It is the only branch of history which gives pride of place to the whole population, and through the study of the economy we can understand the everyday lives of working people. The economy was important. All other human endeavours depended on the production of food and other goods, which means that any investigation of non-material things must take into account the material base. Economic history is a unifying subject, not taking us into an obscure byway of the past, but acting as a crossroads from which we gain access to the history of the environment, culture, politics and thought.

Economic historians are concerned with two types of change. One focuses on the ups and downs of economic life, both the short-term fluctuations in prices and trade, and the long-run movements of growth and decline. The other is concerned with the structural changes, such as the emergence of towns, or the shifts in the distribution of land and the control of farming between social groups. Both are necessary for understanding the course of history.

Why go back to such a remote period? The past has always attracted our curiosity, and there is no reason to think that the period before 1520 offers us any less interest than the twentieth century or any other period in between. Medieval people were as lively, active and complicated as at any other time, and they are as worthy of our attention as those of later centuries. They pose at least as many dilemmas and puzzles of interpretation. Indeed there is a particular fascination in revealing the thoughts and actions of people living in an age unlike our own, when most people worked on the land, and were dominated by an aristocracy and an all-embracing church. The past fascinates us because it was different, and the middle ages were very different. Lastly, but not least, later periods cannot be fully understood if we do not appreciate their predecessors. We owe the majority of our villages and towns, boundaries, roads and institutions to the middle ages. The words that we use to describe economic life, such as farmer, wages, fees, capital and interest were all used (often with distinct meanings) in the middle ages. Our world is based on foundations laid before 1520, and we consequently need to know about that phase of our development.

Choosing the dates for the beginning and the end of a historical period always presents dilemmas. The economic history of the middle ages could be said to have begun with the large-scale clearances of land in the third millennium BC. Much land under the plough in 850 had been cultivated since prehistoric times. It might be tempting to start with Roman Britain, when cities and lines of communication of lasting importance were established. The barbarian invasions of the fifth and sixth centuries offer another convenient point to begin, when English-speaking settlers arrived, and embryonic states and the Christian church developed. The ninth century has been chosen because it marks the beginning of a great formative period, when essential elements in the political, social and productive structure were put in place. The pattern of villages and towns which provided the place of residence and work for many medieval (and modern) people was established in the period 850–1100. The basic principles of the social hierarchy, with a dominant aristocracy living on the rents and services of a subordinate peasantry, and a network of exchange based on towns, all owe their origins to this period. The Norman Conquest of 1066 had economic repercussions, but it cannot be regarded as an important turning point in economic history. Choosing an ending point creates less difficulty. The two centuries after 1100 can be summed up as a time of expansion, followed by a profound crisis in the fourteenth century, marked by the Great Famine (1315–17) and the Black Death (1348–50), but we could not end the story at that point because a combination of contraction and new developments flows from the crisis, and these must be followed through until the early sixteenth century. A new era began with the end of a long period of low population in about 1540, the price inflation which is visible just before 1520, and the redistribution of property associated with the Reformation from the 1530s.

This book deals with Britain, that is the whole island including England, Scotland and Wales. Some common factors united all three countries, such as the influx of northern French or 'Anglo-Norman' elites in the eleventh and twelfth centuries. However, for most of the middle ages the three countries were separate political entities, which makes generalization difficult or impossible. But this is not political history, and the varied regional economies prevent us from generalizing about the experiences of any single kingdom or principality. In many ways this is the history of a collection of regions. East Anglia had its own patterns of settlement, agricultural methods and hierarchy of towns, which were totally different from those of the west midlands or the Lake District. Indeed, the Lake District had much more in common with parts of southern Scotland than with southern and eastern England. A broad distinction can be made between those parts of Britain which by the thirteenth century were characterized by extensive cornfields, a disciplined dependent peasantry and strong urban influence, and the highland regions such as northern and western Scotland and part of central and north Wales, where lords collected tribute from an independent, pastoral and scattered peasantry, and exchange based on money was slow to develop. Regional differences were also important on the small scale, and we can identify a close patchwork of different types of countryside, including the champion or felden districts where large villages and great open arable fields dominated, the woodlands with dispersed hamlets, enclosed fields and a good deal of pasture as well as woods, the wolds and chalk downs which combined extensive hill pasture with cultivation, and the wilder moorlands and marshlands. A traveller through the midlands in 1300, in the 60 miles from Oxford to Lichfield, would have been acutely aware of a succession of varied landscapes: woodlands in west Oxfordshire, the low hills of the Cotswolds, the flat open fields of the Vale of Evesham, and the woodlands again in the Forest of Arden in north Warwickshire. In each case the size and layout of the fields, the balance between cultivated land and grassland, the local road system, the size and distribution of settlements would have offered sharp contrasts. These environments had at least as profound an influence on the productive activities, social organization and mentality of the inhabitants as their location in one kingdom or another.

National differences still had an impact on the economy, especially in such matters as the coinage and international relations. For two centuries the silver coins of England and Scotland were essentially the same, but they diverged in the late fourteenth century when the Scottish money was debased. Scottish and English merchants exported their wool to different continental ports as the result of political decisions about the location of staples. Often the differences cannot be easily explained, such as the absence of records of peasant revolts in Scotland, or Scotland's apparent growth in settlement and farming in the late fifteenth century, when in much of England there was no great expansion. Unfortunately these questions are difficult to answer because the evidence, both written and material, is relatively scarce for Scotland and much of Wales.

We might say that 'Britain' is too big to be easily understood because of regional differences. But in a significant dimension it is too small, because the economic history of the offshore island of Britain cannot be separated from that of continental Europe. This is not just because of the importance of overseas trade, which made the economies of Britain and Flanders in particular interdependent. Nor is it because of continental invasions and migrations which brought new ideas and institutions to Britain between the ninth and eleventh centuries. Continental European culture was a vital influence on mentality and administration, from the ideas of chivalry and crusade among the secular aristocracy, to the religious orders and methods of church government which spread through the international church. Much more significant for economic history were the characteristics that were common across Europe, which meant that people solved problems in similar ways, such as adopting open fields with intermixed strips. All parts of Europe experienced the same trends and setbacks, notably the expansion of the thirteenth century and the crisis in the fourteenth. These parallel developments affected regions in different ways, which helps to identify the special character of each.

Any book on 700 years of complex and varied developments must be built on the work of generations of scholars, and this work reflects the body of knowledge and thinking which has accumulated since the birth of economic history in the 1880s. The early writers on the subject were primarily interested in law and government, so they tended to focus on institutions, such as the manor, serfdom, boroughs and guilds. They often shared the prevailing view that mankind had progressed, and so they looked for evidence in the middle ages for the origins of the modern economy. They thought that the towns were early islands of freedom and capitalism within a more backward agrarian society, and believed that the use of money, trade and the middle class grew in importance, and from that growth emerged the industrial revolution and the modern capitalist economy. A similar strand in the thinking of historians from the United States drew them to study peasants and villages because they traced the origins of American democracy in the communities of the English countryside.

In the middle decades of the twentieth century, the progressive 'Whiggish' view of economic change was challenged by M. M. Postan, who questioned many of the assumptions of his predecessors. He showed that there was no 'rise of a money economy' because the use of money both expanded and receded, and he emphasized the cyclical nature of economic change. There had been growth up to about 1300, and then contraction, and he believed that the roots of change lay in the countryside. The key determinants of economic growth and decline were the level of population and the productivity of the land. The great expansion in numbers of people in the thirteenth century put excessive pressure on land, which created the conditions for the catastrophes of 1315–17 and 1348–50. He argued that much production was for direct consumption in the peasant household, and therefore the market, towns and trade were peripheral to the rural economy.

Postan's interpretation of the changes in the later middle ages was influenced by the ideas of the classical economists, such as Malthus and Ricardo, both of whom predicted contraction as the inevitable consequence of growth. Postan was in no sense a Marxist, and yet his ideas bore some resemblance to the Marxist theory that a feudal mode of production reached its peak of development in about 1300, after which internal contradictions led to a general crisis of the social order. The most eloquent advocate of this view, R. H. Hilton, sees the struggle between lords and peasants for rent as a key factor in precipitating the late medieval crisis. R. Brenner has pursued the Marxist view that demography was not the determinant of economic change, and that class relations explain the circumstances which enabled the gentry around 1500 to impose capitalist agriculture by expelling peasants to create large farms.

The generation of historians that grew up in Postan's later years, and since his death in 1981, have developed alternative ideas which have eroded his great thesis without replacing it with some new grand narrative. The Cambridge demographers have argued for essential similarities between early modern and medieval population structure, which implies that adjustments in marriage rates and fertility caused population growth and decline, replacing the rather cataclysmic view of excess populations and crises of mortality. Postan thought that medieval cultivators could not escape from a cycle of falling yields and fields damaged by repeated cultivation because of an inability to improve their technology. Now we appreciate that the period was one of constant innovation, in the use of mills, in the rotation and mix of crops, in methods of drainage and water management, and in the use of draught animals. Instead of the gloomy views of nineteenth-century classical economists, who argued that excessive numbers of people would be an unsupportable burden, economists like Boserup have shown, using observations of the modern third world, that labour can be used to increase production, and indeed we can see this in the most densely populated English regions. Finally, towns and trade have been rediscovered as an important dimension of the medieval economy. The towns were early to develop, became large by around 1300, acted as a stimulus to production, and promoted specialization. The influence of the commercial world penetrated deeply into the countryside, affecting every region and all levels of the social hierarchy.

The flourishing of archaeology in the last thirty years has made an especially valuable contribution to the period before 1100. Excavation and fieldwork have shown that villages formed between about 850 and 1200, not in the fifth and sixth centuries as was once thought. Work on towns of the tenth and eleventh centuries reveals their large size and concentration of crafts and commerce – in other words, they were real towns. In the later middle ages material remains tell us about housing, trading patterns and the shrinkage of settlements. Archaeological interpretation makes us aware of the social meaning of material things, such as conspicuous consumption or the emulation of social elites, and archaeology demonstrates continuities and technical achievements. Archaeology has altered thinking about economic history in the last few years, but economic historians have always been influenced by other disciplines, especially the social sciences, which include anthropology and sociology as well as economics, and by literature and cultural studies.

The approach to the economic and social history of the middle ages which is represented in this book is based on the assumption that the period mattered. The modern economy owes something to its medieval predecessor, and we should note the emergence within the period of, for example, shareholding or industrial mechanization. But the middle ages should not be studied merely to seek the origins of more recent developments. Those who lived a thousand years ago are worthy of investigation in their own right, and we can learn from their differentness, as well as from the similarities with our experience. For example, medieval lords devoted a large amount of resources to building and maintaining ponds for freshwater fish. Their ponds now lie abandoned, and the rearing of freshwater fish has played a negligible role in modern Britain. Yet the ponds and their management are worth our attention because they meant a great deal to those who built and used them. Once we have appreciated that species such as bream and pike were regarded as a luxury food, the ponds tell us much about dietary preferences and medieval status seeking.

There is always a tendency to belittle the achievements of the past and to assume in a patronizing way that medieval people were primitive and ignorant. For example, the yield of corn in the fifteenth century was low by modern standards, and indeed had fallen since the thirteenth century. Does this mean that the people who grew the crops were stupid and lazy? In fact, if we look at the price of grain and the consumption of bread we find that food was cheap and plentiful. Corn production was adequate for society's needs, and as it was unnecessary for cultivators to strain themselves to increase their output, we should not criticize them for their imagined failings. Recent experience of technological failures, such as the BSE epidemic and the threat of climate change, has perhaps made us rather less confident of our superiority, and a little more appreciative of common sense and skilful management in the middle ages. Scottish economic history has suffered in particular from assumptions about that country's backwardness before modern 'improvement'. Scottish agriculture was not very productive, but the country was thinly populated and not especially prone to famine. In the thirteenth century the abundant Scottish currency and urban growth suggest that the country participated in the general European expansion.

As we adopt a more sympathetic approach to medieval economic management, we appreciate that people had to make a series of difficult decisions about which crops to grow or which type of cloth to weave. As the economy became more complex, the decisions included the raising of credit, marketing strategies and investment plans. Historians once tended to determinism, which means they believed that circumstances forced society along particular channels, and that events unfolded with a certain inevitability. Now we recognize an element of choice. For example, we do not know why some rural communities in the early middle ages lived in scattered hamlets with fields irregularly disposed around them, while others moved into large villages with well-organized open fields. They were influenced by the soils which they worked and the social pressures around them, but we must doubt if the decision was predestined.

It is sometimes believed that the crucial decisions were taken by powerful elites of rulers, aristocrats and merchants. We often find, however, that when kings or great lords initiated some change, the results were unplanned and unforeseen. At the beginning of our period King Alfred ordered the building of a system of forts to keep the Danes out of his kingdom of Wessex. Many of those forts would become towns, but it is not certain that the king intended that result. More often change emerged from the combination of thousands of uncoordinated actions, involving people at all levels. Formal descriptions of medieval society imply the subordination of the masses. Yet even serfs had some use of property, and had some choice in the management of their holding of land, though they were of course restrained in many ways. One of the dynamic forces in medieval society, and the motive force behind many economic changes, was not dictatorial decisions, but the opposite – the competition and frictions between different groups, not just between lords and peasants or merchants and artisans, but also between laymen and clergy, higher aristocrats and gentry, and subjects and the state, and between individuals within those various groups. A society that appears to be governed by rigid laws and customs, in reality allowed people to take initiatives.

Change was based on combinations of interconnected movements, such as the simultaneous emergence of lordship, villages, towns and the state in the period between 850 and 1050. Selecting which came first, or which dominated over the others is often a fruitless exercise. Those who advocate a single explanatory mechanism, such as changes in population, or innovations in technology, or climate change, are usually oversimplifying. We know the difficulties in tracing the origins of the industrial revolution, or the slump of the 1920s, and the argument that single causes can be applied to an earlier period again suggests a patronizing attitude which underestimates the varied and interlocking nature of the medieval economy.

Finally, because we are dealing with a culture and economy very different from our own, various terms and concepts are used which cause problems for modern readers. These are terms in use in the middle ages, and also those coined by modern historians, which as much as possible will be defined when they are first mentioned. Some modern words are so fundamental, and yet have been subject to so much controversy, that they need brief discussion here.

It has become commonplace to describe medieval society and economy as 'feudal'. Some historians regard this as a misleading modern invention to describe an ideal type of society which never existed. The word will be employed here as useful shorthand for a social organization in which lords had powers over others, through private jurisdiction and other non-economic means, which enabled them to extract rents, services and other dues. Feudalism in a more specialized sense refers to the ties between lords and their aristocratic vassals, based on the granting of land (fiefs) in exchange for military and administrative services. Here the word 'aristocracy' will be used to describe the whole landed elite, from the gentry to earls and dukes, but also including the higher clergy. 'Nobility' is used on the continent but is not easily applied in Britain, and the aristocracy can be recognized as a coherent group from its landed incomes and style of life. 'Peasant' refers to small-scale cultivators, who possess land, and are subordinated to lords and the state. There has been a move to deny the existence of an English peasantry, on the grounds that they were not as closely bound to family groups as in other cultures, but peasantries differ, and the economic position of those dependent on small holdings of land (usually below 60 acres) is a defining characteristic. This excludes farmers (who had large holdings) and those entirely dependent on wages. 'Serfs' were peasants who were legally unfree, that is they were judged in their lord's court and could not usually appeal for justice to the king's court. The term 'serf' derives from legal status, and tells us little about wealth. 'Towns' and 'urban' refer to places with a dense and permanent concentration of people who pursued a variety of non-agricultural occupations. The population need not have been very large – a town could have had 300 inhabitants – and many towns were unwalled, and had not been granted a borough charter or other privileges.

PART ONE

Origins of the medieval economy, c.850–c.1100

The late ninth century saw the first stage of a great formative episode in history, when key elements in society and economy such as villages, manors and towns were created and states were forged. Of course people had been organizing production and consumption for a very long time before the ninth century. The whole of mainland Britain up to central Scotland had been brought into a sophisticated urbanized and commercial economy as a Roman province in the first and second centuries AD. The villa estates, cities, industries and tax system had largely collapsed in the fifth and sixth centuries when the Roman army withdrew and the province was taken over by its native British population, some Anglo-Saxons from across the North Sea and migrants from Ireland. The legacy of the Roman empire can be seen in the survival and later re-occupation of many of the towns, and the continued cultivation of much of the land. Changes in England in 650–850 had long-term importance: towns and coinage were revived, and major churches were given property rights over extensive lands. But the main features of the economy at that time – great estates, rural settlements and towns such as the predecessors of London and Southampton – did not survive in their original form or on the same sites.

Understanding the economy in the period 850–1100 is surrounded by difficulties, not least being the shortage of written sources. Two thousand charters, some law codes, narrative sources such as chronicles and the lives of saints, and religious literature such as sermons provide some fragmentary information. Fortunately, at the end of our period we have the unique and comprehensive survey of England (except its most northern counties) made in 1086 and recorded in Domesday Book. Domesday and later documents mention thousands of place names, most of which were formed before 1000, and can tell us about settlements, people and the use of land. Archaeological evidence, accumulated mainly since the 1950s, has provided information about the plan and size of settlements, houses, churches and other structures, graves, artefacts such as pottery and metalwork, and the remains of animals and plants which allow the past environment and its use by man to be reconstructed.

The evidence is difficult to interpret. The most satisfying results are often obtained by bringing together information from different sources. Each type of evidence has to be understood and approached critically. The documents were produced by the elites of church and state, and so reflect a partisan 'official' view. The material evidence which at first sight appears 'objective' has in fact been selected, by the accident of survival, and by the choice of particular sites for excavation.

There is much room for disagreement in making historical sense of this period. Some scholars doubt whether much economic activity existed at all, suggesting that apparent sales of goods and land were really exchanges determined by social and political relationships. Even when we assume that there was an economy as we understand the term, the time scale of change is open to many interpretations, with some putting more emphasis than is shown here on the period before 850, and others regarding the Norman Conquest as having important economic consequences. Archaeologists point to continuity: the same agricultural land, defined by similar boundaries, remained in use for many centuries, even millennia. The processes that underlie economic change are just as controversial, with some favouring the formation of the state as the key to understanding change, while others give more attention to shifts in climate, or the growth and decline of population. Here emphasis is placed on decision-making in all sections of society.

CHAPTER ONE

Living on the land, c.850–c.1050

Most medieval people made their living from agriculture, and had to arrive at decisions about the best methods of production. Their choices were not made freely, because they worked within the limits imposed by their social circumstances and technical knowledge, and by the soil, terrain and climate. Their resources were more restricted than those of later cultivators, but that did not leave them at the mercy of nature. They moulded and exploited the landscape, and indeed were the inheritors of a countryside already changed by centuries of human intervention. It was once believed that great tracts of primeval woodland survived into this period, which made the clearance of trees so that the land could be used more productively one of the main tasks of early medieval cultivators. We know now that in much of England the area under trees was not much greater than at the present day. Patches of 'wild wood' had survived since early prehistory, but some woodland was quite new, the result of the regeneration of bushes and trees on former cultivated land since the end of the Roman period. Woodland was not left as wilderness, but was managed to produce timber or fuel, and feed for livestock. Bears had been hunted to extinction throughout Britain by the eleventh century, and in the following century beavers were to be seen only on a few rivers in Wales and Scotland. Wolves still survived, but only in the more remote parts of England and other parts of Britain. Wild animals which were valued as food and for sport, such as deer and boar, were protected and nurtured. Nature had been tamed.

i. *Farming*

In managing the earth, vegetation and animals, the first priority of medieval men and women was to produce food, but they also expected to receive the benefits of their work in the foreseeable future, so they practised (to use the modern term) 'sustainable' agriculture. They planned for the same land to yield crops regularly, and they appreciated that well-managed resources renewed themselves. They anticipated the changeability of the seasons and the harvests, and hoped that their farming methods would allow them to survive in a year of unusual weather, for example by planting a variety of crops. At no time or place within our period can they be described as 'subsistence farmers', in the sense that they ate only food that they had grown, or that they produced solely for their own consumption needs. They always expected that their land would yield a surplus, whether for the benefit of the state, the church or their lords, or for exchange for goods and services which they could not obtain from their own land.

These aims were most easily achieved in the favourable environments created by the wide river valleys, such as the Wye, upper Thames, Warwickshire Avon, Nene, Great Ouse and upper Trent, and in low-lying districts such as eastern Norfolk, as well as on coastal lowlands in Kent, Sussex, south Wales, and eastern Scotland. Here were light soils that could easily be turned by the plough, which gave a good seedbed for cereal crops. The level ground gave easy access, and implements could be used at all times, as the free-draining soil did not become waterlogged. The topsoil on flat land or gentle slopes was not easily washed away by the rain. The fields were sheltered from extreme weather and in the south there was a long growing season, so that crops would ripen even in a wet summer. In the most favoured locations water was near to hand, and the land adjoining rivers and streams yielded long grass for haymaking. Cultivation extended over much larger areas, which offered many, if not all, of the advantages of the river valleys. The limestone hills like the Yorkshire wolds and the Cotswolds gave good opportunities for growing corn, as did the heavier clay and marl lowlands which prevailed in much of the country from central Scotland, through eastern and midland England, to Somerset.

In these regions which offered fertile land for cultivation the inhabitants devoted their main productive effort to growing large acreages of grain – wheat, rye, barley and oats, together with legumes, mostly peas and beans. This was the most efficient way of producing basic foods. Wheat gave the most nutritious and palatable bread; barley and oats could be made into an inferior bread, or could be malted and brewed into ale, or, like the peas and beans, be boiled for pottage; oats and beans could also be fed to animals. The cultivators had to be careful to combine their arable with grassland and wood. The best way of maintaining the quality of the soil – or even of creating a decent seedbed in the case of the heavier clay soils – was to keep a good proportion of land as grass or hay meadow, so that animals could be fed and their manure used to spread on the fields. Sheep were especially efficient sources of fertilizer, because they could be fed on pasture land in the day, and penned at night on the land on which crops were to be sown. Not only would they deposit their manure, but their small sharp hoofs would tread the droppings into the surface. Animals were themselves an important source of food – medieval people lived not by bread and pottage alone – and their muscle power was essential for ploughing and hauling. Woodland was also a vital asset for fuel, timber for building and making implements, and acorns and beech mast for fattening pigs. So those who lived in the regions with the best potential for grain-growing kept a balance between different types of land. If they extended the arable, they rested it regularly with fallow, on which animals found stubble, grass and weeds to eat, as well as keeping some land as permanent pasture. The descriptions of boundaries attached to the charters of the tenth and eleventh centuries of the Vale of the White Horse in Berkshire reveal the local concentration on arable. The writers of the charters defined the edges of estates not by the usual trees, stones and ponds, but instead by reference to parcels of cultivated land – acres (meaning strips that had been ploughed), furrows and headlands (the strip at the end of a field where the plough turned). If the outermost fringes of these territories were fully occupied by arable, the centre was also likely to be cultivated.

Not everyone was so heavily involved in growing corn. Across the southern counties, from Essex and Kent to the Chiltern Hills and north Wiltshire, and in much of western England, the arable land was interspersed with patches of pasture and woods, some of them commons to be shared among a number of settlements (Map 1). In north Worcestershire, for example, the local informants quoted by the clergy who wrote boundary clauses for charters often mentioned hedges and crofts (meaning hedged fields) as landmarks. In East Anglia much land was given over to arable, but important features of the landscape were the large greens, consisting of uncultivated land used as common pasture. Around the Wash, and along both sides of the Severn estuary, in the Somerset Levels, on the south coast at Romney Marsh and the Pevensey Levels, south of the Humber estuary, and in the south-west of Scotland were fens and marshlands around which communities combined cultivation with summer grazing, peat-digging and fishing. The people of the uplands of western and northern England, Wales and Scotland aimed at a very different balance in their management of the landscape, cultivating arable as much as possible, but inevitably depending on pastures for their main livelihood. An extreme example is provided by the people who

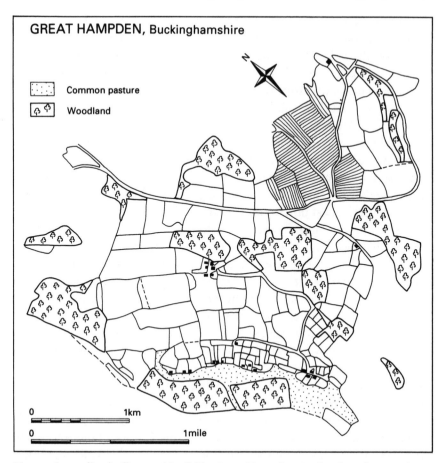

Map 1. A woodland village and its fields: Great Hampden, Buckinghamshire. In the Chiltern Hills, as in much of Britain outside the 'village belt', people lived in dispersed settlements (in this case stretched along a green and scattered among the fields). They cultivated land in limited areas of open field, and also in enclosed fields. Grazing land and wooded areas were plentiful. This map of 1741 reflects a much earlier landscape.

Source: A. H. R. Baker and R. A. Butlin (eds), *Studies of Field Systems in the British Isles* (Cambridge, 1973).

lived in the ninth century on Gauber High Pasture above Ribblehead in the Pennines, in a house at 1,100 feet above sea level, who in spite of the adverse climate were able to grow a few acres of oats, as well as grazing sheep and cattle. In environments lacking easily cultivated land, as in the Scottish islands, soils suitable for growing corn were created by concentrating all of the manure, and other sources of compost such as turf and seaweed, on to small fields. Barley and oats could be grown, but people made much of their living from keeping sheep and cattle, fishing and catching sea birds.

One means of making use of varied types of land was to lay out territories which included hill and valley, wood and arable, so that natural resources would complement one another. The boundaries of an estate or a village would run in parallel across the contours from the crest of a hill to a river bank some miles away, encompassing hill pasture, wooded hill slopes, lowland arable and riverside meadow. Sometimes arable and woodland could be associated only by abandoning the ideal that an estate would consist of a single block of land, and attaching to the main arable-based estate a piece of woodland, even if the two properties were ten miles or more apart. A balance could also be achieved among the possessions of a monastery, for example, which might include among the land scattered over a region some specialist woods and pastures as well as manors devoted to corn-growing.

ii. *Expansion*

The landscapes and territories of the tenth and eleventh centuries were often very old. Much of the arable had been cultivated continuously since Roman times, and some field and estate boundaries dated from that period or even earlier. Building on these foundations, the peasants and estate managers were imposing some major changes on the landscape. Two tendencies can be identified – one to change the use of land in woodland and pastoral regions, and the other to restructure the regions which already contained much arable. The first tendency led them to fell some woodlands and turn them into either arable or pasture, or to bring them under more intensive management. The weald of Kent, one of the largest wooded areas in the country, was divided among the inhabitants of the north of the shire, who gained their main living by cultivating the fertile lowlands. In the autumn, herds of pigs had traditionally been driven to the south-west along well-marked tracks from the Isle of Thanet or the settlements around Faversham to feed on beech mast and acorns, and at the appropriate seasons firewood and timber were cut and carried back considerable distances – often between 8 and 20 miles. The wealden denns, which consisted of pastures and small settlements, some of them occupied seasonally by swineherds and woodcutters, by the late eleventh century had expanded into quite large and permanent communities. The denn attached to Thanet, for example, became the permanent settlement of Tenterden. The use of the land shifted towards arable, though this did not necessarily involve wholesale removal of woods. In a similar way the wolds of the midlands, relatively high ground with limestone or clay soils, which had gained their name from their wooded appearance in the sixth or seventh century, were being brought into more extensive cultivation. On the uplands of Cornwall and the Lake District, shielings occupied in the summer by herdsmen accompanying cattle and sheep on to the high pastures were being converted to permanent farmsteads. The ploughed area was being extended in parts of northern England, south-west Scotland and the isle of Arran at the expense of woodland and pasture, the change in vegetation having its effects on the proportions of pollen of different plants preserved in peat deposits. In the fenland and Somerset Levels, land was being drained and brought into agricultural use. A number of these local changes were not necessarily designed just to expand the bounds of cultivation – often they also increased the amount of pasture, as in East Anglia where intensive grazing turned woodlands into large open greens. The hay meadows of the upper Thames valley were being enlarged by ditch-digging at this time.

Not everyone welcomed this growth in the productive capacity of the countryside. Kings and aristocrats were devoted to hunting, which they valued above all other pastimes. The game, especially deer, would flourish only in a well-wooded environment, and those in authority were anxious to conserve the habitats that still survived. A rigorous forest law of continental type was not applied – that is, the king could not restrict landowners hunting on their own land, but areas of woodland seem to have been put under special protection by kings and major landowners, and they enclosed areas of wood and grazing land into parks. The charters mention 'hays', which in some cases were enclosed woods and in others 'deer hedges' designed to assist in the hunt. Near Oxford, at Shotover, in opposition to the normal trends, the area under trees was actually increasing around the tenth century, presumably in response to royal orders to improve the hunting, and after the Norman Conquest the area became a royal forest. Concern for maintaining areas of wood and pasture was probably a reaction to the prevailing tendency towards its reduction. Outside the aristocracy few people ate venison (deer bones are relatively scarce in excavated rubbish deposits), perhaps because it was reserved for the elite social groups, but also reflecting the domination of the landscape by agriculture.

The main changes in the rural landscape were not on the fringes of woods, moors and marshes, but in the well-developed arable lands, where the tenth and eleventh centuries were an important phase in the creation of villages and their associated fields. Before the tenth century almost everyone lived in small and scattered settlements. These are known from archaeologists' finds of groups of pottery fragments on modern ploughed fields – sites located in this way in the east midlands are usually dated before *c.*850. Excavation reveals ditched enclosures round fields and paddocks, pits for rubbish, and the remains of rectangular buildings with walls consisting of rows of vertical posts set into the ground, which were used for dwelling houses and barns. The houses occasionally seem to have stood alone, and are assumed to have been isolated farms, or sometimes are found in groups. One site with more than sixty structures, at Catholme in the Trent valley in Staffordshire, at first looks like a large village, but the buildings were arranged in farmsteads, each containing a dwelling and agricultural buildings such as barns and cowsheds, and not all of these were occupied throughout the life of the site from the sixth to the ninth century. At its height the settlement consisted of five households, which means that it rates as a hamlet rather than a village.

Dozens of pre-tenth-century settlements have been discovered in eastern and midland England, the majority of them in the fields of the medieval and modern periods, not under modern villages. So people have not lived on the same sites throughout history: a sharp break came when peasants abandoned farmsteads and hamlets, and moved into larger villages. The new settlements which emerged in the tenth, eleventh and twelfth centuries had populations of between twelve and sixty households. They were stable, as the majority are still inhabited; they were compact, consisting either of rows of houses along a street or green, or of a cluster of dwellings; and their inhabitants usually cultivated land in adjoining open fields.

Why was there this remarkable change in the size, site, layout and durability of rural settlements? No contemporary wrote about the transformation that was going on, perhaps because it was so commonplace that no one thought it remarkable, and in any case the literate members of society had their minds on higher things, such as religion and government. Rather we have to reconstruct thought processes from the material evidence of the hamlets and villages. Any explanation of the move into nucleated villages must take into account their localized distribution. The villages were confined mainly to a belt of Britain from eastern Scotland through Northumberland and Durham, broadening to include most of the midlands and central southern England, and ending in Dorset and Hampshire (Map 2). To the east and west of the 'village belt', in south-east England and East Anglia, and in the whole of the west of Britain from Devon and Cornwall up to the Highlands and Islands of Scotland, people lived in various types of hamlet, or in single farms. In these regions of dispersed settlement the farms may have persisted for centuries on the same site, as in the western and northern isles of Scotland; by contrast, hamlets and farms in East Anglia migrated even more than in the midlands, and many of the late medieval and modern hamlets of western England do not seem to sit on sites going back earlier than

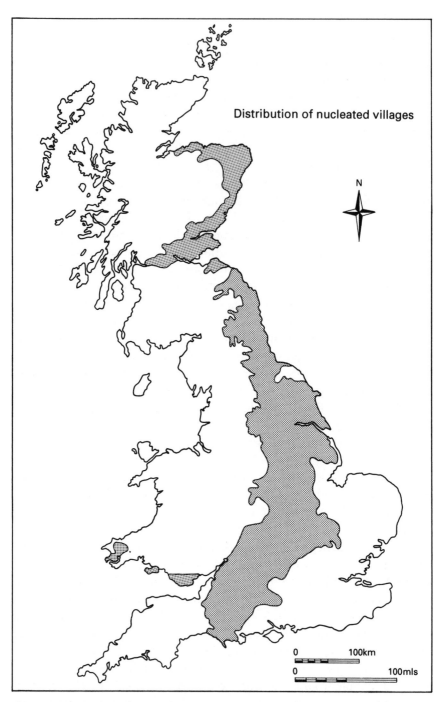

Distribution of nucleated villages

N

0   100km

0   100mls

Map 2. Distribution of nucleated villages. The shading shows the regions where nucleated villages, rather than hamlets or single farms, were the main form of settlement in recent times. This distribution reflects, approximately, the settlement pattern of the middle ages.

Sources: B. K. Roberts and S. Wrathmell, *An Atlas of Rural Settlement in England* (2000); B. K. Roberts, *Rural Settlement in Britain* (Folkestone, 1977).

the eleventh century. So the settlement pattern underwent widespread upheaval, but it was only in the central belt that the inhabitants ended by living in large nucleated villages.

Perhaps the term 'village revolution' exaggerates the speed of this change. While hamlets of Northamptonshire were abandoned soon after 850, signalling the beginnings of village formation, the first phase of occupation in many villages came no earlier than the eleventh century, and the whole process may not have been complete – in north-east England, for example – until about 1200. Precise dates often cannot be assigned to the origin of many villages, and much of the evidence consists of plans recorded in recent times. Perhaps we should see the formation of each village in evolutionary terms. As the density of farms and hamlets increased, the amount of land under cultivation grew, and fields fragmented as a result of inheritance, marriage and other transfers. A crowded and complicated countryside was inconvenient to cultivate, and generated disputes. Meanwhile, the house of the lord, his church and the cottages of slaves and servants provided the nucleus for a large settlement. More and more peasants found it efficient to move their dwellings to the centre, and gradually they organized their landholdings in more systematic ways, ending with all of the houses in one central grouping, and the fields laid out and regulated by the community. This reconstruction of events is supported by some villages which seem to have stuck at intermediate phases of development, notably the 'polyfocal' villages where there may be three groupings of houses in close proximity – as if people had never brought their movement towards a single centre to its final and logical conclusion. Occasional single farms or small hamlets lay interspersed among the large villages, as if a few individuals managed to avoid the general trend towards living in groups. The evolution continued with the replanning of some villages, or their enlargement with new groups of houses. And villages might split into two: as a settlement became large, its inhabitants might decide to form a new nucleus nearby, which helps to explain why we find so many twin villages, called Upper and Lower, or Great and Little, or East and West.

Another explanation of village formation is based on the formal and disciplined nature of many of the settlements, which appear to be the product of a deliberate act of those in authority. Villages were planned, with each house occupying a plot identical in size and shape to its neighbours: the houses were regimented in rows along a street or beside a green, and each was attached to a standard holding of 15 or 30 acres also set out in dozens of strips in strict order in the surrounding fields. Such a planned settlement, it is said, could only have been accomplished by orders from above, most likely from the lord, whose motive was to

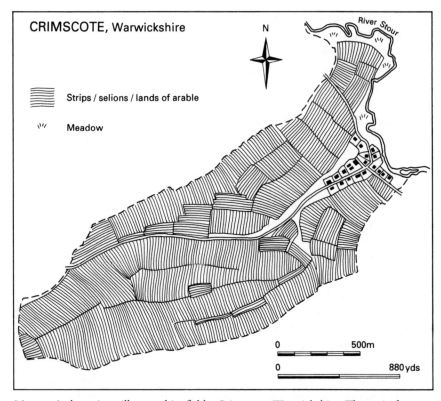

Map 3. A champion village and its fields: Crimscote, Warwickshire. The main features
of this village, though not recorded on a map until the nineteenth century, developed
in the early middle ages. Its characteristic features were the houses closely packed into
the settlement, its high proportion of land under the plough, and limited area of
pasture and meadow. There were *c.*1,500 strips, gathered into 46 furlongs, and divided
(along the road into the village) between two fields.

Source: A. H. R. Baker and R. A. Butlin (eds), *Studies of Field Systems in the British Isles*
(Cambridge, 1973).

impose his control on the peasants. This must have taken place in a short
time, perhaps a single year. In fact the two reconstructions of events
could both have occurred – a gradual nucleation in the tenth century,
followed by a reorganization into a more regular plan in the twelfth. The
measuring and allocation of land necessary for all of these changes is
most likely to have been the work of the villagers themselves, as they
alone would have had detailed local knowledge. Indeed the whole process
could have been initiated by them.

Though views vary about the formation of the village, everyone agrees
that behind these new large settlements lay an economic logic (Map 3).
They are located in regions with a strong commitment to arable farming,

and there was a close connection between the villages and their fields. The fields had a rational purpose. Each peasant household ploughed and harvested its own holding of land, which was regarded as its property. The holding was scattered evenly over the whole territory of the village, in the form of strips, called 'acres' at the time. The working and cropping of the land was regulated by common rules. Everyone had to fallow part (often half) of the land each year, while cultivating the rest. The fallow ideally formed one block of land, a single field consisting of hundreds of acres belonging to each of the villagers' holdings, so that animals could wander over it after harvest and until the next sowing, finding grazing in the stubble. The fallowed land after its rest and manuring should have been more productive when it was its turn to be cultivated and cropped in the following year, and the former arable turned over to fallow. If these rules were not observed, animals would not have been able to graze over the whole fallow field, and crops were in danger of being eaten by wandering animals. In the same spirit, the areas of permanent grassland were available to everyone, and restrictions had to be put on the number of animals lest the community suffer from the effects of overgrazing. Similarly, meadows were carefully allocated to each holding in proportion to the holders' other assets. The details of these arrangements are not recorded until the twelfth and thirteenth centuries, and it may well be that the whole package of rules was not in place until then, but the references to land in intermixed strips (it was said to lie 'acre under acre'), to common land, and to land being divided into two blocks implies that some of the main elements of the open-field system were functioning in the tenth century.

This package of regulations had advantages and restrictions for the individuals. The routine of cultivation and fallowing was designed to maintain a balance which ensured that the grain gave reasonable yields from one year to the next. No one participating in such a system was likely to become very rich, but neither were they liable to starve. All the shareholders in the village felt that they were fairly treated, as everyone lived in the same place, equally near to their strips and the other facilities such as streams and woods. The scattering of the strips ensured that everyone worked some of the best and worst land, and if there was a poor harvest everyone would have the same chances. Each peasant was committed to the common fields – there was no way in which they could withdraw. The village was by no means unchanging, as its size could be increased, by ploughing up pastures for example, or by adding to the number of cottagers by subdividing holdings, or by lords granting out parcels from their land. But in some senses the formation of a village signalled that expansion was coming to an end. Villages developed within fixed limits – many

of the boundaries detailed in tenth-century descriptions coincide exactly
with those of modern parishes. And by the tenth century, as we have seen,
the ploughed land reached up to the edge of the territory. The village provided a means of rationalizing an already full countryside. The standard
peasant holdings served the interests of lords because rents and services
were levied from them, but they also protected the families who occupied
them from impoverishment. Land and people were working together in
equilibrium within the village, and any future transformations would be
more likely to occur outside the village regions.

The field systems which grew alongside the villages represent one of
the principal technological changes in the early middle ages. We do not
have precise information about agricultural methods at this early date,
but the two-course rotation, by which half of the arable was fallowed
every other year, was used. This could well mark a stage in the intensification of farming, because we might expect that in earlier periods when
arable was not fully extended the land would have been cropped only
intermittently or occasionally, or that 'infield–outfield' husbandry would
be practised, whereby a small area (a much-manured infield) was cropped
every year, and the remainder of the territory intermittently. Ploughing
techniques varied from region to region. The light plough, the ard, which
stirred the soil with an iron-pointed share attached to a beam, was being
used in some parts of the country, while illustrations in manuscripts show
heavy ploughs with both shares and coulters, and sometimes wheels,
which were capable of turning furrows and creating the ridged fields
which have been recognized by archaeologists, for example near Montgomery on the Welsh border. Ploughs were cumbersome implements,
drawn by teams of eight oxen in some cases, and in order to turn them
round as infrequently as possible the parcels (acres) in the fields were
long and narrow. One early type of strip field was so extended that it
might stretch for hundreds of yards from the edge of the settlement to
the boundary of its territory. In villages in Northamptonshire smaller
parcels, each containing between a quarter- and half-acre, but retaining
an elongated shape, were formed by subdivision and reorganization of
the original long strips.

Place names, charters and preserved vegetation found in excavations
reveal the main crops that were planted in this period. Rye increased in
importance in East Anglia, probably reflecting an extension of cultivation on the light, sandy soils of the region. Old wheat varieties, spelt and
emmer, were being replaced with bread wheats which were more easily
threshed. While such field crops represent one of the main priorities of
cultivation, much effort went into growing vegetables and fruit, probably
by women, and their husbandry was probably also responsible for
crops used in textile manufacture, notably flax, hemp and dyestuffs,

which were grown everywhere, but with special intensity on the edge of the growing towns.

The methods of livestock farming are reflected in the bones found discarded on settlement sites, most plentifully in towns, and these varied from region to region: for example, cattle were especially important in the vicinity of York, but a higher proportion of sheep grazed in Norfolk and Lincolnshire. Sheep were kept for the sake of their wool rather than meat, so that most of them were slaughtered as mature adults. Some cattle were killed young, for meat, and others kept for many years for dairying and haulage. Animals were not very large. At York, the sheep resembled in size the rather small breed now kept on the Welsh mountains, and the cattle were by modern standards stunted – they probably weighed live about 440 pounds, half the weight of even a small modern breed. This lack of stature may be partly a comment on the cattle owners' failure to breed animals selectively, and partly on the feed and shelter available. One indication of careful management is the lack of many signs of disease on the bones.

Managing woods, in order to ensure a steady supply of both large building timbers and the smaller underwood for fuel and fencing, was not a new technique at this time. But growing demand, especially from towns, must have led to a closer and more systematic control of a limited resource. Many woods were coppiced, that is cut on a rotation in order to crop each new growth of underwood every few years. This must lie behind the deliveries of hundreds of cartloads of wood fuel to the salt works at Droitwich in Worcestershire, recorded as a well-established practice in 1086. Larger trees, which grew either among the coppiced wood or in 'wood pastures' where stock grazed, would be conserved for eventual use as timber. Another woodland product exploited at this time was honey, which is mentioned so often in documents that it must be rated a major product of the countryside. Its plenty reflects the abundant flora, and the skilful management of many hives. In regions where woods were less plentiful, notably eastern Norfolk, turbaries (peat diggings) provided towns like Norwich with fuel as well as supplying the needs of a dense rural population. The pits were on such a scale as to create eventually the pattern of inland lakes now known as the Norfolk Broads. In other parts of East Anglia, and in Somerset, the wetlands were being reclaimed by means of dyke systems, suggesting that drainage methods, knowledge of which had lapsed since Roman times, were being learned again.

Technical advances depended on small-scale cumulative improvements, rather than dramatic new inventions. The story of water mills suggests that we should not always assume that 'improvements' moved in one direction. The 6,000 English water mills that we know existed in

1086 need not have been installed in the previous two centuries – a considerable number were built before 900. Nor should we assume that the more efficient vertical-wheeled mill (in which the power was connected through cogs to the millstones on the floor of the mill building) expanded at the expense of the horizontal mill (where the wheel was fixed in the channel of water, and turned the millstones directly). At Old Windsor in Berkshire, a horizontal mill was built in about 900 on the site of a mill with vertical wheels which had been recently destroyed. Mills were growing in number and efficiency, freeing labour from the time-consuming drudgery of milling by hand for more productive purposes, but a great number of hand mills were still in use.

The tendencies that we have reviewed so far – the growth in towns, the filling up of the countryside implied by village formation, the extension of cultivation and the more efficient exploitation of resources – could be seen as stimulated by a growth in population. Were people living longer, marrying younger, rearing more children to adulthood? Our sources are capable neither of telling us the intimate details of family life, nor of giving exact global population figures. Roman Britain could have had a population of 5 million, and by 1086 a figure for England in the region of 2.2 to 2.5 million seems likely (see pp. 94–5). The main decline of the early middle ages probably occurred in the three centuries after 400, when the collapse of the Roman economy, social disruption and recurrent epidemics were likely to have been linked with low fertility and high mortality. Population numbers may have fallen well below 2 million, so the tenth and eleventh centuries would have been a period of recovery, a preliminary episode in the great population increase which quickened in pace in the two centuries after 1086 (see Figure 2 below, p. 235). If population levels were not rising very rapidly, we should not think of those who moved into towns or restructured the countryside as impelled by some urgent crisis caused by high levels of population. Perhaps they were able to make radical changes precisely because they did not feel the pressure of rapid growth in numbers, but were free to innovate and experiment. They were having to adapt to increased demands from their rulers and lords, and they were encouraged to adopt more intensive methods of production as they became enmeshed in the market.

iii. *Estates and lords*

How did the various sections of society gain a living from the land in the two centuries after 850? At the beginning of the period the magnates and major institutions depended on very large holdings of land, to which various terms are applied: in the north the word 'shires' appears in 'Richmondshire' or 'Aucklandshire'. In Scotland, at a later time they were known as 'thanages' as well as shires. 'Multiple estate' and 'land unit' are terms currently used, but here they will be called 'great estates'.

As with so many aspects of society and economy before 1050, we are dependent on later evidence. Most of our knowledge of the boundaries and subdivisions of the great estates comes from the survival of a few of them in the centuries after 1050, or of traces of their former existence. Occasionally a charter gives a description of a great estate. In 959, for example, King Edgar, quite soon after the northern counties had been taken from Scandinavian rule into the English kingdom, granted to a woman who was evidently a great landed magnate the estates of Howden and Drax, adjacent places in Yorkshire. The land thus conveyed was characteristically extensive – from north-east to south-west it measured more than 10 miles. Also typical of the 'multiple estate', it had a federal character: the charter lists the dependencies of Howden – Knedlington, Barn Hill, Caville, Thorpe, Hive, Eastrington, Belby and Kilpin, most of them settlements still flourishing today in the neighbourhood of Howden. Finally the charter describes the boundaries of the estate, which was easily done because they consisted mainly of rivers – the Ouse, Derwent, Foulness and Aire. It therefore had a geographical coherence with 'natural' boundaries, which has led to the speculation that great estates had very early origins. Great federated estates like that based on Howden have been found throughout Britain. In Scotland, many thanages had a dozen or so constituent 'touns', and the thanes (lesser aristocrats with service functions), who had their own holdings on the estate, made sure that the estate worked. The estate centre in Wales, the *llys*, stood at the head of a group of hamlets or *trefi*. The *maenor* of Meddyfnych (now Llandybie in Carmarthenshire) is recorded in sixth- and ninth-century documents, and in the later middle ages contained seven *trefi* (see Map 4 below, p. 28). The estate measured 7 miles across, and its boundaries included both upland and valley land, which gave the lord access to cornfields, meadow and hill pasture.

The kings, bishops, monasteries and nobles who controlled the great estates expected from them regular supplies of food and rent. Lay lords and bishops would travel from estate centre to estate centre, lodge with their servants in the residence that was maintained there, and order delivery of enough food to keep the household for a specific amount of time: the king with his huge following would demand one night's food only, whereas lesser lords who had fewer estates to visit would stay longer. A typical food rent for an itinerant household in England consisted of

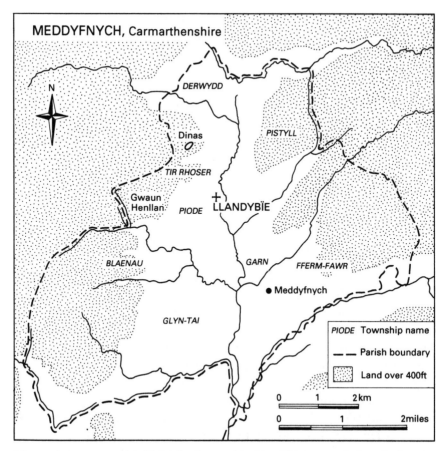

Map 4. A great estate: Meddyfnych, Carmarthenshire. This *maenor* is described briefly in *c.*800. Its boundary coincided roughly with that of the modern parish of Llandybie, which contains about 12 square miles. In the later middle ages it included seven townships (*trefi*) and its varied resources (arable land and meadow in the stream valleys, and upland grazing) would have been exploited from a number of settlements in the early middle ages also. The church is now at Llandybie, but an earlier church is recalled by the place name *Gwaun Henllan* ('meadow of the old church').

Sources: G. Jones, 'Post-Roman Wales', in *AgHEW*, vol. 1, part 2; W. Davies, *Wales in the Early Middle Ages* (Leicester, 1982).

hundreds of loaves of bread, many barrels of ale, cattle, sheep, bacon and dozens of cheeses. Monasteries demanded specified quantities of food from their estates, rather like a bishop or lay magnate, but as their residence was fixed, made arrangements for the food to be sent to them. A food rent attached to Hickling and Kinoulton in Nottinghamshire when the estate passed to Ramsey Abbey in about the year 1000 consisted of 80 bushels of malt (for brewing), 40 bushels of oatmeal, 80 bushels of flour (for bread), eight sides of bacon, sixteen cheeses, two fat cows and eight salmon in Lent. This was enough to feed the monks and servants of a large monastery for a week or two. In Wales food rents consisted of loaves of bread, oats, cattle, sheep, pigs, butter, ale and honey.

The estate was not geared to squeezing the land and its people with any great intensity. The food rents represented a tiny fraction of the produce of the areas of land in the estate – the grain element in the rent from Hickling detailed above, for example, represents the produce of about 30 acres of land. Howden or Meddyfnych could have produced many thousands of bushels of grain and dozens of surplus animals for meat, but its lord would have received only a fraction of these. The estates themselves played a limited role in actual production, because much of the food that was sent to the lord had been gathered as tribute or rent. Descriptions of ancient tenant obligations often include services such as feeding dogs or helping in the hunting field which, though troublesome to perform, cannot be compared with the burden of continuous heavy labour services found in later centuries. There was probably a piece of land, a home farm of some kind, attached to the residence, and the local peasants would have been expected to labour on this land as part of their obligations, with work also provided by slaves. Certainly bond hamlets supplying labour services to cultivate land under the lord's direct control formed part of the idealized Welsh scheme – though as descriptions of estates were written down in the thirteenth century, they may not reflect accurately earlier conditions.

An estate was organized for production in the sense that it contained complementary resources, and different parts of the federation had functions assigned to them, which are commemorated in place names recording their specialisms, like Shipton (which means 'sheep settlement') or Wootton ('wood settlement'). At the estate centre various craft activities were concentrated, such as iron-working. Co-ordinating the estate's activities depended on officials who were granted holdings of land: thanes in Scotland, riding men in western England, and drengs in the north. In Wales the settlement called the *maerdref*, where agricultural work was concentrated, was appropriately the home of the reeve, who supervised agricultural work. However, the emphasis on tribute means that the great estate resembles not a farm, but a unit of government, an agency for collecting rents.

In the period after 850 the great estates were often broken up. For example, Bampton, which had dominated the south-west corner of Oxfordshire, had its outliers granted away one by one, including Chimney, Ducklington and Brighthampton, in 955–84. The formation of smaller units of landholding was not entirely new. The great estates had never covered the whole countryside; relatively small estates lay in the interstices of their larger neighbours. In any case the estates had always been 'multiple' or 'federal', consisting of a number of smaller blocks of land. Some of these had been held on tenancies in the eighth and ninth centuries, and so were already becoming detached from the estate centre. But after about 850 the tendency to fragmentation accelerated. Some of the small estates were entirely new. In regions with extensive arable the new unit of landholding was defined by means of a zigzag boundary turning a series of right angles as it was drawn through the strips and furrows of a well-established field system. In others it was impossible to detach a single piece of land, and the new lord received dozens of strips scattered through the common fields (he might be awarded 'every third acre'), with a separate parcel of meadow or pasture to complete the holding.

The great estates were split up by inheritance, or parcels were granted by will, or they were given away as part of a marriage settlement, or pieces were acquired by the church. Most important of all, the followers and retainers who had previously lived in the household of a magnate or bishop expected to be rewarded with a holding of land, which they could call their own and pass on to their descendants. The English thegns were taking part in a Europe-wide process by which the lesser nobility were receiving landed endowments, and were to become a numerous and influential group of smaller landowners – later known as the country gentry or the squirearchy in England. The lords of the great estates did not make these grants for nothing – they expected that the thegns would give loyal service, in administration and war, for example. The more fortunate received their portion of an estate as bookland, which gave them complete security, but many of the thegns gained *loenland* (leasehold), usually in the form of a grant for three lives, supposedly then to return to the lord, though in practice the lease was renewed. Some of the land was simply sold. In eastern England a great upheaval in landholding was caused by the growth of the estates of the newly reformed or founded monasteries at Ely, Crowland, Ramsey and Thorney in the late tenth century, when the monks bought land, some of it in relatively small units. The transactions recorded by the monks were just part of a busy land market already operating among the laity. Finally, some land was stolen, when powerful individuals, especially in troubled times, put pressure on churches to make leases, or converted a temporary tenancy into permanent possession.

Over much of England, then, the great estates were being fragmented. The wider consequences were firstly the change in the whole scale of landholding. The old estates were often rated at 20, 30 or 40 hides, while the new thegns' landholdings, and many of the grants to the new monasteries, had an assessment of between one and six hides. The hide had originally meant 'land for a family', but it came to be an assessment, a means of apportioning liability to tax and service. In terms of more modern measurements, the great estates like Bampton and Howden might stretch over 50 or 100 square miles, while the new units of landholding covered no more than 2 or 3 square miles. Secondly, the exploitation of the land was transformed: instead of delivering produce for the occasional visits of a household, we have an estate fulfilling the daily needs of a lord. The great estate was one among many of a magnate's possessions, while a thegn would often depend on a few pieces of land, or even a single property. The new lord would expect to be a resident, and indeed we find aristocratic houses being built in the ninth and tenth centuries on previously unoccupied sites. These dwellings became castles or manor houses in later centuries.

There could be no question of living on tribute – the thegn would develop an area of land beside his house as a home farm which under his direct supervision became the main source of produce for his household. He would hope to squeeze labour from his peasant tenants, but later evidence suggests that the land under the thegn's direct control, then called the demesne, was worked mainly by slaves or servants. Land detached by the early eleventh century from the great estate of Stratford-upon-Avon in Warwickshire, at Luddington, consisting of only about 200 acres of arable, was provided with twelve slaves. The great estate had balanced its resources, but when the constituent parts were broken away the combination of contrasting types of land could no longer be guaranteed. Some of the parts consisted almost entirely of arable, others mainly of wood and pasture, so the new lord either had to change the use of land to make it more self-sufficient, or continue with the specialism and sell surplus produce. In either case the new small scale of landholding led to more intensive use of the land. New lords would add to their profits by investing in a water mill, which would pay for the effort and cost of construction from the tolls paid by the local peasants to grind their corn. Attitudes to property and management changed. The thegns in particular now regarded the land as their own, as the ideas about property rights originally designed by the church to protect its endowments became more widely diffused through society. Laymen saw their lands as long-term investments, which would pass to their children and grandchildren. Many new place names were coined at this time which identified the place by its owner: Ardwick in Lancashire, for example, means the farm of Aethelred. In contrast with the rather relaxed regime of the great estates, production and rent-gathering were

watched hawk-like by the resident lords, anxious to protect their
interests and gain the maximum returns.

We can see how the new regime may have worked in the case of a thegn
called Haehstan, who was granted a three-life lease of Pendock and
Didcot in Worcestershire in 967. Haehstan was something of a carpet-
bagger, as he came from eastern England, where his family had been
founded by a Danish immigrant in the late ninth century. One of the
Dane's descendants, Oswald, became bishop of Worcester, and he looked
after his relatives, including Haehstan, by granting them pieces of land
from the church's estates. Pendock and Didcot may have been Haehstan's
only possessions. They were both quite small, rated in total at three
hides, and they were quite awkwardly placed 13 miles apart. Didcot,
located in the valley of the Carrant Brook on the edge of the Avon valley,
consisted entirely of arable land. Indeed, when Didcot was detached from
the parent estate of Overbury, a single block of land could not be defined,
so it was formed of scattered strips in the open fields. Pendock, on the
other hand, was easily carved out of a relatively underdeveloped woodland landscape. It included a small amount of arable, with a good deal
of marsh, open pasture, enclosed fields, a hedged pasture for pigs, and
woodland. Haehstan could have supplied his household with corn,
mostly from Didcot, and meat, dairy produce and fuel mainly from
Pendock. The properties complemented one another in production as
well as consumption, because pigs bred in the valley would have been
brought to the woods to be fattened on acorns, young cattle reared at
Pendock may well have have been sent to Didcot to work as plough oxen,
and if a barn was to be built at Didcot, Pendock would have been the
source of timber.

Didcot offered limited opportunities for expansion, as the land there
was fixed in a routine of cultivation as part of an established field system.
At Pendock, however, there was more scope for development, as its
pastures could have been ploughed to extend the arable under Haehstan's
direct management. New tenants could have been found land there.
People were already established in Pendock, whose names – Osric,
Eadred and so on – were used to identify points round the boundary in
967. But a mainly pastoral landscape would be bound to be thinly
peopled, and the lord could only increase his revenue from rents and gain
labour for his own cultivation if more tenants were recruited from Didcot
and its neighbourhood. Another strategy for developing Pendock would
have been to take advantage of its special resources, to stock it with more
animals, or manage its woods with the intention of producing a saleable
surplus of bacon, cheese or honey which could be taken by road to
Gloucester, the nearest town. The purchaser of a Kentish swine pasture

similar to Pendock was willing to pay £2 40d for it, suggesting its potential to earn money from the sale of produce. Thegns like Haehstan would expect to have cash to spend on aristocratic luxuries like a fine horse, armour, weapons and cloth. A thegn's heriot (death duty paid to his lord) was set at £2 soon after Haehstan's time. So he needed to earn cash from his land.

The lords of the great estates were also forced into new attitudes and policies by fragmentation. As places like Bampton and Overbury lost their former dependencies, their lords had to compensate themselves for the loss of revenues by focusing their efforts in a more concentrated way on the lands remaining under their direct control. The lords had the advantage that they were often located on the best land, and had plenty of peasant tenants capable of doing agricultural service. They emphasized the efficient cultivation of the land, while putting pressure on the peasant tenants to contribute more labour.

The greater landlords seem not to have been driven by the same energy as the lords of small estates. Their assets were so great, and their power over tenants so well established, that they may have felt no need for radical innovations. The wealthier churchmen worried about encroachment on their estates by acquisitive laymen, and the charters that they kept and the boundary clauses that were recorded in so much detail were clearly intended to protect their properties. On the other hand, unlike their contemporaries on the continent, they did not write surveys of their estates, containing the names of peasants and lists of their obligations. The omission may reflect their lack of administrative flair, or a rather complacent attitude towards management. But the existing customs and practices delivered the right results, and would not be helped by a time-consuming bureaucracy. The lay magnates seem not to have put any effort into keeping records. Their estates were so extensive that they may not have been greatly concerned with the details of agricultural profits. Their chief means of expanding their wealth was to add more land to their holdings through their political skills, and they expected to grant away many of their assets in pursuit of patronage. They wished to protect their estates from unnecessary losses, and many of the new acquisitions made by the new monastic estates of the late tenth century had to be fought through the courts as relatives of the donors disputed the legality of the church's possession of their family property.

Magnates of all kinds – kings, earls, bishops, monasteries – faced a dilemma about who would be responsible for the details of cultivation, enforcing service and selling produce. Were these difficult tasks to be supervised by an official appointed for the purpose, a reeve? Or should each estate be leased out for a fixed farm of food, or cash, or a combination of the two? Both direct management and leasing ('farming') are recorded. Farming out their manors would have suited the major lay landlords best, as their estates were often widely scattered, and management would be greatly simplified if it consisted essentially of making a bargain with a lessee, and then ensuring that the farm was paid promptly and in full.

Lords of all types had coped for centuries with the problem of finding the best way to translate their control of land into the revenues of food, fuel and money. As tribute played an important part in the running of the great estates, in theory the practice could have continued and intensified with lords demanding higher proportions of the crops of their tenants. The church received the ancient tax of churchscot, usually levied as grain, and in addition imposed the much more onerous tithe, by which a tenth of all produce – grain, wool, young animals, fruit and so on – was paid to the local clergy. Lords also continued to demand payments in kind, which on the estate of the Winchester monks at Hurstbourne in *c.*900 involved the peasants (the word *ceorl* was used to describe them) paying wheat, barley, ale, firewood and sheep to their lords. As a principal method of taking revenue from an estate, however, payments in kind were rather inflexible and clumsy.

The most effective way for lords to gain income was to develop a demesne, land set aside for their exclusive use, with a core of workers directly employed either as slaves or as hired hands, but which could also draw on the labour of the local peasantry. The whole organization consisted therefore of tenant land, on which peasants were settled on condition that they paid rents and worked for the lord, linked to the demesne on which the labour services could be used. At the centre stood the buildings of the manor, where the lord could live and his officials were based. Both the produce of the demesne and any rents in kind could be collected and processed at this centre of management. Manor (or hall in English) meant a dwelling, but by extension came to refer to the administrative unit which gathered revenues from demesne and tenants.

The concern for the effective management of the demesne was expressed in a treatise written in the early eleventh century known as 'The Reeve' (*Gerefa*), which advised an estate official to know the best seasons for ploughing and mowing, to look after all of the manor's assets, remembering to mend hedges and ditches and clean out sheds. The reeve should be acquainted with a long list of equipment, from an axe to a mousetrap. The section on labour relations advised that the lord's authority should be kept, but that the servants (hired men) should be treated fairly. The treatise resembles a literary exercise rather than a practical handbook, the list of implements being designed to show off the author's encyclopaedic knowledge and wide vocabulary. The subject matter is, however, a guide to the preoccupations of its author, a churchman. Like many of his contemporary landlords, he needed to take an interest in practical agricultural matters. The main message of 'The Reeve', though dressed in rather bookish language, was that anyone in charge of a demesne should protect his lord's interests by paying attention to detail.

The growth of towns, especially in the south and east, influenced the management of estates, as even the 800 inhabitants of a town of modest size would eat and drink the produce of 1,000 acres of arable land, and over a large area would generate demand for livestock and wool. The penetration of cash into the rural economy by the end of the tenth century stimulated a land market which enabled the monasteries of eastern England to build up their estates. The monks of Ely kept a book that recorded for posterity their acquisitions. They proudly entered payments of £15 for a two-hide manor here, £60 for ten hides there, and a purchase of two hides and 37 acres for £11 (see p. 75).

The close connection between the growth of exchange, more intensive production, and the fragmentation of the estates is underlined by the lack of these developments in Wales and Scotland. Here, in countrysides which persisted in traditions of self-sufficiency and tribute payments, the great estates continued to function in the eleventh century, though they soon changed as towns and new political and social formations exercised their influence after 1100.

iv. *Peasants*

The peasant tenants provided much of the labour on many manors, a typical burden according to one early eleventh-century treatise being two or three days each week for a peasant with a yardling, a substantial 30-acre holding, and one day per week for a cottager, but with another day each week during the harvest season. Lords were anxious to gain as much labour as possible, but they were also interested in the payments of rents in cash and kind. They were able to create a dependent peasantry by two routes, one by reducing the independence of tenants, and the other by settling slaves on the land. Lords cajoled lightly burdened peasants to do more work on the demesne. In troubled times, such as a famine year, peasants would have been willing to make concessions for material help, while in times of political troubles the lord could offer his protection in exchange for a promise to labour on the demesne. Perhaps he imposed his protection, and bullied the tenants into doing more work for him. But we should not necessarily envisage such dramatic circumstances, but rather see the lord putting a slow and relentless pressure on his tenants, sometimes threatening them with some loss of privilege, such as access to pasture, sometimes acting as their benefactor, but expecting material returns from that friendship. A lord would, for example, provide food if the whole peasant community turned out to help with the harvest or haymaking.

The freeing of slaves provided another route to a dependent labouring peasantry. Slaves seem to have been very numerous in the ninth, tenth and eleventh centuries. Modestly sized estates were provided with as many as twelve or thirty 'men'. A will written in 992 mentions no fewer than seventy-two of them. In some ways they resemble chattel slaves, like those in the American south in the nineteenth century, as they were listed along with the animal livestock of an estate, and could be bought and sold, the price of a man in the tenth century being £1, eight times that of an ox. They were expected to work in jobs requiring continuous labour, especially as ploughmen, each plough requiring two workers, one to drive the oxen and the other to hold the plough. Many were employed on herding sheep, cattle and pigs, and women worked as dairymaids. Their owners fed the slaves on bread, mutton, beef (for males only) and beans. Slaves, however, seem to have had rather more independence than this picture of subjection and constant work might suggest, as we find them occupying plots of land, marrying and rearing families, attending markets, and accumulating goods and money.

Slaves were being freed in the tenth and eleventh centuries in such numbers that the institution had virtually died out soon after 1100. Various explanations have been offered for this development. Slavery was undoubtedly regarded as morally tarnished, and freeing a slave counted as an act of charity, but this had been the case in earlier centuries. Churchmen disapproved of aspects of the slave trade, and at the same time kept slaves on their estates like other lords. Perhaps difficulties were encountered in recruiting new slaves, with a shortage of war captives. There were other ways of gaining new slaves, among those who sold themselves in times of famine, for example, and in any case married slaves would help to maintain numbers, as the children of slaves were themselves slaves. The conventional view that slaves were lazy and inefficient and that granting them holdings of their own would motivate them does not accord with recent research on the productivity of slave labour. They were, however, difficult to discipline, and tended to run away, or disobey orders. Those who did manage to sell goods and save money would buy their manumission, and so escape legally. Perhaps the estates found the administrative burden of managing the slaves unsupportable, and decided that it was much simpler to settle them on holdings, while still retaining a claim on their labour.

Thousands of slaves were granted tenant holdings, and so they joined the ranks of the peasantry. The descendants of the freed slaves of the tenth and eleventh centuries can be identified after 1100 because they held small tenements in return for heavy services, such as carrying out full-time tasks as ploughmen or shepherds. The manorial tenants owing labour services therefore consisted partly of people who had come 'up from slavery', and partly of an older stratum of dependent tenants pressurized into doing more work for the lord, and perhaps peasants previously free of major obligations who had been caught in the manorial net. We will never know for certain which route into dependence on the manor was more important, and indeed this must have varied with the region or type of estate. Our view is partly obscured by the versions which lords liked to believe. Just as they presented an image of themselves as the friends and protectors of their tenants, they also justified their dominance by claiming that peasants had been granted parcels of the lords' land, together with livestock and equipment, in exchange for heavy services, making the whole arrangement seem like a reciprocal exchange. But very rarely were lords filling up an empty piece of countryside. A more common situation was that they took over an inhabited territory, and then had to subject it, and above all its population, to their control. In these circumstances they had not given their peasants their holdings, but took away lands they already held, and granted them back on more oppressive terms.

Some lords were much more successful than others in forcing the peasantry into manorial discipline. The regions which have produced the best early evidence for a regime of heavy labour service tend to lie in the west, in Worcestershire, Gloucestershire, Hampshire and Somerset, and the documents come from the archives of the major church landlords. To the north and east social organization seems much looser, with large manors provided with relatively small demesnes, associated with outlying dependent parcels of land, known as berewicks when they were under manorial control, and sokes when the peasants enjoyed a great deal of independence. These groups of free peasants may have come under the jurisdiction of lords as late as the tenth century, when kings granted rights over them to English aristocrats moving back into territory formerly held by the Danes. In Kent we find some peasants under close lordly control, and others who were much more independent, who were able to practise partible inheritance into later centuries. In Wales and Scotland, although details survive only from a later period, bond tenants owed services to estate centres, but there were also numerous lightly burdened peasants. The latter were expected to pay rents in cash and kind, or contribute occasional labour dues, but were exempt from the more oppressive routine of manorial labour. These differences to some extent reflected varied types of agricultural production, as pastoral husbandry did not need so much labour, and peasants travelling with their herds were much more difficult to tie down. The different types of landlord had a strong influence, as large church estates were better established in western England than in the north and east.

Peasants' reactions to all these changes are not recorded, but we can attempt to reconstruct their views from the comments of their superiors and their overall behaviour. To begin with the slaves, they clearly felt the disadvantage of their status, and sought to escape from it. In the words put into the mouth of a slave ploughman by a monastic writer, Aelfric, in *c*.1000, 'Yes, the work is hard, because I am not free'. We have seen that slaves contributed to their own liberation in a small way by buying their freedom, or by flight. They welcomed the grants of land which gave them at least a measure of economic independence, and an inheritance for their families. Slave specialist workers such as swineherds and beekeepers were contracted in the eleventh century to deliver to the lord a fixed quota of produce – fifteen pigs or five sesters (a sester weighed nine pounds) of honey – after which they could keep or sell any surplus. They were gaining some control over their working lives.

The smallholder, sometimes called the *cotsetla*, was recorded in the *Rectitudines* (rules), a description of peasant conditions in western England written near to 1000. He contributed relatively small amounts of labour service to the manor – a quarter of his working time was spent on the demesne. As their holdings were probably too small to feed their families, we can deduce that these people formed part of the force of hired workers who were employed on the demesnes, or in towns if they lived nearby, or most often by the wealthier peasants.

The peasant with a yardland (30-acre) holding known as a *ceorl* or *gebur* formed the key figure in the manorial structure, providing the bulk of the labour service and rents in cash and kind. The obligation to work on the lord's demesne for two or three days per week was undoubtedly a burden, and a drag on his ability to produce from his own holding. One imagines in particular the problems he experienced when the sun shone in the haymaking or harvest seasons, but the days had to be spent working for the lord while the crops on his own holding were damaged by neglect. Although technically free, in the sense that he attended the public courts of the hundred, he was subject to manorial discipline, which prevented him from moving without the permission of his lord. We can also glimpse behind the descriptions of peasant obligations the *gebur* and his household as substantial producers in their own right, with a holding of arable, and access to grazing and woodland. The house, judging from peasant buildings that have been excavated, measured 15 feet by 30 feet and was built of substantial timbers, as were the barn and other outbuildings. At least 15 acres of crops were planted each year, and peasants kept oxen as draught animals, and cows, sheep and pigs, from which in normal years the family could feed itself, pay the rent and have a surplus to exchange. The holding was associated with others in a hamlet or village, which was essential for agricultural production, as each *gebur* usually owned two oxen; it would only be through joining with neighbours that the full team of eight could have been assembled. It was also from his neighbours that he gained the labour for harvesting and other seasonal work, employing the cottagers who needed earnings to supplement the produce of their smallholdings. The *gebur* or *ceorl* emerges then not as a mere appendage of a manor, but as a producer, trader, member of a community, and as an employer.

More obviously independent was the *geneat*, a peasant without a heavy commitment to labour services, whose obligations to his lord often involved riding, carrying messages, escorting his lord, helping with the hunt and general carriage work. A *geneat* had a larger holding than a *gebur*, and therefore enjoyed better opportunities to sell produce. He was less burdened with time-consuming labour services, and gained in status from his light and honourable duties.

The manor played a significant part in the economy, but rural society was not entirely dominated by lords and their officials. The village had responsibilities to the hundred court, and the peasant community managed its fields and pastures. Where the village was divided between two or more manors – a common situation at the time of Domesday Book, but going back to much earlier times – the villagers protected the unity of the community, and ensured in the absence of any other single authority that the rules of husbandry were obeyed.

The peasants' ability to conduct their own lives emerges from an examination of their involvement in buying and selling. They paid cash rents to their lords, for which the usual figure given in the tenth and early eleventh centuries was 10d or 12d per yardland, though at the estate of Tidenham in Gloucestershire each *gebur* paid another 6d. In addition, the geld payments to the king were paid in cash, and though not demanded every year, they could amount to 6d or more per yardland. This money could only have been obtained by selling produce. Certain crops, notably wool, bacon, cheese and other animal products, may have been available in quantities beyond the subsistence needs of the family, and were suitable for the market. We find peasants employed in non-agricultural occupations aimed at yielding a cash income, such as the large-scale fishing at Tidenham, presumably reproduced all round the coast and along major rivers, and wood-cutting and transport. They worked in rural industries such as pottery manufacture at Michelmersh in Hampshire and quarrying at Taynton (Oxfordshire) and Barnack (Lincolnshire). Near towns, peasants worked the hemp and flax gardens which kept an important urban craft supplied with raw materials. It could be said that peasants were forced to produce for the market to pay rents and taxes. They paid some of the money that they earned to lord and state, but they also had to buy essential goods for their farming and domestic lives, and wished to indulge in expenditure for pleasure, status-seeking and other familiar motives. In eastern England they bought pottery manufactured mainly in towns, and all over the country they acquired functional iron implements and hand mills, ornamental bronze belt attachments and brooches.

Contact with the market meant that peasants travelled into towns or the less formal gatherings outside churches or estate centres. These visits sometimes turned into longer stays and permanent migrations, hence the growth of the urban population. The manorial authorities attempted to control the movements of the *geburs*, but they could not be prevented from taking opportunities outside their native village. A list of *gebur* emigrants from Hatfield in Hertfordshire was compiled by officials working for the monks of Ely around 1000. Among others they found that three of the peasants had sons – their names were Duding, Ceolmund and Aethelheah – who had moved to Walden (now King's Walden), which would have involved a journey of about 10 miles, perhaps in a concerted move by a peer group of ambitious young men. Marriage provided the motive for a number of Hatfield migrations. Peasant society of the tenth and eleventh centuries was clearly not rooted in one spot or unaware of the wider world.

There are hints in documents written by their superiors about peasants, and in the traces of peasant culture that still survive, in the naming of minor features in the countryside, that tell us a little of peasant mentality. They were aware of local myths and legends, but to some extent they were practically minded, knowing the crops for which a piece of land was best suited (for example 'beanfield'), and had a detailed appreciation of the subtleties of the landscape, so that they had numerous words for 'valley' and 'hill'. They had strong family attachments, and could remember their ancestors; they had a memory for custom, which estate managers were warned to ignore at their peril. This was not just a matter of mindless loyalties to familiar people and old ideas, but a necessary means of protection against dangerous forces in a world that was not always changing for the better. For the same reason they valued the collective organizations like the village community which regulated cultivation, but also offered companionship and support among those of similar status and common economic interests.

A development in the countryside which brings together all of these varied but connected trends was the building of local churches. In the days of the great estate, a few widely scattered rich minster churches provided the main centres of religious life. When the great estates fragmented, hundreds of local lords founded churches on their manors, which became the parish churches that still exist as institutions, even if their fabric has been renewed in later centuries. By 1086, and mainly in the previous century or two, 416 churches had been established in Suffolk, three-quarters of the total that ever existed in the middle ages. These new churches reflect the change in the pattern of lordship, and the ambition of the lesser lords to gain the status symbol that a church represented: it was often built on land adjacent to the manor house. The lords profited from church dues, and like a mill, the church generated valuable revenue for the manor: spending on its construction was an investment. The new pattern of churches also reflects the expansion of the rural landscape, as many were sited on the edges of the old estates, on land that had been brought into intensive use in the previous century or two, as in the weald of Kent. The churches were built for congregations in rural communities, and often stood near one of the relatively new nucleated villages. We do not always know whether the church or the village came first, and perhaps they were built simultaneously. The actual construction, furnishing and decoration of the church shows the growing division of labour and craft specialization. The mason's craft as a major occupation for hundreds of workers was born in the wave of church-building in this period, as these were the main stone structures. Other crafts found employment too. Quarrying new stone seems to have developed around 1000, earlier churches having often been built from reused masonry. Carpenters made the roofs of the stone churches, and the whole of the structure in the numerous churches which were built entirely of timber. Painters, stone carvers, bell founders, goldsmiths, embroiderers of vestments and other specialists equipped and ornamented the interiors of the buildings. Not just the furnishings and fittings were traded over a distance – the building materials could have been brought from far off, like the stones used for the tower of Sompting church in Sussex, which came from Quarr in the Isle of Wight and Caen in Normandy. Here was a society co-ordinating itself at every level, which at the same time was generating disposable wealth. (Plate 1)

The rural economy in the period 850–1050 was growing in the sense that overall production expanded, and was stimulated by changes in institutions and the market. The aristocracy undoubtedly benefited from these developments, emerging at the end of the period more numerous and wealthy. The peasantry had more mixed experiences, with the freeing of slaves balanced by the extension of the power of the manors, and the opportunity of gains in the market being offset by the increasing burden of rents, services and taxes. One guide to the overall health of agriculture may be the incidence of hunger. The *Anglo-Saxon Chronicle* reported famines in 975–6, 1005, 1039 and 1044. These reflect the problems of variable weather, or even the desire of a partisan cleric to emphasize the depth of crisis in times of political troubles. It is surely significant, however lacking in objectivity the reports may be, that the chronicler chose to indicate the severity of the food shortage in 1039 and 1044 by quoting the very high prices paid for grain – 55d and 60d for a sester (quarter) of wheat. The unconscious assumption that this was the best way to measure shortage reveals the strength of the market's influence, not just on agriculture, but also on people's minds.

CHAPTER TWO

Crisis and new directions, c.850–c.1050

Economic history often deals with slow and even imperceptible changes in population or trade, and dramatic events are the concern of political history. Sudden upheavals were sometimes so profound that they had an impact on economic and social life. The Viking invasions were a cataclysmic episode of this kind, when people from Scandinavia surged into the rest of Europe. We need to consider whether an influx of settlers, who certainly regarded themselves as brave, innovative and resourceful, changed the economy, or whether their main impact was to energize the existing population.

i. *The Viking invasions*

The Viking attacks shocked the people of Britain. The first recorded violent contacts came in the years 789–95, when monasteries were sacked at Lindisfarne off the north-east coast of England, and at Iona in western Scotland. In Dorset a group of intruders killed the king's local official who rode to meet them. They moved swiftly and purposefully by sea and along the major rivers, in well-designed ships propelled by both sails and oars, which could carry between thirty and sixty men. In the ninth and tenth centuries people from Norway took over the northern and western isles (Orkney, Shetland, the Hebrides and the Isle of Man) and parts of the mainland of Scotland such as Caithness. The raids against England, mainly by Danes, built up in scale and intensity through a phase of attacks in the 830s. In 850–1 an army stayed over the winter, and from 865 until 896 (with some lulls) armies ranged over the whole country. At the end of that period of warfare the south of England, thanks to the efforts of the inhabitants of Wessex, co-ordinated by its king Alfred

(871–99), retained its independence, but in the north and to a lesser extent in East Anglia, the land was ruled by Scandinavians. The former English kingdoms of Northumbria, Mercia and East Anglia ceased to exist. York became for a time the capital of a Viking kingdom.

In the tenth century successive kings of Wessex conquered the areas under Scandinavian rule, finally capturing York in 954. Northern and eastern England, the Danelaw, retained distinct customs and culture. In a new phase of attacks beginning in earnest in 991, well-organized forces from Denmark extorted tribute from the English (Danegeld) and ultimately in 1016 the king of Denmark, Cnut, became king of England, to be succeeded by two of his sons. At about this time, between about 975 and 1025, the earls of Orkney were leading raids in the north and collecting booty and tribute. Wales was subjected to sporadic raids in the ninth century, and the south of the country was invaded in 914. In the late tenth century north Wales, especially Anglesey, was vulnerable to incursions from the Scandinavians then dominating the Irish Sea.

This brief recounting of events does not convey the full impact of the Vikings on Britain. They had their effects throughout Europe, and played some part in precipitating the breakdown of the Carolingian empire which had brought together much of western Europe, including the territories now called Germany, the Netherlands, Belgium, France and Italy. In addition, they had a role in the formation of the embryonic Russian state based on Kiev, and they explored the north Atlantic, colonizing the Faeroes, Iceland, Greenland and, briefly, Newfoundland. But nowhere felt the force of Viking activity as intensely as did the British Isles. In the north and west, virtually independent Norse colonies were created, including a state based on Dublin, and the isles around Scotland and the Isle of Man were settled intensively. For a time in the late ninth century England faced the full force of Danish aggression, and around 1000 the attacks and invasion were organized by the Danish state.

We often presume that medieval warfare concerned only the political elites, who fought battles and made peace with little direct influence on the rest of society. But the Viking attacks left no one untouched. Their raids were directed against wealthy establishments, such as churches, but their tendency to descend on a monastery when people were gathered to celebrate a special saint's day, which attracted worshippers and would have been a suitable occasion for a market, shows that they intended to plunder the goods and money of the assembled laity as well as the chalices and ornaments of the monks. Captives were carried off into slavery, so poverty gave no protection. Those who lived in the areas of Scandinavian colonization, whether the Picts of Orkney and Caithness or the northern English, were liable to violent expulsion from their homes, or (more commonly) subjection to new lords. Hoards of coins were hidden through fear of the invaders: eighteen of them have been found in England alone from the period 868–75, and no doubt many more still lie undisturbed in the ground. The fact that they remained to be discovered in modern times demonstrates the real social disruption which prevented the recovery of the money by the person who deposited the hoard. The many English who never encountered a Dane face to face were drawn into the conflict because of the demands that were made by the kings of Wessex for labour and cash to sustain the war effort. Under Alfred, conditions near to 'total war' prevailed in southern England, especially in the programme to build a chain of burh fortifications: these were strong points to provide a protective chain along the south and west coasts, and in the Thames valley. Peasants were drafted in to dig defensive ditches and heap earth, to haul timber to make the ramparts, and to take part in related construction projects such as road- and bridge-building. Once a burh was complete, the local population contributed to its maintenance, and to the manning of the walls. A fifth of the adult male population of Wessex was required to garrison the burh system by *c.*900. A century later, under Aethelred (978–1016), new burh works were under way, this time sometimes with stone walls, but above all a heavy burden of taxation was needed to pay Danegeld. The Danes expected to receive even more cash once they had become the masters in 1016, and heregeld (silver to pay troops) was levied until 1051.

This effort was sustained partly by compulsion, but also by the conviction among the population, fostered by rulers and churchmen, that the Vikings were pagan barbarians who were especially cruel, destructive and ruthless in their pursuit of plunder and captives. This demonization of the enemy went further than in other wars, and was established so effectively that it is still widely believed, hence the familiar modern image of early medieval Scandinavians as helmeted warriors leaping from their ships to spread havoc. Here I have followed common custom in referring to all the migrants as 'Vikings', though the word was used in Scandinavia to identify those who went on expeditions, not the whole people. The hostile perception of the Vikings was a real factor in the political and economic life of the period, and it helped to mobilize resources against them.

Did the Scandinavian invaders themselves make a contribution to the economy? Their activities are commonly divided into piracy, trade, settlement and organized invasion to collect tribute and conquer territory. In practice these different sources of profit were closely connected. In the ninth century the Vikings operated as raiding parties, acquiring goods such as precious metals, ornaments and slaves, either by direct seizure or by demands for tribute. These goods could be exchanged, so the raiders became traders. Scales and weights are found as part of the equipment for the afterlife buried with the dead in Scandinavian graves. These could have been used in the course of trade, to weigh gold and silver or precious commodities, or to share out booty after a raid. They are also found in women's graves, so these transactions were not confined to the warriors. Raiding could lead to settlement, as the attackers observed attractive opportunities for farming. The settlements could serve as bases for further plundering expeditions.

In the rural economy, they played a role as colonists. The *Anglo-Saxon Chronicle* says that the Danish 'great army' shared out the land in northern and eastern England in 876–80. 'Great' armies were not very large in the early middle ages, but this suggests that at least a few thousand men took land, and these numbers were swelled later by wives and children and other colonists, who came to account for a substantial proportion of the population of counties such as Yorkshire and Lincolnshire. The place names of the northern and eastern counties of England, the northern and western isles, and parts of north-east Scotland and Galloway, reflect the presence of many people speaking Scandinavian languages. Names like Grimsby (Lincolnshire) combine a Danish personal name with the Danish word *by* that means a village; and in north-west England names ending in -thwaite indicate a Norwegian presence. Norwegian speakers also named many places in Orkney, such as Grimbist, which derives from the word *bolstadr*, meaning a farm.

Linguistic contact with the native population produced hybrid names like Grimston, which combine a Scandinavian personal name with the Old English word for an estate or village. In all, more than a third of the place names listed in Domesday Book in the East and North Ridings of Yorkshire contain Scandinavian elements. These were applied to places of all kinds, both key administrative centres and minor hamlets on poor land. The Grimsby type of name is especially important, because it implies a Scandinavian presence not just in the place itself, but also in the surrounding district, because it would only be a local population of speakers of Danish who would need to distinguish one 'by' from another. The numerous field names in north Lincolnshire based on Scandinavian words points also to the presence of Danish-speaking villagers. In the eleventh century and later we find that the northern English counties have distinctive institutions, such as subdivisions of the shires which are called wapentakes: this derives from a Scandinavian word for an assembly where those attending indicated their will by brandishing their weapons. The most intense colonization occurred in the northern and western isles, where the language was transformed, and a dialect of Norwegian persisted for centuries. Settlements were established there which modern excavations have shown to consist of long houses of Scandinavian type with benches built along the side walls and a hearth in the centre.

While all of this provides compelling evidence that much land was taken over by Scandinavian immigrants, we need to be cautious about assuming a wholesale transfer of population from Denmark and Norway. The process by which a new language was imposed is difficult to understand, but it would certainly be wrong to assume that everyone who spoke a dialect of Danish in Lincolnshire or Yorkshire in the tenth century had come from Denmark or was descended from a Danish settler. Danish words spread eventually throughout England, into regions where virtually no Danes ever set foot, like the word 'toft' meaning a plot of land on which a house was built. Personal names, for example, do not necessarily prove the ethnic origin of their bearers, as a fashion developed among the native English of giving their children Scandinavian names. Place names like Grimsby do not prove that everyone in that part of north Lincolnshire was of Danish origin, and the Grimston type of name shows that English speech persisted: place names indicating a Scandinavian influence are often mingled with those deriving from the native languages of England and Scotland.

The Scandinavians are unlikely to have played a major role as pioneering developers of new land. They found a countryside already cultivated, and took over existing settlements, or infiltrated local communities. The more powerful took over the centres of the great estates, while their followers acquired the attached hamlets, and hastened the break-up of the estate by making these outer parts independent. This is most likely to have led to a renaming of the more remote sections of an estate in the language of the invaders, hence the tendency of Scandinavian place names to be attached to the less desirable land. Many of the settlers took over not as groups of peasant cultivators but as a conquering elite: a contemporary chronicle says that they put East Anglia 'under the yoke'. They seem not to have imposed new agricultural methods or new ways for extracting money and goods from the peasant population. Types of estate organization in northern England are recorded in the eleventh and twelfth centuries in which sokes – outlying parcels of land – were attached to estate centres. The inhabitants of the outlying places, sokemen, were lightly burdened and were once thought to be the descendants of free Danish soldiers. But these free peasants and the distinctive ways of exploiting the resources of the countryside had been established before the Danes arrived, and were also changed by the process of reconquest by the English in the tenth century. So the Danes may not have introduced their own methods of land management. In general the newcomers, far from stamping their customs on the land that they occupied, accepted the culture of their new country, converting to Christianity within a generation or two. The characteristic styles of decoration developed in Scandinavia are most commonly encountered in England on stone crosses and church monuments, so even when they were bringing their own ideas they worked within a framework of existing institutions.

Even in the northern isles, where the Scandinavian presence seems so dominant, not many new settlements were being founded. Jarlshof in Shetland shows that a ninth-century settler built a farmhouse of distinctively Norwegian type, with stone foundations, benches and a long hearth in the main room, and this then expanded into a hamlet of houses either through subdivision of the land among the succeeding generations or the arrival of more colonists. Birsay and Buckquoy are more typical of Viking colonization in that houses of a Scandinavian type were constructed on top of Pictish buildings. The immigrants seem to have been attracted to existing settlements, from which they continued to farm land already under cultivation. The animal bones found in the deposits of the pre-Viking and Viking periods show that there was no abrupt change in the methods of agriculture. Fish formed part of the diet in both periods, but after the Scandinavian migrations more deep-sea species, notably cod, were consumed, suggesting that the newcomers brought with them techniques for fishing expeditions beyond the shore. The inhabitants' use of ornamental metalwork of 'Celtic' type suggests a period of coexistence and cultural contacts between the natives and immigrants, and they may have intermarried.

If the Vikings' innovations in the countryside were on a limited scale, perhaps they brought new life and vigour into the towns? Their raids were linked closely to exchange, as we have seen. Church plate and ornaments which had previously been hoarded were now put into circulation, and stimulated trade. The Vikings have a reputation for technological innovation, especially in the design of ships. They built not just fast, light ships for warfare and raiding, but also heavier trading vessels able to carry bulky cargo. Helped by colonizing ventures, sea routes were developed around northern Europe, linking Scandinavia with Iceland, the British Isles, the Low Countries, the Rhineland and northern France. Scandinavian products, such as soapstone and amber, were imported into York. Towns grew in areas under Scandinavian rule, at Dublin, York and Rouen, as well as in the homelands at such places as Haithabu, Birka and Kaupang. Eastern routes connected the Baltic through the Russian river systems with Byzantium and the Arab states of the middle east. The

Vikings' network of trade brought distant economies into contact, so that 'kufic' coins, minted in the east with Arabic inscriptions, were owned by residents of northern England and Scotland. A hoard buried at Golds-borough in Yorkshire in the 920s contained coins minted at Samarkand in modern Uzbekistan. The Viking rulers of York minted high-quality silver pennies, and thereby brought northern England into the monetary system prevailing throughout western Europe.

By such activities Scandinavians were contributing to economic growth, but this statement needs some qualifications. Expansion in towns and trade was not confined to the Scandinavian sphere of influence; rather they were participating in a general tendency of the period. For example, a community of Scandinavians lived in eleventh-century London, where churches were dedicated to saints such as St Olaf of Norway and St Clement Danes, and the chief legal assembly was known by a Scandinavian word, the Husting court. But they were just one element among a number of groups of continental merchants who traded in the city. The successful town foundations tended to lie in territories already showing signs of growth in exchange before 850, like York, and in some of the areas of most intensive Scandinavian settlement, in the Northern Isles or the Isle of Man, they may have founded trading centres but no real towns. The Vikings looted and damaged towns; the trading settlements at Southampton (Hamwic) and London (Lundenwic) were abandoned in the ninth century, and were re-established, eventually, on more secure sites. The stimulus to exchange which is said to have flowed from Viking activities may not always have worked very rapidly. In the 'five boroughs' of the Danelaw, at Derby, Leicester, Lincoln, Nottingham and Stamford, much of the urban growth may have come in the late tenth century, after they had come under English rule. The number of objects of 'Viking' character found at York, or goods which were imported from Scandinavia, are limited in quantity. The construction of the buildings was not based entirely on Scandinavian types. No doubt the Viking rulers of the city gave the impetus for the growth of new towns, but most of the people who moved in to work as artisans and traders were likely to have been of local origin.

The Scandinavian invaders cannot be dismissed as barbarians but their background ensured that they could influence, but not transform, the economy. Scandinavia had no experience of Roman rule, and had escaped inclusion in the Carolingian empire. Centralized monarchies were developing during the Viking age, and were assisted by the conversion to Christianity in the tenth and eleventh centuries. But the Scandinavians lacked the state institutions, social hierarchy and literacy which had evolved in the English kingdoms between c.600 and 850. They were receptive to influence from the cultures and economies which they encountered. In Yorkshire, they joined in the processes of urbanization and developing the use of money. When they operated in less complex economies, they adopted different attitudes towards acquiring and exchanging wealth. This is apparent from the silver hoards deposited in Scotland between about 940 and 1065, which contain 'hack silver' (pieces of metal resulting from cutting up jewellery and other objects), ingots, coins and arm rings or ring money which were made in standard weights. Clearly these objects had been used in exchange because they had often been pricked or nicked with a knife point to ensure that they were made of pure silver. Coins are found with these marks also, showing that they were accepted for their silver content, not at face value. The population had apparently not become accustomed to the use of money, but weights of precious metals were being bartered. People acquired quantities of bullion and stored it as proof of their status, or used it in the exchange of gifts rather than in commercial transactions, or even handed it over in payments to compensate the relatives of someone killed in a feud. Similarly in the countryside the Vikings adopted the farming methods and settlement patterns which already existed. Economic activity was unlikely to be determined by ethnic make-up or national character. Enterprise and invention arose, as at other times and places, from a combination of circumstances, pressures and incentives. (Plate 2)

ii. *The growth of the state*

Important economic changes followed the Viking incursions. The economy before the Viking age was not very productive or sophisticated. The great estates were designed to gather foodstuffs for consumption by the itinerant households of kings, nobles and bishops, or to send to monasteries. The lords were not exploiting their rural resources very intensively, judging from the fixed quotas of produce, in rather modest quantities, which they expected to receive from each estate. Peasants did not enjoy any great plenty, and their tendency to move their dwellings suggests an unsettled and shifting agricultural system. Slaves did much of the agricultural work, and may not have achieved high levels of productivity. Trade was conducted from a few towns, which were very unevenly distributed. The imported goods were aimed at a luxury market, the small scale of which can be judged from the normal method of unloading ships by hauling them on to beaches. Manufactures were produced by itinerant craftsmen, or by non-specialists. The only potters who made high-quality ware on a large scale seem to have been those working in Ipswich, and their products had a restricted distribution, mainly in East Anglia.

The Vikings shook society, and one indirect contribution that they made to economic growth was to unify and animate the machinery of the state. The Vikings destroyed weaker states, and galvanized others into effective action. They contributed to the unification of the Scottish kingdom by weakening Pictish rule in the east of the country, and by putting pressure on the Scots in the west, which led to the king of the Scots, Kenneth Macalpine, taking over the territory ruled by the Picts in 843. Scandinavian incursions did not pose such a major threat to the rulers of Wales, but nonetheless a prince who vigorously opposed the invaders, Hywel Dda (922–50), enjoyed greater authority than any of his predecessors.

In England, the kings of Mercia in the eighth century, and especially Offa (757–96), had increased state power to build a system of fortifications on the Welsh border (Offa's Dyke), and to defend centres such as Hereford, Tamworth and Winchcombe. They mobilized manpower by insisting that landowners should contribute to military service, and to the building of fortifications and bridges. Similar demands were made on a much larger scale by Alfred and his tenth-century successors as rulers of Wessex and then England. A chain of forts was built around Wessex, and then extended into the midlands, at such places as Bedford, Buckingham, Warwick and Worcester. With the conquest of Danish territory the system was pushed further north, and Leicester, Lincoln and York were taken under English royal control. Forts were also built along the Welsh border, as far west as Rhuddlan.

Before this surge of burh-building, government was based on the king's *tuns*, which were estate centres, usually provided with a residence, where food rents and dues could be collected. A burh was often sited at or near a king's *tun*, but was larger and more strongly fortified, enclosing an area of between 40 and 300 acres, enough space for an army to be based and to provide shelter for the population of the district. A burh was originally conceived as a military strong point, to block off a river or road route, such as the fort which occupied an island in the Thames at Sashes near Cookham in Berkshire. A number of these strategic defences, including Sashes, fell into disuse once the Viking emergency had passed. But many of the forts in the tenth century became formidable centres of royal authority, and behind the security of their ramparts, sited on main roads and river crossings, officials (the king's reeves) could hold courts, enforce law and order, levy troops, supervise the minting of coins and collect taxes. The burh became the basis of a new system of local government, most readily apparent in the twenty shires north of the Thames, each of which took its name from a burh at its centre – Nottinghamshire from Nottingham, Herefordshire from Hereford, and so on. The shires were not entirely new, because they were often formed from putting together many old administrative districts. Henceforth the kingdom of England would be a centralized state, because the burh network gave the king authority in every part of his kingdom. Through the officials in the shires – the ealdormen and shire reeves – the king had a direct line of communication with the provinces. The shire courts, run by the king's representative, dealt with a wide range of business: administrative, military and financial. With the gradual development of written documents in government, the king could send a brief letter of instruction authenticated with his seal, a writ, to the shire authorities to ensure that his will was done. A further tier of government below the shires, hundreds in the south, wapentakes in the former Danish territories, ensured that royal government functioned in every locality. The hundred courts met regularly, settled disputes and enforced law and order, being charged with catching thieves and recovering stolen goods. Each household and community was responsible for the good behaviour of its members, and the smallest unit of government of all, the village, was represented by its reeve and leading men at the hundred court.

The state planned for resources to be assessed and obligations apportioned in a systematic fashion. Every piece of land had for centuries been assigned a hidage – the typical village would be rated at five hides. Hides had ceased to mean 'family land' but had come to be a unit of assessment which bore some relationship to the resources available. Assessments were built up into wonderfully elaborate statistical edifices, so that a model shire like Worcestershire (recorded in the eleventh century) consisted of twelve hundreds each of 100 hides, making a round total of 1,200. If troops were levied at one man for a hide to defend the burh of Worcester, 1,200 would be assembled. If taxes (geld) were levied at 2s to the hide, the king could expect to receive 2,400s. The larger and richer shires in the south owed much more – Hampshire, Wiltshire, Berkshire and Surrey together had originally consisted of 120 hundreds, and perhaps therefore 12,000 hides. The hides went back to very early times, but the system of assessment could be adapted to new needs. When a navy was needed to repel the Danish attacks at the end of the tenth century, hundreds were grouped in threes, and each of the resulting 'shipsokes' of 300 hides was expected to find a crew of sixty men at a rate of one man for each five hides.

The hierarchy of administrative units at the king's command, allowing rational deployment of money and manpower through universal fiscal assessments, resembled in many ways – and indeed was modelled on – the arrangements within the continental Carolingian empire that reached its high point a century before the reign of Alfred. Like the Carolingians, kings of Wessex and England, notably Alfred and Edgar (957–75), as well as developing their practical powers, allied themselves with churchmen. Alfred had a programme for education, to improve the quality of the clergy and to spread literacy among the lay aristocracy. Edgar encouraged the foundation of new monasteries and the reform of existing communities of clergy. Clerics aided government through their literacy, but more importantly for the rulers they gave secular government a moral basis, and held out an ideal of a harmonious society that could develop under Christian royal rule. Bishops, as in the Carolingian system, supported the state as advisers at court and provincial governors. The Carolingian institutions, for all of the official propaganda, had many flaws, and perhaps the same is true of the apparently logical and efficient English royal government.

One gap in the administrative symmetry is apparent in the north, where the large and clumsy shires of Lincoln and York were clearly not formed according to the midland model, and in the far north shires were not created until after the Norman Conquest. The state was no bureaucracy. The king's household probably contained a professional writing office, a chancery, on the lines of continental practice. However, its main task was to produce charters and writs, and there is little evidence that the state kept any quantity of written administrative documents. Geld rolls, recording tax liability, were evidently held in the eleventh century in an archive at Winchester. Law codes and special documents, like the 'burghal hidage' detailing the arrangements for defence in c.900, were compiled occasionally. But the main operations of the state depended on oral instructions, custom and memory. The absence of detailed evidence for the day-to-day running of government means that we do not know if it worked as intended. A group of 'agents of the state' have been identified – minor aristocrats and small landowners who delivered messages, collected money and carried out other government tasks. But even this group would have been hard pressed to conduct all of the work required. In the end, the whole machine depended on the co-operation of subjects, and no doubt the rulers were able to call on their loyalty, persuading them that their self-interest coincided with that of the central government. Everyone with property wished to maintain order, and those who helped the state would find that some of its authority rubbed off on them. Still, we cannot avoid some scepticism about the efficiency of government. Why, for example, was the legislation of the period so concerned with theft and dishonesty, unless it was a major problem that the hundred courts were unable to control?

Finally, the main problem that had faced the Carolingian empire was the necessity for the rulers to delegate power to the local nobility, who at a later stage could become independent rulers. While the centralized monarchy was developing in England, political power on the continent was coming under the control of counts, dukes and castellans whose predecessors had been the 'faithful men' of the Carolingian dynasty. This has become known to historians as the 'feudal revolution'. Such an extreme devolution was prevented in England by the king's continued grip on the shires. The landholdings of the great magnates were usually widely scattered, so unlike their continental contemporaries they lacked a local power base. There was still a degree of delegation of authority, which meant that royal rule could be challenged and undermined by members of the nobility. At the end of Edgar's reign a group reacted against the growing influence of monks, so that monasteries lost land and new foundations ceased for a time. In 1007–17 a great magnate, Eadric Streona, was said to rule like a 'sub-king' in the midlands, and from 1016 to 1066 the earls, bearing a newly created title, were prone to plots and rebellions. The great landowners were able to count on the support of numerous followers among the lesser aristocracy, who formed part of their households, or who held land from them on leasehold or some other dependent tenure, or who were 'commended' to them in a bond which obliged them to provide service. The English magnates did not enjoy the privileges of private jurisdiction which allowed counts and dukes across the Channel to wield a great range of royal rights, from capital punishment to the minting of coins. The English were granted minor legal powers, known as 'sake and soke', though we do not know what this meant precisely in terms of their treatment of the tenants on their estates. An apparent disadvantage of the English aristocracy was their lack of private castles, as the major fortifications, the burh system, were retained firmly in the hands of the king. The aristocracy, however, built some defences around their houses so the idea of a private fortress was not entirely absent from England (see pp. 75–6 and 80). Nor was the strong English state immune to persuasion and lobbying in the interests of individual landowners. The universal hidage assessments for judging taxable wealth could be manipulated through patronage, resulting in reductions in hidage for favoured subjects. No doubt the courts of hundred and shire were also strongly influenced by the local lords.

The English and continental aristocracies inhabited the same world of extensive privileges and private power. We can conclude that the English state that had been formed out of the turmoil of the Danish invasions was a very incomplete organization, in which kings and aristocrats had to work together. But the kings could do more than any of their European contemporaries, and in particular commanded more effective machinery for tax collection than any polity in Europe since the decline of the Roman empire.

The growth of the English state contributed to economic change by providing a plentiful and reliable coinage. Kings kept close control over the currency, much of which was minted in burhs. In the late eighth century the penny had been produced for the first time, and this was to be the main type of coin minted and circulated in England throughout the middle ages. Silver of a high degree of purity (that is with 8 per cent or less of base metal alloyed with the silver) was beaten into flat sheets and out of these were stamped discs of the right size, 18–20 millimetres in diameter. Each disc was placed on an iron die, on which the design of one face of the coin had been cut in reverse. The moneyer held a punch bearing the design of the other face of the coin on top of the disc of silver. A sharp blow with a hammer would impress the relatively soft metal of the disc with the design on both faces simultaneously, and a coin would result. The process was repeated thousands of times, depending on the supply of silver.

Minting practice indicates the kings' aims in managing the currency, which are especially clear after Edgar's reforms of 973. Anxious that the coins should be widely distributed, the kings set up mints all over the kingdom. By the end of the tenth century seventy mints had been established, not just in the obvious centres of population and trade such as London and Canterbury, but also in small places such as Bruton in Somerset and Horncastle in Lincolnshire. No one could claim that they could not pay their taxes because coins were unobtainable, as almost everyone lived within 15 miles of a mint. Kings ensured that only their coins were available by insisting that any foreign currency that entered the country was handed in for minting. Indeed, only new money was in circulation, because every few years (not more than six) the pennies were called in and recoined, which was mainly for the king's profit, as he gained revenue from each recoinage. This involved the trouble of making large numbers of new dies at frequent intervals, but had the advantage of reassuring the users because all of the coins had a standard appearance. Coins were maintained at a good weight (around 1.4 grams on average) and were made from pure metal. Moneyers who cheated were threatened with severe punishments. The reverse face of the coins recorded the name of the moneyer and the place where the coin was minted, so the producer of a bad coin could be immediately identified. The weight and purity of pennies was reduced in the stress of political upheaval and Danegeld payments at the end of the tenth and in the early eleventh centuries, but even this relaxation of high standards was co-ordinated from the centre. The coins carried messages – the king's head and name made clear whose authority lay behind the issues, and the representation of the head often mirrored Roman coins, in a delib-erate bid to associate the monarchy with imperial grandeur. Religious images on coins such as the 'hand of providence' symbolized the divine origin of royal power.

The kings' efforts in controlling the issue of coins seem to have worked. Good-quality coins had beneficial economic effects: buying and selling could be conducted in confidence if both parties to the transac-tion knew that the money could be trusted. This went with a number of other measures, such as the regulation of markets, insistence on the pres-ence of witnesses when a sale was agreed, and the punishment of thieves and frauds. Concerned to maintain law and order, kings recognized that markets were potentially dangerous sources of quarrels, and special measures had to be taken to prevent disputes. Kings also appreciated the contribution of merchants, who brought luxury goods for royal con-sumption, but also performed a vital task in spreading the cash in which taxes would be paid. Realizing their vulnerability when travelling with valuable goods, the kings made a special point of taking them under their protection. Each burh, though built mainly for military purposes, pro-vided shelter for a market. Bridges were often associated with them, partly because the burh often stood at a river crossing, and partly because bridges had a military function in blocking passage up and down nav-igable rivers. The bridge-building and rebuilding of the decades around 900 helped the flow of peacetime traffic once the Viking threat had receded. We might wonder also if the various naval initiatives from Alfred onwards had some impact on sea transport, perhaps increasing the number of vessels available in peacetime, or spreading shipbuilding and sailing skills. In short, then, royal policies which were mainly directed to military, political and fiscal ends smoothed the path for commercial growth. A modern economist looking at the period sees two forces at work. The first was 'emergency conversion' in the periods of threat from the invaders, which brought hoarded precious metals into circulation. The levying of taxes and mobilization of resources by rulers increased economic activity and stimulated exchange in general. The other development was the longer-term reduction in 'transaction costs', as improvements in the network of markets, availability of money and reduction of risks taken by purchasers all encouraged people to trade.

Calculations of the volume and circulation of currency confirm that this was a period of expansion in the economy. The most striking figures for the amounts of money in circulation are the *Anglo-Saxon Chronicle*'s statements that £137,000 was paid in Danegeld between 991 and 1012, and a further £82,500 after the Danish victory in 1018. These seem incredible sums when we remember that £5 was the annual income of a lesser aristocrat, and that cattle cost 24–30d each. Chronicles are notorious for overestimating figures. Perhaps there was not enough money in England to send so much out of the country? Some of the payments, however, may have been spent by Danes in England, and so came back into the economy. Undoubtedly a great number of silver pennies were paid in Danegeld and were taken overseas, as reflected in the 30,000 English coins of the late tenth and early eleventh centuries discovered mostly in hoards in modern times in Sweden. Estimating from the number of dies used by moneyers, and the quantity of coins produced by each die, 20 million pennies could have been minted in six years, 979–85, worth £83,000. The modern discovery of coins as single finds provides evidence for their actual circulation. More than 150 have been found in England dating from the reigns of Aethelred (978–1016) and Cnut (1016–35), an impressive figure when compared with earlier periods. These were lost in towns and villages, showing that they were really used. Many have signs of wear caused by being 'passed from hand to hand on a daily basis' (D. M. Metcalf) and they reflect the real economy of buying and selling. Although the rulers of Scotland and Wales did not mint their own coins, pennies minted in England circulated in limited numbers in those countries, and made some contribution to the growth of exchange.

Concentrating on a sequence of political events with economic consequences may give the false impression that politics determined the history of the economy, or even that economic expansion was part of a master plan. It has been said by R. Hodges that this period shows that 'great men . . . alter their cultural circumstances to their own ends'. But a more plausible interpretation is that rulers like Charlemagne and Alfred pursued military, political, religious and fiscal objectives, and usually in the short term; any economic effects resulted from the backwash of the main flow of policy. The writings of the kings and their advisers make little reference to economic matters. At least as important as the policies of rulers were the quiet actions by millions of their subjects, which in combination, reacting to a range of circumstances, changed patterns of production and exchange. The significance of broad social and economic movements can be seen by comparing developments in Britain and on the continent. As we have seen, the fragmentation of the Carolingian empire coincides with the centralization of the English state, yet both sides of the Channel experienced some similar economic tendencies, such as the growth in towns and trade.

iii. *The origins of towns*

An examination of urban origins and growth should help to define the respective roles in promoting economic change of the state (or even great men) and the underlying shifts in the economy. The term 'town' needs definition. In the early middle ages there were many settlements which had some administrative or religious function, such as king's tuns, burhs, cathedrals or minster churches (which housed a group of clergy to serve a district). These centres must be carefully distinguished from towns. The usual definition of a town or urban settlement is that it should have a permanent concentration of population, some hundreds at least, who made their living from a variety of non-agricultural occupations. These people might include officials and clergy, but usually in order for a large population to find employment the inhabitants would be occupied in trades and crafts. A town would also have a range of institutions, a complex social structure, and would be closely involved in the economic and cultural life of a rural hinterland. But occupational diversity was its most distinctive hallmark. Very often the town grew in or around a fortress or church (the 'pre-urban nucleus') and our task, made difficult by the small quantity of evidence, is to determine when, how and why the place acquired a commercial and manufacturing community.

Some features of early English towns suggest that they were conceived as part of the royal policy of fortress-building. The ideal site for a burh was on a route that was used for the movement of armies, but trade goods were also carried on main roads. Some of these towns were provided with a street plan as well as walls. The best examples are found in Wessex, such as Wallingford and Wareham. At Winchester the Roman walls were refurbished by Alfred to create a burh, and soon after, by about 900, a rectilinear pattern of cobbled streets was laid out. A series of side streets at regular intervals joined the long High Street to a road that ran inside the circuit of the walls. The arrangement suited the defence of the burh, allowing troops rapid access to any part of the walls that was under attack. The layout of streets defined a series of rectangular blocks of land that could be allocated to various Wessex landowners, and the blocks in turn were subdivided into small plots suitable for the houses, outhouses and workshops of traders and artisans. During the tenth century the fortified space filled up and became a thriving city (Map 5a).

The transition from fortress to town in dozens of places was fostered by the siting of mints, and by legislation that required the sale of valuable goods to be conducted in a burh or 'port' (trading centre, often also a burh) before witnesses. Some of the town's inhabitants were recruited by kings and aristocrats: the royal officials and moneyers, the clergy serving new or reformed monasteries, and craftsmen who were settled in the town to serve their lords' needs, and who eventually made goods for general sale. The kings defined a rural territory for each burh, from which defenders of the walls were levied, or which were administered from the burh, and when trade developed, this piece of countryside would form the commercial hinterland of the town. Sometimes a burh had no hope of becoming a town because it was sited in an inaccessible place. Pilton was founded on a hilltop to defend the north Devon coast, but a town developed on lower ground nearby, at Barnstaple. The creation of a fortress was not always a single act: at Worcester there were two phases of burh foundation, one in the 890s and another about a century later, so the authorities seem to have been responding to the growth of the settlement by giving it additional secure space. On the basis of such evidence it is argued that Alfred and his successors intended that the forts they founded would become towns, and ensured that this happened by their initial planning and subsequent encouragement.

The complexity of the history of different towns does not support the idea that kings alone founded them. A few were 'greenfield sites' where the story began with the building of the fortifications, so it is fairly easy to show the connection between the burh and the town. In many cases the town had begun to grow around the 'pre-urban nucleus' that had existed before the late ninth century, and continued within the burh fortifications, which served only as a secondary focus for urban development. In Oxford, crafts like linen-weaving and shoemaking that would be expected in a town were being practised in a settlement near the monastery of St Frideswide (a pre-urban nucleus) in *c.*750–850, well before the burh was fortified. If the burh marks only an intermediate stage in urban development, the royal founders of these fortifications seem less important as initiators of towns.

Most towns do not conform to the Winchester model, in that they lack a single, regular street plan. Instead they were subject to piecemeal development. In the towns of the east and north of England the lines of some streets wandered like country lanes, and did not form a grid, but

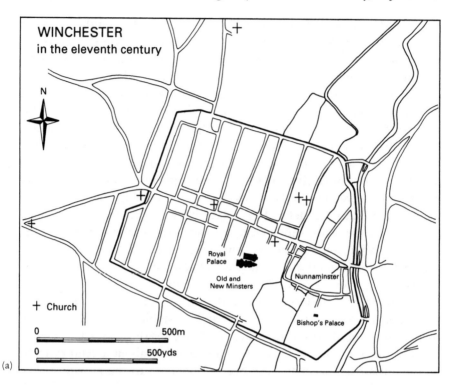

Maps 5a and b. Town plans of Winchester and Northampton. The modern streets of these towns developed in the period 870–1000. Winchester's regular layout contrasts with Northampton's more piecemeal and less coordinated plan.

Sources: D. M. Wilson (ed.), *The Archaeology of Anglo-Saxon England* (Cambridge, 1981); E. Jones, J. Laughton and P. Clark, *Northampton in the Late Middle Ages* (Leicester, 2000).

converged on points within the town. Northampton, Lincoln and York each have this type of 'organic' plan (Map 5b). In both Lincoln and Norwich the town seems not to have been conceived as a single entity, as at Winchester or Wallingford, but was created from the growing together of a number of once separate centres of settlement. These towns were not necessarily unplanned, but were formed out of a series of small-scale planning ventures. When there was a plan, it did not always work: Cricklade, a burh site with considerable potential, failed to attract settlers, and the extensive walled area never filled up with townspeople.

Where the town was a success, the process of urbanization seems to have been a slow one. In London, taken over by Alfred and fortified in the 880s, many of the subsequent developments within the walls, and the building of wharfs along the Thames waterfront, were delayed until the late tenth and eleventh centuries. The stimulus provided by those in authority apparently met with a delayed reaction.

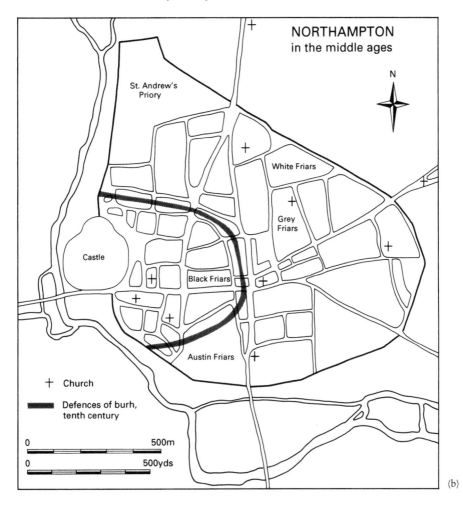

NORTHAMPTON
in the middle ages

St. Andrew's
Priory

White Friars

Grey
Friars

Castle

Black Friars

Austin Friars

+ Church

▬▬ Defences of burh,
tenth century

0   500m

0   500yds

(b)

The inhabitants of towns who are recorded in documents tend to be
the elite of officials, aristocrats and clergy. The way in which they
contributed to the filling up of the urban space can be reconstructed at
Worcester, where initially the burh was laid out in large blocks of land,
called *hagae* (literally, enclosures) on which houses were built. Pieces of
property in the town were attached to estates of land in the surrounding
countryside and granted to thegns, clergy and other landowners. They
no doubt sold produce and bought goods from their houses, but the
initial blocks of land were larger than was necessary for this purpose,
and they split them up and rented them to incomers who intended to
trade and practise crafts. The entry of such obscure people into the town

can scarcely have been planned and co-ordinated by higher authorities: it arose from the migration of people seeking opportunities in the urban economy. Kings undoubtedly arranged for moneyers (who also worked as goldsmiths) to settle in towns, and magnates like Bishop Oswald of Worcester (962–92) granted land in the city to two goldsmiths, Wulfhelm and Aethelmaer, who worked on the ornamentation of his church. Most townspeople were not prestigious enough to attract such patronage. No aristocrat arranged for the arrival on the streets of the one-eyed garlic seller who was the subject of a riddle written at this time:

> A creature came where many men . . . were sitting . . . ; it had one eye, two ears and two feet, twelve hundred heads . . . Say what is my name.

Yet the pursuit of many such mundane occupations was as vital a part of the urban economy as the better-rewarded work of the goldsmith. Towns began from a combination of official initiatives and the response of migrants who saw a chance to make a living. If a burh lacked commercial advantages, it remained a fortified place and no more.

While the role of the state in town origins is a matter of debate, we can all agree that this was an important period of urbanization. Towns achieved a considerable size. At the end of this phase of urban growth, Domesday Book gives a very incomplete picture of towns, but still allows us to glimpse their distribution and size either in 1066 or 1086 or at both dates. A conservative estimate based on its statistics is that England had more than 100 towns, of which at least seventeen contained 2,000 or more inhabitants. London, York and Winchester each probably had a population of 10,000 or more (in the case of York in 1066, but not twenty years later) (see Map 6 below, p. 63). If all of the urban figures are added together, and compared with the national total for peasants, slaves and other country dwellers, we arrive at the conclusion that near to 10 per cent of the English population lived in towns in 1066–86. The towns that existed before 850 could be quite large, notably the predecessors of London and Southampton, but much of the country lacked such centres, and a reasonable guess would be that less than 2 per cent of the population lived in towns.

The main period of town growth, with perhaps a fourfold increase in the proportion of town dwellers, lay in the years 850–1066. In towns that were flourishing in the tenth and eleventh centuries where there have been extensive excavations, and systematic records have been made of casual finds of pottery, coins and other evidence of occupation, the area settled at this time was large – 200 acres in Norwich, and at Cambridge, York and Winchester the built-up area seems similar to that

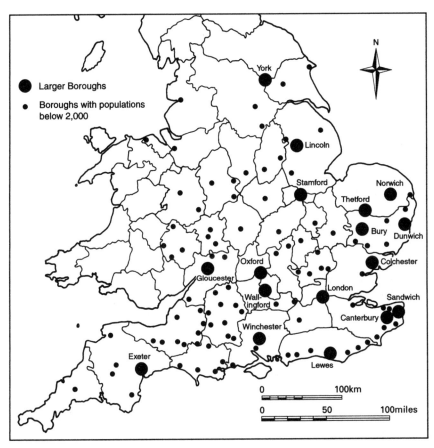

Map 6. Boroughs in Domesday Book (1086). Those boroughs with populations likely to have exceeded 2,000 are named. The larger towns were concentrated in southern and especially eastern regions.

Sources: R. A. Dodgshon and R. A. Butlin (eds), *An Historical Geography of England and Wales* (1990); D. Palliser (ed.), *The Cambridge Urban History of Britain*, vol. 1 (Cambridge, 2000).

of the thirteenth century. Towns like Worcester were spilling outside their walls into suburbs, and by the eleventh century communities of cottagers had formed outside some towns, who were making their living from working in the town or selling garden produce in the market.

Not only were the towns large, but space within them was arranged in distinctive patterns. Land was divided into long narrow plots, with houses towards the street. Such was the demand for building room in the centre of York, along Coppergate, that the width of the plots was only 18 feet. A more open plan prevailed in Thetford, but in general the

density of housing was increasing in the larger towns. One clue comes
from the destruction of buildings when castles were built in towns soon
after the Norman Conquest. At Shrewsbury, for example, fifty-one
houses or plots for houses were lost to the castle, implying perhaps ten
houses to the acre. The concentration of people into a limited space
caused a number of familiar environmental problems. Rubbish disposal
on the plot led to the accumulation of middens and the digging of
pits for cess and other household waste. At Durham some attempt was
made to contain the smell by shovelling layers of sand periodically over
a midden. But the inhabitants of York had a remarkable tolerance of
rotting organic material, which sometimes lay scattered over the floors
of houses, together with the scavenging insects that the rubbish attracted.
Mice, rats, jackdaws and ravens moved in to take advantage of urban
waste. Fish bones recovered at York show the disappearance of shad
and grayling during the tenth and eleventh centuries. These freshwater
species were especially sensitive to the pollution of rivers, so it seems
that they were driven from the Ouse by the effluent of York. The
close-packed wooden houses were vulnerable to fires, which are recorded
both in chronicles and in excavation. No fewer than six phases of
occupation on the early medieval site at Flaxengate in Lincoln ended in
fires.

The large size and high density of urban populations could only
be sustained by a lively economy. The full variety of non-agricultural
occupations has only become apparent from the archaeological research,
especially where waterlogged soil has preserved organic materials.
Excavation at such towns as Lincoln, London, Stamford and York has
produced plentiful evidence for crafts, not just the finished objects themselves, but tools and pottery kilns, raw materials and the residue from
the process of manufacture, such as pieces of leather and bone discarded
by the artisans, or broken crucibles containing traces of metal. The range
of activities includes food-processing and sale, for example by butchers
who have left bones bearing the marks of their work. Woodworking
involved the carpenters who built houses and applied their skills to furnishings and boats, and the turners who made wooden cups and bowls
on lathes. Smiths forged a variety of tools, locks and weapons, and
workers in copper alloys and precious metals cast or hammered ornaments, jewellery and coins. Beads were made from glass, jet and amber,
and stone was carved for gravestones. Leather was processed by tanners,
and cut and stitched, probably by different craftsmen, into shoes, scabbards and belts. Furs were cured for use as clothing. Wool, flax and hemp
were spun, woven into cloth and dyed, and then made into garments.
Fine embroidery work satisfied a specialized luxury demand. Potters

made cooking pots, pitchers and oil lamps, while bone-carving resulted in the manufacture of elaborate combs, as well as simpler pins and toggles, and ice-skates.

The remarkable feature of these craft activities is not just their number, but the evidence they provide for the relocation of industry in towns, and the economic consequences of that shift. Pottery before *c.*850 was manufactured largely in the countryside, on a small scale, the clay being shaped by hand and the resulting vessels fired rather unevenly. In the late ninth and tenth centuries we find pottery being produced on a large scale in Stamford, Thetford and Norwich, and in significant quantities at Lincoln, Northampton, Torksey and York. In the west, where pottery-making had scarcely existed previously, it began at such centres as Chester and Stafford. Stamford ware catches our attention among these new urban products: one type involved the striking innovation of applying a yellow or pale green glaze to a hard cream or pink fabric. The technique may have been invented in the Lincolnshire town, but is more likely to have been introduced by a migrant from Huy, now in Belgium. The wares produced in other towns, and indeed the ordinary cooking pots from Stamford, were unglazed, but they were turned on a potter's wheel and fired in efficient kilns. Towns were not the obvious place to make pots – the fuel had to be carried in from the country, and the kilns posed a fire hazard. On the other hand, there was plenty of labour, and the pots were easily marketed and distributed in the town's hinterland and further afield. Clothmakers also seem to have moved into towns. Archaeological finds of clay weights from vertical looms dating from before the tenth century show that much weaving went on in rural settlements, at Goltho in Lincolnshire in a large shed beside the lord's house. By the eleventh and twelfth centuries weavers appear in numbers in towns, and the vertical loom gave way to the horizontal treadle loom. Similar concentration of crafts in towns probably occurred in the case of metalworkers, and the larger urban communities gave employment to specialists serving the food market, such as bakers and fishmongers.

The move from country to town had implications for the organization and productivity of the industries. The concentration of artisans practising different crafts in close proximity gave them the opportunity to work together. Knife blades could be forged, fitted with bone or wooden handles, and provided with scabbards by specialists working side by side. Although all larger towns supported a variety of crafts, a degree of specialization, like large-scale iron-working in Northampton and Stamford, may have increased the efficiency of production. The whole process of migration into new towns and the adoption of new styles of working was clearly conducive to technical innovation. Artisans sometimes adopted methods from abroad, as in the case of glazed pottery, or ideas spread from one town to another, leading to the manufacture of pottery in Norwich and Ipswich that imitated wares originally made at Thetford. If workers turned out a standardized product, which was especially the case for pottery, their productivity would be raised. Located near markets, they could be sure that the wares were available to the largest possible number of customers, both within the town itself and in its hinterland, and they were well placed to respond to changes in demand. In short the newly urbanized industries could make new and better products, in greater quantities, more efficiently and more cheaply; and these were more readily saleable.

Long-distance trade, especially international commerce in high-value goods, was the most prestigious and profitable part of the urban economy. It was alleged by an early eleventh-century writer that a merchant who travelled three times overseas at his own expense was eligible for the status of thegn (see p. 73). English merchants went to northern Italy, presumably in pursuit of spices and silks, and paid tolls at Pavia. Merchants from Germany, Flanders and northern France are recorded in the port of London in the early eleventh century, bringing cloth, wine, fish and timber. Chester traded with Wales and Ireland, and handled such goods as furs. Imports in eastern towns included millstones and pottery (the high-quality Pingsdorf ware) from the Rhineland, soapstone, amber and walrus ivory from Scandinavia, silk from the Mediterranean, and figs, also from the south. Exports included cloth, the prestigious embroidered garments for which England was famous, tin, lead and agricultural produce, notably cheese and wool.

Trade, particularly in luxury goods, had been going on for centuries, but urbanization was associated with changes in the size and character of cargoes. Although no statistics for the volume of trade are known, it is worth mentioning the development of ships able to carry bulky goods, which included wider, slower, heavier versions of the famous Viking ships, and another type of merchant vessel, the hulk. At London, new techniques of handling cargoes are evident in c.1000, when a jetty was built at the place later called New Fresh Wharf, which would have allowed ships to be unloaded. A shift in the character of trade may also have occurred at this time, because if the imports and exports included herrings, planks, wool and other high-volume and relatively cheap goods, this must point to international trade aimed at a wide market.

Most urban trade, and the basis of the growth of towns at this time, involved carrying quite mundane goods over short distances. Organic deposits from urban excavations show how much was brought into the towns from the surrounding countryside – not just grain and animals to keep the townspeople fed, but also fruits and nuts, together with hay for animal feed, and straw and bracken for their litter. Wood and turf were needed for fuel, and flax, hemp, wool, dye-plants, timber, antler and skins as raw materials. The townspeople depended on the flow of trade from the country, and in turn they had their impact on the rural economy. Land near the town would be turned into garden plots and hemp fields, and over a much larger area husbandry would be influenced by urban demand. Sheep, for example, would be sent to the towns' butchers not as lambs, but when they had yielded an annual fleece for three or four years to help to satisfy the demand from the cloth industry. The trade in urban manufactures is best traced from the distribution of pottery such as Stamford and Thetford ware. Stamford ware is found on numerous rural sites in the town's region, concentrated within a radius of 15 miles. It is also found at York and Northampton, reflecting the traffic between towns at greater distance. Much of this trade was carried by the roads which radiated from every town, some of them of Roman or prehistoric origin, but also new routes: Stamford was served by major north–south roads diverted from the course of the Roman road, Ermine Street. Cheap and easy communications were provided by navigable rivers such as the Thames, along which Londoners were supplied with pottery (shelly ware) made in Oxfordshire. The pottery was probably carried in boats, with grain and fuel as the main cargo. The river was judged so important that at one point south of Oxford a new channel was dug in 1052–66 to aid navigation. The sea brought both vessels from the continent and coastal traffic. Small ports and landing places developed, for example along the coasts of Sussex and Kent, and Hastings from small beginnings grew into a town.

Urbanization transformed the lives of thousands of migrants who worked in trade and crafts. The countryside exchanged agricultural produce for traded and manufactured goods from the urban markets. Did town growth have some more profound effect on the workings and outlook of society? Continental historians used to believe that the merchants and artisans of the towns were separated by a great gulf from the land-based, aristocracy-dominated feudal world. The townspeople were thought to have originated in the marginal elements of society and to have acquired their capital for trade by accumulating small profits. Town dwellers were said to be hostile to the traditional aristocracy. But in fact many leading townspeople were descended from officials and lesser nobility, and they launched their trading careers on the basis of landed wealth. In English towns the aristocracy had a key role, owning houses attached to rural estates, and on occasions they lived in the town. At

Thetford, a large hall appropriate to a thegn was built in the town not far from potters' workshops. A number of guilds for thegns and cnihts provided occasions in towns for convivial assemblies of the local landowners. Great lords encouraged towns, like the monastery of Bury St Edmunds, around which 310 households (*c.*1,500 people) had gathered by 1066. The upper classes in general were not distrustful of towns, but valued them for practical reasons as sources of rent and traded goods. No doubt they appreciated that they had cities which resembled in some ways those on the continent.

The lower classes in the towns were recruited from peasants who had migrated, or whose villages had been absorbed into the town's economy as it expanded, like Stepney in London or Holywell on the edge of Oxford. Many towns were provided with some agricultural land – Colchester in the late eleventh century had an average of 8 acres per household, and ploughs worked extensive fields outside Cambridge, Derby and many others. Few towns had enough land to feed the population, and the inhabitants still had to gain much of their living from trade and crafts: even at Colchester less than half of the households had any land. The towns' agricultural interests, like the investment in urban land by the aristocracy, show that they were not cut off from rural society.

Townspeople developed a distinctive culture and style of life. They built houses appropriate to their restricted living space. In York they lay end-on to the street, and were inevitably quite small – those at Coppergate measured 14 feet wide and *c.*25 feet long. In other towns a type of urban house was built with a sunken floor, perhaps serving as a cool store for ale or cheese. A number of institutions gathered within town walls, like the fifty parish churches at Norwich, or ten each at Cambridge and Gloucester, founded in many cases by wealthy individuals or groups. In terms of privileges and rights of self-government, English towns seem less developed than those on the continent. Holders of urban property had the advantage of paying rents in cash rather than labour services, but towns had no political independence – the king and lords remained firmly in charge. Laws and customs made concessions to the needs of urban living, and leading townsmen would play a central role in running the courts. The firmness and stability of town government is suggested by the fixed nature of property boundaries: once established in the tenth century, these remained on the same line until modern times.

At the end of the eleventh century, English towns had grown impressively, and had a key part in the economy. The foundations that had been laid were remarkably durable, so that the leading towns in 1086 remained important in later times. Urbanization had certainly begun, but still had some way to go, because town dwellers accounted for a minority, and the urban system was still immature. This latter judgement is based on the hierarchy of towns, which in a fully formed urban system consists of a series of ranks, with regional capitals and provincial towns at the top, and numerous market towns below. In England the upper range of a hierarchy can be readily identified, with London at the apex; York, Winchester, Norwich and Lincoln occupied the next tier, followed by about twenty-nine towns below them with more than 1,000 inhabitants. When we turn to the bottom rank, we can see a fair scatter of small towns in Somerset and Wiltshire, but none at all in some midland shires, so that places like Derby and Leicester stand apparently in lonely isolation (see Map 6 above, p. 63). The people of these regions cannot have regularly trekked long distances into their shire town to buy and sell. More likely there were occasional local markets, for example when groups of traders and artisans had gathered at centres of administration or minster churches (see p. 59), such as Chesterfield in Derbyshire or Breedon in Leicestershire. Still, these trading occasions were no substitute for a network of permanent towns in view of their transient and unstable character.

In Scotland and Wales centres of exchange are known. The monastery at Whithorn in Galloway, on a peninsula jutting into the Irish Sea, had become a 'monastic town' in the seventh century, with evidence of crafts and overseas trade. This role continued in the period 850–1100, when a settlement of small buildings clustered around the monastery, and trade contacts were maintained with Ireland and northern England. One speciality among the craftsmen was the manufacture of elaborate bone combs. Whithorn was too small and restricted in its range of occupations to be called a town, and a conventional town did not develop on the edge of the church precinct until the thirteenth century. Scottish towns which gained formal status as burghs (the equivalent of boroughs north of the border) in the mid-twelfth century, such as Dunfermline and Aberdeen, may well have begun to show signs of development as towns around 1100. A site with trade contacts across the Irish Sea in the ninth and tenth centuries has been excavated at Llanbedrgoch in Anglesey. In south-east Wales, Monmouth may have been a centre of trade before 1000, judging from the number of charters granting land in its vicinity, and a find of tenth-century pottery brought from Chester. A later saint's life recalls a tradition that at around 1050 a trading place existed at the mouth of the River Usk, probably at or near Newport. By the 1080s rents and tribute in that region were being paid in cash, and a mint had been founded at Cardiff.

England in the eleventh century has been described as a wealthy country, by which is meant that it was able to pay vast sums in Danegeld and heregeld, and that an abundant coinage circulated. The silver cannot have come from mines within the country, as these were few and small, so it is said that much silver flowed in from the continent, specifically in return for exports of wool. The evidence for this is entirely circumstantial, notably the large sheep flocks recorded in Domesday Book, and no document tells us that their fleeces were carried in bulk overseas. We cannot be sure that the cloth industry of Flanders was really working on large enough scale to need so much wool. In addition, England was importing luxury goods, like wine, which must have absorbed a high proportion of the money paid for goods sent abroad.

The real wealth of a country should be measured not by the amount of silver issued by its mints, but by its ability to produce sufficient goods to give its people an adequate living. It was in the countryside that most people lived and most income was generated.

CHAPTER THREE

Conquest c.1050–c.1100

The English suffered a shocking defeat in 1066, when an army from northern France under William, duke of Normandy, won a decisive battle near Hastings and conquered the whole kingdom. The invaders were soon to penetrate into Wales and Scotland. The humiliation reverberated through the centuries. From the seventeenth century onwards the myth of the 'Norman yoke' fostered the misconception that social inequality and political oppression began with the imposition of Norman rule. These ideas influenced modern historians, and in the twentieth century it was possible to attribute the origins of towns, serfdom, the manor and feudal services to the Norman invaders. We have already seen that urban growth and the imposition of heavy burdens of service on peasants can be traced back to the ninth and tenth centuries, and indeed earlier, and so we cannot regard the Norman Conquest as having a transforming effect on the grass roots of the economy. Our assessment of the impact of the Conquest must therefore be focused on the aristocracy. Here we will analyse the elite in the two centuries before 1066, before examining the subsequent upheaval, and then make some overall judgement of the economic importance of the Conquest.

i. Old aristocracy

'Aristocracy' is used here to mean the whole social elite, both the laity and the leading churchmen. In English writing of the tenth and eleventh centuries the use of the catchy phrase '*eorl* and *ceorl*', meaning 'lord and peasant' or 'noble and commoner', indicates clearly enough the fundamental division in society. A slightly more refined approach to describing social structure comes from the pens of two writers at the

beginning of the eleventh century, Aelfric and Wulfstan, one the abbot
of the monastery at Eynsham in Oxfordshire, the other archbishop of
York. Both refer to an idea first mentioned in English by King Alfred,
that society can be divided into those who fight, those who pray and those
who work. All of these groups supported the monarchy, and their separate and reciprocal functions provided the basis for a harmonious society.
In the real world disharmony prevailed, as churchmen often complained,
but their suggested ideal of mutual support and co-operation was based
on a very unequal distribution of obligations and rewards. Half a million
or more peasant households worked to support a few thousand of the
fighting elite, yet the aristocracy signally failed to carry out their protective function in 991–1016. The peasants were exposed to Viking
attack, and were expected to contribute large sums to the Danegeld.
Churchmen could deliver their obligation to pray for the rest of society
with more consistency. Although they emphasized the differences
between the functions of those who fought and those who prayed, we
cannot avoid noting that the top churchmen and secular nobles enjoyed
similar landed wealth, and that the upper clergy were often recruited
from high-ranking families.

The 'three orders' idea took a very masculine view of society, yet
women played a more prominent part than the theory suggests. Among
the aristocracy women could hold landed property independently of
men. They were granted land, managed it, and from their surviving wills,
bequeathed it, even to other women. Sometimes they were carrying out
the wishes of their fathers or husbands, but they could also follow their
own judgement. They were not just the transmitters of property to the
next male generation. Wulfwaru, who made her will in *c.*1000, held a
considerable landed estate in Somerset. She left goods and lands to the
monastery at Bath, but also made bequests of land and moveable wealth
to her two sons, and to her daughters Aelfwaru and Gode. She reveals a
lower stratum of women of some standing, as she remembered in her
will four male high-grade servants, and her household women who were
probably of similar status. At any one time a sizeable proportion of
landed estates lay in the hands of women, and this is reflected in a
number of place names which still bear the name of a female owner of
this period.

An aristocracy can be defined by reference to its special characteristics – birth, legal status, functions, wealth and style of life.
Contemporary members of the group liked to believe that birth was all
important: they prided themselves on belonging to a race apart, and
could justify their position by reference to their illustrious ancestors. It
was said that marriage into a noble family was restricted to nobles. In

practice the aristocracy could not be so exclusive, but had to admit new recruits to replace the families which died out. Much clearer was the definition of the upper rank, called ealdormen in the tenth century, and earls in the eleventh, because these titles were granted to individuals by the king. The ealdorman was assigned a shire, the earl a larger province (Wessex, Mercia, East Anglia, Northumbria), in which they carried out government functions, such as leading the shire's contingent in the army. They were entitled to a third share of some revenues, and could profit from estates belonging to their office. Bishops and abbots, like the ealdormen, were appointed to specific positions in the church hierarchy, and were expected, in addition to their duties in governing the church, to lend their support to the state by attending local courts and advising the king. Permanent and substantial landed endowments were attached to their church offices. Members of the second lay aristocratic rank, the thegns, also performed various tasks in local government, such as running the hundred courts and collecting taxes. The superior group of king's thegns had a special status and greater wealth, and can be found at the king's court and acting as his advisers. 'Thegn' originally meant 'servant', and they were often called on to perform administrative tasks for kings and greater lords, but men in this rank did not have specific offices assigned to them. Consequently the status of thegn was not granted by any superior authority, but was gained by reputation and the judgement of society.

The ealdormen, earls and thegns had a military function, as the theory of 'three orders' noted. This role is celebrated in heroic poetry, most notably the *Battle of Maldon* which recorded the last stand of Byrhtnoth, ealdorman of Essex, with his band of household retainers, against a Viking attack in 991. A more practical indication of the universal involvement of the aristocracy in war comes from the rules about the heriot, the death duty, by which the earl was expected to render to the king when he died the equipment of eight soldiers (horses, spears, shields and so on), the king's thegn four sets of military gear, and the thegn one. Bishops paid heriots too, because they were responsible for the military service owed from their estates, and the death of a bishop of Hereford in battle against the Welsh in 1056 shows that in emergency the division between those who prayed and those who fought was not strictly observed. Unlike the situation of their contemporaries on the continent, aristocrats' privileges did not include exemption from the justice of the local courts, but when geld (tax) was levied, the 'inland', that is the demesne or land under the direct control of a lord, did not pay.

The landed wealth of the aristocracy provides the clearest way of characterizing the whole group and subdivisions within it. The minimum qualification for a thegn was five hides of land. This was the assessment of an average village, so if it was organized along conventional lines the thegn with five hides would have had a demesne of at least 200 acres of arable land, and perhaps twenty peasant tenants paying rents and doing services. According to Domesday, in 1066 (and values had not changed radically during the previous century) a five-hide manor generated an annual revenue of £5, or the selling price of forty cattle. A monk writing in the early eleventh century at Ely believed that to be a 'noble' (*procer*) you needed to hold forty hides, and on the eve of the Norman Conquest there were at least eighty-eight people with that much land (and presumably an income of £40 per annum or more). But these were modest landholdings compared with the huge accumulations of the ealdormen and earls. An ealdorman of Hampshire, Aelfheah, who made his will in about 970, had land stretching over six shires, including some very large estates, and totalling at least 700 hides. The earls of the eleventh century acquired even greater tracts of property, and Godwin, earl of Wessex and his family gathered lands worth more than £5,000. The lands of both ealdormen and earls, while often including a good deal of property in their shire or province, were widely scattered, over a half-dozen shires or even more. The more modest landed fortunes tended to be more localized. Eadric of Laxfield, for example, in 1066 had assets in thirty-three villages, most of which lay in Suffolk and the adjoining shires. Some of these more concentrated groups of land were the result of a deliberate policy of consolidation, by which a thegn would dispose of outlying properties, and acquire (by purchase or marriage) parcels nearer to the family's base. Bishops, whose landed fortunes can be compared with those of ealdormen and wealthier king's thegns, often held most of their estates within their dioceses, and like their lay counterparts travelled from one property to another to consume the produce. Monasteries developed estates in which a number of food-growing manors lay within convenient carting distance, because the community could not move. Lesser thegns might hold a single piece of land, on which they lived.

With the growth in towns and a market for agricultural produce, lords' demesnes could yield revenues in money from the sale of surplus foodstuffs and cash crops such as wool. Lords could expect their peasants, who also had access to the market, to pay some rent in money. The aristocrats of the tenth and eleventh centuries disposed of large sums in cash, and we can add monetary to landed wealth as one of their distinguishing characteristics. The heriot payments, already quoted as evidence of their military role, included a cash payment, of 200 mancuses of gold in the case of earls, and 50 mancuses for a king's thegn, which, converted into silver pennies at 30d to a mancus, means that an earl paid £25 and a king's thegn £6. Lesser thegns contributed £2. These payments to the king at death did not by any means exhaust the cash reserves of many magnates, who made large bequests of money in their wills. Ealdorman Aethelmaer, for example, when he made his will at some time between 971 and 983, bequeathed 500 mancuses of gold (£62), four gold armlets worth another 300 mancuses, and £56 in silver coin. A further guide to the monetary reserves of the great landowners comes from the purchase of land, which often required expenditure in excess of £10, and for major monasteries like that at Ely, which were building up their estates at the end of the tenth century, these totalled hundreds of pounds.

The magnates also mentioned in their wills goods which reflect their wealth and provide insights into their lifestyle. The value of the weapons lay in the specialist skills and great amount of time that went into making a sword blade or a mail shirt (birnie), and also in the decoration of military equipment with precious metals. Military display figured prominently in the culture of aristocrats who did not always distinguish themselves in war itself. Cups and dishes of silver, often mentioned in the wills, showed off the riches of the host at the lavish meals for numerous guests which played a central role in the lives of the great families. They built residences which accommodated their following and provided the setting for social gatherings.

Houses have been excavated at Goltho in Lincolnshire and Netherton in Hampshire, which belonged to families below the level of the magnates. In the tenth century each contained complexes of buildings, a hall for public meals and drinking, together with 'chambers' or 'bowers' – rooms, separate from the hall, where the lord and the household slept – and service buildings such as a kitchen and a latrine. The buildings, like those found in towns and peasant settlements, were of wooden construction, but they were quite large: the hall built at Goltho just before 1000 measured 42 feet by 29 feet. They sometimes used lavish quantities of timber, and the chamber at Netherton had stone walls lined with plaster on the inside. Fortifications were expensive ways of securing protection and obtaining prestige. Those at Goltho, enlarged early in the eleventh century, enclosed a space 325 feet by 270 feet with a ditch and earthen bank 6 feet high, pierced by two gates. At about the same time the lord at Netherton was building a church on a site adjoining the house: at this time local churches were seen as useful estate assets, and another means of asserting the superior status of their owners. A sign of luxurious consumption comes from the presence at Netherton in the tenth century of a craftsman working in bronze and gold, probably an itinerant worker attracted to the house by the promise of patronage;

here he made ornaments and jewellery commissioned by the lord and his family. We have seen that much of the countryside was set aside for hunting, and this is reflected in the consumption of quantities of venison by the households who stayed at the two residences. Of the bones left over from their meals which have been excavated and analysed, 6 per cent of those from Goltho and 10 per cent of those from Netherton came from the various species of deer, which contrasts with the much smaller quantity known from non-aristocratic sites. (Plate 3)

The aristocracy went through important changes in the pre-Conquest centuries. Their growing numbers are immediately apparent. This is not so true of the highest rank of the laity, as the twenty or more ealdormen of the tenth century were replaced by only four earls in the eleventh, but as the earls' landed wealth was shared out among brothers, wives and other family members the size of the top rank did not diminish so much. The thegns increased in number: not so much the hundred or so king's thegns, but the lesser thegns who must have risen to 4,000 or more by the mid-eleventh century. New landed endowments were found for them from the fragmented great estates, as inheritances were divided or those who had previously lived in the households of the magnates were provided with their own lands. Others could make their way upwards in a society in which the land market and patronage offered increasing opportunities. There were also the invaders to be accommodated – the new wave of Danes who arrived with Cnut, a significant element among whom were the huscarls, the troops who had originally formed the king's retinue.

The church aristocracy was growing at the same time. The bishoprics did not change much, apart from some rearrangements in the south-west and the trend for two sees to be held simultaneously, such as the bishopric of Worcester and the archbishopric of York: this was thought necessary because the latter, despite its grand title, had low revenues. The dramatic change came in the reform or foundation of Benedictine monasteries, which numbered sixty-one by 1066. There had been no shortage of monasteries before the reform movement: hundreds of 'minsters' were well-endowed local churches, served by a group of clergy, some of whom who were married and who might each hold separate pieces of land. These arrangements did not accord with the strict rule of St Benedict, now reinterpreted by continental monks. The new reformed monasteries, like Glastonbury, Winchester, Abingdon, Peterborough, Ely and Bury St Edmunds, were based on large landed estates, often exceeding 300 hides, which were held by strictly celibate monks committed to a collective life in both economic and spiritual matters.

It could be said that these communities were scarcely aristocratic, because the monks possessed very little as individuals and their ethos was based on a rejection of worldly materialism. Monasteries are, however, best regarded as a dimension of the aristocracy, as collectively they received vast revenues and lived in grand buildings, and were provided with sumptuous vestments and precious church ornaments. They were closely bound in to the secular elites, who patronized a monastery as a matter of family prestige, to ensure that they would be remembered in the monks' prayers and buried in an honoured place in the church. Byrhtnoth, for example, the ealdorman who died in a celebrated battle against the Vikings in 991, had close associations with Ely, and his headless bones are still buried in the cathedral there, in his day a monastery church. Needless to say, the monks tended to be recruited from aristocratic families. The clergy who were attached to the new dense network of local churches were often poor and badly educated, the sons of peasants, but those who served the survivors of the old minster churches might still be rich enough to be equated in wealth and style of life with the lesser thegns. To some extent monastic reform involved no more than the reordering of existing church property, and changes in the conduct of the monks within the religious house, but in eastern England significant quantities of lay property were transferred to the new monasteries in the Fens.

Contemporaries who observed the increasing numbers of thegns felt unease at the threat that they posed to the old social order. Conservatives like Archbishop Wulfstan and a number of anonymous writers of law codes and statements about social rank, mainly in the early eleventh century, were concerned at the rise of parvenus. One said that it was not enough for a *ceorl* (peasant) to acquire flashily ornamented arms to become a thegn – he had to have land as well. Another celebrated statement of the qualifications for thegnly status was written in the past tense, so it was referring back to the customs of the 'good old days'. It said that a *ceorl* needed to acquire a bell (or in another version, a church), a fortified house, a seat in the king's hall (an official position) and five hides of land – of his own. The implication is that *ceorls* were in reality achieving social promotion without all of these attributes, above all by acquiring money. At the same time, disloyalty and irreligion were being criticized, and the whole of society, but particularly its highest rank, was seen as declining into a corrupt morass. The word *ceorl* is used to describe these unworthy candidates for higher status, which perhaps, if we translate it as 'peasant', gives an exaggerated impression of the speed of social mobility. We are aware of a group below the thegns with sizeable holdings – a hide or two – who might be called cniht, *radman* or sokeman, who were in a much better position than an average peasant to aspire to thegnly status.

The background to these complaints of excessive dilution of the aristocratic ranks lay in the Danish attacks that began in 991. The whole episode amounts to a profound political and economic trauma for the English aristocracy. They failed to prevent the invasion, some families died out in the struggle, and Danes acquired land even in regions like the west midlands which had not seen any earlier Danish settlement. The heavy taxation, initially to pay the Danegeld and then owed to the conquerors, strained the resources of lords, who may not have contributed very much themselves but were still damaged by the demands made on their peasants. Churches complained that they had to sell their ornaments. Further signs of social tension were the attempts by lay families to prevent transfers of land to the church. The upheaval in 1066 repeated for the English (who strictly speaking should be called 'Anglo-Danish' because of the various Scandinavian migrations, but will be called English here for convenience) the crises which their parents and grandparents had faced. In the early eleventh century there had been not just a drastic change in the personnel of the aristocracy, but also a shift in the structure of landholding with the rise of the enormous fortunes of the earls.

Continental society, particularly in France, was also apparently going through a great transformation around the year 1000, but that was associated with the fragmentation of state power and the rise of territorial lordships, in which the former servants of the Carolingian state, the counts, dukes and castellans, seized control of their localities. They wielded judicial powers that had formerly belonged to the state, and dominated the local population from castles with the aid of mounted knights. This was the 'feudal revolution' or 'feudal mutation' of modern historical writing. In England, we can recognize some similarities in the energy and aggression shown by the elite, for example in the factional struggles of the reign of Edward the Confessor (1042–66), and the proliferation of the thegns who bear some resemblance to the knights. But the cohesiveness of the kingdom, though sorely tested by both the Danish conquest and the independent spirit of the new earls, was not destroyed. The centre held, and at the end of the reign of Edward the Confessor we find a relatively stable hierarchy of earls, including the successors of Godwin of Wessex, and below them in the scale of wealth and status the hundred or so middling lay aristocrats with forty hides or more, and then some thousands of thegns of various ranks. The church elite, though troubled by individual scandals, had settled down at the end of the main period of the reform and foundation of monasteries. The king's own new Westminster Abbey, which was acquiring lands partly at the expense of other religious houses, stands out as a notable exception.

The aristocracy was held together by ties of kinship, well illustrated by the numerous members of earls' families recorded as former land-owners by the compilers of Domesday Book. Their common acceptance of the superior power of the monarchy, and their participation in the running of the state, also helped to maintain the aristocracy's cohesion. They could not contemplate directing their political energy towards the creation of independent lordships, because their lands were dispersed and they lacked a concentrated territory over which they could rule. This did not prevent the ealdormen, earls and superior thegns pursuing their own interests, and forming a clientage among the lesser aristocrats. Thegns were expected to perform political, administrative, military and legal services for the king, but they were often committed also to serve greater lords. This could take the form of commendation of a thegn to a lord, by which the lesser man accepted a personal obligation of loyal service. This did not necessarily mean that the client held land from the lord, or if he did he was sometimes able to sell it as he wished. On the other hand, a thegn or cniht might hold property on a three-life lease, often from a bishop or monastery, under the restriction that the land still belonged ultimately to the church and should be returned at the end of the third life. Occasionally we have direct evidence that the subordinates held their land from a lord and were under a personal obligation to serve him, like the thegns in Gloucestershire who had 'submitted themselves and their lands under the power of Beorhtric (son of Alfgar)'. Everyone contributed to the king's army, and if a magnate owed military service from his estates, he would organize those who held land from him, or who were commended to him, into a contingent of soldiers, as when bishops were required to assemble ships' crews on the basis of sixty men from every 300 hides. The lord could offer to his followers, as well as grants of land, protection if they were involved in disputes or lawsuits, and influence in high places.

All of these bonds within the ranks of the aristocracy bear a strong resemblance to the feudal structure of service and authority found on the continent, though the flourishing of a strong state made English society distinctive. It is sometimes said by those who emphasize the contrasts between England and the continent that the absence of the castle in England shows that royal authority was all important, exercising con-trol through public fortifications (the burhs) while on the continent the nobility could build private strongholds, from which they could compel the local peasantry to obey their commands. But on closer examination the differences do not seem so great. A specific type of castle, in which a tower was built on an earth mound both as a vantage point for observing the surrounding countryside and as a defensive citadel in the event of a siege, is not found in England before 1066, but lords like those at Goltho or Sulgrave in Northamptonshire threw up banks, ditches and palisades around their houses, and may have used timber gates with their superstructures as strong points. English lords may not have had the legal and political power of continental castle owners, but their defended houses bolstered their status and authority. (Plate 3)

Aristocrats, both in England and the continent, are often represented as being mainly concerned with the relationships between superiors and inferiors – magnates had clients among the lesser aristocracy, and all of them depended for their living on their domination of the peasants. But they also developed associations among equals, most readily identified in the guilds of thegns and cnihts which met in towns such as Cambridge and Canterbury, but no doubt also based on more informal contacts when thegns attended hundred courts, or gathered to carry out official duties in the shire towns, or at some religious ceremony, or in the household of a magnate. They had interests and a culture in common, shared similar duties and privileges, and intermarried. While they might sometimes be in competition, they could also eat, drink, worship and deliberate as a group.

ii. *New aristocracy*

The Norman Conquest brought disaster to the old English aristocracy. The government of the country continued to function in the former style, as the well-run state could deliver to William, duke of Normandy and his followers the financial benefits of an efficient tax system. But the years between 1066 and 1086 also saw the largest transfer of property ever seen in English history. Virtually a whole upper class was displaced, as in the revolutions of 1789 in France and 1917 in Russia, but we cannot properly call the events after 1066 a revolution because the property was not seized by the lower orders: the new rulers were aristocrats themselves. How was this done? Was this just a change of personnel, or was there a shift in the structures of landholding? Were any economic changes involved? What was the state of England at the end of the upheaval?

In the autumn of 1066, having defeated King Harold and his army near Hastings, and taken over London, William and his men expected to enrich themselves. One of their first objectives was to secure military control, notably by building castles at strategic points, and then to take over the land. This was inevitably a slow process, but the task was made easier by the decisiveness of the victory. Many English thegns died in battle, either at Stamford Bridge (fighting the Norwegians just before the Norman invasion), or at Hastings. The widows and heirs of the dead, and those who fought and lived, were deprived of their property by application of the argument that William had been the rightful king, so that those who had supported the usurper Harold were traitors. Those who resisted the new regime by joining the many rebellions in the first five years after Hastings shared the same fate. Those who were left could be forced out by financial exactions. They were compelled to pay cash to redeem their lands, so that a thegn might have to find £5 to £12, a year's income, in addition to the heavy tax that was immediately demanded by the Conqueror. The English landowners had to borrow money, and then became so burdened by debt that they needed to sell or abandon their lands, and many went into exile abroad. Others were submerged because they sought the protection of the powerful newcomers, but found that their lords treated them harshly. Whether through debt or other pressures, former thegns or lesser aristocrats were pushed so far down the social scale that within two decades after the Conquest they joined the ranks of the freemen or sokemen as rich peasants. English churchmen were squeezed out under the new archbishop of Canterbury, Lanfranc. A few survived, and even prospered, like Colswein of Lincoln, who was promoted as a major landowner after the Conquest, and a scatter of thegns and their widows, like Ketel, Osward, Edith and others in Gloucestershire. But in general the lesser lords named in 1086 reveal their origins across the Channel by their names: Geoffrey, Henry, Hugh, Ralph, Roger, William and the rest.

As the English were removed or gave up the struggle, newcomers from northern France acquired their lands (the conquerors came from Picardy, Brittany, Flanders and other provinces, as well as Normandy, but for the sake of convenience here they will be called Normans). In the most straightforward method of transfer, the king granted all of the lands of some pre-Conquest lord to a newcomer. This is apparent from Domesday Book, which records in 1086 that, in a typical case, the lands of Asgar the Staller, who had a strong base in Essex, had been made over to Geoffrey de Mandeville. An estate with a western focus, held in 1086 by Queen Matilda, had previously belonged to Beorhtric, son of Alfgar. Such a transfer could have been achieved in some cases by forcing an heiress to marry a Norman, but most commonly lands were confiscated and then granted by the king. If a Norman succeeded an English lord in this way, he was more likely to continue the management of the estate in the former style. This simple transition would not help the Norman who deserved a particularly large quantity of land to establish his status or to reward his contribution to the Conquest, which must explain why some incomers received the lands of two, three or more English predecessors. Sometimes we find that in 1086 a Norman was holding land previously belonging to a dozen Englishmen, scattered over the length and breadth of a shire. One explanation could be that after the king had granted more coherent groups of land to followers, he granted to a latecomer all of the leftover pieces. A rather special example of the creation of a new landed fortune from the properties of a number of English predecessors is provided by the royal estates, as William held lands worth double those of Edward the Confessor, valued at £11,000, or a sixth of the landed revenues of the whole kingdom. This was not just a question of increasing the income of the crown, but involved a strategy of extending the king's direct influence throughout the country. Sections of rural England which did not belong to the royal estate were placed under forest law. This continental concept was designed to protect game animals and the woods in which they lived, and restricted hunting by the forest's inhabitants. The forests included settled and cultivated land as well as wilder country, and in the long run were to yield the kings valuable, but much resented, revenues.

Another dimension of royal policy gave Norman lords the lands of many pre-Conquest owners because the Conqueror decided that in contrast with the normal pattern of scattered possessions, consolidated lordships should be created in strategic positions on the Welsh border and along the south coast. Trusted lords like Roger of Montgomery, who was given much of Shropshire, or William of Warenne, who acquired a large section of Sussex based on Lewes, were set in place in the first case to keep the western boundaries of the kingdom free of Welsh attack, and in the second to secure vital lines of communication with Normandy. On a smaller scale, local castleries appeared, in which the lords of strongholds like Tutbury in Staffordshire or Tickhill in Yorkshire were granted groups of adjacent lands.

Sometimes landholding before and after the Conquest shows a complete transformation, with the properties of English lords being broken up and distributed to many Normans. This absence of central planning or policy in the transfer of land points to the activities of Norman lords which have been called 'private enterprise'. Individual incomers did not wait for grants from the king, but took advantage of the troubles of the English owners to grab their land. They may have forced a widow or daughter to enter into marriage, or they took on a supposedly temporary lease and extended it indefinitely, or used their control of the courts to force out those with debts or disputable legal claims. Such activities would be aided by the connivance of the new Norman officials, especially the sheriffs, who in some localities earned a reputation for ruthlessness and partiality, and indeed for enriching themselves with the lands of the conquered. When disputes were reported to the Domesday commissioners in 1086, the parties would refer to the use of the king's seal to legalize the questionable transfer, and to the role of a 'liberator' (deliverer), that is someone using the king's authority to convey land to a new owner. This freebooting pursuit of landed wealth after 1066 resulting in completely new estate structures was especially characteristic of parts of eastern England.

A further extension of 'private enterprise' took the Normans of the Welsh border into Wales itself. Herefordshire, initially under the lordship of William fitz Osbern, threatened south Wales, and fitz Osbern's subordinates, who included such formidable families as the Lacys, penetrated a considerable distance to build castles at Caerleon and Brecon. Along the north coast, where the threat to the Welsh came from Cheshire under Hugh of Avranches, the kingdom of Gwynneth lost a great deal of territory, though by 1100 the Normans had been pushed back to the River Conwy. In the north of England the Normans began to put in order the shires north of Yorkshire, with the development of Carlisle both as a stronghold and as a bishopric, but the movement into southern Scotland was delayed until the early twelfth century.

Historians debate which change in landholding predominated: the transfer of whole estates from a single English predecessor (antecessor), or the more complicated assembling of new estates from many previous lords. If the latter was normal, then the Conquest seems more 'revolutionary' than if estates were handed over intact. The evidence is incomplete, because our main source for the process, Domesday Book, does not give complete information on the various layers of lordship before the Conquest, so it will tell us that the pre-Conquest holder of a manor was 'Wulfwine', and not mention Wulfwine's overlord. The overlord's dozen manors may have been granted to a Norman successor in a single, coherent transaction, but the record suggests that the new lord had scrambled together a new combination of manors from Wulfwine and eleven other minor English thegns, as they, the subtenants, are named as the holders in 1066. The eastern counties seem to have experienced more complicated and 'revolutionary' transfers of property than those in the west. The conservation of old estates in some regions resulted partly from the continuity of the holdings of the major churches, which held a high proportion of the countryside in the south and west, from

Kent to Worcestershire. They survived the Conquest, and helped to preserve an important dimension of the old economic order into the new
post-Conquest world.

In the reconstruction of the policies and behaviour that lay behind the
upheaval of property-holding after 1066, Domesday Book has been used
as our main source. The enquiry which assembled the information for
the book demonstrates conclusively that the old state machinery was
functioning efficiently, but at the command of new masters. No other
comparable documents exist in Europe, not because they once existed
but have been lost, but because no other government was capable of
such an ambitious project. The basis of the survey came from the tax-
gathering rolls containing the names of places and landholders. This
skeletal information was then greatly expanded by enquiries in local
courts, and by the seven groups of commissioners who went off to the
shires (each group was assigned four, five or six shires each) to gather
from lords and from local juries details of manors, the numbers of
ploughs, peasants and mills, and the size of woods. Animals were
counted too, though these statistics were discarded for most shires during
the process of abbreviation and collation when the data from the shires
were assembled into the main record, 'Great Domesday'.

The survey had three main aims. First, it was designed to provide a
comprehensive picture of the landed assets of the aristocracy, with a calculation of annual value for each manor, so that if they came into the
king's hands on the death or disgrace of their lord the potential revenues
would be known. A short-term objective arose from problems when
troops were assembled to counter a threat of Norwegian invasion in
1085. Information about the resources of landowners would enable the
billeting of soldiers to be shared out efficiently. Secondly, the pleadings
that accompanied the survey were intended to settle some of the disputes
that had arisen from thousands of grants and seizures of property – the
twenty years after 1066 had seen an upheaval in landholding, not just
through the replacement of the English, but also because some of the
new Norman lords had died or rebelled, which meant that the holders
of land in 1086 were often the third in succession in a relatively short
period.

Thirdly, the king wanted an overview of resources which could in the
long term be used to reassess the tax system. The well-established
method of collecting geld levied the tax at a rate, for example, of 2s on
the hide, so that a five-hide manor paid 10s. The Domesday survey
included for some shires a calculation of 'ploughlands' – 'there is land
for eight ploughs' a typical entry reads – and the figure often bears little
resemblance to the number of ploughs said to be working on the demesne

and in the hands of the peasants. One possible explanation was that the ploughlands, which like the hides were designed to reflect the overall taxable capacity of the land, would replace the hidage to form the basis of a new tax, but if this was the case it was not implemented. Another objective that was never realized may have been a plan to extend the tax system to lords' demesnes, which explains why the Domesday enquiry paid such close attention to demesne assets, even to the point of counting pigs, which the English monk who wrote the *Anglo-Saxon Chronicle* regarded as 'shameful'.

As well as changing the people at the top, the Conqueror was distributing landed wealth in quantities which would forge a new social hierarchy. At first William apparently contemplated rebuilding the very large and rich earldoms that he found in 1066. But the political dangers were soon appreciated, and earldoms that developed in the 1070s were conceived on a smaller scale. The new earls resemble the tenth-century ealdormen in their attachment to a shire, which we now call a 'county' after the continental 'count', the equivalent of an earl. In fact the English and continental institutions cannot be equated exactly. The county in the old Carolingian empire had once been a unit of royal government, but by the eleventh century it had become a virtually independent small state, of which the county (later duchy) of Normandy is an outstanding example. The shire/county in England remained under the control of the monarch, with a sheriff appointed by the king. The landed fortunes of most earls were not confined to their shire/county. Some of the great landowners were adding English possessions to large estates in Normandy, but other newcomers made their fortune through their English lands – Bigot, Mandeville and Warenne had only modest properties across the Channel.

In place of the pre-Conquest hierarchy of wealth consisting of a few super-magnates towering over many modestly well-off thegns, the new social order established about 200 substantial tenants-in-chief, earls and barons holding directly of the crown, who together owned about half of the land. Below them were another 1,000 landholders with land worth at least £5, and 6,000–7,000 lesser men, some resembling pre-Conquest thegns, many with only a hide. The overall effect of the Conquest had sometimes been to increase the landed wealth of the higher ranks. In Cambridgeshire, for example, of the seventy-four landholders in 1066, only three were worth £100 per annum or more, while in 1086 the forty-three tenants-in-chief included five with £100. This impression of a changed distribution of land must be qualified by the problem of Domesday's incomplete record of landholding before the Conquest. Its tendency not to refer to overlords may lead to an underestimate of the number of rich lords in 1066. One of the major lords in Cambridgeshire throughout was the monastery of Ely, and stability in the church's share of property is typical of the whole country. Various pressures were applied on the church to grant land to Norman lords, resulting in some losses, but on the other hand the Normans made pious gifts, both to monasteries across the Channel and to a handful of new foundations, such as the priory of Lewes in Sussex.

Conquest, and the continuation of Norman rule, depended on armed power. The numerous new castles had to be garrisoned, and both the aristocrats and the king needed the ability to summon armies to suppress rebellions and counter threats from overseas. The key figures were the knights, who included both well-off aristocrats with lands assessed at between five and twenty hides and people who were called 'country knights' on the continent, with only a hide or two of land. In addition, many knights still lived in the households of the greater lords. The king gradually assigned quotas on the tenants-in-chief by which they were required to provide a set number of knights, later known as the 'due service'. This figure was only loosely based on the landed resources of the lord, and indeed sometimes seemed to reflect political loyalty. So the rich monastery at Evesham was expected to provide only five knights, while Peterborough Abbey was burdened with sixty. Wealthier lay lords were usually assigned a quota of forty or above, giving a total potential over the whole country of an army of 6,000 knights.

These arrangements, by which a social hierarchy of king, tenants-in-chief and knights were bound together by obligations to provide military service in exchange for landholdings, have been seen as a major change, introducing continental feudal notions of social and political dependency. Indeed, the social vocabulary was new and largely French. We have seen already that the top rank of aristocrats were called counts and the second rank barons; the sheriffs were known as viscounts. Knight (cniht) is an English word, but the terms *miles* (Latin) and *chevalier* (French) were commonly used. The lands and rights of a magnate, an honour, included among its tenants knights who held fiefs in the continental style, though in English this later became a 'fee'. Tenants symbolized their subordinate (yet still honourable) relationship to their lord by swearing an oath of fealty (faithfulness) and performing an act of homage. They owed him, as well as service, 'aid and council', meaning that they might be expected to pay money in emergencies, and attend his private court to make judgments and offer advice. On death and inheritance the English paid a heriot, but under the new arrangements the heir paid a relief. In important respects the new language was describing old practices, and before the Conquest thegns held tenancies, commended themselves to lords, and served in the army in their lord's contingent.

All of this has significance for economic history because the definition of rights and obligations established a relationship between crown and magnates peculiar to England, in which the central state maintained control over the localities, while still delegating a great deal of power to the aristocracy. Everyone in England could regard the king as an ultimate authority, in spite of the import from the continent of a strong tradition of private justice. Much was made of tenancy, which defined the conditions on which land was held, and the rights of lords. Even the greatest earl was a tenant-in-chief, and his land could be confiscated if he was disloyal; in the event of any tenant's death without a male heir, or if the heir was under age, the lord could take over, and either marry off the daughter, or act as ward of the young heir and exploit the lands. But the recognition of hereditary rights ultimately made the tenant, even the lowliest knight, the effective owner of his land. As the pre-Conquest custom of divided inheritance was replaced by the succession of a single heir, it was possible for property to be accumulated and passed on to future generations. Tenants could also expand their landholdings by acquiring properties from the tenants of other lords, which obliged them to serve two or more lords. The tenants could use the land in the way that they thought most effective, and had lordship over the peasants living there, and they made the decisions about extracting revenues from their manor.

All of these changes in the upper levels of society had a limited impact on the economy. The new lords were anxious to make a regular income from their newly acquired estates, and their best course at first was not to disrupt the existing customs and practices, but to let the routines of production and rent collection continue. The officials who ran the manors or groups of manors, the reeves, remained in office. The main impact of the conquerors can be seen in the destruction of selected parts of the country, and in the reordering of manors in order to expand their profits. There were also some new developments in the towns.

Destruction refers both to the incidental consequences of military operations, and to the deliberate wasting of rebellious districts. The first type of damage affected the area around Dover, where the conquering army moved after the victory at Hastings, and then along the line of march from the south coast to London. Presumably the troops took animals and grain to feed themselves and their horses, and like armies at all times intimidated the inhabitants by burning houses. Manors on this route dropped in value after 1066, but usually had recovered again after twenty years. Deliberate devastation was concentrated in the north after the rebellion of 1069–70, apparently reflected in Domesday in more than a thousand villages described as 'waste', notably in the West and North

Ridings of Yorkshire, with 267 and 367 reports of 'waste' respectively.
We cannot take the statements in Domesday at face value, however. A
puzzling feature is the concentration of 'waste' in the uplands, on the
slopes of the Pennine hills. Perhaps the rebels lived in the wilder country?
Or the destruction had originally covered the lowlands, but the more
attractive villages on the most fertile soils could be repopulated more
quickly, even at the expense of the uplands? Another explanation is that
while destruction undoubtedly occurred, it was followed by reconstruction which also involved the reorganization of estates, and that when
places were absorbed into some new unit of lordship, they were described
as 'waste', which therefore had an administrative rather than a physical
meaning. Parts of towns were destroyed to make space for royal castles,
the number of houses affected varying from four at Warwick to 166 at
Lincoln. The reality of the demolition is proved by modern excavations
beneath castle earthworks which have revealed the remains of the houses.

These acts of destruction were compatible with the conquerors' aims
of profiting eventually from their newly acquired territory. The short-
term loss of revenues in a few parts of the countryside could be justified
if the shock convinced the English as a whole of the futility of rebellion.
The castles in the towns kept the inhabitants, and the surrounding
country, under observation, and the prominent towers made everyone
fully aware of the potential violent power of the new regime. The remarkable continuity in the flow of revenues proved the value of the display of
ruthlessness and military might. A limited amount of pain inflicted at
the beginning of the process of Conquest ensured long-term gain for the
invaders.

The Conquest must have been regarded by the peasants with mixed
feelings. They may have felt a strong loyalty to the lords it displaced.
More likely they had found the restrictions imposed by their English
lords irksome, judging from the pre-Conquest lists of peasants who had
left the manor, and the hints in the treatises on estate management on
the need to avoid trouble by observing custom and ruling with a firm
hand. Before 1066 they would have had limited opportunities to form any
bond with the many lords who were infrequent visitors to their manors
or even total absentees. The replacement of their former superiors may
not have been regarded as a disaster. They had often changed lords
before, especially after 1016, and although they would have had some
sense of nationality, they may not have reacted with hostility to 'foreign'
Normans. Again, they were used to being ruled by strangers – Danes, or
aristocrats from remote provinces. But whatever their initial reactions,
they would soon have good economic reasons for regretting and resent-
ing the Conquest. For a start they faced heavy tax demands, like the geld

demanded in 1067, and contributions to the redemption payments that their English lords were expected to pay. The new Norman lords kept up the pressure for rents and services to maintain a high level of profit from the manor.

When we know the changes in the values of manors between 1066 and 1086 they often show an increase. This must have been achieved by lessees or farmers to whom the running of manors was delegated for a fixed annual rent or farm. These middlemen were squeezed by lords, and in turn would have passed on the demands to the peasants below them. As the lords' demesnes do not seem to have expanded, the extra revenue must have come from the peasants. The jurors who reported to the Domesday commissioners sometimes expressed an opinion on the high 'renders' or values that they recorded, and made comments such as 'it cannot bear it'. The manor of Coggeshall in Essex was reported as having been worth £10 per annum in 1066, but in twenty years the sum had increased to £20. Its actual value was judged at £14. These statistics tell us much more than the mechanics of estate administration: the high sums that had to be found each year must have entailed stress for the farmer and anguish among the peasants. Specific methods by which lords or their farmers could increase revenues included, in the east and north, pressing the sokemen to pay more. One group of sokemen in Norfolk found their annual payments rising from £2 to £20 in the ten years after 1066. In Yorkshire a 'sokeland', where the inhabitants enjoyed consider-able independence, might become a 'berewick', an appendage of a lord's demesne manor, with consequent increases in the services owed by the peasant population. Numerous former sokemen and freemen had by 1086 been reclassified as villeins and bordars: presumably this was not just a change of name, but committed them to more rents and labour. In 1066 there had been eight free men at Frostenden in Suffolk. Twenty years later, under the lordship of Ralph Baynard, only three were counted, but the number of bordars – smallholders closely subjected to the manor – had increased from fourteen to twenty. In the north, such developments may have been associated with more radical changes whereby new manors with demesnes were formed out of sokelands, and the peasants were required to provide labour services. This was not just part of recon-struction after the devastation of the north, but can be linked with a longer-term reorganization of the countryside, as the great estates were breaking down in Yorkshire at a later stage than in the south and the midlands.

Many of the tendencies after the Conquest disadvantaged the peas-ants, as lords' control was extended and everyone had to pay more to the manor. The decline in slavery might suggest that there was some compensatory improvement. At Frostenden the two slaves of 1066 had disappeared twenty years later: perhaps one of them had joined the bordars. In general the ex-slaves reappear as oxmen or bordars, having gained a tenancy of land, but were still required to work on the lord's demesne, so the lord had not lost a great deal. The lords of eastern England in particular were pursuing a policy of reducing all the different categories of peasant to a common state of subjection, which involved loss of independence for some, and a token liberation for others. All of this had been a long-term tendency, and the phase of social change after 1066 may not have been a consequence of the invasion. The Normans took over existing manors, working demesnes and dependent peasants, and made the most profitable use of them, observing local customs and no doubt taking advice from the English reeves and farmers who dealt with the detailed running of the manors. Occasionally changes were made on the initiative of a Norman lord, notably in the case of Ernulf de Hesdin, who held land in ten shires. He enjoyed a reputation in the twelfth century as an agricultural improver, and in 1086 his manors had unusually large demesnes, some of them, such as Chipping Norton in Oxfordshire and Kempsford in Gloucestershire, exceeding 500 acres in area, and were well provided with slaves to man the ploughs. He was rewarded for his apparent vigour in management with increases in values, which in view of the size of the demesnes must have partly derived from the sale of produce.

The invaders recognized the importance of the towns that they found in England, and made sure that they acquired urban property. For example, the list of owners of houses in Leicester – Hugh de Grentemaisnil, the earl of Chester, the bishop of Lincoln, and so on – echoes the distribution of rural manors among the tenants-in-chief in the county. The town dwellers remained mainly English, though an influx of migrants from across the Channel established separate 'French' boroughs, notably at Norwich, Southampton and Wallingford. These newcomers were presumably attracted by commercial opportunities, and their presence made a contribution to the expansion of towns. The towns along the south coast – at Chichester, Pevensey and Sandwich – prospered from the increase in cross-Channel traffic and trade, but reports of poverty and vacant holdings are found in East Anglia, at Norwich, Thetford and Ipswich, and towns such as Huntingdon and York suffered from destruction after rebellions. Elsewhere the reports of waste and destroyed houses – at Shaftesbury and Dorchester in Dorset, or at Oxford – might suggest that the urban economy was going through a difficult patch when Domesday was being made, perhaps unrelated to political events. On the other hand, small towns seem to have been growing to fill the gaps between larger centres, sometimes encouraged by the patronage of monasteries, such as Battle in Sussex (the religious house founded on the field of victory by William I). Some developed at the gates of new castles, and therefore presumably under the stimulation of the new lords, like the forty-two men gathered at a market 'around the castle' of Tutbury in Staffordshire, or the forty-three burgesses who had been established at Clare in Suffolk, the stronghold of Richard fitz Gilbert.

The setbacks suffered by the towns, as well as the examples of growth after 1066, provide one set of guides to assessing the overall effects of the Conquest. We might expect that by putting pressure on their manors to generate more revenue, by squeezing free tenants to produce more rent, and by granting to slaves land on which they could produce their own food, the newcomers would have been giving some stimulus to the economy in terms of both productivity and the increase in exchange. More money was spent than ever before on building work: perhaps the local inhabitants were compelled to dig earth and haul timber for the new castles in the initial assertion of power, but the continued work on aristocratic construction, such as the great stone White Tower that dominated the east of the city of London, must have given employment to masons and the carters and boatmen who brought materials to the site. More widespread was the rebuilding programme on the major churches, both cathedrals and monasteries, which were now to reflect more closely continental Romanesque styles (which we now call 'Norman' architecture) and were conceived on a larger scale than their predecessors. Many small local churches were also rebuilt. (Plate 4)

The undoubtedly negative effects of the invasion on the economy included not just physical destruction, but the disruption of trade and estate management by violence. High rents and taxes may in some circumstances have pressurized peasants to grow and sell more actively, but when we are told that a manor that had doubled in value 'cannot suffer it without ruin', the peasants were apparently being impoverished by excessive demands. Some of the money that the Normans gained in this way was carried out of the country and not spent to the benefit of English merchants or artisans.

iii. *England in 1086*

We can sum up both the aftermath of the Conquest, and the longer-term developments in country and town discussed in the last three chapters, by examining the state of England in 1086, an analysis made possible by the Domesday survey.

Before looking at the wider picture, the nature of the evidence and its meaning can be examined through a single manor, Pinbury in Gloucestershire, which lay on high ground to the north of Cirencester. It had been given to the nuns of Caen in Normandy in a pious act by King William. We are told that in 1086:

> There are 3 hides. In demesne are 3 ploughs. 8 villeins and a smith with 3 ploughs. There are 9 slaves. A mill at 40d. It was and is worth £4.

The information is so compressed, and the terms so unfamiliar, that it seems to be written in code. Fortunately we can use other, less enigmatic evidence to help to decode the message, in the form of a survey made by the Caen nunnery for its own purposes as landlord thirty years later, in about 1120. This later survey contains similar information, confirming the essential accuracy of the Domesday entry, but it supplies more details. The three hides need not detain us, as this was an assessment, used by the state in determining tax liability, which shows that Pinbury, falling towards the lower end of a range which mostly lay between two and ten hides, was rated as a small but not insignificant manor. Such assessments were inevitably artificial and archaic, but other information is based more closely on agricultural realities. The three ploughs of the demesne were real implements of wood and iron, pulled by teams of eight oxen each, which was almost the case in c.1120, when Pinbury was provided with twenty-two oxen and two cows, the latter perhaps substituting for the missing pair of oxen. The number of ploughs gives a clue as to the amount of land in the Pinbury demesne, as a plough could, according to later records, cultivate about 100 acres in a year. In fact at Pinbury in c.1120 205 acres were recorded as under crops (wheat, wheat mixed with rye, and oats) which means that the demesne totalled 400 acres, of which half was planted each year while the other half lay fallow. Extra ploughing was provided by the villeins, who had three ploughs between them, suggesting that each peasant owned two or three oxen, and they joined together to make complete teams, mainly to work their own holdings, but with spare capacity for the demesne. The contribution of the villeins to demesne cultivation has to be presumed from Domesday, but it is confirmed by the later survey which tells us that they each owed the lord five days' work each week. The smith presumably had a holding of land, but his main task was to make and mend the lord's ploughshares, iron bindings on carts, sickles and other implements. The nine slaves worked full time for the lord, six of them as ploughmen, as each plough needed a crew of two. The other three would have looked after the animals on the demesne, which are not recorded in 1086, but in c.1120 there were seventeen cattle, a horse, 122 sheep and ten pigs. The mill made a profit from tolls on grinding the corn of the peasants (toll corn), and perhaps those from neighbouring manors as well.

Both surveys suggest a self-sufficient system of production, in which the lord could obtain all the labour for the demesne from the villeins and slaves, and did not even have to go elsewhere for the specialized skills of a smith. In fact the long distance between Pinbury and Caen meant that the produce cannot have been used by the lord, except perhaps for cheese and wool. The value of £4, that is the annual payment from the manor to the lord, could only have been achieved if the main product of the demesne, grain, was being sold in the locality, perhaps at the market in Cirencester, in the same way that the miller could obtain money for the toll corn. Judging from the small numbers of sheep in c.1120, which at other times formed the main Cotswold cash crop, there was a limited demand for wool.

While surveys give the lord's view of the manor, they must be used cautiously to reconstruct the lives of the peasants. Pinbury had a single manorial lord, so the numbers of peasants and slaves suggests a village with eighteen households, if we think of the slaves as married and having their own dwelling. The figure would be nineteen if we include the priest, who is mentioned in c.1120 but not in 1086, which might mean that the church had been founded in the intervening years, or more likely was omitted from the Domesday survey. The village consisted therefore of 80–90 people, if the average family contained between 4.5 and 5 individuals. The villeins each cultivated 30–40 acres, so their fields totalled about 300 acres, less than the demesne. If their farming resembled that of the lord, they concentrated on corn, with wheat as the main crop, and kept a few cattle, sheep and pigs as well as their plough oxen. We can begin to visualize the village surrounded by about 700 acres of cornfields, but with some pasture and meadow for feeding the animals, and perhaps a small wood, which would not be mentioned in Domesday if it did not provide revenue for the lord, but was a source of fuel and pasture for the peasants. The villeins grew their own food, but sold the surplus if they grew more corn than they needed to eat, and part of the lord's £4 annual income would have come from rent. The smith would not have been fully employed making and mending the lord's implements, and no doubt sold his services to his neighbours and in the surrounding villages. In the thirty years after 1086, the main change seems to have been the 'freeing' of six of the slaves who were called oxmen, who still manned the three demesne ploughs, and the appearance of four cottars, who may have been provided with land from the subdivision of one of the larger peasant holdings, as the number of villeins had fallen from eight to seven.

By decoding the information for a single manor, we can apply it cautiously to the thousands of manors recorded in 1086 to give a more general picture. Having calculated the population of one place, can we now estimate the population of the whole country? Domesday records a total of 269,000 individuals (villeins, cottars and so on) in its descriptions of manors, and a little more than 20,000 people, houses, plots and other indications of urban households. If we multiply these combined figures by 4.5 or 5 to allow for whole families, the result is between 1.3 and 1.5 million. However, many people were omitted from the survey, such as the households of the lords, which each contained officials, servants and soldiers, the garrisons of the new castles, monks and nuns and their servants, and the population of the four northern shires, together with a considerable proportion of those living in Lancashire. Large towns – London, Winchester and Bristol – were not described in detail; nor were smaller ones like Coventry and Tonbridge. Other towns were clearly not as systematically surveyed as the rural manors, and we sometimes have near-contemporary surveys which show that hundreds of households were omitted. At Gloucester, for example, more than 600 properties are implied in a survey in c.1100, but fewer than 150 houses and burgesses are mentioned in Domesday. The actual number of townspeople throughout the country may have been near to double the recorded figure.

In the countryside the record was also incomplete, as can be suspected from the small numbers of slaves listed in some northern counties, which might suggest that the officials there did not collect information about that social group. A more widespread problem arose from the concentration on the peasant tenants who made the main contribution to the demesne economy, the villeins and bordars, so that those who paid money rents were not counted. Judging from those known to have been living shortly after 1086 on one Staffordshire estate, that of Burton Abbey, and not mentioned in Domesday, their numbers could run into many thousands over the whole country. Priests were recorded inconsistently, as were officials and craftsmen. There were at least 6,000 mills, but apparently only eight millers or mill-keepers; demesne sheep must have numbered well over a million, but only ten shepherds are mentioned; similarly, the hundreds of square miles of woodland must have been supervised by more than four foresters and one huntsman. An important category of people, who would not appear in Domesday because they held no land, were the servants who worked on demesnes when slaves

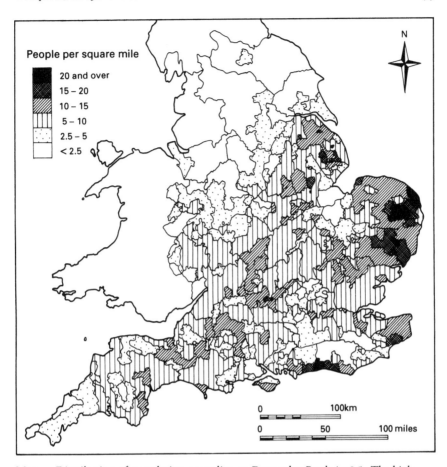

Map 7. Distribution of population according to Domesday Book (1086). The high density of population in the east persisted throughout the middle ages. There was a band of districts with relatively high population densities running from the Humber south-west to southern Somerset and Dorset.

Source: H. C. Darby, *Domesday England* (Cambridge, 1977).

were in short supply, and indeed were employed by the better-off peasants. Their presence must explain how the numerous small manors were operated which had a plough and a single tenant or slave, or even a plough and no recorded population at all. Making conservative allowance for these gaps in the Domesday survey would give a population figure of 2 million in 1086, but a more likely estimate would lie somewhere between 2.2 and 2.5 million (Map 7).

The example of Pinbury shows how the acreage of arable and patterns of land use can be calculated. For the country as a whole, the cultivated area probably lay in the region of 7 or 8 million acres, while woodland took up perhaps 4 million acres, or 15 per cent of the total available land. The arable was concentrated in a belt across the middle of the country, from Herefordshire to Norfolk. The woods were most extensive in the west and the south-east.

Comparing these statistics with those from other periods, we arrive at the conclusion that the population in 1086 was about half of that in 1300 or 1700, but the numbers were comparable with those of the period 1377–1540, that is after the Black Death and other epidemics. William I ruled almost as many English subjects as did Henry VIII. The cultivated area in the mid-twentieth century, when the population was twenty times greater, was 8.3 million acres, and 1.8 million acres were used for forests and woods – figures which are remarkably similar to those of the eleventh century. Domesday mentions 13,000 places, and the great majority exist now as hamlets, villages and towns with similar names. The general impression we gain is of a country with few very large empty spaces, in which agriculture, though not intensive, had attained a high level of development. The regional distribution of arable and pasture bears some resemblance to the patterns of land use in modern times. Another way of looking at the statistics is in terms of the experiences of those living in 1086. The cultivated area amounts to three acres or more per head. If half of the land was actually producing crops each year and yields were comparable with those recorded 150 years later, the land could have provided everyone in normal years with about 2 pounds of grain per day, more than sufficient to sustain healthy life if combined with other foods. Each person needed an acre of woodland for fuel for heating and cooking. This would have come from managed coppice woods, of which there were many among the 4 million acres of woodland, and together with the peat in East Anglia and the north, the supplies were ample for the population.

The survey of 1086 was mainly concerned with describing manors, and these provide a huge amount of evidence for the management of human resources. At Pinbury the demesne and tenant lands were fairly evenly balanced, which is characteristic of small manors in general. Minor lords, both monastic, as in our example, and the much more numerous laymen and women, kept quite a high proportion of their land in demesne, in some cases to feed their households, in others to produce a saleable surplus. As they did not have numerous tenants, and many of them were not burdened with very heavy labour services as was the case at Pinbury, they depended on slaves, or in eastern England, where slavery was dying out, they employed a good deal of hired labour. On the larger manors a higher proportion of the land was held by the peasant tenants, so that on many of the well-established church manors only a fifth of the land was held in demesne: in terms of Domesday statistics, peasant ploughs exceeded demesne ploughs in a ratio of 4 to 1. Such manors were therefore amply supplied with labour services from the peasants, especially the villeins. On very large manors, and particularly those in the king's direct control, the demesnes were relatively small, and as the numerous tenants were superfluous to the labour needs of the demesne, they were evidently paying rents in kind and cash.

The varied distribution of the different types of landowner gave each region its own social and economic character. Church estates were especially numerous in parts of the east midlands, notably in Huntingdonshire, and also in the west midland counties of Gloucestershire and Worcestershire. They also formed a large part of the southern shires of Hampshire and Kent. But other factors influenced the manorial regime, such as the large manors with their many dependencies and high proportions of sokemen and freemen in the old Danelaw, which gave rent payment a prominent role. Slaves were especially numerous in the west.

Domesday tells us much about villages and peasants as well as manors and tenants. The village had a part to play in law enforcement, and sometimes the peasants were sufficiently well organized to take on collectively the farm of the manor. The cohesiveness of the peasant community was not always reflected in compact nucleated villages, which were still being formed at this time, and in many parts of the country the settlement pattern remained dispersed. The Domesday survey of Devon records numerous tiny named manors which clearly represent a scattered spread of farmsteads.

The most numerous category of peasant tenants was that of the villeins, who account for about 40 per cent of the recorded rural population. On average they owned about three oxen each, and held yardlands or half-yardlands of 30 or 15 acres. They were important producers from their own holdings, had a surplus for exchange, and contributed much labour to the demesnes. The bordars and cottars, with holdings of 3 to 5 acres, accounted for 30 per cent of the rural population. They did not have enough land to feed themselves, and acted as hired workers for the demesnes and their better-off neighbours. They were most numerous in woodland and pastoral counties, where they could keep animals and find employment in such work as wood-cutting and turf-digging. In East Anglia they may have found paid work easier to obtain because of the commercial influences on the region, and more intensive farming systems. This was also an area with little slave labour, and bordars probably did the full-time work on the demesnes. Although villeins, bordars and cottars were tenants on manors, and in many cases had heavy obligations to their lords, they were carefully distinguished by the Domesday survey from the slaves. The words used to describe them by the Domesday clerks were derived from a continental vocabulary, in which 'villein' meant villager, and 'bordar' a tenant of a small house or smallholding. These names did not imply that they were servile, and indeed, like the pre-Conquest *gebur*, *ceorl* and *cotsetla*, these peasants were still legally free. The balance of public and private jurisdiction was beginning to change, as in continental style some of the hundreds were taken under private jurisdiction.

Domesday depicts an economy in which money and commerce played a central role. Its pages are littered with references to small payments of cash in rent, whether the valuations of mills or the obligations of groups of tenants, like the twenty-two sokemen of South Leverton in Nottinghamshire who together paid 20s. Above all, every manor could be assigned a render or value related to the annual income from that property to the lord. The whole country was thus valued cumulatively at £72,000, which cannot all have been paid at once, as the evidence of coins suggests that the total of pennies in circulation came to no more than £37,500. In the real world many lords obtained little or no cash from a manor, but took delivery of foodstuffs for consumption by the household. The values show that estate managers and the compilers of the survey envisaged that every manor was capable of producing an annual revenue in cash. Lords had to pay out in order to obtain these profits: for example they invested in 6,000 mills, which contained machinery built by specialists, and materials such as steel and the stones for grinding the corn which had to be purchased. Some of the demesne crops were put on the market, but much grain, together with cheese and meat from the animals kept, was consumed directly. Not so the wool from the sheep which, judging from the 13,000 to 50,000 listed in each of the south-western and eastern counties in the Domesday survey, would have numbered more than a million for the whole country – and that accounts for demesne flocks only. Some fleeces may have been processed and woven on the estates, but much of this production was sold to the increasingly specialized urban cloth industry both in England and overseas.

Town dwellers accounted for almost a tenth of the English population. Such a figure implies that the countryside was producing a substantial surplus for consumption by townspeople with limited access to land of their own, and that the towns were producing or trading goods and services that the country could buy. Towns were not just centres of population, but also generators of wealth, which the state recognized and exploited when it could extract annual sums of £50, £60 and more from individual towns. The interaction of town and country encouraged the development of property relations which bound urban centres to rural manors – boroughs belonging to a single lord were intended to serve as markets for the produce of the nearby estates, and for the larger and more complex royal towns, urban houses were attached to the rural manors of various landholders within the hinterland. Towns, as well as providing points of sale and processing facilities for agricultural produce, also specialized in expensive goods for the wealthy, like the furs traded at Chester. Country dwellers, as well as producing agricultural surpluses, extracted raw materials by quarrying, and by mining iron and lead, and also processed goods for sale, such as salt on the coast and pottery inland. Fishing was sometimes concentrated in towns, such as Sandwich with its large herring catches, but was also widely distributed along the coast and on the major rivers. In addition to the fully urban communities, markets were held in administrative centres, such as Luton (Bedfordshire) and King's Sutton (Northamptonshire).

This account of Domesday has focused on its picture of a rationally organized, well-populated and productive country. There were many weaknesses, including uneven development, with thin populations, low values and pastoral economies in the north and west. The lack of basic security on the Welsh border, to take an obvious example, and political instability everywhere discouraged investment. The activities of a predatory aristocracy who were still disputing the ownership of land and seeking short-term profit at the expense of the long-term interests of their tenants damaged confidence. The incomplete hierarchy of towns, in which the smaller towns were absent, and the limited marketing network, meant that much production was either for direct consumption, or surpluses might be wasted. Weaknesses in technology condemned many to such drudgery as milling by hand, and gave low agricultural returns. To some extent the problems of the eleventh-century economy were general difficulties felt before the industrial revolution, and we should still be impressed by the changes in the two centuries before the Conquest which had created many of the structures that would endure in subsequent centuries – villages, field systems, manors and towns.

PART TWO

Expansion and crisis, c.1100–c.1350

Many of those who lived between the time of Domesday and 1300 experienced varied types of economic growth. If they lived in the countryside they saw the number and size of settlements increase, and they were aware that land was being brought into more productive use through clearance of woodland, scrub, moors and heaths, or the drainage of fens and marshes, or the enclosure of open land and woodland. Town dwellers realized that new houses and streets were being built around them, and many new towns were being founded, sometimes in rivalry with existing places. By 1300 the numbers of towns can be estimated at around 700 in England, 80 in Wales, and over 50 in Scotland, compared with little more than 100 in Britain in 1100. Urban and rural workshops were making more goods, and demanding increased supplies of raw materials. By 1212, for example, a million pounds of tin were being smelted each year in Devon and Cornwall, and the extraction of ore was scarring the landscape. Carts and pack-horses were moving along the road system in ever greater numbers, and by 1300 hundreds of ships were passing in and out of the ports annually, with the fleeces of 12 million English sheep among their cargoes. Observers in the thirteenth century were conscious of the growing numbers of people, without feeling the need to calculate how many, but we can make some estimate for 1300 of about 6 million in England, a million in Scotland, and 300,000 in Wales, about three times the totals in 1100. These people carried in their purses the silver pennies minted in especially large numbers by Edward I of England and Alexander III of Scotland, and indeed the amount of money in circulation had grown more rapidly than the rise in population. In England more than £1 million in coin was circulating in 1320 compared with £37,500 at the end of the eleventh century. In Scotland from about £20,000 in the middle of the twelfth century the total had grown to between £130,000 and £180,000 in 1280. From the point of view of individual adults that meant 4–5 shillings each at any one time.

The strengthening of the state in part provided a secure environment for an expanding economy, and in part was made possible by growth. In England Henry II (1154–89) made legal reforms which extended the jurisdiction of the royal courts, and the extension of powers to judge and tax the king's subjects reached its high point under Edward I (1272–1307). Frictions with the aristocracy in 1212–16 (during which time Magna Carta was issued by King John) and 1258–65 (when Simon de Montfort sought to reform the rule of Henry III) were part of a process by which the magnates lost some independence, but were brought into close association with royal government, to form a 'community of the realm'. King and barons conquered that part of Wales which remained independent, and unsuccessfully attempted to subdue the Scots. The Scottish kingdom entered a new era under David I (1124–53), who introduced the main features of a west European state: a local government structure based on sheriffs and sheriffdoms; royal castles; burghs; and a penny coinage. He reorganized the church with a system of dioceses, and founded monasteries belonging to the main European orders. He encouraged outsiders, especially Anglo-Norman aristocrats, to settle, granting them lands in exchange for service. His successors continued the same policies, extending royal rule of the new type into the north and west of the country. Although troubled by rebellions and problems of succession to the throne, the country enjoyed relative peace under Alexander III (1249–86).

The reign of Stephen (1135–54) was a political episode which probably disrupted the English economy. As two rival claimants competed for the allegiance of the aristocracy, the normal processes of government were interrupted. Lands were confiscated from enemies, and used to reward supporters. Monasteries were granted lands to which the donor had dubious title. Coins of inferior quality were issued, some from unofficial mints. In the civil war, armies ravaged sections of the countryside and towns were damaged, especially during sieges of castles. The prevalent insecurity and lack of stable property rights were reported by chroniclers at the time, and were remembered long after order had been restored in the 1150s. The extent of the destruction is apparently reflected by the amount of geld (tax) collected by the officials of Henry II in 1156. The sum had fallen by 24 per cent since 1130, and the local officials blamed 'waste', especially in the midland counties. This word could refer to administrative disruption rather than physical devastation, but Henry II's officials did have to pay very large sums to restock royal manors, apparently because cattle had been stolen and other damage done. Some of the places complaining of waste are known from chronicle accounts to have been the scene of fighting. This period of insecurity and sporadic damage to property may have contributed to the rather slow growth in landed incomes in the twelfth century (see below, p. 121). Kings had a direct influence on the economy of substantial parts of the kingdom through their administration of the royal forests. These reached their maximum extent in the early thirteenth century.

The increase in written documents represents for historians an especially important aspect of growth in administration. Economic activity and record-keeping were directly connected. First, an economy with a large surplus was better able to pay for an educational system, and to reward specialist writers such as administrators, clerks and poets. Secondly, such documents as accounts were desirable as transactions became more numerous and complicated. In an age of rapid change, property owners needed the assurance of written proof of their title, and customs previously entrusted to the memory of old people were now preserved in more durable form. Finally, and most importantly, those in power found that, when different groups were competing for wealth and privilege, documents increased their authority and efficiency. Before Domesday a relatively small number of charters, law codes and chronicles give us a very patchy and imprecise glimpse of economic life, and we are not sure about the main long-term trends. From Domesday onwards the records accumulate in ever greater quantity. The first surviving financial account for the English kingdom relates to the year 1129–30, and records of the royal court begin in 1193; detailed tax lists survive from 1225. The earliest estate surveys were drawn up in the teens of the twelfth century; the first manorial accounts relate to the year 1208; and lords' court records have survived from the 1230s. The earliest urban court proceedings begin at the end of the twelfth century. From the 1270s onwards we can gather information from thousands of charters and deeds, and hundreds of surveys, tax lists, court rolls and bishops' registers. Most adult males alive in 1300 in England, even lesser peasants and ordinary artisans, must have had their names written in documents a number of times, often when they paid a rent or tax or because they came before a court on some routine matter. In spite of the destruction and loss of documents, enough have survived for a good proportion of those names to be known to us.

Now, these documents were produced by and for governments, and they can only give us a very incomplete and even misleading picture of economic activity. They tell us much more about the thirteenth century than the twelfth, which retains rather an air of mystery. About southern, eastern and midland England we have much more information than about the north and west. Wales was partly incorporated into the English state and eaten up by English lords, so it is quite well represented in the archives, especially after its conquest in 1282. Many Scottish charters survive, but there are few detailed local surveys, accounts or court records. Even when the documents are abundant, the poor and under-privileged are under-represented. The peasant economy has to be reconstructed from indirect evidence, and those who lacked land are almost hidden from view. Women and children are much less prominent than adult males.

The records tell us often about how things should have been, viewed from the perspective of those in authority. A charter issued by the king may grant to a lord the right to hold a weekly market on his land, but it does not tell us that trading has been taking place on that spot unofficially for many years, and that the charter is merely confirming an existing event. To take an opposite possibility, the charter will not explain that the grant was a speculative venture which failed dismally – no one wished to trade there, and the market existed only as a theoretical privilege. The purpose of the charter was to record the grant from king to subject, not to describe the local economy. Fortunately we are not entirely dependent on written evidence, and the mass of material remains from the period provides welcome confirmation that settlements were being founded, towns were growing in size, goods were being manufactured and traded in bulk, and large quantities of rubbish were accumulating. The archaeological evidence is also selective, because more substantial remains survive of the public works of the crown (such as Edward I's great Welsh castles), or cathedrals, than of the houses of the peasants and townspeople. But the material remains have been selected in different ways, and so we gain greatly from putting the written and unwritten evidence together.

The documents, and to some extent the buildings and artefacts, have a value beyond giving us routine information such as the figures for industrial production and levels of population that have just been quoted. If we are to glimpse the outlook of those who lived and worked in the medieval economy, to have some notion of their motives, intentions and ideas, then the 'bias' of the evidence is valuable to us. Medieval people have left us few explicit explanations for their behaviour, and when they did we should be suspicious because they were often seeking to justify their actions for some political or moral purpose. We must reconstruct their intentions from their actions, and attempt to understand the thinking behind the documents or the artefacts. The market charter mentioned above, which reveals so little about the realities of trade, speaks volumes about the pretensions of kings and lords, in their desire to regulate and profit from the activities of their inferiors.

The main theme of the first three chapters of this section is growth. The fourth deals with the early fourteenth century, when expansion faltered and ceased. This crisis deserves our attention as a significant episode in itself, but also compels us to re-examine the period as a whole.

CHAPTER FOUR

Lords, c.1100–c.1315

The lords had established themselves in a strong economic position after the upheavals of the eleventh century, and here we need to consider their involvement in the age of expansion. Did they develop their control over property and expand their landed assets? How successful were they in managing their estates and incomes in a time of rapid change? And did they make their own contribution to growth?

i. *Aristocracy and property*

To begin with property, the word is linked in our minds with ownership, but such modern concepts cannot be applied to the world of the twelfth and thirteenth centuries without reservations. The English magnates, that is the earls and barons among the lay aristocracy, and the bishops and larger monasteries in the case of the churchmen, thought of their collection of lands and rights as an 'honour'. By this they meant a great lordship, at the core of which lay demesne manors yielding great quantities of food and cash. Dozens of tenants of substance held their lands from the magnate in 'fee', and therefore owed military and administrative services. Some were themselves known as barons, with perhaps five or more demesne manors, but most of them were knights and lesser landholders with a single manor. At the centre of an honour in secular hands lay a castle, as much a centre of government as a military stronghold. Visitors would be impressed by the nucleus of buildings and people around the castle, as at Tutbury in Staffordshire or Pontefract in Yorkshire, because next to his stronghold the great lord would have founded a monastery, where his family would be buried and their memory perpetuated in the prayers of the monks, and a planned town was laid out at the castle gates. Nearby, to confirm the high status of the lord, there would often be a park full of deer and great ponds for fish. The appearance of wealth and power was not just show, because the honour was run like a small state, with officials like the steward (originally in charge of the household), the butler (who supplied the wine), the marshal (who looked after the stable, and had military duties) and chamberlain (who managed the finances), just as in any kingdom. The more advanced honours had their own exchequers, where the revenues from land, towns, profits of justice and feudal dues were collected and any debts noted. The lord's judicial authority was exercised through the honour court, in which the tenants in fee assembled to deal with any disobedience in their ranks, such as failure to do services, and to settle internal disputes. The tenants could be summoned to advise the lord: the foundation of a monastery, for example, might be approved at such a gathering. Revenues came to the lord from his rights over the tenants, whose lands, if they died leaving a young heir, would be managed in wardship by the lord for his own profit while he acted as guardian. If the lands came to a female, her marriage was arranged by the lord, often for a considerable sum of money. When an heir succeeded, he paid a relief in cash to be accepted as tenant, and on certain occasions lords could demand financial help from the tenants, the aid.

The honour appears to stand as a denial of the property rights of the tenants, who formed the great majority of the aristocracy. This powerful organization, especially in the twelfth century, enabled a few magnates to exercise a very real control over their subordinates. The honour might seem to have provided the basis of the social and political lives of the tenants in fee. It was said that they could not grant away their land, or let land to subtenants (subinfeudate it), without the lord's permission. The lord was able to take their money, in reliefs for example, and through his rights of wardship and marriage he was making crucial decisions about the future of his tenants' families and lands. In short, everyone was a tenant – even the magnates held their honours of the king. Can words like property and ownership be applied in a feudal world where society functioned on the principle that land was held in exchange for service?

If we adopt this view of twelfth-century society we are in danger of accepting the image that the magnates projected. They claimed great powers and dramatized their social position, but their authority was limited from many directions. Crucially, they were never independent of the king. In the later twelfth century the royal courts extended their jurisdiction and offered to all free tenants, that is to the tenants of the honours, protection from eviction through the assize of novel disseisin, by which aggrieved tenants could bring a complaint against anyone who deprived them of possession (seisin); in addition, the assize of mort d'ancestor enabled a tenant who was deprived of his inheritance to reclaim the land. This was not an unprecedented attack on the honours, as the royal courts had always been there, and had dealt with cases involving the tenants of honours for decades. Even in the late twelfth century the kings and their lawyers thought that they were seeking to force the magnates to remedy abuses and judge their tenants fairly, not to undermine the honour courts. Whatever the intention, the opportunity to use the royal courts was welcomed by the tenants, and private justice was weakened. The growth of the common law exercised in the king's courts marks an important stage in the development of a state in which citizens depend for their security and property rights on a single authority.

The upper ranks of tenants, even before 1100, had not been entirely under the thumb of the honours. Many of them lived on substantial estates, had built castles and held their own courts, and so rivalled the jurisdiction of the honour from within. The Tourville family, for example, held lands from the honour of Leicester, and were close to the Beaumont family who were earls of Leicester in the early twelfth century. Geoffrey de Tourville based his considerable wealth and power on his castle at Weston Turville in Buckinghamshire, and in c.1150 was owed service of castle guard by the knights who held land from him. The tenants like the Tourvilles formed a group who met regularly, could co-operate in their own interests, and exercised influence in the honour court. Judgments often took the form of compromise settlements and arbitrations rather than the lord handing down orders. In the ladder of tenures which made up a feudal society, magnates could not behave as dictators, because they were the king's tenants, and if they expected their lord to behave reasonably and listen to their advice, they could scarcely adopt a different standard in their own lordship. When King John assented to Magna Carta in 1215 he was accepting limitations on his feudal powers, on such matters as marriage, wardship and reliefs, but at the same time the barons who imposed the charter had to concede that they could not treat their tenants in an arbitrary way. For example, the standard relief of £5 for a knight's holding became normal throughout the feudal hierarchy.

The main obstacle to the power of the honour came not from direct challenges from above or below, but from the independent attitudes of the tenants, which eroded the authority of the magnates. They, like the magnates, thought that they had earned their lands as rewards for past service. They expected to enjoy hereditary succession by right. There had always been an element of fiction in the notion that they performed

military service in person for their lands, because at any one time a proportion of them would have been too old, too young, too ill or disabled
to ride and fight, and so they paid for a substitute. More often than not
in the twelfth century the tenants paid money (scutage) and the lord or
king engaged professional soldiers for wages. In the thirteenth century
the principle of military service was kept going, but each magnate was
expected to provide a much smaller quota of knights, and soon after 1300
armies were paid entirely from tax revenues. Similarly the ideal that lords
and tenants enjoyed a close personal bond had probably never been true,
and was certainly receding, in view of the scattered nature of the great
estates.

In practical terms, by the early twelfth century lords had limited
powers over the tenants in fee, who could do much as they wished with
their holdings. The exploitation of resources was left entirely to the
tenant. Land could be sold or given to the church on the tenant's initiative, and no one questioned that when a tenant died the successor in possession of the land would be the heir, ideally the eldest son. The custom
developed by the middle of the twelfth century that if there were no male
heirs, and the tenant had more than one daughter, the inheritance would
be divided between them. Only in exceptional circumstances, such as
total disloyalty, would a lord step in and take the land away. If the tenant
wished to sell the land, he would 'subinfeudate' the property, that is make
the buyer his subtenant, which added to fragmentation of holdings and
the complexity of the honour's tenures. Alternatively the tenant could
convey land by substitution, that is by asking the lord to accept the buyer
as a tenant instead of the seller. These alienations of land were allowed
on condition that the tenant looked after the interests of those who might
be damaged by the transaction – members of the family who might be
deprived of their inheritance would give permission, and the lord would
be guaranteed that any change to the tenancy would not result in a loss
of service.

Tenants acquired land from a number of lords, by purchase or marriage. This was not a deliberate policy to create divided loyalties, but
the inevitable consequence of expanding landholding in localities where
there were normally a number of overlapping magnate lordships. Lords
in search of political or military support, who may at one time have
depended on their tenants, instead sought the services of those with skills
(as lawyers for example), or influence among their neighbours, and rewarded them with money payments or promises of protection. In other
words they built up a retinue of supporters, and this rather than the
honour became the basis of lordly power and influence. This process
extended over a long period. Lords were recruiting supporters among

people who were not their tenants before 1200, but they still expected their tenants to attend their private courts and to form an important element in their circle of allies and helpers as late as the 1260s.

The English aristocracy did not have the full control over their land that we associate with modern concepts of ownership, but nor can we regard the majority of the aristocracy as living under the overwhelming restrictions of an overlord's honorial authority. In the long run the magnates' political power was completely overshadowed by the state. Edward I asserted royal power when he enquired into the franchises of his subjects, and objected if they were claiming (for example) hunting rights (free warren) or supervision of the sale of bread and ale, but could show no written evidence for those privileges. He was still willing to sympathize with their complaints that their tenants were depriving them of feudal rights of wardship and marriage by subinfeudating their lands, or by granting land to the church without permission. The Statutes of Quia Emptores (1290) and Mortmain (1279) forbade these practices. In future if land was sold a new tenant should be substituted who would recognize the rights of the overlord, and gifts to the church required a royal licence which was granted after an enquiry to establish that other interests would not be damaged. The crown's self-interest was served by these measures, but they show that at least some dimensions of lords' interests in their tenants' property still survived at the end of the thirteenth century. But the aristocracy regarded themselves as the owners of their land, and we can confirm that they were the effective masters of their own estates.

The secular aristocracy took a lofty view of their obligations. They justified their position by the services that they owed to overlords and ultimately the king, but also claimed a more general role as the protectors and defenders of the whole community. They believed that this function on earth was sanctioned by God. Their collective sense of duty was given a more specific focus in the twelfth and thirteenth centuries by the growth of ideas of chivalry, which in some versions emphasized the close link between knights and the church – knights were portrayed as soldiers of Christ, protecting the weak and defending Christendom against the heathen. More often, knights regarded themselves as uniquely skilled practitioners of the arts of war, and in peacetime found a place in the households of the lords and kings, winning the praise of women with their civilized accomplishments. In the same period the higher clergy also gained in self-confidence, as the church reform movement separated more clearly the clergy and the laity.

The aristocracy had more selfish aims. The laity were attached to their lineage, so they were conscious of their debt to previous generations of their family, and of their responsibility for the well-being of their offspring. They competed for land that could be added to the main inheritance, ultimately for the benefit of the eldest son, and also for land which could be handed on to younger sons and daughters. In a comparable fashion, monks focused on the landed assets of their monastic house, and they took a long-term view. Many monasteries kept a chronicle, which perpetuated a collective memory of any 'bad' abbots whose mismanagement caused debt or the loss of land, and recorded the virtues of those who had been successful in running the estate and adding to its resources. Monastic houses competed with rivals. Benedictines, who were well established, not to say complacent, by the twelfth century, resented the austerity of the Cistercian order (which seemed to smack of hypocrisy) when they were attracting patronage, and were affronted in the thirteenth century by the enthusiastic and fashionable orders of friars. Their hostility to the latter was sharpened by the friars' preaching of a doctrine of poverty, which included criticisms of the wealth of the traditional religious orders.

There were acquisitive individuals who advanced themselves by using their talents and good fortune, like William the Marshall, a younger son of a minor baronial family who embarked on a career under royal patronage fighting in wars and tournaments from 1168, until eventually he received the reward of loyal service in marriage to the heiress of a rich marcher lordship in 1189. His counterpart among the clergy was one of the great pluralists, like Walter de Merton, who served successive kings as chancellor in 1261–3 and 1272–4, and ended his days as bishop of Rochester. In the course of his career, which began in 1233, he drew income as a cathedral canon at Wells, Exeter, Lincoln, London and Salisbury, and was either vicar or rector (in name) of ten churches. In 1270 his income from these offices alone must have been near to £400 per annum.

These two extreme examples show that aristocrats became richer most rapidly by gaining political favour, as the patronage of magnates and kings could be translated into acquisitions of land, or offices which would yield the profits in cash with which land could be bought. The aspiring careerist had to show appropriate talents and find the right patron. Backing the losing side, as those who supported Simon de Montfort's cause in 1258–65 found, could lead to confiscation of land, and to ruin. The important chances for an up-and-coming courtier or soldier came when old families died out in the male line, leaving the lands to a marriageable heiress. In the late twelfth and early thirteenth century, risk-takers could 'proffer' money to the crown – often hundreds of pounds – for a wardship or marriage, calculating that the income they gained would cover the investment.

One route to success lay in moving into frontier territories, where lands of conquered enemies could be acquired, but also where underdevelopment in the economic and administrative sense gave the opportunity for carving out new lordships. Norman lords can be seen taking risks by moving into Yorkshire and the other northern counties after the pacification of the region in 1071: here they could build castles like that at Richmond and develop the surrounding countryside. The Welsh marches provided such opportunities, and lords established themselves there by seizing land and building castles as the basis of their lordships at such places as Wigmore (Herefordshire) and Grosmont (Monmouthshire). Anglo-Norman lords were welcomed by David I and his successors in Scotland, where they were granted feus (fiefs). Intervention in Ireland extended the colonial territories from the late twelfth century, and many English and marcher lords acquired lands there. Often the occupation of new territory was followed by a colonizing movement by monasteries belonging to the new orders of the twelfth century, especially the Cistercians and Augustinians.

Once established, the land accumulated by aristocratic families had to be protected against erosion. There were constant pressures to detach pieces of land as rewards for deserving followers, or to endow the local monastery. Children who had no formal claim on the main inheritance expected to receive some land – daughters to take it with them into marriage, or younger sons who could be made subtenants or under the prevailing custom could be given land that had been acquired during their father's lifetime, as distinct from the property that he had himself inherited. The most successful operators looked after the whole family, made good marriages which would bring useful alliances for the future, and endowed monasteries, without ruining their estates. As old families faltered, or most likely when the careful calculations of successive generations were frustrated by biology and the main inheritance went to a female, there were plenty of new men anxious to acquire land and establish their families. Lesser barons like William Marshall sought promotion into the ranks of the magnates, and replacements for losses among the lesser aristocracy came from officials, soldiers, merchants or rich peasants. The aristocracy was always an 'open elite', proclaiming that only high birth and long ancestry qualified them for their privileges but accepting that in the real world landed wealth was the main qualification.

Individual aristocratic families rose and fell, and some died out and were replaced by new recruits, but we might expect to see an overall pattern. There are so many examples of magnates prospering – such as the constant accumulation of land, mainly through a successful marriage policy, of the Clares, earls of Gloucester, throughout the twelfth and thirteenth centuries, or the purchase of land from indebted lay families by monasteries in the thirteenth century – that contemporaries commented on the growth of larger estates, which they sometimes deplored. Soon after 1300 a chronicler complained that 'the earls and other magnates who could live according to their status on their inheritance ... pester their poor neighbours to sell what they have inherited'. Because the surviving documents come from the successful landowners, the land market may appear to have worked in favour of the large estates.

The routine records of enfeoffment, however, and the emergence of new small manors, can leave no doubt that land became more fragmented and the lesser aristocracy multiplied. Magnates rewarded their supporters and officials, and indeed renewed old obligations of service by granting land to families already endowed with fiefs in an earlier generation. The new estates were not always the result of splitting existing units, but were also created by the clearance or drainage of new land. In the same way lesser aristocrats multiplied especially rapidly in the frontier areas, such as the north of England or the Welsh marches in the twelfth century, when there was not so much room for new manors in the older countries of the midlands and the south. In Scotland at this time, magnates who had benefited from the initial grants of feus were using part of their estates to reward lesser aristocrats. In the monastic world, as well as the growth in the size of the large estates, we should not ignore the hundreds of new small foundations – priories and nunneries in the twelfth century, friaries, colleges and hospitals in the thirteenth, many of which were provided with annual revenues of less than £100. The proliferation of small units of landholding was not always controlled by superior lords, but often resulted from initiatives among the knights and gentry, who were carving out new manors for themselves by buying parcels of land or making clearances. They were using as capital money acquired from their office-holding or profits gained from farming and trading. Throughout our period most land was in the hands of the lesser aristocracy, and their share increased through time.

An example of the multiplication of small manors is Hanbury in the wooded country of north Worcestershire. In 1086 it was described in Domesday Book as being divided between two large manors, one belonging to the bishops of Worcester and the other part of the royal demesne. A minor lay lord held one very small sub-manor. By 1300 the territory was divided into ten or eleven units of exploitation. The king kept a fragment of his original estate, a 1,000-acre park, and his park keeper held a small manor in keeping with his gentry status. The bulk of the former royal land had been granted to Cistercian monks from Bordesley Abbey, who farmed it in two separate granges, one of which was formed by clearing new land from wood and rough grazing. The bishop retained a much-truncated manor, having ceded a large section of underdeveloped land to a lay family who then granted it to the Knights Templar. Four other gentry families had created small manors by a combination of grants from the bishops, purchase and clearance, which joined the small manor surviving from the time of Domesday. The bishops were not left out of the move to expand, as they had developed a detached area of former woodland into a virtually separate manor, and they also bought up an area of newly cleared land from one of their tenants, but the general tendency clearly favoured the multiplication of small manors in the hands of gentry and the new religious orders.

The balance of landholding between the laity and the church moved in two directions immediately after 1066. Bishops and monasteries were required to provide landed endowments for knights perfoming military service. The opposite tendency of lay families endowing the church was probably on a larger scale. It began slowly with a few new Benedictine houses such as Lewes in Sussex and Much Wenlock in Shropshire, both initiated by Norman magnates, and the royal foundations at Battle in Sussex and Reading in Berkshire. A significant wave of monastic expansion came with the arrival of the new monastic orders in the twelfth century, of which the most important were the Cistercians (with various allied orders such as the Premonstratensians), the Augustinian canons (including the Arrouasians and Victorines), the native English order, the Gilbertines, and the military orders of the Templars and the Hospitallers. They attracted enthusiastic aristocratic support. A prominent family would wish to be associated with a particular monastery, and would gain spiritual benefits and social status from the size of the endowment and the quality of its monks and buildings. A typical example would be the new earl of Leicester, Robert de Beaumont, founding on a lavish scale Leicester Abbey, an Augustinian house, in 1138 or 1139, which would ever after be regarded as an asset to his earldom.

The greatest number of new monasteries were founded in the north and the marches, where older Benedictine monasteries were relatively few, and where new lay families were anxious to make their mark. The numbers are impressive – there were more than sixty Cistercian houses by 1200 in England and Wales and at least 150 Augustinian foundations. In Scotland, where new monasteries were founded later, twenty Cistercian, seventeen Augustinian, seven Tironian and six Premonstratensian houses had been established by 1300. They were not given many great manors occupying prime agricultural land in the fashion of the earlier Benedictine establishments. Cistercians and some branches of the Augustinians attracted lay benefactors by their preference for occupying wild places (deserts, as the monks called them), in order to contemplate spiritual matters away from the corrupting influence of secular society. They could be established in remote valleys like Rievaulx in Yorkshire or Llanthony on the Welsh border, and their colonizing effort would contribute to the development of the whole region, without great cost to the founder. (Plate 5) The Augustinians sometimes occupied former minster churches, so they had some landed basis for the new monasteries, and they were often given parish churches with their glebe lands and tithes, which laymen were being discouraged from owning in the new climate of the church reform movement. Monasteries added to their estates by purchase, especially in the thirteenth century. The new centres of religious life of this time, such as the orders of friars and the foundation of colleges of priests to pray for the souls of the founder, added yet more property to the church's considerable possessions, but were not as well provided with land as the monasteries had been. We can estimate that the church's share of landed wealth in England had grown from about a quarter of the total in 1086 to almost a third in 1300.

Finally the king lost land. The 'royal demesne' had been inflated by the Conquest, but was then granted to loyal subjects as part of the crown's patronage, and was used to endow religious houses. The land said by Domesday in 1086 to have been held by the king, at £11,000, amounts to about a sixth of the total value of land in the kingdom. Around 1300 the royal demesnes yielded £13,000–£14,000 annually, a small increase in money terms, but after a major inflation and much general economic growth, the king's share of landed income had fallen to about 2 per cent. A king such as Edward I suffered no great hardship from this loss – his predecessors had gained valuable political support from the grants of land, and the monarch disposed of many other sources of income such as taxation.

The landowners of the twelfth and thirteenth centuries had made great efforts to increase and keep the amount of land under their control, and as a result estates rose and fell in size, and parcels of land large and small were constantly moving through inheritance, marriage, purchase and gift. In the long term the church acquired land from the laity in general, small church institutions multiplied, and among the laity the knights and gentry gained at the expense of the magnates and the crown.

Scottish landholding deserves some separate consideration. The language of continental feudalism arrived in the reign of David I, when the crown began to grant feus to immigrant aristocrats from England and Normandy, who grew in numbers and influence during the late twelfth century. One of these 'infeftments' gave Robert de Brus, from a family which originated near Cherbourg, a great tract of country in Annandale from the Solway to the source of the Clyde in 1124 for the service of ten knights. The charters issued at this time, and those that they in turn used to grant lands to their supporters, give the impression of a pyramid of landholding for service, which has been seen to mark the 'feudalization' of the kingdom. The Scottish common law came under the strong influence of English law, with its concern to regulate property relations within a framework of lordship and tenancy. The grants of feus (many of them much smaller than Annandale, and for the service of a single knight) to the Anglo-Norman elite was concentrated in the south and east of the country, where royal power was most securely established and which contained the most developed agricultural land and urban centres. Gradually the new form of tenures was extended into the west and north, where more traditional forms of lordship tended to persist and royal rule remained a more remote influence.

During the twelfth and early thirteenth centuries, magnates built up great accumulations of land which ignored the frontiers of kingdoms, and in some cases combined estates in Scotland and England, and Ireland. So David, earl of Huntingdon (1152–1219) held Garioch, a great compact lordship north-west of Aberdeen, with smaller holdings in the east and in Midlothian, near Edinburgh. He was also a considerable lord in the east midlands of England (Map 8). He did not see these lands as separate but ran them as an integrated enterprise. He recruited in England some of the lesser aristocrats whom he established with grants of land in Scotland, and one of his Scottish estate stewards came from his midland properties. A handful of great magnates can be compared with the earl of Huntingdon, including the Stewarts, hereditary stewards to the Scottish kings and major lords in the west, with a base at Renfrew

---▶

Map 8. Examples of estates in the twelfth and thirteenth centuries. The map is designed to show the characteristic estate patterns of different types of lord: a bishop's manors tended to be concentrated in his diocese, though in the case of the very rich bishopric of Winchester there were important outliers, from Taunton in the west to Southwark in the east. An earl's estates were much more scattered, for the earl of Huntingdon in his English honour, the manors were stretched across the east midlands and, in addition, he had a string of lands, some of them very extensive, up the east coast of Scotland. Monastic lands tended to lie within carting distance of the monastery, but the granges of Margam Abbey (a Cistercian house) were more tightly concentrated than those of the older and richer Norwich Cathedral Priory. The rich knightly family the Longvillers had scattered manors in one region, mostly in Yorkshire, but stretching into Nottinghamshire and Lincolnshire.

Sources: J. Z. Titow, *Winchester Yields* (Cambridge, 1972); K. Stringer, *Earl David of Huntingdon 1152–1219* (Edinburgh, 1985); D. H. Williams, *Atlas of Cistercian Lands in Wales* (Cardiff, 1990); I. Atherton et al. (eds), *Norwich Cathedral* (1996); C. Clay, 'The Family of Longvillers', *Yorkshire Archaeological Journal*, 42 (1971).

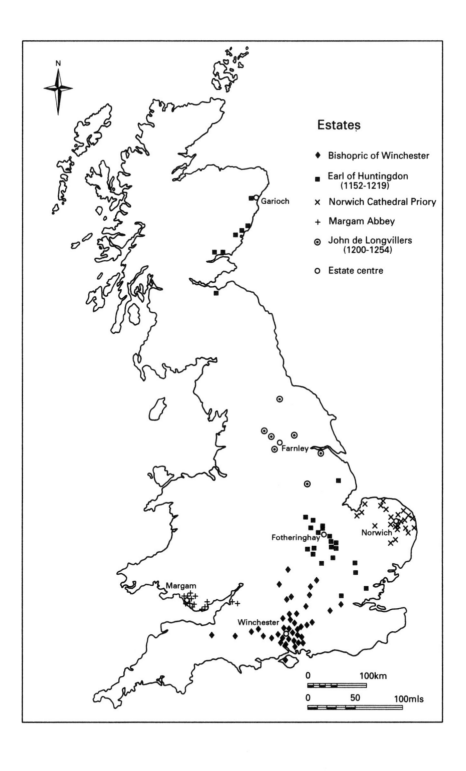

Estates

♦ Bishopric of Winchester

■ Earl of Huntingdon
  (1152-1219)

✕ Norwich Cathedral Priory

✚ Margam Abbey

◉ John de Longvillers
  (1200-1254)

○ Estate centre

N

Garioch

Farnley

Norwich

Fotheringhay

Margam

Winchester

0   100km

0   50   100mls

but also with land in the Lothians and on the borders. The power of such lords is likely to have exceeded those of the English lords in their honours. Like the lordships of the Welsh marches, Annandale, Garioch and their like stretched over a single, large territory, and gave the lord complete and exclusive control. The ties between magnate and tenants were relatively new, hereditary succession was not always established, and the tenants looked for continuing patronage. In a very large lordship the tenants were less likely to acquire land from a number of lords. Royal control was a less inhibiting factor, though royal justice was being extended in the thirteenth century.

This view of a 'feudal' Scotland may be a product of surviving documents, and charters apparently recording simple grants concealed social and economic complexity, such as sales of land and loans of money. During the thirteenth century the tenants of the great magnates seem to have gained more independence, especially in the more commercial envronment of the south and east.

While broadly common patterns of economic and social developments among the aristocracy of England, southern Scotland and south Wales can be seen from the late twelfth century, Welsh Wales as well as the north and west of Scotland present a poorly documented and very different picture. English observers at the time regarded these as alien territories, inhabited by wild and barbarous people. Feudal tenures provided a veneer of influence from a more settled world. Lords were the heads of kin groups, and ruled over men rather than lands. They received from their subordinates not rents and services, but payments of tribute, in kind, which were acknowledgements of superiority rather than rents calculated on a holding or an acreage. The word for lord in western Scotland, *mormaer*, and in Welsh the *pencenedl*, both refer to chiefs or heads of kindreds rather than territorial lords in a feudal state. They did not gather possessions like the English aristocrats in order to enrich future heirs to their estates. Without towns, commerce, production for the market, rents and the other elements of the infrastructure, they lacked the means to accumulate wealth in the manner of their counterparts in Lothian or the English midlands. Coins were not minted in north-west Scotland. And any cattle or goods which they did gather together would tend to be distributed among the kin rather than kept in a single line of descent. They sometimes gained wealth by plunder. Lords in the Western Isles in the early and mid-thirteenth century went on raids to gather booty (especially cattle) in Ireland, and with few openings in landed society young men from the Isles were hired by Irish rulers as galloglasses (mercenaries). The prince Owain Gwynedd in 1162 took a plundering expedition to Arwystli (Montgomeryshire). These freebooting societies were introduced gradually to the feudal world through migration, inter-marriage and the cultural influence of such western European concepts as knighthood, but also in the case of Wales through conquest.

ii. *Managing the estate*

In addition to the decisions that had to be made over acquiring and losing property, landlords had to consider various options is relation to the exploitation of their estates. For the greater lords – the earls, barons, bishops and larger monasteries – these decisions became more urgent as time went on. In the eleventh century, both before and after the Conquest, the landholdings of the greatest magnates seem so enormous that we cannot imagine that they had to worry about their incomes. But we know from our own times that even the greatest millionaires seek new ways to expand their fortunes, and they justify themselves, as would the medieval earls, by pointing out their expensive responsibilities. A handful of families belonged to the super-rich category, and among the leading 200 in 1086 were many lords with perhaps a dozen manors in demesne worth in total about £50 per annum who understandably felt a need for more income.

Estates consisted partly of land held directly by the lord, the manors in demesne, and of lands held as fiefs by tenants. Even in the midlands and the south, where the bulk of grants in fee had been made before 1100, parcels of land were still being given out to tenants during the twelfth century. They were lost to the lord as sources of substantial income, so lords hung on to their largest and richest manors, and tended to grant to subordinates or to the church smaller, outlying and less valuable prop-erties. The Lacy family, based at Weobley in Herefordshire, illustrate the point. They kept in demesne large manors located on fertile soils, like Stanton Lacy in Shropshire, and Weobley itself. Here they had their main residences, and so their household could be fed directly from their own produce. They also kept large and valuable demesne manors further east, such as Painswick in Gloucestershire, which were safe from devastation if war broke out on the Welsh border. Land out on the border itself, further west than Weobley, which was not very productive and which was vulnerable to attack, was either granted to knights who could give valuable service defending the border, or was used to endow the remote Augustinian monastery of Llanthony.

Lords' resources of land were constantly diminishing, and there were limits on their other sources of income. They were prevented from demanding large sums in feudal dues, as custom developed to protect the tenants in fee – for example, the £5 maximum relief on a knight's fee, which was becoming customary in the late twelfth century, was fixed by Magna Carta. Profits of justice were limited as the royal courts became more active at this time. The franchises which allowed lords to take fines and charge tolls on their subordinates – in markets, for example, or from the regulation of ale-selling, or by seizing the goods of those convicted of felonies in the royal courts – were defended by lords against royal enquiries in the thirteenth century, but even when their rights were upheld under the Quo Warranto investigations of Edward I's reign, they were not very lucrative. In the lordship of Holderness in east Yorkshire, for example, which was especially powerful, the franchises were valued at £14 annually, a small fraction of the income from land.

The magnates felt beleaguered in the 1190s and in the reign of John (1199–1216) because the royal courts were attracting business, to the long-term damage of their own honorial courts, while at the same time the crown was subjecting them to demands for very large sums of money. In 1213–14 William fitz Alan, a Shropshire baron, was an extreme example of a general trend when he was expected to pay a relief of 7,000 marks (£4,666), a sum well in excess of the annual income from his estates. The sums demanded for a wardship or marriage rose to near impossible levels. To make such payments, the magnates had to borrow money on the strength of their future income. On top of these problems came severe inflation. A load (later known as a quarter) of wheat had cost on average 2s for most of the twelfth century, but soon after 1193 it had increased rapidly, soaring as high as 8s, and settling to an average of between 3s 8d and 4s 10d in 1210–50, nearly double its old price (see Figure 1 below, p. 230). Oxen, the main source of pulling power in twelfth-century agriculture, increased in price by a similar amount, fetching 3–4s before 1200, and an average of 6s 8d in subsequent years. Foot soldiers in the king's army had been paid a penny a day in the reign of Henry II but by 1200 their wages had doubled. The rate of pay of agricultural workers probably also doubled at the same time, from a halfpenny to a penny per day.

Unlike the soldiers and labourers, the incomes of the landed aristocracy did not rise in the general inflation. Those lords who supplied their households directly from their estates were at least protected from the increase in the price of basic foodstuffs, but the cost of any grain and meat bought on the market, and of other goods and services, was rising, while many of their demesnes were leased out for fixed rents. Demesne leases were recorded by some church landlords, but were apparently generally employed throughout upper landed society. The canons of St Paul's Cathedral in London in 1152 leased their manor of Kensworth in

Bedfordshire to a farmer, Henry Bucvinte, a member of a local lesser aristocratic family, for an annual rent of £10 for the rest of his life (they helped him to become established with lower rents in his first four years). For this he received farm buildings including a manor house, barn and housing for animals, 220 acres of arable land, and enough pasture for at least 24 cattle and 120 sheep, together with the labour services of the peasant tenants – sufficient assets to enable him to pay £10 to the canons and to make some profit for himself. Such an arrangement was based on the assumption that prices and profits remained relatively stable. In 1181 the rent of Kensworth had risen to £13 annually, but such an increase would not have protected the canons against the effects of inflation if Bucvinte's successor had lived through the 1190s while prices were doubling. Many farmers found themselves in the happy position of holding a lease of a demesne for quite a long term – for the remainder of their lives, or for twenty years – paying a fixed cash rent, while their profits increased.

The landlords had grown up with stable prices, which meant that they thought of land values as fixities – a farm, in Latin *firma*, a leasehold rent, was described by a twelfth-century official as so-called because it was firm and unchanging. Many manors between the late eleventh and late twelfth century increased their annual revenue but not by a very large margin: Charing in Kent, for example, was worth £34 in 1066, and £40 at the end of the twelfth century. Lords on the eve of the inflation received much the same income as their predecessors at the time of the Domesday survey. The archbishop of Canterbury, one of the great church magnates, had estates valued at £1,246 in 1086 and £1,375 in 1172. The landlords' world fell apart when these apparent fixities in their lives shifted. Between 1184 and 1214 the greater lords converted their system of management from leasing of demesnes by taking over each manor as the farmer's term ended, and putting it under the control of officials directly responsible for the profits. Apart from the shock of inflation, the lords may have had other motives for the change; they may have solved the problem of the price rise by leasing out the demesnes for very short terms of a few years, negotiating a higher rent at each renewal. More likely they were concerned about the improvement in tenants' security which had resulted from the legal reforms of the late twelfth century, and became worried that leasehold tenants, like tenants in fee, would be protected by the royal courts. Bringing demesnes into direct management would certainly prevent such a disaster.

Lords were taking a far-reaching step when they brought demesnes under their direct control. It involved other developments which were still having repercussions two or three generations after the initial decisions were made around 1200. One of the advantages of the old system of leasing lay in its administrative simplicity. Once a suitable farmer had been found, and the bargain struck with him, the central estate officials had no more complicated task than collecting the money or agricultural produce when it was due (often at four dates through the year), checking that payment was made in full, and ensuring that the buildings were not being neglected.

Under the new system, the lords' officials were working full time on the detailed supervision of agricultural tasks. Each manor was put under a local official, a reeve, sergeant or bailiff, who either served as a condition of holding land or was in receipt of rewards in cash and kind. These officials took charge of a large agricultural enterprise, as each demesne on a large estate usually consisted of between 200 and 500 acres of arable land, with meadow, pasture and wood. The official had to assemble a labour force of full-time servants, hired workers and tenants, supervise their work, and pay and feed them. On a mixed farm the tasks on the arable of ploughing, harrowing, sowing, weeding, harvesting, threshing and grain-processing had to be conducted alongside mowing and making hay, milking cows and shearing sheep, as well as the daily routines of feeding and caring for animals. Decisions had to be made about marketing – when and where and what quantity of grain or animals should be sold. The local official was often expected to collect rents and other dues. The reeves who carried out these tasks in the thirteenth century were servile peasants with experience of cultivating a holding of perhaps 10, 20 or 30 acres. They brought to the management of the demesne a wealth of detailed local knowledge about the soil, the crops which grew best, the most suitable animal breeds, the nearby markets, and the tenants and workers on the manor. It was this expertise which made the reeve such a useful asset for the lord, but he had no experience of large-scale agriculture, and he took a great risk in venturing into an operation of such size and complexity.

The lord took an even greater risk, as he was entrusting his valuable assets to a peasant who might prove incompetent or dishonest. Accordingly the lords created a new central management to supervise the reeves and bailiffs. There would be regular visits to the manors by the lord or members of the household. On a monastic estate monks would call in, and some of them established a system of monk wardens who looked after a group of manors. The steward would arrive regularly as he went round the manors to hold the lord's courts, and the receiver or treasurer, or a representative, came to collect money. These higher officials would not expect the reeve to make major decisions; such matters as wool sales or large items of expenditure would be arranged centrally. Their primary concern was to check on the reeve's conduct, which could be done through informal observation, but more officially through the manor court. One accusation made to the court was that the reeve used the lord's servants, ploughs and seed to cultivate his own holding.

The main check on the reeves' honesty and efficiency was made by the lords' auditors. They sometimes held an interim 'view' of the account, but their main meeting with the reeve came after the end of the farming year, at Michaelmas (29 September), when they examined the account that he had compiled with the help of a clerk. The audit involved a search for inconsistencies which would expose the reeve's tendency to exaggerate expenditure and minimize income. In the first part of the account the reeve would list the rents that had been received and the money gained from the sale of grain, cheese and other produce, and in the second part show how much of this income had been spent on wages, repair of buildings and implements, and purchase of animals or goods such as a new bucket for the well. Most of the surplus money would already have been sent to the treasurer or receiver. The auditors would check the reeve's figures by referring to a survey of the manor, which, for example, listed the rents, and they consulted the accounts for previous years. They would keep themselves informed about local conditions such as the performance of crops and the price of corn. The reeve could answer some of their sceptical enquiries because he kept evidence of transactions: written records or at least tallies on which the sum paid would be recorded with notches on wooden sticks. If the reeve could not provide a satisfactory answer the item on the account would be crossed out, the auditors would substitute their version, and the reeve would be expected to pay the difference. A clever reeve would make a profit from his term of office, but skilled auditing prevented him from lining his own pocket too lavishly.

The auditors, and the other estate officials, were helped in their work by a number of treatises, textbooks as we would call them, on the philosophy and practice of estate management, which carry such titles as the *Husbandry* or *Stewardship*, though the most famous, written around the 1280s, is always known by the name of its reputed author, *Walter of Henley*. These were mainly in French, and clearly aimed at an educated readership of clergy and aristocrats. *Walter* addresses itself to the lord himself, and gives rather moralistic advice about the need to calculate the resources of an estate, and to match expenditure to those assets. Such books dispense some useful agricultural knowledge, but they are mainly concerned with management, including the choice and control of employees, and above all calculations about yields of grain and animals, which would help auditors to make informed judgements about the performance of the reeves and their manors. *Walter*, for example, informs its readers that every two cows on salt marsh pasture will produce every week enough milk to make a stone of cheese and a half-gallon of butter, while three animals grazing ordinary pasture – in woodland or on meadows after haymaking – yield the same amount of dairy produce. The authors take a rather pessimistic view of the staff of lesser officials and farm servants, who are assumed to be potentially dishonest, lazy and malicious. Another type of textbook from the thirteenth century contains formularies which demonstrated to clerks the correct form of accounts, surveys and other records. These books were used in schools, at Oxford for example, where clerks who had received a conventional education were given a more practical training in producing the documents needed for running an estate. The change from leasing to direct management created thousands of new administrative jobs for clergy and gentry.

In addition to employing staff to run their estates from year to year, lords needed advice on more strategic matters, such as the purchase of property, or the clearance of new land, or major new building works. This was provided by a council of officials and lawyers. Monasteries recognized the need for expert management, and some of them took manors away from the individual departments of the monastery (the office of the almoner, precentor, sacrist and so on) and put the bulk of the land under a single powerful official, often the cellarer or the treasurer.

Did the lords and their advisers make the right decisions? They clearly believed that direct management was the right way to increase their revenues, because this method was employed by all types of lord over a large section of the south, east and midlands of England for the best part of two centuries. The combination of local responsibility and checks from the central officials overcame the problem of running a large scattered estate. Indeed, scattered estates had their advantages, because manors on different soils were less likely all to suffer crop failure in the same year. Also they could be linked to complement each other's resources: sheep and cattle from lowland manors could spend the summer on hill pastures, or pigs might be driven to woodland to be fattened on acorns and beech mast. Dispersed manors could also be convenient for providing food for the household, if they lay in districts which an itinerant lord (such as an earl or a bishop) might wish to visit. Lords and their households would stop for a few days or weeks at each residence, conduct local business, entertain their supporters, and consume the food from the demesne. Provincial lords who held a manor in the vicinity of London often made regular use of it when travelling to the capital, and it would serve as a retreat if the city became too uncomfortable (see Map 8 above, p. 117). Many estates inherited their geography from the remote past, but they modified their structure in the interests of efficiency and profit. An inconveniently remote manor would be sold or leased out. Large productive demesnes would be divided into two to create more easily manageable units of production. A small demesne could be increased in size by purchase.

In view of the relative uniformity of the accounting system, and the widespread knowledge of the textbooks such as *Walter of Henley*, we might expect to find that different demesnes were exploited along similar lines. It is true that mixed farming was usually practised, and most demesnes planted four different types of corn, and kept the main types of livestock – horses, cattle, sheep and pigs, with some poultry. A degree of centralization was practised in the management of sheep. Large estates would place all of the scattered flocks under a stockmaster or master shepherd, who orchestrated their movements from one manor to another according to a central estate strategy. One of the richest heiresses of the late thirteenth century, Isabella de Fortibus, had a stock-keeper for the lordship of Holderness in eastern Yorkshire, a lowland district with a tradition of mixed arable and pastoral farming. From a base at the manor of Keyingham he supervised shepherds at eleven places on the estate, who looked after more than 7,000 sheep. He would arrange for the flocks to move to the best pastures at the right time – for example on to rich grazing on the Humber estuary in the summer. The stock-keeper could assemble all of the wool together in order to sell it in bulk to a major merchant. The Holderness clip was bought between 1260 and 1280 for as much as £200 in a single year by the great international trading company, the Riccardi of Lucca. They provided a banking service for the lady, so they would not give the money to the estate officials in Yorkshire, but would credit it to Isabella's account.

Further west in northern England, on the Scottish border and in Scotland itself, hilly country was ill suited to much arable farming, and on the slopes lords set up specialist stock grazing centres, vaccaries (for cattle) and bercaries (for sheep). On the estates of the Lacy family based on Pontefract in 1295 a stockman called Gilbert de la Legh was in charge of twenty-seven scattered vaccaries in Lancashire, in such places as Accrington, Pendle and Rossendale, each with local keepers with more than eighty animals in their charge, making a total of almost 2,500. The estate invested in buildings to shelter the stock, which were moved frequently as a precaution against disease. They bred oxen for sale as draught animals and for beef in the markets of northern England.

Stock-rearing, whether managed separately within a mixed farming estate or practised as the main agricultural activity on remote hillsides, shows that estates were capable of specialization. On the lowland manors that made up the bulk of the great estates the managers left the choice of crops and agricultural methods largely to the reeves and bailiffs who knew the local conditions. In some districts wheat was chosen as the main winter-sown corn, but in others rye or a mixture of rye and wheat, maslin, was preferred. In some districts, notably in parts of Norfolk and Suffolk, barley occupied a very large acreage and not much wheat was grown. Oats and pulses (peas and beans) varied a great deal in their importance as a crop. Oats in some districts (parts of Essex, for example) were sown on more acres than barley, and in the south-west, the north-west and parts of Scotland the crop was grown almost as a monoculture.

The combinations of crops were chosen by the managers in the light of a number of complicated calculations. They were influenced by the local environment, so oats, which tolerate acid soils and have a short growing season, were grown in upland regions, while rye, which is well suited to light soils, was cultivated in gravelly river valleys and the sandy districts of East Anglia. The managers also had an eye on market opportunities, and would grow wheat for the urban market, though they also devoted land to oats and rye near to large towns, because traders used horses a great deal, for which they needed oats for fodder, and the poor ate rye bread, though these relatively cheap grains could only be carried relatively short distances. Manors sited away from towns, and from waterways which could be used for relatively cheap transport, had more limited opportunities to sell crops. A high proportion of the crops were consumed on the manor, which encouraged the cultivation of at least a small acreage of oats for the horses, even when the crop did not yield very highly. Similarly, if the demesne was to supply the lord's household, wheat for baking and barley for brewing would be produced. The demesne managers grew peas, beans and vetches partly for their value as animal feed, but also because of their beneficial effect on the following crop, as these legumes helped to add nitrogen to the soil.

The same mixture of motives governed the choice of animals, and while certain environments suited the various species – sheep were kept on hilly country, cattle in river valleys and pigs in woodlands – livestock also complemented arable cultivation, so many lowland manors practised sheep and corn husbandry, in which the flocks spent much of the time in the stubble and fallow fields, finding grazing in the vegetation that grew with the corn, and contributing their manure to the next year's arable land. Some demesnes found ways of feeding animals without relying on the natural resources of the locality. Manors which had limited access to woodland could still keep pigs, allowing them to feed on grain or peas and beans. The managers were aware of the ecological importance of selecting the right balance of arable and livestock, and of different crops and animals. They also insured themselves from complete failure in the event of bad harvests or diseases among the animals. At least part of the demesne's range of products would be likely to succeed even in a disastrous year.

The frequency of cropping varied from region to region. Through much of north-eastern, central and southern England, demesnes sowed crops on half of the arable land each year (following a two-course rotation) in step with the field systems operated by the peasants; while many other demesnes were organized on the basis of a three-course rotation, by which a third of the land was fallowed each year. In parts of the south-east and in Norfolk the land was cropped more frequently and nine-tenths or an even higher proportion of the land was cultivated. The managers of some manors, such as South Walsham on the earl of Norfolk's estate, had by the 1260s given up fallowing entirely, and cultivated all of their arable every year. Such intensive methods were adopted in north-east Norfolk not just because the soil was naturally fertile, but also because the high population density allowed labour to be concentrated on the land, with repeated ploughing, weeding, and spreading of manure and marl. Peas were cultivated in quantity, which added nitrogen directly to the soil, and provided fodder for animals fed in stalls, which was a good source of manure. Seed for grain and legumes was applied thickly; oats on one demesne were sown at 6–8 bushels to the acre rather than the 4 bushels which was normal in most of lowland England: the purpose was to smother the weeds. The ploughs were pulled by horses, which worked more quickly and efficiently than oxen. These methods were designed to raise the productivity of the land as much as possible in a region where towns such as Norwich and Yarmouth generated a high demand for foodstuffs, and there were many rural consumers. The demesne managers achieved the highest level of production of grain per acre recorded in medieval England, in good years climbing above 20 bushels per acre.

Most lords away from the agricultural hothouse of north-east Norfolk were content to leave a half or a third of the land to lie fallow, to plough the land with slow ox teams only once or twice before sowing, to sow only 2 to 4 bushels per acre, and to harvest between 8 and 16 bushels from each acre. Therefore their crops achieved only a three or fourfold increase over the seed sown. They were not betraying conservative attitudes in following this agricultural system – it was well suited to the conditions, and gave them acceptable returns.

It has been said that the level of investment in buildings, equipment and other assets on the large estates was often low, with only 5 per cent or less of income being spent in this way. The productivity of the demesnes' arable seems generally unimpressive. Even the profitable sheep was so small and ill-fed that its fleece often weighed little more than a pound and a half. For comparison, modern grain cultivation achieves a yield ratio of twenty-five times the seed, and a modern sheep's fleece weighs 4–6 pounds. The great lords could be seen as rather complacent because of the scale of their resources, like the successive bishops of Winchester whose estate contained more than forty manors with demesnes with a total of 10,000 to 14,000 acres sown each year (see Map 8 above, p. 117). Such lords did not need to be so concerned about the productivity of the land per acre, and were slow to learn from better practices in other regions or on other estates. Also, they gained much of their revenues from rent, and indeed a proportion of the labour supply was obtained as labour services of peasants.

We ought not to be censorious and over-critical in making judgements about medieval demesnes. It is not appropriate to compare their yields with those of the twenty-first century, because modern farmers have the benefit of chemical fertilizers, machinery and veterinary science. The manorial managers had limited opportunities to invest, given the level of technology, and in their society great benefits flowed from the status and patronage associated with high expenditure on entertainment and high living. Rather than judging them by modern standards, we should appreciate the way in which they managed their affairs in difficult circumstances. It was, for example, an impressive achievement for the demesnes of Norfolk to produce yields around 1300 which are comparable with the performance of farmers in the same county in the eighteenth century.

Demesne managers were capable of innovations in their farming. Monastic lords who were active around 1300, such as Henry of Eastry of the cathedral priory of Christ Church Canterbury, or John of Laund of Bolton Priory in Yorkshire, have enjoyed a reputation as improvers akin to that of Coke of Norfolk in the agricultural revolution of the eighteenth century. Modern historians have applied the term 'high farming' to the great estates of the late thirteenth century, again borrowing an idea from recent agricultural history. The estates under their energetic lords were administered in more effective ways, and they reacted to the stimulus of the market, as demand for produce of all kinds increased and pushed up prices.

England had the most agriculturally minded aristocracy in Europe, who were prepared to innovate. Among their triumphs of administrative ingenuity was the second phase of manorial accounts which appears from the 1270s. Earlier accounts tend to be very formal records compiled centrally for all of the manors of an estate, but the 1270s saw some decentralization, in which the reeve gained more responsibilities but also more freedom of action than before. The accounting officials in the late thirteenth century were calculating profit (*proficuum*), which included not just the gains that the lord made in cash, but also valued the goods that were sent to the household. They understood the concept of productive investment, as they regarded the cost of building a barn or spreading marl on the fields as expenditure contributing to the profitability of the manor. There were different methods of calculating profit, but at this time the officials were anxious to know if agricultural activity was making adequate returns. Any manager examining long-term profitability found his task complicated by the fluctuations from year to year as yields and prices rose and fell with changes in the weather. The fellows of Merton College, Oxford, for example, found that their manor of Ibstone in Buckinghamshire returned no profit in 1299–1300, but in the following accounting year made about £8. It was difficult in these circumstances to make long-term plans, or even to decide that direct management was the most profitable method of running the estate, but we must appreciate their efforts to make rational calculations.

The managers knew of good practices, and these methods spread from estate to estate. Often they were adopted in particular regions, where they were appropriate to specific social and economic circumstances, like the package of intensive methods that developed in northeast Norfolk. These practices were not confined to Norfolk. Increased acreages of legumes, mainly for fodder, were grown in many regions. Horses were used for ploughing in Kent, the Chiltern Hills and south Hampshire, while mixed teams with both horses and oxen were adopted by some manors in south-east England and the east midlands. The trend toward the use of horse power had begun in the twelfth century and gathered pace in the thirteenth; it had a universal impact on transport, as carts pulled by horses replaced ox wains. Horses and carts carried goods by road more quickly, and therefore could cover greater distances, which was especially useful for travelling to market. As plough animals the horses also gave more speed, so that while an ox team could plough only a half-acre in a day, a mixed team could plough a full acre. While a plough team of oxen often contained eight animals, a horse team consisted of six at most, and often four or even two, which compensated for the higher cost of feeding the horses with oats: oxen usually managed on grass. Particular types of plough were appropriate for the different draught animals, so horse teams tended to haul wheeled ploughs, while ox teams or mixed teams pulled swing ploughs or ploughs with a 'foot' and no wheels.

Demesnes participated in the expansion of cultivation by ploughing up pasture and clearing woods, and by draining areas of marsh and fen.

The work often involved adding a few acres to an existing demesne, but estates could carry out reclamation on a large scale. The bishop of Winchester, for example, spent £44 in two years in 1251–3 on an assart near Downton in Wiltshire. More than two miles of ditches were dug around the new enclosure, and at least 500 man days were devoted to spreading marl to improve the newly cleared land. Such additions to the arable could contribute to the productivity of land in the short term, as new ploughing of pasture released nutrients for the benefit of grain crops, as has been observed on another Winchester manor, at Rimpton in Somerset. In the long term, of course, reducing the amount of grazing might not be good for productivity, as there would be less manure for the arable. A reclamation project was carried out in the early thirteenth century by the monks of Glastonbury Abbey in the Somerset Levels around the villages of Chedzoy and Westonzoyland. The scheme to build dykes called the Aller Wall and the Lake Wall, and to divert the courses of the Rivers Parrett and Cary, reveals remarkable surveying and con- structional skills and an audacious ability to conceive of transforming the landscape over many thousands of acres. One of the main results of the drainage scheme was not to extend cultivation, but to raise the quality of grassland, allowing meadows with abundant hay crops to replace rather soggy marshland that was only available for grazing in the summer. (Plate 9) Any means of increasing the supply of fodder aided the whole farming system. We also find lords cropping their woods more efficiently, by extending the coppices from which fuel could be cut on a rotation, for the benefit of their own household supplies, and for sale to local peasants and to industry and towns. Woods do not represent land kept in its natural and unproductive state: on the contrary, they provided valuable grazing, timber, fuel and raw materials for crafts.

The demesnes' main contribution to technology lay in the manage- ment of resources rather than in new inventions or mechanical devices. They realized that they could maintain and improve yields by finding ways to combine arable and pasture to the advantage of both, through changes in rotation or combinations of crops. *Walter of Henley* advised them to carry out experiments – to show that seed brought in from outside gave better yields, he said, plant a strip with your own seed alongside another strip sown with purchased grain, and observe the results. That spirit of trial and error was practised. An Oxfordshire manor of Merton College, Cuxham, appears to have followed the tedious routine of a three-course rotation, in which winter-sown corn was followed by spring-sown corn and then fallow in repetitive sequence, but in the 1280s quite radical changes were made in the crops on the spring-sown field, with a reduction in the quantity of oats sown; instead more peas and dredge (a mixture of barley and oats) were cultivated.

Agricultural buildings achieved a higher standard in the thirteenth century, with more use of stone foundations and advances in carpentry. The greatest care was taken in building barns which, by providing secure and dry storage, prevented losses to crops after the harvest. The building costs appear on the manorial accounts, and monks sometimes boasted of new barns in their chronicles, but the robust nature of construction is signalled most emphatically to us by the survival of barns, some of them still employed for their original purpose: for example, two barns at the manor of the Knights Templar at Cressing Temple in Essex, which had an exceptionally large demesne of 1,000 acres. The barley barn was built in the 1230s, and the wheat barn in about 1290; the differences in the timber framing and the joints used in the construction show that the techniques of building these large structures was developing during the intervening half-century.

Mills were built at considerable cost for the sake of the revenue that came to the lords either in tolls collected by a miller employed by the lord, or as rents paid by a tenant miller. The number of water mills was already high in 1086, when Domesday records more than 6,000, but many were valued at such modest sums that they must have been small, weakly powered 'horizontal' mills (see pp. 25–6). In the next two centuries these were upgraded as vertical mills, which needed much more investment, both in machinery and in the building of ponds, weirs and leats to provide a sufficient flow of water. As well as improving the performance of existing mills, lords built them on new sites, and in the west midland counties of Gloucester, Warwick and Worcester the number increased from about 500 in 1086 to 800–900 in 1300. If lords in the rest of the country behaved in a similar way, the total of English mills by 1300 probably exceeded 10,000. Some of this increase came from new corn mills constructed on streams which had not previously been harnessed for this purpose. Corn mills driven by wind, and water-powered fulling mills were introduced in the late twelfth century. The fulling mills enabled lords to take some profit from the growing cloth industry, much of it in the countryside, which had developed outside the control of the manor. Windmills proliferated in districts where streams were few and small, or where the flat landscape, notably in eastern England, made the water flow so sluggishly that it gave insufficient power for water mills. These new machines, invented either in the east of England or on the shores of the North Sea, were the product of the daring imagination of craftsmen who raised the machinery on to a post above the ground, and designed sails which would turn the mill but not make the whole structure topple. Lords spent about £10 on building a new windmill, and would have to make regular outlays on repairs, but could expect to gain an annual return of a pound or two. (Plate 7)

Mills contributed to peasant production as they freed for more useful tasks labour which had previously been spent on milling by hand. The peasants resented attempts made to force them to use the lord's mill, and objected to the rate of toll that the miller charged, but nonetheless took their grain to be ground. Lords seem on occasion to have behaved like entrepreneurs in their management of mills: when complaints were voiced that their tenants were not using the manorial mill, the peasants were often not grinding the corn at home, but taking it to the mill of a neighbouring lord which offered lower tolls, less queueing, or a less dishonest miller.

Lords also aided the commercial economy by building bridges. Bolton Priory, for example, spent £90 mostly in the years 1304–8 on Kildwick Bridge across the Aire in Yorkshire, naturally for the convenience of their own carts, but indirectly the whole neighbourhood benefited. All of these changes show that lords were not conservative and hostile to technological innovation, but they cannot be seen as leaders. Such developments as the introduction of horses were taken much further by peasants. And the brilliant carpenters or millwrights who invented the windmill in about 1180 had to wait a long time for the new machine to be taken up on a large scale by lords. The bishop of Ely, whose East Anglian estates were ideal sites for windmills, did not begin to build them in any numbers until the 1230s and 1240s.

The lords were part of a society undergoing economic growth. They participated in that expansion, gaining from such trends as the specialization in crafts, and interacting with others involved in production and marketing. Their great contribution lay in the resources that they could mobilize, and their ability to pay for major projects, though they were often reluctant to commit themselves too heavily. The aristocracy were not the directors and controllers of change, but sometimes joined with enthusiasm, and sometimes held back with caution.

Landlords were faced with dilemmas in the deployment of labour on their demesnes. The manor had grown up by combining the productive capacity of the demesne land with the labour of the tenants. We have already seen that at the time of Domesday manorial structures with a high proportion of land in the hands of peasant tenants gave some lords much more abundant peasant labour services than others. In the east midland counties covered by the Hundred Rolls of 1279, the only general survey of lords' resources in this period that can be compared with Domesday, 13 per cent of manors can be described as large, and were served by numerous customary (servile) tenants owing heavy labour services. These manors must not be ignored, because by virtue of their size they accounted for a high proportion of the English countryside, and they are most likely to have kept records. But most lords held land on a limited scale, and two-thirds of manors were small (with 500 acres or less). These manors tended to have a small proportion of tenant land, and in particular lacked servile tenants and labour services. Even on the larger manors, the labour services would not have supplied all of the needs of the demesne even if they had been demanded in full, and often much of the lord's income from tenants came in the form of cash, not labour service. Around 1300, many lords decided to collect rents, commuting a proportion of the service for cash, and used the money to pay labourers to do the work. Throughout the twelfth and thirteenth centuries lords relied on a group of farm servants (*famuli*) as the core of their labour force. Some of them were tenants, usually of small holdings, who were obliged to work full time in a vestige of slavery, but most were contracted to serve for a year in exchange for a cash wage and an allowance of grain.

The monks of Crowland, for example, in the 1290s employed on their Northamptonshire manor of Wellingborough eight ploughmen (enough to man four ploughs throughout the year), two carters, three shepherds, a dairymaid and cowherd. With the addition of various part-time servants such as a swineherd and tithe collectors for the harvest season, these workers accounted for about a half of the labour needed to cultivate the 300-acre demesne of the manor. Extra occasional wage earners were hired for specialized and skilled work. At Wellingborough in 1292–3, smiths and woodworkers mended the ploughs and carts, and for 6d the piglets were castrated. But in addition workers were hired to carry out routine tasks that might have been performed by tenant labour services – a modest 2s 2d was spent on weeding the corn, and 24s 3d on threshing. On other manors at this time, wages were being paid for mowing hay and harvesting corn. The best estimate is that around 1300 only 8 per cent of tasks on demesnes came from tenant labour.

The demesne managers should have welcomed labour services. The labour owed was directly related to the peaks of demand in the agricultural year. A peasant who owed two days per week through the winter, spring and summer might be expected to do three days per week in August and September when the corn was cut and carried, and additional 'boons' when the whole community was expected to turn out in the harvest field, including older children and servants. Lords were able to harness not just the labour resources of the peasant household, but also its equipment, as some services expected the peasants with middling and larger holdings to plough and cart with their own implements and draught animals.

Labour services, however, were not without their problems for the managers. They were fixed by custom, which made them inflexible. Smallholders often were obliged to work on Mondays, but if bad weather prevented work on that day, the lord lost the work. Sometimes a 'work' was defined as labour for a full day, and sometimes only until noon. There was much ground for dispute about working hours, and other conditions such as the quantity and quality of the food to which workers were entitled when they attended a 'boon'. The feasts provided on these occasions had been established by custom at quite a generous level, and at a 'meat' boon the workers would consume large loaves, meat and ale. The accountants would sometimes find that the food and drink cost more than the wages of hired workers, and questioned the benefit of enforcing the service. The main problem lay with the compulsion by which the work was obtained.

The workers approached their task without enthusiasm, especially when by the mid-thirteenth century they were well aware of the alternative of commutation of service. Working on urgent seasonal tasks, such as haymaking or harvest, would be especially resented because these interrupted the completion of the same job on the peasants' own land. There would be problems of absenteeism, even of co-ordinated boycotts, and when the workers attended, as they normally did, they did not work as carefully and efficiently as the lord would have wished. At the haymaking at Wisbech in Cambridgeshire in the mid-fourteenth century, the productivity of tenants doing their services can be compared directly with that of hired workers. An average day's labour service produced one-third of a cartload of hay, while a wage earner doing the same task yielded a half-cartload. More precisely, hired labour was 36 per cent more efficient. Presumably this discrepancy, though its extent may have varied in time and place, was found throughout the country, and the demesne managers must have been aware of the problem. This helped them to decide that in some circumstances it was more profitable to let the tenants pay their commutation money – to 'sell' their works, to use the language of the accounts – and to use wage earners instead. This decision was made in the light of the knowledge that the commutation money, fixed before the thirteenth-century inflation, did not cover the full cost of the hired workers.

Demesnes were run on rational lines, and were not trapped in a mindless routine. Managers made investments and adopted new methods in the interest of greater profits. But we must beware of exaggerating the achievements of agriculture under the control of lords. The Cistercian

order of monks seems to represent a special case. They appear as a
radical force sweeping with a new broom through the orthodox world of
estates and manors. The monasteries were founded mostly in the early
to mid-twelfth century, inspired by an austere conception of religious
contemplation set apart from the distractions of the world. They sought
out sites remote from existing settlements, and rejected endowment with
parish churches which provided other orders with an income from glebe
land and tithes. Their desire for a self-contained religious life led them
not just to choose isolated and remote sites for their monasteries, but
also to found on their estates granges which consisted of blocks of land
under the monks' exclusive ownership, and which were separated from
the common fields of villages. They selected sites for their granges on
moors, marshes and woods, which often involved them in enclosing,
clearing and draining land and earned them an enduring reputation as
agricultural improvers. If they acquired land on the edge of a village's
territory, they would set about extending it, consolidating scattered
parcels by buying up land or by making exchanges, and even arranging
for any peasants who lived on the land to move elsewhere. These
processes took some time, and it was not until the middle of the thirteenth century that the Cistercians (together with orders with similar
ideals, such as the Gilbertines and Premonstratensians, together with
some Augustinian houses) had developed their grange system fully
(see Map 8 above, p. 117). By 1300, confining the calculation to the
Cistercians, there were almost a hundred houses in Britain, many of
which had provided themselves with between ten and twenty granges.

The granges resembled modern farms, and have been represented as
agricultural enterprises ahead of their time. With their compact group
of buildings on a new site, surrounded by land free from the restraints
and complications of communal farming, the 'grangers' who managed
them could use their compact group of fields as they and the central
monastic adminstration wished, ignoring conventional crop rotation,
and specializing if appropriate. The size of the granges, often about
300–400 acres, was chosen for reasons of efficiency. In the early days
the labour force consisted of lay brothers (*conversi*) – laymen who
had chosen to live a religious life, but without becoming fully-fledged
monks – and later hired workers, full-time farm servants and day
labourers. No labour services were available, because the grange often
had no peasant tenants attached to it. Setting up the grange involved
much investment in buildings, enclosures and land clearance. Sometimes
industries such as tanning were sited on the granges. The whole unit of
production was integrated into the market, as the land was often purchased, the labour hired, and the produce, such as the famous Cistercian

wool, was sold. The Cistercians rarely founded towns on their lands, as this would not accord with their ideal of isolation, but they acquired houses in urban centres such as York where wool could be stored and sales negotiated. They acted as middlemen in the wool trade, buying up fleeces from their neighbours and putting them up for sale with their own produce.

The granges' reputation for modernity is supported by the belief that Cistercians stood apart from feudal society, because their ideas about the religious life and the world prevented them from receiving services, or even tithes, and they were exempted from the usual obligations to do military service for their lands, or to pay tithes. But on closer inspection the order does not seem so distant from the rest of medieval society. Their estate management was intimately bound up with lordship. They held much land outside their granges, from which they collected rents, and where they held courts for their tenants in much the same style as other lords. The lay brothers bear a close resemblance to types of servile workers, and the institution developed in the early twelfth century as a replacement for slavery, like the tenants who acted as full-time farm servants on conventional demesnes. Indeed, the *conversi* recognized the anomaly of their position, resented the inadequacy of their quasi-religious status as a reward for their hard work, and rebelled. Their ambiguous situation was so difficult to sustain that the *conversi* were phased out in the thirteenth and fourteenth centuries.

The Cistercians represented themselves as heroic settlers in 'deserts', where they transformed unproductive land. But when their houses were founded in really bleak places, they persuaded their patrons to move them to more hospitable sites. A group of monks established at Barnoldswick in the Pennines in 1147 survived five years of hunger and cold before migrating to a fertile valley at Kirkstall near Leeds. Similarly most granges were not carved out of windswept moors, but were assembled out of parcels of already cultivated land near existing settlements. The exploitation of a compact block of land was by no means confined to the Cistercians, as many demesnes consisted of fields separated from the common fields of the village. On the hills Cistercian vaccaries and bercaries resembled those belonging to other lords, both churchmen and laity. Demesnes of conventional manors, as we have seen, could specialize in husbandry systems, such as sheep and corn, or they might concentrate on particular crops, such as barley in East Anglia. Demesnes and granges of all kinds produced partly for consumption in the household, and partly for sale. The Cistercians were not uniquely wedded to the market, except that their location in northern and western hills naturally encouraged their involvement in the wool trade. They certainly developed a commercial relationship with overseas merchants, judging from the lists of those selling wool to Italians in 1294, which included two-thirds of the Cistercian houses in England. This was not always a very advantageous arrangement for the monasteries, as the merchants from the great financial centres of Lucca and Florence were lending them money and contracting to take the wool in the future for fixed prices which no doubt benefited the buyers in a rising market. The granges do not seem to have been technically more sophisticated than other demesnes. In short, the Cistercians' 'progressive' farming and their supposed separation from feudal society seems to have developed as a modern myth, as indeed has the belief that monks in general were unusually inventive and efficient.

We can appreciate the quality of aristocratic management of agriculture without accepting the excessive adulation sometimes accorded to those involved in 'high farming' or to the Cistercian order. The achievement of aristocratic direct management has to be kept in perspective. Demesnes in general occupied a great deal of land in the midlands, south and east, but still only a third of the land in some regions, and a fifth in others. In the south-west and the north-west of England, and throughout Scotland, demesnes could be very small, or even non-existent. Many English lords leased out their demesnes, and either failed to adopt direct management, or abandoned it before the end of the thirteenth century. Neither should we exaggerate the commitment of estates to the sale of produce. We can find large scattered estates, like those of the bishopric of Winchester or the earldom of Cornwall, where the most convenient policy was to sell valuable crops like wheat, and indeed between half and three-quarters of wheat went on the market. On others, even in *c.*1300, where the manors were grouped around a monastery, such as Norwich or Durham Priories, most of the wheat went for consumption by the monks, their servants and their guests (see Map 8 above, p. 117).

iii. *Lords and peasants*

Direct production on demesnes after *c.*1200 attracts attention because it was new, because it shows lords responding to wider economic changes, and because it distinguishes the English aristocrats from those of continental Europe. But lords continued to gain most of their income from rents. Even at the peak of 'high farming' at the end of the thirteenth century, English estates striving to maintain and increase their demesne profits were deriving 50 or 60 per cent of their income from rents of various kinds. In Scotland, where there is little evidence for direct management of demesnes, rents were even more prominent. In the south and east of Scotland, tenants' rents in cash yielded a high proportion of lords' revenues, and in the north and west where the great 'multiple' estates dominated the countryside, peasants paid traditional rents in kind, which were sometimes commuted for cash, known as cain and conveth. At Strathearn in *c.*1200, tenants contributed payments in grain, malt, cheese, fowls and game.

Landlords could raise more revenue by increasing the number of tenants, or by taking more from them in cash rather than in kind or labour, or they could squeeze more from each peasant household. None of these routes to gaining higher rent was straightforward, and every policy decision encountered obstacles, but lords were helped by the growth in population and the expansion of the market which made land a valuable asset. An obvious means of creating new holdings was to clear woodland or waste. Land-hungry peasants would be eager to occupy new land. Lords did not, however, control large areas of such underdeveloped land if their estates lay in districts where the arable area was already extensive. Loss of woodland and pasture endangered the livelihood of the existing population, even in areas with large areas of uncultivated land, so a lord who encouraged colonization of the wastes might find himself facing vociferous opposition, and even if he succeeded would risk impoverishing, and therefore reducing the rent-paying potential of, tenants already established. The tenants of new land were not always major sources of income, as the normal custom was to grant assarts on free tenure for modest cash rents. Another way of expanding tenant numbers, subdividing holdings, could result in a numerous but poor body of tenants who could not pay as much as those with large holdings, and would not be able to bring ploughs and carts to their labour services as they could not afford to buy and maintain implements, or own oxen and horses. Land could be taken from the demesne for peasant holdings, but surely the land gave a higher return under direct management? The calculation of advantage was not always easy, especially in the long term. Changing the form in which rent was paid, or raising its level, would again risk peasant resistance. Free tenants might take the lord to the king's court, and those governed by the customary law of the manor could cause trouble in the lord's court, or in some circumstances appeal for protection to royal justice.

The lords steered round these restrictions and made substantial increases in rents. In the twelfth century the bulk of lords' income came from rent because the demesnes were often leased to farmers. In addition, some lords shifted the balance between demesne land and tenant land by granting out parcels of demesne land to tenants for cash rents on hereditary tenures. At the same time, partly because of the reduction in the demesne area, but mainly in view of the growing opportunities to sell produce, holdings that owed labour services were converted to paying money rents. Lists of tenants sometimes divide tenants into those owing works (*ad opus*) and those paying rents (*ad censum*). Both developments are recorded in a survey of Blockley in Gloucestershire in about 1166, when a tenant called Girard held 12 acres formerly in the demesne for 2s and six labour services, and a cotland (a smallholding attached to a cottage) which had previously done labour services was rented for 18d.

In both the twelfth and thirteenth centuries lords took advantage of the expansion in cultivation by taking rents from the newly cleared or drained land. In some cases the lord may well have caught up with settlers after they had taken over the new land, but some clearance ventures were planned and encouraged by lords. A typical group of such tenants was listed by the canons of St Paul's Cathedral at their manor of Navestock in Essex in 1222 under the heading of 'New assarts'. Over the previous forty years the holdings of twenty-five tenants had been established, most of them smallholdings – an acre, a half-acre, a curtilage and so on. The tenants paid the usual moderate cash rents – in this case at an annual rate of 6d per acre, but these gave a total of 12s 10d per annum, a useful addition to the value of the manor which yielded £7 7s 1d for its lord in 1181.

Most manors added to the number of free tenants paying cash rents in the twelfth and thirteenth centuries, not all of them holding newly cleared land. One group consisted of servants and clients of the lords who were granted the land as rewards, but their rents brought in modest sums of money. The main benefit for lords came from additions to the numbers of customary tenants who owed heavy burdens of labour service and cash payments. The well-established standard units of land holding, were called virgates or yardlands in southern England, bovates or oxgangs in the north, and in parts of Scotland. Lords often agreed to their subdivision, so that by the late thirteenth century many customary tenants held half- or quarter-yardlands, or half-oxgangs, which usually produced for the lord more than half or a quarter of the rents owed by a full unit. Lords were reluctant to allow excessive subdivision lest the rents and services attached to the original holdings be forgotten, and the tenants be impoverished. No such inhibitions seem to have applied in parts of East Anglia, where the original 'tenements' were highly fragmented as a result of partible inheritance, a lively land market and weaker control by lords. Landlords in that region may even have favoured the splitting of holdings into very small acreages: at Gressenhall in Norfolk, a manor of the Stuteville family, it was believed in 1287 that a steward called Crowe some time before 1259 had changed the custom from inheritance by the eldest son to division among all sons 'because he wished to have more tenants'.

Lords faced a serious problem in their relations with tenants around 1200. Their most privileged tenants, the tenants in fee, had become virtually independent, helped by the protection of the royal courts. The king's common law was being extended to all free tenants, preventing lords gaining any more income from them. But where could the line be drawn between the free and unfree? Before about 1180 the distinction had been imprecise, and a tenant could be described as 'more free' than another. A clear distinction was now essential, so that the royal courts could decide who fell within their jurisdiction, and so that lords could be reassured that there were to be limits on the king's encroachment on their powers. The lawyers in the royal courts developed means of testing the legal status of individuals. If a tenant owed the heavy labour services known as week-work, or paid marriage fines (merchet), or was liable to serve as reeve, then the individuals and their families were judged to be of villein or servile status. Words changed their meaning, so that 'villein', which had once described a villager with a middling or larger holding of land, came to mean an unfree tenant, holding by a servile tenure – in villeinage. A customary tenant, that is someone holding land under the custom of the manor, which was enforced through the lord's court, was excluded from the common law of the royal courts, and therefore categorized as servile in status. The term 'neif', in Latin *nativus*, had meant someone born into servility, and this stigma was now being attached to many of those who held by customary or villein tenure. It was still possible for a personally free individual to hold land in villeinage, but increasingly legal status was being equated with the tenure of land.

Take for example the case of William, son of Henry of Pilton in Rutland, who complained to the king's court in 1224 that he had been deprived of his free holding by Bartholomew, son of Eustace. He was bringing an action under the assize of novel disseisin, as free tenants had been doing for more than forty years. Bartholomew responded with a claim that William was a villein, and he had no right to appear before the royal court. The case had been heard before, in the reign of King John (1199–1216); reference back to the earlier hearing showed that William owed heavy labour services and that neither his daughter nor son could marry without his lord's permission. This proved that William was unfree, and that he would have to take his case before the court of his lord, Bartholomew, son of Eustace, where he may not have been heard with much sympathy.

There were distinct advantages in establishing the villein status of tenants. Certainly it confirmed the labour services which were becoming so valuable to lords when they were introducing direct management of demesnes. But they were always conscious of the financial benefits from villein tenants. The many restrictions on the unfree, such as those controlling their marriage and movement from the manor, became opportunities to levy fines in money. The lord would happily give permission, or lift a restriction, in exchange for a few shillings. The tenants in villeinage, because they were not 'free men', were not subject to the provision in Magna Carta of 1215 that new tenants should pay only a 'reasonable' relief. Free tenants would therefore pay one year's rent, usually no more than a few shillings, but when a villein wished to take over a holding, including when he inherited after the death of his father or mother, the lord demanded an entry fine or *gersuma*. On some manors this became fixed by custom – perhaps at a mark or half-mark (13s 4d or 6s 8d) – but most lords resisted any move towards such a restriction, and levied fines that varied with the demand for land, the size and quality of the holding, and the capacity of the new tenant to raise the money. Entry fines around 1300 commonly rose to three times the annual rent of the holding. A yardland of about 30 acres of arable could command a fine of £3.

The acute shortage of land made it possible for lords to make these demands, and the profits that could be made from the sale of agricultural produce enabled the peasant to pay, or at least to borrow the money and eventually pay it back. Servile tenants were also expected to contribute to collective payments, notably tallage or aid, which often amounted to £5 or £10 on a large manor, to which the more substantial tenants in villeinage contributed 2 or 3s each. The recognition fine, again a collective sum of a few pounds, was demanded from servile tenants when a new lord took over an estate. Heriots, or death duties, were often owed by free tenants, but in the north-west midlands, where rents and services were not usually very onerous, lords compensated themselves by demanding from customary tenants not the usual heriot of the 'best beast' but a number of animals, pots and pans, beehives and other goods.

Powers of private justice were given a new lease of life in the thirteenth century. The manorial courts administered the customs under which serfs lived, and many of the dues such as marriage fines and entry fines were collected through the court. In addition, the courts dealt with matters of tenancy and services, such as failure to do labour services or to maintain the buildings on the holding. Trespass on the demesne land, whereby tenants pastured their animals on the lord's pasture, or even on his crops, was punished. The courts also gave the tenants an opportunity to settle disputes by hearing small claims for debts, trespasses and detention of chattels: if one peasant bought a cow from another and failed to pay the agreed price, or a straying animal trampled the plants in another's garden, or if an axe was borrowed but not returned, the court would help the injured party to recover the money, goods or compensation for damages. The courts provided a forum for community matters to be discussed – by-laws might be issued relating to the protection of grain in the harvest period, or to regulate the grazing of animals on the commons. The contribution that the court made to good order in the community came at a price, as each stage in the inter-peasant lawsuits or each breach of the by-laws resulted in the lord collecting a few pence in amercements (a money payment in order to gain the lord's mercy). In a single court, dozens of amercements, each of 2d, 3d, 4d or 6d, accumulated to a few shillings, and as the courts were held regularly through the year, sometimes every three weeks, and rarely with an interval of more than three months, the profits of justice amounted to a few pounds over the whole year. In lowland England the 'perquisites of the courts' could amount to a tenth of the income of an estate, but in the Welsh marches, where lords enjoyed much wider powers of justice and could use the courts to levy substantial collective fines, lords were gaining as much as a third of their revenues from this source.

From a lord's point of view the dues arising from servile tenants or from profits of justice had a special value because they were variable and not supervised by any other authority. Lords could imagine themselves as independent rulers, boasting that they could tallage their tenants 'high and low, at will', that is they could demand as much payment, and as often, as they wished. In practice they received the same sum annually, so the rhetoric was not applied. The state exercised some restraint on lords, for example in reviewing their franchises and in providing channels for tenants to appeal against injustice. Some payments, like entry fines, reflected the growth in land values and the scarcity of land.

A typical tenant of a yardland on a large church estate in the early thirteenth century, Jordan de Legh of Street in Somerset, a manor of Glastonbury Abbey, had his obligations recorded in 1241. Jordan was expected to pay a cash rent of 2s 6d, together with 'lardersilver' of 14d, on 11 November, when the lord could claim that he needed help with stocking his larder with salt meat for the winter. He also paid 1d for 'hurtpenny' (called Peter's pence elsewhere – a contribution supposedly for a tax to the pope, though in practice part went to the lord) and 2 bushels of wheat for churchscot (payment originally to the local church). But his main obligation was to work for three days each week through the year, with extra days in the harvest, making an annual total of 170 days, that is two-thirds of the working days in the year. These customary obligations were written into a formal document kept by the abbey, and etched on the memories of the peasants, and any move by the lord to increase them would breach custom and provoke a storm of protest that even the monks would have found uncomfortable. However, the lord could decide to take part of the labour service in cash, and by the end of the thirteenth century many tenants of Jordan's type would be paying 10s rent, and working on the demesne for 100 days or less. In general, tenants seem to have preferred to pay cash rather than do labour services.

Some lords would arrange for some of the holdings that owed labour services to pay cash only. For example, at King's Ripton in Huntingdonshire the lord of the manor, Ramsey Abbey, increased the number of holdings carrying a rent entirely in cash from three to nine between 1250 and 1275, while still requiring labour services from fourteen others. Rents in kind were also converted into cash payments. These figured especially prominently in the dues owed by peasants in north Wales. In the commote of Ardudwy in Merioneth, for example, 200 bond tenants were expected to do only one day's labour service each per annum, but were obliged to pay cattle, pigs, milk and flour, and to entertain the prince's men when they visited the district. But in the decades before the English conquest in 1282, many of these dues were rendered in money – the rent in animals, for example, was valued at £10 18s and paid in cash.

Ways were found to increase tenants' obligations, not just to move from one mode of payment to another. Occasionally lords could establish new villein holdings. The manor of Cuxham in Oxfordshire was undersupplied with villein half-yardlands, which were the main source of rents and labour services. The number was more than doubled from six to thirteen between 1276 and 1293, by converting cottage holdings with additional acres from the demesne. Lords could find ways of taxing activities not covered by the customary rules. In the thirteenth century peasants were anxious to sublet land, which enabled lessors to raise money or reduce the size of a holding that was becoming burdensome, and allowed lessees to add to their acreage. Lords were ambiguous in their attitudes to subletting, as it threatened the unity of the holding and contributed to the remoteness of the lord from those actually working the land. On the other hand they saw in this a source of profit, and so some lords insisted that sublettings, especially those for more than a year or two, be reported to the court and be subject to fines.

Another route to extra profit for lords came from the conversion of both free and customary holdings into leasehold, a form of tenure in which a contract was made between lord and tenant which fixed the rent in relation to the market for land. This could be used when lords bought up freeholdings, which produced low rents, and then let them to new tenants on short terms. This was a policy pursued on the estates of the Berkeley family on the rich valley land between Bristol and Gloucester. The land that the lords recovered was rented out for 9d per acre, even 20d per acre, reflecting local demand for fertile land, but acquiring the holding was expensive for the lord. On the nearby estate of Gloucester Abbey villein tenants would offer substantial lump sums – £6, £8, even £16 13s 4d for their tenures to be converted from customary tenure to leasehold. William the reeve of Coln Roger, for example, with Agnes his wife, was able by an agreement of 1289 to hold his half-yardland for 8s per annum, and be exempt from all labour services. Leasehold made its greatest advances in Cornwall, where 'conventionary' tenure gave tenants a seven-year term. The cash rents were not very burdensome, but each renewal was agreed with a large fine, payment of which was spread over the first six years of the term, and therefore became an extra rent. On the largest estate in the county, that of the earls (later dukes) of Cornwall, conventionary tenure was introduced in the 1280s and became widespread by the 1330s. Parcels of demesne were also leased out in growing quantities around 1300 as lords became more doubtful about the profits they were gaining from direct management.

There were obvious advantages for lords in extending leasehold, so why did they not lease land on a larger scale? The answer must be that leasing was often seen as a short-term measure, and serfdom represented a fundamental institution, at the very centre of their way of life.

Lords may have had a strong regard for custom and their ancient rights over their peasants, but their outlook was not entirely conservative and inflexible. They introduced ways of maintaining control through written records. Admittedly the surveys that church landlords in particular compiled seem very formal: each tenant was named, the holding described, and the tenant's services and rents listed in considerable detail. These were useful for auditors checking accounts, and could be consulted in the event of tenants querying their duties. They carried such authority that the title of 'Domesday' was sometimes given to them. But gathering the information was troublesome, and the circumstances that they described quickly changed. The matters that might be disputed with tenants, such as the customs governing the transfer of holdings, were not usually recorded in surveys.

Much more effective were the court rolls, which estates of all kinds, including those of knights and gentry, were writing and preserving in the last quarter of the thirteenth century. Instead of making a formal list of tenants at one point in time, the court roll recorded each change of tenant. Settlements of disputes, declarations of customs and statements of inheritances and transfers of land provided precedents, and lords and peasants alike respected the rolls as evidence. Peasants had some regard for the court and its deliberations, because they participated as jurors and pledges, and their interests were in some ways served by its judgments. They would give money to have items written into the court rolls – for example, John and Alice Tonestal of Weedon Bec in Northamptonshire in 1296 paid 5s to occupy 2 acres jointly, and for the new tenancy to be 'enrolled' as a permanent record of the arrangement. The procedures of the courts were going through continuous development partly under the influence of the common law in the royal courts, but also because lords and their officials were anxious to make their courts efficient. Around 1300, greater use was being made of juries for settling disputes, which was a more decisive and speedy way of arriving at judgments than depending on the deliberations of the whole court. The courts compelled tenants to attend, but new procedures were also designed to attract business. The joint tenancy of husbands and wives, as in the Weedon case mentioned above, was wanted by peasants. It made no difference to the lord – he would gain his rents and services whether or not the land was held jointly – but agreeing to the change yielded an extra 5s.

iv. *Lords and towns*

Lords took a number of initiatives in order to profit from the growth in trade: they promoted new towns, founded markets and fairs, and invested in urban property. A few new towns founded by lords are recorded in Domesday Book, but their numbers increased dramatically in the succeeding two centuries. A common procedure was to create a borough by conferring on the tenants the privileges of burgesses, which gave them the right to hold a plot of land (usually less than a half-acre) for a fixed money rent without any labour services or servile dues. They were able to sell, sublet or mortgage their land, and could trade in the borough market without paying tolls. Some boroughs were formed by attaching new privileges to an old settlement, some were entirely new towns, laid out on greenfield sites and depending on migrants to inhabit the plots. In England the hundred or so boroughs recorded in 1086 had increased to 218 by 1200, and to more than 500 by 1300. The king had founded the majority of boroughs before 1086, and another seventy in the next two centuries. Between 1086 and 1300, church landlords accounted for ninety-five, a little more than their fair share in view of the proportion of land that they held, while lay lords (mostly the higher ranks) founded about 170. Boroughs appeared for the first time in Wales in the late eleventh century, but they then proliferated quite quickly, with twenty-eight recorded between 1070 and 1200, and another fifty-five in the thirteenth century. In Scotland royal burgh foundations dominated, with thirty in the twelfth century, and eleven created by church and lay lords. In the thirteenth century ten of the nineteen new burghs were non-royal (see Map 9 below, p. 189).

The obvious advantage to an estate from a borough or burgh founda-tion lay in the rents paid by the burgesses, which would often yield £4 even from a small place with eighty burgage plots paying a shilling each. But with the market tolls, profits of the borough court, and tolls from a mill the profit could easily rise to £10. The area of land on which the borough stood would have been worth no more than £1 if it was still in agricultural use. Lords could always hope for a booming success and the growth of a large town like King's Lynn, originally Bishop's Lynn from its founders, the bishops of Norwich. After shadowy beginnings around 1100, Lynn had at least 800 inhabitants by 1167, and by 1300 it ranked twelfth among all English towns, and its judicial profits alone brought the bishops £40 per annum. Towns were often founded in stages, as at Ludlow in Shropshire where five or six new planned extensions and suburbs were added to the initial foundation of about 1090 adjoining the castle. In a number of towns there would in effect be twin new towns, as a borough foundation by one lord would encourage a neighbour to foster urban development nearby – Chelmsford in Essex, for example, founded by the bishop of London in 1200, stimulated the growth of a suburb on the other side of the bridge over the River Chelmer at Moulsham, a manor of Westminster Abbey. Durham developed as a complex of four or five small adjacent boroughs founded at different times by two lords, the bishop and the priory.

Lords calculated that the growth of a town would add to the pros-perity of their nearby rural manors by giving the peasants easy access to a market and allowing them to pay money rents. David, earl of Huntingdon on his Scottish estates achieved a notable success with the promotion of Dundee, but also founded a burgh next to his castle of Inverurie which brought an opportunity for exchange to the remote and thinly populated lordship of Garioch. A town also conferred a sense of importance on its lord. A castle or Benedictine monastery would have seemed incomplete without a town outside its gates, and a 'city' was an essential setting for a cathedral – a bishop's main church and throne were expected to be located in an urban place. Both Lichfield (Staffordshire) and Wells (Somerset) lost their standing as the seats of bishops because they were too rural, and had to be founded in the twelfth century as new towns in order to reclaim their old position against rivals at Coventry and Bath.

Every borough had a market and most were granted at least one fair, but many lords by acquiring a market charter from the crown founded these privileged occasions for trade in villages. Perhaps they hoped that the market would attract a permanent population of traders and the settlement would become a town. Some achieved this without acquiring borough status, such as Stowmarket in Suffolk. In most cases the place remained a village, and the lords had to be content to receive the tolls from the market, and presumably to enhance the prosperity of their rural estates. More than 1,000 market charters were issued in the thirteenth century, mostly to lords of all kinds promoting either boroughs or centres of commerce in villages.

In larger towns lords owned urban property, either exploiting the houses which had been attached to rural estates since pre-Conquest times, or buying houses as an investment. These were sometimes intended as bases, perhaps for warehouses and accommodation for officials trading on behalf of the lord; this explains, for example, why the bishop of Moray (in the north of Scotland) bought a house in the wool-exporting town of Berwick-on-Tweed. Lords also acquired houses which could be rented out profitably to merchants and artisans, and we can find lords like Coventry Priory, which already held much of the town at its gates, buying yet more property in the thirteenth century. New institutions founded after 1200, such as hospitals, chantries and colleges, were often located in towns, and depended for a high proportion of their income on urban property. For most lords, their rent from towns was no more than a useful supplement to their main income from rural manors. Urban revenues were appreciated because when agricultural profits were stagnating, expanding towns provided avenues for investment and profit. This was especially true of lords in the poorer regions. The number of boroughs in upland districts with low populations and restricted agricultural opportunities, such as north Devon, the Welsh marches, Staffordshire and south-west Scotland, reflects their founders' desire for a few more pounds of income. Presumably the concentration of fulling mills in western England and Wales can be explained in the same way.

v. *Knights and gentry*

To what extent did the lesser aristocracy, the knights and gentry, participate in economic growth in the same way as the bishops, abbots, earls and barons who have been our main focus of attention so far? They were numerous, with perhaps 10,000 families in England in 1300, and at that time they varied in wealth from rich knights on the verge of the baronage holding a half-dozen manors which yielded more than £100 per annum, to freemen (they might be called franklins) with a single manor or scattered pieces of land valued at £5 annually (see Map 8 above, p. 117). Together, they held more land than the magnates, so that the management of their estates is of great importance in the economy as a whole. They were vulnerable to sudden changes in prices, bad harvests and political upheavals, as their finances were fragile at the best of times. Their manors often lacked servile tenants and customary labour services, so rents tended to come from free tenants who paid fixed sums in cash, which lost value in the inflation. Many small manors had a high proportion of their land in demesne, which allowed the lord to profit from the sale of produce, but demesnes with less than 200 acres of arable could not make a very large profit if most of their surplus grain was being delivered to the household for consumption by the lord's family and servants.

Another trap for the small landowner lay in the purchase of goods and services, which also rose in price in the inflation. The gentry felt insecure about their status as they aspired to be aristocrats on a modest income, and so felt social pressure to consume at a high level, or even to increase their expenditure. For example, in the counties north and east of London, and in the north-western midlands, the standing of lesser lords depended on surrounding their houses with moats, which were usually linked with new building work, in all costing much more than a year's income. A horse suitable for warfare could be bought for £2–£4 in the early thirteenth century, but was more likely to cost £8 towards the end of the century. Small and insecure incomes, the temptation to increase spending, and family loyalties which persuaded families to provide for non-inheriting children from meagre landed resources, all tended to pull gentry families into debt. They could well have developed an optimistic view of their circumstances after a run of good agricultural years, spent too much, and then regretted their commitments when the crops yielded poorly and disease spread among the sheep. They lived on credit at all times, but a minority fell into serious debt, whether to Jewish moneylenders before the expulsion in 1290, or to wealthier aristocrats. 'In my urgent need' as troubled small landowners would explain in their charters, they turned to a wealthy monastery or layman, and this 'friend' paid off their debts, but in exchange would take over the land. Families ended their days living on handouts from a monastery, having ruined the future of their family. In 1219 Stephen de Fretwell came to an agreement with the abbot of Eynsham whereby he surrendered his land (some hundreds of acres) in the Oxfordshire village of Woodeaton, in exchange for which he and Sarah his wife were assigned a house at a low rent at Eynsham, and a corrody, consisting of a daily allowance of bread, ale, pottage and dishes of food from the monastery kitchen. The abbot would pay his debts in order to recover land in eight villages around Woodeaton which Stephen had surrendered to his creditors as pledges, after which the abbey would keep half of the land, and return the other half to the de Fretwells. Stephen and Sarah were clearly bankrupt (to use a modern term), and this was not a case of decline in old age, as they had daughters of marriageable age, one of whom would have her marriage arranged by the abbot, presumably at a profit. We can only imagine the humiliation of this once-proud aristocrat, who had been forced to move from his manor house to a modest dwelling in the town of Eynsham, specified in the agreement as 30 feet long, in the same street as tradesmen and abbey servants, and depending on food from the abbey.

Only a minority faced ruin, but some more general crisis must lie behind the rapid upheaval in status in the early thirteenth century. In the time of King John about 4,500 people were identified by the title 'knight', but in the following twenty years the title was restricted to a wealthy minority: only about a thousand individuals were dubbed knights by the middle of the thirteenth century, leaving thousands of lesser landowners, most of them holding land in fee, that is for military service, but without a specific title. This change must be related to advancing ideas about chivalry, which identified knights as an elite group with special qualities. It had an economic dimension, because it was expected that knights would have incomes from land of at least £20 per annum, and by the later thirteenth century £40: we know this because the government attempted to insist that all those with such incomes or above should be dubbed knights. Many relatively wealthy landowners preferred to pay the fine: not, we may suspect, because they felt themselves unworthy of the great honour, but because they knew that it would commit them to spending time and money on ceremonies and official duties. Each county's grand jury, for example, consisted of twelve knights, and as some small counties could barely muster a dozen, those who had been dubbed were expected to attend regularly. In time of war the knights would be required to turn out properly equipped with armour and weapons, riding a warhorse, which together could cost £20 in the 1280s and 1290s. They received pay, at a higher rate than other mounted soldiers if they were dubbed knights, but the initial expense was still formidable.

Despite all the difficulties of matching income and expenditure, fear of debt, and the problems of keeping their status, small landowners were given many opportunities in the twelfth and thirteenth centuries. They received grants of land from magnates, and were able to acquire land by purchase. Knights and gentry gained in two ways from the growth of state power, as the protection of the common law confirmed that they were no longer controlled by the magnates, and bigger government gave them employment opportunities as officials and lawyers. Initially the crown granted such offices as that of sheriff to trusted household officials, but during the thirteenth century these influential posts were occupied by the local landowners. At the same time, large numbers of gentry were employed in the direct management of magnate estates, and it became more common for magnates to recruit officials, advisers and supporters, sometimes by means of a written contract, and often with a regular payment of money as an annuity. The sums involved were not very large – but even a few pounds each year was a valuable addition to the £10 or £20 which most gentry received from their lands. Rewarding service with money rather than land has been called 'bastard feudalism', meaning not an illegimate or disreputable version of feudalism, but a system of clientage resembling feudalism. As the law increased in complexity a legal profession emerged, and recruited many of its practitioners from the gentry. Already by the 1240s a group of sergeants of the Bench can be identified working in the royal courts, and by 1300 the local courts had their groups of professional pleaders, such as the fifteen who worked in the county court of Warwickshire.

Talented and well-connected administrators and lawyers could move between private and public office. Geoffrey Russell, from an obscure gentry family on the estate of Peterborough Abbey, became the abbey's steward in 1250–63, and then moved on to work for Isabella de Fortibus and other magnates. By the late 1270s he had been appointed a royal justice, and also steward of Wallingford on the estate of the earldom of Cornwall. The fees and perquisites of office gave him the resources to acquire land in the vicinity of Peterborough. Russell's contemporary, Sir Geoffrey de Langley, a royal official whose landed base lay in Warwickshire and Gloucestershire, expanded his property by purchases from lesser families suffering from debt. As a result of the failure of gentry families to manage their affairs, land did not flow just from them to the monasteries, but also to other more successful members of the lesser aristocracy. (Plate 6)

Office-holding and its profits gave some knights and gentry useful incomes in cash, but as the purchases of the successful officials show, their ultimate goal was to acquire land. Land provided a stable and enduring investment, and if well managed, could yield a high income. The gentry were committed to direct management of demesnes long before the magnates were converted by the circumstances around 1200. They often held a single demesne and lived nearby, so that leasing the land to farmers would have been unnecessary. Duties to superior lords or the king might take them away for long periods, but their wives could then take over the supervision of agriculture. Such was their interest in management that smaller landowners also became farmers of the manors of the great estates. So when the magnates went over to direct management, they were imitating the knights and gentry, and indeed a constant cross-fertilization between large and small estates continued through the thirteenth century as the new breed of officials brought to the manors of the magnates the experience they had gained on their own lands.

The management style of the small landowners would have differed from that practised on the larger estates. The structure of gentry manors, with their high proportion of land in demesne, forced them to rely less on rents, and put more emphasis on production. With few servile tenants owing labour services, the gentry depended on wage labour. A relatively small manor would need to spend a higher proportion of its income on investment in buildings and equipment. The lord would supervise all of these activities in person – he would practise hands-on management. There was no need to employ officials or keep a large archive of surveys and accounts, which is a loss for us, but probably made for greater efficiency as the lord knew exactly what was happening, and could conduct business orally. This might give the impression that the gentry were behaving like modern entrepreneurs, but there was still a great deal of direct consumption of produce, so the market had a limited influence, and there is not much indication that gentry manors used more advanced techniques than those found on the large estates. We can see a gentry manor at work occasionally, when accounts were kept by a wealthy knight. William de Curzon's sergeant, Hugh, presented his account for the manor of East Carlton in Norfolk in 1274–5. Rents, at £3 10s, were not very important compared with the sale of grain, which brought in £30. The lord derived little profit from his powers of justice, which produced only 2s 6d. The volume of sales was limited by the need to supply the household, which took half of the wheat, a third of the barley, and two-thirds of the oats. Few animals were sold: they were mainly used in the lord's kitchen. Curzon spent about 7 per cent of his receipts on farm buildings and equipment, a higher level of investment than would be found on many larger estates, and much of the labour, in the harvest for example, was hired. But this expenditure did not result in higher productivity, as the grain mostly yielded only two, three or four times the seed sown.

In a key respect, knights and gentry can be identified as innovative in their estate management, in their ability, like the new religious orders, to create new units of landholding. By a combination of land purchase, clearance of new land and exchange, the Segrave family built Caludon near Coventry into a new manor, with a 200-acre demesne, a small park and a few tenants, which gave the family an income of £20 per annum from the sale of produce in the mid-thirteenth century. This construction of new manors was especially characteristic of woodland regions, where gentry were numerous, and the assarting and fluidity of settlement and landholding gave them better opportunities. Minor lords had to use their ingenuity, because with their limited resources there were some projects that they could not envisage. They do not figure prominently in the lists of borough founders, for example, because they did not have enough land to attempt such large-scale ventures; but they established a good number of markets. Knights and gentry profited from the expansion of trade and other social, economic and political changes of the twelfth and thirteenth centuries. They took risks, and there were casualties, but these formed a minority. A sample of thirty-one families from Oxfordshire shows that five of them lost land, nine gained it, and seventeen remained in much the same position.

vi. *Aristocratic achievement?*

The overall impression must be that the aristocracy at all levels adjusted to the rapid changes of the period 1086–1300 and profited from them. They enjoyed high incomes in 1300, with perhaps 20,000 households living comfortably on between £10 and £100 per annum – that is the gentry and the beneficed clergy. At least 200 households – of the barons, earls, bishops and the greater monasteries – were equivalent to modern millionaires, with incomes of between £200 and £6,000.

But was their achievement so great? We can find estates which recorded leaps in annual income, like Bolton Priory which doubled its cash revenues, from £240 to £460 between the 1280s and c.1310, as a result of prudent investment and skilful management. But many of the estates with rising revenue, like that recorded for the Clare family, earls of Gloucester, between 1267 and 1317, came more from acquiring additional land than developing existing resources. Bishoprics and Benedictine monasteries, which tended not to add much to the size of their estates, increased their incomes in the period from the late twelfth century to c.1300 between two and three times – Ely bishopric from £920 to £2,550 for example, and the bishops of Worcester from

£330 to £1,200, while Westminster Abbey rose from £739 to £1,641. This was keeping pace with inflation, but only just. In the same period wheat tripled in price.

The aristocracy were held back in many ways. The magnates were not free agents: from above, the state was bleeding power away from their courts in the twelfth century, and setting limits on their franchises in the thirteenth. From below, their tenants in fee were wriggling out of their control in the twelfth century, and even the unfree peasants in the next century were able to limit their demands by defending their customs. Their demesne management was flexible and efficient, but they could not always exploit the resources of the land to the full. Better-off peasants and townspeople made more from the economic growth of the thirteenth century, but lords could not, for all of their bluster about their serfs owning nothing but their bellies, take away the full profits. Because they were inhibited in appropriating their serfs' wealth directly, lords resorted to indirect measures to make some money, like building fulling mills or founding boroughs in poor regions.

Most lords gave higher priority to war, politics and the government of church and state. The literature of the period, which presumably expresses their interests and concerns, has much to say about religion, courtly love and knightly prowess. The treatises on estate management were greatly outnumbered by books on these spiritual and chivalric themes. The cultural preoccupations of the aristocracy are reflected in the amount of land and resources they devoted to their hunting reserves. A few richer families held chases, or private forests, which could cover dozens of square miles. But more often the aristocracy, both churchmen and laity, and including knights and upper gentry, made parks, and most of the 1,900 known to have existed in the middle ages were created in the thirteenth and early fourteenth centuries. Parks yielded profits, as sources of venison, timber and wood, and grazing. But they were valued not for their economic benefits, but for the pleasure of hunting, the opportunity to make alliances with visitors who came to hunt, the chance to send gifts of venison, and as status symbols.

The wealth of the aristocracy cannot be measured entirely in acres or coins; they were not just money-grabbers. Status and reputation counted as well as wealth, but this reinforces the impression of them as a competitive and acquisitive group. They were not just rivals within their peer group: there was also a competition between the magnates and the lesser aristocracy, and between the churchmen and the laity. There was friction between the elites of different regions, particularly between the expanding rulers of the Anglo-Norman world and the chieftains beyond the frontiers. The aristocrats were not in complete control of the rest of society; they were inhibited by the power of the state, and did not always have their own way with the peasantry. The constant shifts within the aristocracy, and in their relations with others, provided one of the dynamic forces in medieval society and economy.

CHAPTER FIVE

Peasants, c.1100–c.1315

We rely on documents produced by peasants' superiors, and material evidence, to reconstruct their lives, because they did not write. They gained their education from the practical training given to them by their elders in house and field, which does not mean that they lacked intelligence. They were actively involved in the growth and innovations of the twelfth and thirteenth centuries. They perceived that some changes were to their advantage, and that others were against their interests, and behaved accordingly. For example, they cleared land, and sold produce, but resisted those technical changes which might involve them in more work for few benefits. In pursuing their interests they lacked power, especially as individuals, but in acting collectively they could have a significant influence.

i. Families and population

The growth in population in the twelfth and thirteenth centuries was largely the result of increases in the number of peasants. The population in towns expanded especially rapidly, but an important part of that growth came from migration from the countryside. We have seen that in England the number of people rose by between two and three times in the 200 years after 1100. The precise time scale is not clear, as twelfth-century surveys of manors record more tenants – sometimes twice as many – than were described in Domesday Book, but this was sometimes the result not of a real change but of under-counting in 1086. Some surveys of the 1160s, 1170s and 1180s show that recorded numbers had grown by a modest 50 per cent or by an even lower figure, which might suggest that the expansion came at the end of the twelfth century or after 1200, and in some places the most rapid acceleration seems to have occurred in the late thirteenth century. But regardless of its timing, the increase is plain to see from the growing ranks of tenants, or the many people who came before lords' courts, or the long lists of contributors to the king's taxes. The remains of hamlets in the Scottish Highlands and in isolated farms on the Welsh hills bear material witness to the extension of settlement. The process by which Britain had become as densely populated in 1300 as it was to be in the eighteenth century could be seen as the result of accidents in biology and the weather. The number of epidemics was reduced, and seriously deficient harvests became less frequent: for example, there were relatively few really bad years between 1260 and 1290. But changes in population are rarely the result of a single factor, and as well as the temporary easing in mortality, fertility rose as peasants were making decisions about marriage which had an impact on the birth rate.

Peasants traditionally approached marriage with great caution. For them, as for us, it was an event of great personal importance, but in the middle ages the alliance had profound implications for the two families, as transfers of property were involved: initially the goods given as a dowry with the bride, but in the long term the marriage and its offspring would determine the descent of land. Peasants assumed that marriage could be contemplated only if the couple had property of some kind, even if it consisted of no more than a cottage and garden on which they could establish a new household. The land might be obtained by inheritance, but it was often gained by purchase, or as a gift from a father or other relative.

In our period the legal basis for marriage changed. The church was especially active in the eleventh and twelfth centuries in defining marriage law. In the eyes of the church the consent of the marriage partners was all important, and if a couple agreed to marry, even if the exchange of promises (the troth-plight) took place in private, this was recognized as a binding contract which could be enforced in the church courts. In the real world the agreement to marry was often negotiated between the families. The parents weighed up the suitability of the intended partner, and the alliance was settled only after some haggling over the dowry. The families probably took some account of the feelings of the marriage partners, but their individual choice did not carry as much weight in practice as the church's doctrine might imply. The material implications of marriage are recorded only when the contracts went wrong and aggrieved parties brought actions to the secular courts. For example, some time before 1312 at Duffield in Derbyshire Avicia Maud married John Wade. John complained that Richard Maud, Avicia's father, had agreed to give with her a cow worth 10s and clothing valued at 13s 4d, and to build a house in which they could live at a cost of 40s, but this contract had not been carried out. Though not in dispute, and therefore not mentioned in the case in the manor court, a transfer of land may also have been involved, as the house was to be built on a plot belonging to John Wade.

Marriage, a public event, concerned not just the couple and the families, but the lord and the whole community. Servile women (and men too on some manors) needed a licence to marry from the lord, which was given in exchange for the payment of a fine. Women who were not married but who were sexually active had to pay leirwite (literally a fine for lying down) and childwite (a fine for giving birth out of wedlock). Lords were not just levying taxes, but had a real interest in the marriage of their serfs and their choice of partners, as serfs and their offspring contributed so much in cash and labour to the profits of the manor. Lords wished to see an orderly succession of heirs as tenants of the peasant holdings. They intervened in specific cases when on occasion they attempted to compel their serfs to marry, most often requiring men to marry widows, whose holdings they believed would be more effectively cultivated if they were in the tenancy of an able-bodied man. The lords even expected to gain a small benefit from wedding festivities, as on some manors they insisted that their farm servants (*famuli*) should be invited to the feast.

Neighbours kept a close eye on the marriage and the subsequent conduct of the partners. The more substantial householders and tenants had a direct interest in the marriage of their sons and daughters, and in the descent of land to the next generation. They also had a general concern for the maintenance of order and efficiency in the village – everyone cultivated land in the fields, and contributed to rents and taxes. A good marriage would ensure that these obligations were carried out effectively and would not put extra burdens on to other villagers, who expected stability and decency in the family life of their neighbours. No doubt they would bring informal pressure to bear on those behaving improperly, and if necessary would report such offences as adultery to the church courts. The loose behaviour of servile women would be made known to the manor court, where leirwite and childwite payments were enforced.

All of this demonstrates that peasants did not enter lightly or easily into marriage. Behind all of the restraints and regulations that surrounded the institution lay the practical principle that only couples with resources, and specifically some land, should be rearing children. This would help to prevent a population explosion, because those without land would remain celibate. Those who did marry had to wait, and this served as a mechanism by which the ups and downs of the economy affected the birth rate. If couples married in their mid-twenties, for example, rather than their late teens, the number of children born to them would be considerably reduced. Another influence on fertility, both outside and within marriage, may have been the contraceptive practices which were discussed in the writings of churchmen who heard the confessions of the laity. Through such non-mechanical methods as coitus interruptus and the deliberate prolonging of breast-feeding of infants, peasant couples could lengthen the intervals between births.

In addition to the favourable climate, economic changes in the thirteenth century may have had an influence on increasing the number of marriages, and encouraging couples to marry at a younger age. More intensive methods of cultivation or better storage of crops may have made people feel that the supply of food was more plentiful and secure. The better-off peasants lived in improved houses and enjoyed an adequate diet, which enabled them to bring up more children in spite of the hazards of disease. At Halesowen in Worcestershire in the late thirteenth and early fourteenth centuries the wealthier peasants had large families, with a mean of 5.1 children in each household, compared with the cottagers' 1.8 offspring. The 'average' peasant family therefore contained parents and two or three children, with a tendency for more families to have three or more offspring during the thirteenth century. The 'average' conceals many variations in family life and structure. There was much remarriage after bereavement, and many households included children from more than one union.

A major factor in raising the population was the formation of many new households provided with small quantities of land. In areas of partible inheritance, mostly in East Anglia and Kent, when a peasant died his holding was divided among his sons. Many families had only one son, but when subdivision took place a good number of sons evidently used their fragment of land as the basis for marriage. In harder times they might have accepted that a few acres did not provide a secure basis for married life, and sold the land, perhaps even to their brother in order to reunite the parts of the original holding. In the areas of impartible inheritance, where the holding descended intact to a single son, usually the eldest (primogeniture) but in a number of villages the youngest (ultimogeniture), fathers went to much trouble to provide the children who were not inheriting any of the main holding, both sons and daughters, with parcels of land acquired by clearing new land or by purchase. Again, sons who in earlier generations might have remained celibate were enabled by gaining a modest property to contemplate building a cottage and finding a marriage partner. Many young men, perhaps on their own initiative, were able to acquire land in the same village, typically by marrying a widow who had a holding. At Chesterton near Cambridge a sixth of sons obtained land during the lifetime of their fathers, demonstrating that the younger generation did not have to wait until their parents died before they were able to possess land.

The peasants' dilemma of choosing between loyalty to family and prudent notions about landholding as a precondition for marriage was shifted in the thirteenth century by the availability of an income from employment or a trade. These apparent opportunities tipped the balance in the argument in favour of allowing the setting up of married couples on smallholdings. There were more wage-earning jobs, both in agriculture and in crafts. Opportunities were growing for people without much wealth to enter into retail trade, such as brewing and selling ale. The wages of the male head of household would not have been very high, but his wife could add her earnings – from selling ale, for example, or spinning yarn – to the total income of the family. Children could contribute a little, and when they reached the age of twelve they could go into service in another household. Smallholders had various makeshifts to gain a little extra income: they practised a 'cottage economy'. Depending on the local custom, they could graze a cow on the common pasture, and gather fuel, bracken, broom and other useful materials from the commons. They could gain some profit from the growing market – they might sell rushes. Pieces of land might be acquired by subletting from neighbours, and livestock, such as a cow, could be hired. Such people lived on credit always, and could hope to borrow enough to survive in bad harvest years.

Peasant fathers were anxious to help their children without a customary right to land. They may have been aware that the cruel law of primogeniture had been forced on them by their lords, and they certainly knew that lords still resisted moves to divide holdings on the grounds that these were the tenurial units on which rents and services were assessed. Behind this family sentiment lay practical self-interest, because parents expected their relatives to help them in their old age. A kind gesture to a son early in life would be reciprocated in the parents' declining years. A typical arrangement was agreed at Cranfield in Bedfordshire in 1294, when Elyas de Bretendon granted his half-yardland (15 acres) to his son John, in exchange for a promise that John would supply Elyas and Christine his wife with a residence on the holding and 'suitable food and drink' for the rest of their lives. Such agreements were normal customs of the manor, but in this case the two generations distrusted one another, and the father felt the need of a formal contract and a special clause guaranteeing adequate quantities of food in case the relationship soured. Parents would wish to keep on good terms with all of their children, because the uncertainties of mortality might mean that when they needed help only one of their offspring had survived.

Peasant choice was always restricted. The size of some village populations did not increase in the two centuries after 1086. For example, Compton Verney in Warwickshire contained forty-eight households at the time of Domesday, and supported forty-five in 1280. Such examples of stability were not uncommon in the 'champion' country, the midland belt dominated by open fields and nucleated villages. A decision must have been made by the lord not to form any more smallholdings, which could only have been carved out of existing tenant land or the demesne as there was no new land to clear. The peasants, most of whom held full yardlands of 40 acres, may have accepted that their interests and their heirs were well served by preserving these larger holdings, which gave their tenants an adequate living and a saleable surplus. Smallholdings were created more readily in regions where new land was being reclaimed, or which came under strong commercial influence. For example, the numbers of tenants increased sixfold and more on such manors as Bromyard, Ross-on-Wye and Ledbury in Herefordshire, where towns grew and nearby woods and wastes gave opportunities for assarting, especially by smallholders. Even in these zones of opportunity, population growth slowed down at the end of the thirteenth or in the early fourteenth century as harsher times prevailed, though some communities continued to expand until the great catastrophe of 1348–9, the Black Death.

Having examined the rising population and the influence of the market, we can explore some of the ways in which peasants accommodated themselves to economic growth, and indeed encouraged it: the extension of cultivation and changes in the structure of landholding; and peasant contributions to the market in selling produce, technical innovation, and involvement in crafts and trades.

ii. *Peasants and their holdings*

Peasants played an important part in extending the quantity of agricultural land in the twelfth and thirteenth centuries. Some of the largest projects, such as the reclamation of a large part of the Somerset Levels in the thirteenth century, were funded by as wealthy a lord as Glastonbury Abbey. Some lords give the appearance of having cleared substantial areas of woodland, when they paid fines to the crown for offences against forest law, but this was often on behalf of their tenants who had carried out the work. They could also co-ordinate and encourage assarting by renting out parcels of uncultivated land at rents designed to encourage new tenants. In special circumstances, lords organized colonization on a grand scale, as with the new villages founded for English and continental immigrants in south-west Wales in the twelfth century. These settlements had a strong political dimension, and though they led to the land being occupied in a new way, with large villages and open fields which had been previously unknown in the region, the land had previously supported a native population, so cultivation was not greatly expanded.

Lords may have directed and orchestrated clearance of new land and the founding of settlements, but the initiatives taken by thousands of peasants cumulatively accounted for a much larger area of land. Peasants expended great effort to assart from woodland or scrub, because as well as cutting down trees, roots had to be dug out of the ground, and the land enclosed against animals. Often peasants could tackle an acre or two at most at a time. When they had brought the land into production, their lords required them to pay a rent – usually a few pence in cash. If the assart was located in a royal forest – which was often the case because in Hampshire, Wiltshire and Staffordshire, for example, forest law extended over a half of the county – a fine had to be paid to the crown: a typical record from the enquiry into assarts in Cannock Forest in Staffordshire in 1286 reads 'Robert Broun assarts and holds there one rood (a quarter-acre) enclosed with a ditch . . . sown twice with spring corn and twice with winter corn . . .' These small efforts accumulated into hundreds and thousands of acres – 1,286 acres in Rockingham Forest in Northamptonshire in the early thirteenth century, to take one example. Peasants' drainage schemes in the fenlands and marshlands provide a contrast with the individual clearings in the woodlands, because the only effective method was to build large walls or dykes collectively, in collaboration with lords and other villages. The village territories were extended progressively by a series of reclamations beginning before the Conquest and continuing into the thirteenth century, resulting in long strip-shaped parishes which stretched up to 16 miles towards the coast. Once protected from flooding and drained with ditches, the land was divided into small plots, so that individual peasants gained parcels on a similar scale to their contemporaries in the woodlands. On the uplands, too, the peasants were responsible for thousands of piecemeal encroachments and enclosures, by which hillsides and moorlands were taken into more intensive agricultural use. The expansion of cultivation was often accompanied by the foundation of new settlements, like the isolated farmsteads established next to areas of still visible plough ridges on the Lammermuir Hills in southern Scotland. In the Pennines of Yorkshire and on Dartmoor in the thirteenth century, both individual farms and small hamlets were settled among new fields.

The movement to convert woodlands, wetlands and rough grazing land into arable and improved pasture could be seen as evidence of peasant irresponsibility. The ecological balance of the countryside depended on the pasture, woods, marshes and moorlands on which animals grazed, and which provided fuel, building materials and other raw materials. If peasants, anxious to increase production of cereals for feeding their families, extended the arable, they would deprive themselves and their neighbours of valuable assets. Ultimately the arable would yield badly, as it was poor land at the outset, better suited for pasture, and because it was deprived of nutrients by the shortage of grazing for animals by which manure was produced. By their reckless assarting, it could be said, peasants displayed either short-sighted greed, or desperation.

Peasants were under pressure at this time, which may well have led them to make mistakes. But in general their assarting activity was pursued cautiously. The clearance of land might involve bold pioneering in remote places, but more often it resulted from gradual intensification of settlement and agriculture. In the uplands of Scotland and northern England, land was cultivated continuously in a small infield near the settlement, and occasionally in parcels of the much larger outfield, most of which was grazed. Assarting (or making a purpresture or encroachment) was often a matter of adding acres to the infield, or cultivating larger sections of the outfield, or pushing the boundaries of the outfield further into the moor. These regions remained thinly populated and with a limited area of arable, showing that the inhabitants sensibly chose not to endanger their livelihoods by over-ambitious expansion. As in the pre-Conquest period, some of the 'new' settlements were established on sites previously occupied seasonally as shielings, so again the changes were not as radical (or foolhardy) as first appears.

Communities practising more intensive arable farming in the midlands and the south were acutely conscious of the need for conservation of scarce resources. When the peasants of Oldbury in Worcestershire realized in 1301 that their lord was proposing to enclose and rent out an area of pasture, they paid a fine of 6s 8d and promised an annual rent for the land to be left as common grazing. In the 'champion' areas, where most land was already cultivated, a protective line must have been drawn around the surviving woods and pastures at a much earlier date. This was done through community action, but the peasants perceived their livelihood in terms of the balance of types of land in their own holdings. Each yardland, oxgang, wist (in Sussex) or other unit of tenancy combined dozens of arable strips scattered over the fields with rights in common meadows, pastures and woods, and the well-being of the whole unit would depend on maintaining enough grazing to complement the corn-growing land.

We have already seen that lords were willing to divide holdings into halves and quarters in their own interests, as more tenants meant more rents and services. This was in response to demand from the peasants, who wished to provide holdings for their offspring, and indeed would-be tenants were willing to pay substantial entry fines to gain access to such a newly created holding, even if it was rather small. By 1279–80, in a large sample of midland peasants listed in the Hundred Rolls, less than a quarter of peasants held full yardlands, and 40 per cent were in possession of half- and quarter-yardlands. In the north, tenants had often held double oxgangs, which broke down into single oxgangs and occasionally half-oxgangs in the thirteenth century. This meant that a diminishing minority of peasants belonged to the elite with about 30 acres, which gave the average family plenty of food, a saleable surplus in all but the worst years, and would need the labour of at least two full-time workers. A substantial minority of peasants held about 15 acres (a half-yardland or an oxgang) which would feed a family, provide a suffi-cient surplus to pay the rent, and could be worked by the tenant alone if he was able-bodied. Those with a quarter-yardland or half-oxgang would need to have an alternative source of income to supplement the produce of the holding, as it would not be fully sufficient for the family's food, let alone rent payments.

Some traditional units of tenure were fragmented. In East Anglia the old tenements survived as ghosts, because they were still used to levy rents and services, but in practice they were split up among many tenants. Throughout Norfolk, Suffolk and south Lincolnshire, and to a lesser extent in Essex and Kent, while a fortunate minority might hold as much as 20 acres of land, on many manors the majority of tenants had only 5 acres or less. Smallholdings had proliferated everywhere, as assarts, or fragments of demesne, cottage tenements carved out of yardlands or oxgangs, or parcels put on the market were joined to the already sub-stantial minority of bordars and cottars recorded in 1086. Lords played a part in this, granting cottages to former slaves, encouraging small-scale assarting, or even changing the inheritance custom so that holdings were partible.

iii. *Peasants and the market*

Peasants changed the management of their land, and their way of life, in response to the growth in the market. They had moved away from simple self-sufficiency before 1100, and they were producing for sale on a considerable scale by the late thirteenth century. The landlords ran their

demesnes in order to take advantage of higher prices, but still a high proportion of demesne produce went to supply the household, or to feed
animals and servants on the manor itself. Peasants had small households
and few servants, and sold a high proportion of their crops. A yardlander
in the midlands in about 1300 could hope to harvest 23 quarters of grain,
and after reserving 6 quarters for next year's seed and 10 quarters to feed
his family and animals, was able to sell 7 quarters, for which he could
expect to receive a sum of between £1 and £2. The choice of crops was
partly influenced by the local soil and climate, and by the needs of their
families, but also by market opportunities. The people of the large woodland manor of King's Norton in Worcestershire in about 1300 paid tithes
which reveal that oats accounted for two-thirds of their grain. No doubt
they used some of this relatively cheap corn for brewing and baking, and
as fodder for horses, but they would also have sold a good deal, as there
was demand from the district immediately to the south which produced
few oats.

Niches in the market could be occupied by peasants. Demesnes tended
to concentrate on the staple, bulky products such as grain, wool and livestock. This left the peasants to cater for steady demand for the smaller
and troublesome items, such as poultry, eggs, fruit and vegetables, honey
and wax. Peasant gardens and yards were usually tended by peasant
women, and it is no accident that when we hear of the sale of these goods
in towns, they were often being hawked in the markets and streets by
women with baskets, like the fourteen women who paid a toll of a halfpenny each to sell beans, peas and apples in Bristol in 1282–4. Peasants
grew industrial crops in small plots and gardens, most commonly flax
and hemp, but also dyestuffs such as madder, all of it for sale. Demesnes
used most of their hay and straw for feed and litter within the manor, so
much of that sold in urban markets came from smaller producers.

Livestock were kept on peasant holdings mainly for the revenue that
could be obtained by selling wool, dairy produce and surplus animals.
Some of the cheese and bacon, and pieces of salt beef and mutton for
the wealthier peasants, went into the peasants' larders, but most wool
was destined for the commercial cloth industry, not domestic weaving.
The potential for surplus is most easily demonstrated for the more
pastoral regions. For example, when David Fychan of Marchros in Merioneth was assessed for the tax of 1293 (and no doubt was under-assessed)
he owned four oxen which he would have used for ploughing, and also
had six cows and twenty sheep. The 500 pounds of cheese and butter that
he could have expected to obtain from the cows would have been well in
excess of his family's consumption, and the cash (about 10s if he sold
half of it) was needed to pay rents and taxes. Fychan's flock of twenty

sheep was fairly typical in size, and throughout Britain there were many thousands of these modest flocks, an enormous number taken together. The scale of peasant sheep-keeping can be appreciated from the total of 46,382 sacks of wool exported from English ports in 1304–5, the peak year. If each sack contained 260 fleeces, the wool came from at least 12 million animals. We can estimate that at least two-thirds of wool production for export came from peasant flocks. At East Meon in Hampshire in 1302, the lord kept 1,300 adult sheep, which in the course of the year had produced 555 lambs. In the same year, the rector of the parish collected in tithes 150 new lambs, implying that 1,500 had been born in the parish. The peasant flocks in the parish therefore contained a cumulative total of about 4,000 adult animals.

Peasant producers were stimulated by rising prices. Wool from a dozen sheep (weighing a stone, that is 14 pounds) fetched about 2s in 1209. In 1302 the same quantity could be sold for almost 4s. In the same way a quarter of wheat (approximately the crop of an acre of land) was sold for 2s 7d in 1209, and 5–6s a century later (see Figure 1 below, p. 230).

Peasants responded to market demand by changing their farming practices. They worked within local farming systems, so there can be no generalizations which apply to the whole country. Each system varied in the proportions of enclosed and common land, and between private and public control of resources. They had different balances of arable and pasture, and cultivated with varying intensity, specifically the extent to which land lay fallow between crops. The choice of crops and animals also varied.

In western and south-eastern England were the districts sometimes called 'old enclosed', 'woodland' or 'wood/pasture', which often had areas of open field, sometimes with a dozen or more 'fields', combined with much land enclosed in crofts and closes (see Map 1 above, p. 16). Peasant holdings commonly combined both enclosed and unenclosed land. With the assarting movement the proportion of enclosures tended to increase, as newly cleared land was usually surrounded by a hedge and held initially by a single tenant. In the long run assarted land might be subdivided with inheritance and the sale of strips, and come to resemble an open field. The balance between different types of land often shifted towards arable in order to meet the subsistence needs of the cultivators, but peasants from these regions were able to sell surplus grain, dairy produce and livestock, such as pigs.

In the 'champion' or midland landscapes stretching from southern Scotland to south-west England the fields were under strict communal control, which maintained either a two-course or three-course rotation (see Maps 2 and 3 above, pp. 20 and 22). Every peasant produced both winter-sown crops (wheat, rye and maslin, a mixture of the two) and spring crops such as barley, oats and legumes. The fields were designed to provide adequate grazing for animals, mainly sheep and cattle. Changes included the rather rare conversion of a two-field to a three-field system, involving a new layout of the whole village territory in a single operation, but the much more common and more informal arrangement was that of inhoks, by which parts of the fallow field were temporarily fenced and planted. Both led to an increase in the planted area, and more frequent cropping. The cultivators intended to increase their output partly in order to send more surplus corn to market.

In hilly country, with its restricted area of arable, often in an 'infield', and extensive pastures, more land could be taken into cultivation by extending the infield or by cultivating the outfield more frequently. The quality of the arable was improved on uplands in Devon and Cornwall by applying sea sand (which contained lime) and beat burning (paring turf, burning it, and speading it on the land), but these methods, though recorded for the first time, may not have been new.

Some practices were adopted in a number of regions. Manure from the yard and animal houses of the peasant holding, as well as household waste and the contents of cesspits, was carried by cart to the fields, and was concentrated on the best land. Large quantities of marl, that is subsoil containing lime, was dug out of pits in the fields and spread on the land. Demesnes did this, but it was especially characteristic of peasant farming. The acreage under legumes expanded, to provide food for humans and animals and to benefit the next crop from the nitrogen in the roots. Peasant buildings, like those of the lords of the manors (see p. 131), were constructed with stone foundations and timber frames, which allowed crops to be stored in barns where they were protected from rats and damp, and byres, stables and sheepcotes also gave shelter to animals. Peasants increasingly used horses rather than oxen as draught animals. In the twelfth century most better-off peasants owned ox-drawn wains, which were effective, but were slow and best suited to carrying heavy loads around the fields. During the thirteenth century, mainly in the east of the country, peasants adopted horses and carts, which could be used for hauling around the village, but also were well suited by their comparative speed to carry sacks of grain or sides of bacon to market at distances of five or ten miles. (Plate 8) Horses were sometimes employed as plough beasts by peasants while the demesnes still relied on oxen.

The market encouraged greater intensity of cultivation. This trend was taken to extremes in north-east Norfolk, which was densely populated

and came under strong urban influence. Peasant holdings were very
small. In the manor of Martham in 1292, 220 of 364 tenants held an acre
or two, and only ten had more than 10 acres. If the peasants followed
the pattern of husbandry found on the local demesnes (see p. 127), which
seems very likely, they worked their fragments of land with great care,
cropping the arable with few or no periods of fallow. They prepared
the land for sowing by ploughing (or digging in the case of the smallholders) the land repeatedly, and sowed the seed thickly. As the corn
grew they hoed and weeded. They planted quantities of legumes. They
used horses for ploughing as well as hauling. We do not know if the
peasant land was as productive as the demesnes, with yields as high as
20 bushels per acre for wheat, but in order to support so many people
on smallholdings they must have obtained better results than their
contemporaries in the midlands. Throughout the country intensive
methods were applied to the tiny plots used for horticulture, and
although gardens accounted for a small percentage of total output, in
some regions they made a significant contribution to peasant incomes.
Again, in parts of East Anglia flax and hemp, though grown in small
plots, contributed as much as 6 per cent of total agricultural production
in the early fourteenth century, measured from the tithe revenues.

While capable of adopting new methods, peasants were understandably reluctant to make more radical changes. The Norfolk methods were
appropriate to local circumstances: midland peasants would have been
impressed by the grain yields, but would not have been envious of the
amount of work that was expended to achieve them. Resistance to change
was not necessarily the result of ignorance, but was based on rational
calculations of advantage. For example, the Oxfordshire village of South
Stoke, which had two fields, in about 1240, apparently on the initiative of
its lord (the monastery of Eynsham Abbey), recast its fields to make three.
The surrounding villages, which also cultivated their land in two fields,
would have observed the results with great interest. South Stoke had
trouble with its new third field, which proved too small, and the change
led to a dispute over pasture. Even if the transformation had been better
planned, the people of the neighbouring settlements would have been
deterred from following South Stoke's example because the apparent
increase in each holding's cultivated area by 33 per cent each year would
not give them a proportionate increase in production. They would lose
some grazing, and the new system tended to push yields down as
the land was rested less often and deprived of some manure. The same
reservation applied to the inhoks. The central concern of peasants
throughout most of lowland England was their difficulty in keeping

enough animals to bring high returns in the market and to maintain the arable in good heart. Many peasant flocks of sheep consisted of a dozen or two dozen animals, and many smallholders had none at all, judging from the inability of the lords' officials to find a beast which could be taken as a heriot when a cottager died. They would not have known about the deficiency in minerals, such as phosphorus, but they would have been fully aware from practical experience that extra cartloads of manure on the ploughed land made a difference to the subsequent harvest. Some of the technical changes which might be seen as far-sighted improvements seem to have been makeshifts in difficult circumstances. Peasants may have appreciated the speed and strength of the horses that they owned, but judging from the sums of money at which some of their old nags were valued, their chief virtue was their cheapness.

Although they were influenced by the market, peasants did not develop a fully commercial mentality. Very rarely did peasants at this time have sufficient confidence in the market to specialize in a cash crop and buy their main foodstuffs. The holding was expected to provide a proportion of the family's food, and most of the labour came from family members. They would make decisions on the basis of their needs rather than calculations of cash profits, expending much effort on a crop such as dredge, a mixture of barley and oats, which yielded well, was versatile in use, but did not fetch a high price. They were not free agents, but were bound by the rules of the village. For example, a yardlander could not in theory expand his sheep flock beyond the maximum fixed by the customary stint; in a typical village the limit was forty animals. Lords reduced their tenants' ability to invest in buildings, equipment or livestock by their rent demands, especially for high entry fines. And the lords enjoyed many advantages in the marketing of crops. Rents collected at Michaelmas (29 September) and the following months pressured peasants into selling corn when the price was low. Lords could keep their corn back until the price rose in the following spring and early summer. A modern economist would sum up the peasants' position by saying that at this time they were only 'partly integrated' into the market.

Agriculture had never been the sole source of peasants' incomes. In the early middle ages they had gathered and hunted around their settlements, and made their own utensils and clothing. In the twelfth and thirteenth centuries they continued to exploit the sources of food and raw materials that were locally available. On the coast they fished and made salt. In the Fens they caught wildfowl and fish, collected rushes, reeds and sedge, and dug turf (peat) for fuel. In woodlands they had access to fuel and timber, collected nuts and fruit, and when the opportunity came, poached deer for meat. But as market demand increased, peasants used these assets to generate a cash income, and in the woodlands burnt charcoal, made potash, and participated in a dozen crafts, from wood-turning to glass-making. Towns consumed ever-growing supplies of salt, fish and rushes. The population of London in about 1300 burnt about 140,000 tons of wood to warm their houses and cook their food, as well as to provide fuel for industries. This had repercussions for dozens of rural communities within easy reach by cart or boat (in practice 30 miles), especially those near to the Thames. In the Chiltern Hills on the north bank of the river, and Surrey to the south, peasants could exploit their common rights to woods, or cut wood in groves that they rented. Many smallholders found employment from the lords of the manor, or richer neighbours, in cutting wood and then carrying the faggots and 'talwood' (logs) to the river bank for loading on to boats.

The market not only intensified gathering activities, but also promoted a greater degree of specialization among peasant craftsmen and encouraged the spread of complex industrial processes in the countryside. Sometimes mining for minerals and smelting ore was carried out on such a large scale, like tinning in Cornwall and Devon, that most of those employed were full-time wage earners rather than peasants. Iron, lead and coal workings, which did not attract the same level of investment, gave opportunities for peasants to engage in mining as a part-time activity. Coal miners at Longdon on the edge of Cannock Chase in Staffordshire, for example, paid 6d per pick per week, in one case for seventeen weeks from May to September. These were small bell pits no more than 100 feet deep, which were sunk into the coal seam where it lay near to the surface; typically these were worked by two men using little equipment apart from a pick and shovel, and a windlass to haul the coal to the surface. Quarrying for building stone or millstones was another intermittent activity that could be fitted into the less busy times in the farming year.

A number of crafts which had been located mainly in towns in the early phases of urban growth spread into the countryside after 1100. It made sense to make pottery near to abundant supplies of clay and fuel. Villages gained such a reputation for pottery-making that their names changed, to Potters Marston (Leicestershire) and Crockerton (Wiltshire). Clothmaking continued as an urban activity, but was supplemented by an important rural industry. Lords noted the number of weavers on their manors, and from about 1180 built fulling mills in order to exploit the demand for mechanical cloth finishing. These are found especially in the south-west, the west midlands and the north-west, but judging from the distribution of occupational surnames such as Webb (weaver) and Walker or Tucker (fuller), the industry was also well established in the east in the thirteenth century, in such counties as Essex. A scatter of craftsmen are found in many villages. Smiths were often established by lords of manors, though they would also sell their services to their neighbours. Many leather workers (tanners in particular), and building workers (especially carpenters and thatchers) were widely scattered in the countryside. The number of tailors, one of the commonest non-agricultural occupations by c.1300, demonstrates the degree of craft specialization that had been achieved. The country tailors held land, but in order for them to make even a modest living from their craft a significant number of their peasant neighbours must have had their clothing made by a professional.

Cottagers and smallholders took up industrial employment because they could not make a living from their modest acreage of land. The whole landholding population of the Wiltshire potting village of Crockerton in 1234 consisted of tenants with 4 acres of land at most. But potting offered low status and rewards, and many other peasant-craftsmen had a stronger base in landholding. The manorial smiths were often tenants of a medium-sized peasant holding, a half-yardland or oxgang. Two charcoal burners who worked in Inglewood in Cumberland had goods (probably livestock) valued for tax purposes at between £2 and £3, which means that they formed part of the peasant elite. And peasants with their own carts were able to sell their services as carriers. As is so often the case, those who were already well off were in a better position to make the maximum from non-agricultural activities.

The same social and economic variety can be found among those, mostly women, who worked in the most widespread of medieval village trades, the brewing of ale. In every village in the late thirteenth century a high proportion of the women brewed for sale. Some were providing for their own households, and occasionally sold the surplus, perhaps only once or twice in a year. For others it was a more continuous, full-time occupation. The economic circumstances of these brewsters varied considerably. Some of them were the wives of wealthier or middling peasants, who used grain from the holding, while others were cottagers, widows and single women for whom brewing was their main source of income, based on malt that had been purchased. Of thirty-eight regular brewsters at Brigstock (Northamptonshire) before the Black Death, twenty came from settled middle-status peasant households, and eighteen were poor cottagers, recent immigrants and women on the margins of the community. Brewing is a well-known activity because it was regulated through the manor court, which enables us to calculate profits. The sale of 22½ gallons of ale brewed from 3 bushels of malt in about 1300 should have left the brewster with a surplus of 5d. On this basis, a brewster could have kept herself and her family if she brewed and sold ale from 6–8 bushels of malt each week. This was a feasible total, if she was working in a community with dozens of consuming households.

Peasants may have been only 'partly integrated' into the market, but this still enabled them to buy a wide range of goods and services. Everyone was handling money, whether it was gained from the sale of produce or earned in wages. A substantial proportion was earmarked for rents, taxes and church dues, but some could be devoted to consumption. A yardlander in southern England would have had £1 to spare in a good year, and wage-earning cottagers may well have spent more, though in their case the main call on the money would have been the purchase of foodstuffs. At least 40 per cent of rural families bought at least part of their basic supplies of grain, because they could not grow enough on their land. The middling and wealthier peasants tended to provide for their own food need from their holding, hence the strong regional traditions in diet, with wheat being the main bread corn in the south; rye and barley were baked in Norfolk. Ale was usually brewed from barley, but in Essex and the south-west malted oats were used. On the other hand, they did not rely entirely on their own crops for food and drink. Often they found it convenient to obtain ale from ale wives as we have seen, relying on the informal rota of brewsters within the village. Bread, joints of meat, cheese, puddings and pies were available from retailers in towns and often in the country too. For those who lived inland, sea fish, a regular item in their diet, came from the network of local markets.

The main calls on peasant cash, after food, came from their need for housing and clothing. To begin with their houses, modern commentators have sometimes assumed that these were built by the peasants themselves, using materials available in the locality at little cost. No doubt the peasants contributed to building work, by hauling materials and preparing the site, but they employed specialists, and in particular carpenters, to assemble the timber frame. Their handiwork can be seen in peasant houses that still stand, and indeed are inhabited at the present day, at Aston Tirrold and Harwell, both in Berkshire, which have been dated quite precisely, to 1282–4 and 1285–95 respectively. Many more houses have now gone, not necessarily because they were flimsily built, but because they became redundant in later periods. Their foundations have been excavated, and these show that between about 1180 and 1320 the rural building tradition went through an important change with the adoption of stone foundations. Builders used the local materials – granite, chalk, flint, limestone – or just set the timber frame on twenty or thirty padstones where stone was scarce. The stone added to the cost of construction, but helped to prolong the life of the timbers which now were raised above the damp ground. The dimensions of the foundations suggest that the timbers were assembled in frames in two or three bays, according to a convention that each bay measured about 15 feet by 15 feet, giving the houses a length of 30 or 45 feet. The use of standard sizes again points to the work of professional craftsmen, as do the distinctive local styles of building. Cruck construction predominated in the midlands and western and northern Britain, which meant that the main vertical elements in the timber frame consisted of pairs of curved timbers, often formed by splitting a single tree. In the south and east buildings the framing tradition was based on vertical posts.

Some materials used in peasant buildings – straw or reeds for thatch, and clay and dung to daub over the wattled walls – came easily to hand. But timber in sufficient quantity to build a whole house – at least twenty trees – and the timbers of the right size and shape to make crucks, were not to be found in every wood; they had to be carried from a distance, and often were purchased. The combination of paying craftsmen's wages and buying materials ensured that peasant houses were not cheap. We have seen (p. 157) that in 1312 in Derbyshire building a house, which may not have been very large, was said to have cost 40s. In the uplands, dwellings and byres were built in line under a single roof, which reduced total expenditure. Most houses, however, were specialized dwellings, which were divided between a hall and chamber. The dwelling was often accompanied by separate agricultural buildings, such as barns and byres, and as these could also be built with stone foundations and timber frames, the cost of an entire complex could have exceeded £6. The peasant demand for decent, secure and weather-proof accommodation, with adequate living space and shelter for crops, implements and animals, had repercussions throughout the rural economy. To afford the buildings peasants were stimulated to grow and sell more produce. Their expenditure encouraged the growth of a specialized and skilled labour force, and promoted trade in timber and other materials. Their houses also tell us something of peasants' attitudes to property and privacy. Often they lived close to neighbours in communities which enjoyed a collective identity based on shared assets, but the tenants of individual houses guarded their privacy. They were surrounded by hedges and ditches or walls, and their outer doors were secured with locks. Windows were small, barred, and protected with shutters. If outsiders penetrated into the house, they would find that clothing and other valuables were locked in stout chests in the inner private room, the chamber.

Clothing, like housing, was largely the work of specialists, and peasants bought their textiles: woollens for clothes, and linen for undergarments and household use, such as sheets and towels. A peasant from Walsham-le-Willows in Suffolk, William Lene, died in 1329, a little after our period, but his possessions were acquired earlier and are unlikely to differ from those of his predecessors in the late thirteenth century. He was a rich peasant, with 37 acres of arable, and he owned 10 yards of russet cloth valued at 9s, clothing worth 13s, four sheets and carpets (14s), two tablecloths (2s) and two towels (16d). His chests contained more textiles than most peasants had, but when thefts of clothing are reported, or reference is made to the provision of clothing in agreements to maintain old people, it is clear that there was widespread ownership of wool and linen cloth of some quality and value by peasants of all kinds. For example, when peasants on the Dorset manor of Sturminster Newton were summoned to have their Christmas dinner in the manor house, they were expected to bring their own tablecloths. These purchases created a mass market for relatively cheap textiles – William Lene had bought russet at 11d per yard, towards the lower end of the price range. Lene's inventory does not mention shoes, but peasants wore leather shoes and boots made mainly in towns, typically costing 6d per pair.

Even small-scale producers were also consumers of farming equipment, domestic utensils, furniture and objects for personal use. Most households contained dozens of manufactured items. Their number and quality varied with the wealth of the peasants, and there were great disparities between regions. One indication is provided by the objects found when peasant houses are excavated. At Cefn Graeanog in Gwynnedd, on a ridge between Snowdonia and the sea, a house, barn, stable and byre were occupied by a peasant family in the thirteenth century. The buildings, with their stone foundations and (probably) cruck frames, suggest owners of some substance, but they left behind for discovery by modern archaeologists only an iron spade, two knife blades, a horseshoe, a few pieces of scrap bronze and lead, seven stone objects, including whetstones, and four fragments of pottery. Perhaps they disposed of their rubbish away from the house, but more likely they based their domestic and farming activities on wooden and leather objects, and were careful to recycle any broken or worn-out metal tools or artefacts. A house at Upton in the Gloucestershire Cotswolds was occupied from the twelfth to the fourteenth century, but the thirteenth century marks the peak of occupation. The dwelling house and farm buildings were constructed with high-quality stone foundations, a timber frame and thatched roof. The twenty-one iron objects that were found included a billhook, a 'spud' for weeding, knives, horseshoes, door fittings, including a lock plate, latch and key. There were three bronze buckles from clothing, and a score of stone objects including pieces of hand-mills and whetstones. The pottery fragments exceeded 5,000 in number, and included pieces of cooking pots, jugs and bowls, which were mainly suitable for preparing and serving food and drink, but also were used in dairying and other activities on the farm. The contrast in their material possessions reflects the poverty and wealth of the two regions, partly because of their natural resources, and partly because of the unequal development of the market economy.

Small and quite cheap objects acquired by peasants were almost all produced at a distance, in specialist centres of manufacture, and a few were imported. Pottery at Upton came from rural industries 20 or more miles from the village, in western Worcestershire, north Warwickshire and Buckinghamshire. They reached their eventual owners through markets and fairs held in the local market towns, as did the hand-mills of German origin. The metal objects would have come from urban workshops, though some of the ironwork could have been made by country smiths. Urban craftsmen probably made the wooden and leather goods which are not preserved but are known from documents, such as ploughs, carts, harrows and harness for the farm, furnishings such as tables, benches and chests, and the tubs, troughs and vats used in preparing food and drink.

While they bought goods and employed artisans, peasants could ill afford luxuries, and often made do with old, worn-out and mended utensils. They were short of cash, so their purchases were usually based on credit rather than immediate payment. Nonetheless they had some spending power, and must often have faced difficult choices about whether to put their money into consumption, or to invest their limited funds in buildings, equipment and livestock on the farm. In general, even the most successful peasants did not opt for high levels of personal consumption. Their houses seem sparsely furnished, and their most valuable possession was a cart with wheels fitted with iron tyres.

The market for land was not always directly connected with the trade in produce and goods. Many transfers of land took place within the family, whether by inheritance after the death of a tenant, or by grants between family members, for example when an elderly tenant retired. In any peasant society there would be elderly people and widows who lacked labour and the need for large quantities of produce, and young and vigorous households which had more capacity to work and many mouths to feed. These inequalities could be resolved if parcels of land passed from one tenant to another. Such adjustments and exchanges had probably gone unrecorded in the early middle ages.

In the thirteenth century, with extended use of written documents and the growing value of land, transfers between peasants were more commonly recorded. In the case of free land the conveyance was made by charters or deeds. A typical deed concerns a grant of 2 acres of land in Elbridge in Kent which was made by Peter son of Nigel and Godeva his wife to William and Robert sons of Simon, in about 1200. The 2 acres of land were described in relation to the land of other tenants, and the rent specified as 9d. William and Robert gave 18s 6d for it. The grant was witnessed by a small group of local people.

Sales of customary or servile land were supervised by the manor court: a tenant would come into court and surrender a holding to the lord; a new tenant would then appear and be granted the land. In fact the parties had agreed the transfer before the day of the court session. This is made more explicit in the common procedure by which a tenant surrendered land to the lord for the use of (*ad opus* in Latin) another tenant. Sometimes the outgoing tenant paid a heriot to the lord, as this 'death duty' was often demanded on surrender of land as well as on the death of a tenant, and usually the incoming tenant paid an entry fine. A typical record in the court roll for King's Ripton in Huntingdonshire in 1294 reads 'Nicholas Hall in full court surrenders into the lord's hands for the use of Henry son of Simon a half-acre of land lying in Westcroft', for which Henry paid a fine to the lord of 6d. He would also have paid money to Nicholas Hall, but arrangements between tenants were no concern of the lord, and not normally recorded. The purchase price at that time of high demand for land would have been considerably higher than the entry fine. Such transfers were permanent alienations, in which the hereditary right to the land passed from one tenant to another. A short-term transfer could be made by means of a lease, which was handled by different lords in various ways. Some lords allowed leases, especially if they lasted for only a year or two, without insisting that they be registered in the court. Others attempted to forbid them, or required that they be reported to the court (at a price). Such controls encouraged the tenants to arrange them clandestinely, which created an illicit land market that was very difficult to police. The authorities sometimes discovered horrific examples of a yardland that had been divided among a dozen tenants, and in consequence had almost escaped from the control of the estate administration. When we have a systematic record of subtenancy, like the survey of the royal manor of Havering-atte-Bower in Essex in 1251, the normally hidden layer of subtenants is revealed to have consisted mainly of smallholders with a few acres.

A further area of controversy concerned the difficult border territory separating free and customary land, and between people of free status who held servile land and serfs who acquired freeholdings. Free land attracted the unfree, because it gave them more complete rights of ownership and carried light cash rents. They aspired to be able to buy and sell customary land in the same fashion as free tenants, without the oversight of the manor court, by means of charters and deeds. Lords like Peterborough Abbey would allow the serf to acquire free land, but only if the deeds were surrendered to the lord. On some estates the land was surrendered and granted back to the tenant by the lord, which allowed the lord to control the serfs' land acquisitions, and to make some profit from them. Lords would not compromise at all on attempts to hold customary land by charter, and communities that attempted this, like Barnet in Hertfordshire, met with stout resistance.

The changes in the land market in the thirteenth century extended beyond the introduction of better records. With the rise of market production, and a more lively commercial economy, successful peasants bought land, not in order to provide for the subsistence of their family, but as part of a strategy to expand their profitable agricultural production, or to gain rents by subletting land. A few entrepreneurs were building up their wealth at the expense of their less able, fortunate or ruthless neighbours.

A commercial land market developed most intensely in eastern England, where most manor court rolls contain dozens of records of land changing hands every year. Analysis of the manorial court records of Coltishall (Norfolk) and Redgrave (Suffolk) in the late thirteenth and early fourteenth centuries shows that 91 and 87 per cent respectively of the land transfers were made between people who were not related. Many of these transactions, like the example of a surrender given above, concerned small parcels of an acre or two. Larger holdings were more likely to be inherited or passed from one relative to another, so that if the quantity of land changing hands is being calculated, as distinct from the number of transfers, about half passed within the family. In the midlands and the west an active land market existed, but a higher proportion of land was kept within the family and a smaller proportion was sold to people who were not relatives. At the very well studied manor of Halesowen 63 per cent of transfers were between family members, and 80 per cent of the land was conveyed by inheritance or was granted by fathers to children, or from brother to brother, or between other family members.

Many motives lay behind the land market. We can be confident that some of those accumulating land were seeking to profit from the rents that could be collected from subtenants. An acre might be liable to pay the lord of the manor 3d annually, but could be sublet for 12d in regions of high land values. This is the most likely reason for townspeople penetrating the rural land market, like the burgesses of Dunstable in

Bedfordshire who held land in nearby villages in 1279. Active cultivators were probably acquiring land in order to maximize grain production. This is most likely to lie behind the marked tendency for land to be gathered by a few wealthy tenants from poorer neighbours during periods of bad harvests. At Hinderclay in Suffolk in the difficult years of bad weather and poor yields between 1294 and 1299, of the 112 people involved in transfers of land, thirty-nine were buyers, fifty-five were sellers, and another eighteen both bought and sold. Poorer people, who no doubt were already in debt, sold land in order to buy food, and a minority of better-off peasants took advantage and expanded their holdings. Cultivators with larger acreages were in a better position to produce a saleable surplus and to profit from the prevalent high grain prices.

If the number of sellers consistently exceeded the number of buyers, especially in the succession of bad harvests and cattle disease for thirty years after 1294, very large holdings would have developed and the smallholders would have lost their land. Such an extreme polarization did not take place, even in eastern England. The accumulations of land were rather fragile, and disintegrated soon after they had been created. To some extent this reflects the general economic instability of the times, with individual entrepreneurs who made some gains, but who failed to found dynasties of rich peasants. The lands were bought in an opportunistic fashion, and there is little evidence of a strategy by the purchasers to buy adjacent plots in order to cultivate with more efficiency. A further explanation of the breakdown of the larger holdings reflects the fact that their tenants were not ruthless economic men: often they divided their lands among their family. This provides further confirmation of the generalization that peasants were only partly integrated into the market.

Although East Anglia saw the most flourishing land market, it developed everywhere. In Wales, tenants were restrained by their lords from making permanent alienations of their land, but they found ways around these institutional obstacles, in the form of the pridd. By this device land was leased for a fixed term of years, but this was constantly renewable, so in effect the grant had been made for ever. The purchaser enjoyed considerable rights over the land, and could, for example, bequeath it.

The earliest document recording a pridd dates from 1286, and subsequently these arrangements multiplied until they became the basis for wealthy and successful tenants to build up considerable landed fortunes.

Those who bought and sold land were also involved in lending and borrowing money. The purchase price for a holding, and the entry fine, were often paid in instalments. In the same way, the purchase of goods or animals was invariably based on credit, in that the purchaser would not pay the full price for some months. Peasants would borrow from Jews, but Jewish communities were localized, and even before 1290 the main sources of peasant credit would be wealthier neighbours, the parish clergy, and urban traders, who might (for an advantage) pay money in advance for crops not yet harvested or wool not yet clipped. When creditors pursued those who owed them money in the manor courts, the 'pleas of debt' suggest that most debts resulted from sales of goods that went wrong, or non-payment of wages. But peasants did make loans of cash to one another, and in some cases a land transfer resulted from a failure to pay which forced the debtor to sell his or her holding.

iv. *Peasants and lords*

The growth in the commercial activities of peasants had important implications for their relations with their lords. We saw earlier the many ways in which lords increased their revenues from peasants (pp. 137–45), but how did these change the peasant economy? It would be easy to represent the period as a disastrous one for peasants, as their legal status was diminished by the imposition of villeinage, the new more precisely defined serfdom, making them liable to pay large sums in tallage, marriage fines and entry fines. The higher payments had the potential of milking the peasants of their profits in the market, and preventing them from accumulating money for consumption or investment. Servile peasants were restricted in a number of ways – in buying and selling free land, or in moving from their manor. The ability of their lords to behave in arbitrary ways, such as charging higher entry fines or imposing new dues, made serfs feel insecure. The growing rural population raised land values, allowing lords to increase rents and entry fines, and the shortage of land reduced the bargaining power of tenants.

In fact the tide did not always run against the peasants. The twelfth century brought an end to slavery, with the settling of slaves on landholdings by lords. Some holdings owing labour services were converted to pay cash rents, and freeholdings with no obligation but money rent multiplied with the clearance of new land. Once fixed, an annual free cash rent could not be changed, and the inflation around 1200 reduced its value to the advantage of the tenant. Free tenants accounted for the majority of the peasantry, and many of the most successful producers for the market were freemen (sometimes called franklins) who could accumulate large holdings without the expense of entry fines and without restriction from lords' courts. The most commercialized and prosperous regions, such as East Anglia and Kent, contained a high proportion of free tenants.

Even after the imposition of the new serfdom, lords exaggerated their arbitrary power over their villeins. When the lawyers claimed that an unfree tenant would not know when he went to bed what he would be doing the next day, this implied that the lord's officials could summon tenants to labour services as they pleased. Some boon works could be announced at short notice, but most labour services were fixed in terms of day and season. The conditions of tenure in many respects were defined in written surveys, and in unwritten customs that were declared and modified in the manor court. Lords could make increases in services or rents, but usually had to do so in indirect and subtle ways or they would provoke troublesome reactions among the tenants. Again, in legal theory, a servile holding was the property of the lord, and some lords would announce in a grandiloquent gesture in their manor courts that the villein holdings had been seized. In practice the holdings grew to resemble the property of the villein. Their hereditary rights were respected by the lords, who rarely interfered with the succession of land to heirs according to the local inheritance customs. Customary land could be bought and sold, providing that the transaction passed through the lord's court. Lords disapproved of peasants who made wills, but came in practice to accept bequests. For example, a device was used by which a tenant on his deathbed could surrender land to beneficiaries, preferably in the presence of an official of the lord, who could then report the transfer to the next court. Lords were always anxious to gain money, so that many of the rules that restricted serfs would be set aside for a payment.

Peasants achieved these advantages by vigilance and pressure. They were in continuous dialogue with their lords, employing a variety of strategies for defending their interests, from negotiation to outright rebellion. They had an opportunity to have an influence on the running of their manors because lords depended on peasant officials such as the reeve and the jurors in the manor courts. Peasants would use these positions in their own interests: for example, when they were asked to decide some disputed question of the custom of the manor, they would employ their collective memory selectively. The prominent peasants who occupied the responsible positions in the management of the manor negotiated directly with the lord. When labour services were commuted for cash rents, an agreement would be made for all of the tenants in a particular category (all of the yardlanders, for example) which must have resulted from some form of collective bargaining. Sometimes tenants found that they could buy a concession from the lord – they could escape from some irregular payment, or preserve their rights to a pasture, by offering a sum of money.

A characteristic clash between lord and tenants broke out at Bourton-on-the-Hill and Todenham in Gloucestershire. The customary tenants were supposed in the late thirteenth century to do labour services on certain days of the week. If one of these days coincided with one of the numerous religious holidays, their lord, Westminster Abbey, lost the day's work. A zealous abbot who came into office in 1315 insisted that they work on another day in compensation. The tenants resisted the change, and were charged money for the days' work that were lost, which they failed to pay. The abbot won, but offered in a gesture of reconciliation to cancel the money owed by the tenants. He imagined that this was a generous act, but the tenants thought that the money had been demanded unjustly in the first place. The abbot was enraged when the reeve of Todenham, Henry Melksop, 'of fair face but an ugly snout', 'did not deign to open his mouth to thank us'.

Tenants could register their resentment of customary works by not attending when summoned, sometimes in a co-ordinated withdrawal of service. Or they could work badly. They evaded the penalties of servility, most commonly by concealing the marriage of their daughters so as not to pay the fine, or by transferring land without going to the court (and paying the entry fine) or by illicit subletting. They showed their lack of respect for the lord by grazing their animals on his land, even in his corn, and by stealing corn and taking wood without permission. They took their corn to be ground at a mill other than the lord's, or used their own hand-mills. Lords responded to these offences by amercing (fining) them in the manor court, the revenues of which could provide a twentieth, or even a higher proportion of estate income. In Scotland lords took forfeitures from their tenants in compensation for offences, often in the form of valuable livestock, a cow or a sheep.

The protests and agitations of tenants could become purposeful and well organized. The men of Penrhosllugwy in Anglesey had suffered a harsh assessment of the obligations in 1294, in the aftermath of the English conquest of north Wales. A very heavy burden of labour services, which they had not previously owed, was valued for the whole community at £21, which came on top of payments for various dues and service worth £27. The tenants felt a strong sense of injustice, and mounted a legal campaign which lasted for forty years, including a petition to parliament in 1305.

Serfdom provoked the most consistent opposition from those who were judged to be of villein status after the legal reforms of the late twelfth century. Individuals defended their free status in both manorial and royal courts, and their actions led to the more precise definition of villeinage in terms of liability to pay specific dues such as marriage fines and tallage. More troubling from the lords' point of view were the collective actions brought by communities against their lord, alleging that if their manor had once belonged to the crown, as tenants of 'ancient demesne' they enjoyed a privileged status which allowed them to appeal to the king against any attempt to increase their rents or dues. These pleadings took place within the framework of the law, and show that the peasants believed that the king's courts would be capable of protecting them. Sometimes more direct action was involved, as lords would seize their tenants' animals to bring pressure on them, and tenants would sometimes become involved in violent confrontations, though rarely resulting in serious injury.

The tenants of South Petherton in Somerset in 1278–80 hired a lawyer to bring an action against their lord, Ralph Daubeny. They argued that their complaints had provoked the lord into seizing their goods to a value of £100, an exaggeration but indicating serious antagonism. These disputes raise key questions about the economic implications of serfdom. Tenants clearly resented the burdens that were imposed on them, but often their protests were directed against demands by the lord which appear relatively small-scale. The South Petherton tenants were upset because the lord attempted to seize the goods of widows who committed adultery – not an everyday event. In other cases the issue was pannage of pigs (a few pence paid to allow the pigs to eat acorns in the lord's wood), or some modest customary obligation. To remove these payments tenants were prepared to collect a large fund, £5 in the South Petherton case, in order to pay a lawyer. Usually the better-off peasants played a leading role and contributed most of the money. This was not a case of starving peasants who were being reduced to abject poverty struggling for their very existence. They were concerned with matters of principle – one arbitrary imposition might lead to other, more costly demands, which would be a particular concern for those with larger holdings who feared that their market profits would be lost to the lord. Behind some of the actions lay the belief among serfs that they had once been free, and that the king's power could restore their ancient liberty.

'Ancient demesne' pleas were usually unsuccessful. The courts were not impartial sources of royal justice, but tended to side with landlords. Small victories were registered, as in Battle Abbey's attempt around 1300 to declare the peasants who lived around the Sussex monastery to be serfs. John atte Doune, a tenant of customary land, brought a successful lawsuit in 1305 in the king's court which resulted in a declaration by the abbey that he was simply a tenant, not a serf. However, even in the cases that the lords won, their tenants had shown their solidarity, skill and persistence in fighting an unequal battle, and put their lords to great legal expense. The anger of the lords is displayed in the narratives they wrote about these conflicts. After they were over, both sides still resented the situation, and lords usually did not attempt any further imposition. In other words, the peasants had helped to draw a line on further extensions of their lords' power, and these messy and troublesome disputes served as a warning to other lords not to push their tenants to the limits of their patience.

Two other forms of direct action were used by peasants in conflict with their lords. One was flight, which is well attested in both Scotland and England in the twelfth century when legal measures were available to lords pursuing the escapees. The other was provoked by lords who sought to enclose land on common pastures, or to grant to tenants parcels of common land previously grazed by the whole community. The tenants sometimes attempted legal action, though the law favoured the lord, especially after the Statute of Merton in 1236 strengthened lords' rights over commons. Alternatively they might gather to remove fences and fill in ditches, like the 'malefactors and disturbers of the king's peace' who destroyed a hedge and ditch of Henry Baret's at Lydlynch in Dorset in 1279 'with force of arms, by night'. This could have served its purpose, either removing the enclosures or at least preventing any further encroachments, though the lord usually prevailed and the enclosures were restored.

Lords worked quite hard to increase their revenues from their tenants, but they were not able to extract as much money as they wished. The peasants paid more towards the end of the thirteenth century than they had a century earlier. Money rents were levied as labour services were commuted, and occasional payments such as entry fines could increase threefold. Nonetheless, the demands of lords rose less than the prices of primary products that the peasants sold. Lords could not override custom in order to make major increases in rents, and we have seen that they were slow to convert tenancies into leaseholds that would have reflected more accurately the value of land. The efficient running of estates was constantly held back by the surliness of their tenants. The better-off peasants were therefore able to keep some of their profits won in the market, though they still felt restricted by the ties of serfdom. At an earlier period the demands for cash from lords had helped to simulate peasants' trading by forcing them into the marketplace. By c.1300 the peasants had accepted the commercial habit with some enthusiasm, so were irritated by restrictions which did not drive them into poverty

1. Church of the tenth/eleventh centuries, Duntisbourne Rouse, Gloucestershire. This parish church stands as an example of the hundreds of its kind of this period, when the lords of the new small manors provided places of worship for their households and tenants. The walls are strongly constructed of large stones, so even such a small and plain church was built at considerable cost.

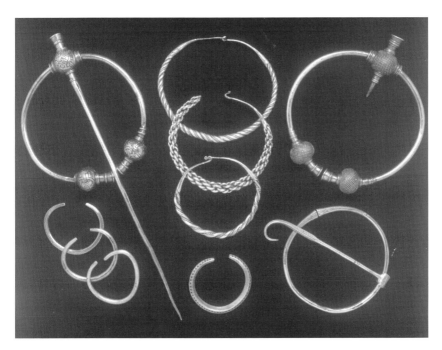

2. Viking silver hoard of the late tenth century from Skaill in Orkney. The objects shown here are large and ornate penannular brooches, together with neck rings and arm rings. These were worn as showy jewellery, but also served as stores of wealth. The chief who owned them may have concealed them when he left on an expedition, or at a time of danger, and did not return to recover them.

3. Reconstruction of an aristocratic house at Goltho in Lincolnshire, tenth century. A ditch and bank provided defence, with a gatehouse which is thought to have been high enough for a vantage point. In the hall, in the foreground, the household ate its meals. The long building near the gate appears to have been a weaving shed. The smallest structure was the kitchen, and nearer the hall stood the bower, or sleeping quarters.

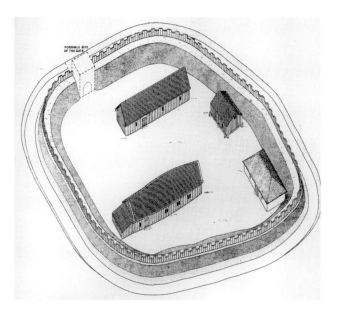

4. The White Tower in the Tower of London. The most impressive secular building from the late eleventh century, the White Tower demonstrates how the Norman conquerors from a site on the edge of the city observed and threatened the largest town in England. A building on this scale kept a labour force of considerable size employed for some years. The stone was brought by water from Caen in Normandy and from Kent.

7. (*facing page*) A windmill, from a fourteenth-century manuscript. These ingenious machines were invented towards the end of the twelfth century, and spread in the thirteenth. The mill and its machinery were mounted on a post firmly fixed into a timber framework. The pole to the left was used to turn the mill and its sails into the wind. In this illustration the miller is carrying a sack of corn, while a customer arrives by horse.

5. Tintern Abbey, Monmouthshire, from the south-east. A Cistercian monastery, founded in 1131, the site is typical of the order's preference for remote, wooded and hilly places away from the distractions of the secular world. The monastery was rebuilt in the thirteenth century, when its income was rising from the sale of wool. The monks sold 25 sacks of wool, much of it of the highest quality, to an Italian merchant in 1294.

6. A gentry house: Markenfield Hall, North Yorkshire. Built *c.* 1310 by John Markenfield, then chancellor of the exchequer, this opulent house reflects the profits of a royal official. Though surrounded by a moat, defence took second place to prestige and comfort. This view from the north shows the hall, lit by two ornate windows, with a chimney for a large hearth between them. The plain structure to the left of the hall contained the garderobes (lavatories).

8. A cart, from a manuscript of *c*. 1300. Carts were used in growing numbers in the thirteenth century. This is being loaded with sheaves of corn, and the artist accurately represents the construction of a light vehicle with two, well made, spoked wheels. The cart is being pulled by a donkey or mule in this mythical scene – in medieval England horses were invariably used.

9. Reclaimed land in the Somerset levels. This part of the valley of the Parrett was reclaimed as part of a large scale drainage scheme mounted by the monks of Glastonbury Abbey in the thirteenth century. In the foreground is the edge of a rhyne, a drainage channel, and behind the cows are shallow ditches dug across the field. All English landscapes are man made, but this was an especially audacious creation, showing technical expertise and an ability to think ahead.

10. A new town of the twelfth century, at Burford in Oxfordshire. The lord of the manor realized that this site, on the main road between London and Gloucester, had potential for making a town. In about 1100 his officials planned the main street, wide enough for a market place. They laid out rows of narrow plots on either side, and many of their boundaries are visible on this photograph. The venture was a success, settlers were attracted, and houses were built on the plots along the street, on the sites of those existing today.

11. The interior of a town house at Perth in *c.* 1300, reconstructed from excavated evidence. These small houses (often 25 by 12 feet) were built with wattle walls covered with clay, and the insubstantial upright timbers supported a roof of straw or heather thatch. Food was cooked over an open hearth in ceramic pots, and served on wooden bowls and plates. This living room would also have been used as working space by artisans.

12. (*right*) Abandoned fields on Bodmin Moor, Cornwall. The plough ridges and field boundaries stretched across this high moorland at Garrow show that arable cultivation extended, by the thirteenth century, over land which has not been ploughed since. The fields were worked from hamlets and isolated farms. Former fields on uplands in many parts of the country were abandoned at various times between *c.* 1300 and the late fifteenth century.

13. The Black Death cemetery at East Smithfield, London, during excavation. Two new cemeteries were opened in London in 1349 to cope with the sudden demand for burial space. The centre of the photograph is occupied by a long trench containing an orderly row of burials. It was later believed that 50,000 Londoners died in the epidemic, and this is not impossible. The well-organized burial arrangements do not support the view that panic led to social collapse.

14. A 'corner shop', at the junction of King Street and Broad Street, Ludlow, Shropshire, of 1403–4. This imposing three-storey building occupied a prime commercial site in the centre of Ludlow, the second largest town in its county. It was built very well of substantial timbers, both to fulfil its functions as a retail outlet and residence, and to impress. It was subdivided among a number of traders, including a mercer, fishmonger and a goldsmith.

15. Pottery from Southampton, *c*. 1490. The potters were using new techniques to satisfy consumer demand. A variety of wares were available in the port of Southampton: local products include the cooking pot and the 'Tudor green' drinking jug on the right, and the large bowl in the centre at the back. The other glazed and colourful vessels came from France, Spain, Italy, Germany and the Low Countries. The jugs and mugs reflect the importance of drink.

16. Sleeve of a fourteenth-century garment, found near the Thames waterfront at Baynard's Castle, London, preserved in water-logged conditions. It was made of wool, and was woven in a check pattern with some yarn dyed red and other yarn left undyed. The row of twelve buttons fastened into button holes in facings made of silk. This expensive garment demonstrates the skills of both clothmakers and tailors.

17. Ships of the late fifteenth century. These drawings, made in about 1485, show ships incorporating the new technical features of the period: the hulls are carvel built; two masts in the stern are fitted with lateen sails; and guns on the deck fired over the gunwale. These ships were designed to be efficient to build and sail, and were capable of crossing the Atlantic.

18a. A peasant house in the western, cruck tradition from Llanarth, Monmouthshire. The timber frame of Pit Cottage was based on four pairs of sturdy, curved timbers – crucks – of which one pair is visible at the gable end. This three-bay house contained a hall, a chamber and two small rooms. Hundreds of these houses, mostly dating from the fifteenth century, survive (and are still inhabited) in eastern Wales and western England.

18b. A peasant house of wealden type, from Plaxtol in Kent. Spoute House was built in two phases, dated from tree rings. The two-storey end to the right belongs to *c.* 1424, and the part to the left, containing the hall and the other end of two storeys, was built in 1445. One end is jettied – the first floor juts out. There are many surviving medieval houses in Kent – thirteen in the parish of Plaxtol alone.

19. The site of a deserted medieval village at Coates in Lincolnshire. Coates had about twenty households in *c.* 1300. It halved in size by 1377 and was not recognized as a separate village after 1428. The photograph shows the former village street as a long hollow running away from the camera. The figure stands on one of a series of platforms which mark sites of peasant houses.

but held them back from the full enjoyment of the fruits of their enterprise. A new dimension after 1275, and especially after 1294, came from demands for taxation. The better-off peasants who were assessed for the lay subsidy were often paying between 10s and 20s per annum in rent to their lord, and were now presented with a demand for an additional 2–4s to the tax collectors. It was not demanded every year, but it ate into their disposable income.

v. *Individuals and communities*

The peasant economy contains many paradoxes. Peasants produced for the market, yet practised self-sufficiency when possible; they made technical innovations, while continuing with many traditional practices; they were consumers, but on a modest scale; they developed a lively land market, but avoided extreme polarization; they had to pay more to their lords, but were still able to keep a proportion of their surplus. The final paradox of the peasantry concerns the collective nature of their agriculture, while they retained a high degree of individual autonomy.

In many ways the rise in population and commercial activity threatened to weaken the community. The village seems to have had an egalitarian basis in the sense that the tenants were ranked according to their standard holdings of yardlands, half-yardlands and oxgangs. Every yardlander was treated equally by the lord, with the same services and rents. However, individuals responded with varying degrees of skill and talent to the opportunities of the market, as is demonstrated by the varied tax assessments, based on the goods and especially animals that they owned – one yardlander might pay 2s, and another 6s. Similarly, when entry fines were charged they varied from holding to holding, depending on how well they had been managed, fences repaired and buildings maintained. Many of the changes of the period, such as the growth of the land market, encouraged selfishness among a minority, who took advantage of the weakness of their poorer neighbours. Even if they were not always acting for their personal benefit, they were clearly motivated by a strong attachment to their families and kin, and these groupings could be seen as detracting from the unity of the community.

Even more damaging was the gap between those with holdings adequate to feed a family, and those with insufficient land who needed an income from wages or non-agricultural activities. That divide had existed for centuries, but population growth tended to swell the ranks of the smallholders and landless. By the late thirteenth century an underclass had grown of workers without land, either servants living in the household of their employer, or casual labourers leading a more precarious existence. A fifth of the population of some Wiltshire villages were called 'lads'(*garciones* in Latin) who were listed by the lord because they made a small payment to him. In eastern England they were known as *anilepimen*, and in Scotland *gresmen* because they were allowed to graze animals. In the period 1270–1320, when yardlanders could sometimes make good money from the sale of grain at high prices, the labourers were receiving miserable rates of pay, often 1d per day, which in the years of high prices must have made life almost impossible. They were in danger of spending periods in unemployment because there were few employers, and they had limited needs for workers. The better-off villagers benefited from this cheap labour, and indeed villages like Newton Longville (Buckinghamshire) in 1290 issued by-laws aimed at preventing harvest workers from earning more than 1d with food. Market forces, arising from abundant labour and scarce foodstuffs, had driven real wages to a low level, and the village community still sought to limit the one opportunity that these people had to earn a little extra.

Migration was encouraged by the combination of rising population and varied employment opportunities. Peasants' sons and daughters might need to leave if they had no inheritance of land, and the landless workers would always hope that better earnings could be obtained elsewhere. Successful towns, and rural areas that were industrializing or intensifying agriculture, would attract labour. In the villages of Weston and Moulton in Lincolnshire, where the lord, Spalding Priory, compiled lists of serfs and their offspring in the mid-thirteenth century, between a third and a half of adult children had left their village, and two-thirds of women married partners from outside the village. In Essex in the early fourteenth century, where males aged twelve and over were listed each year to pay a small sum to their lord, between 3 and 5 per cent of them moved each year. Villages were not inhabited by a static population, and migration is only one symptom of the wide horizons of peasants who knew a great deal about the outside world beyond their village.

In spite of this growth in individual initiative, self-interest and inequality, the community still showed signs of health. At its heart lay the management of the common land, especially when all of the arable in a midland field system (see pp. 21–4 and 165–6) was subject to common grazing. The pressure on land meant that rules had to be observed or neighbours would suffer. The village elite, acting through the manor court, issued by-laws especially to regulate the harvest. Animals trespassed in their grazing into forbidden places, such as gardens and cornfields, and tenants encroached on their neighbours' strips with the plough, but there is remarkably little evidence of flagrant indiscipline in cultivation at this time. Evidently everyone realized that there was a common interest in keeping agriculture running smoothly. The court records show that villagers were failing to pay their debts, or not returning animals and implements that they had borrowed. These were probably a minority of cases in which relationships had broken down, and there was a great quantity of co-operation which worked to mutual benefit, and was therefore unrecorded.

To some extent, village self-government was created by superior authorities, as it suited lords, the church and the state to have a system whereby local people collected their own rents and taxes, mended the roads, built the church, and maintained law and order. As government was becoming more complex, the functions of the village community were extended. But this was not always to the advantage of the authorities, as the people and the mechanisms that carried out official tasks could also organize petitions and lawsuits against their lords, as we have seen in the case of the pleas of ancient demesne.

The potentially divisive effects of the gap between rich and poor were bridged in a number of ways which helped to reduce tensions within the village. The harvest by-laws which bore down so heavily on the labourers were of course not observed, as can be judged from their constant repetition. Individual employers, anxious to secure workers at a time of peak demand, paid a higher rate. Wealthier peasants may have established long-term clientages among the cottagers, helping them out in hard times in exchange for guarantees of labour at peak times. At Redgrave in Suffolk in 1289–91, John Kyde, who held only an acre and a half, worked as a labourer for the relatively wealthy Oky family. Simon Oky acted as his pledge in the manor court. One way in which the poor came into contact with their richer neighbours was by living and working in the household as young servants, which must have made it difficult for them to express bitter resentment at their plight. The harvest by-laws included provision for the poor, who were allowed to gather beans and peas in the summer, and to glean ears of corn in the harvest field, providing that they observed regulations about the time and place of these activities. The community showed its interest in social security again when maintenance agreements for retired peasants were made in the manor court, inviting neighbours who were present when the contract was agreed to make sure that the old people were not subsequently neglected (see p. 159).

This period favoured individual initiative, but the peasants who showed these entrepreneurial and selfish tendencies were still contained within highly cohesive communities. No doubt some individuals were held back by the restrictions of common agriculture, but many more welcomed the security that came from belonging to a group with many shared interests. While small-scale enterprises took advantage of the market, under-employed smallholders lived in impoverished conditions. Those numerous villagers with a few acres or a cottage were dependent for their living on wage-earning. The increased numbers seeking work ensured a low level of pay, and the high price of grain reduced real wages. A calculation of the purchasing power of the daily wage – the amount of food that a worker could buy after a day's work – shows that a very low point was reached in the 1270s, and there was no sustained recovery until after 1320. The danger of the proliferation of families attempting to live on small amounts of land was becoming all too obvious by the 1290s.

CHAPTER SIX

Towns and commerce, c.1100–c.1315

The two centuries up to *c*.1300 transformed the urban scene in Britain. The total number of towns increased from 100 to 830; in England the proportion of the population living in towns rose from nearly 10 per cent to almost 20 per cent, and in Scotland and Wales from virtually none to more than a tenth. This chapter is concerned with exploring the significance of that urban expansion, and how it changed the lives and outlook of those who lived in towns and those who had contact with them. We have already seen the decisive contribution of the lords who founded many of the new towns as part of a policy of estate development (pp. 145–7). Now we can turn to examine the upheaval that led so many individuals to leave their homes in the country to swell the urban population. In order to understand that process of migration, we will need to define the anatomy of the towns, and the relationship they had with their rural surroundings.

i. *Urban expansion*

None of the hundreds of thousands of migrants has left a personal record of their move, but we can attempt to understand their motives. The rural economy could not give everyone an adequate living. The underprivileged, such as many young people and those with smallholdings, were faced with long-term impoverishment in villages already well supplied with labour, and in which land was scarce. A crowded countryside, occasionally threatened with food shortages, pushed its population into leaving, but towns also pulled in newcomers by offering them positive advantages. We define towns as permanently established concentrations of people, who were pursuing a variety of non-agricultural occupations, in which crafts and trades would predominate, but which also included administrators, clergy, schoolteachers, prostitutes and other specialists. To would-be migrants, the towns beckoned because they gave opportunities for different skills and talents.

Some towns that attracted immigrants at this time were brand new. David I of Scotland (1124–53) set up fifteen burghs in the first phase of Scottish urbanization, and encouraged traders and artisans to settle in them by offering the privileges of fixed cash rents and free disposal of land, which were based on the benefits enjoyed by the tenants of an English new town, Newcastle-upon-Tyne. The new arrivals who took up a plot in a burgh were given a five-year respite on paying their rent while they built a house and set up a business. The king and his successors founded most of their burghs in the eastern part of the kingdom where royal rule was firmly established. The burghs were associated with castles, and they were made the centres of new shires, thereby giving the towns political and administrative importance. Later they acquired religious houses, like the friaries founded in the larger towns in the thirteenth century. The towns also enjoyed the advantages of a region with a developed rural economy, and royal grants of the privileges of holding markets and fairs made them the commercial centre of their sur-rounding countryside. The most successful foundations were those best able to take advantage of overseas trade, notably Berwick, Edinburgh, Perth and Aberdeen. Permanent urban settlements, albeit small in size, grew across the west of the lowlands and in the borders, in places such as Renfrew, Lanark and Jedburgh. In addition to the royal foundations of David I and his successors, prominent churchmen encouraged and planned towns in the twelfth century at such sites as Glasgow and St Andrews, and lay aristocrats fostered towns on their estates, such as Dundee (Map 9).

The Scottish new towns of the mid-twelfth century recruited from scratch, so their settlers were real pioneers without experience of urban life, though some may already have been practising trades and crafts in the countryside. Most newcomers in the thirteenth century were not making such a leap in the dark, because towns were already familiar as centres for the surrounding countryside. They acted not just as hubs and meeting places where produce was sold and goods bought, but also often served as centres of administration, religion and entertainment. Country people would go to towns to attend courts, to participate in ceremonies, to watch a bull baited, or to hear musicians, and the move to live in towns often followed from such visits.

Contemporary attitudes and behaviour towards towns would have been influenced by their position in the urban hierarchy, which depended on their size, location and functions. At the top stood London, without

Scottish burghs in existence by 1300

N

Cromarty   Cullen
Dingwall   Elgin   Banff
        Nairn Forres
        Inverness   Fyvie

                    Inverurie   Newburgh
                        Kintore
                            ABERDEEN

                Brechin
                Forfar   MONTROSE
                            Arbroath
        PERTH   DUNDEE
    Auchterarder   St. Andrews
            Newburgh   Crail
        Inverkeithing
        Stirling   Kinghorn
    Kirkintilloch
Dumbarton Linlithgow   Dunbar
    Renfrew   EDINBURGH   Haddington
        Glasgow   Canongate
        Rutherglen Lanark Peebles   BERWICK UPON
    Irvine   TWEED
    Prestwick   Kelso
    Ayr   Selkirk   Roxburgh
            Crawford   Jedburgh

            Dumfries   Lochmaben
            Urr   Annan
        Wigtown

● Burghs of the king

□ Burghs of other lords

◉ Burghs passing between the king
    and private lords

BURGHS in capitals were important
trading ports in the early 14th century

0   100km
0   100 miles

Map 9. Scottish burghs in existence by 1300. The larger towns were established mainly in the east, but smaller burghs were distributed across the central belt and to the south into the borders and Galloway.

Source: P. G. B. McNeill and H. L. McQueen, *Atlas of Scottish History to 1707* (Edinburgh, 1996).

any doubt the leading town in Britain, and indeed one of the largest and most important cities in north-west Europe. With a population by 1300 which may have been as great as 80,000, it was smaller than Paris, but probably exceeded in size any one of the great cities of Flanders or the Rhine valley. It towered over the main provincial capitals in England, and was at least three times as large as Bristol, Norwich or York. Norwich in the early fourteenth century may have reached 20,000. In the next rank lay the provincial towns, which could be as large as Winchester with its 10,000 people in c.1300, but most, like Canterbury, Gloucester, Oxford, Bury St Edmunds, Coventry and Lincoln, had populations in the region of 5,000. The major ports attained similar size, most of them on the east and south coasts, at Newcastle, Hull, Boston, King's Lynn, Sandwich and Southampton. Chester served the north-west of England and parts of north Wales. In all, about fifty English towns had 2,000 or more inhabitants, leaving the great majority, more than 600, which can be rated as market towns or small towns. The more important of these provided a living for a thousand or two, like Banbury, Chelmsford, Louth, Peterborough, Ludlow and Doncaster, but the majority, with populations measured in hundreds, like Tenterden, Petersfield, Lostwithiel, Lechlade, Newmarket, Bradford, Cockermouth and Alnwick, still contained a concentration of traders and artisans, and served as centres for the surrounding countryside.

The line between towns and other types of commercial and industrial community is sometimes difficult to draw. Hundreds of markets were founded, especially in the thirteenth century, in villages where the inhabitants were mainly peasants, and which did not build up a permanent population of people pursuing non-agricultural occupations. Some of these market villages provided useful venues for buying and selling, but these were just occasions on one day of the week, after which the community returned to the routines of cultivation. Some rural markets attracted a handful of butchers, smiths and carpenters, and began to resemble a town. Similarly, most industrial villages consisted entirely of weavers or lead miners or fishermen, and so lacked the variety of occupations that was so essential to a town, but again food traders and craftsmen might gather in the village, and create a community with town-like qualities.

The hierarchy had a different character in the less densely populated parts of Britain. In Devon and Cornwall, amid numerous very small towns, Exeter, the capital of the region, attained a modest size of about 3,000–4,000, smaller than the provincial towns 100 and more miles to the east. In the north-west of England, Carlisle served as a centre of administration, defence and religion, with its castle and cathedral, and provided an important channel of exchange across the border to Scotland, and yet was no larger than many market towns of the midlands and the south-east. In Wales a handful of towns, notably Cardiff, Carmarthen and Haverfordwest, rose a little above the 2,000 mark, and the great majority of Welsh market towns fell below 1,000. In eastern Scotland there was more of a hierarchy, with Aberdeen, Perth and Berwick probably above 2,000, and Edinburgh falling into the second rank. Western Scotland resembled the rest of western Britain in its very small towns.

The larger the population of a town, the more complex and varied its life became. The larger places provided a living for people pursuing numerous occupations, more than 100 in the case of a provincial capital. You would be more likely to encounter craftsmen making luxury or specialized goods in a large town – a bell founder or armourer, for example. Only large towns contained a group of really wealthy merchants, who traded either in luxury goods (such as wine), or in large cargoes for distant markets, such as wool being carried by the sack to Flanders. Small towns were full of artisans and petty traders supplying a limited range of relatively cheap and ordinary goods.

The larger towns were more likely to serve as centres of local administration, and to have powers of self-government. You would find in such towns institutions, like the half-dozen religious houses (mostly friaries) which were established in Newcastle upon Tyne, and two or three hospitals; the older towns were divided into many parishes, with a dozen parish churches in most larger provincial towns, and more than 100 in London. Many small towns could boast of no more than a chapel and a fraternity. Visitors would be struck by the large town's skyline dominated by impressive buildings – a castle keep, and church towers and spires. This emphasis on the vertical was continued by the houses in the main streets, which rose to three or four storeys, compared with the two- or even one-storey buildings and single church tower in market towns.

Every type and rank of town interacted in a different way with its rural surroundings. Each had an immediate hinterland extending for a radius of 6 or 7 miles, within which the rural population could easily and habitually travel to market. The towns formed a network, with market centres distributed over the land at regular intervals. This complementary system was to some extent the result of political decisions, as the lawyers said that neighbours might object if a new market was proposed within a radius of $6^2/_3$ miles. Markets (in towns and in villages) were held on different days, which reduced the amount of direct competition and allowed traders to move from place to place through the week. Large towns might have markets at the end of the week, so that a grain dealer, for example, could visit a succession of small town and village markets, buying up small quantities and then selling his accumulated purchases. In south Nottinghamshire, minor markets held at Wyssall on Wednesdays and Granby on Mondays could have fed into the large market of Nottingham. The even distribution of markets was often interrupted in the immediate vicinity of the larger towns, where both small towns and village markets were notably absent, whether through political influence, or recognition by would-be promoters that small ventures would not flourish in the shadow of a large town.

The larger towns had long-distance contacts for specific commodities and customers, and they dominated the smaller centres of trade within their spheres of influence. So London drew its grain supplies from ten counties, in some cases from a distance of more than 50 miles. Many small towns and markets served as collecting points for grain which would eventually reach the capital. Strategically placed small towns, notably Faversham in Kent, Ware in Hertfordshire, and Henley-on-Thames in Oxfordshire, were dominated by London traders, under whose control crops within carting distance were collected, stored in granaries, and loaded into carts and boats for carriage to the city. The dependent relationship worked in reverse when merchants from the larger towns supplied imported or luxury goods to small town retailers, like the wine from a Bristol vintner which was sold by the gallon in a tavern in the small Herefordshire town of Leominster. A large town's commercial reach crossed administrative and cultural boundaries. So Bristol had a strong influence on the towns of Glamorgan and Monmouthshire, just as those in north Wales looked to the merchants of Chester.

The traders of the large towns sold luxury items, or foodstuffs in bulk, direct to wealthy customers at a considerable distance. The bishop of Hereford, Richard de Swinfield, in 1289–90 bought wax and spices in London, and obtained most of his parchment at Oxford. The advantage of such dealings lay in the ability of the merchants of the major towns, especially in London, to supply quantities of luxury goods, to offer a wider choice, and to be able to sell in bulk at a good price, which did not include inland transport costs and the profits of provincial middlemen. Magnate consumers in the thirteenth century often bargained with the merchants at the great international fairs, where quantities of spices, wax, preserved fish and cloth were available at 'wholesale' prices. The merchants who sold these goods at such fairs as Boston and St Ives (Huntingdonshire) tended to come from the larger towns and especially London. The London merchants had the great advantage that as the city (together with neighbouring Westminster) emerged as the permanent seat of government, the magnates of church and state acquired grand houses in the suburbs of Holborn, Southwark and along the Strand, where they could stay on their visits to the royal household, the law courts and parliament. These residences contained storage space, and some magnates also set up separate 'wardrobes' in the city, where purchases could be kept for future use.

The size of the towns' trading zone varied from one commodity to another. Cheap and bulky goods could not be carried very far, or the cost became prohibitive, and so most towns, even large centres, obtained their fuel within a short distance, often 12 miles. Cattle, on the other hand, could transport themselves, with the encouragement of a drover, so herds came out of Wales to supply the butchers of major towns such as Gloucester, and some of them eventually made their way to London. Water transport enabled heavy goods to be carried long distances. The fine building stone quarried at Caen in Normandy was used for castles and churches in London and the south-east, and stone from Barnack in Lincolnshire, where the quarries lay near to navigable rivers, was taken by boat over much of eastern England. In the same way, metals such as iron and lead travelled many miles.

The hinterlands, with all of their variety depending on the town, the customers and suppliers, transport routes, and the goods being carried, had a considerable influence on the pattern of migration. A place that was already familiar from visits to market or carting journeys was likely to be the first choice of destination for those intending to find work in a town. In some cases the local rural population had more formal links with the town, because they paid a fee to have access to the market without paying tolls. In Wales, 'censers' who had attachments to such places as Caernarfon and Aberystwyth, often lived within 10 miles of the town. Half of Shrewsbury's 'foreign burgesses' in 1232 lived within a radius of 8 or 9 miles. Wealthier country people could also establish links by joining the town's religious fraternity. But most of the associations between town and country depended not on any institution but on the constant to and fro based on the weekly market.

Just as London had the largest hinterland, so it drew migrants from considerable distances, frequently from the east midlands and East Anglia, over 50 miles and more. Take an incident in a street in the capital on 11 November 1300. John de Bois, from Suffolk, was accidentally killed when a piece of wood, used to dry saddles during their manufacture, fell from the upper storey of a house in Cheapside, the busiest thoroughfare in the city. He was carried to the house of Adam de Drayton. The sudden death was investigated by the alderman of the ward, Walter de Finchingfield. Various people living nearby were required to give evidence, including Nicholas de Gotham, and among those appointed to ensure their co-operation in the investigation were William de Kent, William de Kemesing and William de Assington. De Bois came from Suffolk, and may have been a visitor to the capital, or a recent immigrant. The Londoners who became caught up in the events had names deriving from Middlesex, Essex, Suffolk and Nottinghamshire, with two from Kent. Names were becoming fixed at this time, and they may have been coined to identify the fathers or even grandfathers of those alive in 1300, but they still demonstrate past migrations; from this small sample of six, four had travelled more than 30 miles, and one had made a journey of about 100 miles. The larger towns often attracted immigrants from a distance of more than 20 miles. Exeter, which was an important place in its region, though of no great size, pulled in more than half of its population from within 20 miles, but 27 per cent came between 20 and 40 miles. Small towns drew most of their inhabitants within 20 miles, and commonly from a 10-mile radius.

Young people, including a high proportion of women, were most likely to make these moves, often in order to become servants in towns. An example is Emetina, daughter of John, son of Robert, of Moulton in Lincolnshire, who some time shortly before 1268 had moved 20 miles into the town of Stamford. Her father was quite prosperous, with a holding of about 22 acres, but her two brothers would have taken priority in the inheritance of the land. The family were serfs, so Emetina would acquire her freedom by leaving the control of her lord, the priory of Spalding. She showed her adventurous spirit in seeking her fortune in a relatively large town. Perhaps a friend or relative from the village had moved to Stamford earlier, and helped subsequent migrants to find jobs. She may even have been in contact with employment agents. The advantage of moving to a large town was the greater range of openings, both in service in households and in the cloth industry.

A different type of migrant moved into new towns, where the tenants of burgage plots were not penniless young peasant women, but mature men with the capital to build a house and set up business in such trades as smithing or tanning, and the skill to make a success of their trade. An example is Alexander de Hatton, who appears in the new town of Stratford-upon-Avon in 1251, just fifty-five years after the town had been founded. Either he or his father had moved from Hatton-on-Avon, a village within 4 miles of the town. Alexander's family in Hatton had some spare resources from their holding of a full yardland, and their servile status gave him a reason for migrating. The de Hattons in Stratford made a success of their new urban life. Already by 1251

Alexander had acquired a larger than average amount of property – a plot and a half – and his son thirty or so years later gained more land and joined the elite of the town, acting as bailiff and witnessing the deeds by which his neighbours conveyed property. Another type of relatively affluent migrant is represented by those who moved from one town to another. Having presumably acquired skills or capital, an artisan or trader might hope to make a better life in a different town. Often these men were seeking promotion by moving from a small town to a higher level in the hierarchy, which presumably explains the presence in Chester in the 1290s of Thomas de Manchester and William de Flint. Indeed, quite a high proportion of the migrants in the regional capitals and London had come from smaller towns. Those who had experience of a major centre would sometimes move down to a market town, like the people called 'de London' who lived at Baldock in Hertfordshire in 1185. Perhaps they hoped to play a larger role in a small place, or perhaps they failed to cope with the competition of the big city, or the move may have resulted from an accident of marriage or business.

A special case of movement between towns is found in Wales, where English influence was deliberately spread by town foundations. Recruits were gathered in western English towns, and so we find names like 'de Stratford' and 'de Warwick' in Carmarthen. Other migrant groups influenced by political events were the French colonists who moved into English towns soon after 1066. The most easily identified group, the Jews, came mostly from Rouen. They settled in dozens of towns, but formed especially strong communities in Lincoln and York, and by 1200 the Jewish population in England exceeded 5,000.

Towns attracted clergy, doctors, administrators and lawyers. The professionals were well placed to meet clients, or to travel out to them in the hinterland. The clergy were established in the towns from an early stage to serve the many parish churches, and as chantries and fraternities increased in number in the thirteenth century more chaplains were employed to say masses. By 1300 perhaps one in twenty of town dwellers was a clergyman, and many of them were migrants. Their economic contribution was mainly as consumers and as redistributors of wealth, as they took revenues from the laity in tithes and offerings and then often spent the money within the town. They contributed more directly as developers of church land. They also provided education, and wrote deeds and bonds. Towns could gain importance if the local church became a centre of pilgrimage. Every major church encouraged visitors to venerate relics or images, but a few pulled in large crowds, most notably Canterbury with its cult of the tomb of Thomas Becket, who had been murdered in 1170. Finally, some very well-heeled settlers are found in towns. The landed gentry did not acquire town houses just for temporary occupation or as bases for selling and buying, rather as the magnates did in London, but sometimes became almost permanent residents, like the knight John Sampson at York in the 1290s. And some successful merchants found it convenient to have houses and businesses in more than one centre.

Moving to a town was a risky venture. Some of the new foundations failed; migrants who moved hopefully into Skinburness in Cumberland found that not enough people followed them to make the town work, and so they had to move again, judging from the fact that the royal charter granting borough status in 1301 was cancelled only four years later. Not all of the large towns were expanding – Winchester was probably smaller in the early fourteenth century than it had been in the twelfth. One factor in its reduced size was the centralization of royal government at London, and another the rise of successful rivals such as Salisbury, which was founded in 1219. Political factors disrupted towns in Wales. Under English rule new towns were founded as part of the process of imposing alien rule, which damaged the existing towns set up by Welsh rulers. The population of the active port of Llanfaes on Anglesey was displaced when Edward I founded a new town under the walls of his castle of Beaumaris at the end of the thirteenth century. The Welsh directed their resentment against these instruments of foreign control, and Caernarfon, built under the walls of Edward I's castle in 1283–4, was burnt in the rebellion of 1294. Towns on both sides of the Anglo-Scottish border suffered in the fighting which began in the 1290s. The Jews encountered resentment in England, partly arising from hostility to their religion and culture, but also owing a great deal to their role as moneylenders under royal protection. The Jewish community endured periodic persecution, most savagely at York in 1190, and a century later the whole episode of medieval Jewish settlement came to an end with the expulsion of the Jews by Edward I.

But these setbacks and episodes of destruction were exceptional. Most migrants stayed, and hundreds of towns achieved some success. Behind the global increase in the urban population are many stories of growth in individual towns. Cowbridge in south Wales doubled in size between 1281 and 1306. Many of the larger English towns with 1,000 to 2,000 inhabitants in 1086 had 5,000 or more by 1300, and some had risen into the leading fifty towns after being founded in the twelfth and thirteenth centuries – Newcastle, Hull, Lynn, Boston and Salisbury all achieved success in a few decades of sustained growth. Migrants were needed in all towns, even those which did not grow very rapidly, because families in towns raised relatively few children to adulthood.

ii. *The urban environment*

The fabric of the town changed as the population grew, with consequences both for living conditions and the property market. The lords made the initial town plans. Kings were the leaders before the Conquest, and continued to take initiatives. Edward I, a great town founder in Wales, also showed a personal interest in establishing Berwick-upon-Tweed, Hull and Winchelsea, and indeed summoned a gathering of advisers on town planning in 1297. In the twelfth and thirteenth centuries the majority of towns were created by lords, with lay lords outnumbering bishops and monasteries by a ratio of two to one. The purpose of the planners was to establish a framework which would encourage trade and crafts. At the heart of the town was the marketplace, often outside the church or at the entrance to the manor house or castle. The market was equipped with stalls, and a toll house or market hall. Often a separate cattle or beast market was established on the edge of the town, large enough to take the animal pens. The planners would divert roads in the vicinity to make sure that traffic passed through. They laid out streets wide enough for carts to pass, and to provide space for overspill of stalls and selling points from the main marketplace. The more elaborate plans included side roads and back lanes so that deliveries could be made to the rear of properties. (Plate 10)

Plots were set out with houses and shops fronting on to streets to make contact with customers, sometimes with an entry from the street to allow vehicles to have access to the plot behind, and a large enough plot (often about a quarter-acre) for outbuildings, workshops and storage space. The plan was flexible: if demand for premises increased, the plot could be split down the middle, or even divided three or four times, with narrower houses fitted end-on to the street, to maintain the vital direct contact with the customers. If necessary the rear of the plots was used more intensively, even to the point where these were filled with cottages and workshops. Another response to growth was to add sections to towns, with new streets and rows of building plots. These extensions have left their mark on the modern town plans, and the successive phases of growth can be reconstructed by close study of street plans and property boundaries. Many of the 'New Streets' and 'Newlands' (to the surprise of their modern inhabitants) date from the thirteenth century. The planning could be the result of further initiatives by lords, or sometimes a neighbouring lord would set up a separate suburb (see p. 146). The new phases of development could also come from townsmen who had become landlords by buying up property, or from the urban community itself, like the rows of houses and shops, in effect a new street, which were built on both sides of the first stone London Bridge when it was constructed between the late twelfth century and 1209.

The incentive to plan towns, extend them, and to build on the plots came from the money that could be earned from the renting and sale of urban property. Lords usually received an annual ground rent of between 6d and 18d, often 12d for each plot, which was many times the value of agricultural land, but did not reflect the full income generated by an urban economy. The burgesses or freeholders would sublet plots, or subdivide them and rent out a fraction, and if the demand for land was high could expect to make 20s from renting a house with its plot, and even 5s for a small cottage. A growing proportion of the subtenants would be leaseholders, and might pay their rents monthly. Such investments could provide acquisitive town landlords with large rental incomes, like the £22 per annum which a Bristol merchant, John de Cardiff, gained from property in the town in the early fourteenth century. Monasteries, which had in some cases founded the towns in which they stood, bought up land and houses in order to profit from the higher income that could be made by subletting. In Canterbury in 1199, houses and shops in the city worth £25 per annum belonged to the cathedral priory, but by 1300 it owned about a third of the town and enjoyed an income from rents of £110. As the urban economy expanded, and the demand for property increased, so the sale price and rent of urban land and buildings rose. The amount of money paid by buyers to acquire land in Coventry rose from about £1 in each transaction at the beginning of the thirteenth century to about £4 by the 1280s and 1290s. Urban landlords invested in buildings, and most of the houses in towns were rebuilt at some time in the thirteenth century. A minority of houses in the twelfth century had been constructed entirely in stone, and a few houses of this type were added after 1200, but most often stone was used in modest amounts to build a few courses for foundations to support timber-framed superstructures. A modest new house could cost £10, and landlords could certainly justify such construction costs, as they would quickly recover the money in rents.

Town houses incorporated workshops, and rooms where customers could inspect goods and make their purchases, but there were also premises given over entirely to commercial use. These were the stalls and shops built in marketplaces and along the busier shopping streets. In even the smallest market town the space set aside in the marketplace for temporary stalls was quickly covered with permanent structures, sometimes of two storeys, with a chamber above the shop where goods could be kept, or which came into use as accommodation for people. Some rows of stalls were dedicated to the use of a particular group of traders. The butchers would commonly have their 'shambles', segregated in order to keep the more unpleasant sights and smells away from other retailers and shoppers. A marketplace would commonly have a 'drapery' where woollen cloth was sold, or a 'mercery' for linen. To hold and build a stall could be very rewarding, judging from the rents they commanded; a stall covering only 100 square feet at a prime selling point could be rented annually for 10s, the same as 20 acres of good agricultural land. The busiest shopping street in Britain was Cheapside in London, where a shop in 1300 cost the tenant £3 per annum: this had doubled over the previous half-century.

The concentration of opportunities to make wealth, or at least earn a living, led people to be packed into the confined space where manufacture and marketing were focused. While in modern cities the rich live in the suburbs, leaving the central business district empty at night, with the poor living in other parts of the inner city, in the middle ages everyone, including the rich merchants, wished to live in the town centre, and the less fortunate were left on the outskirts. This created problems for those crowded in the densely built environment. It is true that even in large towns those at the centre could walk to fields and open spaces in a few minutes. At Ayr and Denbigh and many other places, most of the burgesses held some acres of land in the fields attached to the town. Larger houses often had gardens at the rear, even in the middle of London. But this access to space cannot alter the fact that most townspeople lived in cramped conditions. The less affluent often occupied houses with a floor area of 15 feet by 15 feet, though with two storeys to provide a sleeping room separate from the living and working space on the ground floor. Alternatively, labourers and servants lived in larger houses, but occupied only a room or two, commonly on an upper floor. These problems of overcrowding were not confined to the largest towns, as smaller places, such as Durham or Edinburgh, were often built on a restricted site. The inhabitants of Perth occupied very narrow plots, and their wattle-walled houses (revealed by excavations) lay near to cesspits, middens and manure heaps. (Plate 11) Here as in other towns animals lived close to people. Horses were essential for transport and many townspeople kept a cow or a few sheep on the land outside the town, but the typical urban animals were the pigs which were fed on household waste, though they also scavenged on rubbish. Trades such as butchery fouled the streets, and tanning put effluents into the rivers and streams. Almost every industrial process, from brewing to smithing, contributed to the smoky atmosphere, and some towns suffered from continuous fumes and air pollution, such as the salt-boiling centres of Droitwich in Worcestershire and Northwich and Nantwich in Cheshire. As coal production grew, the inhabitants of towns such as Newcastle and Nottingham experienced especially severe smoke problems.

The town authorities aimed to create a decent environment. The elite, after all, lived in the town centres, so there was an element of self-interest in their policy, but they were also concerned with the reputation and general well-being of their town. They were beginning to provide piped water supplies, and by *c.*1300 refuse disposal was changing so that less use was being made of middens and pits in the back yards of houses, and more rubbish was being carried to tips on the outskirts. The town governments were also concerned about the obstruction of the streets by manure heaps, stacks of firewood and building timber, and stalls jutting out of the front of houses and shops. In London these problems were resolved through the 'assize of nuisance'. For example, in 1301 William de Betonia complained that the cesspit of his neighbour, William de Gartone, lay so close to his cellar that the sewage dripped through the wall. This was investigated by the mayor and aldermen, who did not accept de Gartone's argument that he was a free tenant and that his predecessors had always had a privy. Instead, the offender was given forty days to build a stone wall $2^{1}/_{2}$ feet thick between the pit and his neighbour's cellar.

Those governing towns were also concerned about the hazard of fires, which occurred not infrequently when houses were closely packed and built of inflammable materials, especially thatch for roofs. A town with a healthy economy, like Boston which was burnt in 1288, could recover quickly enough, but Carlisle, in its vulnerable position on the Scottish border and in a relatively poor and thinly populated region, suffered a more serious setback from its great fire of 1296. One remedy adopted at this time was to insist that houses be roofed with slates, tiles or shingles.

Towns may have reached the limits of the size that could be sustained by about 1300. The proportion of the population living in towns, and therefore dependent mainly on the agricultural production of the rest of society, was nearing a fifth, which was not very different from the proportion in 1500 or indeed in the early eighteenth century. The urban population could be fed in normal years, though special measures had to be taken when harvests were severely deficient. One sign of strain was the difficulty in the supply of fuel, apparent in London at the end of the thirteenth century. The woods of the region were managed to provide a continuous flow of 'underwood' suitable for use in domestic and industrial hearths, but prices were high, and transport costs would not allow wood fuel to be brought from further afield. Some mineral coal was already being carried by ship from Newcastle, and the long-term growth of the capital depended on increasing use of this more efficient (if more polluting) fuel from the north-east.

iii. *Urban occupations*

People crowded into towns, in spite of the unhealthy living conditions, because they offered a means of making a living. At the bottom of the heap were the very poor with no stable source of income. Because they had no property and no formal role in society or government, we know little about them apart from the accusation in court records of their criminal or apparently anti-social behaviour. In London no 'whore of a brothel', according to an order in 1277, was allowed to live within the walls, and in York in 1301 it was stated that women living in the city and keeping brothels were to be imprisoned. Beggars were attracted to the cities by handouts of free food or cash from monasteries and wealthy households. The royal household fed 20,000 paupers at Westminster in 1244, suggesting the very large numbers of poor in and around the capital.

Most migrants hoped for a better life than was available on the fringes of urban society, and their first toehold in towns came from gaining employment as servants. These accounted for a high proportion of the population of towns in the late fourteenth century, when servants commonly made up 20 to 30 per cent of urban poll-tax payers. The proportion is unlikely to have been any less a hundred years earlier. The majority of employers would have no more than a servant or two in their houses, either carrying out domestic tasks or working in a particular trade or craft. The servants usually lived in the household, and part of their pay consisted of food, drink, accommodation and clothing. Apprentices were rewarded in a similar way, but their masters had an obligation to teach them the skills of the craft, and could expect some reward from their parents for their instruction. At the same time they required a high standard of behaviour from the apprentice, and the master provided something resembling parental care.

While apprentices and some servants could expect to acquire a skill, many townspeople worked as labourers. This meant that they might keep their own household in a rented house or cottage, and walk to work each day. Many tasks in towns required little training, such as carrying water to houses, and removing rubbish. For every skilled building craftsman there were two labourers, digging foundations, hauling stone and timber, and mixing and applying daub to wattle walls. Their period of employment was often short-term and and precarious, and they might go in the morning to a meeting place to be offered a day's work, like those at Bedford who were said in 1305 to have 'stood at the Cross to be hired'.

As the labourers were ill-paid and their lives uncertain, those entering towns had the ambition to take up a craft, either in manufacture or retail trade, or in the service sector. The number of crafts increased with the size of the town, so that we know of 175 occupations practised in London, but no more than twenty in a small market town. The descriptions attached to an individual or group or used as surnames give an air of precision, as if people could be placed in a specific pigeon-hole. In practice their lives were more complicated. The male head of the household had a sideline, and his wife would commonly have her own trade, typically as a brewster. For example, Adam de Stretton, a butcher of Shrewsbury, who was assessed for tax payment in 1297, owned meat worth 20s, as would be expected, but he was also in possession of 5 quarters of rye, which was a greater quantity than his household would have eaten, and suggests that he dealt in grain. His supply of malt worth 10s could represent another part of his corn-dealing stock, or it might have been stored for use by his wife in brewing ale for sale. Material remains indicate a number of small-scale or part-time occupations. At Perth, the inhabitants of two adjacent plots on the High Street, in addition to working leather and metal, removed horns from cattle slaughtered by the town's butchers, in order to make transparent panels for lanterns, and skinned cats (there were many strays in towns) for their fur. We have already seen that many townspeople held some land, or at least a garden, which was not their main source of income but provided a valuable supplement. In spite of these dual or mixed occupations, the record of crafts and trades still gives a valuable impression of the range of activities to be found in each town.

In most towns the food and drink trades provided more employment than any other activity. Townspeople could produce only a fraction of their food needs, and in many cases their working lives allowed them little time to prepare meals. In addition, numerous visitors – travellers, customers, pilgrims, those attending courts – expected to eat and drink during their stay. In particular the sellers of food and drink catered for the country people who attended markets. In Winchester in about 1300, eight millers ground grain and malt for consumption in the town. There were twelve bakers, sixty brewers, eleven butchers and seven fishmongers. Counting the families and households of these traders alone, about 500 people were gaining a substantial part of their livelihood from preparing and selling food and drink, and this does not take account of the cooks and innkeepers who prepared and served meals, or the dealers in fruit and vegetables, dairy products, poultry, honey and salt. At the luxury end of the trade, vintners and taverners sold wine, and spicers and grocers dealt in expensive imports of condiments such as pepper and ginger, and dried fruits and nuts. A more basic living was earned by the hucksters, women with baskets of bread or eggs, vegetables and other foods, who obtained their supplies from the bakers and other well-established traders, and then sold their wares for meagre profit in the streets or from door to door. In a similar fashion, women called variously gannockers, tapsters or tranters would sell ale that they had obtained from the brewers. As in any branch of commerce, when demand reached a large scale in a major city, trade became more specialized, and a living could be made by a 'stockfishmonger' (dealing in dried cod from Norway) or a 'garlickmonger'.

Every town had some section of its workforce devoted to manufacture, which can be divided into branches depending on the products, and the materials used: leather (including sheepskins and furs), textiles (wool and linen), clothing, metalworking (iron, copper alloys, lead and tin) and wood. Building should be mentioned as an important sector of employment in towns as well as in the country. The balance between the different crafts depended on the supply of raw materials, local demand, the opportunities for wider distribution, and the traditions of skill that might develop in a town.

Making woollen cloth probably employed more people in towns than any other industry. The separate processes included combing and carding the wool, spinning the yarn, weaving and various stages of finishing – dyeing, fulling and shearing. It was well suited to larger towns where enough people were concentrated to practise the different crafts, particularly in the preparatory stages, when dozens of combers, carders and spinners were needed to supply a few weavers. The preparation of the wool and spinning of yarn were often carried out by women, who were paid relatively little for unspecialized tasks. The larger towns, such as Beverley, Leicester, Lincoln, Oxford, Stamford and York were important centres for clothmaking in the thirteenth century, and the presence of weavers' guilds in many of them suggests that the industry had become well established in the twelfth. Clothmaking was also a source of employment in smaller towns, such as Banbury, Cricklade and High Wycombe and, as we have seen, in many rural locations.

One element in the growth of clothmaking was the higher demand from a rising population. But the industry was very complex, and its ups and downs reflected fierce competition in both domestic and continental markets. The producers had to make difficult calculations about demand and customer preferences, because ultimately success depended on consumer choice. The very wealthy required a well-finished cloth, like Lincoln scarlets, the appeal of which depended on the quality of the shearing as well as the colour. The cloth producers of the English towns such as Lincoln and Stamford won continental customers, and exported large quantities of relatively expensive cloth in the thirteenth century. In the mass market, consumers demanded cheap textiles known as burrels, or cloths which were either undyed, or dyed grey or russet. Those who bought textiles were conscious of the price, so the producers might use coarse cheap wool, or they could economize on the wages needed to finish the cloth, with the danger that the consumers would notice the difference. There were always the continental producers, and especially the famous clothmakers of Flanders, waiting to take over the continental market, and indeed to make inroads among English customers.

Migrants into towns would find that opportunities for finding jobs depended on the amount of skill and training, and on the extent to which the craft required expensive equipment and premises. Yarn was often spun in the country, and a woman who moved into the town could continue in that activity. Finding an opening in the more skilled, and better rewarded, end of clothmaking was more difficult, not only because of the skill needed, but also because weavers' looms, or dyers' vats, or fullers' tubs and cloth shears cost money, and could only be used in a house or outbuilding with adequate space.

Other crafts were similarly closed to all but the well-prepared and properly funded. Tanners, for example, occupied yards with a series of pits lined with timber. They needed working capital in order to buy the raw hides (sometimes directly from the butchers) and materials such as oak bark from which the chemical tannin was extracted. Their investment was tied up in the long process of treating the hides to produce a supple and long-lasting leather. A similar scale of investment was normal in the metal trades. The raw metal was produced in the country: in forges for iron, in smelting furnaces for tin, and bole furnaces for lead, all located near the mines. The smiths, based in both country and town, worked the iron into implements, tools, weapons, nails and horseshoes, using bellows and anvils which again needed capital and extensive working space. Workers in non-ferrous metals – such as the pewterers who made tin into vessels, or the potters or bell founders who cast brass or other alloys of copper into cooking pots and bells, along with a range of smaller buckles and brooches – constructed furnaces and prepared moulds, requiring both considerable investment and a larger labour force than the two or three commonly working in an artisan workshop.

Other crafts were more open to newcomers in the sense that they needed very little equipment, but some of them depended on high levels of skill which would normally be acquired, if not by a formal apprenticeship, certainly by spending some years as a servant to an established artisan. The clothing trades belong in this category: shoemakers and glovers, for example, could buy their raw materials in quite small quantities, and work them with cutting tools and needles and thread which were not very expensive. The tailors had representatives in every town, and dozens in the larger centres. They measured and cut cloth that was often supplied by the customer, and stitched it, again without any great outlay, though with considerable skill. In the building trade, the materials and working space were generally supplied by those paying for construction, so the workers provided a few tools – trowels and chisels for masons, and saws, axes and augers for carpenters. The numerous coopers who made wooden barrels and other vessels, or those who made bows and arrows (bowyers and fletchers), or the ropers and stringers who twisted fibres into ropes, cord and string, used quite cheap raw materials and a limited range of equipment.

The variety of occupations gave towns their defining characteristic. They did not usually specialize in a single craft or group of crafts, and individuals and households were not tied to a single means of gaining a living. Occasionally a town did gain fame for a particular product, and a thirteenth-century list mentions a number which can be confirmed from other sources, such as the 'knives of Thaxted' (Essex), the 'scarlet (cloth) of Lincoln', and the 'cord of Bridport' (Dorset). These products provided employment for only a minority of artisans, but they allowed small towns like Bridport and Thaxted to sell their distinctive products over long distances, beyond the limited hinterland in which their butchers, tailors and shoemakers traded.

One of the specialities included 'herring of Yarmouth', a product which employed a very large number of people and was widely traded. The fish migrated seasonally, and so an intensive short-term effort was required to catch them. The industry was typically small in scale, as the fishing vessels, rarely exceeding 30 tons, cost between £3 and £27 in about 1300, and were often crewed by five men. The expeditions to the North Sea usually lasted for a day or two, with intervals between voyages for the catch to be unloaded, the crews to rest, and the boat and nets to be prepared for the next sailing. Each vessel would make ten to fourteen trips in a six-week season, making about £10 and £20 from its catches of 10–20 last of herring (there were 12,000 fish in a last). The profit would be divided between the boat owners (boats were often shared by a number of investors) and the master and his crew. The fish quickly decayed, and the bulk of them were cured, either by smoking (to make red herring) or salting (white herring). They were traded in huge quantities mainly at herring fairs, as the preserved herring were relatively cheap. They were eaten in great quantities in the households of the wealthy, but could be afforded at least occasionally by the mass of relatively poor consumers. Although this specialism was unusual in its concentration in time and place, it can stand as in many ways typical of medieval industry, with quite low levels of investment in a small enterprise that employed a handful of people in any one part of the production process (in this case both catching and curing) and sold quite cheap basic commodities to a large number of consumers, many of them of modest means. There were, however, profits to be made, and the people who became wealthy from the industry were not the seamen who braved the North Sea, or those who toiled in the smoky curing sheds, but the merchants who handled the barrels of fish.

Merchants contributed much to the economy of towns, and took their rewards in consequence. They traded over long distances both in expensive luxury goods, and in cheaper commodities in bulk. Without their management of the higher levels of the trading system, the larger towns in which they were based could not have existed, but they also had great influence on small towns and country markets, in which the commodities they handled were bought and sold. Merchants reduced risks by diversifying their activities, including the purchase of land, moneylending and holding office. They were the richest people in the towns, played a major role in municipal politics, and advised the royal government.

The wealthiest and most ambitious merchants had wide horizons. The twelfth and thirteenth centuries had been a period of globalization, in the sense that Europe's contacts with Asia grew in importance. This was not so much because of crusading and the establishment of a western Christian colony in Palestine, as through the growth of trade with the eastern Mediterranean and the Black Sea in spices, silks, cotton and other goods, which was mainly handled by Italian and Spanish traders. The Italians led the world in the business methods by which they raised capital in partnerships and companies, and then arranged profitable ventures in distant cities through their factors. The merchants of London and the other towns in Britain contributed to this trade mainly by acting as distributors of the luxuries, enabling rich consumers to indulge in a sophisticated Mediterranean culture. Even in the commerce of northern Europe, English and Scottish merchants took second place to those from Flanders, Brabant and France, with the Italians and the Germans rising in prominence towards the end of the thirteenth century. Nonetheless, native merchants still traded overseas, like Robert of London, who bought pepper worth £183 at Genoa in 1186, and exporters of wool like Lawrence of Ludlow from Shropshire, who went down with his ship in the North Sea in 1294 while taking a cargo to Holland. The English participated in this embryonic globalization when in the twelfth century they developed trade links with Spain, where merchants found an outlet for English woollen cloth, and brought back spices, gold and fine leather. Good-quality shoes were made from Spanish goatskins from Cordoba (cordwain), which gave English shoemakers, even if they worked mainly in locally produced leather, the distinctive occupational name of cordwainers.

When archaeologists excavated a rubbish pit in Southampton, in Cuckoo Lane near the quay, they found a seal bearing the name of Richard of Southwick, a merchant active in the 1270s and 1280s, who lived in a stone house nearby. The pit contained rubbish from Southwick's house, revealing his international contacts. He had business links with a merchant from Normandy called Bernard de Vire, whose seal was found, and he had bought decorated jugs from south-west France and lustreware from Spain, together with more valuable but perishable goods such as wine. The sheath for his dagger was made from Spanish leather, and he ate imported figs and grapes as well as local fruits. The pit also contained the skeleton of a small African monkey, brought to Southampton by a sailor from the Mediterranean and presumably kept by Southwick as an exotic pet.

Merchants aimed to earn maximum profits by handling the commodities which gave the best returns. This meant above all dealing in the most important export, wool. Merchants based inland bought up the fleeces from local markets, like the appropriately named Alexander le Riche of Andover in Hampshire, who in 1270 was buying wool over a range of 50 miles, from Wiltshire and Somerset. By an alternative method, merchants negotiated directly with the producers, and bought the wool in bulk. The celebrated Douai clothmaking entrepreneur, Jehane de Boinebroke, who obtained much of his wool from Scotland and northern England, contracted to buy seventy-two sacks from Newminster Abbey in Northumberland in 1270. The abbey acted as a middleman, and was able to add another twenty sacks to the bargain consisting of the *collecta*, that is wool bought by the monks from other producers, most of them peasants. Non-English merchants were then exporting two-thirds of English wool, but the share of native traders increased towards the end of the thirteenth century, and by 1304–11 the English handled 57 per cent. At this time Thomas of Coldingham of Berwick-upon-Tweed, applying the methods commonly used by foreign traders, negotiated to buy all of Durham Priory's wool. He drove a hard bargain because the priory wanted money in advance – he agreed to buy for the next three or four years, but at the very cheap price of £4 per sack.

He could sell these for £6 or £7 each in Flanders, and even after paying transport costs his profit margin must have been above 20 per cent. The advance of the English into this lucrative trade was helped by political troubles which had disrupted the trade in the 1290s, when Edward I had imposed an embargo on trade with Flanders in the course of his war with France.

Wool, together with wool fells (sheepskins), were the major export from the various parts of Britain in the period. Hides and fish figured prominently among the goods carried from Scottish ports, and metals were exported from England, notably tin from Devon and Cornwall, and lead from north Wales and the Pennines. Exports were closely linked with the import trade, as those who had carried wool to a continental port would have the money to buy goods and the space in their ships to carry them back. In the late thirteenth century when the Italian merchants played a key role in the wool trade, they also brought spices to London, which were then distributed by the London pepperers, later called the grocers. By the early years of the fourteenth century a higher proportion of spice was imported by the English traders. The expensive imported goods bought by wealthy consumers carried high profit margins. These included wine, which during the thirteenth century came increasingly from the English king's possessions in south-west France, the duchy of Aquitaine, and reached their peak in about 1308, when 20,000 tuns (5 million gallons) were imported. Manufactured goods included woollen cloth from Flanders, silks from Italy and Spain and linen from France. The north of Europe, Scandinavia and the Baltic, provided the furs which were used to line the clothing of the rich, and wax from which the best-quality candles were made for churches and the households of the wealthy. Merchants could also make profits by importing quite cheap and bulky goods which were in demand because they were not produced within the country, or obtainable in sufficient quantity. These included the alum, oil and dyestuffs, such as woad, essential for cloth manufacture; Baltic timber, especially in eastern England, for both houses and ships; and pitch, tar, iron and steel. Foodstuffs which were not especially expensive or luxurious, such as preserved fish, came from northern Europe, together with such ordinary domestic implements as whetstones and hand-mills.

Many merchants, especially those living in inland towns, did not trade overseas but transferred goods from one region to another. Some handled luxury commodities ultimately for aristocratic consumption, like the goldsmiths who sold plate and jewellery, or the vintners who distributed wine by the tun or pipe from inland ports such as Gloucester. The skinners were well established in Northampton in the thirteenth century, and from here they visited fairs at St Ives. In much of the inland trade the main opportunities came from the movement of grain, which was bought and sold by bladers and cornmongers acting as suppliers for the larger towns, and sometimes sending boatloads for more than 20 miles down the rivers to London, Bristol and King's Lynn. Raw materials for crafts included hides, iron and wool, which was being carried in quantity to industrial centres within the country, not just to the continent. Finally, manufactured goods were traded inland, notably woollen cloth from centres of the industry such as Lincoln and Stamford, and the linen which was made in Norfolk and sold through the drapers of Norwich.

The merchants traded from their houses, and just as artisans had workshops on the premises, so merchants' accommodation would include warehouses and counting houses where bargains would be struck and records of transactions kept. Merchants often travelled with their goods and negotiated deals in person, hence the occasional tragedy like the shipwreck in which Lawrence of Ludlow died. They also used agents or factors, often simply called 'servants', who represented their interests in remote places. This period marks the heyday of the English fairs, occasions when the maximum number of merchants and customers came together to conduct business for a few days of intense commercial activity. Almost every town acquired its chartered fair during the thirteenth century, and many changed the time of year when the fair was held, or added new ones, with the intention of finding the moment which would attract the maximum number of buyers and sellers.

The really successful fairs had established themselves by the mid-thirteenth century mostly in eastern England, and they followed each other in a sequence through the year, with the Stamford fair in Lent, St Ives at Easter, Boston in July, Winchester in September and Northampton in November. These were the fairs regarded in the 1250s by merchants in Douai and Lucca as especially important, though others such as those held at Bury St Edmunds, King's Lynn and Westminster attracted a great volume of trade. The fairground would be transformed temporarily into a small town as dozens of booths were erected, and within a few days hundreds of pounds' worth of goods would be sold. Agents from the great households attended and bought their supplies of wax, fish and cloth at wholesale prices. The archbishop of York, for example, regularly spent £60 per annum at St Ives in the 1280s. But most of the trade at the fairs was between one merchant and another. English drapers would lay in stocks of cloth from Flemish merchants at fairs, and sell pieces to customers from their town shops. A characteristic visitor to fairs was a Lincoln draper, Stephen of Stanham, who was especially active in 1299–1304. He bought goods at the fairs of Boston and St Ives, and held a shop in London. He was able to supply the king's wardrobe with spices, wax and cloth, and when parliament met in Lincoln in 1300, could provide the members with sugar and figs.

Those engaged in trade took the risk of losing their cargoes through fire, crime or shipwreck, or they might find that demand had slumped because of famine or war, or they could be defeated by commercial competition. They bought land most commonly to avoid risk and store some of their wealth in a secure asset. They may sometimes have gained capital from their rents from real property, but the amount that they owned does not seem adequate for that purpose – the landed assets of a leading merchant were commonly worth £10–£20 per annum, whereas they traded goods worth hundreds of pounds. Most were reluctant to tie up too much of their money in land. They may have included in their portfolio of interests the profits derived from leases on assets, such as mills or fisheries, or they acted as farmers, by collecting tolls or taxes, and paying a fixed sum to the state or the town government. So a late twelfth-century goldsmith, Terrice of Canterbury, in addition to his private trade in precious metals, acted as farmer of the royal exchange in Canterbury, where foreign money would be brought in to be changed for coin of the realm. He also purchased goods for the king. In addition he was a considerable property holder, with a rental income of £69 per annum. In a similar fashion, members of the Fortin and Isembard families in Southampton in the same period were put in charge of work on the royal castle and farmed revenues from the town.

As the larger towns became self-governing around 1200, merchants commonly occupied municipal offices, sitting on town councils and serving as chamberlains, bailiffs and mayors. These may not have been very profitable jobs, as they were often expected to pay for at least part of their expenses. But whether because of the indirect material benefits (which some contemporaries believed them to have exploited for private gain), or the status that followed from the exercise of public duties, merchants tended to fill the highest offices, and sometimes repeatedly, like the wealthy Selby family in York who served as mayor over three generations between 1217 and 1289.

Mercantile trade depended on credit. Goods were bought without immediate payment, and in selling goods the merchant advanced credit, allowing the purchaser to pay later. Merchants also had opportunities to accumulate cash, and lent money, for example to aristocrats who were incurring extra expenditure on a building project, or to kings embarking on war. In the twelfth century the moneylenders included Flemish and English merchants, notably William Cade, the great Flemish financier who died in 1166, and later in the century the Londoners, Gervase and

Henry of Cornhill. The Jews had come to England after the Norman Conquest as dealers in bullion: they bought and sold silver plate, which for the aristocracy served as the ultimate status symbol but was also a means of storing surplus wealth. Jews changed money, in support of the strict royal policy that foreign coins should not circulate in England, and they also lent cash. When Henry II in 1180 set up royal exchanges in eight selected towns, one of the functions of the Jewish community was lost, and they faced competition from English goldsmiths in the trade in silver plate. In increasing measure from the late twelfth century they made their living from moneylending. They could provide this service over a large area as Jewish communities developed in most of the larger towns in eastern England, in the most commercially active regions, and also extended to the west as far as Exeter, Hereford and Shrewsbury. The crown had always offered protection to Jews, who tended to live in towns near to the royal castle.

After a wave of anti-Jewish violence in 1190, which was especially savage at York where almost the whole community was massacred, the Jews were bound even more closely to the royal government. Chests containing records of Jewish loans were kept in selected towns under official supervision, and Jewish affairs were regulated by the Exchequer of Jews. Some Jews had become rich in the twelfth century, notably Aaron of Lincoln who died in 1186 with debts owing to him of £15,000. Under royal patronage they became even more wealthy in the early thirteenth century, when many aristocrats, unable to pay their way in the face of inflation, royal financial demands and expectations of a grander style of life, borrowed money on the strength of their landed assets. The Jews obliged, but at a cost. One type of loan imposed as a penalty on late payers an annual interest charge of 43 per cent. In 1241–2 the total amount owed to Jews can be estimated at near to £80,000, and the king, fully aware of the possibility of raising money from a vulnerable minority, collected £73,000 in taxes from the Jews in the years between 1241 and 1256. Not every debtor was aristocratic; indeed many peasants and artisans figured more prominently among Jewish clients after 1260.

The Jews were a means by which the crown taxed landed society indirectly, as the Jews passed on to their clients the costs of the Jewish tallages and other financial burdens. The Jews declined in numbers and wealth in the 1260s and 1270s, through a combination of royal taxation and Christian prejudice, and were eventually expelled in 1290. The demand for ready cash continued, however, and the gap was filled partly by Englishmen with spare money, like the notorious government official, Adam de Stratton. Thomas of Coldingham, who has already been mentioned for his advance of money to Durham Priory on the strength of a guarantee of cheap wool (pp. 207–8), also lent money to landowners, and at one point in his career had taken over a manor from which he drew an income, which allowed him to profit from the loan. The greatest sums were advanced by the Italian companies, which were also taking over sections of the trade in wool. Edward I borrowed from the Riccardi of Lucca, but towards the end of his reign, after 1294, he developed a relationship with the Florentine company of the Frescobaldi, who were rewarded with trading privileges.

iv. *Techniques of trade and manufacture*

The growth in the population and in exchange increased the volume and value of trade with the continent. Records made in the course of assessing and collecting English royal taxation allow an estimate that in 1204 the combined value of exports and imports was worth between £55,000 and £75,000, and that the equivalent sum a hundred years later lay in the region of £500,000 per annum. Allowing for inflation, these figures suggest a threefold increase in overseas trade, and a growth in the quantity of exports and imports per head of population. The total value of inland trade cannot be estimated, but its growing importance is indicated by the higher proportion of rents paid in cash by 1300 and the section of the population which obtained most of its living from non-agricultural activities, which by *c.*1300 amounted to well over 20 per cent, counting those working in rural industries as well as the town dwellers.

Was this merely a growth in quantity, or was it accompanied by changes in technique and business methods? Perhaps those who made their living in manufacture or trade could expect to benefit from cheap labour and higher demand, and so were not impelled to make savings in labour costs or to improve the efficiency of their operations. No 'industrial revolution' can be identified at this time, but there were technological advances, designed to expand production and to increase profits. Water power was applied to a number of industries, notably clothmaking, with the first reference to a fulling mill in 1185. The water wheel operated wooden hammers which rose and fell rapidly on to cloth in a trough containing water and fuller's earth, a naturally occurring detergent. Traditionally the process had been performed laboriously by fullers agitating the cloth with wooden clubs, or more often by trampling it underfoot – hence the name 'walker' by which fullers were commonly known. By the end of the thirteenth century about 800 fulling mills had been built in England. The main motive for investing in the mills, as we have seen, was the local lord's desire to make some profit from a local industry, and as fulling represented only one operation in the many stages of cloth manufacture, these mills cannot be compared with the textile factories of the eighteenth and nineteenth centuries in which a number of processes were mechanized. On the other hand, the mills would not have been built unless the local clothmakers could have been persuaded to use them. Lords' attempts to use compulsion had limited effects, and the main motive for people to bring their cloth to be fulled was the labour and money that could be saved. It was said that fulling by foot produced better results than the new machinery, so efficiency seems to have been the main consideration.

Water mills could also be used to power heavy metal shod hammers to forge iron after it had been smelted, or to work up wrought iron into implements and tools. At Bordesley Abbey in Worcestershire, for example, a triangular pond was constructed in the valley of the River Arrow in about 1175 to provide a flow of water for machinery housed in a timber-framed mill. The first mill burnt down, but was soon replaced, and the building and machinery went through a series of alterations and rebuildings throughout the thirteenth and early fourteenth centuries. It was clearly regarded by its monastic builders and owners as a good investment that repaid its heavy initial costs and the expense of maintenance. The operation of the mill resembled a small factory, because a number of metalworking processes were carried out, including bronze casting, as well as the central activity of forging iron. In a fashion typical of the Cistercian monks who funded the mill, a venture which may originally have been designed to serve the internal needs of the monastery and its estates became a commercial enterprise satisfying the local market, producing a variety of implements and equipment, including weapons and armour as well as nails and the tenterhooks on which cloth was stretched after fulling. Human smiths wielding hammers would have done this work more slowly and, one suspects, less thoroughly, than the water-driven machine. The adoption of this technology undoubtedly advanced productivity.

In most industries the new methods were not as expensive or as far reaching as mill-powered machinery. Instead, modifications were made to the process or the product which aided the artisan or the consumer. In building, the adoption of stone foundations and improved methods of timber framing created structures with a high degree of durability. Construction cost more initially, but maintenance and rebuilding expenses were greatly reduced. In towns, the replacement of thatched roofs by tile or stone slates was similarly expensive, but saved in the long run as the roof did not require such frequent renewal, and was less likely to burn down. The fact that houses built in the early fourteenth century for renting to the lower grades of artisans in York have survived and are still in use is a remarkable tribute to the technical accomplishment of medieval builders.

In the English pottery industry, glazed jugs were made in a few kilns before 1100, but by the late thirteenth century almost all of the dozens of centres of production were making these vessels, often in attractive designs. They were bought in large numbers for wealthy households, but peasants and artisans served ale in them. In Scotland, pottery manufacture was introduced in the twelfth and thirteenth centuries, and while the ownership of decorated jugs was more restricted than in England, locally manufactured cooking pots were in widespread use, especially in towns.

The techniques of trade were also being adapted to make the process easier and less costly. Inland transport was improved by building bridges and roads. Fords, which took many roads across rivers, were replaced by bridges; timber bridges were rebuilt in stone; the roads approaching bridges were built on causeways to raise the traffic above the level of river valleys that were liable to flood. A high proportion of bridges were sufficiently wide to allow carts to cross – they were not mere pedestrian or pack-horse bridges. By 1300 bridges had been built on the main crossing points, and on many rivers no new bridges were added until new routes were developed and new demands made of the transport system in the eighteenth century. On the River Severn below Montford Bridge, for example, eight bridges had been built by the early fourteenth century, compared to ten after a passage of another 400 years. Edward I had new roads made for his armies when he invaded north Wales in 1277, from Chester to Diganwy through Flint and Rhuddlan. Throughout England, road-building was being carried out by town governments, or by landlords and village communities, mainly on short stretches, but cumulatively this work helped the passage of traffic over long distances. Some roads were rerouted, and new sections – of the Great North Road, for example – constructed. At a local level, roads and tracks were more numerous than they are today, serving every field or house, so that even a small parish would contain 20 miles of road.

Traders who were organizing the transport of goods often chose to use pack-horses, which could negotiate steep and narrow paths but carried relatively small quantities of goods. We have already noted the gradual replacement of the ox-drawn wain by horses and carts for transporting bulky goods. Cart journeys over longer distances seem painfully slow to us: it could take eight days for a loaded cart to cover the 150 miles between Gloucester and London. Anyone contemplating carrying goods over such a distance had to allow for the expenses of feeding the horses, shoeing them and repairing the cart, as well as the hire and living expenses of the driver. Costs for transporting wheat from Huntingdon to London in 1305 amounted to 1$\frac{1}{2}$d per mile for each ton of grain. If corn prices were high, then the expense was worth it, but if wheat was selling for 5s per quarter, a quarter would gain 7$\frac{1}{2}$d in cost if it was carried for 20 miles, which might not be profitable. On the other hand, a tun of wine which was worth £5 could be transported many miles without an unacceptable addition to its price. Land transport was dependable, and even long journeys were made in the winter, contrary to modern myths about impassably muddy and potholed roads.

Carriage by water was much cheaper, at a halfpenny per ton/mile, but England's inland waterways served only a small proportion of the country. A network of rivers in the east midlands and East Anglia, such as the Trent, Nene, Witham, Welland and Great Ouse, supplemented by the Foss Dyke (a canal originally built in Roman times to join the Witham to the Trent), served such inland towns as Nottingham, Lincoln, Stamford and Cambridge, joining them and their hinterlands to the ports of Hull, Boston and King's Lynn. The south was served by the Thames, the west midlands by the Severn, and Yorkshire by the Ouse and Hull. Coastal shipping often provided a cheaper and more convenient alternative to roads, which allowed Cornish tin, Purbeck marble from Dorset, and coal from Newcastle upon Tyne to make the journey to London relatively cheaply. But these important and useful arteries for commerce left large parts of the country dependent mainly on roads.

Among seagoing vessels, bulky cargoes were carried by the hulk and the cog. The advantage of these vessels was their carrying capacity rather than speed, so they were wide in relation to their length. The larger cogs were 65 to 100 feet long, with a capacity of 200 tons. In the ports, the town authorities built timber-faced waterfronts where ships could be loaded and unloaded, and sometimes docks were constructed, as in Hartlepool in the thirteenth century. Cranes were being used at the larger ports before 1200.

The business methods of English merchants lagged behind those employed by the Italians, but they were developing partnerships as a means of raising capital and extending the scale of their trade. We tend to hear about their arrangements when they went wrong, which led to revealing court cases. One such deal was made in 1304 between John Chigwell and William de Flete, both Londoners. This was not an isolated alliance, as the two men, and their relatives, had been trading in partnership for many years. Both men employed servants to travel to foreign ports, to collect goods and pay for them. The two merchants agreed each to put up £40 as trading capital for a year, and then to divide the profits equally. Although the partnership agreement mentioned sums of money, they invested goods rather than cash, which were actually worth more than £40. De Flete contributed a consignment of wine, beans and salt, which was carried to Scotland and sold, probably to supply the castle garrisons in the area of English occupation. The profit on that transaction, once transport costs and other expenses had been allowed, gave a return of 25 per cent. Chigwell was offered a consignment of wool and hides by a Scottish magnate, John Comyn. To raise the money, the London merchant made another partnership with an Italian who had travelled with him to Comyn's castle. They paid £220 for the goods, and £125 to carry them for sale at St Omer, and they were sold for £396. After other expenses this transaction made a profit of £51. Meanwhile some mishap overcame a cargo of woad from Picardy which was Chigwell's contribution to the partnership, and the two fell out, mainly because de Flete thought that he had contributed all of the capital, but had to share his profits with Chigwell.

Most partnerships and business transactions are not recorded in any detail because they were conducted successfully, even though one suspects that they were just as complicated as the Chigwell/de Flete arrangements. They bore some resemblance to Italian practices of their day, in the sense that, like the Italian *commenda* contract, the parties agreed to share the investment and the profit. In the Chigwell/de Flete case the parties both contributed capital and personal participation in trade, but some partnerships involved a 'sleeping partner' who put up the money and an active merchant who did the negotiations. In England, groups of traders were known in the Latin phraseology of the documents as a 'society', but there were no large companies of the Italian type. Those embarking on complex business ventures needed some assurance that money would be paid and debts recovered. A common way of recording a debt was to use a bond, in which the borrower promised to pay by a certain date. These documents were often linked to a grant of land which provided some guarantee that the creditor could recover something of value. Recognizances recorded an obligation, and this method was standardized and given the backing of the state in 1283 when by the Statute of Acton Burnell certain towns were given the authority to maintain an archive in which the documents could be kept. In 1285 the Statute of Merchants clarified the earlier law, and strengthened the measures for forcing the debtor to pay.

Much medieval business was not recorded in writing. Bargains were made between the parties directly, and promises to pay were mainly oral. Written accounts were not apparently kept, and were certainly not preserved. The whole system depended on word-of-mouth communication and informal agreements. Traders had reputations which were made by personal recommendation and could be damaged by gossip. Successful trading decisions depended on the spread of intelligence, whereby news would be conveyed from one town to another on which decisions would be based. In 1319, for example, the price of wheat in England was quite low, at about 4s 6d per quarter, but for some reason, probably a harvest failure caused by bad weather in the south-west, Exeter wheat prices rose to 6s. Ships arrived within a few months from eastern England and northern France loaded with grain, proof of the rapid and accurate flow of information.

Many of the commercial techniques were developed to aid 'business to business' dealings, but the end of the process involved traders selling goods to customers. Here the main object was to bring as many consumers as possible into direct contact with the commodities and the sellers, and to tempt them with a wide range of goods at competitive prices. To some extent this aim was achieved by the proliferation of markets, fairs and towns in the twelfth and thirteenth centuries, so that no one needed to travel for more than a few hours to find a place to trade. It was important there should be plenty of space for marketing, and numerous stalls and shops. The rational arrangement by which trading was fixed for particular days and times, and the stalls in the marketplace, or the shops in the streets, were grouped so that all of the butchers, drapers, ironmongers and shoemakers could be found together, was a convenience for customers and traders alike. Trade was not restricted to market days, and medieval people could 'shop' throughout the week. Efforts were made to maximize the concentration of retailers. One strategy was the seld, the medieval version of the shopping mall, which reached its most developed form in Cheapside in London. In this central street dozens of selds were built, which consisted of rows of stalls or even chests from which goods could be displayed and sold; by 1300, 4,000 shops, stalls and other points of sale were operating there. Selds were introduced on a smaller scale into many provincial towns.

An especially high density of shopping outlets was provided in Chester, which was almost the regional capital of north-west England and north Wales, and a port for the Irish trade. It expanded within a confined space, as its walls were essential for security in a border area, and there was limited land for suburbs. The Chester townsmen devised a means by which the number of shops could be doubled by building houses along the four main streets with the usual shops on the ground floor, but also with galleries at first-floor level. Shoppers could move along the streets to see the wares below, and by flights of steps at frequent intervals gain access to covered walkways along which were ranged a further row of shops. The successful planning of the 'Rows' depended on compromise between the private interests of the individual owners and builders of each house, and the public authority of the town government which regulated the arrangement.

v. *Urban government*

The reduction of 'transaction costs', the modern economist's phrase for measures to make trade more convenient and efficient, took place within a framework of security provided by the state and town governments. Townsmen were normally of free status, so their lords could not make arbitrary demands of them, and their rights to landed property were protected in the king's courts. The English legislation of 1283 and 1285 ensured that credit arrangements could be officially recorded, and aided the recovery of debts. Criminals would steal goods and merchants could be waylaid on the road, but the state kept some control over disorder, as much as was possible in an age before a professional police force.

The English government maintained a high-quality currency. Admittedly the silver pennies, struck at a rate of 240 to the pound of silver, were a rather clumsy means of conducting both large and small transactions. If a merchant wished to pay £100 at once he had to assemble a bulky collection of 24,000 coins; if a consumer of modest means wished to buy a loaf of bread or a quart of ale for a farthing, small change was in short supply. Kings like Edward I made some effort to answer the demand for small denominations by minting halfpennies and farthings, and pennies were often cut into halves and quarters, but there were never enough. However, the inconvenience of the penny coinage was of small account compared with the problems on the continent posed by debasements and manipulation of the currency by states pursuing short-term profit. The weight and the silver content of the coinage were usually maintained by English governments through their financial crises. There were problems of price inflation, as we have seen, occasioned at the end of the twelfth century and in the early fourteenth by influxes of silver from the continent, and there were periods when coins were in short supply, notably between the 1070s and the 1160s. Edward I had to cope with an influx of foreign coins (crockards and pollards) in the 1290s, which he finally resolved by a major recoinage, but in general the principle that only English coins could circulate was maintained. The English kings were continuing a long tradition, while the Scottish royal coinage began, together with the burghs, in the twelfth century, and from the first striking of pennies in 1136 until 1367 the Scottish kings maintained a standard of coinage closely linked to that south of the border. The majority of coins circulating in Scotland were in fact English, and the two currencies seem to have coexisted: unlike any other 'foreign' currency, Scottish coins were tolerated in England.

Medieval people seem rather inconsistent in their recognition of towns, as the words 'town' and 'toun' in both English and Scots had a very general meaning, and could be applied to a wide range of rural settlements as well as the larger non-agrarian places that we regard as towns. The Latin word *villa* ('vill' in English) was equally ambiguous, and the term *villa mercatoria* (market town) was coined in the thirteenth century to identify settlements with a trading function. 'Borough' in England and Wales and 'burgh' in Scotland, *burgus* in Latin, meant a place where the tenants enjoyed the privileges of paying fixed cash rents and free disposal of land – in short, holding defined plots by burgage tenure. Modern historians compile lists of English boroughs on the basis of references in documents to burgage tenure, burgesses or burgage plots, but contemporaries seem less precise about the whole notion. When officials were deciding on the taxation of boroughs, or selecting places to be invited to send borough representatives to parliament, they made some very unpredictable judgements. A number of 'boroughs' were summoned to Edward I's parliament in 1295 where there is no evidence for burgage tenure, and only 221 places with such tenure, out of a total of about 600, paid tax as boroughs in any of the lay subsidies between 1294 and 1336.

Perhaps remote officials were uncertain about the status of a place, and those who lived in towns were more conscious of the rights and privileges which affected their daily lives. Lords granted tenants burgage tenure because they believed that a borough provided the right institutional framework within which a town could develop. They would offer packages of privileges based on those enjoyed by other towns, such as Newcastle or Hereford. The 'laws of Breteuil', deriving from an obscure town in Normandy, were widely conceded to new boroughs throughout England and Wales. Many lords continued to encourage their new towns – having granted burgage tenure in one charter, they might offer new privileges in a second. Lords were often ready to co-operate with the urban elite; for example, the leading townspeople would fill the offices of bailiff, or serve as jurors in the borough court. The townspeople farmed the market tolls, which in effect gave them the management of the market. High Wycombe in Buckinghamshire paid a fee farm of £30 for all of the revenues from the town to its lord by an agreement of 1226, an important step towards running its own affairs. The same end was achieved at Burford (Oxfordshire) when it was allowed to have its own guild merchant, that is, its traders were able to regulate the commerce of the town. In general, judging from the absence of any evidence of friction, the inhabitants of towns ruled by their lords were willing to go along with the arrangements made, which often involved some practical compromise between the interests of the lord and of the most influential townspeople.

The tenants in some towns were freeholders, but lacked the special privilege of burgage tenure. This did not prevent the development of an urban economy. In the west, towns which were not boroughs tended to be relatively few and small: they included places like Bridgend in Glamorgan and Rugby in Warwickshire. But in the east they were numerous, and included large market towns like Wymondham in Norfolk, and as important a place as Westminster, which in spite of its prominence in servicing the great abbey and royal palace had the status of a 'vill', no different from any rural community. The implication of these 'informal' towns is that they began from initiatives taken by traders and craftsmen, who created their own town without a lord's active patronage. On occasion a town struggled for its lord to recognize its borough status. Burgesses were acknowledged at Cirencester in Gloucestershire when the town was ruled by the crown, but after it was handed over to the new abbey which was founded in 1131, the canons treated its tenants as if they were villagers. At Bury St Edmunds the monks accepted that the settlement at the gate of their monastery was a borough, but resisted the townspeople's foundation of a guild merchant which would have allowed them to control access to the market. A number of monastic towns resembled these two places in their long-term disputes with their lords, at Abingdon, Dunstable and St Albans, and towns under the lordship of bishops were capable of occasional outbursts of discontent, notably at Wells in Somerset. Townspeople who were unable to run their own affairs found ways of meeting and working together by forming their own institutions, often a religious fraternity, which would acquire property, employ chaplains, and exercise at least some influence over the government of the town. At Henley-on-Thames by the 1290s the fraternity which maintained the vital bridge over the Thames had become a *de facto* town government, appointing a warden, two bailiffs and two bridge-wardens, who collected and spent a considerable annual income.

The form of self-government which townspeople desired was usually only acquired by the larger royal towns, which by charters granted between around 1189 and 1216 were allowed to pay rents, tolls and other financial obligations by a fee farm. They managed their own affairs through a mayor and council, they held their own borough courts, and expressed their separate legal identity by holding a common seal. Their right to hold a guild merchant meant that the townspeople decided who could trade toll free. All of these institutions, but with some different nomenclature – feu ferme, provost and bailies, guild merchant – were acquired by the leading royal burghs at rather later dates in Scotland. Those who received these rights clearly valued them, as towns were willing to pay substantial sums of money for their charters of privilege. Lincoln, for example, gave King John £200 for its charter in 1200. The townspeople, above all the elite, felt that they would enjoy economic advantages from self-government. They could decide how to levy the money to pay the fee farm; by-laws could be framed to advance the common good; the borough court would be run by people who understood trade and the disputes that might arise from it; the guild merchant would be able to make and enforce regulations for the general economic well-being of the town.

We can see the importance townspeople attached to controlling their space. They resented the existence of separate jurisdictions, like the precincts within the walls that belonged to cathedrals and religious houses. At Norwich a section of the city belonged to the cathedral priory, and it was suspected that criminals could escape justice by hiding there. The economic interests of the townspeople were thought to be damaged because the monks did not enforce strictly the rules of trade, such as the regulation of the price of bread and ale. And those who lived in the priory's enclave did not contribute their fair share to the municipal budget. These suspicions and grudges came to a head in 1272 when, after a dispute in the marketplace of Tombland adjoining the priory, a servant of the monks shot and killed a townsman with a crossbow. In the ensuing riots part of the priory was burnt. The list of rioters shows that they included the whole Norwich community, from the civic elite to craftsmen and servants.

Perhaps people at the time were right to think that their towns would prosper if they achieved the special status of a borough, or gained the more advanced rights of self-government. The opposite is almost impossible to prove, but we can only point out that places which were not boroughs – three-quarters of the towns in the highly urbanized county of Norfolk, for example – seemed to flourish in spite of their supposed disadvantage. Lords often gave borough charters to places where economic opportunities were uncertain, to give an institutional stimulus to a new town in a region like north Wales or Cumberland, where the population was rather thinly spread and the agricultural surplus meagre. Towns like Attleborough or Aylsham in Norfolk could grow without the need for such artificial stimuli.

The same reasoning can be applied to the higher stages of self-government, because for all the grumbling and rebellion of the people of Bury, their town was the second largest and richest in the county of

Suffolk at the time of its most bitter conflicts with the monastery in the early fourteenth century, and indeed it ranked twenty-fifth in the country as a whole, ahead of places like Northampton which had all of the desired privileges. Boston in Lincolnshire was ruled by officials appointed by its lord, yet it was placed in the top four provincial towns by wealth. The suspicion must be that contemporaries did not distinguish between the political advantages of self-government and the economic gains. Political autonomy allowed a section of society to order the affairs of the town in ways that favoured themselves, and this was the most pressing reason for campaigns for independence. We think that a charter of liberties freed those who received it from restrictions, but freedom in the middle ages meant privilege in an exclusive sense: charters often gave the recipients the right to rule over others.

The same problems of assessing the ideas and attitudes of contemporaries are apparent when we consider competition between towns. In the twelfth and thirteenth centuries new towns were founded which carved out hinterlands from the commercial territory of existing centres. This caused no great problems in the early stages, when towns were still widely spaced, but by the mid-thirteenth century the rivalries became more acute. Some newcomers faded rapidly back into obscurity, but some old established places were damaged, such as Hedon in east Yorkshire, founded in *c.*1170, but overshadowed by Beverley and Hull, and temporarily eclipsed by the mushroom growth of Ravenserrodd, a town which was built on a narrow peninsula of temporary dry ground off Spurn Point in the mouth of the Humber estuary. Towns which felt threatened searched for legal and political remedies. The law allowed English market holders to object to a new market which might damage their trade, and the lawyers adopted the rule that markets should lie $6^2/_3$ miles apart. The monks of Bury St Edmunds in 1201–2 resisted a newly founded market at Lakenheath, which was more than 15 miles from Bury, and sent a band of its supporters to demolish the stalls, in effect claiming a monopoly.

Welsh towns were granted monopolies like Carmarthen's privilege of selling wax and tallow in its vicinity. Transactions of all kinds within 15 miles of Cardigan had to take place in the town. In Scotland, towns also claimed monopolies, like the exclusive right of the inhabitants of Lanark according to a grant of 1285 to buy wool and skins in Lanarkshire. Guild merchants attempted to extend their powers beyond their own town. Lincoln, for example, campaigned against the traders of Louth, and Leicester objected to the purchase of local wool by traders from Melton Mowbray, Loughborough and Lutterworth, all of them towns within

Leicestershire. Guild merchants more often brought pressure to bear on their own members, prohibiting them from trading outside the town, or requiring them to discriminate against outsiders. The butchers of High Wycombe were ordered in 1313 to offer hides firstly to their fellow townsmen, and only then to sell them to 'foreign' traders. Occasionally it is possible to show that these regulations were enforced, but even then we suspect that those who were fined for trading, for example within 15 miles of a Welsh town, or the member of a guild merchant who was punished for selling forbidden goods to outsiders, were unlucky. Medieval governments did not have the resources or police force to protect monopolies or supervise markets, especially over long distances. In the same way, townsmen expressed prejudice against their rivals from overseas. The Lombards (Italians) and Hanseatics (Germans) probably attracted more hostility than any other groups, though like the Jews they received royal protection. More general regulations sought to restrict traders from overseas by insisting that they be 'hosted' by an English merchant, and foreign merchants were forbidden to trade retail. These restrictions in practice did not prevent the foreign trade on which the towns depended.

Attempts to control the economy were more likely to succeed within the town, where the powers of self-government gave wealthy minorities the ability to manipulate the regulations and the borough courts in their favour. The town authorities often used the rhetoric of the common good, but self-interest had a strong influence on their actions. The general privileges granted to burgesses or freemen or citizens were confined to a minority. In a borough governed by a lord, only the tenants of the burgages were eligible; in a town with a guild merchant, entry into the guild was by inheritance or apprenticeship, or by purchase. To join one of the fraternities which acted as unofficial town governments a fee was usually required. Entry fees alone excluded many artisans from full membership of the urban community. Discrimination against weavers in particular was a feature of the regulations governing trade in the larger towns. At Winchester, the guild merchant forbade weavers from dyeing or selling cloth, and Leicester weavers were ordered not to work for country employers except when no one within the town had work for them. Here we clearly see the influence of the drapers, whose main interest was to secure for their warehouses a steady supply of cloth, of reasonable quality and at the lowest possible cost.

Often regulation was used by the merchants to secure their control of commodities and exclude competition. At Southampton only members of the guild merchant could sell herring or millstones, or keep a tavern, or sell retail outside the marketplace, in their shops, on days other than market day. The big London companies emerged in the thirteenth century, and some of them performed the apparently innocuous and public-spirited function of inspecting and checking the quality of goods for sale. We can be sure that as the fishmongers inspected the fish markets, and the goldsmiths made sure that silver and gold plate were of good materials and workmanship (by a rule of 1238), defective goods were most commonly identified on the stalls of rivals or on those of members of their own companies who were not co-operating with a ruling faction. Opponents of the ruling groups alleged that they managed the tax system so that the poor paid a disproportionate share (at York in 1305, for example), and lists of assessments show hundreds of taxpayers contributing a few pence who, if the payments had been made under the officials of the royal government, would have been exempt.

Elitist manipulation of urban government was not always effective. Towns sought to curb excessive profiteering, especially by food traders. Perhaps this was a further example of self-interest, because those who sold cloth, leather, ironware and other products of urban artisans, or who employed labour themselves, did not wish to have the cost of living of workers pushed up to the point where they demanded higher rates of pay. But town governments had some commitment to good government, and were also anxious to avoid the trouble that might be caused by blatant exploitation of consumers. Accordingly they attempted to prevent forestalling and regrating, that is the purchase of goods, especially grain and fish, before they entered the public market, so that middlemen could create scarcities and sell at a higher price. The assize of bread and ale was enforced everywhere, but was particularly contentious in towns where the volume of sales was much greater and a higher proportion of the population were dependent on the market for prepared food. This regulation fixed the weight of a penny, halfpenny or farthing loaf of bread on a sliding scale which depended on the price of grain; similarly the price of ale varied with the cost of barley. Although this restricted the free market in food, and allowed a fixed amount to the bakers and brewers for the cost of production and profit, the regulation respected the market price, as the key variable was the price of grain, which depended mainly on the quality of the harvest. The town governments seemed to believe that in an ideal world consumers of foodstuffs would buy direct from producers, without the intervention of middlemen, at a price fixed by supply and demand. In the real world corn dealers and other entrepreneurs sold much of the food, and a number of traders, such as the cooks, lived by buying food and selling it at a profit.

vi. *Towns in a feudal economy*

The special status of towns gave many of their inhabitants privileges. Burgesses and citizens had their own courts, and many were governed by local laws. Their involvement in the market set them apart from the traditional agrarian economy. Among them lived groups even more distant from the mainstream of society, such as the Jews, communities of foreign merchants, and the mendicant friars. Historians have understandably regarded medieval towns as an alien growth within a feudal society and agrarian economy. Indeed, the urban economy can be seen as the economy of the future, a modern, capitalist implant, and even a subversive force, spreading ideas about freedom, individualism and the participation by citizens in government.

This conception of the modernizing role of towns in medieval society is of limited value. Towns were fully integrated into the political and social structure. Kings certainly gave them special treatment, valuing them as sources of tax revenue and appreciating the expertise of merchants. At times of war, the towns were called on to make extra efforts, above all in their financial contribution, but also to provide practical assistance, such as the ships of the Cinque Ports which aided Edward I's campaigns in Wales. They recognized their political strength, especially that of the Londoners, who at a number of crucial moments gave support to the king's baronial critics. The towns were supposed to rule in the king's name, and if they were ineffective, for example in maintaining order, their governments were suspended and the king took over direct rule, as happened in London in 1285–98. When parliaments were developing in the late thirteenth century, representatives of the boroughs formed an important part of the commons, primarily because their consent was necessary for the acceptance of the taxes to which towns contributed such a large share.

Feudal lordship and urban life were also fully compatible. Lords of all kinds founded towns, promoted them and invested in urban property. They appreciated that towns added to their revenues directly from rents and tolls, but also had a beneficial indirect influence on the revenues from their rural estates. They and their tenants sold rural produce in urban markets, and lords enjoyed the good things that could be bought from merchants. The elite in seignorial towns co-operated with their lords' government by serving as officials. Leicester showed deference to its lords, the earls of Lancaster, by greeting them with gifts on their visits to the town: they obviously regarded them as patrons as well as overlords. Monastic lords were more likely than others to quarrel with their towns, but that reflected their conservatism as landlords, and the townsmen were not generally opposed to lordship on principle, or to organized religion. Indeed, the towns were the scenes of exceptional devotion, with their processions and well-attended sermons. Town dwellers gave a great deal of financial support to the religious institutions which were especially attuned to the towns' needs, such as parish churches, friaries, hospitals, and of course fraternities.

Both the countryside and the towns were dependent on money and trade. There were many parallels between the urban and rural worlds, in both of which the household served as the main unit of production. The values of the town dwellers were not markedly different from those found in landed society. The aristocracy provided role models; they set the style for dress, and heraldic devices were in widespread use in decorating metalwork, floor tiles and textiles. Towns were not democratic, as the rulers, like the London aldermen, emphasized hierarchical distinctions, and kept the majority of townspeople out of elections and municipal office. The political and social ideas found in towns tended to favour authority, by maintaining that decisions should be made by the 'greater and wiser part', that is, the wealthy minority who ran the larger towns. Even the urban rebels aimed at nothing more revolutionary than a share in the privileges enjoyed by those in power. The respectable merchants who led the agitations against the abbey of Bury St Edmunds suppressed a movement of hot-headed youths calling themselves the 'bachelors' in 1264, but these young people did not wish to overthrow the existing social order, merely to replace one guild with another. The peasants who in the thirteenth century were inspired by an imagined ideal past of universal freedom were expressing more radical ideas than those put forward by many rebellious townsmen.

The aristocracy looked down on mere traders, who did not appreciate the finer points of chivalry or courteous behaviour, and the church condemned the avarice of the urban rich. But the landholding elite knew that towns represented civilization and provided an appropriate setting for their castles and cathedrals. In Wales, new towns were part of the process of colonization, which brought a wild countryside and its unruly inhabitants into the mainstream of Christendom. The shape of the town mattered as well, as a regular plan projected a rational image, reflecting in its geometrical forms the symmetry of the divine order. The church's teaching on economic matters reflected the accommodation between Christian values and the urban way of life. Rather than the traditional belief in the sinfulness of personal wealth, which presented an obstacle to salvation, theologians showed that private property and moderate affluence, if accompanied by charitable giving, accorded with the law of nature. Trade and exchange were socially useful, providing they were not exploited for greedy and selfish ends. The just price at which goods should be sold was the market price. Workers should be rewarded for their efforts. Money was a useful means of exchanging and storing wealth, so long as its acquisition did not become an end in itself. Usury was a serious sin, because the lender profited from the passing of time, and time belonged to God. Lenders found legitimate ways of gaining interest, such as taking the income from a piece of land surrendered by the borrower as a gage, or seeking compensation for the damage caused by the temporary loss of the money.

A more numerous and affluent aristocracy, a peasantry involved in the market, and urbanization were all linked together, and developed simultaneously. The urban sector was not competing with 'feudal' society or undermining it, but formed part of the feudal order. The interactions of town and country developed their own momentum and the lords became less important players in the market economy, which they sought to manipulate, but could not control.

CHAPTER SEVEN

Crisis, c.1290–c.1350

Those who experience turning points in history are not always fully aware of the great movements around them. This is especially true of changes in economy and society, which tend to develop inexorably but gradually. An exception to this rule was the first half of the fourteenth century, which was punctuated by two sudden natural disasters: the Great Famine and agricultural crisis of 1315–22, and the epidemic of 1348–50, usually known as the Black Death. The famine affected the whole of northern Europe, and the plague spread over virtually the whole continent. These disruptions of economic and social life coincided with momentous political events, when two English kings, Edward I (1272–1307) and Edward III (1327–77) fought wars within Britain, in an attempt to subdue Scotland, and also against France, the year 1337 seeing the beginning of the Hundred Years War. Edward II (1307–27) faced a number of episodes of opposition from the aristocracy, and in the last of these he was deposed and killed. Scotland was disrupted by disputes over the succession to the throne and the wars with the English. This was also a troubled period in religious life, when the papacy left Rome and settled at Avignon. A general sense of unease throughout western Europe may have been expressed in the persecution of minorities. The notion of a 'general crisis' of the whole social and political structure may help us to see the developments in Britain on a broader canvas, but our first concern must be to establish when economic expansion came to an end, and in particular to identify the turning point – did it come after the Black Death, or in the decades before 1348?

i. Great Famine and Black Death

A first question must be to ask if the Great Famine was a really momentous event, or just a transient episode. It began with the poor harvest of

1314, succeeded by two years of wet weather and disastrous crops. The good harvest of 1317 did not bring the level of prices back to normal until 1318. Another bad year, especially in East Anglia, followed, in 1321–2. The deficient grain harvests coincided with disease among sheep, and an epidemic affecting cattle in 1319–21. The shortfall in cereal crops can be calculated very precisely from the yields recorded in manorial accounts. On the bishop of Winchester's manors in the southern counties, from Somerset to Surrey, wheat yields fell to 60 per cent of average in 1315, and 55 per cent in 1316. This meant that the bishop's officials were taking into their barns in the autumn about twice as much corn as they planted, not four times as much, as was normally the case. After they put to one side the seed for the next year, this left them with very little to spare for feeding animals and servants on the manor, or for supplying the lord's household, or for sale. The harvests on the estates of Bolton Priory in Yorkshire suffered more acutely, with rye crops on the land adjoining the monastery in 1315 and 1316 down to 28 per cent and 11.5 per cent of normal. The north generally suffered more severely than did the south. Parts of East Anglia, and Cornwall were spared the worst effects. The same problems of low returns affected peasant crops, reflected in the amount collected in tithe. A number of chroniclers reported that wheat prices reached a high point of 40s per quarter (instead of the normal 5s or 6s), and that they remained at 26s 8d per quarter for two and a half years. This was an exaggeration, but a quarter of wheat on average over the whole country cost a very high 16s during the two worst famine years, and a quarter of barley 10s to 11s instead of its usual price of 3s or 4s (Figure 1).

Cereals were not the only foodstuffs affected. The rain spoiled the supplies of peat and reduced salt production, and high salt prices affected the supply of butter, cheese, and preserved meat (such as bacon and salt beef). Hay production was also damaged by the weather, which in turn affected the health of animals. The only reductions in price were for oxen and cart-horses in 1316–17, but that was another symptom of crisis, because peasants were selling their draught animals to obtain cash to buy grain, and few people could afford to buy them. The peasants who reduced their ploughing capacity presumably suffered further hardships when the time came to prepare the land for the next year's planting. Their difficulties continued after the bad harvests when cattle died of disease in large numbers in 1319–21.

Everyone lost income as the famine cut into production. The large cultivators, the managers of the lords' demesnes which ran to hundreds of acres, could profit from poor harvests if they could sell their smaller surplus at a very high price. But a really bad harvest left some manors

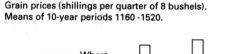

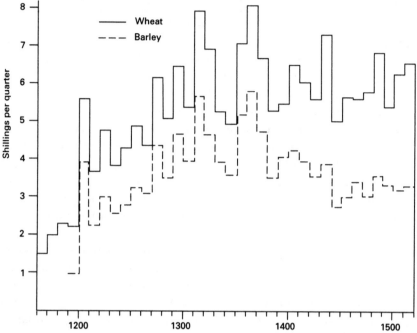

Figure 1. Grain prices in England, 1160–1520. Prices in shillings per quarter of 8 bushels. Means calculated in ten-year periods, for wheat and barley.

Source: *AgHEW*, vols 2, 3 and 4.

without much to sell, and so they made no money out of the shortages. Some smaller monasteries had to reduce their food consumption. The lords and their companions would not starve, but workers on the manor were sometimes deprived of their payments of corn, and lords, such as Bolton Priory, dismissed servants. The wage earners were doubly hard hit: grain prices were very high, and peasants as well as demesnes cut down on their employment of labour. Traders and artisans found that demand for their products fell as household budgets at all social levels were squeezed by the high price of food, which left little to spare for clothing, building or manufactured goods. Brewing and selling ale, one of the most widespread of commercial occupations, declined as malt shortages pushed up the price and most consumers saved their money to buy bread. In terms of a household budget, enough barley (a cheap grain) to feed a family for a year cost 60s, but a labourer would be lucky to gain in wages as much as 30s. The earnings of wives and children contributed something to family budgets, but even small-scale casual employment became hard to find.

The famine caused much social and economic stress. The chronicles exaggerated, or rather reached for the literary clichés which were commonly used to describe extreme hunger, when they reported that the poor ate dogs, cats, horsemeat and even human flesh. More objective evidence reveals less lurid but still significant symptoms of hardship, in that peasants were selling land in great quantities. In most years at Redgrave in Suffolk before 1315 no more than sixty-five transfers of land were made between one living tenant and another, but in 1316 there were 188 transfers, and in 1317, 135. Small amounts of land – less than an acre on average – were being sold on each occasion, and there were more sellers than buyers. Relatively poor peasants sold parcels of land to their richer neighbours. It could be simply said that the smallholders were selling land in order to buy food, and that the better-off peasants were able to take advantage of their poverty to acquire more land. A more complex sequence of transactions may lie behind the sales of land, suggested by the large number of debts that peasants were attempting to recover through the manorial courts. Many of those selling land had probably borrowed money or grain, and had been forced to surrender the land when they could not repay the loan.

On the Yorkshire manor of Wakefield the court records of the famine period are filled with references to the acquisition of new land by tenants through assarting. In a typical entry of July 1316, Richard, son of John Bete of Sowerby gave the lord 5s for permission to take an acre of new land, paying thereafter an annual rent of 6d. This wave of land clearance appears to show peasants expanding the size of their holdings in the hope that they could produce enough to feed their families at the next harvest. It reveals another dimension of the social stress arising from the famine, as the lord's officials, realizing the profits that could be made from the desperate plight of the peasants, charged high fines for the new land. They may even have been discovering a backlog of land clearances made over many years and were charging retrospective fines for them.

The records of manor courts and royal courts throughout England during the famine years contain the names of thousands of people accused of crimes, especially the theft of foodstuffs. Hungry people were turning to crime as the famine reduced their ability to make an honest living. Another factor may have been a shift in the attitudes of those in authority. As their incomes diminished, they felt threatened by the poor, reduced their charitable giving, and were not prepared to tolerate or condone misbehaviour by the lower orders. The famine strained the normal social bonds by which poverty was alleviated. For example, in April 1316 at Wakefield, John, son of Adam Bray, who had previously been accused of stealing 14s in cash, was said also to have taken a bushel of oats worth 12d from his father. The information about the new (petty) crime must have come from the father, who in normal years would surely have helped his son, or at least turned a blind eye to a member of his family 'borrowing' some grain.

The links within communities, as well as family ties, were tested at this difficult time. For example, the lord of Eldersfield in Worcestershire in 1316 heard sympathetically the complaint that the wealthier villagers, when they gathered money to pay collective fines imposed by the lord's court, insisted that those without land should contribute more than their fair share. Whether this was a new abuse provoked by the famine, or an old practice which attracted complaints only at this time of stress, is not known, but in either case relations between the upper and lower ranks of village society had deteriorated. Illegal gleaning posed a more widespread problem. In normal years village communities (according to by-laws which were approved and enforced by the manor courts) allowed the genuine poor to collect ears of corn left in the fields after the sheaves had been carried. The able-bodied were not permitted to glean, and care was taken that it did not serve as a front for sheaf-stealing. In the famine years complaints multiplied that the various rules governing gleaning were being broken, perhaps because the hungry poor were stretching the rules to the limit, and also reflecting the intolerance with which the better-off regarded their less fortunate neighbours.

Lords in general seem to have made some profit from the plight of their tenants, as the increased business in their courts and above all the fines paid on land transfers gave their revenues a temporary stimulus. Occasionally the difficulties of tenants were recognized, and they were let off payments, like the labour services at Ibstone in Buckinghamshire which Merton College did not demand 'on account of the poverty of the tenants'. The royal government reacted to the threat of famine in 1315 by making an ineffective attempt to regulate the prices of animals, and by collecting a lay subsidy in 1316 which it was thought the taxpayers could afford. More constructive efforts were made to encourage the carriage of grain from areas less severely affected, such as Cornwall.

A test of the severity of the famine must be the extent to which it led to an increase in mortality. A rising total of deaths can be observed in manorial court records of the tenants who died, the reduced numbers of males over twelve years old who were liable to pay an annual head penny, or the gaps in the lists of landless, unmarried wage earners, the *garciones*, found on the manors of the Glastonbury Abbey estate. From places in different regions come estimates of mortality of 10 per cent, 15 per cent, and in the case of the *garciones* of Longbridge Deverill in Wiltshire, 17–18 per cent. An unusually high death rate is not found everywhere – for example, Coltishall in Norfolk, in a region which escaped the full effects of the famine. Not all deaths in the famine years were caused directly by the food shortage, as there was also an epidemic of disease. This may have been typhus, which spread from those deprived of food to the more affluent: parish clergy and members of the gentry died, though not in the number found among peasants and wage earners.

The troubles of 1315–22 disrupted social and economic life, and were associated with severe mortality which affected much of Britain, together with a large section of northern continental Europe. Analysis of tree rings shows that unusual climatic conditions prevailed beyond Europe, which suggests that the events recorded here formed part of some major natural disaster. For England this was the worst famine in recorded history.

The impact of the Black Death of 1348–9 will be discussed in more detail below (pp. 271–81). It caused much higher mortality than the Great Famine. Peasants died in very large numbers, varying from 40 per cent to 70 per cent of the observed population, and it would be reasonable to estimate the death rate in 1348–9 at about half of the English population. Its effects were universal, and no village, town or region for which records exist escaped. If the total population stood at about 5 or 6 million, there were 2½ or 3 million casualties. As we will see, lesser but repeated later epidemics, and underlying shifts in fertility, reduced the population for the next two centuries, so there was no sustained recovery from the Black Death.

We are faced with the evidence of an almost unimaginable catastrophe. The Black Death on a global scale exceeded in mortality any other known disaster. By the standard of the events of 1348–9, the deaths in 1914–19 from war and the Spanish influenza, in relation to the total population affected and in long-term consequences, seem of lesser significance. The case for regarding the Black Death as a momentous episode seems stronger than can be advanced for the Great Famine. By the rather macabre yardstick of the number of corpses, the famine was responsible in England for no more than a half-million dead, a mere fifth or sixth of those who died in the plague. Yet in identifying turning points, we ought to search in the decades before 1348. The famine may not in itself have been the key factor, but the Black Death's role seems to have been to confirm, deepen and emphasize tendencies which had begun earlier. The expansion that had been such a pronounced feature of the thirteenth century came to an end in the first two decades of the fourteenth century, and contrary tendencies of contraction in important areas of the economy had at least begun in the period 1320–48.

We cannot appeal to contemporaries' comments to confirm this view, so the argument must be based on the information gathered together from year to year in administrative documents, and the unspoken testimony of the physical remains.

If the Black Death had been a turning point for the population of England, we would expect to find that the population growth of the thirteenth century, after an interruption in 1315–17, continued up to 1348. In some cases this seems to have happened. At Halesowen in Worcestershire, for example, the number of males mentioned in the manorial courts stood at 331 in the five-year period between 1271 and 1275, and increased to 485 by 1311–15; after falling mainly because of the famine to 412 in the early 1320s, the total climbed back to 470 by the late 1340s. After the famine at Halesowen much land came into the hands of young people who were able to marry and produce children, and these children in turn were of marriageable age and adding another generation in the 1340s. At Coltishall in Norfolk the number of tenants increased from 141 in 1314 to 198 on the eve of the Black Death, without mortality in the famine. But these places experiencing growth are outnumbered by the examples of falling population after the famine, notably in Essex, where the total of males aged over twelve fell, at Chatham Hall, from seventy in 1320 to fifty-five in 1346, while at the much larger manor of Great Waltham, the peak of 320 in 1306 was reduced by the famine to 254 in 1319, and then was further eroded to only 200 in 1340. On the Northamptonshire manor of Brigstock the number of adult males resident in the manor can be estimated at about 500 before the famine, and was reduced to about 400 on the eve of the Black Death. A similar tendency to decline after the famine can be observed among the *garciones* of Longbridge Deverill in Wiltshire.

Harvest failures and epidemics both before and after the Great Famine help to explain the population decline. The severity of an episode can be judged by the rising cost of grain, in which prices which were 25 per cent above the average can be regarded as a significant threshold, or by low yields, especially those 15 per cent or more below the average, or by signs of social stress such as an increase in mortality, a peak in the sale of land by peasants, or an increase in illegal gleaning cases. These hard times affected different regions unequally, reflecting the variety in the climate, soils and local economy. Bad harvest years were concentrated between 1293 and 1296, followed by an episode of high prices and a rising death rate in 1310–11, and after the famine, in 1321–2, 1322–3 and 1331–2.

There were also epidemics when the death rate increased in years when the harvest was not especially deficient, in 1304 for example. Sometimes an abnormal number of deaths is found in a particular locality, such as Downham in Cambridgeshire in 1327–8. In east Sussex there were fourteen deaths among the townspeople of Battle in the late autumn of 1331, and six tenants of Beddingham died in the same year. The numbers seem small because it is only the deaths of tenants that were recorded – for every adult landholder who died, there could have been four deaths among relatives and dependants, as young people, women and the elderly are consistently under-represented in the documents. We should not assume that they were the only factor behind the fall in population, as changes in the birth rate are likely to have played their part. We have noted that the famine could have stimulated long-term population growth by giving young people the opportunity to acquire land, and to marry, at an early age, but it would be over-optimistic to think that every mortality peak was followed by a compensatory baby boom – the troubled times of frequent harvest crises and epidemics cannot have created the confidence and optimism to encourage early and universal marriage.

In the light of the successive short-term food shortages and bouts of mortality, the episode of famine and disease of 1315–22 appears to form part of a pattern, and a longer period, beginning in the mid-1290s, can be identified as bringing to an end in most regions the thirteenth-century growth in population (Figure 2).

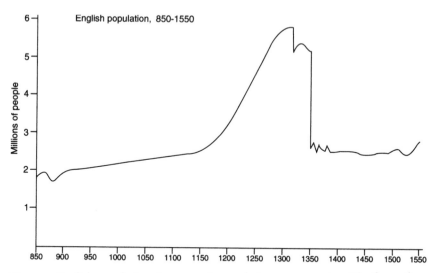

Figure 2. English population, 850–1550. A speculative reconstruction. The figures from 850 to 1086 are pure speculation. The subsequent figures are based on Domesday (1086), the Poll Tax (1377), the subsidies (1524–5) and the military survey (1522), and by extrapolation from manorial records of tenant deaths and payments of headpennies and common fines.

Sources: J. Hatcher, *Plague, Population and the English Economy, 1348–1530* (1977); R. M. Smith, 'Human Resources', in G. Astill and A. Grant (eds), *The Countryside of Medieval England* (Oxford, 1988); E. A. Wrigley and R. S. Schofield, *The Population History of England, 1547–1871: a Reconstruction* (London, 1981).

ii. *Contraction and change*

Both peasants and lords were reducing the scale of their farming operations in the early fourteenth century. There had been earlier threats to
agriculture, such as the outbreak of sheep scab in the 1270s and 1280s,
but significant reductions in the area under cultivation came after 1300.
The heroic phases of large-scale reclamation in the fens and marshes
were over. Small-scale drainage projects continued after 1300, such as
those in the Isle of Axholme in Lincolnshire. In the 1330s and 1340s
throughout the country thousands of acres were lost to agriculture from
flooding. Such episodes as the tidal surge in the Wash in 1338 played their
part, but this was a long-term deterioration in the whole system of water
management, not just a series of accidents. The extension of cultivated
land by the clearance of woodland and scrub, and by breaking up
pasture, had accounted for a large proportion of the new land of the
twelfth and thirteenth centuries, and again in some regions this assarting had come to an end by 1300. Clearances can still be found in the early
fourteenth century, like the inroads into the Weald in the south-east as
late as the 1330s and 1340s. But these assarts were not raising the global
total of cultivated land, as at the same time a large area was falling out
of cultivation. The reports of uncultivated or 'frisc' arable, of holdings
lying unoccupied, and of houses abandoned by their inhabitants come
from all parts of the country in the 1320s. To take an example from the
borders of eastern Staffordshire and western Derbyshire, a wooded area
which included Needwood Chase and Duffield Frith, the officials who
were managing the estates of the earls of Lancaster, after Earl Thomas
was executed for treason in 1322, reported that 6,000 acres of land were
vacant, and 167 houses and cottages unoccupied. They explained this
sorry situation, which reduced the rent income from these manors, partly
as the result of recent events, such as the political upheaval and the cattle
plague. They also mentioned as long-term problems the poverty of the
tenants and the poor quality of the land. The importance of these more
structural problems is suggested by three phases of decay in rent income
of which they gave details, which stretched back to before the famine.
This is confirmed by documents produced for the earl nine years previously which mention falling rents and abandoned land.

　　The tax assessors in 1340–1 listened to complaints which showed that
parts of England were experiencing widespread decline in cultivation.
The parliament of 1340, in order to provide money for Edward III's
French wars from an already tax-weary country, experimented with a
grant of the ninth lamb, fleece and sheaf of corn, in effect an extra tithe

of agricultural produce after the church had taken its normal share of a tenth. The grant met with much opposition, and the reasons given for non-payment (recorded in the 'Inquisitions of the Ninth') might be dismissed as the usual excuses of reluctant taxpayers. We would expect to find that taxes were disliked in equal measure over the whole country, but the grumbles are found in particular places, and mentioned appropriate local problems. For example, in coastal parishes in Sussex they blamed flooding for the loss of productive land. In inland counties they complained of sterile and infertile soil and sheep disease, all of which caused land to fall out of cultivation, the inhabitants to become poor and on occasion to leave their homes, even to go off to beg. More than half of the villages in Buckinghamshire were said to have suffered shrinkage in arable land. In that county, and in Bedfordshire, Cambridgeshire, Gloucestershire and Oxfordshire, the villages that were affected were in the main corn-growing belt of the midlands, not precarious upland settlements which might have been vulnerable to changes in climate. There were reports of poverty and declining cultivation also on higher ground, in Shropshire and north Yorkshire. It therefore appears that the abandonment of land was widespread, both on the sandy soils of Bedfordshire and on the clays of Buckinghamshire, land that had been cultivated for many centuries, and on recent assarts. (Plate 12)

Perhaps the complaints of 1340–1 were a temporary episode, after which cultivation resumed and the villagers returned and prospered? When individual cases are examined in detail, it can be shown that the assessors of 1340–1 were reporting events which belonged in a sequence of long-term changes with permanent results. For example, when they came to Aston Blank in the Gloucestershire Cotswolds they found that the full amount of tax could not be paid because seven families from the hamlet of Little Aston had given up their holdings and left the parish. As Little Aston contained fewer than a dozen households, this meant that it had lost most of its population, and indeed soon afterwards it ceased to exist. The landlord, a small nunnery, lost all revenues from the place for a time, and eventually received 40s per annum from Little Aston instead of its normal income of 66s 8d. The arable fields belonging to the hamlet were turned into pasture, and were not cultivated again for centuries. The remains of peasant houses can still be seen on the site of Little Aston, and deserted farms and hamlets are also found on much more exposed and difficult soil on Dartmoor. One of them, Hound Tor, had developed in the thirteenth century, when new settlers ploughed up some of the moor and kept livestock on the rough pasture, but in the early fourteenth century the inhabitants retreated down into the valley. A similar upland site at Cefn Graeanog in north Wales was probably abandoned at this time, and a settlement on the south Wales coast at Rhossili was covered with blown sand, though it was probably abandoned because of agricultural problems before the sand took over.

The compilers of estate surveys in the early fourteenth century described the deficiencies of the land that they were valuing in the same language used by the enquiries of the tax assessors in 1340–1. They said that the soil was stony or sandy, or simply poor or infertile. The fields did not acquire these characteristics suddenly, so these criticisms must have come to the minds of officials because they were conscious that land was not giving sufficiently abundant or consistent crops, and needed to justify valuations as low as 2d per acre. The concern about soil fertility is difficult to verify. Although the accounts kept by manorial officials contain many thousands of figures from which yields can be calculated, they vary so much from year to year that long-term trends cannot be easily identified. On the estate of the bishopric of Winchester over the period 1209–70 the average bushel of barley that was sown produced 4.32 bushels of grain at the harvest, after the tithe had been deducted. This ratio declined to 3.36 in 1270–99. This downward movement was not continued; in the early fourteenth century the ratios increased slightly, to 3.57 in 1300–24, and 3.74 in 1325–49, though still remaining well below the pre-1270 figure. Yields may not have recovered after 1300, however, because the amount of land cultivated by the bishopric was reduced, as the lord leased parcels of demesne land to local tenants. The estate officials, it has been suggested, probably selected inferior plots of land to be rented out, in order to concentrate the lord's crops on the better soils, hence the apparent recovery in yields. Had the information on the missing acres been available, the yields would have remained at a low level or even deteriorated. At Cuxham in Oxfordshire, where the area of demesne was reduced only slightly, an underlying downward movement in productivity can be detected between 1298 and 1348, which did not affect barley and oats, but which reduced yields of wheat per acre by about 18 per cent. This has been explained as a result of the gradual loss from the soil of the essential mineral phosphorus, caused by the annual removal of crops without an adequate return of nutrients to the soil.

Information about yields derives from demesnes, which covered perhaps a quarter of the cultivated land, and the crucial question is whether the peasant cultivators, who managed most of the land in the country, experienced similar changes in the productivity of their crops. Occasionally a lord's officials harvested a tenant's grain, when he died or left the holding. The crops on tenant holdings at Bourton-on-the-Hill (Gloucestershire) which were harvested after the plague in the autumn of 1349 suggest peasant yields of less than 8 bushels per acre, well below demesne production, but this was a year of unusually bad weather as well as plague. It can be argued that each acre of peasant land would produce less than an acre of demesne, because it was likely to receive smaller amounts of manure, and peasants would have inferior equipment, buildings and draught animals. Lords had greater control of their land, and were not always bound to follow the routines of common field farming. Peasants would be taken away from vital seasonal tasks such as harvest by labour service.

There were some advantages for the peasant in compensation: the labour force, consisting largely of the peasant family, was committed and hard-working, in contrast to the unenthusiastic spirit in which labour services were performed (see p. 134). Peasants could afford the time to carry out those jobs requiring close attention to detail, such as weeding. Demesne managers, conscious of labour costs, were tempted to reduce the amount of time spent on such tasks. Estates may have been managed by men who had read the books which gave farming advice, such as *Walter of Henley*, and the reeves and bailiffs who ran the manors knew that the auditors would make them pay for any errors. But peasants had the advantage of the accumulated wisdom of many generations, and intimate knowledge of their holdings. Above all they knew that their well-being and even survival depended on their decisions. The advantages and disadvantages of peasant cultivation probably cancel each other out, with the result that their yields were rather similar to those of the demesnes. They probably followed the same tendency to stagnate or even decline in the first half of the fourteenth century, as suggested by the many reports of poor tenant land and abandoned holdings.

Total cereal production declined in the period 1300–48. The acreage under the plough diminished, and the productivity of the land that remained under crops stagnated or fell. The prices of grain were declining in the long term: wheat was sold on average for 5s–6s per quarter in the period 1270–1310, but had dipped to about 5s in the 1330s and 1340s. The change in the same period took barley prices from 3s 6d–4s 8d in 1270–1310, to 3s 6d–3s 11d in 1330–47 (see Figure 1 above, p. 230). There are many ways of explaining that downward tendency, one of them being an improvement in the weather. An underlying influence could have been the reduced number of consumers. That this was a factor is supported by the apparent rise in wages at the same time. A carpenter's daily wage before the famine (1280–1310) moved around 2½d to 2¾d, but between 1320 and 1347 the average wage rose just above 3d (Figure 3).

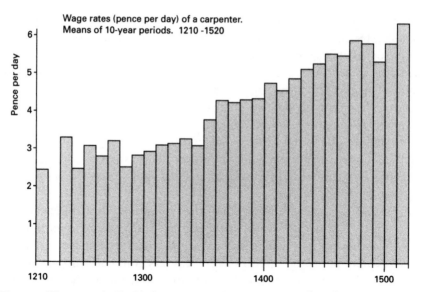

Figure 3. Wage rates in England, 1210–1520. Wages, pence per day, of a carpenter.
Means calculated in ten-year periods.

Sources: AgHEW, vols 2 and 3; J. E. Thorold Rogers, *A History of Agriculture and Prices in England*, vol. 3 (Oxford, 7 vols, 1866–1902).

The increase in cash wages was slight – less than a halfpenny per day – but when combined with the reduced cost of grain, the purchasing power of a skilled worker's wage rose by about 15 per cent. Real wages can be measured directly, confirming that the rising wage was not just a statistical illusion. When estate officials in Norfolk and other counties gave food as part of the wages of harvest workers in the late thirteenth century, bread, often baked from cheaper grains such as barley, bulked large in the diet. For each pound of bread, the workers received only a half-ounce of meat, which was often bacon. In the early fourteenth century a higher proportion of the bread was baked from wheat or rye, more ale was allowed, and the amount of meat increased. More fresh meat was included in the meals. The most likely explanation of the tendency for rewards to workers (both skilled and unskilled) to rise must be that a decline in population, combined perhaps with the broadening opportunities for employment created by industrial expansion, was making labour a little more scarce.

These were harder times for some lords and for those who managed their estates. The era of 'high farming' was coming to an end. The policy of maximizing demesne production, with land purchases, reclamation, marling, new building and other improvements, often gave way to dif-

ferent strategies, especially after the famine. Since the late thirteenth
century some estates had been making calculations of the 'profit of the
manor'. They must have become aware that the prices of grain (and also
those of wool and livestock after the diseases of the 1320s), were in
decline, and labour costs were beginning to rise. The estate officials introduced further accounting devices to allow them to monitor grain yields,
and to recover some money if poor performance could be blamed on the
mismanagement of the reeve. These involved setting targets for yields –
it would be stated that wheat should have returned four times the seed
planted, and the reeve would be required to pay the difference if the crop
fell below that level. Sometimes the auditors' target became a quota,
and the reeve who was required to produce 300 eggs would then return
that figure each year, selling any surplus for his own profit. When they
adopted this method of securing a minimum fixed income, the estate
managers were starting on the road to leasing their assets.

Lords, no longer believing that profits would increase, were beginning
to focus on reducing their losses. The next stage was to rent out an
acreage of the demesne to peasants, who were anxious to acquire parcels
of land and would pay good rents. Lords were strongly attached to direct
management of their demesnes, and in East Anglia they often kept them
intact and under cultivation throughout the early fourteenth century. In
the midlands and the south, estates such as those of Westminster Abbey,
the bishoprics of London and Worcester, or the lay lords of the Welsh
marches, in addition to renting out piecemeal parts of demesnes, also
leased out the whole demesne of a few manors. These were often selected
because they were small, or detached from the main estate. In the south-
west and north-west directly managed demesnes were scarce even in the
late thirteenth century, and leasing of demesnes was far advanced by
1320.

As lords began to doubt the value of land, they stopped buying it as
an investment. Some, like Quarr Abbey on the Isle of Wight, acquired
little after 1300, and others went on into the 1320s and 1330s, such as
the Lincolnshire abbeys of Crowland and Thorney, which had bought a
great deal in the thirteenth century. Church estates had been restrained
in buying lay land by the Statute of Mortmain in 1279, but they could
still acquire land legally if they bought a licence from the king. Church
estates ceased to grow mainly as a result of economic calculations
rather than legal restrictions. Lay magnates who bought a great deal of
property, such as the Beauchamps, earls of Warwick, also acquired less
in the early fourteenth century. Some lords continued to buy urban property, suggesting that it was agricultural land in particular that was seen
as unprofitable.

The scaling down of demesne production changed the relationship between lords and peasants. A movement from labour service towards rent is found in all parts of the country, on the scattered manors of the Abbey of Bec, the estates of the monks of Westminster, which were mainly near London, and the lands of Ramsey Abbey in the east. A different story is found in Kent, where labour services were limited in number, and those few were demanded by such lords as Canterbury Cathedral Priory.

In general, peasants in *c.*1320 were paying more cash to lords than ever before: they owed leasehold rents for parcels of demesne and cash payments in lieu of labour service, as well as the usual assize rents, entry fines and other dues. Lords attempted to make as much as they could from tenants, especially as their demesnes seemed less profitable. The variable payments such as entry fines and marriage fines which were negotiated by individuals offered the best chance of profit, and they are also helpful to us in understanding the rise and fall in demand for land. They rose on the Ramsey Abbey estate until the monks' officials could collect 66s 8d for a yardland, and 40s for a half-yardland in the 1310s – though the fines were lower in the 1320s. Thanks to the long series of documents compiled for the bishops of Winchester, the successive fines paid for individual holdings can be traced over long periods. A yardland at Bishop's Waltham was acquired in 1227 for 20s, and when it changed hands in 1328 cost 80s, but then fell back to 40s in 1331 and 20s when it was sold again in 1333, 1338 and 1341. This suggests that the would-be tenants of this holding were making a pessimistic calculation of the profits of land after 1330, and were unwilling to pay the higher sum which was no doubt sought by the bishop's officials. A similar insight into changes in the market for land comes from Cornwall, where the estate of the earl of Cornwall adopted conventionary tenancies in 1333. This was a form of leasehold by which tenants paid a fine for a seven-year term, after which the whole tenancy was renegotiated. The first payment of these 'assessionable' rents in 1333 yielded a large increase in revenue, which was partly the result of the introduction of the new system, but partly an indication of the high demand for land. There was, however, no increase in the 1340s, suggesting a levelling in the demand for land as tenants recognized the limits on their profits.

The peasants were not entirely gloomy about their circumstances, however, judging from the continued liveliness of the land market. Lords could lease out parts of their demesnes profitably because peasants were anxious to acquire extra acres. The decline in cultivation did not leave land derelict, but gave the peasants the chance to acquire more animals:

individual flocks of a hundred sheep were reported in a number of midland and southern manors.

The aristocracy had problems in managing their expenditure as well as their incomes. They began to experience the 'price scissors', as the price of the goods which they sold, such as grain and wool, tended to fall after about 1320, while their cost of living began to edge upwards. We have seen that wages were rising slightly, making building in particular more expensive. Wine from Gascony, a major item of household expenditure for the magnates, was sold commonly for 3d or 4d per gallon at the turn of the century, but by the 1330s and 1340s the price had risen to 4d and 5d. Lords were concerned to control their spending, and household accounts were compiled with more care and sophistication. From about 1310 the more complex accounts included in their calculations not just the money spent each day, but also valuations of the goods used from stock. An unusual budget compiled in 1346 for Thomas III, Lord Berkeley, summarized the expenditure for a year (which probably took up too high a proportion of his income) and noted various savings which had been made by substituting cheaper meat and malt. Monasteries, especially smaller and poorer establishments, were prone to overspending and indebtedness, and reports of monastic debt are concentrated in the period 1329–48.

Towns, trade and industry were naturally caught up in the crisis as they were so closely integrated into the rural economy. Commercial life had its own dynamic forces leading both to decline and new growth. The foundation of new towns had already begun to slow before 1300, and it virtually ceased in the first half of the fourteenth century. New markets and boroughs were still founded, but in reduced number, and with diminishing chances of success. New Eagle in Lincolnshire is an example of the fate of optimistic hopes in an unfavourable economic climate. Its founders, the Knights Hospitallers, obtained a charter in 1345 which justified the creation of a new town because of the lack of stopping places for travellers on the Fosse Way between Newark and Lincoln. The charter authorized the building of a chapel, the planning of plots for houses, and the holding of a market and fairs. The site is now marked by a single inn and empty fields, and there is no evidence that anyone ever settled in the new town. The economy of older and larger urban centres was evidently slowing down. Rents were reduced in the centre of London, and in its suburbs of Southwark (after 1320) and Westminster (in 1317–41). Falling rents are also found in the provinces, at Oxford for example. At York, which enjoyed some economic advantages in the early fourteenth century, new rows of houses were being put up in the 1330s, but new building slowed in some towns, and some old properties decayed. There are hints of a scaling down of food and drink production at Colchester, where one of the eight mills went out of use after 1311, and the number of ale wives was reduced. There were some disasters, as towns as well as arable fields were subject to flooding and the inroads of the sea. Dunwich on the Suffolk coast lost 209 houses, a quarter of the town, between 1278 and 1326. But in general the signs of urban decay before the Black Death were on a modest scale.

Underlying the waning fortunes of many towns were reduced levels of trade and industrial production. Wine imports probably reached their highest point in the whole medieval period in 1308. Wool exports peaked, at 46,382 sacks, in 1304–5, and remained at between 20,000 and 30,000 sacks in 1315–30 (see Figure 4). The mining of tin in Cornwall had been in the doldrums in the first decade of the fourteenth century, but then increased to a remarkable total of more than 1.6 million pounds of metal in 1332, followed by a decline which became a serious slump after the plague. Major building projects on cathedrals and large monasteries seem to have reached their highest level of activity in the 1270s, and had entered into pronounced decline by 1320. Each product had its own momentum, and its own special reasons for expansion and contraction. All goods which crossed the English Channel in time of war were subject to embargoes, piracy or new taxes. But there were also underlying long-term economic rather than political influences, such as aristocratic need to check spending which damaged the wine trade.

Clothmaking was an important English activity in the late twelfth and thirteenth centuries. Weavers, fullers, dyers and other specialist artisans

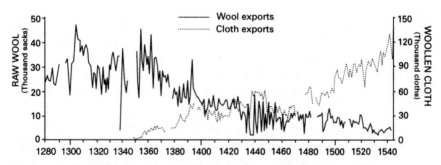

Figure 4. English exports of wool and cloth, 1279–1544 (cloth exports are only consistently recorded from the mid-fourteenth century).

Sources: E. M. Carus-Wilson and O. Coleman, *England's Export Trade 1275–1547* (Oxford, 1963); E. M. Carus-Wilson, *Medieval Merchant Venturers* (1954).

are found in many towns, notably in the larger towns of eastern and central England. Their products, such as 'stanforts' (probably referring to a distinctive weave rather than the town of Stamford), 'haberget' (made at Stamford among other towns), and Lincoln scarlets were well known on the continent. The English made light, quite cheap cloth which sold well in the Mediterranean world. A list of cloths compiled in Portugal in 1253 mentions 'Northamptons'. Between about 1290 and 1320 various complaints are heard that the numbers of weavers and looms in such major centres of the industry as Leicester and Oxford had declined drastically, and continental documents make no mention of English cloth.

Town-based clothmaking may have collapsed because the guilds and urban governments were too restrictive, and the high costs of urban life, such as taxation, pushed up the price of English cloth. Part of the industry relocated in the country, and a large share of the cloth market, it is said, was seized by the Flemish who outdid their English rivals in both quality and price. This cannot be entirely accepted, because the number of cloths from Flanders, Brabant and other parts of northern France and the Low Countries imported each year in the early fourteenth century amounted to 10,000–11,000, but many of these were quite expensive, and were clearly aimed at the wealthier consumer. To replace their worn-out clothing, each year the English needed at least 200,000 cloths (each measuring about 25 yards in length). The Flemish industry was going through its own troubles, and was not in a position to supply the English market with more than a fraction of its requirements. The bulk of England's cloth must have been supplied internally, and its manufacture continued in places such as Winchester and York and was growing in towns like Colchester and in the countryside. The worsted industry in Norfolk, based in villages and small towns, notably at Worsted and Aylsham, expanded at this time. Native cloths, both cheap and more costly, gradually and almost imperceptibly took over the domestic market, helped by the taxation of wool exports which made English wool much more expensive for the clothmakers across the sea. By 1347–8, 4,000 cloths were being exported, and the industry was entering a new phase of growth as English cloth became an article of international commerce. The industry had gone through severe problems, but had emerged even before the Black Death in a healthier state.

Lords, peasants and townspeople were caught up in the complex and inconsistent movements in the economy of the early fourteenth century. In parts of East Anglia the upheaval was not so pronounced, but generally the trends, not merely of a few decades but of the previous two or three centuries, were checked, and went into reverse. A similar pattern of events is found over much of continental Europe. There was indeed a crisis of the fourteenth century, which had profound effects before the Black Death.

iii. *Historical debate*

Such a remarkable change in direction demands an explanation which takes into account the long-term as well as the immediate symptoms of crisis. An ambitious model was created by M. M. Postan, and received support from the continental historians W. Abel and E. Le Roy Ladurie. Postan's interpretation emphasized the changes in population as the main dynamic force in the economy, and the impact of expanding agriculture on the ecology of the countryside. He saw all of the changes as inter-connected, and all flowed from the great expansion, which had to stop because it was unsustainable. The premise of Postan's thinking was that in a peasant society the balance between the cultivators and the land pro-vided the crucial variable factor. At the level of the individual and the family, he saw landholding as being adjusted to suit the needs of larger and smaller households. As a young family grew, its food needs and labour capacity were satisfied by transfers of parcels from the holdings of the elderly or disabled. This was a 'natural' land market, with the sub-sistence requirements of each household being met by the exchange of land between neighbours. In the same way, whole populations depended on land for their living, and any movement in population would have an impact on the use of land. In England, by 1200 the population was quite high and the land extensively cultivated. Yet the numbers of people more than doubled in the following century. At Taunton, where each male over twelve years old paid a penny to the lord of the manor, the numbers rose from 506 in 1209 to 1,359 in 1311. Almost every local calculation based on the recorded tenants or taxpayers reports different rates of growth, but the same upward trend.

As more people crowded on to the limited areas of cultivated land, holdings fragmented, leading to the proliferation of cottagers and tenants living on small parcels. Postan put together a collection of estate surveys, mostly of the thirteenth century, from different parts of the country, and found that 45 per cent of tenants had a quarter-yardland of about 8 acres, or smaller amounts of land. This substantial minority of smallholders could not feed their families from their land alone, and sup-plemented their crops with earnings, at inadequate rates of pay which reflected the abundance of labour. The demand for land increased in the late thirteenth century, and the lords could sometimes demand very high entry fines for their holdings – as much as £40 for a yardland on church estates in Somerset. Rising land values and high corn prices encouraged the extension of cultivation at the expense of woodland and grazing land, which created imbalances between arable and livestock husbandry. The high rents paid for pasture and especially meadow indicated the shortage of land for feeding animals. Peasants did not own enough animals to keep the land well manured. For example, the tax records of a group of Wiltshire manors from the year 1225 show that a countryside ideally suited to sheep farming suffered from a shortage of sheep. The total number of peasant animals, according to tithe records, was diminishing in the late thirteenth and early fourteenth centuries.

These imbalances helped Postan to explain why grain yields, such as those on the estates of the bishopric of Winchester (see p. 238), were so low, and were becoming even lower in the course of the thirteenth century. The 'metabolism of the field system' had been disrupted by the misuse of land. The cleared woodland and ploughed-up grassland did not benefit the cultivators in the long term, because the land was often of poor quality and had been left unploughed by previous generations of farmers for good reason. Comparison of the yields of crops on 'colonizing' manors with those from old cultivated manors shows that the recently assarted marginal lands gave poor returns. Eventually these newly won lands were given up: there was a 'retreat from marginal land'.

As growing populations were trapped on their limited holdings of land which produced ever smaller quantities of crops, Postan considered their inability to make technical changes, such as those introduced in the eighteenth century. He concluded that peasants were too poor to innovate, partly because of their subordination to lords, and because the lords themselves were too preoccupied with impractical learning and with expenditure on display. The lords were unwilling to invest capital in their manors. The population was, in the view of Postan and his supporter Titow, poised on a knife edge of subsistence. Every time a deficient harvest pushed up the price of grain, peasants died in unusual numbers, as is reflected in the extra heriots recorded in the accounts of the bishopric of Winchester. The famine period was merely the worst among many years of high mortality. The expectation of life among peasants declined from an already low level. In the late thirteenth century, at the age of twenty a peasant could expect to live for another twenty-four years; in the early fourteenth the figure sank to twenty years. In short, according to this account of events, the fourteenth-century crisis was man-made. Too many people produced too many children in the thirteenth century, the population outstripped resources, and the land could no longer feed everyone. Death and economic contraction followed as night follows day.

This coherent theory, made plausible by supporting evidence, has been a valuable stimulus to thought about the period, and alternative inter-pretations of it have been developed. These lead us to question both Postan's underlying assumptions, and the evidence that underpins them. If we begin with the growth in population, this was thought by Postan to be the normal pattern in a peasant society, especially in the absence of epidemic disease or serious famine. As we have seen, from an early date there was an inbuilt restraint against rapid population growth, in peasants' acceptance that marriage should be based on the possession of land. These restrictions were modified by the land market and the growth in non-agricultural employment. An increased rate of marriage, perhaps with a reduction in the number of celibates, a lower age for marriage, as more young people were able to acquire a cottage or parcel of land, and a subsequent rise in the number and frequency of births all helped to promote population growth. Children had a better chance of survival as the quality of houses improved, and as food became relatively plentiful in the middle decades of the thirteenth century. Population growth was a product of economic change, not an independent factor which caused other developments.

Nor should the population increase be seen mainly in a negative light. People were assets: they could make a positive contribution to their own well-being and that of society as a whole. We have noticed, for example, the small landholdings and high density of population in north-east Norfolk, which led not to immediate mass starvation, but to the careful and thorough application of labour to the land, from which came higher productivity. Smallholdings had been numerous long before the popula-tion growth of the thirteenth century – Postan's calculation of the high proportion of those without adequate quantities of land included figures from surveys of the Shaftesbury Abbey and St Paul's estates of the late twelfth and early thirteenth centuries in which smallholders accounted respectively for 33 per cent and 48 per cent of tenants. This substantial minority of wage earners and craft workers provided a flexible labour force that was essential for lords' demesnes, larger peasant holdings, and industrial workshops. They were often a disadvantaged group with meagre earnings, but the economy would not have functioned without them. They were not a miserable underclass acting as a drag on the rest of society. To be specific, they brought in much of the harvest, as both demesnes and larger peasant holdings lacked a permanent labour force capable of handling the intense work pressures of August and Septem-ber. They also gathered the fuel necessary for domestic and industrial use: wood-cutting, charcoal-burning, peat-digging and coal-mining were largely carried out by the smallholders.

The intense demand for land was a significant feature of the thirteenth-century economy. The very high entry fines found in Somerset were rare elsewhere, but many lords charged as much as £3 for a yardland. Tenants were willing to offer a great deal of money to acquire scarce and valuable land, but they must have made the realistic calculation that the returns from cultivation would enable them to pay back the moneylenders. The lenders must also have judged that the cash they advanced could be repaid. Entry fines give us evidence for the squeezing of the resources of peasants by lords and moneylenders. But in the scale of fines we can also find some positive signals about the state of the peasant economy.

Postan was aware of the dangers of formulating reliable statistics about village livestock on the basis of tax records from which so many peasants were omitted, and which were subject to a great deal of evasion and manipulation. Although the figures are questionable, no one would argue that peasants in general had an abundance of animals, because many fragmentary sources, such as heriot payments, lists of animals straying on to lords' demesnes or feeding in royal forests, and lists of stock seized by lords from rebellious or absconding tenants, support the general proposition that peasant holdings were under-stocked in lowland England. The balance between arable and pasture was an ever-present problem, going back to the origins of the open-field village. Peasants had limited access to fodder, both from grassland and from crops such as beans and vetch, because they had to give priority to producing crops for human consumption. But were they trapped in a deepening spiral of expanding arable, manure shortages and lower productivity? The existence of some open-field villages with much the same population and cultivated area between 1086 and c.1300 suggests that the inhabitants had found some sustainable agricultural system with limited amounts of pasture, which did not lead to disaster over many generations – though such villages often encountered difficulties in the fourteenth century.

The 'retreat from marginal land' can certainly be observed in the abandonment of hamlets and farmsteads on Dartmoor and Snowdonia. But its importance was exaggerated by Postan. Much of the land that fell out of cultivation in the early fourteenth century lay in good corn-growing districts such as mid-Buckinghamshire, which suffered from no major physical disadvantage apart from the heavy soils which were by no means confined to that county. In districts with more severe limitations on cereal crops, such as those on high ground, or which were densely wooded, or surrounded by marshes and fens, peasants had devised means of balancing resources, cultivating a limited area and taking advantage of the pasture, wood, turf, reeds or fish to supplement their income from cultivation. In the Breckland on the borders of Norfolk and Suffolk, for example, the sandy soils were cultivated occasionally, not continuously. Much use was made of the extensive heathy pastures, and of the nearby fens. The concept of 'marginal' land varies greatly with such human factors as the level of rent and proximity to markets. A moorland field was worth cultivating for its meagre crop of oats if the rent had been set, as was often the case, at 2d per acre. Poor land could be profitably cultivated as a garden, provided that it lay near to a large town where fruit and vegetables were in demand.

The methods of making productive use of different soils and landscapes were just part of the range of technologies applied to agriculture at this time. This was a period of innovations, such as the extended use of horses as draught animals and the planting of legumes (see pp. 166–7). Peasants lacked capital, and their lives were insecure, so they were limited in the techniques that they could use. But they should not be regarded as trapped and unable to adapt.

Peasants were vulnerable to disease and hunger, but not to the extreme degree that Postan suggested. The calculation that peasants died in every poor harvest, and that their expectation of life sank to twenty years at the age of twenty, was based on the evidence of heriots, but heriots were sometimes paid on the surrender of a holding, that is a sale of land, as well as on death. In years of scarcity peasants felt hardship, but sold land to survive. Their life expectation, based on tracing individuals through the series of Halesowen court records, can be estimated for the early fourteenth century at 30.2 years at the age of twenty for better-off peasants, and 20.8 for the smallholders. These are higher figures than those calculated by Postan, but are still much lower than those found in the era of parish registers, in the sixteenth and seventeenth centuries. Halesowen's adults were dying young, and of course we know nothing about the deaths of those aged under twenty, but we suspect that they suffered great losses. If the population of Halesowen was rising at this time, as seems to be the case after the famine, to compensate for the heavy mortality there must have been a very high birth rate. This leaves us with a further unsolved problem, as one view of the demography of this period represents it as a 'high pressure' system, in which people married young, produced many children but also suffered high rates of mortality. This has been identified at Halesowen, and might support the view that this was a period of overpopulation and careless reproduction. Another interpretation suggests that the demographic system of the fourteenth century resembled that of the early modern period, in which marriage was

delayed until both partners were in their mid-twenties, and a proportion
of people remained celibate. Such a system meant that levels of population followed changes in the economy: in hard times people married very
late, or not at all, and the size of the population was reduced through
the mechanism of the birth rate rather than mortality. We simply do not
have enough information about marriage and births to know which of
these best describes the behaviour of the population before the Black
Death.

iv. *Crisis in Scotland*

The early fourteenth century in Scotland is not so well documented as
in England, but it still provides a helpful comparison. Scotland seems
to have gone through the same sequence of growth and contraction as
occurred in England and the rest of Europe. In the thirteenth century
there is a recognizable pattern of expanding cultivation, increase in the
size and number of towns, growth in the export trade in wool and hides,
and a rise in the amount of coinage in circulation. Monastic foundations,
some of them new, built up respectable incomes, so that by about 1290
Newbattle Abbey was worth at least £267 and Holyrood near Edinburgh
£774. The secular magnates, numbering about fifty families, prospered,
and the earl of Fife, for example, was worth £500 per annum.

Between 1296 and 1328, and again in 1332–5, the economy was
disrupted by war with the English, but in addition we can detect
underlying problems. Long-term economic changes in Scotland are
signalled by three documents which valued the property of the church
for taxation purposes. From the early thirteenth century comes the
'ancient assessment' (*antiqua taxatio*); Bishop Halton's assessment dates
from about 1300; and the 'true value'(*verus valor*) of 1366 reflects the
situation after the Black Death. The valuations recorded in the 'ancient
assessment' doubled by the time of Bishop Halton's survey: in the diocese
of St Andrews they rose from £8,000 to almost £14,000, and for the
Glasgow diocese the increase was from £4,000 to a little more than
£11,000. After 1300 came a collapse in values, with the 'true value'
recording much lower figures than in Halton's survey, even below the level
of the 'ancient assessment'. A local survey of the bishopric of Moray
allows us to trace the decline in a little more detail: the value in about
1300 of £2,496 was cut to £928 in the mid-fourteenth century, and then
sank to the very low £559 in 1366.

In interpreting these figures, the effects of the fighting, the plague and
any longer-term economic malaise cannot be disentangled. Tithe revenue

contributed a high proportion of these church valuations, and the ups and downs in tithe are a good indicator of the fluctuations in general economic activity. It was therefore not just the Scottish church, but the whole country which apparently suffered from a profound recession in the fourteenth century. This is confirmed by the royal accounts of the 1350s which refer to waste and lost revenues on a more damaging and widespread scale than would be expected from the plague epidemic alone. Settlements in the countryside were abandoned in the fourteenth century, such as farms and fields on the Lammermuir Hills, and a hamlet at Springwood Park on the edge of the burgh of Roxburgh. The economy of the towns suffered a setback, if we consider the way in which a site in the centre of Perth, where there was plentiful craft activity in the thirteenth century, shows little sign that goods were being manufactured there in the early fourteenth century. Some of the new burghs that were founded in this period, such as Tarbert and Staplegorton, initially failed to develop as towns. The export trade in wool and hides in 1327–32, of 5,700 sacks of wool and 36,100 hides per annum, declined to an annual 2,450 sacks and 17,900 hides in the early 1340s. Both sets of figures probably reflect a period of depression, judging from the known productive capacity of the great estates, and the larger amounts, which were traded in the early 1370s – 7,360 sacks and 39,500 hides.

The Scottish economy contracted in the fourteenth century, though there is little direct evidence of the effects of the Great Famine or the Black Death, and the date of the turning point remains uncertain. The country could have experienced some problems resulting from the over-exploitation of land. Settlement and cultivation were unevenly distributed, with much of the population living on the best agricultural land in the east. In the south-east, nucleated villages cultivated open fields and displayed a bias towards arable farming similar to that found in much of England and continental Europe. Yields would have fallen in the Isles if there had been a reduction in the regular spreading of manure such as seaweed on the infield. In addition, fields were cultivated on hillsides at altitudes in excess of 1,000 feet which were especially vulnerable to episodes of bad weather. Some wheat was grown in the south-east, but much of the Scottish population was dependent on oats and barley to a dangerous degree. In times of bad harvests consumers in more favourable climates could switch from wheat and rye to barley, oats and other inferior corn, but if the spring-sown crop failed, many Scots had no alternative cereal. Disputes over grazing rights between monasteries and other lords with rights to upland pasture suggest some pressure on land, and overstocking may have contributed to the outbreak of sheep disease, like that in 1294.

In spite of these disadvantages and weaknesses, it would be hard to maintain that this was a countryside in which an excessive proportion of the land was under the plough, or where grazing had been reduced to the point that the arable was deprived of manure. The *sourning* (allowance of animals allowed to landholders, called a stint in England) for an oxgang of about 15 acres of arable on the estates of Arbroath Abbey was fifty-two sheep, five cows, two oxen and a horse, which does not suggest any shortage of pasture – a peasant in the English midlands would have been allowed half of this. Much of the arable lay in outfields which were cultivated occasionally. The suggestion that land was over-exploited, or that the pressure of population damaged the rural ecology, would be difficult to apply to Scotland, which even after the growth of the thirteenth century must be regarded as a thinly populated country.

Many medieval peasants were compelled to hand over a high proportion of their surplus production in rent, which deprived them of their potential capital and sometimes of their food, and contributed to the crisis. Again, there is little evidence that this was a serious problem in Scotland. Lords did not usually cultivate large arable demesnes, so it was unnecessary for them to demand heavy labour services from their tenants. Many lords kept extensive flocks of sheep, but these did not require much peasant labour. Peasants often paid a rent in cash by the early fourteenth century, and while these could be as high as 18s for a husbandland on the Kelso estate, they were not usually so burdensome. The extra dues that were extracted in cash and kind do not seem very heavy, judging from the earl of Fife's revenue from his whole estate of 40s from marriage fines, 33s from heriots and 16s for forfeitures. Scottish lords were oppressive, in their restriction on their peasants' freedom of movement, for example. Tenants were not allowed hereditary succession to their holdings, which led them to petition Edward I in 1305 (when he was occupying the country) to allow them the same rights of inheritance as their counterparts in England. Scottish peasants often lacked material possessions, as can be seen from the finds from excavations of rural sites, and sections of the peasantry were servile in status, but they did not apparently suffer increased privations at the end of the thirteenth century which might have precipitated the crisis that overtook the Scottish economy.

If Scotland went through a turning point in the fourteenth century without an ecological crisis, this must create doubts about whether the imbalance of arable and pasture, the shortage of manure, and the 'metabolism of the field system' in England and elsewhere were the main reason for the economic setbacks of the period.

v. *Explanations*

The crisis may have been caused by some external change (an exogenous factor) which jolted the economy and turned it downhill. One of these could have been the climate, which played an important part in the harvest failures, the flooding of reclaimed wetlands, and the Great Famine. The climate went through a period of instability between 1290 and 1375, which was particularly damaging to cereal production because a number of wet summers prevented the ripening of crops. The hay harvest was disrupted, which affected livestock, and damp ground could encourage diseases such as foot rot and liver fluke in sheep. Wet conditions created a favourable environment for pests and plant diseases. However, although the climate undoubtedly contributed to the crisis, its role was surely to expose economic weaknesses. Today, third world countries are vulnerable to natural disasters such as flooding because they do not have the capacity to repair the damage, while more advanced economies can shrug off these problems. In the history of western Europe the most adverse weather conditions in the last 2,000 years created the 'little ice age' of *c.*1550–1850, in which the economy sometimes went into recession, but also entered the first stages of the industrial and agricultural revolutions. Bad weather does not necessarily lead to disaster and recession. In the later middle ages, the climate returned to stability and allowed a succession of good harvests after 1375, but the economy did not resume the growth patterns of the thirteenth century.

In a similar vein, another disruptive influence came from fluctuations in the supply of money. The later middle ages saw a long-term decline in the amount of silver in circulation throughout western Europe, partly because the mines did not produce enough to compensate for the loss of precious metal which was hoarded, used to make plate and ornaments, or sent to the east in the course of trade. In the first half of the fourteenth century, silver was liable to move from one country to another because of changing government policy on monetary matters. In 1305–10, for example, the authorities in the Low Countries temporarily ceased minting in silver, and the king of France overvalued his gold coins, which caused continental silver to flow into England, leading to a temporary sharp inflation in prices. Much more serious was the loss of bullion in the late 1330s, when Edward III taxed the country heavily to pay for the opening of the Hundred Years War, and specifically to make gifts to rulers to persuade them to become his allies. At that time there were complaints that goods could not be sold because of the shortage of coin, and the tax granted by parliament in 1340 was to be levied in kind. These episodes were disruptive, but the troubles of the period must have had deeper roots, because they continued in times of monetary stability.

Perhaps the crisis began because of stresses and strains in the social and political structure? The power of lords over peasants has already been mentioned as an explanation for their poverty. The number of demands made by lords seem particularly high, and little reduction was made during the critical years in the Welsh marcher lordships, which enjoyed relative independence from the crown and could exploit inhabitants ruthlessly. The marcher lords – that is, aristocrats such as the earls of Arundel, Gloucester and Hereford, who also held extensive English lands with conventional rights as lords of the manor – gained a small proportion of their income in the Welsh march from demesnes and labour services. They also exploited their powers as lords, such as their right to revenues from mills, and in particular their judicial authority, to extract money. The courts were used to levy large quantities of cash. For example, in 1321–2, 700 people in Caernarfonshire were fined a total of £27 for failing to attend the lord's court. The right of tallage was also enforced in an arbitrary way – a 'gift' could be raised if the lord incurred some unusual expense, such as serving with the king's army in France. In 1324 in the lordship of Chirk the tenants paid 1,600 marks (£1,066) for a charter which gave them hunting rights, access to pastures and woods, and exempted subtenants from the obligation to pay heriot. The suspicion that this bargain benefited the lord more than the tenants is confirmed by the issue of another charter ten years later confirming the first, and allowing free tenants to build mills, again for 1,600 marks.

Arbitrary exactions, however, were confined to particular regions and particular types of tenant, and the fourteenth-century crisis was universal. A high proportion of English peasants, probably the majority, were free, and for many customary tenants increases in dues had not kept pace with thirteenth-century inflation. A more intangible influence arose from the aristocracy's position of social leadership. They provided the lesser ranks with role models, and their example did not set much store by thrift and industry. But peasants were capable of forming their own ideas, and were by no means uncritical admirers of the aristocracy. The conclusion must be that social inequalities and lordly power were a contribution to, but not a prime cause of, the crisis.

The disruption and draining of the economy by war played some part in precipitating the crisis. Wars were being fought in Britain or by the rulers of England or Scotland for at least forty of the years between 1290 and 1350. Armed conflict was a normal activity in the middle ages, and it usually made no extraordinary demands on the economy. But in this period it was organized more systematically, on a larger scale, and on a long-term basis. Edward I's campaigns in Wales had established new methods of war, in which the armies received wages and which aimed at the systematic and permanent conquest of territory. Roads and harbours were constructed, and the troops were kept supplied with food and weapons by land and sea. Once the enemy had been defeated, massive castles were built at strategic points to control the population, and colonies of English settlers established. All of these activities cost money, and when English aggression was turned on Scotland and France, the long lines of communication, the large armies (some containing 20,000 men), the support of ships and sailors, and the complex diplomacy, added still more to the expense of war.

The most direct economic impact of war was the destruction of the countryside and towns by armies, which was not an unforeseen accident of campaigning, but a deliberate policy to damage enemy resources and to force opponents to abandon the conflict, or to accept a settlement favourable to the attackers. The Scottish borders were especially badly devastated. The country around Carlisle was attacked by the Scots in 1297: mills and barns were burnt, and peasants killed and driven away. Another raid led to the burning of villages and seizure of cattle in 1314, and more raids followed in 1315, 1316 and 1322. In 1345, after more incursions in the same district, sixty-four villages were judged to be unable to pay their taxes in full. The Scots found that the eastern side of the border offered richer pickings, and penetrated in a series of attacks into Northumberland, Durham and northern Yorkshire. The revenues received by Durham Priory from churches on the eastern side of the border, in south Tweedsdale, came mainly from tithes, and their fluctuations indicate general changes in agricultural production. Before 1297 the priory received above £400 per annum from these churches, but in 1297–8 the figure sank to £35, as a direct result of Scottish destruction. After full recovery, from 1318 with the Scots back on the offensive, revenues fell back to £20, but in the subsequent period of relative peace they failed to climb higher than £269, in 1338–9. English pillage of the Scottish countryside is not recorded in such detail, but this was not confined to the border area, and in 1337 a destructive invasion reached as far north as Aberdeen and resulted not just in the burning of that town, but also in the ravaging of some of the best agricultural land, such as the Mearns to the north of Montrose. The threat of raids caused distress to the border population, because they had to pay for fortifications, and the English were sometimes able to pay the Scots not to attack. The presence of English soldiers supposedly defending the border was a dubious benefit, as they tended to rob the local population, and even to turn to brigandage. The events at Flint in 1294 indicate the vulnerability of towns. The English authorities, fearful of an attack by Welsh rebels, themselves burnt the town which had been built next to the castle, to prevent its use as a shelter for a besieging army. The seventy-five burgesses were paid £521 in compensation for the loss of their houses and goods, which probably did not cover the full value of their property. Towns in the south of England were raided in 1338–40 by the French, which caused not just much damage to property, but afterwards the expense of building a more effective town wall at Southampton. In general, as in the case of Flint, a programme for reconstruction followed the destruction of war, and no permanent setback necessarily resulted. More serious economic consequences followed repeated attacks, especially in districts like the Scottish borders or north Wales which were not agriculturally rich, and where town life was still rather precarious. The most northerly counties of England changed their character in the early fourteenth century: the atmosphere of insecurity became a dominating feature for centuries.

Armies destroyed specific localities, but war affected everyone who paid taxes. Direct taxation in England was raised only in time of war, and the almost continuous series of campaigns between 1290 and 1348 resulted in the levying of successive lay subsidies, which brought to the government a total of £1,055,300. Additional measures to swell government coffers included the taxation of the clergy, which yielded £551,000 in the same period, the taxation of international trade, from which the king obtained an income in most years in excess of £10,000, and a number of measures such as purveyance, by which the king's agents made compulsory purchases of supplies for armies or the royal household, for which the 'sellers' received a poor price only after long delays.

Was this of real economic significance? It could be said that the total wealth of the country was sufficient to provide these sums without undue strain. If the king took £80,000 (beyond his regular income of about £30,000) in a year of active campaigning, for example in 1297, this amounted to just under 2 per cent of the estimated Gross Domestic Product. It was a small sum compared with the total of rent that lords collected: for example, each year the lay aristocracy and the higher clergy and monasteries received incomes totalling £600,000. The money was not taken away completely – much of it was used to pay English soldiers, or to buy food, equipment and weapons with benefits for the English producers. The administration of taxes, it might be said, was not harsh or oppressive. The taxes were granted by parliament, so that consent had been given, and unlike the French, the English taxpayers did not usually rebel on a large scale. All social classes were included within the tax system, including the aristocracy and clergy. The only exempt categories were those of tin miners in Devon and Cornwall, the men of the Cinque Ports, and the inhabitants of Cheshire and Durham, who paid taxes in a different form. No one could have had a strong sense of resentment that some wealthy groups were not paying anything. The assessments, based on valuing moveable goods (for most peasants this meant livestock) were carried out by local people who did not include every item, and who used some generously low valuations. The rules allowed the poor to escape, by stating that those with goods worth less than a certain sum (commonly 10s) would be exempt. Large numbers of people with goods worth much more than 10s were given a sympathetic low valuation which took them below the tax threshold. The tax was administered with some sensitivity to the feelings of the taxpayers, so that although the rate, that is the fraction of the value of goods, could be as high as a ninth or as low as a thirtieth, the amount collected did not change greatly, suggesting that officials turned a blind eye to large-scale evasion and under-assessment.

In spite of these reservations, we must accept that some people suffered from war taxation. A great lord like Canterbury Cathedral Priory paid so much in the mid-1290s that it sank into debt and was forced to reduce wine purchases and cease building operations. The better-off peasants, who paid a high proportion of direct taxes, were required to find 2–4s in many years, which was a considerable sum on top of their obligations to their lord. A peasant born in 1270 and acquiring a holding of about 20 acres by 1293 would find himself contributing for the first time in 1294, followed by further payments to the taxes granted in rapid succession in 1295, 1296, 1297 and then in a further nine years between 1301 and 1322. If his son succeeded him in the mid-1320s, during a brief respite, he would pay in 1327, 1332, 1334, 1336, and contribute to three subsidies in 1337–40. In all, the two generations of this family paid about 60s to the lay subsidy, which may not seem very much, considering that their saleable surplus over forty-six years would have amounted to at least £40, and their rent payments to more than £20. The tax demands would have been a nuisance because they appeared unpredictably – they fell in the years that suited the king, not the peasants, and they tended to come in concentrated groups, notably in 1294–7 and 1337–40. Nor did the grants take much account of adverse circumstances, such as the bad harvests of the mid-1290s, and we have seen that a subsidy was collected in the midst of the famine in 1316–17.

The official records tell us of the payments that were returned to the central government, but other sources show that tax collectors were bribed. Those who were making their contribution would also be liable to purveyance, which fell unequally across the country, with counties such as Lincolnshire bearing more than their fair share. On occasion the king also demanded quotas of foot soldiers from the shires, which under the system of array meant that each large village, or groups of smaller ones, would find and equip a recruit and pay him until he reached the main army, towards the cost of which again our better-off peasant would have had to pay a few more pence. In addition, the taxes on wool, which helped to push down the price to the grower, would reduce the profit of many peasants' main cash crop. The smallholders may at first sight seem to have slipped through the tax net, but we should take account of interdependence in the village economy. If money was taken from the wealthier peasants, they had less to spend locally, which reduced the employment opportunities of smallholders, or diminished the market for such non-essentials as ale. When, in response to complaints of corruption and mismanagement, the administration of the subsidy changed in 1334, tax collectors no longer assessed each individual, but instead each village and town was given a quota of taxation to raise as it saw fit. The peasant elite passed some of the burden on to their poorer neighbours, who had previously been exempt. So hard-pressed smallholders did feel the effect of taxation, both indirectly and directly. Finally, the king's taxes were alleged to have caused such poverty among peasants that they left their holdings. This was said during the collection of the ninth in 1340–1. In Shropshire at Clungunford the existence of waste land was blamed on the king's many taxes, and all but two of the inhabitants of the hamlet of Cold Weston, on the slopes of Clee Hill, were said to have abandoned the settlement for fear of taxation.

Having weighed up the arguments for and against regarding direct taxation as a major influence on the economy, the conclusion must be that it had a considerable impact, but not on a scale sufficient on its own to have precipitated the crisis of the fourteenth century. War and taxes had universal effects. Most other changes, such as those in the policies of landlords, or the climate, or the long-term consequences of land clearance, varied from place to place and region to region, whereas government demands were felt everywhere – and this applies in particular to taxes on international trade. The wool export trade attracted the attention of government because its high profits could be tapped without immediate economic damage, and as the wool was carried through a small number of ports there was limited scope for evasion. In addition, the clothmakers of Flanders depended on supplies, and therefore political pressure could be applied by cutting off the trade, or directing it elsewhere. The 'great custom' on each sack of wool from 1275 stood at 6s 8d (sacks varied in price from £4 to £8). In the time of Edward I's wars, and in later episodes, a *maltolte* ('bad tax') was imposed which in some years brought the level of tax up to £2 per sack. The most ambitious scheme to allow the king to enjoy the full profit of wool sales was that launched in 1337, when a consortium of wool merchants advanced a loan of £200,000 to Edward III in return for a monopoly of the bulk of the wool trade. The operation was over-ambitious and badly organized, and it ended in tears, with royal officials selling the wool cheaply in 1338 at Dordrecht in the Low Countries and paying off the merchants with bonds that would enable them to recover money – eventually. The government continued to intervene in the wool trade in the 1340s, and in 1343 a 'company' of thirty-three merchants, who may have been representing a much larger group, took over the whole customs system on wool in exchange for grants of money to the crown. One explanation of their move was that this removed the provision in an earlier law that wool merchants had to bring back bullion from the continent for each sack sold.

The government's manipulation of the wool trade – with its taxation, embargoes and monopolies – was bad news for the producers of wool, because it disrupted the marketing of their product to varying degrees. The high levels of taxation could not be passed on entirely to the foreign customers, so taxation probably contributed to the long-term drop in the prices that the producers received. Trade in general suffered from the emergency measures of wartime, such as the requisitioning of merchant ships to carry armies, and the increased danger of piracy, which forced ships to carry an extra crew of soldiers and to sail in convoys. Fear of the loss of ships, and of the unpredictable shifts in politics, cannot have helped business confidence.

Warfare is often credited with some positive economic benefits, for example, the acceleration of technical innovations. Some people did benefit from the military expeditions of 1290–1350. The traders of York, for example, enjoyed prosperity because the city at times served as a temporary capital of the whole kingdom. The urban and industrial life of north Wales was transformed by Edward I's conquest, to the benefit of the new urban colonists. Even the coal mines of Flintshire experienced a boom as fuel was needed for the smiths making the tools, nails and other ironwork used in castle-building. Members of the aristocracy expected to profit from war. They would contract to bring a contingent of troops, and make a small surplus from the pay for the men under their command. The general expansion of government activity and expenditure increased the number of official positions; those who performed well were rewarded with titles and the lands and grants of money to support them, like the new crop of earldoms created by the youthful Edward III. The campaigns in France in the 1340s brought plunder and ransoms for those on active service, and the earlier conquest of southern Scotland resulted in English nobles enjoying temporary profits from confiscated Scottish lands.

The indirect effects of war deserve our attention. Taxation on wool exports pushed up the cost of the raw materials used by continental manufacturers and made their cloth more expensive. The taxation was applied only to exports, so the wool available in England was relatively cheap. Cloth made in England was cheaper than that produced by its continental rivals, which helped it to capture the home market and begin to make inroads once more among the consumers across the sea. English commerce also gained from the growing proportion of trade handled by English merchants. Aliens paid a higher rate of tax on wool exports, and various protectionist measures, such as a prohibition on foreign merchants buying wool directly from the producers, helped local traders. From 1313 a staple was introduced, by which all wool was supposed to be carried to a single continental port. The choice of town depended on diplomatic considerations: the staple was initially located at St Omer, and then moved to Antwerp and on to Bruges, but later in the century was fixed at Calais. The staple policy was primarily meant to keep control of the trade for political and fiscal reasons, but it also had the effect of favouring English exporters, as the whole system was sponsored by the government and managed by an English mayor. The wool trade was closely connected with substantial loans to the crown. All three Edwards had used as their bankers big Italian companies: the most prominent names were the Riccardi, then the Frescobaldi, and finally the Bardi and Peruzzi, and these hard-headed businessmen gained trade privileges, and especially access to wool exports, as a reward. The last two firms failed in the 1340s – not entirely because of the inability of Edward III to honour his debts. Increasingly the king relied on loans from English merchants, such as William de la Pole who came originally from Hull and acquired a large landed fortune from the profits of trade and financial dealings with the crown and the aristocracy. In Scotland, by the 1330s a staple had been fixed for wool at Bruges, which was linked with royal taxes, including higher rates for alien merchants. In the thirteenth century most Scottish wool had been exported by continental merchants, but now 85 per cent of the wool trade was in the hands of Scots.

In general then, the wars of the period had a profound effect on the economy, resulting both from the disruption of agriculture and trade by military operations, and from taxation, but some of the positive developments of the period in the cloth industry and the advances by native merchants also owed something to short-term government policy. Perhaps this was intended, but it is more likely to have been an accidental by-product.

The crisis of the fourteenth century cannot be given a simple cause, any more than we can easily explain other turning points in history, such

as the fall of the Roman empire or the decline of the European colonial
powers in the twentieth century. The economy and society of *c.*1300 had
become complicated and interlocking, and growth had added tensions
and pressures. We cannot unpick the complexities and identify a single
internal problem, such as population growth, or a single external change,
such as climate, and give these a privileged place in our interpretation of
the period. We can indicate a number of points of weakness in the structure that had been assembled in the period of growth before 1300. Each
area of achievement had its limitations, or its negative repercussions.
Such was the success in agriculture that in most years there was sufficient
food for everyone, including the substantial minority of town dwellers
and country people employed in industry. In times of stress, townspeople did not necessarily suffer most hardship, as the urban authorities
were able to secure supplies, in which case the rural poor went hungry.
Migrants into towns were often looking for chances to better themselves,
and many succeeded, but at this time a migration of the desperately poor
in search of charity or casual work was of no benefit to the town or to
the migrants themselves.

The size of the towns created ecological difficulties, as we have seen
in the case of London's fuel supplies. But towns also had economic problems if the demand for traded and manufactured goods was levelling off
soon after 1300. The spiral of demand, and of interaction of the urban
and rural economies, was flattening at this time. Country people who
sold food and raw materials to the town found that as demand for these
goods declined, they could not spend so much on urban manufactures.
The turning point in the cycle of trade may have come in the years before
the Great Famine, and the economy was certainly not recovering after
that event. The many peasants' sons and daughters who had founded
new households on the basis of opportunities in the non-agricultural
economy were experiencing difficulties in the 1290s and were among the
casualties in 1315–17. Perhaps it is not just the population that had
grown as far as was possible by the early fourteenth century, when Britain
was as populous as it was to be in about 1750. The whole commercial
economy and level of urbanization – in the relatively thinly populated
parts of Scotland, Wales and northern and western England, as well as
in the south and east – had reached their upper limits.

The aristocracy had been drawn into participation in the trading
system when they took their demesnes into direct management in the
early thirteenth century, and in the next hundred years they improved
both production methods and administrative techniques. By the early
fourteenth century, having specialized to some degree, and made some
technical innovations, they realized that their profit margins were not

very high. After the instability of 1295–1332, they experienced a fall in grain prices and a rise in labour costs which discouraged them from continuing with high farming. They could not squeeze more out of the peasants, because these small producers were affected to some extent by the same problems, such as low prices, and could not afford to pay any more rent. They also resisted demands, or suffered hardship from royal tax collectors. The lay aristocrats welcomed the opportunity of war and royal service as an additional source of income, but not all of them made great gains, and the general extension in the authority of the state tended to close off avenues of profit for the landlords, such as their powers of private justice. The aristocracy cut back on expenditure, with further dampening effects on trade and manufacture.

The surge of economic activity which had begun in the tenth century was losing momentum. The nucleated villages, the open fields dedicated to extensive grain production, the manorial structure based on binding peasant rents and services to demesnes, the magnate estates, the larger towns, were all running into stagnation or decline after 1300. But even at this decisive moment when these organizations reached their peak and began to falter, we can see signs of growth in the reviving cloth industry, especially in the countryside and small towns, greater confidence and more trading activity among English merchants, and a rise in the importance of London and some provincial towns such as Coventry. The peasant land market and peasants' larger sheep flocks are signs of vitality. The crisis of the early fourteenth century, like the period of 'recession' that followed, had its dimension of innovation.

PART THREE

Making a new world, c.1350–c.1520

In this period the sources change, as those who once dominated the economy lost their active role. The manorial accounts kept by reeves and bailiffs, which tell us so much about agriculture under the management of the lords, become less informative after 1400, and are quite rare by the late fifteenth century. This was because lords, and especially those with large estates, pulled out of direct involvement in growing corn and rearing animals. We know something about the new activists of the economy, especially the wealthier peasants and entrepreneurs, from the growing number of wills. Some documents are informal and full of insights into human reactions, notably the letters in English written by the gentry. The English language, newly emerging from its inferior status in relation to Latin and French, was the vehicle for much social and polit-ical criticism in the half-century after the Black Death, when poets such as Chaucer, Gower and Langland, together with many writers whose names are not known, expressed their perceptions of a shifting, often troubling world. Their depiction of the age supports modern historians' view that the crisis that began before 1348 continued and deepened, to the point that articulate observers thought that the old order was threatened.

Contemporaries realized that they lived in a material world that was contracting, because most villages and towns bore the scars of collapsed buildings, and settlements as a whole or in part were abandoned. A fifteenth-century book of school exercises, in which commonplace com-ments were to be translated into Latin, refers casually to a hazard of urban life: 'The roof of an old house had almost fallen on me yesterday.' At the time, it was not known that the population of England had been reduced from about 5 million on the eve of the Black Death to 2.5 million in 1377, and it was to remain around that level until after 1520 (see Figure

2 above, p. 235). But employers and landlords were fully aware of the scarcity of labour and tenants, and there was much disquiet in the early sixteenth century about the shortage of manpower for the armed forces. After the mid-fifteenth century, the changes in population in parts of the continent, notably France and Italy, where numbers were growing quite rapidly, contrasted with the persistence in England of low levels of population until about 1540.

Those who lived through these years were very conscious of the short-term fluctuations from year to year in the quality of the harvest, reflecting the patterns of weather, and they would refer to 'good' and 'bad' years on the basis of the price of corn, though sellers and buyers had different views on shortage and plenty. Prices were mainly low, as our school-book suggests when it sets passages for translation such as: 'All manner of white corn, as wheat and barley, was never sold better cheap [cheaper] than it is now . . .', and 'there is no man now alive who can remember that ever he saw wheat or peas or other corn or any other foodstuff that is brought to the market to be sold cheaper than we see now . . .', leading to the comment put into the schoolboy's mouth that he is sorry for the peasant producers ('poor husbands') who 'sell much things for little silver'. In terms of average prices, wheat in England retained or even surpassed in most decades between the 1380s and 1490s the figure of 5s per quarter at which it settled after the Great Famine. But barley declined to only 3s to 3s 6d per quarter in the same period and oats fell below 2s for much of the fifteenth century (see Figure 1 above, p. 230).

Contemporaries also commented on the shortage of coin, and especially on the lack of coins of small denominations. This reflects the 'bullion famine', as it has been dubbed by historians, which meant that the outflow of silver to the east was not matched by new supplies from mining. Governments were faced with hard decisions on how to keep the economy running on diminishing quantities of silver. In England, the mint which had been accustomed to producing coins worth at least £1,000 in a year was striking £182 in an average year in the early fifteenth century. The authorities supplemented the silver currency with gold coins from 1344, the most frequently minted being the noble, worth 6s 8d. Gold accounted in the late fifteenth century for half of the total amount of cash in circulation. Debasement, in which coins were minted with a lower silver content, was another option, though by the standards of other countries the reduction of the silver content of the penny in the 1340s, again by one sixth in 1412, and in 1464, was on a modest scale. The amount of silver available for minting increased after 1465. The English government showed some concern for the needs of those using coins, and introduced the groat (worth 4d) in the 1340s, and then the half-groat, which were quite convenient after the Black Death because rises in wages meant that employers needed to pay 4d per day to skilled workers, rather than the 3d that prevailed in the 1330s and 1340s, and in the fifteenth century craftsmen commonly earned 6d per day. But, as in earlier periods, the mintings of halfpennies and farthings were insufficient to meet the demand for small change.

In Scotland, which had a sterling currency closely matching that of England, the debasement route was followed from 1367, after which Scottish coins were no longer accepted in England, and English pennies were driven out of use in Scotland. The initial decision was taken for the profit of the state rather than in response to the shortage of bullion, but further reductions in the quality of the coins were encouraged by the lack of silver. In the late fourteenth century, an English pound sterling was judged to be worth 26s 8d in Scottish money, but by 1483 was equivalent to £5. Gold was minted in Scotland, and in the late fifteenth century low-denomination coins made from base metal were issued. The fluctuations confused those who used the coins, leading to formal statements of rent payments or other obligations as being payable in 'the usual money of Scotland', a phrase which acknowledged the changeable nature of the currency. Rents and prices were affected by the shifts in the money, and to further confuse the issue there were changes in the measures, such as the 'boll' in which grain was sold. Prices of grain, of which oats were the most important, rose in the long term, while lower prices were paid in the fifteenth century for the ever-plentiful livestock.

The conventional historian's view of the period is one of contraction, a trough between periods of growth in the thirteenth and sixteenth centuries. A concern of those alive at the time was the moral and social deterioration that followed the Black Death. John Gower wrote in the 1390s that:

> The world is changed and overthrown
> That it is well-nigh upside down
> Compared with days of long ago.

He was ostensibly contrasting the world of antiquity with his own times, but when he went on to refer to former wealth and plenty, and to an age when knights were honoured, aristocracy received proper respect, and cities were not divided by contention, he clearly had in mind the changes of the previous half-century. Gower and other poets of the late fourteenth century made much use of the 'three orders' idea, which explained that society could function in peace and harmony if each order – those who fought, those who prayed and those who worked (aristocrats, clergy and peasants) – pursued its God-given duty, while receiving services from the other two orders. Workers should carry out their tasks and pay their rents, confident that they would be protected by the military skills of the aristocrats, and benefit from the prayers of the clergy. Everyone agreed, however, that each order failed in its obligations, and threatened the unity of society. Another member of the elite, the Norfolk esquire John Paston, complained in 1462 that tenants 'hoped to have a new world', referring to their reluctance to pay rents. The estate officials of the bishop of Worcester in 1450 gloomily compared the 'ancient' rents and servile dues of the thirteenth century with the lower sums prevailing 'in modern times'.

The long-term trends of the period worked against the interests of the aristocracy. The low population reduced the numbers of tenants and the demand for land, and therefore rent income declined. The price of primary products, especially grain, fell because of slackening demand, while the costs of scarce labour rose, together with the prices of manu-factured goods, to which wages made a considerable contribution. So the incomes of lords decreased while their cost of living increased: they were caught in the famous 'price scissors'. But these tendencies are apparent only when we survey the evidence over fifty or a hundred years, while the lifetimes of individuals were often influenced by short-term movements sometimes in one direction, sometimes in another. The period between 1349 and 1375 was one of generally expensive grain, so the picture of falling prices applies after 1375, and even then was interrupted by peri-odic shortages, notably in the late 1430s, the early 1480s and in 1519–22. The commercial economy was subject to fluctuations, the most signifi-cant being the quite high levels of trade around 1400, the depression of the middle years of the fifteenth century, and the new expansion after about 1470. In addition there were sudden shocks like the slump in the early 1520s. The end of the period saw the first stage of the inflation in prices that was to become such a dominant feature of the sixteenth-century economy.

The contractions in the period should not dominate our view of it. The lower orders of society have left us no accounts or letters to inform us of their experiences, but we can appreciate that high wages, reduced rents and cheap food may not have done them great harm. Also, while it is important to understand the ups and downs of the economy, structural changes in the control of production and the distribution of wealth deserve our attention. The old cliché that this period saw 'the rise of the middle class' has no validity, as no middle class existed. If the phrase refers to townspeople, they multiplied in number, and some of them became prosperous, before 1300, and after the Black Death they recovered, but were scarcely 'rising'. But different social groups were repositioned, with a weakening of those sections of the aristocracy dependent on traditional manorial revenues, the decline of some towns, and the greater prominence of new social and occupational categories, such as gentlemen, yeomen, farmers and clothiers.

Regions had varied fortunes, with the densely populated grain-growing, village-dominated English midland claylands falling behind the more dynamic industrializing pastoral areas, such as southern East Anglia, Kent, the south-west, and west Yorkshire (see Map 11 below, p. 359). The position of England in relation to the continent of Europe also underwent a transformation. Large towns, international trade and intensive agriculture had been located in north Italy and Flanders, and these regions remained key points in the European economy, but in the fifteenth century the centres of gravity shifted to the north and west, with the rise of Castile and Portugal, Holland, the port of Antwerp, and England. England became an industrial and maritime power, as its woollen cloth was exported in quantity all over Europe, and a growing proportion of overseas trade was organized by English merchants and carried in English ships.

The political upheavals of the period have been seen as providing the appropriate setting for economic contraction. In England, dynasties of kings were overthrown when Richard II, Henry VI and Richard III were forcibly removed from their thrones, and the Wars of the Roses broke out sporadically in the period between 1455 and 1485. Scotland has also been seen as dominated by 'over-mighty subjects' who caused so much instability that James I was assassinated in 1437 and James III deposed and killed in 1488. Nonetheless in both countries an underlying community of interest between aristocracy and monarchs has been identified, and recent writing has emphasized the desire for peace which prevented anarchy. For example, the contracts between aristocrats secured by the bonds of manrent in Scotland, and the alliances between English magnates and gentry based on 'bastard feudalism', aided cohesion and harmony rather than disorder and civil conflict. The Wars of the Roses had a limited direct impact on the economy, and they were brought to an end because aristocrats were reluctant to continue with disruptive internal warfare. The rulers at the end of our period – the Tudor dynasty in England and the Stuarts James IV and V in Scotland – brought stability, albeit using increasingly autocratic methods.

For contemporaries, the main impact of the state on the economy came from demands for taxation, which in England were heavy in the 1370s, and in the early fifteenth century, when Henry V resumed aggressive policies towards France. Taxes ceased to be a serious burden after the English defeat in the early 1450s and English rulers gave up the war.

In Scotland money had to be raised to pay David II's ransom in the period 1357–77. The heaviest incidence of direct property taxes, the 'contributions', lay between 1358 and 1373, and in 1424–5 to pay another ransom, this time after the capture of James I by the English.

CHAPTER EIGHT

The Black Death and its aftermath, c.1348–c.1520

i. Plague and population, c.1348–c.1520

The epidemic of plague which spread from Asia into western Europe reached Britain in 1348. It was in effect a new disease, as an interval of six centuries had passed since the previous major epidemic. The plague moved through the population of black rats, colonies of which surrounded human settlements, even in remote places. When the rats died, their hungry fleas moved on to human beings and infected their new hosts when they bit them. The bubonic plague was a warm-weather disease, so it was most active in the summer, but in the winter it developed a pneumonic strain which could be spread directly from person to person by coughing. Most of those who contracted bubonic plague died after a few days, but almost all of those who caught the pneumonic form succumbed very quickly.

Plague spread inexorably from its entry point in south-west England in the late summer of 1348; it reached the midlands in 1349, and probably did not end in northern Scotland until 1350. Its movement to villages and hamlets indicates the completeness of the commercial network, as every place was visited regularly by travellers, cartloads of grain or hay, and packloads of goods, all of which might contain infected rats or fleas. Once the disease had begun, its passage through the community was aided by the sociable and charitable impulses of a society in which neighbours entered afflicted houses in order to visit the sick, mourn the dead and comfort the bereaved. The official procedures of will-making, and the distribution of bequests of grain and clothing, would help to maximize the number of contacts. The mortality among the privileged sections of society could be quite low – 27 per cent in the case of the tenants-in-chief of the English crown (earls, barons and some knights and gentry). They lived in stone houses and at a distance from the rats. Among the parish clergy, who were also relatively affluent, between 42 and 45 per cent died. The proportion of peasants who died, according to manorial court records, was usually above 40 per cent, and could reach 70 per cent, which gives the basis for an estimate of a 50 per cent mortality overall. A very high mortality, admittedly from a small sample, is provided by the twelve tenants of the demesne lands of Llan-llwch near Carmarthen, eleven of whom died.

Those who survived the epidemic had to struggle with appalling problems. Most families lost at least one member. Others came near to being wiped out. For example, the monks of Stoneleigh in Warwickshire, when they recorded in the 1390s the histories of different properties on their estate, recalled that a substantial freeholding, amounting to about 50 acres, had belonged to Robert le Heyr, and 'in the first pestilence' Robert, both of his sons Henry and Richard, and Robert's grandson all died, leaving the land vacant. The first task facing those who still lived was to bury the dead. The tradition that 50,000 corpses had to be buried in London may not be an exaggeration, and two new cemeteries were opened, with communal graves. Then came the legal problems: proving wills, arranging for the transfer of property, and providing for widows and orphans. The task was complicated if, as in the case of the le Heyr family, the succeeding generation had died as well. Faced with such horrors and difficulties, the economy and system of administration might have broken down, but with remarkable resilience people returned to work, and the whole system held together.

At Longdon in Worcestershire, the manor (which belonged to Westminster Abbey) was being managed in the year before the plague by the reeve (a tenant of the manor), Andrew Eyloff. He continued in office for another term, beginning in September 1348, but he died halfway through the year, on 14 April 1349. Seventeen other tenants also succumbed to the epidemic, and the manorial officers collected their heriots, the death duties of the best beast on each holding, amounting to two oxen, five cows, two horses, two sheep and two pigs, the others being too poor to contribute. A superior official, a sergeant, was appointed to fill Eyloff's place in the emergency. He had to cope with an acute labour shortage on the manor. The dairymaid died, as did the carter, and a ploughman left his work through illness after six months. Another ploughman temporarily took over carting jobs 'because no one could be hired to carry (corn) this year because of the pestilence'. In spite of the difficulties, there are only a few signs that the routines lapsed, for example, when we are told that a payment was made 'by a certain man, whose name the clerk does not know'. At the end of the year, in October or November 1349, the written account was compiled as usual, showing that the agricultural work had been completed, and the rents collected. Everywhere officials, clerks and tenants died, but substitutes were usually found. In the surviving documents the handwriting may abruptly change, as a new clerk takes over. The royal courts resumed their work after a brief interval, and the number of cases was understandably reduced. The institutions were clearly sufficiently robust to withstand the stress of the epidemic. The mass graves of the London plague cemeteries revealed by modern excavations provide an excellent demonstration of this ability to cope. 'Plague pits' in our lurid imaginings suggest corpses being tipped hastily into great holes, but instead the authorities dug long trenches, and the bodies, some in coffins, were laid in an orderly and dignified fashion side by side. A body may sometimes show signs of decay before burial, perhaps after lying unnoticed for some time after death, but the main impression is of a civilized and organized society doing its best to make decent arrangements in desperately difficult circumstances. (Plate 13)

Having dealt with the immediate effects of the plague, people returned to their usual tasks. Some activities were temporarily halted. Lead mining in Denbighshire stopped in 1349; building operations on the parish churches of Ashbourne in Derbyshire and Patrington in east Yorkshire, and on the west front of Exeter Cathedral, all seem to have ceased, either because of deaths among the workforce, or a sudden shortage of funds. These interruptions lasted for some years, but work was eventually resumed. All of the potters at Hanley Castle in Worcestershire were reported to have died in 1349, but the industry flourished again later in the century. Cornish tin mining did not apparently cease, but it suffered a severe setback, as in 1338–42 more than a million pounds of the metal was presented annually for taxation (coining), but in 1351 less than a quarter of that amount, 237,408 pounds, were recorded. Production climbed back to pre-plague levels by 1386.

On many landed estates, peasant holdings were left vacant in the 1350s, lying, as the court records say, 'in the lord's hands', but over the years they were rented out, if only on short-term lettings. The new tenants were in many cases the younger generation who acquired their inheritance more quickly than expected. Some previously landless labourers and servants took advantage of the situation to rise into the more substantial peasantry, but these opportunities were limited, because capital was needed to acquire the land, and to buy equipment and livestock. Many holdings were taken by tenants who survived, who were given the chance by the death of their neighbours to expand their acreage. In these circumstances, houses surplus to the tenants' needs were neglected, and the countryside was dotted with even more ruined houses and empty plots. These decayed holdings were distributed over all settlements, however, and very few whole villages or hamlets were abandoned as a direct result of the first plague. Quob, a hamlet in Hampshire, was reported deserted immediately after the Black Death, as was Tusmore in Oxfordshire, but the latter was in severe decay in 1341, so the epidemic did no more than seal the fate of an already declining village. Some parts of the economy seem to have proceeded almost unscathed, such as wool exports, which, at 35,000 sacks in 1350–1, were at much the same level as in the 1330s and early 1340s (see Figure 4 above, p. 244).

Perhaps the statistics of production and landholding are taking too cold a view, and we should suppose peasants, miners and shepherds continued their tasks in a traumatized state? Contemporary witnesses, such as the chroniclers, do not suggest that society was paralysed by the loss of life. The writers worked within the conventions of their age, which meant that they tended to express stock moral judgements. They linked the plague with the sins of mankind, and exaggerated the effects, claiming in some cases that the mortality rate was 90 per cent, that there were scarcely sufficient survivors to bury the dead, and that many villages were deserted. They also remarked on the disruption of the social hierarchy. The Rochester chronicler noted the inversion, whereby those formerly at the top could only afford to eat bread and pottage, while labourers whose wages had risen could buy more expensive food. In addition, he claimed that there were so many funerals at which free bread was distributed (a normal show of charity on such occasions) that the poor did not need to work. 'Those who were accustomed to have plenty', he said, 'fell into need', and 'those accustomed to suffer want' experienced abundance. There may have been despondency after the plague, but the survivors appreciated the new opportunities.

In the next one or two generations people referred back to 'the first pestilence' as a landmark, but reactions to that event are difficult to disentangle from responses to changes over a longer span of time. The fall in population and the continued low numbers into the early sixteenth century were part of a process rather than a single event. A catastrophic epidemic need have had no more than temporary effects as the young survivors married and replaced the losses. But the Black Death came after a period of declining population, and was followed by more obstacles to growth. A series of plagues after the first outbreak, in 1361–2, 1369 and 1375, caused fewer deaths than the epidemic of 1348–50, in the range of 10 to 15 per cent, but they were severe and frequent enough to cut back any recovery after 1350. They were succeeded by more localized episodes of disease, which visited most parts of England once in every ten years from the 1390s until well after 1500. In a very similar pattern, chroniclers recorded eight plague years in Scotland between 1349 and 1420, and in Wales there were nine in 1361–1415, and again they continued into the late fifteenth century. Plague became an endemic disease, which was liable to appear sporadically and locally.

Terms used by observers at the time, like 'pestilence', are difficult to identify precisely, but the number of episodes of mortality in the late summer suggests the presence of bubonic plague, the warm-weather disease. In 1473 the chroniclers describe an epidemic with the symptoms of dysentery, and in 1479 this was followed in many places by the worst mortality of the fifteenth century. From 1485, the 'sweating sickness', perhaps a form of influenza, caused further rises in the death rate. Towns may have suffered more frequently and severely than the countryside, though rural populations also experienced regular epidemics. These were dangerous times, when people understandably feared for their safety; those who could afford to do so kept clear of large towns in times of plague. Everyone would have been endangered by infectious diseases, both those which killed large numbers in a few months, and ever-present threats such as tuberculosis.

The expectation of life can be calculated by investigating the length of adult active existence. Lives were shorter than they were to be after 1540 (when parish registers provide abundant evidence) and life expectation tended to fall during the fifteenth century. Monks at Westminster lived after the age of twenty for twenty-nine to thirty years in the early fifteenth century, and in the later part of the century for only twenty years after reaching twenty. At Canterbury Cathedral Priory the comparable figures were thirty-two at twenty, falling to twenty-four at twenty. These monks were privileged people, with an ample diet and comfortable accommodation, but they lived in unhealthy towns. The townspeople of Westminster, for example, experienced very high mortality at the end of the fifteenth century, so their infections evidently spread into the monastic community. Peasants of the late fourteenth century, who were poorer but had a healthier lifestyle, judging from Essex examples, could expect to live for forty-two years after they reached the age of twelve. Those born in the early fifteenth century had an expectation of life of thirty-nine at twelve, and later in the same century of thirty-six years at twelve.

The general health of the population should have been improving at this time. Few should have died of starvation, as cheap bread was available in most years after 1375. The last great medieval famine, from 1437 to 1440, caused hardship as yields fell and prices rose, just as they had done in 1315–17. But unlike the earlier episode, there was no great increase in mortality, except in regions where a plague epidemic coincided with the food shortages. In normal years, not only were basic foodstuffs cheap, but more people enjoyed a balanced diet with a higher proportion of meat and fish. Diseases associated with a poor diet, such as leprosy, were in decline. Rural housing improved in quality; in the south-east, for example, a house would commonly have a chamber at first-floor level, which gave living space separated from the dirt of the street and the farmyard. In the towns, the authorities often provided piped water, and rubbish was carted to communal middens. Disease seemed to have an independent ability to kill a higher proportion of the population, regardless of their improved standard of living.

Was mortality the main cause of the low population which prevailed from before 1348 until about 1540? Changes in population usually arise from a combination of the death rate and the birth rate, but in our period deaths were more carefully recorded than births. Fifteenth-century families were small – they often contained no more than four people, that is, two adults and two children. It would have seemed an ageing society, which lacked an abundance of children and young people. This may reflect high rates of mortality among children, though these are not known precisely. Disease could also influence the birth rate by creating a 'gashed' age structure, in which potentially fertile age groups were reduced in number by epidemics. So the first plague tended to kill older people, but still caused some mortality among those aged between twenty and forty. Twenty or thirty years later there would have been a reduced number of births because of the 'missing generation' who would otherwise have been born in the 1350s and 1360s. Still more serious for future generations was the tendency for the epidemic of 1361–2, the 'children's plague', to kill young people, and therefore to have a negative effect on the birth rate in the 1380s and 1390s. Towards the end of the period the numbers of children recorded in a sample of Kent wills declined from 2.08 in the fifteenth century to 1.90 in 1501–30. Did this reflect a rise in mortality affecting children, or did changes in the age of marriage reduce the number of births?

The main cause of the lower birth rate could have been late marriage. If it became customary for couples to marry, say, at the age of twenty-six rather than twenty-two, then this would reduce the number of children surviving to make up the next generation. A further influence would have been an increase in the number of those who did not marry at all. A feature of the population history of England in later centuries is both late marriage and the significant proportion of celibates, but for our period there is not enough evidence to reconstruct marriage patterns with any certainty. The period of servanthood which often preceded marriage for those in their late teens and early twenties may have been prolonged. It has been argued that this was partly a choice of employers, because in the countryside the move from arable towards pastoral farming created an increased need for full-time shepherds, cowherds and dairymaids. It may also have been a decision made by the young employees. Women in towns, for example, had better job opportunities and greater earning power after 1348–50, so they may have spent more time in employment before they married. This is not entirely convincing, because while it is true that young servants were an important part of the labour force in both town and country in this period, employees expressed a strong preference for short-term employment, and women had no great incentive to remain single as they could continue to earn after they had married. Women seem to have valued marriage: quite apart from emotional and other intangible benefits such as enhanced status, it offered them security and access to property.

An alternative approach is to note the changes in the peasant family at this time. These did not follow immediately after the plague, but developed over a number of generations. The rising rate of migration, and the loosening of bonds of kinship, meant that land was less likely to pass from one generation to another. At Halesowen in Worcestershire in the two or three generations after 1349, land stayed within the family because relatively remote relatives, such as nephews and cousins, took on the inheritance in the absence of sons. In the long run, by the early fifteenth century, not even these heirs came forward, and high proportions of land passed from one family to another. Even when sons did inherit their parents' land, they immediately sold it. The old family solidarities no longer worked. Fathers did not acquire land for the benefit of sons, and old people could no longer be sure that their children would look after them in their declining years. This greater individualism might have encouraged early marriage, as young men could find cheap holdings of land very easily, especially if they were prepared to move from village to village, and the possession of land gave them the basis for marriage and starting a family. But perhaps early marriage did not follow automatically. This became a restless and rather unstable society, with its lack of kin solidarities and with a reduction in family support. Social pressures to find a partner may have been relaxed, and the negotiation of marriage more difficult.

In terms of economic logic, there should have been an era of early and youthful marriage in the early fifteenth century, and easily available land and jobs would have led to a high rate of fertility and population growth. Something of this kind did happen in parts of continental Europe, suggesting that an English family culture had emerged which prevented population growth. Whether by accident or some hidden and presumably unconscious design, the English peasants avoided a repeat of the rapid increase that caused problems around 1300.

ii. *Low population, c.1348–c.1400*

While the explanation of the long period of low population is uncertain, its consequences are better understood. Here we will focus on the late fourteenth century. After the Black Death, all of those 'accustomed to suffer want' (to quote the Rochester chronicler) expected improvement in their conditions. This was a time of liberation, when old restraints were removed and new freedom of choice opened. Scottish serfdom seems to have faded away, though an occasional reference to fugitive serfs, for example from the estates of the Bishop of Moray in the 1360s, suggests its persistence if only on a small scale. The lack of evidence for unrest suggests that serfdom ended without great contention. Servile peasants in England could not easily persuade lords to give them their freedom, but an increasing number of them left their lords' manors, especially in the 1380s and 1390s, and were able to acquire employment or land on manors where their servile origins were either unknown or quickly forgotten. At Hemmingford Abbots in Huntingdonshire in the 1370s, Simon Duntyng, a serf, had moved to the small Northamptonshire town of Daventry, while the daughter of Thomas Clarell had gone to London. The lord of Hemmingford, the abbot of Ramsey, ordered their relatives who still remained to bring them back, with threats of financial penalties, but serfs who had departed stayed away and became free by the fact of their separation from their lord. Peasants negotiated reductions in the costs of tenancy, with a continued move towards the conversion of labour service into money rent, and some reductions in rents and entry fines. They avoided some servile and occasional payments by concealing marriages or land transfers. This process was very uneven and partial, however, and in many cases rents did not fall as much as might be expected in view of the sudden reduction in the ranks of would-be tenants.

A second liberated group were the wage earners, who to some degree were freed from low wages and poor conditions of employment. Their behaviour was described at length by employers who resented their new-found freedom. They would not accept a contract to work for a year, as had been normal before 1348, but preferred shorter terms such as three months, or insisted on working by the day or by the task. Richard Tailor of Legsby in Lincolnshire chose freedom, when on 31 July 1374 he was required to continue to serve William Lene of nearby Lissington as a ploughman for a whole year. He refused the offer, and left to work 'in the district' (moving from job to job) for higher wages. Short-term employment was preferable because it was abundant, with dozens of employers anxious to hire labour, and work by the day was much better paid. In the harvest season, when Richard Tailor significantly made his decision, the going rate in Lincolnshire was 4d per day, that is the same wage as a skilled craftsman (a carpenter, for example) earned. His total reward for his work in August and September could have been 15s. A ploughman would have been lucky to receive 13s 4d for the year, together with an allowance of grain worth twice as much, and a few minor perks equivalent in total to less than 2d per day. Workers also insisted on increases in rewards in kind: the grain allowance for servants contained a higher proportion of wheat, and harvesters received meals with bread wholly or mainly baked from wheat, as well as ample supplies of fresh meat and ale.

Wage earners gained more freedom to choose their occupation. As the gap between skilled and unskilled workers narrowed, a common result of an overall labour shortage, it sometimes paid a skilled artisan to move into agricultural work, especially in the harvest. Likewise, less skilled workers took up specialized work, like the ploughman who became a carpenter, and another who went to sea as a mariner. Skills, training and experience were evidently not being given a high value. Workers also chose for whom to work, and frequently moved from one employer to another. Above all, they sometimes took breaks from work, for example in order to travel to a new workplace. They took more holidays, worked shorter hours, and insisted that they should still be paid – the old custom was discarded that winter work (limited by the hours of daylight) received less pay than summer work.

A third dimension of the liberation of the disadvantaged after 1348–50 was the freeing of many of those afflicted by poverty. The numbers of smallholders were drastically reduced, as heirs did not take up vacant cottages and some tenants acquired extra land or moved to larger holdings. We have already seen that wages, especially the wages of less skilled workers, rose, and real wages increased decisively after 1375, when grain prices fell. The area cultivated with cereals did not shrink as much as the population, so that when the run of bad harvests ceased, corn became abundant, and the purchasing power of agricultural wages expressed in bread, meat and cheese increased by 40 per cent between the 1340s and the 1380s. The unemployment and under-employment prevalent in the early fourteenth century no longer blighted the earning capacity of the poor, which helped to exasperate social commentators, who saw no excuse for begging by those capable of work. Charity was not withdrawn because of the criticism of the idle poor, but instead was focused on those thought to be in genuine need.

After the plague, individuals found that they were no longer tied so closely to the social groupings which had previously been so powerful.

The family was a less dominant influence, as young people were able to find work and land away from their homes, though the peasant family was too strong to crumble even under the shock of the first pestilence. Similarly the village community had rallied to protect the interests of its members during the hard times of the early fourteenth century, and had acquired new powers in 1334 when it became responsible for the assessment and collection of the king's main form of taxation, the lay subsidy. Again, it was too firmly founded to break apart after the plague, but it was put under some strain as individuals sought to claim their independence in such matters as the use of the common pastures. Thomas Baldwyn of Shuckburgh in Warwickshire, for example, refused to accept by-laws drawn up by his neighbours, and defied them for thirteen years until his death in 1400.

The Black Death liberated the women who asserted themselves in a male-dominated economy. Many still worked in the less skilled and less well paid preparatory processes in clothmaking, such as wool-combing and spinning. They seem to have expanded their role in the better-rewarded craft of weaving. For their traditional tasks, such as weeding and harvesting, they demanded higher pay, like the male labourers who closed some of the gap between their wages and those of skilled craftsmen. Women improved their rewards, but rarely received pay equal to that of men. Women also entered occupations from which they had traditionally been excluded, even such heavy tasks as metalworking. Joan Edwaker, a married woman of Eynsham in Oxfordshire, was driving a cart pulled by two horses in 1389. We know that she was doing this 'man's job' because she was killed by a fall, and her death was the subject of a coroner's inquest. Towns had always provided more economic opportunities for women, sometimes to carry on their own trade, notably in preparing and selling food and drink, and sometimes as participants in their husbands' craft or trade. Their role in the 'family' business became apparent when widows took over when their husbands died, showing that they had acquired the necessary skills and experience. In the 1360s Margaret Hogg of Edinburgh went on trading expeditions abroad with her merchant husband, and was involved in the business. When he died, she continued by marrying his business partner. As wives, they negotiated with customers, sold goods and managed the servants; as widows they took over credit negotiations, purchase of raw materials, training of apprentices and production. Emma Erle had established herself as a major dealer in cloth in the Yorkshire town of Wakefield by 1395–6, when she sold forty-eight cloths in a year, worth at least £50.

Women gained more rights over property, not just as widows entitled to their traditional 'free bench' (the right to hold all or part of their dead husbands' land for life, providing that they remained single), but also as joint tenants with their husbands, which gave them more extensive rights to land in widowhood. In this period we find that more women made wills; they reveal themselves from their bequests as owners of much moveable property. Women were still at a great disadvantage in a man's world; for example, they were excluded from political office, including positions of authority in fraternities and guilds, and found it difficult to gain full trading privileges in towns. The achievements of women tended to be gained informally. They acquired skills by experience, often without serving an apprenticeship. They traded on their own account, but their husbands appear in the records, as when men paid the routine penalties for selling ale at too high a price when it was their wives who were brewing and managing the alehouse. An all-female craft, silk-weaving, was developing, and though the silk women had a collective organization in London, they did not form a guild of the kind found in male-dominated crafts.

These new freedoms were not acquired without cost, and those who felt threatened by them struggled against the changes. The poet William Langland represents one point of view, that of a cleric of strong religious convictions who was offended by the immorality of the new social order, but he also reflects more widespread prejudices. Langland spent his adult life writing and then rewriting his great poem, known to us as *Piers Plowman*. The second version, the 'B' text of about 1380, brings his social and economic views into sharp focus. Piers, the central figure, is presented as an ideal peasant, diligent, frugal, dependable, loyal, honest and blunt in speech. The poem shows this admirable worker on a spiritual quest for salvation, and the poet puts into his mouth plain and virtuous comments on the sinful world. He is depicted within the conventions of the 'three orders', as a hard worker who is committed at one key point in the poem to the cultivation of a half-acre of land. He makes a contract with a knight, promising to work for the benefit of his superior, providing that the knight upholds law and order and hunts harmful animals. This model of mutual obligation was depicted in order to underline the failings of the real world. Piers had to remind the knight not to oppress his tenants, and while he could arrive at an agreement with the knight, he was unable to make a contract with a priest. Langland steps outside the conventions of the three orders by introducing a fourth estate of wage earners, beggars and petty criminals. Piers attempts to set this unruly labour force to work on the half-acre, but they soon stop. Piers criticizes them harshly, and the poem argues that only the threat of hunger will drive the idle back to work. Elsewhere in the poem Langland comments on the greed of labourers, who insist on the best food and drink, and makes especially harsh comments about beggars, both the secular vagrants and their clerical equivalents, the friars.

Piers Plowman was a bestseller in its time, in that numerous manuscript copies were made and many people heard it being read. Peasants knew of its contents, and naturally appreciated the favourable picture it gave of them, though of course Langland also portrayed a greedy and envious peasant, who criticized his neighbours behind their backs. Members of the social elite, both laymen and clergy, read the poem, because they could agree with many of its sentiments. In particular they shared Langland's belief that the social order had been dangerously undermined by the bargaining power of labourers, who demanded too much, used their newly acquired wealth in excessive consumption, and did not contribute enough to taxes. Beggars made the problem worse, because they lived on alms and refused to work.

Prejudices (formed well before Langland expressed them) led to legislation and changes in government policy, as they informed the thinking of the king's advisers, and of the landed magnates, gentry and wealthier townspeople who attended parliament. The Ordinance of Labourers (of 1349) and the Statute of Labourers (of 1351) made it illegal to demand or to offer rates of pay above those prevailing before the Black Death; it was also against the law to refuse to work, for example for a servant to decline an offer of a year's employment, or to break a contract by leaving before the term of employment was completed. Prices were also fixed. The Ordinance prohibited giving alms to those capable of work, 'so they may be compelled to labour'. The law was redefined by the Statute of Cambridge in 1388, which paid particular attention to those wandering in search of work, who were expected to carry documents, and beggars, who were supposed to stay in their place of origin. The laws were enforced by the local gentry, the specially appointed Justices of Labourers in the 1350s, and then by the Justices of the Peace, who had a general responsibility for law and order in the localities.

The labour laws have a superficial air of fairness in the sense that employers as well as employees were liable to prosecution, and the cost of foodstuffs was supposed to be regulated as well as wages. Enforcement was not just carried out by the gentry, as local people were drawn into the process. The constable of each village or town (mostly peasants or artisans, serving part-time out of duty) were expected to make workers swear an oath to observe the laws. The juries which gathered information for the courts and reported wrongdoers contained leading peasants, and some of the complaints must have come from peasant employers. Villagers were encouraged to bring offenders to the notice of the justices because the money collected in fines would be deducted from their quota of taxation for the next lay subsidy. The village of Beauchamp St Paul in Essex, for example, owed 75s in tax, but when the lay subsidy of 1352 was collected the 'fines of workers' came to 60s, which meant that the better-off villagers who normally paid the tax had to find only 15s. The tax burden was being shifted on to dozens of small-holders and labourers without land.

Despite the participation of those below the gentry in the courts, the law was used in a very one-sided fashion to defend the interests of the employers, and in particular the larger employers, such as the lords of manors and their bailiffs. In a court session held at Braintree in Essex for the administrative district of Hinckford Hundred in June 1378, the bias of the court is obvious. Only three cases were brought against employers, and in each case they were described as 'labourer' and 'mower', so they were leaders of groups of workers, subcontractors as we would call them, who carried out a task such as mowing a meadow for a lump sum, and then paid individual workers out of the proceeds. Not a single member of the gentry, lord of the manor or bailiff came before the court, yet we can be confident that they were paying wages above the legal rates. Instead, twenty-six labourers and other workers, such as a ploughman, a disabled carpenter and a roofer, were accused of taking high wages, especially in harvest time, or were said to be wandering from village to village 'for excess'. A typical case was Nicholas Thressher, labourer of Halsted, who 'takes 2d per day, both in winter and summer, and 4d in the harvest'. Gilbert Rougge of Sturmer was fined 5s for refusing to take the oath and therefore being 'a rebel against the constables'. No food traders were pros-ecuted in this session. The gentry justices who presided over the court were punishing a selection of workers from the hundreds of men and women who regularly broke the law each year. They may have hoped that their actions would help to depress wages, and therefore reduce the costs of production on their own manors. But they were probably not acting so directly in their own interest. They resented the earning power of the lower orders, and wished to make an example of some of them.

The Sumptuary Law of 1363 was not enforced, but it indicates the frustrations of those represented in parliament. The law complains of the 'excessive apparel' (extravagant clothing) that was being worn, and sets maximum levels of expenditure on cloth and accessories. Agricul-tural servants (ploughmen and shepherds, for example) were not allowed to wear cloth worth more than 12d per yard. This piece of unenforceable legislation was prompted by the rising price of manufactured goods, which those in parliament believed was being pushed up by demand from the lower orders. Another motive, however, clearly expressed in contemp-orary literature, was that as the visible symbols of social rank ceased to have their former meaning, the whole hierarchy of society was being threatened. If silk clothing, silver buckles and fur linings had previously been worn only by knights and great lords, it was feared that aristocratic privilege as a whole might be compromised if merchants or minor gentry wore such finery.

The aristocracy's role was to fight, and this became a serious problem in the 1370s, when the war with France was resumed after a truce in 1360–9. In the late 1340s and 1350s English armies had been successful, winning famous victories at Crécy and Poitiers, at modest cost for the taxpayer because the soldiers to some extent paid for themselves by living on the French countryside and making profits from ransoms. After 1369 the victories were elusive, the war came to England with raids on coastal towns, and the taxpayer was required to pay for the ineffective military effort. In the opinion of those in government, the tax system was not tapping effectively the wealth of the country, and an unfair burden fell on the contributors to the lay subsidy, including the peasants with middling to large holdings of land. After an experiment with an ill-planned parish tax in 1371, the poll taxes of 1377, 1379 and 1381 were seen as a useful supplement to the lay subsidies. They brought into the tax system a large section of the population previously exempt, that is wage earners without large quantities of livestock or other goods, both servants living in the households of their employers, and labourers who had their own cottages or smallholdings. The first poll tax of 1377 expected everyone over the age of fourteen to pay 4d, without any attempt to match income to payment. The second assessment of 1379 showed some awareness of criticisms, by raising the age to sixteen, and by using a sliding scale by which the rich paid more than 4d. The third, granted in 1380 but collected in 1381, demanded 12d from each person over fifteen, but within each village and town the rich were encouraged to help the poor.

The tax was clearly motivated by the belief that the wage earners whose rate of pay had risen since the 1340s should contribute to the national war effort. The labour laws may have failed to prevent wage increases, but at least those who broke the law could pay a part of their extra earnings to the state. The new tax was bitterly resented by those who had to pay for the first time. It was thought particularly unfair that young servants, including females, whose modest rewards reflected their limited productivity, should have to pay. In practice, their employers or parents must have found the money. The taxpayers' response was to evade payment, mainly by concealing young people, whether servants or children, and especially females. This could be done by denying the presence of adolescents in the household, or more commonly by claiming that young people were under fifteen or sixteen. The number of those paying throughout the country fell from 1,355,201 in 1377 to below 900,000 in 1381. These figures alone point to a high level of discontent. As often happens when groups do not speak to each other and nurse grievances, rumours spread which helped to poison the atmosphere. After a rash of lawsuits mounted by peasants in forty villages in southern England to claim the privileges attached to 'ancient demesne' (see p. 181), a petition in 1377 from the knights in the lower house of parliament claimed that if the French invaded, the peasants would support them. This accusation was not justified by later events, when peasants, even those exasperated with the government, remained fiercely loyal to the crown.

Such measures as the Statute of Labourers meant that the government was intervening in the economy in a new way. Before the Black Death the state had an interest in maintaining law and order, which lay behind laws regulating merchant debt, or in rewarding the king's supporters with such economic benefits as market charters, or in economic measures that would raise revenue, such as Edward III's wool monopoly. After the Black Death the ruling groups temporarily closed ranks, and used the power of the state to defend the interests of the rich in a blatant manner. Members of landed society (both laymen and churchmen) made up the personnel of government, as civil servants and members of the king's council and household, and their membership of parliament allowed them to bring their influence to bear. One of the most important developments strengthened the role of the local gentry as the agents of the state by giving the JPs more responsibility and power. The ranks of society below the gentry felt that the state was losing any claim to impartiality as it became so closely identified with the landed interest.

Landlords influenced state policy, and at the same time took measures in their private courts. While the local justices enforced the labour laws, a 'seigneurial reaction' was being mounted in the manors. Manorial courts had always provided useful profits, but after the Black Death their revenues increased, a remarkable development as the numbers of tenants had fallen drastically. Lords whose income from rents was tending to diminish stepped up pressure on local officials to search out breaches of manorial discipline, such as peasants who allowed their animals to stray on to the demesne land, or who failed to carry out their labour services. Each offender was charged an amercement of 3d, 4d or 6d for the offence, and the totals on a large manor could amount to £5 or £10 by the end of the year. On some manors each peasant was paying on average twice as much to the courts as his predecessors had done before 1348. The lords' courts also clamped down on those who evaded payments or broke the rules governing tenancy or servility. If servile women married without paying a fine, or if customary tenants sold land without informing the court and paying an entry fine, or if they allowed their buildings to fall into ruin, the court would eventually catch up with them, exact the payments that had been avoided, and make them pay extra in amercements. Take the case of John Hamond of Earl Soham in Suffolk, who was attempting to build up a larger holding by buying land, keeping this secret so that his lord would not interfere with his activities or charge entry fines. In 1379 the manorial officials discovered that he had acquired a servile holding in 1377 and was failing to repair the buildings. For ten years he had held 7 acres by free tenure, but had ingeniously assigned them to a trust to avoid the difficulty of a serf acquiring free land. It must have been well known in the village that he was in possession of the land, but his neighbours kept quiet. In such cases, the peasants who were supposed to report such matters to the lord's court, the chief pledges or the jurors, might be made to pay an amercement for the offence of 'concealment'. The peasants or artisans who had been pushed into accepting offices in the manorial administration felt divided loyalties, as they were members of a community and wished to remain on good terms with their neighbours, yet they had an obligation to serve the lord and present to the court 'well and faithfully' those who broke the rules. It is not surprising that substantial peasants like Thomas Gardiner of Little Barton in Suffolk refused in 1380 to take the oath as chief pledge, even when ordered to do so four times. On some occasions in Essex and Suffolk, the friction between lords and tenants reached such a pitch that all of the tenants boycotted the court.

iii. *Revolts*

The rising of 1381 (the 'Peasants' Revolt') shows that the ordinary people of south-east England sought political solutions for their grievances, but their complaints were rooted in economic and social problems. The rebellion was provoked by official enquiries into the evasion of the third poll tax in Essex and Kent. The poll tax was not the cause of the rising, but it served to highlight the whole issue of taxation and misgovernment. The burden of taxation was already heavy: it amounted to £382,000 collected from the laity in the ten years before 1381. The taxpayers, that is mainly the more substantial peasants and artisans, were each contributing more than their predecessors had done before the Black Death. The quotas of the lay subsidy had been fixed in 1334, and these sums now had to be shared out among fewer villagers, who by the 1370s were no longer benefiting from the fines paid under the labour laws. Many households were having to find 4s for each lay subsidy, which meant that a

middle-aged couple with two children in their late teens would have paid
8s in 1378 (when parliament granted a double subsidy), 6s in 1380 (a
grant of a subsidy and a half), as well as 1s 4d in 1377 for the first poll
tax, rather less in 1379, and a threat of another 4s in 1381. Their dissatisfaction was provoked partly by the amount to be paid, but also by the
suspicion that the money was being wasted through incompetence and
fraud within the government. There had been widespread support for the
faction in the 'Good Parliament' in 1376 which persuaded the assembly
to refuse a grant of taxes, and to prosecute corrupt officials. That wave
of enthusiasm turned to bitter disappointment when subsequent parliaments, influenced by the richest and most powerful magnate, John of
Gaunt, Duke of Lancaster, reverted to a policy of futile military campaigns funded by more taxes, including the poll taxes.

The rebellion was directed initially against local government officials,
such as the sheriffs and escheators, and against the local properties
of the 'traitors' in central government who were held responsible for
the failure of policy. These included John of Gaunt, Simon Sudbury (the
chancellor, who was also archbishop of Canterbury), and Robert Hales
(the treasurer, also prior of the Knights Hospitallers). Such was the level
of political consciousness in the south-east, and the rapid spread of news
and rumours, that the rebels were sufficiently well informed to know the
name of a relatively minor figure in the government, John Legge, who
had proposed the enquiries into tax evasion. The rebel bands assembled
at meeting points in their counties, and then converged on London,
acquiring on the way a leader, Wat Tyler. They presented themselves as
agents of the king, calling themselves the 'true commons', that is the
king's loyal subjects, seeking to replace the 'traitors' who had misled
him. They recruited men and collected money as if they had taken over
the government, and they advanced under banners and pennons like a
legitimate army.

When the rebels reached London they demanded to see the king,
and met him on 14 June at Mile End to the east of the city. The young
Richard II issued charters of freedom, and appeared to agree to the
removal of the 'traitors'. The rebels had already attacked property
belonging to their enemies in and near London, such as Gaunt's palace
of the Savoy and the headquarters of Hales's Hospitallers at Clerken-
well, and now they captured Hales, Sudbury and others and killed them
in what they believed was a judicial execution. On the next day Tyler met
the king at Smithfield, presented a list of demands which appear to have
envisaged the removal of aristocratic privilege and the church hierarchy,
and the creation of a popular monarchy in which the king ruled over self-
governing village communities. Shortly afterwards Tyler was killed and

the rebel bands dispersed. Rebellions in Cambridgeshire, Norfolk and Suffolk continued for some time after the collapse of the Kent and Essex risings, with gatherings at Bury St Edmunds, Norwich and Cambridge. The whole country was brought under control after fights at Billericay in Essex and North Walsham in Norfolk. Dozens of rebels died in those confrontations, and in a flurry of executions.

The political actions of the rebels reflected their perception that the government and the landlords were bound together in the same corrupt system. They resented the dual role of the king's justices, such as John Bampton, whose enquiries in Essex set the revolt in motion, and Sir John Cavendish, the Chief Justice of King's Bench, both of whom lent their legal expertise to major church landlords for profit. We understand the rebels' thinking better when we can identify them as individuals and examine their lives before the revolt. They included every type of person, from servants to a few gentry and clergy. Townspeople joined in, from London, Bury, Canterbury and St Albans within the central region of the revolt, but also in pursuit of their own specific quarrels at Beverley, York and Scarborough in Yorkshire, and at Bridgwater and Winchester in the west.

The majority held land, often with middling holdings of between 5 and 20 acres, and owned herds of cattle and flocks of sheep. The majority in Essex, Suffolk and Norfolk were customary tenants. William Smith of Ingatestone in Essex can serve as an example. He was accused of joining the revolt at the beginning, of attacking John Bampton the justice, and also of taking part in the killing of the escheator of Essex. He was a serf and a customary tenant, and owned at the time of the revolt at least six cattle, five calves and some pigs. The rebels included a significant number of craft workers, such as carpenters or tailors, or those who were involved in trade, though these people often held land as well. Many who attracted the attention of the authorities, that is the local leaders of the revolt, had served in official positions in their manors or villages, as chief pledges, jurors, reeves and constables. William Smith of Ingatestone served as an ale taster, and as his daughter was married by 1387, he must have been at least in his late thirties at the time of the revolt. The rebels were middle-aged, responsible people, who were moved to rebellion not by poverty or despair, but by hope. They had observed the changes in the world since 1349, which potentially benefited them, in terms of cheaper land, the opportunity to increase their livestock, and an expanding market for ale, meat and manufactured goods. Individuals who joined the rebellion are known to have acquired extra land before the rising. These better prospects were opening for peasants and artisans everywhere, but the south-eastern counties seemed to offer particular advantages, as London's economic influence was strong, towns like

Colchester were prospering, and rural industries flourished. Yet in parts of this commercial and mobile society the old institution of serfdom was still strong, and both lords and the state found ways to take their cash. The leading peasants and artisans who served as local officials felt acutely in 1350–80 that their lords were pushing them one way, and their neighbours pulling them in another. They knew something about law and the working of local government, so they could criticize lawyers and government officials on the basis of experience.

The rebellion drew strength from the ability of the local elites to organize contingents from each village and co-ordinate their movements. The bands made rapid progress across the country because they were riding on their own horses, a further indication that they were not desperately poor. The letters which circulated encouraged the rebels to stick to their cause and complete the task by emphasizing the solidarity and loyalty of the rebel bands: 'stand manly together in truth'. The rebellion was a serious matter, and those who took part must have realized that they were risking their lives, but an air of festivity emerged, perhaps because the time of the revolt coincided with summer games when village communities normally celebrated and drank ale.

The leading rebels' aims flowed from their experiences and frustrations as subordinates in a world that offered a prospect of improvement. Their ideas were well established. Some of them, such as the people of Harmondsworth in Middlesex or Mildenhall in Suffolk, came from villages which had a long history of resisting serfdom, especially by appealing to the king for protection as tenants of former royal estates. The strategy of the 1381 rising was based on the correct assumption that only the authority of the state could set aside the property rights of lords and free the serfs. These convictions were encouraged by the message of the renegade preacher, John Ball, who reminded them of the Christian doctrine of the equality of all men, and the injustice of aristocratic privileges. The letters that were sent out by Ball or like-minded associates urged the moral justification for rebellion: 'do well and better, and avoid sin'. In the localities rebels burnt manorial records, an act which symbolized their rejection of serfdom and the authority of lords, but which also had the practical effect of removing the written evidence for their unfree status.

When the rebels met the king, they did not mention the poll tax, but instead demanded their freedom. At Mile End they declared, according to a chronicler, 'no man should be a serf, nor do homage or any type of service to any lord, but should give 4d for an acre of land'. The sum of money mentioned was quite low, but not absurdly low. They also insisted that service should depend on contracts that had been agreed freely (a reference either to labour service, or to the compulsory contracts under the Statute of Labourers). Other demands that are reported to have been made at Mile End included free buying and selling. The central importance of serfdom for most rebels is suggested by their willingness to return home once they had been granted the royal charters of liberty which were issued at Mile End. Other rebels remained, realizing that they had scored a notable victory and could press their opposition to the power of lords yet further. When they met the king again at Smithfield they repeated their demand for freedom, and added that 'no lord should have lordship in the future, but it should be divided among all men'. They were envisaging removing the lords as intermediaries between king and people, and empowering themselves to run their own affairs. Their demand that there should be no law except the law of Winchester would have dismantled the royal courts, removed the lawyers and deprived the lords of their jurisdiction, placing the maintenance of law and order in the hands of each village community.

Many of the local actions and demands of the rising pursued this hostility to lords. At St Albans and Bury St Edmunds the rebels insisted that ancient royal charters of liberty had been hidden by the monks who ruled over those towns, and at St Albans they claimed common rights to pasture animals and to take game in the local woods and pastures. One chronicler reports the extension of hunting rights as a rebel demand in London, which would show the rebels envisaging the removal of lordly privileges in a concrete and practical form. The rebels generally focused their attacks on individuals who oppressed them, either particular agents of central government, or specific lords. They did not assault or kill lords in general, perhaps because this would be unnecessary as they expected to abolish their powers as a group. The reasons for their choice of victims sometimes remain a mystery, and in particular we do not know why they hunted and killed Flemish immigrants in London and the provinces. The rebels were not 'anti-foreigner': they caused no problems for German merchants, so clearly they had some grievance against the Flemings, perhaps because they competed with English textile workers.

Was the revolt of any significance in the long term? The first impulse must be to regard it as a transient episode. The revolt's collapse was complete and sudden, after only two months. Many rebels were killed or put to flight, and the charters of manumission were declared invalid. Lords held courts in the late summer or autumn of 1381, sometimes headed 'the first court after the rebellion', which had to cope with the practical problems caused by the destruction of the records. The tenants made their submission to their lords, after which their names, holdings and terms of tenure might be written on the court roll, and a fine demanded. The lords were anxious to reimpose their discipline, and to resume normal life and the routines of rent collection as soon as possible. The crown granted rebels who had escaped initial capture the chance to buy a pardon, and lords allowed them to return to their holdings. William Smith of Ingatestone, the typical rebel mentioned above, returned to his manor and was serving again as ale taster by 1386.

Although the rebellion was short-lived and normality swiftly returned, it left a profound sense of shock. The chroniclers who wrote about the revolt all reacted strongly to an event that seemed so sudden and unprecedented. Some of them emphasized the sinfulness of the rebels, who had offended against the divinely ordained social hierarchy by refusing to accept their role in the three orders. Some observers compared the rebels to animals; like mad dogs and unnaturally fierce oxen they behaved savagely and without reason. Others did not condemn the rebels only, but blamed the errors of government and the sins of the aristocracy. The severity of the shock made the royal ministers abandon the poll taxes, and the expensive campaigns against France. Among the peasants, artisans and wage earners, the ideas expressed in the revolt could not be erased. William Smith, our Essex rebel, continued to cause trouble in his lord's manor, refusing to pay a common fine in 1386, and in the following year he had to be bound over to be well behaved towards the lord's bailiff. New small-scale rebellions broke out throughout the 1380s, 1390s, and into the following century. They raised the same issues of freedom and the power of lords, as for example at Barnet in Hertfordshire, where tenants of the monks of St Albans rose in 1381, and in 1417 renewed an old demand that they be allowed to buy and sell customary land by charters, rather than having to take such transactions to the lord's court.

When peasants between the 1390s and the 1440s came to negotiate with lords for conversion of labour service to money rents, or for rent reductions, or the removal of archaic servile dues and collective payments such as tallages and common fines, their hand was strengthened by both sides' memories of 1381. They did not need to use violence, but merely had to show their determination by refusing to pay, or by threatening to leave the manor to find land elsewhere. The lords' officials usually gave way. Serfdom withered away in the fifteenth century, together with high and unpopular rents, partly because the economic realities made it essential for lords to make concessions to keep tenants, but also because the 1381 rising had demonstrated the potential strength of the peasants.

Twenty years after 1381, a revolt shook Wales even more profoundly. It was led by a member of the gentry, Owain Glyn Dŵr, and its objectives were overtly political: the end of English rule. The rising attracted much support from peasants and artisans, and an important reason for their participation was the extreme 'seigneurial reaction' in the Welsh marches. The marcher lords did not feel inhibited by the restraining power of the state or by local custom. When their rents began to stagnate or decline in the fourteenth century, the great lords were able to compensate themselves with other sources of revenue. While every English manor's revenue was shrinking after the Black Death, the Arundels increased their income from the lordship of Chirk in North Wales from £300 to £500 per annum in the sixty years after 1322. They pushed up leasehold rents, which were partly based on their power as lords, as mills were one of their main assets and they profited by maintaining a milling monopoly. They could also, like the other marcher lords, impose collective fines, aids, tallages and 'mises' on the inhabitants. At Chirk, the lords demanded a collective payment of £500 because the tenants failed to carry timber as a labour service. These impositions caused distress to tenants because they were unpredictable both in their timing and in the amount of money levied. There was a particular concentration of demands at a time of political instability when a number of marcher lordships changed hands after Richard II confiscated the estates of his opponents in 1397. Henry, duke of Lancaster used the occasion of his succession after the death of his father John of Gaunt in 1399 to force the people of Cydweli to pay £1,575. The tenants could respond by paying slowly or not at all, and by 1400 arrears at Chirk, mainly caused by unpaid fines and rents, had built up to £663.

Relationships were made more difficult because the lords were English and the peasants Welsh, and differences in customs caused dispute and resentment. For example, under English law, if a line of hereditary succession to a holding died out (as tended to happen after the Black Death), or if a tenant failed to pay his rent, the land would escheat to the lord, but under Welsh law it went to the kin. Naturally English lords favoured their own custom. A good deal of native Welsh resentment was focused on the towns, which had been founded as English colonies and were given rights and monopolies. As late as 1399 a charter to the Flintshire town of Hope stated that Welsh brewers could not sell their ale within a radius of 3 leagues (4½ miles). These discriminatory measures were still imposed, although they were becoming irrelevant as more Welsh people moved into the towns and the English acquired land in 'Welsh' areas.

Glyn Dŵr rose in 1400, and the war continued for seven years. The attacks of the rebels, especially on towns, and the movement of English armies against them, caused much destruction. Even a century later, the decay of dozens of towns was blamed on the revolt, but there were probably deeper economic problems, as some places burnt by Glyn Dŵr's armies, like Carmarthen, recovered quite quickly. A positive development after the revolt brought more Welsh people into towns, so that they came to dominate even in such a colonial borough as Caernarfon. In the marcher lordships, tenants commonly refused to pay rents, and arrears built up to very high levels. Lords had to accept the situation, and in doing so they were acknowledging the danger of offending tenants to the point that they would again rebel.

To sum up, the Black Death liberated the lower ranks of society; the elite were stimulated into a reaction, which soured relations and provoked rebellion. The revolts established a new balance, in which the authorities adjusted to the reality that the peasants, artisans and wage earners had improved their bargaining power. The fall in population created the environment in which these changes took place, but reduction in rent and the freeing of serfs did not happen 'naturally'. The entrenched institutions would crack only if the lower orders developed ideas which contradicted those of their rulers, and asserted themselves in a coherent and organized way.

iv. *The economy, c.1348–c.1400*

The general economic aftermath of the Black Death and the reduced population was neither simple nor predictable, partly because of other impersonal influences, and partly because people reacted to their new circumstances in unexpected ways. The long-term impact of a smaller population, as we have seen, was to reduce the demand for basic foodstuffs, which depressed corn prices, lowered rents and encouraged the shrinkage of the area of land under cultivation. As the labour force became smaller, wages and the cost of manufactured goods increased. The period 1349–75 does not, however, fit this pattern. Corn prices remained at a high level, probably because unstable weather conditions reduced yields. Real wages, that is wages expressed in terms of the prices of food, were in consequence depressed, and indeed cash wages did not leap forward as much as we would expect after a halving of the workforce. The labour shortage should have been acute, not just because many workers died in the epidemic, but because many smallholders who had been part-time workers acquired enough land to live without needing to earn wages. Wages rose rather gradually in the late fourteenth century, and did not reach their highest level until twenty or thirty years after the first epidemic. Mowing an acre of meadow, for example, cost 5d in the 1340s, between 6d and 7d in the twenty years after the first plague, and 7¹/₂d in the 1370s and 1380s. In many parts of England the daily wage of skilled building workers such as carpenters, which had been 3d before the Black Death, hovered between 3d and 4d in the 1350s and 1360s, and only in the last quarter of the century reached a plateau of 4d (see Figure 3 above, p. 240). The slow rise in wages may reflect the large number of under-employed people in the 1340s, who took the place of the plague casualties. The labour laws may also have had their effect, both by keeping wage rates down for fear of punishment, but also by distorting our evidence, so that higher wages were really paid, but the illegal rates were concealed in the manorial accounts which provide most of our information. Plague mortality was also playing a part in making workers more scarce in the 1380s, as the cohort of young people who then entered the labour market had been depleted by the death of their parents' generation in the 'children's plague' of 1361–2. In addition, urban and industrial growth in the 1380s and 1390s was creating more competition among employers.

In the countryside the persistently low population should have halved the size of villages, and therefore put double the amount of land in the hands of the surviving tenants. The impact on landholding varied from region to region and from village to village. In general, the number of tenants did not fall as much as would be expected. At Alveston in Warwickshire, where there had been eighty-five tenants in the thirteenth century, the number had reduced to fifty-five by 1385. It was not until the next century that the numbers fell to only thirty-two. At Alveston and in the midlands generally lords and tenants kept to the old yardland or oxgang units, but it became increasingly common for two half-yardlands or two yardlands to be put together, or a smallholding or a cottage to be added to a yardland or half-yardland. A rental of the Dalkieth estate of the Douglas family made in 1376–7 shows that the standard holding had become four oxgangs, double the normal substantial tenements of the early fourteenth century. A higher proportion of holdings reached 30 to 60 acres, but very large accumulations of land, containing 100 acres or more, were quite rare. At the south Devon village of Stokenham, the main landholders (as distinct from cottagers) reduced in number between 1347 and 1390 from 147 to 120, and the average amount of land held by each tenant rose from 31 to 45 acres. These relatively modest changes came about because a higher proportion of the rural population acquired land. Young people could gain a holding at an early stage of their lives, and the landless workers, like the *garciones* recorded in the south-west, almost disappeared. Evidently, acquisitive peasants did not pursue the accumulation of very large holdings, perhaps because they had difficulty in finding labour either from within their own families, or by hiring workers. In central Essex a high proportion of smallholders persisted, with nearly half of holdings (both before and after the plagues) containing less than 5 acres, perhaps because so many tenants were employed in industry.

At the other extreme, while relatively few villages were abandoned at this time, a minority went into severe and terminal decline, as tenants left, or died without successors. A handful of small villages in the Cotswolds disappeared, and in many parts of the midlands villages lost more than half of their population. In these cases the land was sometimes acquired by ambitious villagers, and so holdings could grow as large as 5 yardlands. Alternatively, no tenant wished to take it, and it was left 'in the lord's hands'.

Lords took various steps to prevent the loss of tenants, such as drastically reducing entry fines, or converting the former servile land into leasehold, so that tenants could take on a term of perhaps six or nine years with a fixed cash rent, with the reduction or abolition of the uncertain and variable extra payments which caused so much dissatisfaction. There were still tens of thousands of tenants in the 1390s who held their customary land on hereditary tenures in much the same way as their predecessors fifty or even a hundred years earlier. In west Suffolk and Cornwall, some rents were as high towards the end of the fourteenth century as they had been before the first plague. Labour services were mostly being commuted, but that was a continuation of a trend that had begun well before the Black Death. Lords might still be able to charge a few pounds' entry fine for a yardland. The really decisive and universal change through much of lowland England was the leasing of lords' demesnes, which had begun before 1348. The first plague did not push lords into wholesale leasing. Direct cultivation of large acreages paid quite well while the high grain prices lasted, and it was the combination of falling prices and rising labour costs after 1375 which forced lords to accept that it was better to let a tenant worry about the profit margin. In the 1380s and 1390s, one large estate after another embarked on the process of handing over the demesne of each manor as a block to a farmer for a fixed annual rent.

The economy of towns might have been expected to suffer severely from the loss of population: the number of inhabitants should have fallen by a half, partly because of the general decline, but also because of the notorious tendency for towns to harbour disease. Trade and industry could well have contracted after the fall in the number of both workers and consumers. We have seen that industries were disrupted in the 1350s and 1360s, but the general level of commercial activity reached a very high level around 1400. Wool exports were certainly reduced, from about 35,000 sacks annually in the mid-fourteenth century to about 18,000 in

the 1390s, but this was partly offset by the increase in cloth exports, from
about 2,000 cloths just after the first pestilence towards 40,000 in the 1390s
(Figure 4 above, p. 244). Overall production must have been at least four
times this level, because most of the cloth from English looms was bought
within the country. It is therefore not surprising that clothmaking became
widespread in the countryside and in small towns, as in Essex, Suffolk,
Wiltshire and Somerset. Towns which specialized in woollen textiles,
Colchester and Coventry, brushed aside the effects of the Black Death and
actually increased in size from 4,000 to 6,000 in the first case, and from
about 5,000 to 9,000 in the other. Larger towns, which subsequently
declined, such as Bristol, Norwich, Southampton and York, experienced
a phase of prosperity at the end of the fourteenth century, and small
places like Chelmsford were growing, with new shops being built in
1384–1417. Scottish wool exports stood at a high level in the 1370s, and
merchants like John Mercer of Perth (who died in 1380) and Adam
Forester of Edinburgh (who died in 1405) made fortunes at this time.

The tin industry, after going through a trough in the middle of the
century, was booming in the years 1386–1416. Cornish tin miners and
smelters produced more than a million pounds of the metal in a year,
comparable with output in the 1340s. Lead and iron mining were prospering, and imports of wine from Gascony climbed to a peak in 1403
that came near to returning to pre-war levels.

Why did trade, industry and towns do so well when they should have
been depressed? A partial answer might be that the landlords did
not suffer a catastrophic fall in income, and were able to maintain quite
a high level of expenditure. England, notably through its cloth exports,
was producing goods previously made in continental Europe, and so
was prospering at the expense of its rivals. But home demand was all
important, and here the developing consumption of the mass of the
population accounts for much of the health of trade. People who had
previously spent most of their food budget on basic cereals for bread
and pottage could now drink more ale and eat more meat, so the trade
of brewers and butchers was growing at this time. Consumers were also
able to spend a higher proportion of their incomes on non-food items,
such as clothing, houses, utensils and furnishings. They could replace
their clothes more often, and could own a number of garments. Fashion
was influencing the choices of peasants and wage earners, who adopted
the shorter and more closely fitting styles which had been taken up by
the aristocracy in the mid-fourteenth century. The new ideas were
encouraged by the many tailors who worked throughout the country in
towns and villages. (Plate 16) The fashionable lined garments used more
material, and ordinary people wore more colourful clothing, which was

expensive because of the cost of dyeing. In their households, consumers began to replace their cheaper utensils with more durable and attractive materials. Wooden plates were supplemented with pewter, and cups were made from glazed pottery as well as wood. Peasants kept more horses, and probably spent more on ironwork for their shoes and harness, and on the iron fittings on carts. Town-based craftsmen provided cast brass cooking pots, which were now in universal use, and also mass-produced inexpensive buckles, and small metal ornaments for a large market.

The first pestilence confirmed and deepened a downward trend in population which became a characteristic of the next two centuries. The plagues and the low levels of population did not have the immediate consequences that would be expected. Wages, rents, prices, lords' incomes and the fortunes of towns all failed to rise or fall in line with predictions. This was partly because of the manipulation of the economy by those in power. Social tensions built up as the poor glimpsed better opportunities, and the rich resisted. Once the air had cleared after the explosion of revolt, the economy settled down. Lords gave up their role as direct producers, and the peasants cautiously accumulated larger holdings. As the masses, including those depending mainly on wages, spent their new wealth, the urban and commercial economy regained some of the lost ground and grew once more. The low population also failed to produce predicted effects because there were many other forces for change, such as innovations in the organization of production. We will now turn to these developments in both town and country between 1350 and 1520.

CHAPTER NINE

Towns, trade and industry, c.1350–c.1520

In 1462 John Paston remarked in exasperation that his tenants looked forward to a 'new world', but could that phrase be applied in general to economic and social changes in the century and a half after the Black Death? Those who made their living from commerce and manufacture, whether they lived in town or country, encountered difficulties in a time of recession. Yet towns retained their importance, some grew and new ones emerged. There were changes in the flow of trade, and from industry came new methods of production.

i. Urban fortunes

Towns, and large towns in particular, in the fifteenth and sixteenth centuries provided limited opportunities for enterprise, because many were shrinking in population, and their trade was reduced in volume. This was sometimes stated by the inhabitants, at length, when they asked for release from the burden of taxation. The north Lincolnshire town of Grimsby, which supported near to 2,000 people before the Black Death, contained 1,500 in 1377 and fewer than 900 in the early sixteenth century. In the 1450s the town was unable to pay to the crown in full, and on time, the fee farm of £50 per annum which had been fixed in 1256. In 1461, the royal government had been informed that the town was 'greatly impoverished' by the excessive charges laid on it. The complaints do not suggest that the inability to pay was merely a symptom of economic troubles, but imply that the high fee farm was in itself a cause of the town's ills. The annual payment was reduced to £30 in 1464, yet the townspeople still complained, and in 1490 asked for the fee farm to be reduced to £20, giving as an explanation the problem of supporting three parish churches and four religious houses, in addition to the payment to the crown. They claimed that newcomers were discouraged from settling in the town by the financial responsibilities imposed on them. Buildings were falling down, and the number of wealthy people had diminished. Trade had 'gone down', and the harbour was 'wrecked and stopped'. If the fee farm was not reduced, the town would be 'utterly destroyed'.

Taxpayers have always pleaded poverty to justify reductions in their assessments, and Grimsby's claims, like similar excuses made by other towns at this time, were exaggerated. The harbour, though silting up, was still in use, and some trade was continuing. The leading burgesses of fifteenth-century towns in general, though they made much of their troubles, had no difficulty in justifying their arguments, and we can confirm their complaints to some degree. Houses were falling into ruin, and their empty sites were converted into gardens or rubbish dumps. At Oxford, colleges could be built near the town centre because land there was either vacant or cheap. When Robert Cole compiled a rental in 1455 for one of the main landlords in Gloucester, the priory of Llanthony, he found that six houses were decayed or ruined, twenty dwellings were being used as stables, there were twenty-four vacant plots and sixty tofts and curtilages, many of which had previously contained houses and cottages. In many towns, even when houses were still occupied, the diminishing demand for property forced landlords to accept lower rents. The vicars choral in York, a major landowner in the city, received £122 in 1371, but that figure was almost halved, to £68, by 1500. Individual houses in many towns were rented for about 20s before 1350, but these were typically reduced to 15s or 13s 4d after 1400. In Canterbury, the slide in rents began in the 1420s and 1430s, and in Oxford in the 1440s and 1450s, and in both places low rents then prevailed in the late fifteenth and early sixteenth centuries. Rent collectors in Newcastle upon Tyne had difficulties in persuading the tenants to pay, and could not prevent reductions, in the second half of the fifteenth century.

Public buildings were liable to decay. Town walls, which served as much as symbols of civic identity as practical means of defence, were everywhere neglected. At Aberystwyth, where the fee farm had been halved, by the early sixteenth century the walls had fallen into ruin. Parish churches were abandoned in Winchester. There had been fifty-four of them in 1300, but twenty-one had decayed by 1400, and another seven went in the fifteenth century, leaving less than half, twenty-six, that were still in use in 1500.

The physical decay of public buildings could be seen as a symptom of a deterioration in civic loyalties. Towns complained that those eligible for office in the town government refused election, fearful of the personal expense. Finally, some towns could point to the changes in the coastline and the sea level, which caused part of Dunwich (in Suffolk) to fall into the sea, but at Yarmouth and Saltfleethaven, as at Grimsby, silt was being deposited in the harbour.

These problems were by no means universal, and even in the towns which were affected the complaints give only one side of the picture. For almost every apparent symptom of decline there are reasons for doubting the evidence. The fee farm was not such an enormous burden for places which contained many people and much wealth. Often when towns said that they could no longer afford to pay, they meant that specific revenues which had been earmarked for the fee farm (such as rents on particular properties) had diminished. Leading townsmen did not lack a sense of civic duty – individuals had always declined election to such time-consuming jobs as that of chamberlain or bailiff, and some councils nominated candidates who they knew would refuse, in order to collect a fine. The decay of some houses removed overcrowded and cramped cottages, and left space for gardens, which improved the quality of life for those who remained. The rents which decayed were often being collected on behalf of remote institutions, and some of the collectors may not have tackled their work with much zeal or efficiency. Townspeople were sensible not to maintain the walls, which often served no useful purpose. While they saw no point in maintaining parish churches for which there were inadequate congregations, even in shrinking towns they lavished money on the embellishment or even rebuilding of the churches that remained in use. Many towns either rebuilt or added substantially to their parish churches in the fifteenth and early sixteenth centuries, and not just the 'wool churches' of the Cotswolds, or those in the clothmaking districts in Devon or Suffolk. There were many complex motives for church-building, among which local prosperity was one important dimension. But if we take the presence of a large new church as evidence that people had cash to spare for expensive building work, then it reflects not just the wealth of a few individuals, but of the whole community, as fundraising was frequently a collective effort, to which many parishioners contributed.

Towns had to adjust to reductions in the size of their populations, especially after the period of relative prosperity around 1400. Winchester suffered more than most, when its 10,000 to 12,000 people in c.1300 dropped to below 8,000 in 1417, and to about 4,000 in 1524–5. Places which lost about half of their populations between 1377 and 1524–5 include Boston, Lincoln, Lynn and York, while Beverley, Leicester and Grimsby shrank severely. They probably fell more catastrophically between 1300 (before the plagues) and the 1450s, when trade reached a low point. The larger east coast ports were especially vulnerable to decline, as were both large and small towns in the east midlands, such as Stamford in Lincolnshire and Brackley in Northamptonshire.

The towns which ceased to be towns entirely, either because their inhabitants deserted them or because those who remained turned to agriculture, tend to be found in the west and north of Britain. In Wales, at least nine boroughs were completely deserted, and a dozen others, like Caerphilly, ceased to have an urban economy. Failed boroughs are also found in north-west England, for example at Greystoke in Cumberland. At least twenty Scottish burghs, like Auchterhouse and Scrabster, either failed to develop, or by the early sixteenth century had relapsed into rural settlements or fishing villages. Failures are also scattered over the midlands and the south, like the Warwickshire borough of Bretford, and Newton in Purbeck in Dorset. With many of these places we cannot be sure that they had ever been flourishing towns. Often they were granted a market charter, or burghal privileges, but in the fifteenth or sixteenth centuries the burgage plots were vacant or occupied as agricultural holdings.

Changes in the size of towns came about because of inhabitants' decisions about where to establish their homes and businesses, and how to make their living. In towns which did not offer a good income or future prospects, landlords or tenants neglected to carry out work on houses, or allowed them to fall down, or could not see any benefit in building anew. Potential immigrants were discouraged, or moved to a place which promised more jobs and higher rewards.

Towns suffered setbacks when the trade in basic commodities was reduced in volume. The Scottish trade in wool and hides was doing quite well in the late fourteenth century, when 9,000 sacks of wool were exported in 1372, and more than 70,000 hides in 1381, but in the 1460s exports had fallen to 2,000 sacks and 15,000–18,000 hides. Exporters were carrying from England 18,000 sacks per annum in the 1390s, about half of the figure earlier in the fourteenth century, and this slipped to 15,000 annually in the early fifteenth century, and after a period of volatility in the 1440s and 1450s, settled down to 8,000 to 9,000 sacks in a typical year between 1460 and 1520 (see Figure 4 above, p. 244). This damaged the prosperity of east coast ports, from Aberdeen to Yarmouth. A higher proportion of exports went through London, so ports like Boston and Hull were handling a diminishing share of a declining trade. Wool exports were organized by a small number of merchants, but it was not just a handful of rich men who suffered from the loss of trade. The merchants employed labour to cart, load, unload and ship the wool, and the returning ships would bring merchandise into the town. An active port kept the food and drink trades busy, as ships were provisioned before each voyage. The wool merchants spent some of their profits on local goods and services. The recession in trade had effects on the whole supply network, and might help to explain the decline in population of such inland centres as Melton Mowbray in Leicestershire, where wool had been collected for transport to the east coast.

The traders of the east coast ports also suffered because of the decline in their access to the commerce of the Baltic. The merchants of Lübeck, Hamburg and the other north German ports belonging to the Hanseatic League struggled with the English government over reciprocal trading rights. The Hanseatic merchants were able to operate from English ports (where steelyards were established as depots), and the English could trade in Germany. One of the success stories of the late fourteenth century, in addition to the general advance made by English merchants in gaining a larger share of the country's trade, was their expansion into the Baltic. A period of friction in the early fifteenth century was only temporarily settled by treaties in 1409 and 1437, and open hostilities broke out in 1468–74. The English lost in this struggle, and although twenty-one Scottish ships were able to pass through the Sound into the Baltic in 1497, English vessels were absent.

The decline in the Scottish wool exports set back that kingdom's overseas trade: no major substitute commodity could compensate for the loss of the country's most abundant product. The kingdom's customs revenues, which had been running at an annual £9,000 in the 1370s, had fallen to £2,500 in the 1450s, and picked up again, but only to £3,000, in the late fifteenth century. For England, cloth exports filled at least part of the gap created by the fall in the wool trade, but this did not come to the aid of all of the ailing towns. The cloth trade as a whole was subject to ups and downs. The number of cloths going out of English ports between the 1390s and the 1440s expanded from about 40,000 per annum to almost 60,000, but then fell back to 40,000 or even below that figure, and did not recover fully until the 1470s (see Figure 4 above, p. 244). A high proportion of the cloth was exported through London, so that Bristol, for example, did not handle all of the cloth from Somerset, Wiltshire and Gloucestershire. And the manufacture of cloth, which could bring much employment and wealth to individual towns, was subject to fluctuations depending on unpredictable changes in fashion or competition. So Colchester and Coventry based their fourteenth-century success on textiles which did well in continental markets, but went into decline during the fifteenth century. At Coventry, cap-making provided employment as textile manufacture declined, but that did not last. By 1523 Coventry's population had fallen to about 6,000, having reached 10,000 at its peak in the early fifteenth century. York had been famous for its cloth, but its industry declined before the Black Death. After a revival towards 1400, it suffered loss of business and employment during the fifteenth century when demand fell and production was cut back.

Merchants who did not necessarily handle a great deal of cloth could still make money from the import trade in raw materials used in textile manufacture, such as oil for treating yarn for weaving; woad and other dyestuffs; alum which was used in dyeing; soap; and Spanish iron which had the right properties for making the wire used in cards for preparing wool. Many of these goods were imported through London. Individual wealth diminished because of these changes in the pattern of trade. At York, 83 per cent of merchants left less than £50 in their wills after 1460; before that date the figure had been 65 per cent. Five York merchants (for whom we have records) who died in 1379–1415 thought that their estates could afford to pay £300 or more to beneficiaries. In the period 1468–1514 only two could dispose of so much.

In some degree the difficulties of the ports – especially those on the east coast, but also including Bristol and some of the larger inland towns – can be explained by the decline in wool exports, the fluctuations in cloth manufacture, and the growth of London as a channel for exports and imports. But why did the smaller towns, especially in a belt running from east Yorkshire through the east midlands to the western fringes of East Anglia, lose population? This was not so much an example of urban decline as a case of the whole population of the region shrinking, in villages and towns together. This part of England had been devoted to arable cultivation, which brought less prosperity as the grain trade stagnated. Wool was a leading product of the region, but not much of it was made into cloth locally; most was carried into other parts of the country, such as Suffolk. Elsewhere towns stood on the frontier between contrasting landscapes, and their markets would provide a point of connection between different rural economies. In the east midlands there was less variety in landscape, with less need in consequence for local exchange. The towns did not collapse, but continued to serve as useful market centres (see Map 11 below, p. 359).

The successes among towns outweighed the failures, probably leaving the urban sector as large as it had been before the Black Death. The proportion of the English population who lived in towns, according to the tax records of the 1520s, stood at about 20 per cent. This is very similar to the proportion of town dwellers in 1377, and the situation had probably not changed greatly since the late thirteenth century. In other words, England had achieved quite a high degree of urbanization by about 1300, and the towns retained their relative importance two centuries later.

This must mean that the commercial outlook which had been established before the Black Death did not revert to a more primitive economy based on self-sufficiency. The rural population still produced a surplus to feed the townspeople, and still spent money on the goods and services that towns had to offer.

The most successful city in England was London. Badly hit by plague epidemics, in 1377 it contained about 50,000 people, which represents a drop from the estimated 80,000 at the beginning of the fourteenth century. By the 1520s about 60,000 were living in the city, with 3,000 in Westminster and 8,000 to 9,000 in Southwark (much more than in 1300), which together with lesser suburbs made a formidable conurbation. Londoners enjoyed great advantages over the traders and artisans of the provinces. The city lay at the centre of the kingdom in every sense, which drew the magnates to establish town houses, numbering 75 by 1520. Every year hundreds of provincial gentry came to stay at London's inns, to attend parliament and the central law courts, but also to enjoy the social and cultural life of a metropolis. The Thames estuary gave London an excellent port, with easy access to the hub of continental trade in northern France, Flanders, the Low Countries and the Rhine. Coastal trade connected London with Exeter, Yarmouth and Newcastle, the Thames provided a convenient route by boat between the capital and the south midlands, and the radiating network of roads brought trade and travellers from every part of Britain. London merchants, in addition to superior communications, had more capital and more political power than their provincial rivals. Talented and ambitious people in the provinces moved to London because they expected that their aims could be achieved there. Richard Whittington, for example, did not arrive penniless in the city, though as the third son of a Gloucestershire knight he had little prospect of inheriting much land. In the 1380s and 1390s he became a rich mercer, selling silks to the royal household and to landed magnates. Later in life he was lending money to Richard II and Henry IV, and traded in wool on a large scale. He became mayor of London three times, and left money at the end of his life to fund charitable work in the city. The story grew up that he became rich through the intervention of his miraculous cat, because people felt the need to explain how such great wealth came from small beginnings.

Whittington was just one of many London merchants who gained a large share of exports, both in wool and cloth. Sarplers of wool (each containing two sacks) and packs of cloth were brought in growing quantities by road or down the Thames to London. Imports came into London rather than other ports, and were distributed over the country by London merchants. The grocers of London, for example, handled a great variety of goods, including wool and cloth, but their distinctive trade was in spices, dyestuffs and alum: goods that were sold by weight. They visited fairs to sell these commodities to provincial traders, or made direct contact with the spicers of the towns who would sell the goods retail in their localities. Chapmen also played a part in distribution, some of them small-scale traders who bought packs of spices from a grocer and then travelled round the country hawking them in penny parcels. Whatever the method of distribution, we can be sure that the largest profits were made by the Londoners. The major consumers, even those from the northern counties, like the bishop of Carlisle or Durham Priory, bought spices from London grocers, because they had a better choice if they selected their goods from the large quantity on offer, but also because a bulk purchase of pepper, ginger and dried fruits could be obtained more cheaply directly from the wholesaler (see Map 10 below, p. 306).

London was a centre of manufacture, with the range of workers in cloth, leather, metal and wood that would be found in any large town, many of them serving local needs. Consumers came to London from a distance, however, particularly to buy luxury goods, because London craftsmen had a reputation for high-quality workmanship, and the presence of so many specialists in one place gave the purchaser some choice. A provincial town would often have only a single goldsmith, but the London company had a membership of 180 in 1477, and 210 in 1506. If a rich aristocrat wished to buy jewellery or silver plate, or to have a seal engraved, or if a church was seeking an ornate processional cross or chalice, they would go to a London goldsmith. Church bells could be cast in a number of provincial towns, such as Leicester and Nottingham, but the reputation of the Londoners meant that their bells were hung in churches more than 100 miles from the capital. Richard Hill, who flourished between 1418 and 1439, made bells for parish churches at Tixover in Rutland and Shipton Moyne in Gloucestershire. The quality that London craftsmen brought to their work can be appreciated from the brass plates on tombs engraved with figures by London marblers. Those made in the late fourteenth and early fifteenth centuries show a sensitivity, sense of proportion and elegance of line which few provincial rivals could achieve. London brasses were still chosen throughout the country when their quality was not quite so high, so the memorials to gentry such as Robert Eyr at Hathersage in Derbyshire (1463) and Sir Robert del Bothe of Wilmslow in Cheshire (1460) were commissioned from craftsmen in the capital.

The extension of London's dominance over many branches of the commercial economy was partly achieved, as has been suggested, by the advantage of price, choice and quality that the merchants and artisans

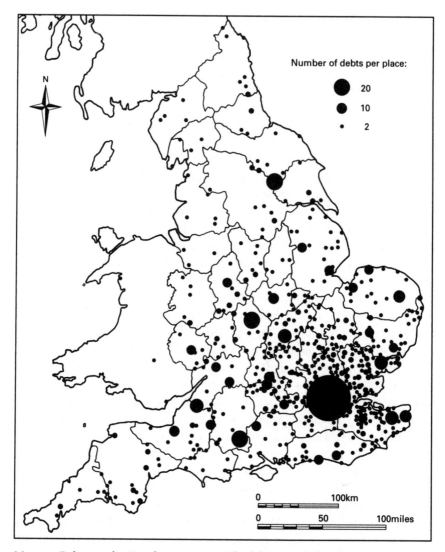

Map 10. Debts owed to Londoners, *c.*1400. The debts recorded in the royal courts, arising from sales of goods, or business dealings that went wrong, demonstrate the extent of London's trading connections.

Source: J. Galloway (ed.), *Trade, Urban Hinterlands and Market Integration c.1300–1600* (Centre for Metropolitan History, 2000).

could offer. But they also drew benefits because of their superior organ-ization and political influence. The London fishmongers, for example, controlled the sale of fish in the city, and excluded the Yarmouth men. The merchants from London were fully represented in the two organ-izations that oversaw the trade in wool and cloth, the Staplers and

Merchant Adventurers, and they used their position to the disadvantage of provincial rivals. There were Merchant Adventurers in Newcastle and York, but the Londoners were given effective control of cloth exports to the Low Countries, and in 1497 northern merchants were forced to join the London fellowship, in spite of strong protests. In 1478 they complained that at the cloth fairs the Londoners took the best stalls, and left them points of sale on the periphery.

Although the rise of London weakened the ports and the larger provincial towns by drawing away their share of trade, some towns in the south-east gained from the association. Southampton and Sandwich served as outports for the capital, so that Italian ships *en route* to Flanders would load and unload at Southampton without making the longer journey up the Thames estuary. Some small town traders in the vicinity of the capital learned that they could profit from the great concentration of consumers in London, and so High Wycombe (Buckinghamshire) bakers produced as their speciality simnel bread which was sold in the city; Walden in Essex grew saffron in gardens around the town, much of it for London consumption. The inns at Newbury in Berkshire and St Albans in Hertfordshire did a busy trade because they provided convenient stopping places for travellers on two of the busiest main roads into London.

Edinburgh expanded its commerce as well as its role as the centre of government. It became the permanent centre of administration under James III (1460–88). A relatively small town in the fourteenth century, overshadowed as a trading port by Aberdeen and Berwick, it developed as the principal exporter of wool in Scotland, handling 57 per cent of the total in the 1440s, partly because it took over much of Berwick's trade after that town was lost to the English. It became Scotland's largest town in the sixteenth century. Another successful Scottish town, Dundee, overtook Perth and Aberdeen. In Wales the largest towns before the plagues were in the south and west, at Cardiff, Carmarthen and Haverfordwest. They were joined by expanding centres in the east and north-east of the country, at Brecon, Denbigh and Wrexham. From relatively small Welsh towns, these moved towards the upper rank with populations near to 1,000. A smaller Welsh town also in the north-east, Ruthin, did well at this time from its cloth industry. Brecon and Wrexham were helped in their rise by their strategic positions on the routes taken by cattle drovers into the English midlands.

Some towns were able to prosper because they replaced another centre within their region. Wrexham increased in size while Holt shrank, just as Reading in Berkshire flourished while Wallingford declined. In southeast Wales, Trellech and Usk went downhill, while Abergavenny and Monmouth improved their relative importance. Sometimes the reasons for these shifts are not easy to explain, but Abergavenny was given an advantage by its clothmaking, while Trellech had depended excessively on an uncompetitive iron industry. Many towns which maintained their position or even expanded were relatively small market towns, and their traders attracted custom away from the small village markets which must always have offered a very limited choice of goods, and may not have given the best prices for those selling agricultural produce. The village markets, which had received charters in such numbers in the century and a half before the Black Death, had mostly ceased to operate by the sixteenth century. In Staffordshire, forty-five markets are known to have been founded, of which twenty were still in use after 1500, and all but one or two of these were located in towns.

An active role in clothmaking undoubtedly protected the vulnerable larger towns from shrinkage. Some revived, or new cloth towns peaked early, as we have seen in the cases of Coventry, Colchester and York, which had all fallen back by 1520. Others benefited from a steadier and more sustained growth in their textile industry. Salisbury, with many weavers and fullers in the town, maintained its position throughout the period. Exeter, at the centre of the dynamic south Devon clothing district, with a population of only 3,000 in 1377, grew to 7,000–8,000 in 1524–5, mainly in the previous fifty years. Worcester also expanded during the fifteenth century and became a major centre of clothmaking, while cloth enabled Kendal to grow in the early sixteenth century to become the largest town in the north-west. These changes meant that in the hierarchy of English towns Exeter moved into the top ten, while an old cloth town which had failed to find a new role, Lincoln, dropped into thirteenth position.

Some traders in the large towns, such as Exeter and Salisbury, prospered because of their association with the spinners, weavers and fullers who lived in the hamlets, villages and small towns in the vicinity. Small towns in these districts based their success on providing goods and service to country clothmakers as well as their own industry. This helps to explain the presence among the fifty wealthiest and most populous English towns in the 1520s of Crediton in Devon, Hadleigh in Suffolk and Newbury in Berkshire. Others with the same basis for their growth include Halifax, which had a cloth hall for the sale of locally made textiles in 1500, and Leeds, where three new fulling mills were built between 1455 and 1499. Tiverton and Cullompton in Devon were the homes of the wealthy clothiers John Greenway and John Lane, both of whom left permanent memorials by paying for lavish additions to their parish churches. At Lavenham in Suffolk, the clothing Spring family, who converted themselves into landed gentry, contributed 37 per cent of the town's taxes in 1524; its many timber-framed buildings and its large and ornate church show how much money came into the town in the fifteenth and early sixteenth centuries. These small towns, founded in the phase of urban expansion before the Black Death, took on a new lease of life in the fifteenth century. Some new towns grew almost imperceptibly at this time, without charters or encouragement from lords, such as Stroud in Gloucestershire and Pensford in Somerset, both housing numerous cloth workers in the heart of busy textile districts.

The traders and artisans of other small towns also took advantage of local industries which were practised in the town and its surrounding countryside. Birmingham by the early sixteenth century was a flourishing centre of a number of crafts, including tanning, but its blades, including scythe blades, were traded over a wide area. Stourbridge, a new town at this time, benefited from the iron industry and pastoral agriculture in its north Worcestershire neighbourhood. The distinctive industries in some towns were directly connected to local resources, like the marble quarried near to Corfe in Dorset. Sometimes the initiative came from an entrepreneur or group of entrepreneurs who, realizing the potential of a particular product, encouraged the skills of manufacture and devised a system of distribution. Walsall in Staffordshire, for example, had nearby resources of fuel, limestone and iron, but so did a number of other towns in the vicinity. The human factor must explain why it became a supplier of lime in its region, and also produced horse bits which were traded beyond the midlands. Nearby Burton-on-Trent was also famous for two products, beer and religious statuary carved from the alabaster quarried nearby.

Most new towns in England are associated with the period of urbanization before 1300, and the concept seems to fit uneasily with the shrinkage and even extinction of towns in the two centuries after the Black Death, but three examples have already been mentioned, and on the coast Brighton and Minehead both seem to have become urban settlements towards the end of the middle ages. In Scotland, again, most of the towns which became important centres of local government, trade and manufactures had been founded before 1348, but between 1350 and 1520 another fifteen burghs, ten of them royal, were created, and a remarkable fifty-nine burghs of barony and burghs of regality were founded from the early fifteenth century onwards, especially in the period 1488–1512. Each was granted a weekly market and annual fair, and the inhabitants acquired trading and legal privileges, but not the monopoly over trade in their district which was enjoyed by the burghs. The burghs of this new generation were speculative ventures, and about half of them failed, but others met with some success as commercial centres, as at

Alloa, Paisley and Hawick. The Scottish burghs received formal grants
of privilege, unlike the unofficial and therefore poorly documented
English new towns of this period.

The expansion of a few of the larger towns, the growth in many of
the smaller towns, especially in the industrial districts, the foundation
and emergence of new towns, all deserve our attention when they take
place against a background of an overall stagnation in population. Most
townspeople, however, lived in existing urban centres which lost varying
proportions of their population. These towns still performed their functions as centres of exchange, production and administration. Coventry,
for example, after the apparent disaster of losing almost half of its
people, in 1520 was still the capital of its region, with trade links extending overseas through the ports of London, Bristol, Chester and Boston.
Even after its shrinkage, it was still larger than it had been in 1300,
and numbered some very rich individuals among its citizens, including
Richard Marler, one of the wealthiest merchants in the whole country.
The experience of living in such towns was by no means one of misery
and poverty. They still attracted immigrants. These are especially visible
in Wales when so many people of Welsh descent settled in towns, even
those formerly regarded as English colonies, that their language and
culture became a dominant influence. High earnings encouraged people
to move to towns. With wage rates at 6d per day in the fifteenth century
for many skilled building workers in the south, a fully employed skilled
mason or carpenter could hope to earn £6 in a year. The profits of artisans who ran their own businesses, as shoemakers or tailors for example,
are difficult to calculate, but they regarded carpenters as their inferiors.
Workers paid by the day would have their earnings limited by the dis-
continuity of employment caused by the search for work, as well as by
illness and bad weather. Those with longer contracts would earn less
but be guaranteed continuous employment, so journeymen cappers in
Coventry were supposed to receive 44s per annum, with meals. The food
would have taken the total remuneration above 60s, and as the regulations were seeking to prevent excessively high wages, the journeymen
presumably received more than the legally defined maximum.

In spite of problems with the flow of trade, mercantile profit could
still be high; this enabled the Cely family, merchants of the staple around
1480, to receive about £100 per annum. Even in Aberdeen, which was
well past its peak as a port for overseas trade, a merchant like Sir John
Rutherford flourished between about 1467 and his death in 1528. He had
a good start as the third generation of his family in the town. Like
merchants everywhere he diversified, protecting himself against failure.
He dealt in cloth, oats, meal, salmon, salt and wine – both luxury goods

and more basic commodities for a broader market. These goods were sold in Aberdeen, in other Scottish towns such as Forfar and Dundee, and overseas to Dieppe. Rutherford invested in property in both town and country as a means of storing wealth, as security for raising future capital, and as a source of income from rents. He rented peat cuttings, fisheries and sheep pastures. He bought jewellery and silver plate, and was accepted in aristocratic society: his first and second wives were both the daughters of local lords.

Artisans often seem to have been a particularly underprivileged group in Scottish towns, but this does not mean that the lesser ranks of Aberdeen did not enjoy some of the fruits of the town's trade. Tax assessments from 1448 and 1472 suggest prosperity among smiths, shoemakers and dyers. Individual craftsmen held property in the town, and owned such prestigious goods as silver spoons. Throughout England and Wales, good-quality timber-framed houses of this period, including both large merchants' dwellings, and many modest two-storey houses appropriate for artisans, are found in towns of all sizes, with different economies and in varied regions, at Salisbury, Stamford, Ludlow, Hadleigh, Winchcombe, and dozens more. The buildings are still used because their original construction and materials were of a high standard, and the successors of the medieval owners did not demolish them and rebuild. The urban property market was less lively than it had been around 1300, but landlords, such as monasteries, found it advantageous to buy up houses and plots and to pay for new buildings for rent. This happened in the vicinity of Westminster Abbey, where the monks developed the town in the interests of increasing their rent income, and enterprising laymen were following suit, behaving in the style of modern speculative builders by acquiring an empty plot and running up a row of houses.

In their house designs the landlords, or indeed the many tenants who also rebuilt their own properties, were following the established tradition of urban building, but they added a little to their expense with a greater number of separate rooms, even to the extent that in Stamford the main public room, the hall, was eliminated and replaced by a more comfortable and intimate parlour. A growing proportion of houses were roofed with tile and slate rather than thatch or shingles, and instead of open hearths, rooms were heated with fireplaces and chimneys. Builders were paid by their clients to make some show of status on the street frontage, with 'close studding' in which a great quantity of timber was displayed, with decorative carving, and jettied upper storeys towering over those passing by. (Plate 14)

Townspeople aspired to increase their domestic comfort by purchasing internal fittings such as wainscoting, as well as painted cloths for the walls, and soft furnishings such as carpets and cushions. Artisan house-holds would be equipped with a range of metal cooking and table ware, and plentiful ceramic pots, cisterns, jugs and cups. One small town artisan, John Symond of Wickham Market in Suffolk, when making his will in 1481, described himself as a barber, but he also traded as a wax chandler. He does not seem to have had very much cash, as he left £2 10s mainly to the church, and allowed his wife, as well as the use of his house and land, an income of 13s 4d each year for five years. However, in his life he had bought a range of household goods, as he bequeathed twelve silver spoons, a feather bed and bedclothes, six pewter plates and at least two pewter salts, a brass pot, fire irons, a chest made of spruce wood, four candlesticks of latten (an alloy of copper and zinc), rosary beads and a saddle and bridle for his horse. These were only the goods that Symond thought worthy of mention. Other wills and inventories show that a prosperous artisan's possessions would have included furni-ture, household textiles such as towels and tablecloths, and many garments. In addition to increasing their purchases of consumer goods, townspeople also enjoyed an improved diet, with greater quantities of meat, fish and ale.

Towns attracted the poor, who could obtain casual employment there, and because surplus food was handed out both by religious institutions and by better-off private households. The most generous doles were pro-vided at funerals, when townspeople making their wills assumed that a large crowd of paupers would assemble. For the indigenous poor, that is the townspeople who were unemployed, ill or old, the arrangements for social security probably improved at this time. The number of places in almshouses and hospitals grew, certainly in relation to the population, and private charity, some of it channelled through the churchwardens or religious fraternities, was directed at the 'deserving poor', that is widows, sick, old and poor householders with children.

The urban scene changed significantly between 1350 and 1520, but not out of all recognition. The numbers of towns throughout Britain prob-ably fell from 800 to 740, but then a handful of new towns pushed the figure up again above 750. The population of towns fell overall, though at different rate, and some places were larger in 1520 than they had been in 1300. The urban share of the whole population did not change. Towns moved up and down the urban hierarchy, but the leading towns of 1300 were still quite highly placed in 1520. The shifts in trade and industrial output had a significant influence, especially on the east coast ports and the clothing towns. The stability of the network of towns in some regions is suggested by the way that the same market towns served the same hin-terlands as in the early fourteenth century, and indeed were strengthened by the disappearance of the village markets. The clothing districts saw some changes, as small places became more important; some new towns even grew up. But the pattern that had emerged before the Black Death, both in terms of the proportions of large and small centres and in their geographical distribution, stood the test of time (see Map 11 below, p. 359). In parts of England the urban system had reached maturity. Wales and particularly Scotland were not so stable, with a crop of new burghs in Scotland at the end of the period, and more casualties than can be found in lowland England. Of course, individual town dwellers went through hard times as their town shrank or their trade failed, and they fell into poverty or moved out, but most townspeople were enjoying a higher standard of living than their predecessors.

ii. *Urban economies*

Did the quality of town life and the character of the urban economy change? Townspeople seem more articulate and assertive in this period, partly because there are more records and more of them were written in English. But the creation of documents, and the use of the vernacular, was part of the desire to reflect the importance of their town, and to communicate positive messages to fellow townsmen and to outsiders. A characteristic statement of civic pride and responsibility was the 'Mayor's Calendar' written by Robert Ricart, the town clerk of Bristol, in 1478. The book celebrated the liberties of the 'noble and worshipful town of Bristol', which were the same as those enjoyed by the city of London. Ricart provided a history of Bristol, including a myth of the town's foundation, and then went on to describe civic ceremonies, and to give the text of the oath to be sworn by a new mayor. The mayor's duties included holding courts, meeting with the masters of the guilds, supervising the bakers and brewers, and regulating the markets. The ideas expressed in the 'Calendar', which were shared in varying ways in all of the larger towns, emphasized the duty of officials to provide good government and celebrated the unity of the town, which suggests a closing of ranks in times of uncertainty.

The leading townsmen, which in large towns usually meant the merchants, aimed to exercise close economic control. They accepted the aspirations of the artisans and small-scale traders to have some representation in the government of the town through the common council. But the key decisions were usually made by a group of councillors (in most towns numbering twelve or twenty-four), together with a small group of officials: the mayor, sheriff, recorder, bailiffs and chamberlains in England, or the provost and bailies in Scotland. They represented the town's interests in the outside world by sending burgesses to parliament, petitioning the crown and pursuing cases through the courts. They sought patronage from aristocrats who might help them in their political and legal negotiations. In Scotland, towns would enter into formal agreements to gain the influence of local lords through bonds of 'manrent' (see p. 269). Their concerns remained much as they had been before 1350, such as disputes with rivals, as when Brechin, Forfar and Montrose worked out their conflicting interests in the late fourteenth century, or Yarmouth at about the same time pursued its quarrel with Lowestoft. Towns still resented the enclaves of jurisdiction held by the church; Exeter, for example, unsuccessfully challenged the power of the clergy to rule in their cathedral close in 1445–8. Londoners were exercised by Southwark's independence, which they thought allowed criminals and rogue traders to carry on their dishonest practices south of the river. And foreigners were distrusted at best, and occasionally persecuted, as when a wave of violence was directed against the Italians in London in 1456–7.

The elites who ran the towns were concerned to maintain peace and order. They used the traditional system of courts to do this, but also sought to extend their control over society in a manner reminiscent of the later puritans, as they passed laws against prostitutes, eavesdroppers, gossips and night walkers, and made desultory attempts to forbid the playing of illicit games, from football to dice. In a more positive spirit, they founded or refounded hospitals as shelters for the poor who were (as they saw it) genuinely in need. They were also concerned to follow social policies that would prevent unrest, hence their legislation against forestalling and regrating, the rule in the markets that corn be sold for the first few hours to the consumers, not the grain dealers, and the enforcement of the assizes of bread and ale (see p. 224). At Aberdeen, oatmeal could not be bought in bulk, and the sale of oat bread was forbidden. The bakers could produce wheat and rye bread for the better-off, but the basic food of the poor was to be kept out of the hands of the dealers and processors. There was concern about the creation of monopolies by the linking of crafts, so that, again at Aberdeen, butchers were not allowed to make candles for sale, as they controlled the supplies of tallow. In many towns the poor were expected to be able to buy cheaply the brewers' dregs and the butchers' offal. The rules were not kept, but they must have had some effect when the town took determined action. At Aberdeen, the butchers (fleshers) were constantly before the courts between 1505 and 1509 for selling meat at an excessively high price, and the authorities decided in 1511 to expose the fleshers to competition by allowing anyone within the burgh or the countryside to sell meat as they wished in the town.

Their food policies might suggest that the governing minority ruled in a public-spirited fashion, upholding the common good against profiteers. However, in many ways they protected their own interests. The freedom of the town was restricted: it could be acquired only by inheritance, apprenticeship or purchase. The cost of buying the freedom, which carried with it full access to the market, was often fixed at a high level which excluded many artisans. At Dunfermline, the fee was set at 40s, which meant that only about a third of the burgesses enjoyed the privilege. The artisans in larger towns belonged to fraternities, or 'craft guilds' as they are now known, which gave them the chance to hold social gatherings for those in their trade, and discuss matters of common interest. But these organizations were regulated by the town's government, which took a close interest in their internal affairs. The authorities supervised the craft's rules, which were approved by the mayor and copied into the town's archives.

The ordinances of the Bristol cobblers were drawn up by eighteen named masters of the craft in 1364. These limited the wages paid by the master craftsman to the servant or servants (journeymen) who worked in his shop to 6d for sewing and 'yarking' (finishing) a dozen pairs of shoes, with more for boots. If a servant was contracted to work for a master, he could earn no more than 18d per week with a bonus of eight pairs of shoes each year. Masters were forbidden to poach workers from other members of the craft. This is a typical example of wage regulation after the Black Death, supporting the restrictions of the Statute of Labourers. It was in the interests of the employing masters to keep down wage costs, but the wider body of consumers would be protected from paying more for their shoes, and the governing elite of the town, who were all employers, would welcome measures to limit wages. The mayor approved the regulations, and may have played an active role in framing them.

The influence of the Bristol merchants is readily apparent in the dyers' rules of 1407, which were focused on the problem of shoddy workmanship and the lack of proper training among the dyers' craft. The regulations allowed for inspection of dyed cloths by two masters approved by the mayor, and the exclusion from work of those who lacked the right skills. The craft was clearly difficult to discipline, and the rules were being imposed against the will of some of the masters, as it was ordered that 'all the masters of the said craft of dyeing . . . ought to come before the mayor to hear the said ordinances, and whether they will assent to and grant the same or not'. The initiative behind this measure came from the merchants, who had seen Bristol's cloth exports fall in the period 1399–1407 and, searching for an explanation, blamed the dyers for giving Bristol cloth a poor reputation.

The authorities wished to have well-ordered towns, where everyone knew their place in the hierarchy. The 'craft guilds' played their role as disciplinary organizations. The contribution of each craft, and its place in the civic body, was symbolically displayed each year in the plays performed on Corpus Christi day, when each craft was assigned a biblical episode, often appropriate to their skill: so the carpenters performed the story of Noah's ark, and the smiths (who made nails) the crucifixion. The plays cost money, for the costumes and props and pay for professional performers, which led to grumbling, and some of the smaller crafts clubbed together. In Scottish towns, artisans were not allowed to form associations in the early fifteenth century. Their 'customary congregations' in 1427 were described in an Act of parliament as conspiracies. They still met, although they were not supposed to trade while pursuing their craft occupations. After 1469, guilds of craftsmen were formed.

Unskilled workers were not allowed to associate. For example, at Coventry the daubers and rough masons were forbidden to form a fraternity. The government of London also clamped down on illicit fraternities of journeymen. Nicholas Symond and eleven other journeymen spurriers were found in 1381 to have been meeting each month in St Bartholomew's church in Smithfield for the previous nine years. They swore an oath to support the fraternity, contributed money to a common box, and made ordinances, which had been written down. The members no doubt saw their organization as a legitimate religious and social body, so much so that when a member failed to attend meetings he was reported to the church court for perjury (an offence under canon law, the church's legal code), which brought the fraternity to the notice of the authorities. The mayor and aldermen of London regarded this little group as a sinister conspiracy to raise wages – they had apparently fixed the minimum reward for making twenty-five spurs at 20d. The city elite reacted strongly to this serious threat to the common good, and ordered them to disband.

Townspeople came together in religious fraternities more often than in any grouping outside their households. They had developed in the thirteenth century, but after 1350 became more numerous, prestigious and prosperous. In self-governing towns the fraternity gave the elite the opportunity to organize a collective chantry, employing priests to pray for the souls of the brothers and sisters. They would arrange ceremonial funerals for members of the fraternity, and they gave alms and founded almshouses. They employed schoolmasters and built schools, and often paid for local facilities, such as bridges and roads. Their annual feasts and other gatherings were important social events for the leading townspeople. In larger towns the management of the religious fraternity provided valuable training in the skills of government, and the master of the Corpus Christi Guild or Holy Trinity Guild would often progress to become mayor a few years later. In smaller towns the fraternity became the primary collective body, which in fact if not in name governed the town. The exclusive and opulent character of some small town fraternities is indicated by the Holy Trinity Guild of Wisbech in Cambridgeshire, which was reputedly founded in 1379, and flourished in the fifteenth and early sixteenth centuries. Its membership was restricted to the more substantial townspeople (the 'better and wiser part', as they were called elsewhere) who numbered sixty-six in 1453. The alderman who presided over them was elected by a jury of twelve to eighteen leading members. The property which the fraternity accumulated was worth £40 annually in the mid-fifteenth century, which was ample to pay for a priest, a schoolmaster and the upkeep of the guildhall. At the splendid annual dinner venison and veal were served, and minstrels provided the entertainment. By a rule announced in 1506, the poor were allowed to eat the leftovers.

These organizations were intended to have an impact on the town's economy. They encouraged co-operation among the elite, by bringing them together at social events and by providing a forum for settling disputes. They gave the leading townspeople pride in their community and opportunities for informal government. Often members were recruited from the surrounding countryside, or other nearby towns, which helped business dealings. If the local gentry could be persuaded to join, they gave useful political and legal advice, added to the prestige of the fraternity, and brought trade to the town. The fraternity provided some measure of social security, especially for the relatively affluent who feared for their future when they became old or ill. The spending of the fraternity's funds on building the chapel, guildhall, school and almshouses, but also on bridges and roads, and on repairs and replacement of the houses in the town with which it was endowed, offered employment and represented investment in the urban fabric. Towns were made more civilized and dignified places by the fraternity's activities. Small towns in particular owed their impressive public buildings, schools, colourful processions, and their standing in the region to the efforts of their fraternities. But, like many other aspects of the collective life of towns, these facilities were devised by elites for the benefit of elites.

Town governments and the lords of seigneurial towns, and individual townspeople, contributed along with the fraternities to town buildings. They realized the need for roads, bridges, quays, marketplaces and stalls for the easy flow of trade, and there are many examples of substantial and useful public works taking place at this time. Occasionally these involved not just the replacement of existing facilities, but new ventures which helped the town's economy, as when the leading townspeople of Abingdon in Berkshire, acting through their fraternity, paid for a new bridge over the Thames at Culham, which brought new trade and helped to seal the fate of Wallingford. As in earlier periods, the authorities were much concerned with public health, which led them to legislate for street-cleaning, and more towns were provided with a public water supply. The battle with the butchers continued, to force them to clean up the squalid mess that they left in the gutters and to carry their waste to some approved dumping ground well away from the town centre.

An ambiguous example of an initiative which changed the public face of many towns was the provision of clocks in church towers or purpose-built 'clockhouses'. In some ways these can be seen as civic ornaments, showing that the town appreciated technical novelties, and often they had no more practical purpose than ensuring that religious services took place at the right time. Eventually they were adopted for measuring the working day, and a journeymen capper at Coventry in 1496 was enjoined 'to come to his work at 6 of the clock in the morning, and to leave at 6 at night'. Working hours had previously been defined with reference to light and dark, which left room for debate, but now precision could enter into a central aspect of work discipline.

Civic elites were skilled image builders, who were capable of creating a sense of community by fostering legends about the early history of the town. They used high-flown rhetoric about the good government they claimed to be practising, praising their predecessors (at Wells in Somerset) for the 'convenient ordinances' which they had made 'wor-shipfully and discreetly'. If we accept that urban economies were closely regulated by town governments we are in danger of believing their prop-aganda. The stream of local legislation gives the impression that the town was run with an almost military discipline, and this has led histor-ians to argue that they created a strait-jacket of regulation, levied heavy taxation to pay for civic building and ceremonies, and helped to drive business away.

In fact, many of the attempts at control were not very successful. The food traders habitually bought grain before it reached the market, as this was an essential part of the long-distance grain trade which kept town populations fed. Direct sale of corn or fish by producers to the consumers was a utopian idea, inappropriate to a complicated market system with its many middlemen. The regulations were not enforced in such a way that they would change the behaviour of the offenders. In small towns we often find that the assizes of bread and ale, or the regulations to restrict profit on the sale of meat and fish, were being broken by members of the leet jury or other officials. Ale tasters presented themselves (or their own wives) for breaches of the assize: they paid the fine, and continued as before.

Attempts to control rates of pay or to ensure that workers were properly trained were no more successful than the Statute of Labourers, because they were attempting to hold back the tide of the labour market. Artisans could not be pigeon-holed into occupational categories. Nor could their journeymen and other wage workers be entirely prevented from forming their own small fraternities. The artisans resented the elitism of the town governments, and voiced their dissent. In London the tailors gave their support in 1438–44 to Ralph Holland when he led an agitation against a city government that was biased in favour of the drapers. They even questioned the assumption that merchants should dominate the city's affairs, and remembered that one mayor, Walsh, had been a cordwainer, and he was said to have been the best mayor that the city had ever had! Individuals, like a series of dissenters from the fraternity which governed Wells, including William Webbe and Thomas Chynnok, were expelled and had to make a humiliating submission to their superiors.

Some towns were managing without much government. Alongside very closely regulated small towns were Bromsgrove in Worcestershire, or Buntingford in Hertfordshire, where there is very little evidence for an active controlling hand, whether from the lord of the manor or a fraternity. Towns had sometimes developed in a number of manors and parishes, so that no single conventional authority could dominate them. Others escaped close supervision because they grew up in a corner of a much larger manor. Those places with small and weak fraternities, and an inactive lord, were also free from much formal regulation. The large suburb of Southwark, which grew to the size of a large town in its own right, had no central government – different parts of the sprawling settlement came under the jurisdiction of a number of lords, none of them very assertive. Modern advocates of the free market might point to these places as 'enterprise zones' which flourished without economic controls. But while it is true that Southwark grew rapidly, many of the smaller towns like Buntingford succeeded only in the sense of serving usefully as a small market town.

In a parallel development traders tended to ignore the formal network of markets. In theory, the royal government had either issued charters to enable lords or towns to hold markets on set days, or had accepted that some markets were old and well established. The country was dotted at regular intervals with these chartered markets, and almost everyone lived within a short distance of one. We might be led to expect that the bulk of buying and selling took place in designated marketplaces on the appointed day, under official supervision and with tolls paid. In practice much urban trade was conducted on days other than those of the official market, in shops or warehouses. Bulk purchases of agricultural produce such as wool and corn were agreed at the farm. Inns, in both town and country, were much used for bargaining over these unregulated sales. There were also unofficial trading places, where small groups of traders, artisans and innkeepers formed embryonic towns, such as Knowle in Warwickshire, at the junction of roads joining Warwick, Birmingham and Coventry. There were markets and fairs which took place without official recognition, but were so well established that their marketplaces were incorporated into the plan of the settlement, and are still visible. Perhaps the general lesson that can be learned is not that regulation was harmful and stunted economic growth, but that it did not make a great deal of difference. The flow of commerce was more powerful than the efforts of government to control behaviour.

Crafts and trades became more specialized. The unit of production remained the workshop based on the household, which normally consisted of a handful of workers: the master, his wife, a child or two if they were of working age, and one or two servants or apprentices. Occasionally a master in the metal trades employed a larger workforce, the greatest number known being the eighteen servants and apprentices employed in Thomas Dounton's pewter workshop in London in 1457. Some official records might suggest that the number of specialisms was increasing. In London, for example, 111 organized crafts were listed in 1422, and the occupational labels used to identify people coming before the courts in the fifteenth century suggest minute subdivisions of skill. For example, among those preparing animal skins, as well as tanners and skinners we find curriers, pelterers and tawyers. But the suspicion must be that these descriptions result from the official desire to fit artisans into categories, rather than real changes in the work they did. In the fifteenth century, as in earlier periods, an individual would pursue a number of occupations, like John Symond, the barber/wax chandler of Wickham Market.

Specialization came about when many people in the same craft settled in one place and dominated its economy. This on the whole had not happened at the time of the poll tax lists of 1379 and 1381, and if we classify the occupations of the taxpayers into the categories of food and drink, leather, textiles, clothing, mercantile, metal, building, wood and transport, we find that in most towns all are represented, but none predominate. The main function of a town was to provide its hinterland with a full range of goods and services, hence the diversity of crafts and trades. An exception is found in the case of the food and drink trades, which, for example, account for 27 per cent of the taxpayers in Oxford and Southwark, reflecting the response of the towns' traders to demand from those attending the university in the first case, and the travellers entering and leaving London in the other. Among the manufacturing crafts, specialists sometimes gathered in small towns, like the 25 per cent of the population of Sheffield who were listed as metalworkers in 1379; already the town was becoming a centre of knife-making. Usually the share of the population in any one branch of manufacture did not rise above 15 per cent.

During the fifteenth century, concentrations of particular crafts in individual towns became more common, especially those producing cloth. At Salisbury in 1421 the numbers of cloth workers attending a meeting to discuss the industry suggest that, with their families, they accounted for about a quarter of the population. By the sixteenth century Worcester's textile workers made up about 40 per cent of the inhabitants. Those acquiring the freedom of larger towns were recorded in registers, which are biased sources because of the exclusion of the poorer workers and other categories. It is still worth noting that the proportion of textile workers among the new freemen at Wells increased from 19 per cent in the late fourteenth century to 31 per cent in the late fifteenth. In another clothing district, the occupations of those assessed for the military survey at Long Melford in Suffolk in 1522 show that clothmakers, weavers, fullers and others in the clothing trades accounted for 37 per cent of those with specific occupations. In the same survey, eighty-three cappers and hatmakers were listed for Coventry, and two years later there were fifty shoemakers in Northampton: together with fifteen tanners and thirteen glovers, this suggests that the town's modern reputation as a centre of leather-working was already beginning.

This trend towards specialization in such small towns as Tiverton, Stroud, Saffron Walden, Walsall and Burton-on-Trent has been mentioned (see pp. 308–9). Its economic importance lies in the implication for the distribution of goods, which were being produced in these centres for distant markets, in greater quantity than would be needed in the immediate vicinity of the town. The products must have been given distinctive qualities which customers would recognize. The workers are likely to have gained in skill and efficiency through working in large numbers in close proximity.

iii. *Consumers*

The flow of trade and manufacture was strongly influenced by the high
level of consumer demand, in spite of the reduced size of the population. Trade in some luxury goods, such as wine and furs, was in decline,
reflecting the reduced spending power of the aristocracy and the difficulties of supply in wartime, which in particular pushed up the cost of
wine from south-west France. The very wealthy altered their choices
because they were concerned that the new rich after the Black Death were
buying goods once affordable only by the aristocracy. Squirrel fur linings
for clothes, for example, were now being worn by the wives of artisans.
The response of the elite was to stop wearing so much squirrel and to
buy small quantities of scarce furs such as marten, which maintained the
distance between them and the social climbers. In the same spirit they
drank expensive sweet wines from the Mediterranean, such as rumney
and malmsey. If the volume of international trade declined, especially in
the middle of the fifteenth century, so did the population, and traded
goods per head had a higher volume than in the thirteenth century.

The sustained demand for textiles from the majority of consumers
kept the economy of some towns buoyant, which meant that clothmakers, as well as making quite expensive broadcloths and such
high-quality brands as Bristol reds, were also producing relatively cheap
woollens at 1s or 2s per yard. Their production of these affordable cloths
helps to explain the large output, especially from Devon, west Yorkshire,
Kendal and Wales. Scotland did not produce cloth for export on a very
large scale, but its cheap products served not just customers of modest
means at home, but also gained markets among the poorer sections of
Flemish society. Peasants and wage earners who had previously bought
minimal quantities of very cheap cloth were now able to afford more
of a better quality. This tendency provoked the Scottish Sumptuary
Law of 1447, which forbade husbandmen and labourers from wearing
dyed cloths on working days; they should wear only grey and white
(undyed) cloth. It was ignored, like all such regulations, to the benefit of
clothmakers. Linen was produced in many parts of the country, and in
quantity in Norfolk, but we can only guess how much. In order to keep
households of all levels of society supplied with shirts, underwear, sheets,
towels and tablecloths, imports of the cloth were recorded at 462,000 ells
in 1390 and 420,000 ells in 1480–1. Only the trade of alien merchants is
known. If estimates for the imports of natives are included, the total
imports in these years could well have exceeded a million yards.

The increase in meat-eating ensured that butchers were an important
group in the urban economy. Their supplies were maintained by the long-

distance cattle trade from Wales and from northern England into the midlands and London, in which a number of Welsh and midland towns played a part. The higher consumption per head of ale and beer encouraged major changes in the urban brewing industry, with a concentration of the trade into fewer hands: this forced out of the trade some of the women who brewed occasionally for sale. At Oxford, for example, the numbers of those brewing and selling ale declined from over 250 in 1311 to about twenty-four in the early sixteenth century, but the total amount brewed probably increased. At the end of the fourteenth century, beer (which contained hops) was introduced from the Low Countries. The spread of this drink in eastern towns had far-reaching consequences, because the hops not only gave a distinctive flavour, but also acted as a preservative. Now, instead of brewing a few hundred gallons of ale which had to be sold and consumed within a few days, before it deteriorated, breweries could produce beer on a larger scale, store it, and carry it considerable distances. It could be used, for example, to provision ships. A domestic industry was being industrialized, with investment in more expensive equipment (the brewing vessels often cost in excess of £20) and larger quantities of raw materials. A rather similar change affected the herring fishery, again under Dutch influence. A new technique for gutting and preserving fish on board the boat made the whole operation more efficient, and gave the consumers a product with a superior flavour.

In the metal industries, the growth in demand for pewter table ware made the pewterers one of the leading London companies, with fifty-six masters, thirty-four journeymen and ten others working in the city in 1457. Among traders, the period saw the rise of haberdashery, which emerged as a specialized trade out of mercery; the specific role of haberdashers was the selling of small items such as hats, purses, pins and buckles, inessential but desirable accessories which a large number of consumers could afford. Some of these items were made by urban craftsmen who were developing techniques for turning out large numbers of buckles and other metal ornaments, not all of them well designed or finished, but cheap enough to enable labourers and lesser artisans to decorate their belts with showy fittings. Such goods were also imported in quantity. When William Mucklow, a clothier from Worcester, exported cloth in 1511 to the Low Countries, he brought back for sale in England hundreds of bells, spectacles, pins, girdles, silk ribbons, sheets of brown paper and pouches.

Demand from individual consumers stimulated industries in the countryside. Rural industries were well established in the early middle ages, so the novelty in the period after 1350 lay in the scale of the operations. In the extractive industries, such as mining for iron, coal, tin and lead, or stone quarrying, the presence of the minerals determined the siting of the industry, but other crafts could be located either in town or country, and the reasons for preferring a rural setting seem to have been the convenience of being near to raw materials and fuel, the presence of water, both for industrial processes and as a source of power, and the relative cheapness and flexibility of the labour force, many of whom were part-timers who also held land or worked in agriculture. The industries often developed in districts with a bias towards pastoral farming, which needed less labour than arable, and left workers with free time for industry. Labour costs were especially important, as they constituted one of the main expenses. In clothmaking, for example a 12-yard piece of cloth in 1391 which was sold for 24s cost 12s 5d in payments to a succession of artisans to do the spinning, weaving, fulling and dyeing, with materials accounting for much of the remainder. Consumers may have had more money to spend, but they still counted their pennies, and the success of an industry in competition with its rivals often depended on providing goods more cheaply. This encouraged the concentration of production, to turn out goods on a larger scale (we have already seen this happen in the urban brewing industry) or to gather producers in specialist centres.

Pottery manufacture was scattered in *c.*1300 over hundreds of mainly rural kilns. By the fifteenth century many of these had gone out of production, and instead potting was focused on a smaller number of centres with a larger output. In Oxfordshire, for example, lesser kiln sites like one at Ascott-in-Wychwood seem to have gone out of use, while the larger industry at Boarstall and Brill, which supplied Oxford as well as much of the north of the county, survived. But a large and enterprising pottery centre outside the county, in Surrey, came to supply an ever-increasing proportion of Oxfordshire consumers together with those through much of the south-east region. English potters competed with the accomplished products from the continent, such as German stoneware, and were successful in producing hard, well-glazed pots, which could be used as table ware instead of wood. There was less emphasis on local variety; kilns in different parts of the country produced similar types, such as 'Cistercian ware', which was light, thin-walled, and finished with a distinctive metallic glaze. (Plate 15)

Consumers demanded more iron, which peasants and artisans used for tools, implements, horseshoes and cart fittings, and in the house for knives, hinges and pothooks. Iron purchased by Durham Priory came mainly from Spain in the mid-fifteenth century, but from the 1480s the bulk was produced in local ironworks, especially in Weardale. Before the Black Death, iron was smelted in many small country bloomeries, which individually had a limited output – one at Tudeley in Kent in the early fourteenth century made between 2 and 3 tons of iron in a year. Water power was being applied to smelting at this time, but its use spread, for example in Yorkshire, where mills powered both hammers and bellows. The machinery and the pond and channels to control the water all required a heavy investment, but the works could produce much more iron, such as the operation at Byrkenott in Weardale (County Durham) which in 1408–9 yielded more than 18 tons of forged iron in less than a year. Mechanization of the most labour-intensive processes increased the output per worker. The next stage down the route to more efficient production came when English ironmasters followed the example of continental smelting processes, and introduced the blast furnace, which depended on a water mill to power the bellows. This made more metal, but also generated high enough temperatures for a new product – cast iron. The first blast furnace was operating in Sussex in 1496.

Capital was invested in clothmaking in a different way. Mechanization had arrived before 1200 in the form of fulling mills; these, as we have seen, spread through some of the clothing districts in the thirteenth century. Mills were built to serve the new needs of the industry in the fifteenth century, with a series, for example, in the stream valleys of Stroudwater in Gloucestershire. A total of 202 are known to have been built in Wales by 1547. Fulling, however, was only one process in making cloth, and some cloths, such as the worsteds made in Norfolk, were not fulled at all. Otherwise clothmaking used much the same equipment as in the thirteenth century, except that there was a spread in the use of the spinning wheel, which made yarn more quickly than the distaff method. The impact of new capital came through the organization of the industry by country clothiers. Entrepreneurs in the industry were not new – urban clothmakers before 1300 had used the putting-out system, by which the merchant or draper controlled the various stages, providing the raw material and selling the finished cloth, sometimes lending money to the artisans, or supplying the weavers with their looms, and therefore making them virtually his employees. Artisans in both town and country were often able to maintain their independence. Half of the weavers in York in 1456–7 owned their own looms, and in the cloth villages of Essex and Suffolk around 1400, most of the weavers made cloth on their own account. Some customers would pay a weaver, fuller and dyer separately for their work, rather than buying the cloth ready made.

In the fifteenth century the clothiers extended their control of sections of the industry. We have already noted the prosperity of John Greenway and John Lane in Devon, and the Spring family of Lavenham. Other figures include Thomas Horton of Bradford-on-Avon in Wiltshire, who owned four fulling mills and whose fine house was admired by visitors to the town. Thomas Paycocke's grand timber house still stands at Coggeshall in Essex, and in his will of 1518 he indicates the extent of his patronage over the local artisans when he asks for 12d to be given to each of his weavers, fullers, shearmen, combers, carders and spinners. No doubt the previously independent artisans lost money when they fell under a clothier's control, but the industry as a whole expanded under their influence. They were able to achieve the 'vertical integration' of which modern economists speak by acquiring sheep pastures, flocks of sheep, fulling mills, looms, dyeing establishments and warehouses, and by dealing in wool, dyestuffs, alum and oil, as well as the cloth, and therefore controlling the flow of materials and products through the various processes, and profiting from every stage. They came near to introducing a small-scale factory system when they built next to their dwellings spinning houses and dyehouses, and employed directly some craftsmen, such as shearmen who trimmed the nap from cloth. They had contacts with London merchants and knowledge of customers' requirements which individual weavers would acquire with difficulty. Their wide horizons enabled them to spot the best markets for buying wool cheaply and selling the cloth for a good price. For example, the Wiltshire clothiers at the end of the fifteenth century found that there was a demand in Flanders for 'white' cloth, which was taken to London to be carried across the Channel, where the Flemish drapers could have it dyed to their own requirements and then exported to Italy.

Coal mining also attracted entrepreneurs, such as the Newcastle merchants who profited from the coal trade of the north-east, with a good deal of investment from landlords such as the bishops of Durham. In the thirteenth century most coal had been dug in small bell pits, in which two men would work, often as part-timers. As demand increased, from domestic consumers but mainly from those in other industries, such as lime burners, brewers, brickmakers and blacksmiths, the scale of production rose. At Coleorton in Leicestershire, miners were working underground using the 'pillar and stall' technique by the late fifteenth century, and elsewhere deep mines needed expensive drainage adits. A horse-powered pump was removing water from a mine at Finchale in County Durham in 1486–7. The labour force of the larger collieries consisted of a dozen men. The scale of operations rose to the extent that Railey in County Durham was producing annually 8,000 tons in the mid-fifteenth century, and Wollaton in Nottinghamshire yielded 9,000 tons in one year in the 1520s. In 1508–11 Newcastle was sending out annually 40,000 tons, much of it to London. Workers at Whickham in

Northumberland and Railey in Durham were achieving productivity comparable with that of the early nineteenth century, with a hewer (underground worker) producing each day between 1.2 and 2 tons.

iv. *Old and new*

We have discussed the influence on the medieval economy of unregulated trade, consumer demand, entrepreneurs' responsiveness to markets, capital investment, mechanization, specialization of production, increased scale of production and productivity of labour. Does this mean that commercial and industrial activity had by about 1520 gone through a transition to capitalist methods of production, and had medieval people adopted a modern economic outlook? Significant change had occurred, but in many ways the traditional economic system still had a powerful influence. The great merchants were not as willing to innovate as the country clothiers or the enterprising artisans who changed the brewing or iron industries. Export of wool and cloth lay in the hands of powerful associations of merchants who were concerned to secure markets and maintain a profitable routine, by which wool was carried to the staple port of Calais, and a high proportion of cloth exports were sold by the Merchant Adventurers in the Low Countries, and increasingly at Antwerp. Their business partnerships continued the type of *commenda* arrangements developed over the previous two centuries (see pp. 215–16), though we can see larger groupings of merchants resembling later joint stock companies launching genuinely adventurous trading initiatives, like the Hull and Lynn merchants who pioneered a new trade with Iceland in the fifteenth century. It was from another port in contact with Iceland, and also with Ireland, Bristol, that an expedition set out in 1480 to explore the west Atlantic, and Cabot made his voyage to Newfoundland in 1497. English merchants visited a wider range of ports than they had in *c.*1300, for example in trading regularly with Spanish ports, but they did not penetrate far into long-distance markets, such as in the Mediterranean. Even in 1500 about 40 per cent of English overseas trade was in the hands of continental traders.

Raising money for capital may in the long run have become a little easier, as interest rates in the fifteenth or sixteenth centuries, at about 5 to 7 per cent, seem to have been rather lower than the 10 per cent prevailing in the thirteenth century. Merchants' credit arrangements still consisted mainly of allowing buyers to pay late, so that everyone involved in business was bound into an endless chain of informal debt. Not uncommonly, when a merchant died, the bulk of his assets consisted of unpaid debts, and his estate was heavily encumbered with commitments to others. Formal recognizances, used as a legal assurance that debts would be paid, which had developed in the thirteenth century, declined in number, perhaps reflecting the recession after 1400. There was a growing use of the bill, by which a simple promise was made to pay, and this could change hands, so that a purchase of goods could be made on the basis of an earlier obligation to pay. The debt could therefore be assigned from one merchant to another, without cash changing hands. The merchants of the Calais staple would receive for their wool letters of payment, by which a continental merchant would give them written authority to receive the money from a third party, often in London. Again, the document could be used in further transactions, and in this respect resembled paper money. English merchants in general depended on verbal agreement and mutual trust to make their bargains. Their account books, of which very few survive, consist of memoranda of transactions with notes of money paid, which were primitive instruments compared with the more precise methods of the Italians.

The ships in which goods were carried abroad underwent major structural changes after about 1410. Until then, ships were propelled by a square sail attached to a yard on the single mast. The hulls were clinker built, from overlapping planks, in the same technique as that used by the Vikings. During the fifteenth century, Mediterranean carracks and caravels were imitated in English shipyards, and vessels were given two or three masts, with a lateen sail on the mizzen (rear) mast; the hull was 'skeleton built', with planks fitted on to a framework, edge to edge in the carvel method. The new techniques allowed the ships to make more efficient use of the wind, and the hulls were rather cheaper to build, requiring less skilled labour and smaller quantities of timber, while gaining in strength. All of these features were being employed by English shipwrights in the 1460s, and the vessels which made the first recorded Atlantic crossing in 1492 used essentially the same design. (Plate 17)

Much else in 1520 maintained the traditional medieval economy. The small artisan workshop and the unspecialized town still predominated. But we cannot dismiss as resistant to change a period which saw the invention, introduction or much wider dissemination of brick buildings, paper mills, drinking glasses, guns, gunpowder, the printing press (innovations that space has not allowed us fully to discuss) as well as blast furnaces, deep mining, beer brewing and carvel-built, three-masted lateen rigged ships.

New attitudes to the economy are demonstrated by public efforts to control disruptive and idle behaviour, and by discriminatory policies adopted towards the poor. This early puritanism applied to personal as well as public life, with more emphasis on privacy in the home and a new value placed on thrift. A work ethic was widely influential: idleness met with disapproval. Ordered working lives began with training and experience in youth, and led to retirement for those with even small amounts of property. Wage earners did not all choose to work fewer days when their pay increased, but maximized their earnings in order to buy better food and desirable goods. Household incomes were increased by the ability of men, women and children to contribute, often undertaking a number of activities during the year. Employment contracts based on lump sums for the completion of a task, such as 20s for the carpentry of a building, encouraged hard and purposeful work. When apparently low rates of productivity are recorded, such as the Hull tiler in the late fifteenth century who laid 300 tiles in a day, compared with 1,000 for a modern roofer, this may reflect the conditions of work and the range of tasks expected of the medieval worker, such as fixing laths as well as tiles, rather than his lack of commitment to the job. Those working on the land also changed their way of life and economic outlook.

CHAPTER TEN

The countryside, c.1350–c.1520

The prejudice that new ideas come from towns, and that country people are slow and conservative, was held to be true in the middle ages, as it is now. The superiority of the towns does not survive close examination. The rulers of large towns clung to old values and attempted to preserve their prosperity by preventing change, while the country and small town clothiers contributed a new energy and expertise to industrial production. Here we turn to the the rural economy, to see how those who made their living from agriculture stood up to the tests of the long-term changes after the Black Death.

i. Landlords

After 1348–50, the higher aristocracy had to make hard decisions about the management of their lands in altered circumstances. We have seen that they hoped that the fall in population, with all of its damaging implications for wages, agricultural profits and rents, would be a temporary problem, and they believed that they could hold back the economic tide until normal times returned. This was not a stupid response. They had experienced setbacks before. They were given hope by the high grain prices for more than twenty years after the Black Death, and the rise in wages that was less rapid than expected. By the late 1350s, holdings were tenanted and peasants were still paying substantial rents and dues. The 'seigneurial reaction', helped by circumstances, worked, and over the generation after the first plague epidemic the revenues of some estates fell by as little as 10 per cent. In some places, such as the Welsh marches, they even increased.

The estate managers in the late fourteenth and early fifteenth centuries continued to make decisions about which crops to grow and how much land to cultivate, just as their predecessors had done. More barley was grown on demesnes, often instead of oats, because of the rising demand for ale, which drinkers preferred to be brewed from barley malt. Many manors also expanded their acreage of beans, peas and vetch, in order to feed these crops to animals, which were being kept in greater numbers. The managers responded to the labour problem by reducing the scale of arable cultivation, so the gradual shrinkage of arable demesnes which had begun before 1348 continued. On a Devon manor belonging to Tavistock Abbey at Werrington, for example, 128 acres had been cultivated in 1298, but this fell to 80 acres by 1350 and 50 acres by 1420. Some of the land that was no longer cultivated by the lord was rented to tenants, but some was used as pasture for the manor's livestock, because lords appreciated that greater profits came from animal husbandry. This was not a response to rising prices; although animals such as oxen fetched more money after 1360 than they had in the 1330s and 1340s, wool slipped down after 1380. The great advantage lay in the relatively small number of workers who could look after flocks of sheep and herds of cattle, compared with the many hands needed to cultivate cereals, and above all to harvest them.

The large estates had to make choices about the use of the crops that they produced. Selling as much as possible could be the right decision if the manor lay a long way from the household, or if the lord did not find it convenient to visit a manor in order to consume its produce. Manors near large towns, where prices would be high and transport costs low, would also sell their grain. Lords were quite ready, even if in earlier times they had become accustomed to buying grain, to provision their households directly from their demesnes. This decision was made by a small and quite remote monastery, Owston Abbey in Leicestershire, which in 1386 was entirely self-sufficient in grain, and also by a large metropolitan establishment like Westminster Abbey.

The magnates had to decide how much of the income from their estates they were prepared to put back into agriculture by paying for new buildings, or fencing, or other productive investments. Routine repairs cost more because of rising wages, but in addition estates which contemplated leasing out their demesnes judged it prudent to offer to the lessee buildings in good repair, in order to obtain the highest possible rent.

Manors derived more income from tenants than from their demesnes, and those assets had to be managed as well. At their most extreme, lords were seeking to keep intact servile obligations, to keep rents as high as possible, and to push up court revenues. They attempted to prevent the migration of serfs, and to compel those left behind to repair their buildings. However, the more realistic estates had to compromise by reducing rents and entry fines, and converting tenancies from customary tenure to leasehold. The demand for land did not usually collapse, so that the influence of the market as well as coercive pressure helped to prevent rents falling immediately and disastrously.

As the years passed, the old conditions showed no signs of returning. The good harvests after 1375 reduced the price of grain and therefore the profit of cultivation. Wages rose in the 1370s and 1380s. Tenants showed by their concerted efforts in 1381, and their truculence as individuals throughout the period, that there were limits to the lords' options in bullying their subordinates to stay put and pay the old rents and dues. The officials of the earl of Warwick decided in about 1400 that labour services on one manor should be commuted into cash rents, 'until the world is restored', which they must have realized was becoming a faint hope. Lords in growing numbers decided to lease sections of arable demesnes, or whole demesnes on individual manors through the fourteenth century, but the movement became an overwhelming tide between about 1380 and 1410. A businesslike monk of Canterbury Cathedral Priory, Thomas Chillenden, taking over as prior from the otherworldly John Vinch, acted decisively and leased all of the monastery's demesnes in 1391–6. A more typical caution was shown by their neighbours, the archbishops of Canterbury, who leased eighteen of their thirty demesnes between 1381 and 1396, more of them in the next few years, and were left with six still under direct management in 1422. The great lords were putting their demesnes into the hands of lessees or farmers, in return for a fixed cash rent.

The end of direct management of agriculture by the great estates represented a sharp break with a long tradition. The decision to lease was made after detailed calculations by the estate's receiver and auditors. These financial experts working for the bishop of Worcester decided in 1393–4 that the profit on cultivating the arable on the manor of Bibury in Gloucestershire amounted to 11s 4¹/₂d on a cash outlay of £6. The amount of profit was not the only consideration, as the managers also weighed up the advantages of a guaranteed regular annual income from a farmer against the unstable returns from direct management. The demesne was farmed out two years later. The change on this manor and thousands of others was much more than just a financial technicality, because it was often accompanied by the final conversion of all labour services to money. The two parts of the manor, demesne and tenant land, which had been held together by the bond of labour service for centuries, were being separated. Occasionally the farmer took on the whole manor, tenant holdings as well as demesne, but usually the demesne alone was rented out, and the lord continued to collect tenants' rents and hold the manor court. Nonetheless the link between lord and peasants was weakened by the break, as the manor would receive less frequent visits from officials, and lords' residence might cease entirely if, as often happened, the manor house fell into disuse. A more remote and impersonal lordship contributed to the long-term decline in rent income.

The break with direct management occurred on many manors before 1410. Sometimes when the arable was leased, pastures were separated from the manor and kept under the control of the lord. This was another blow to an old tradition, which was based on mixed farming with a balance between different types of land. The duchy of Lancaster kept more than 1,000 sheep on its pastures detached from the manors of Aldbourne, Lambourne and Berwick on the Berkshire and Wiltshire downs in the 1430s. The flock was expensive to maintain because, while the old manorial system kept breeding ewes to replenish numbers, the duchy owned only wethers, mature wool-producing animals, and maintained their numbers by purchase. The profits on this operation were reduced by falling wool prices, and in 1443 and 1445 most of the sheep were sold and much of the pasture leased. Many estates gave up their sheep flocks in the middle of the fifteenth century. Some estates continued to manage some arable demesnes directly until the same time, and after that kept one as a home farm for supplying the household. Tavistock Abbey unusually kept four arable demesnes under its own management until 1497. There was less change in the northern counties of England and in Scotland at this time, because they had either not developed large arable demesnes, or they had leased them out before 1350.

The transition of the magnates' estates into organizations for collecting rents did not mean that they were relieved of the problems of management. Without constant vigilance, rents would diminish or even disappear. The great estates continued to recruit talented officials, some of them clergymen but mainly members of the gentry with a training in the common law. As in the days of direct management, receivers, auditors and stewards collected money from reeves and bailiffs, checked accounts, and held courts. The lord's council met to discuss such matters as legal disputes over land. Some lords were constantly in the royal courts, even bringing lawsuits against household and estate officials who owed money. A new official was the supervisor or surveyor, who was charged specifically with negotiating leases and new tenancies. The estates, challenged with the problems of collecting rents, required new types of document, and officials compiled valors, which attempted to show lords how much each manor was worth, together with lists of arrears to identify reluctant payers, general surveys to investigate lost revenues, registers of extracts from court rolls which contained useful precedents, and books of leases to ensure that tenants' obligations were remembered. The documents had a defensive tone, as they focused on preventing losses. Estate management was not just a question of poring over the archives to catch tenants evading rents, nor were the offices of the great estates staffed entirely by grey bureaucrats and lawyers. One of the most engaging characters and original minds of the period was William Worcester (1415–85), who served Sir John Fastolf, the self-made Norfolk knight, as secretary and surveyor. Worcester had been educated at Oxford, which would normally have led to a career in the church, but he remained a layman, and has been described as a gentleman-bureaucrat. He kept a notebook designed to help his master profit from his manor of Castle Combe in Wiltshire, which had become one of the most prosperous centres of clothmaking in England. Worcester anticipated the gentry antiquarians of later centuries in his interest in topography, architecture and local history, and his notes on Castle Combe, in which he analysed revenues over the previous hundred years, bear some resemblance to economic history.

Worcester and his contemporaries devised the most advantageous method of leasing the demesnes. Should they be rented out as single entities, often 200–400 acres at a time, or would there be more money for the lord in breaking the land into parcels? Would the demesne yield a higher rent if livestock and equipment were included in the lease in addition to land and buildings? The officials had to search out farmers, individuals or groups, who would take on the lease and stay the course as reliable tenants. The exact terms of the lease had to be negotiated: the rent, the length of time (usually in years), and detailed conditions such as the responsibility for building repair. Sometimes a lord, concerned that a farmer might neglect the land, would insist that it be returned in good condition, with a minimum area manured and under the plough, for example. The rent would usually be in cash, but some lords might ask for part to be paid in kind, and monasteries such as Coventry Priory required the farmer to send specified quantities of grain, animals, cheese and so on to feed the monks through the year.

Once the indenture recording the agreement had been written, and the farmer installed, the negotiations did not stop. The officials would have to cajole the tenant to pay his rent in full and on time. The tenant in the early phases of leasing would have taken the land for a term of between seven and twelve years, but later in the century this increased to twenty or forty years. He would complain that a rent agreed in 1430, for example, did not take into account declining prices in the 1440s, and would argue for a reduction. Farmers would drive a hard bargain by paying only part of their rent, like Nicholas Poyntz, an assertive member of the gentry who leased the unprofitable demesne at Bibury already mentioned. In the 1430s and 1440s Poyntz successfully pushed his lord, in some years by paying nothing at all, into reducing the rent from £6 16s to £4 16s, and then he paid £4 per annum as if he regarded that to be the just rent.

Most leases required the tenant to repair buildings, though the lord would agree to help with timber or stone. In practice the tenants would complain that they could not afford repairs, and persuaded the lord to take over the work. Lords found it difficult to refuse as they would not be able find a tenant in the future for a demesne with its barns, byres and sheepcotes in ruins. On the estate of Canterbury Cathedral in the middle of the fifteenth century between 7 and 16 per cent of income each year was spent on building repairs, which was a greater level of investment than in the era of Henry of Eastry, the improving landlord of the thirteenth century. Many leases forbade the subletting of the land, but this often occurred, and the lords turned a blind eye, even recording in their accounts that the leasehold rent had been paid by the occupier, who was not the officially recognized tenant. Farmers who were doing well out of a lease (which they did not admit readily) might ask for the term to be extended, or ask at the end of their term for their son to be given the renewed lease.

Other manorial tenants also needed close attention. They often failed to pay their rents, and persuasion had to be used to get them to take a vacant holding. Some entire communities confronted the lord's officials, as when Thomas Huggeford and Nicholas Rody, officials of the earls of Warwick, were told by the tenants of Lighthorne in Warwickshire in 1437 that if they did not reduce the rent the tenants would leave the manor. Huggeford and Rody knew that a ring of nearby villages were in a state of near collapse, and had no desire to see Lighthorne follow the same route, so they brought down the annual rent of 15s 6d owed by each yardland holding to 10s 6d. Most of the bargaining was conducted with individuals, and concerned the terms of tenure as well as rents and dues. Sometimes tenants continued to hold their land by the former unfree or customary tenure, but with no (or very few) labour services, and the cash rent was supposed to incorporate defunct dues such as tallage. Such tenants were liable to pay an entry fine, but this was commonly negotiated down to a few shillings or even a token payment during the fifteenth century as the demand for land slackened. Heriots on death or surrender often survived in their original form of the best animal, but many lords had to accept a cash payment, or a merging of the heriot with the entry fine of the next tenant. Holdings were commonly converted into leaseholds, by which the tenant would be granted the land for a term of between five and twelve years, for a simple cash rent with no other obligations. The short term protected lord and tenant from committing themselves in unpredictable times. Some tenants held their land 'at the will of the lord' or from year to year without any formal, written agreement. Such tenures were common in Scotland, and were used in England to enable the lord to gain an income from land which otherwise would lie vacant. In the north of England 'tenant right' developed around 1500, in which holdings could be inherited, and sold, without the lord's permission. Rents were fixed, but fines were paid when a tenant died, and also on the death of the lord. Military service against the Scots was an important tenant duty.

All of this suggests that the lords had little bargaining power, but tenants did not dictate their terms. English and Welsh customary tenants were supervised by the lords' courts, and pressure could be brought to bear on them to repair buildings, and to observe the rules of the tenancy, such as not felling the trees that grew in the hedges of their tenements. The courts kept alive the memory that some families were of servile status, and the dwindling numbers of serfs were ordered to return if they left the manor without permission, or were required to pay their marriage fines. Stewards were tempted to evict tenants who broke the rules, but did so only in exceptional cases because tenants were usually in short supply. The courts still performed useful functions for the lord, for example in overseeing the transfer of holdings and recording the names of new tenants. They were still respected by tenants, who made by-laws to regulate the fields, but they made less use of the courts than in earlier centuries for recovering debts or for suing their neighbours for trespass or the return of borrowed goods.

On well-run estates, lords kept some control over tenants by making rentals (lists of tenants and rents) at regular intervals, knowing that if enquiries were not made into tenants and holdings, land might be lost and rents would lapse. Arrears of rent payment were a constant anxiety, arising from tenants who paid rents slowly, or who refused to pay selected charges at all. These could build up to very high levels, notably in the Welsh marcher lordships, where a restless peasantry asserted their independence after the Glyn Dŵr revolt. On the Brecon lordship, for example, which produced an annual revenue of about £1,000, a total of £2,453 had accumulated in arrears by 1454. In the marches arrears were an intractable dilemma, but elsewhere officials could contain the problem by cancelling rents and making concessions when necessary, while persuading and pressuring tenants to pay up when that could be achieved. Estates could make a constructive contribution to keeping tenants and cajoling them to pay their rents by helping them with the repair of buildings. They might achieve this end by letting them off their rents, or by providing materials, or in exceptional circumstances by building houses and barns themselves. Help came at modest cost to the lord on the estates of the earls of Northumberland in 1471–2, when at Great Houghton six tenants were given help with pairs of crucks, at a cost to the lord of 18d for each pair. Robert Eldere, for example, received 6s for four pairs, sufficient for rebuilding a whole house or barn. At the other extreme, the duchy of Lancaster at Brassington in Derbyshire in 1441 spent almost £7 on a complete rebuilding of a house and barn with stone walls, a timber superstructure and thatched roofs.

During the first half of the fifteenth century lords found that their lands declined in value. The manors of Canterbury Cathedral Priory produced £2,202 annually in 1419–20, after which the figure fell to £1,907 in 1454 and reached a low point in 1469 of £1,757. Reductions, in the region of 20 per cent, were normal in southern and midland England. In Cornwall, with its favourable economic conditions influenced by tin mining and other industries, the lords lost less ground: the rents for the assessionable tenants of the duchy of Cornwall (see p. 242) had stood at about £600 in the 1360s and slipped down to £500 between 1459 and 1484. The worst effects of the decline in revenues were felt in the northeast of England, which suffered severely in the bad harvests of the 1430s, and where revenues fell by a third. In Scotland lords were able to push up cash rents to compensate for the falling value of the debased currency: in the lordship of Strathearn rents rose by 40 per cent in money between 1380 and 1445, but this represents a decline in real terms. Some lords in effect went bankrupt. A number of monasteries fell into debt so seriously that administrators had to be sent in to make savings on household expenses and to install an efficient estate management. Smaller religious houses were merged with more prosperous establishments and therefore effectively closed down. The dukes of Buckingham had more acute financial difficulties than most landed magnates, and were often unable to pay their bills promptly. The third duke became reckless, and when in 1520 his debts exceeded £10,000 (two years' annual income) he was forced to sell some of his many manors.

Most lords accepted the realities of fixed or diminishing resources, and reduced their commitments. They scaled down the size of their households, introduced budgets to check on expenditure, such as the recommendation at Bury St Edmunds Abbey that each monk could be fed on 2s 6d per week. Lords audited their household accounts in person, signing their names at the end of each page. They made cuts in hospitality, and reduced the number of their houses. Earls and bishops, who before the first plague had maintained and visited twenty or more houses and castles, now focused their expenditure on three or four residences, which they could build and furnish to a higher standard. Houses like Thornbury Castle and Dartington Hall were more opulent and comfortable than the dark and draughty castles of the thirteenth century.

After a long period of retreat, the estate managers took opportunities when they reappeared after about 1470. Most lords increased their revenues in the period 1470–1520, though hesitantly, and with setbacks. Canterbury Cathedral Priory's manorial income reached its low point in 1469 and recovered to £2,056 in the early sixteenth century, which was still a little below its revenues in 1420. When officials negotiated with would-be farmers in that period they found that they could push the rent up a little, or charge a fine for entry. The customary rents paid by manorial tenants were fixed, but entry fines equivalent to two years' rent and more could be levied on manors in prospering localities, especially after 1500. Arrears dwindled as tenants paid more promptly. Direct management of agriculture experienced a revival, with more lords in the north of England and Scotland keeping livestock. Lawrence Booth, bishop of Durham, grazed 1,000 cattle and 1,000 sheep in the 1470s. James IV of Scotland (1488–1513) was pasturing large flocks of sheep, for example 6,300 in Ettrick Forest.

The reason for this modest revival in the fortunes of the great estates, which coincides with a growth in trade and industry, cannot be easily explained, as the level of population remained low and prices did not begin to rise generally until about 1517. One factor seems to have been the recovery in livestock prices. A more assertive, even more predatory style of profit-seeking entered into the mentality of the officials of the great estates at this time. We find the duke of Buckingham's men seeking out serfs who, having left the manor illicitly, had made their fortune and could be blackmailed into buying their manumission for huge sums. The royal estate (including the duchy of Lancaster) was run more efficiently, with surveyors appointed who had instructions to gain the maximum return from leases. Pastures in the Peak District of north Derbyshire were rented out in the late 1490s for sums 25 or 30 per cent higher than those which had prevailed for the previous forty years.

Lords faced with low estate incomes for much of the fifteenth century developed alternative economic strategies. Some acquired more land. This was not so easy for the great church estates, which acquired few new manors, but the monasteries steadily expanded their assets by appropriating parish churches, which allowed the monks to profit from the tithes and glebes. Each church that they took over would add an average of £10 per annum to the monastery's income, though occasionally they picked a plum worth £50. These acquisitions had to be justified, and the monasteries could spin plausible stories of plague and agricultural problems. The losers were the rectors, who when they enjoyed the income of their parishes could live like landed gentry; after appropriation they were replaced by less affluent vicars. New ecclesiastical estates were created by the fashion for founding collegiate churches, not just in Oxford or Cambridge (where Magdalen College and King's College were especially opulent examples), but also at such establishments as Eton in Berkshire and Bothwell in Lanarkshire. Much of the land for these new foundations in England came from the assets of the small monasteries and cells attached to French religious houses, which were confiscated during the Hundred Years War. These tendencies do not mean that among churchmen the units of landholding were generally increasing in size. Large numbers of chantries were being founded, sometimes attached to fraternities or small colleges. In these, one or two priests who said masses for the souls of the dead were endowed with rents often worth £10 or £20 per annum.

Lay families could plan to expand their landed resources by arranging marriage alliances, or attracting political patronage. Some successful families brought together the landed assets of a number of aristocratic estates, notably in Scotland in the late fourteenth century, when the Douglas family had accumulated three lordships and twenty-four baronies, and the Stewarts held no fewer than twelve earldoms. In England during the fifteenth century some of the great accumulators of land included the dukes of York and the earls (later dukes) of Warwick. New legal techniques were devised, above all enfeoffment to use, which enabled the aristocracy to escape from the right of overlords, including the crown, to take over an inheritance and profit from it if the heir was young or female. Aristocrats were also able to decide the descent of property and avoid the restrictions of the normal rules of succession. They could use this to keep an estate intact, for example to avoid the division of the lands among daughters when there was no son to succeed. In fifteenth-century Scotland the magnate families show a remarkable ability to continue through successive generations, which helped them to hang on to their wealth.

In England a number of tendencies prevented the aristocracy from maintaining their fortunes in the long term. Some fathers took advantage of their control of the inheritance to look after younger sons and daughters by dividing the lands. In addition, because families were so frequently dying out in the direct male line, the ranks of the aristocracy were constantly being renewed by new blood as lawyers, merchants and

wealthy peasants acquired a sufficient quantity of land. So although individual families may have gained land and increased their incomes against
the prevailing trend, the aristocracy as a whole did not close ranks and
share the resources among fewer families.

The aristocracy believed that they could add to their incomes by participating in war and thereby gain pay, ransoms and booty. The English
hoped to find especially rich pickings from campaigns in France. As well
as the usual profits from plunder and prisoners, lands and offices were
available to English soldiers in Normandy after Henry V took over that
province in 1415. There were famous examples to prove that profit was
possible, notably Sir John Fastolf who from modest beginnings rose to
become a war captain in the 1420s and 1430s, and sent enough money
back to England to buy lands worth £1,000 per annum. Sir Hugh
Luttrell rebuilt Dunster Castle in Somerset on the basis of his service in
France under Henry V. Others were not so fortunate, and incurred
expenses that exceeded their profits, such as having to pay ransoms to
the French. The whole enterprise ended in the 1450s, when the French
expelled the English. The Scottish aristocracy suffered from similar
delusions. They did gain plunder, ransoms and protection money in their
raids into northern England in the late fourteenth century, but after 1400
the English were better organized. The Scots became the victim of incursions, and the obsessive but incompetent warrior, the fourth earl of
Douglas, who was active between 1398 and 1424, found himself paying
a ransom.

Longer-term profits could be gained by service both in peace and war
through 'bastard feudalism', by which sums of money were paid by the
crown, for example in Scotland in 1389–1406, to such figures as the duke
of Albany, and in turn by magnates to their retainers. These financial
payments among the aristocracy in both England and Scotland were not
new, though they may have increased in number, for example in times of
civil war.

ii. *Gentry*

The landed incomes of the higher aristocracy show adjustment to change
rather than many new initiatives. The landed gentry have more of a reputation for enterprise. The lower ranks of the English aristocracy were
given a new precision in this period when they were identified in legal
records after the Statute of Additions in 1413 as knights, esquires and
gentlemen. Contemporaries could recognize them by their houses, their
numbers of servants, their style of life and their participation in govern-

ment, especially at the local level. But their defining feature was possession of a landed income, which in the case of gentlemen attained at least
£10, with a minimum of £20 for an esquire and £40 for a knight. This
meant that they often held only one or two manors, though rich knights
could have estates with a dozen.

The gentry encountered the same problems as the magnates. They
leased out their demesnes in the search for a steady income, and their
rents from lessees and peasant tenants tended to fall in the first half of
the fifteenth century. They took similar counter-measures, by compiling
rentals and if necessary putting money into peasant buildings. John
Catesby esquire, of Ashby St Ledgers in Northamptonshire, in 1385 and
1386 reviewed the 'state' of his five manors, which were valued at £123
per annum. He found much to worry him. One arable demesne was
calculated to make no profit at all, ten peasant holdings on one manor
lay 'in the lord's hands', rents were in decay or in arrears, and the cost
of reconstructing peasant buildings was calculated at £18. Manors presented the same problems, regardless of the type of lord.

The gentry served the magnates as administrators, so they were
bringing their experience as landlords on a small scale to their work as
stewards and supervisors, and no doubt returning to their own lands
with ideas gleaned from the larger estates. More of their income came
from non-landed sources. They fought in some numbers in the armies in
France, and they were the chief beneficiaries of the payment of fees and
annuities (commonly worth £5 or £10 per annum) by the magnates –
often as a reward for estate management, but also for more general
political and legal work. Above all, they manned the legal profession,
which gave a useful income to many, and allowed some stars to amass
large landed estates. Rich lawyers, like Thomas Kebell who died in 1500
with many manors in Leicestershire, became effective and innovative
estate managers.

As in the case of the higher aristocracy, individual families
united inheritances by making advantageous marriage alliances. Gentry
families in Anglesey, for example, through a combination of skilfully
negotiated marriages, office-holding and the land market, making full
use of the pridd (see p. 177), put together large accumulations of property, like the Plas Newydd estate which was built up by the Griffith family
between about 1442 and 1479. As a whole, however, the gentry did not
concentrate land into the hands of a few families; their numbers
increased in some counties by the early sixteenth century. Small institutions with similar incomes to the gentry reduced their expenditure: in the
mid-fifteenth-century depression the fellows of Exeter College, Oxford,
in view of their declining rents had to discontinue the practice of paying

themselves a bonus at Christmas, Easter and Whitsun. Economies were more difficult for lay families with a handful of servants and very restricted consumption of luxury goods. If they made any more cuts in spending they would lose their aristocratic status.

The manors of lesser lords, as in earlier periods, tended to have a high proportion of land in demesnes, and they obtained a modest income from tenant rents. Those with only a few hundred acres used much of their produce in their households, which left them with limited quantities for sale. Their great advantage over the bureaucratic estates of the magnates lay in the small scale of their operations, often adjacent to or very near to their residence, which enabled these lords to supervise agriculture and rent collection personally. Sometimes they put reeves and bailiffs in charge of manors, in which case formal accounts were submitted and audited, as on a large estate. This was especially likely for a gentry estate with a number of manors, like Catesby's. But some gentry jotted down few financial details, or compiled rough and incomplete accounts, and those with very small amounts of land did everything by word of mouth.

They clearly took a close personal interest in their lands. Gentry audited accounts, authorized payments, and attended the sheep-shearing. Sir Roger Townshend, a very rich Norfolk knight, in his account book of 1480 recorded the smallest detail, recommending that old hurdles should be sent to the household to be used as firewood, or warning shepherds to look out for dangerous dogs. When members of the gentry made their wills they revealed intimate knowledge of their livestock by bequeathing a specific animal, such as 'the black ox' or the horse with a white star. Another wealthy Norfolk family, the Pastons, kept their own sheep but lived mainly from rents. Their letters show that they observed carefully the selection of tenants, and sometimes held their own manorial courts. They received some of their rents in kind, which made them fully aware of the market for barley. John Pennington, a Lancashire knight, records in his books of accounts and memoranda written between 1486 and 1512 that he personally took the money from lessees who paid their entry fines in instalments. If gentry were active in government and service of great lords, or spent much time in the law courts or on military campaigns, their wives managed their lands. Relatives were drawn into administration, presumably because they could be trusted, and the lord's brother acted as rent collector or bailiff. The first treatise on agricultural methods to be written after the era of *Walter of Henley*, which was published in 1523, was, needless to say, not written by a manager who worked for a great estate, but by an esquire, addressing himself to a readership of gentry. John Fitzherbert, from Derbyshire, in his 'Book of Husbandry' assumed that his readers were in charge of their own manors and would profit from advice about types of plough and the best techniques for sowing corn and weeding.

Many gentry, probably a majority, depended mainly on the rents from their demesnes held by farmers and, if they were actively involved in agricultural production, concentrated on a home farm mainly for domestic consumption. They could obtain grain for the household by receiving rents in kind from their tenants, or by themselves acting as farmers for parish tithes. A significant section of them produced on a large scale for the market. They took on the demesnes of other lords as farmers, sometimes with the intention of subletting, but often they ran the demesnes as profitable enterprises. To help in this they selected their acquisitions carefully, for example leasing a piece of land next to one of their manors so as to make a larger unit of production. Usually they focused on pasture, which gave the best returns for low labour costs. The Giffard family who lived in north Gloucestershire leased out the arable demesnes of their home manors of Weston Subedge and Norton Subedge, but in the late 1440s took on lease the nearby grange of Combe from a Cistercian monastery, on which they grazed 2,156 sheep and 55 cattle. At the end of the fifteenth century John Spencer, who began his career below the gentry, accumulated in eastern Warwickshire a string of lands held on lease, most of them demesnes or the sites of villages where the fields had been converted to pasture, and in 1506 became the lord of the manor of Althorp in Northamptonshire. Land held on lease did not carry the same status as the lordship of a manor. When gentry gathered such land they did so for profit, not to gain prestige.

The gentry who were most active in agriculture specialized in livestock. The Catesbys, who after their investigation of their unprofitable arable farming leased out their demesnes, kept one in hand at Radbourn in Warwickshire, converted it entirely to pasture (including the site of the village and the peasant holdings), and added lands leased from other lords to make an even larger block of grazing land. In 1448, when lords were generally at the trough of the mid-century depression, the pasture at Radbourn was stocked with 1,643 sheep and twenty cattle, and they kept a warren which yielded 202 rabbits in a year. The whole operation in 1449 was valued at £64, three times the value of the manor when it was a mixed farming demesne with tenant rents in 1386. Later, along with a number of other midland gentry, the Catesbys bought Welsh cattle that had been driven to markets such as Bromyard in Herefordshire, and fattened them for onward sale, often to end in the hands of London butchers, or to supply the garrison in Calais. The Townshend family of Norfolk must have been the greatest sheepmasters in the whole country at the end of the fifteenth century. Between 1475 and 1490 the first Roger Townshend expanded his flocks from 7,000 to 12,000, which provided a profit of at least £200, far in excess of his income from rents. Under his successor the number of sheep rose to 18,000 in 1516. The wool was sold locally for clothmaking, and to traders in King's Lynn. There was also much money to be made by selling animals to butchers at a time of high demand for meat. Gentry with large flocks economized on cash wages by rewarding their shepherds with the right to keep their own small flock on the pasture.

The gentry also saw the advantage of investment in a wide range of commercial and industrial enterprises. We have noted their presence in towns, where they held property and joined fraternities. This was partly for prestige, as they would be the guests of honour at feasts, and they acted as political and legal advisers, but they also valued towns as outlets for their produce. They invested in a wide range of industries, such as iron-working, tin extraction, tile and glass manufacture, and the quarrying of stone for building and millstones. In Derbyshire, not just the very wealthy Vernon family but also many lesser gentry made profits from the lead industry, and near Nottingham, at Wollaton, one of the largest coal mines in England was developed by the knightly Willoughby family. Members of the gentry also owned shares in ships and invested in trading ventures.

The gentry then were actively engaged in production, but they have also gained a reputation for taking decisive actions to change the world around them in order to make larger profits. They shifted the boundaries and the size and shape of the units in which property was held. Their most notorious actions relate to the removal of peasant tenants and the seizure of village territories to create enclosed pastures, which was recorded in some detail in the reports of the enclosure commissions in 1517. In one incident, on 11 August 1495, Thomas Pigott enclosed the fields of Doddershall in Buckinghamshire with fences and ditches. Twenty-four houses in the village were allowed to fall into ruin, and 120 people left 'tearfully'. These acts of depopulation affected villages of the corn-growing open-field farming districts, and was only possible when a lord had control of a whole village or at least a substantial part of it.

More commonly, the gentry bought up land from peasants, including the customary holdings which had formerly been held by servile tenures. Thomas Tropenell, a rising lawyer and estate official, acquired a dozen holdings in Corsham in north Wiltshire between the 1430s and 1470s. The piecemeal accumulation of holdings, which could merge a number of manors, or create new ones, was a feature of the countryside surrounding London. Avery Cornborough (who died in 1487), by origin a merchant, rose in royal service to become an esquire to Edward IV. He put together holdings in Havering atte Bower to the east of London, making a total of 1,200 acres, and expanded his demesne at the expense of the tenants he inherited with his purchases. The gentry caused particular disruption by taking over areas of grazing land from peasant communities. In Norfolk they bought not the land but the the fold-courses, that is the right to pasture sheep on village fields, to the ultimate damage of the peasantry. When they enclosed common pastures in other parts of the country they were liable to cause violent hostility. A good example is Ralph Wolseley, a south Staffordshire lord, who after political service acquired rights to a large area of woodland near the small town of Rugeley and enclosed it in about 1465, some of it for grazing and a rabbit warren, and partly to provide fuel for a glasshouse. His openness to innovations is suggested by his investment in a beer brewery (in a region where ale was the main drink) and in a dyeworks. His novelties provoked the local population to riot, mainly because the enclosure deprived them of common pasture, but also because the introduction of beer threatened the local ale brewers.

After a review of the activities of the Catesby, Giffard, Spencer, Town-shend, Vernon, Willoughby and Wolseley families, we might be tempted to identify the group as a whole as entrepreneurs, exhibiting all of the hallmarks of capitalists, in their specialization in profitable lines, large scale of production, investment, technical innovations such as enclosures, and refusal to be inhibited by tradition. There would be much truth in this view, but the characteristics of this group cannot be applied to the gentry as a whole, and their acquisitive ambitions are also found among larger landlords and peasants.

Many of the smaller gentry lacked the resources for long-term invest-ment and large-scale enterprises. Humphrey Newton of Newton in Cheshire, who recorded his affairs in a rather unsystematic notebook in 1498–1505, had a finger in many pies, but all on a small scale. He culti-vated less than 100 acres of arable, and bought extra supplies of grain to feed his household. He dealt in cattle and kept about fifty sheep. He repaired his corn mill and built a new fulling mill, which brought in a rent of 26s 8d per annum. He spent money on his ponds as a source of fish for the household rather than sale. Newton, like some of his grander contemporaries, went to market, at the local towns of Macclesfield and Congleton, and the fair at Chapel-en-le-Frith, and he was interested in improving his land, devoting a lot of attention to spreading marl. He showed ingenuity, boldness, a willingness to invest and an awareness of the market, but he cannot be accused of specialization, and his efforts were devoted to keeping afloat on small assets. At Newton he increased his income from £11 to £14. Many of the gentry, of course, relied on rents, and ran their estates without much enterprise or innovation. Nicholas Franceis, with fourteen properties spead over Somerset and Devon, seems to have been content to draw £65 per annum from them in rents. The energies of many gentry were devoted to law and administration, which may well have brought them better rewards than risky investments in production.

Profit-making ventures were not confined to the gentry. Monasteries like Durham Priory kept large flocks and herds throughout this period, and the bishop of Durham invested in coal mines. Many other lords profited from tileworks and fulling mills on their estates. If the gentry were enterprising, it was often through their alliances with non-aristocratic entrepreneurs, and it is to them that we must turn next.

iii. *Farmers*

Farmers – that is the tenants of leased demesnes or granges, so called because they paid a fixed annual rent or farm – appear as a powerful new force for change in the countryside around 1400. As the lords shed their demesnes, they were handing over to the farmers the management of agricultural production of perhaps a fifth or a quarter of the agricultural land in Britain. This was not such a sudden break as first appears, because assets had been leased for centuries before. But it is the scale of the change, in a few decades, which gives it an almost revolutionary quality. Leasing of demesnes put new people in control of landed resources, established new relationships between lords and tenants, and the farmers brought new methods of production and management.

When leasing began we can sense the caution of the lords, as they often rented out their demesnes to the reeves who had already been running the manors under the system of direct management. A lord was not just choosing someone who could be trusted: the new farmer was often a customary tenant, and indeed might be a 'serf by blood', over whom the lord could hope to exercise control. To emphasize this dependency, the lease was sometimes written into the rolls of the manor court and resembled a customary tenancy; the farmer's conduct could be supervised through the court. To add to the lord's guarantee that a rash decision would not do permanent damage, the early leases were often for very short terms, even less than ten years. As the system developed, the farmers became more independent and escaped from such close supervision by the lord. However, in Kent, Warwickshire and Wiltshire, the majority of farmers continued to be recruited from the peasantry. Indeed, these figures understate the proportion of peasants actually working the leased land, as the gentry, clergy or merchants who made up the remainder of the farmers would sometimes sublet the land to peasants.

For peasants who took over the demesne in a group, becoming farmers allowed each of them to add substantially to an existing holding, perhaps to double its size. The Cistercian monastery of Coupar Angus in central Scotland leased Coupar grange in 1468 to Simon Anderson, John Olyver and eight others for five years, in return for a rent of corn, fuel and poultry. Perhaps the lessees, like the monastery, were interested in the crops they would gain for their own consumption. But many individual peasants took over a demesne of 200–400 acres for a cash rent, after their previous experience of cultivating a holding of 30–60 acres. For example, John Hickes of Durrington in Wiltshire leased a 200-acre demesne in 1401–14, having originally tenanted a single 30-acre yardland, though he later acquired three more. Many peasant farmers in the fifteenth century were recruited from outside the tenants of the manor, so they did not even bring to the task detailed knowledge of the fields and labour force. They had to adjust quickly to all of the problems of large-scale farming – raising capital, investing in equipment, buildings and livestock, hiring and managing many employees, and marketing great quantities of produce. Lords went to some trouble to identify suitable candidates to take over a farm, like William Smythe, recommended to the Pastons as 'the most able man to take a farm of land that I know in your lordship'. Most farmers stood up to the test, and stayed throughout their term.

Running a farm presented less of a challenge to the gentry, clerical or merchant lessees. We saw that the gentry might take on other lords' demesnes adjacent to their own manor in order to increase the efficiency as well as the scale of their operations. Sometimes they wished to acquire a type of land, usually extensive pasture, which was not available on their own manors. The proportion of demesnes acquired by 'gentlemen farmers' grew in the late fifteenth and sixteenth centuries, as the profits from agriculture increased. The merchants included woolmongers, clothiers, butchers and others with an obvious interest in using the produce in their businesses, but sometimes the lease was just one of their portfolio of investments.

Leases, which were contracts agreed between the parties, helped to change relationships between lords and tenants. More traditional concepts of lordship and clientage could not be banished overnight. The first farmers were sometimes serfs or customary tenants, and later farmers, like those on the Fountains Abbey estate in Yorkshire in the early sixteenth century, were expected to attend the abbot as his retainers. In essence, however, the indenture recorded a mutually advantageous

contract, and the striking feature is the lack of conditions and restrictions on tenants. They were expected to repair buildings and pay their
rent on time, but even elementary commitments were not kept. Most
farmers were not required to carry out any particular type of husbandry.
The leases after 1450 reflect the strong bargaining power of the tenants
in their length. In the south-east they often ran for fifteen to twenty years,
but in Yorkshire fifteen to forty years were commonly allowed, and in
the midlands they could stretch to sixty years and more. In Scotland,
where short leases were often granted, in the fifteenth century a growing
number were for the tenant's life. Hereditary succession was not
unknown. For example, at the bishop of Worcester's manor of Bishop's
Cleeve in Gloucestershire, Thomas Yardington held the farm from 1471
to 1525 and was succeeded by his son. It was clearly possible for the
possessors of such leases to regard the land as their own, and to do with
it virtually as they wished.

Farmers' adoption of new methods is apparent in the quantity and
layout of the land. When farmers took on leases they bargained for
acreages that they could manage. The least ambitious, like the Coupar
Angus peasants, just wanted a larger peasant holding. Those with
grander aspirations might still be daunted by very large demesnes, and
it was common for lessees of Cistercian granges which tended to run to
300–400 acres to have them divided into two. Similarly, if a demesne consisted of a number of scattered blocks as much as a mile apart, which
was not uncommon in woodland districts where the manor had developed by assarting and purchase in the twelfth and thirteenth centuries,
the lord found it easier to lease out each block separately; this led to the
building of new farmhouses out in the fields, a development normally
associated with the eighteenth century. Farmers often wished to specialize, which led to the break-up of old units, and the leasing of upland
pastures apart from the arable demesnes to which they had once been
attached. We have seen that lords began this process by keeping their
sheep pastures in hand when they first leased the arable demesnes.
The farmers could also create new combinations of land, with the
emphasis on specialization rather than the mixture of land types
favoured by the traditional estates. A good example of this new conception of an estate was John Spencer's group of leased lands on the
Warwickshire/Northamptonshire border, which consisted of extensive
pastures, often formed from the grassed-over fields of deserted villages.
The Nanfan family in Merionethshire also made a new estate out of the
leased granges of Cistercian monasteries.

Needless to say, many farmers converted arable to pasture to increase
their profits. Thomas Vicars of Strensall near York, who farmed two

demesnes, owned on his death in 1451 two ploughs, suggesting he had no more than 200 acres in cultivation, but was grazing 799 sheep, 198 cattle and 92 horses. He was evidently fattening cattle for the urban market, and breeding horses for sale. Wool merchants and clothiers could bring marketing expertise to their management of sheep pastures. Technical changes needed capital, particularly to build new structures such as sheepcotes for the increasing flocks, and enclosures in which to feed the animals. Lords commonly funded farmers' buildings in the difficult times in the mid-fifteenth century. It still happened in 1497–1507 on the bishop of Winchester's manor of Overton, where the lord spent £80 on a new house and barn for the farmer. In general the farmers were paying for their own improvements, and were able to raise loans on the basis of their profits.

The complaints of the local peasantry about the damaging changes made by farmers at this time show the degree to which they were transforming the agriculture of some demesnes by enclosure and changes in the use of land. The tenants at Quinton in Warwickshire, a manor of Magdalen College, Oxford, accused their successive farmers in 1480 and 1490 of depriving cottagers of acres of land which by informal custom they had been allowed to cultivate, of ploughing up common pasture, and generally making life difficult for tenants, who were leaving the manor and threatening the well-being of the peasant community. In this case the remote lord was persuaded to protect the peasants from the farmers. Sometimes a really radical change in the farm, involving the complete enclosure of the fields and the exclusion of the peasants, was accomplished by an alliance between lord and farmer. The Warwickshire manor of Burton Dassett was enclosed in 1497 as the result of co-operation between John Heritage, the farmer, and Edward Belknap, a young and acquisitive lord who expected to gain a higher rent as the farmer's profits increased.

iv. *Peasants*

An interpretation of the period has identified the key promoters of change as the gentry, who saw their opportunity to remove the unprofitable peasantry from their manors in order to create large and efficient units of agricultural production. We have already noted the enterprising character of gentry agriculture, their willingness to make radical changes in the landscape, and their alliance with farmers in pursuit of profits. One theory emphasizes the vulnerability of the English peasantry (in contrast with the security of tenure enjoyed by their French contemporaries), because the leaseholds or tenancies at will by which many of them held their land were easily terminated. Lords still retained arbitrary powers over the copyholders, who were the descendants of the villeins of the thirteenth and fourteenth centuries and who could display a written copy of the entry in the lord's court as evidence of their title. Lords sometimes charged such tenants very high entry fines, which could drive even those with rights of inheritance from their holdings. The gentry were not as enterprising as this view presumes: many lived on rents, and the activists were too scattered to have an overwhelming effect on the agricultural economy. Many peasants still held by hereditary tenure, such as copyhold, and while this in theory was under the control of the lords' courts, the royal court of chancery extended its protection over copyholders in the late fifteenth century. Peasants were well organized, and had recourse to many defences against a predatory farmer or lord – the peasants of Quinton, for example, mounted an effective protest by persuading their parish clergyman to petition on their behalf.

We can test the view that there was large-scale expropriation of peasant holdings by examining the 2,000 or more villages which were deserted in England between about 1370 and 1520. Together with a much larger number of villages which shrank severely, and many thousands of deserted hamlets and farms in all parts of Britain, we have apparent evidence of the lords' deliberate removal of peasants from the land.

In fact most peasants removed themselves. Far from evicting peasants, lords used their courts in often futile attempts to prevent migration and to promote repair to tenant buildings not just in the 'reaction' after the Black Death but right through the fifteenth century and even after 1500. Lords were interested in securing a healthy income of rents, and that was best secured by keeping buildings in good repair and tenants on the land. When a village was abandoned, the estate authorities were sometimes slow to take advantage, and the pasture was grazed by neighbouring villages before money was invested in enclosures and the land exploited profitably.

The villages fell victim in the long term to the fall in population, which through differences in migration affected some villages more drastically than others. Often a village survived the Black Death and later epidemics, and then its people moved away in search of better prospects. The small Oxfordshire village of Brookend which had sixteen tenants before the first plague still had fifteen in 1363, but gradually they left and were not replaced, and by 1441 only three families remained. If the villages were killed off by their lords, we would expect them to disappear rather quickly, but often they went through a long-drawn-out decline, which sometimes began in the crisis before 1348, and continued over the next century. Many villages seem to have reached the point of no return in the early fifteenth century. (Plate 19)

The inhabitants found some villages unattractive, and left them. Villages with an industrial side to their economies were rarely abandoned, and indeed a number of them expanded at the expense of purely agricultural settlements. Peasants drifted away from small villages which were not at the centre of their parishes and which lacked social variety and facilities. Chapel Ascote in Warwickshire in its decline in the early fifteenth century could muster only one brewer. When this last alehouse closed in 1451 the village's fate was sealed.

Acquisitive villagers also made life difficult for their neighbours. We find peasants taking over a number of holdings as their tenants left. At Hangleton in Sussex a peasant built his house on a site which had previously been occupied by five neighbours. These accumulators of holdings tended to behave selfishly, as the scale of their farming set them at odds with the rest of the community. Henry Chandeler of Roel in Gloucestershire, who held five tenements totalling 150 acres in 1400, was accused of overstocking the common pasture with sheep. He probably did not cultivate his large area of arable thoroughly. Such activities threatened the orderly running of the open-field system, on which the livelihood of all of the villagers depended. At Compton Verney in Warwickshire, where the village was in decay around 1400, and finally died soon after 1460, the manor court issued orders for tethering grazing horses and for the control of rooting pigs, but large sections of the arable had been converted to pasture, and tenants were holding blocks of land in the fields as if the old boundaries and rotations had been forgotten. Tenants held fragments of holdings, and the coherent yardlands that had been formed centuries before were being broken up and redistributed. Compton's fields were so ill-managed that neighbouring villages sent their flocks and herds to graze illicitly.

The lords (by no means all of them gentry) who presided over these decaying villages eventually lost patience with attempts to retain tenants or restore them to profitable health. The rents that the rump of villagers paid were very low, and the land would be worth much more if converted into enclosed pastures. Contemporaries complained that 'avaricious men' (as John Rous of Warwick called them) were destroying villages. Rous compiled in about 1486 a list of sixty villages that had been deserted, mainly in Warwickshire, and three years later public opinion had become so alarmed that legislation was passed to prevent the 'pulling down and wilful waste of houses and towns' (town meaning rural settlements, in this context). Concern continued, and in 1516 Thomas More complained that the sheep, once a meek and gentle beast, had become an eater of men.

In 1517, the government, under Cardinal Wolsey, set up a commission to investigate the 'casting down of houses' and the conversion of arable to pasture. The reports of the commissioners and the court cases that followed revealed hundreds of offences, mainly in the east midland counties, from Buckinghamshire to Nottinghamshire. They missed many deserted villages, because they had disappeared before the legislation had been passed, but they tended to catch lords who were removing the last villagers from badly shrunken settlements. For example, the depopulation of Burton Dassett in 1497 by Edward Belknap and John Heritage resulted in the loss of twelve houses, but this had been a very large manor with more than seventy tenants before the first plague. Clearly most of the inhabitants had moved out before the lord enclosed the fields.

Deserted villages attracted the attention of contemporaries like Rous and More, and have continued to fascinate modern historians because their end was so complete: a compact settlement with 100 or 200 people, cultivating complex open fields covering a territory of hundreds of acres, was transformed into a group of enclosed pastures in which the sheep and cattle were herded by a few employees. In fact, more households and land were abandoned as a result of the reduction in size of the great majority of villages from which lords gained no benefit: this was wholly the result of mortality and migration among the peasantry. Similarly, a high proportion of the half-million houses which were abandoned between 1320 and 1520 lay in hamlets and isolated farms in the regions throughout Britain where villages were rare. Often a settlement shrank down to a single farm, like the hamlet of Carneborne in Helston (Cornwall), which had once contained three holdings; by 1486 they had been taken over by a single tenant who was said to hold 'the whole vill'. In the woodlands of the west midlands half of the houses that were inhabited in about 1300 had commonly been deserted by 1520. And the traces of ruined farms scattered over the uplands of Wales and Scotland, which are rarely closely dated, include some abandoned in this period of low rural population. The loss of holdings did not lead, as in the case of the villages, to the total transformation of a section of the landscape, and it was rarely instigated by lords, but it adds to the picture of peasants choosing where to live, and leaving settlements, or avoiding moving into them, because they saw better prospects elsewhere.

Scottish tenants appear to have been more vulnerable than those in England to encroachment by landlords. Many tenants held by short, even one-year leases, but in practice these were renewed, and heirs were allowed to succeed. Similarly 'rental' tenants, whose names were included in a list of tenants, had at least some written evidence for their tenure, and the holdings could be inherited. The convention of 'kindly tenure' meant that lords were disposed to respect the rights of sons and other relatives to take a holding after a tenant's death. However ill-defined the rights of tenants may have been, they were not expelled or denied succession because in general tenants were in short supply, and the Scottish lairds, the counterparts of the gentry, did not pursue aggressive policies of direct management or the incorporation of tenants' lands into their demesnes. A new development from the mid-fifteenth century came with the adoption of *feu-ferms*, which gave tenants property rights over their holdings, if they paid an entry fine and a high annual rent. The lords gained short-term profit, but early sixteenth-century inflation made the fixed rents seem cheap, so the tenants – a third of whom were lairds, but who also included some peasants – gained in the long run.

The abandonment and shrinkage of rural settlements shows that peasants were not the victims of their lords, but decision-makers and initiators. Many peasants did not better themselves or make great changes in their economic roles in this period. In the early sixteenth century thousands of them lived in a style bearing some resemblance to that of their predecessors two centuries earlier. Between a fifth and a third of tenants worked standard holdings of 15 or 30 acres of land. They still practised mixed farming, with a strong emphasis on the cultivation of corn. Millions of acres lay in open fields, and strong village communities regulated the use of land. The techniques of cultivation and stock-rearing had not changed fundamentally. Many were either free tenants whose rents had been fixed before 1300, or in England copyholders who owed their lords rents based originally on the money value of labour which had been calculated when the services of villeins were commuted in the fourteenth century. They paid entry fines to acquire a holding, and a heriot when they died or surrendered it. Many Scottish peasants still held their land from year to year, and the Welsh pridd was used to transfer land. Hundreds of families were called serfs, and could be expected to pay marriage fines if the lord enforced them. The family was the basis of labour on the holding, and some sons worked with their fathers, and looked after them in their old age. In Wales the kin still exercised great authority over landholding. Most produce from the land was consumed within the household and farm, leaving a limited surplus for sale.

The lack of change in the peasant economy could be regarded as proof of peasants' unenterprising outlook, and their contentment with customary ways and modest profits. Rather, the persistence of a traditional peasantry reflects the fact that the economic circumstances were not especially favourable to producers – their corn in particular fetched modest prices. The cost of labour, if they were tempted to expand their holdings above the acreage that could be managed by the household, remained high. Their rents were still a burden, and there was some truth in their complaints that they could not afford certain rents. They asserted themselves, however, showing that they did not accept their lot by refusing to pay selected dues, and by rebelling against new taxes in 1489, 1497 and 1525.

For all of the survival of the old ways, and the adversity of the times, the peasants still took initiatives. The importance of migration in the changes in the settlement pattern is clear, but the constant, even restless, movement of people lies behind many other developments. It was not new for peasants to uproot themselves – otherwise the clearance of new land and growth of towns in the twelfth and thirteenth centuries would not have been possible. But in the fifteenth century three-quarters of the families living in some villages changed every fifty years. It was a rare family which in 1520 had been settled in the same place continuously since 1350. George Underhyll, a serf of Hampton Lovett in Worcestershire moved to Hartlebury, about 5 miles away, in 1479, where he made a successful career as a landholder and seller of food and drink. His son Richard, who was born at Hampton Lovett, migrated 20 miles to the small town of Tewkesbury, where he worked as a tanner, and then went to Hartlebury in 1503.

The role of the peasant family was changed not overnight by the plagues, but in the long run. Everywhere individuals broke free from some of the constraints of family and kinship. In East Anglia the family had always had a limited influence on landholding, with most land transfers being made between individuals who were not related to one another rather than passing though the family by inheritance. By the early fifteenth century the frequent disposal of land outside the family, and apparent reduction in inheritance as a means of transmitting property, had spread to the midlands and the north. Children left home to find work and land elsewhere, so that when their parent died or retired, there was no one to inherit the land, and it passed to another family. In Wales the group of kinsmen, the *gwely*, diminished in importance, and land was held in larger units by individuals. This does not mean that family sentiment came to an end, just that attitudes towards family had always been based in some degree on the state of the market for land and produce. In times of land scarcity it paid to be loyal to one's parents, look after them in old age, and take over the family holding. After a period when land was cheap and plentiful in the mid-fifteenth century, transfers within the family tended to return with rising land values around 1500.

Some historians might say that strong attachment to the family was a basic peasant characteristic, and that the move away from family values shows that the people concerned had ceased to be peasants – they had adopted capitalist notions of individualism and acquisitiveness. But peasants were not ruled entirely by emotion, and had always been motivated by some measure of self-interest. The varying attitudes in different parts of the country, and the changes in different periods, demonstrates that they were rational economic people, whose behaviour was influenced by their circumstances. The decline in family attachments may have some bearing on the greater social and economic role of the village community. After 1334 the village was made responsible for assessing and collecting its own taxes, and it seems to be in association with the collection of money for that purpose that villages developed a common box, from which poor relief was paid. In the early sixteenth century the parish was given the legal responsibility of looking after its own poor, but that function had clearly been developing for more than a century. The community was taking over some of the responsibilities to the old and sick that had previously been the duty of relatives.

At the same time, the churchwardens grew in importance, with a primary task of fundraising for the maintenance of the fabric of the parish church. Often they became ambitious to rebuild the church, or at least to add towers, porches, aisles and clerestories, or to embellish the interior with screens, images and wall paintings. In many parishes a public hall, the church house, was built by the churchwardens next to the church; here church ales could be held at which parishioners gathered to drink, and the profits of selling ale and food went to church funds. Some villages also built almshouses, advancing yet further their charitable activities. And in many parishes, especially in eastern England, religious fraternities were formed, which also raised funds, built substantial guild-halls, and made some contribution to poor relief. A growing proportion of the village's resources was devoted to public spending on these projects, and the wealthier households spent more on community projects than they paid in taxes to the crown.

Peasants knew that their lords possessed great authority and political power, but they were also aware that as the number of potential tenants declined, especially in view of the fright delivered to the aristocracy in 1381, lords could be pressurized to secure better conditions. We have already seen something of the bargaining process at work, and can appreciate that the reductions in rent, abolition of unpopular charges such as tallages, recognitions and common fines, and changes in tenancy such as the introduction of leasehold, came about through negotiations backed up by rent strikes and threats to leave the manors. Peasants still gained strength from their community organization, which meant that collective action, such as a common refusal to pay tallage, was particularly effective. One reason why we know so much about the encroachments on common pastures and other acquisitive behaviour by the gentry is that the peasants were well organized and were able to bring legal action against their lords, including making use of the royal courts. As always, the peasant suitors at the lord's courts were adept at manipulating its machinery, for example by using their influence as jurors to adjust customary laws in favour of the tenant. Peasants were becoming more closely involved in politics, as is suggested by the written programme of reform which the rebels from south-east England put forward in Cade's revolt of 1450. They were attempting to make use of the existing political machinery by agreeing with measures proposed in parliament, such as the demand that the king live on his own landed resources and not by taxing his subjects. They had apparently abandoned their attempt, as in 1381, to seek to change the social and political structure from outside.

Initiatives from the serfs put a virtual end to servile status, not by grand political actions, but by the quiet process of migration. A relatively small number of peasants paid quite large sums (£5–£10) to buy their freedom, which enabled them to live in their native village without the taint of serfdom. But for many, the desire to move from the village in search of economic benefits had the incidental effect of providing an escape from the jurisdiction of the lord: they knew that in a new home servile status would be unknown or quickly forgotten.

In pursuit of a higher standard of living, peasants rebuilt their houses in growing numbers after 1380, with a concentration of new construction in the period 1440 to 1519. Dendrochronology allows us to give a precise date for standing buildings such as the 'wealden' houses of Kent, and the cruck houses in the midland counties of Buckinghamshire, Leicestershire, Shropshire and Warwickshire. The new buildings' quality can be judged from the hundreds which survive and are still inhabited (though no longer by peasants). They were also designed to provide superior accommodation, with two storeys in the end bays of the wealden houses of the south-east, which still retained open halls; even in the midlands and Devon, in the essentially one-storey cruck houses, upper rooms were inserted at least at one end. Houses at Seacourt in Berkshire were built with external staircases against the gable. In west Yorkshire and parts of the midlands, peasant houses were being roofed with stone slates instead of the traditional thatch. A three-bay cruck house in the midlands or the north in the mid-fifteenth century measuring 15 feet by 45 feet required an outlay of about £3 on materials and the wages of craftsmen. Some houses built at this time for prospering yeomen in east and north Wales were substantial, expensive and indicate status seeking. The medieval house which is now called Leeswood Green Farm near Mold in Flint was 50 feet long by 20 feet wide, with a large hall and rooms at each end with lofts. Not only were the family provided with space and comfort, they could also impress their neighbours and visitors with a show of the large quantities of timber used in construction and the decorative carving of some of the timbers. (Plates 18a and 18b)

Peasants bought more clothing, furnishings and household equipment at this time. They also ate better. Harvest workers employed at Sedgeford in Norfolk in 1424 were provided with a pound of meat and at least 6 pints of ale for each 2 pounds of bread. This was not just a reversal of the bread-based diet that predominated before 1300, but much higher-quality ingredients were used, with bread made from wheat flour rather than barley meal, and fresh beef instead of bacon. Many peasants would have eaten as well as the harvest workers during that season of heavy work, and would have expected to eat meat and wheat bread throughout the year. They seem to have been attempting to emulate the material conditions that they observed in towns, and in the manor houses and parsonages. Their diet, arrangement of their houses, and furnishings and clothing brought them closer to the models provided by better-off townspeople, gentry and clergy. In addition to individual consumption, they also aspired to a high level of collective spending on their churches and associated buildings.

The main means for a peasant family to raise their income was to increase the size of their holding. They achieved this by the traditional process of inheritance and marriage, but land was purchased from another tenant, or taken (more cheaply) from the lord when a tenant died or departed without heirs. There were very large variations in the size of holdings, but it was still true, as in the pre-plague era, that midland and northern peasants tended to hold standard units of yardlands or oxgangs, and the wealthier minority could commonly accumulate 45 or 60 acres. Some lords split holdings in response to demand. A typical accumulation was that of William White at Cowpen Bewley in County Durham, who inherited a bondland (30 acres), two cottages, and 30 acres in five holdings from his father in 1480. He brought his total holding from 60 to 80 acres by more acquisitions in 1482. In the east and south-east of England, land was held in acres rather than standard units, smallholders were more common, and the discrepancies between tenants greater. At Ickham in Kent in 1400, forty-one of fifty-one tenants held 9 acres or less, and seven held 30 acres or more, including two with 150 acres. In 1492 the smallholders with 9 acres or less had fallen to thirty, and there were individuals with 240 acres, 141 acres and 80 acres. In England as a whole by the early sixteenth century about an eighth of the rural householders held 50 acres or more, compared with the tiny percentage with so much land before the epidemics.

A new terminology to describe the English peasantry was introduced in the fifteenth century. Instead of the old distinction between free and unfree, which was becoming irrelevant, the new vocabulary was based on economic stratification, with an upper rank of yeomen, who often held 80 acres or more, a middle category of husbandmen, and at the bottom the labourers who held a few acres and had to work for wages. Yeomen of course were most likely to produce a large surplus and to employ labour. The land that defined this stratification was valuable. In Norfolk, in the depression of the market in the mid-fifteenth century as well as in the early years of the sixteenth century, customary land could command a price (that is, the money paid by the new tenant to the outgoing tenant) of 30s per acre. The busy land market meant that holdings tended to change hands in every generation, often outside the family. At Shillington in Bedfordshire, where there were about seventy tenants, 244 transfers were made in 1398–1458, so each holding changed hands about four times, mostly between unrelated parties. This land market was fed by the instability of many accumulations of land: a yeoman might build up a large holding from many parcels, but after his death it would fall apart and the parts would be used to build up new composite units.

Labour posed a serious problem for those gathering these large accumulations of land. The wages of agricultural labourers, which had risen from about 1d to 2d at the time of the Black Death, reached 3d–4d in the fifteenth and early sixteenth centuries. Real wages – assessing the value of the wage in terms of the food and other goods it would buy – increased two and a half times between 1300 and 1450. A tenant could cultivate a 30-acre holding cheaply if he had a son to help. But in the fifteenth century sons were not plentiful, and did not stay at home. One alternative was to hire young living-in servants whose labour was considerably cheaper than workers hired by the day, but again servants were in short supply because no village had a great surplus of young people. There would have been plenty of labour if the effects of the redistribution of land had worked as they did in other economic circumstances, that is to cause differentiation, with a growing number of cottagers and landless at the bottom to complement the larger holdings at the top. But all ranks of the post-plague peasantry expanded their holdings, with a general decrease in the number of cottagers. Many of the descendants of smallholders had been able to pick up a few more acres so that they no longer needed to work for wages. Presumably they were seeking the security that came from landholding rather than the cash rewards of wages. Cottagers were also highly mobile, and travelled to villages and

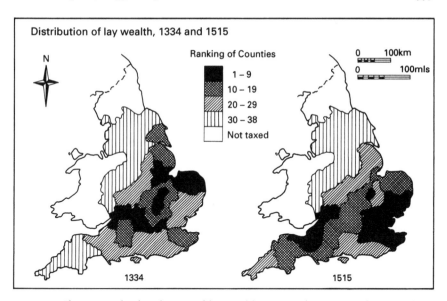

Map 11. Changes in the distribution of lay wealth, 1334 and 1515. One factor in the rise in the relative wealth of Suffolk, Essex, Kent, Gloucestershire and Somerset was the growth of the rural cloth industry.

Source: R. Schofield, 'The Geographical Distribution of Wealth in England, 1334–1649', *Economic History Review*, 2nd ser., 18 (1965).

towns where the wages were highest (Map 11). Some clothmaking settlements were as large as they had been in 1300, or even more populous. While houses everywhere were being abandoned in large numbers, in woodland villages with industrial employment, such as Sedgley in Staffordshire, new houses and cottages were being built on the waste in the late fifteenth century to accommodate the labour flowing into the community. Tenants with larger holdings attempted to solve the labour shortage by taking cottagers as subtenants, and monopolizing their labour. These tied cottages are found at Coupar Angus in the mid-fifteenth century, when ten peasant lessees of a demesne were presumed each to have two or three cottars under them. In Devon the wealthier peasants at villages such as Stokenham in the late fourteenth century gathered up the cottages as part of their larger holdings, in order to sublet them.

Peasants employers economized on labour, just like the farmers and lords, by converting their land from arable to pasture. They preferred to be self-sufficient in food, and so rarely used all of their holdings entirely as pasture. But the proportion of land under grass was increased almost everywhere in England and Wales. In open-field systems the land was put down to leys, which meant that by agreement parts of the arable fields were used for grazing. Where peasants in the woodland and uplands held their land in crofts and closes these were turned over to pasture in growing numbers. Scotland was an exception. Here peasants had always had access to ample pasture, and in this period oats prices were high and cattle cheap, so there was a tendency for cultivation to be maintained, and indeed there were complaints in about 1500 that extension of arable was damaging the hunting in the royal forest of Ettrick. The numbers of animals kept by tenants of all kinds seem larger than before the plagues. In midland open-field villages, flocks of 300 sheep belonging to individuals were not uncommon, and many tenants owned thirty to sixty sheep. Yeomen, especially in upland or woodland districts, kept impressively large numbers of animals. A late fifteenth-century Anglesey tenant had thirteen mares and foals, eleven oxen, twenty-three cows, fourteen bullocks, 176 sheep, two pigs and three hives of bees. In Wales, and also in pastoral districts of England such as the Forest of Arden in Warwickshire, peasants specialized in cattle, especially with the aim of satisfying the market for beef. The increase in numbers of livestock caused a good deal of friction in villages, and there were constant complaints of animals trespassing, and of the overburdening of the commons, leading to overgrazing. Villages responded by fixing stints and repeating these limits on the numbers of anmals that could be kept. Offenders were fined in the manor court.

Conflict could be avoided, and land could be used more efficiently, by changes in the management of land, and peasants in consequence reorganized their own holdings, and the common fields. In the uplands they enclosed more open grazing land; in the woodlands, crofts which had previously been available for common grazing were closed off and neighbours' animals denied access. The open fields could only be restructured after a process of exchange and consolidation of strips, which then formed coherent blocks of land which could be enclosed. We find individuals carrying out this process piecemeal at Stoke Fleming in Devon around 1400, and by 1500 the village was surrounded entirely by enclosed fields. Sometimes there was a collective agreement to enclose, like that made by the sixteen half-yardlanders (tenants of about 15 acres) at Sambourne in Warwickshire between 1445 and 1472, by which strips covering 240 acres were exchanged and fenced off. Peasant enclosures of this kind were much more numerous, and enclosed a much larger area of land, than the enclosures carried out by the lords. They attracted less dispute and attention because they were accepted by the peasants. Once land had been enclosed, it could be converted to pasture, or cropped as each peasant wished, but the common fields could be adapted, again with collective consent. Sometimes cultivation became less intensive, with the introduction of more fallows in districts like north-east Norfolk where fallows in more pressured times had been virtually eliminated. In the same trend to cultivate the land less frequently, it might be left under grass for some years and then ploughed up, with beneficial effects on the yields of crops of the newly cultivated ground. This technique, which was once thought to have been introduced in later centuries, known as 'up-and-down' or convertible husbandry, was already in use well before 1500. Sometimes an infield–outfield system was adopted, by which part of the field system was cropped every year, and the outer furlongs were planted one year in two. This had been typical of upland regions, but now spread to villages in the midlands and East Anglia.

A quiet change in technology led to a further extension in the employment of horses rather than oxen as draught animals. John Davye of Stalbridge in Dorset, a western county where oxen predominated before the first plague, when he died in 1496 owned eight horses and six oxen. The high-quality building methods which were developed for houses were also applied to farm buildings, especially barns. At Caldecote in Hertfordshire a tenant who had absorbed the holdings of a number of neighbours built two very large barns, capable of holding the crops of 160 acres, which dwarfed his house. Peasants searched for products which gave better returns, and we find such novelties as saffron gardens, especially in north-west Essex, and the keeping of goats, which had been discouraged before 1348 because of the damage they caused to trees. In their quest for an alternative source of income when conventional crops gave poor returns, East Anglian peasants turned to sea fishing, and those inland rented fish ponds. Changes in peasant marketing are suggested by the disappearance of the small village markets. Sales were being made further afield, as peasants with vehicles and considerable knowledge of the prices in their region were willing and able to travel longer distances.

The productivity of demesne arable declined in this period. In Norfolk, famous for its high yields, lords produced about 9 to 12 bushels per acre in 1250–1350, but in the range of 8–10 bushels in 1350–1450. Yield ratios, calculated by dividing the amount of grain that was harvested by the amount sown, on the bishopric of Winchester estate reached quite a high average of 3.88 (for wheat) in 1381–1410, but slipped back to 3.66 in 1411–53, below the thirteenth-century figure. Perhaps peasant yields moved in the same direction. Both demesnes and peasant holdings had more animals, and could therefore put more manure on the land, which may have increased returns, but on the other hand both lacked labour, and it was the neglect of such activities as repeated ploughing and intensive weeding which probably lay behind the relatively low yields. The fall in the weight of sheep fleeces in this period has been blamed on the climate and the shortage of grazing, which would apply to peasant as well as demesne flocks. The low price of grain did not hurt the peasants so much, as they were often producing for their own consumption. They may even have responded to lower prices by growing greater quantities so that they could achieve the cash income that they needed. This, of course, helped to ensure that prices remained low as supply outstripped demand. The productivity of labour increased at this time, as peasants worked more land per head than in earlier centuries. Just as shepherds on demesnes were expected to tend larger flocks of sheep, and plough-men to cover more acres, so peasants, their families and employees had to work harder to deal with the tasks on large holdings.

Peasants adapted their way of life in a period of adversity. Their performance does not conform to the gloomy assumption of modern observers that low prices and scarce labour would impoverish them. Peasants in contact with the market had long been acquiring a commercial attitude towards their land and its management. John Mell of Bramfield in Suffolk, who inherited 48 acres in 1461 and through purchase and leasing increased his holding to 150 acres in 1478, managed his mixed farming so well that he could expect his executors when he made his will to raise £26 13s 4d in bequests to the younger sons and daughters of his family. He was hard-headed enough to expect that his son, who was to inherit the land, would buy the goods and chattels from the executors, presumably by borrowing money and paying back from the profits of production. This arrangement opens up a vista of peasants with a tough and realistic view of the economic world in which their offspring could make their own way. In this period the distinction begins to blur between the prosperous peasant like Mell, and many demesne farmers, themselves of peasant origin, who disposed of similar quantities of land. Townsmen who acquired and managed large acreages seem to have had a similar outlook. Andrew Bate of Lydd in Kent leased demesne land in nearby Dengemarsh, and was said in 1468 to have kept excessive numbers of cattle, which encroached on the other tenants' land and sent them away, so that he 'had driven away half [of] Dengemarsh'. This was the brave and ruthless new world at the end of the middle ages.

New ideas and new methods were making large changes in the countryside. The great lords, and to a lesser extent the gentry, were no longer the leading producers. They had to grant better conditions to their tenants, and those tenants – farmers and peasants – were running their own affairs, and changing the countryside both as individuals and as communities.

Conclusion

People in the early sixteenth century tended to depict their world according to traditional habits of thought. Edmund Dudley, writing in 1509, divided the commonwealth into the three orders of nobles, clergy and peasants, as William Langland had done in the 1370s and Aelfric soon after 1000. Little had changed in some respects over the centuries before Dudley wrote. The fundamental structure of manors and villages of his day, which provided the basis for the relationship between lords and peasants, had been formed between 850 and 1050. The urban network had also begun to take shape by about 900, though it did not reach an advanced stage until about 1300. Edmund Dudley would have encountered townspeople, such as shoemakers or bakers, and in the country peasants with middling holdings of 15 to 30 acres of land, whose way of life remained similar to that of their predecessors in the thirteenth century.

Italian visitors in the early sixteenth century saw the country differently. They noticed a thinly inhabited countryside, with expanses of pasture. They remarked on the idleness of the English, presumably in comparison with the intensive work required of Italian peasants and rural workers. Perhaps they did not visit the clothing districts, where they would have seen a busier workforce. Continental consumers showed their appreciation of English industry by their purchase of cloth from Yorkshire or Wiltshire.

The view from the continent should guide us to appreciate the transformation of the economy in the last two centuries of the middle ages. The 'new world' envisioned by the tenants of the Paston family had to some extent come about by the early sixteenth century. Lords had retreated from production, and the farmers and peasants were the main driving force behind change in the countryside. In many ways they were struggling against adversity, because of low prices and high labour costs, but that encouraged them to adopt more efficient methods which put them in a better position when conditions for producers improved in the sixteenth century. Townspeople had their problems too, but the towns maintained their importance in that their population shrank no more than the population as a whole. London strengthened its position as the centre of international trade and much else.

Contemporaries agonized over the social evils they saw about them, of depopulating enclosure and the army of vagrants. But to some extent their anxieties were being awakened unnecessarily. As the population remained low, the loss of houses and cultivation in the countryside was only to be expected. The widespread fear of beggars was provoked partly by a mobile workforce, and partly by the annoyance of employers at any signs of idleness in an economy when booming textile and metal industries were crying out for workers.

While emphasizing the many changes of the middle ages, this book has not offered a single story to explain them. This is because none of the 'grand narratives' can be made to fit the changes we can observe. The onward and upward march of commerce, money and the middle classes was not the whole story, as that movement was checked at key moments, with retreats into a degree of self-sufficiency and problems for many towns in the fifteenth century. The 'transition from feudalism to capitalism' can be applied to the emergence of the clothiers and farmers in the fifteenth century and the weakening of lords' authority at the same time. The survival of lordship, and a middling peasantry, does not accord with a complete triumph for capitalism. Also, there is little evidence for the emergence of a proletariat – a workforce entirely dependent on wages – as about 40 per cent of households lived mainly on wages in 1524–5, which is not dissimilar to calculations for the thirteenth and fourteenth centuries. The view that high levels of population and falling returns for the land precipitated a crisis in the fourteenth century and initiated a long recession fits much of the evidence, except that it is difficult to reconcile with the regions that lack high population densities and over-exploited land. The population should have bounced back once the pressure was removed by the epidemics of 1348–75, so the fact that it remained low requires some special interpretation. The idea that a powerful centralized state promoted economic growth in the tenth century, and continued to provide the framework for a more efficient system of exchange at the end of the middle ages, has something to commend it, but we must bear in mind the limitations on the power of the central government at all times, and in particular note its comparative weakness in the fifteenth century, when the 'new world' was emerging.

If none of these schemes provides a fully satisfactory explanation, some of the crucial ingredients in transforming the medieval economy must be the creation of an enduring framework for production and exchange in the two centuries after 850, and the urbanization of the period 880–1300. The dynamic tension within the feudal regime in the twelfth and thirteenth centuries, with its element of competition among the aristocracy and the lack of strict controls which enabled peasant initiatives, must be accorded great importance. The relaxation of demographic pressure in the fourteenth century and the opportunities that were given to the upper ranks of the peasantry enabled some growth in a period of apparent adversity. As lords did not take all of the peasants' surplus, they could consume enough to enable towns to grow in the thirteenth century, and the problems for producers in the next two centuries again allowed a level of consumer demand which kept industry and trade in a healthy state, especially around 1400 and again after about 1470.

These influences are presented here in an impersonal manner, but we should not forget that the medieval world developed in the way that it did because Haehstan managed his limited estate in an enterprising way (Chapter 1); Wulfhelm developed his goldsmith's craft in a new urban environment (Chapter 2); Stephen de Fretwell mismanaged his affairs and went bankrupt (Chapter 4); Robert Broun cleared new land (Chapter 5); Nicholas Symond the spurrier demanded higher wages (Chapter 8); and Thomas Vicars managed his farm in the most profitable fashion (Chapter 10). These individuals had little impact on their own, but they were part of tendencies involving many others, and their accumulated actions created the 'new world' with which the middle ages came to an end.

Further reading

This list cannot pretend to include all of the works and sources that have contributed to this book. It is a selection of books, articles and documents, but should indicate where a point can be pursued further. Most of the works listed themselves contain bibliographies which will guide readers to more specialized works. To help the reader locate the sources, they are listed in approximately the same order as the topics appear in the text. Unless otherwise stated, the place of publication is London.

Abbreviations:

AgHEW: The Agrarian History of England and Wales, vols I–IV (Cambridge, 1967–1991)
AgHR: The Agricultural History Review
CBA: Council for British Archaeology
EHR: English Historical Review
EcHR: Economic History Review
JHG: Journal of Historical Geography
Med. Arch.: Medieval Archaeology
P & P: Past and Present
TRHS: Transactions of the Royal Historical Society
VCH: Victoria County History

INTRODUCTION   APPROACHING THE ECONOMIC
HISTORY OF MEDIEVAL BRITAIN

General surveys of the economic and social history of England began with the pioneering historians of the late nineteenth and early twentieth centuries, notably J. E. Thorold Rogers, *Six Centuries of Work and Wages: The History of English Labour* (1884); W. Cunningham, *The Growth of English Industry and Commerce* (1882, enlarged in 1890); W. J. Ashley, *An Introduction to English Economic History and Theory* (1893); E. Lipson, *The Economic History of*

England (1915) and J. H. Clapham, *A Concise Economic History of Britain* (Cambridge, 1949). A distinctive American approach to the period is represented by G. C. Homans, *English Villagers of the Thirteenth Century* (Cambridge, Mass., 1941) and W. O. Ault, *Open-Field Farming in Medieval England* (1972).

Historical geography has made an important contribution to the subject, and indeed many of the authors mentioned in subsequent pages were trained as historical geographers. See H. C. Darby (ed.), *A New Historical Geography of England before 1600* (Cambridge, 1973); R. A. Dodgshon and R. A. Butlin (eds), *An Historical Geography of England and Wales* (2nd edn, 1990); G. Whittington and I. D. Whyte (eds), *An Historical Geography of Scotland* (1983). Historical atlases with economic information include P. G. B. McNeil and H. L. McQueen (eds), *Atlas of Scottish History to 1707* (Edinburgh, 1996). There are now a number of county and regional atlases, for example R. Kain and W. Ravenhill (eds), *An Historical Atlas of South-West England* (Exeter, 2000). Postan's revolutionary influence on thinking is best reflected in his essays and articles, reprinted in M. M. Postan, *Essays on Medieval Agriculture and General Problems of the Medieval Economy* (Cambridge, 1973), but see also M. M. Postan, *The Medieval Economy and Society* (1972) and his chapter in the *Cambridge Economic History of Europe*, vol. 1, *The Agrarian Life of the Middle Ages*, 2nd edn (Cambridge, 1966). General books which are broadly sympathetic to Postan's view are E. Miller and J. Hatcher, *Medieval England – Rural Society and Economic Change 1086–1348* (1978) and J. L. Bolton, *The Medieval English Economy 1150–1500* (1980).

Marxist views of the period are to be found in M. Dobb, *Studies in the Development of Capitalism* (1946) and E. A. Kosminsky, *Studies in the Agrarian History of England in the Thirteenth Century* (Oxford, 1956). Significant modifications to the orthodoxy are made by R. H. Hilton, *Class Conflict and the Crisis of Feudalism* (1985) and R. H. Hilton, *The English Peasantry in the Later Middle Ages* (1975). Another strand of Marxist thinking is expressed, and criticized, in T. H. Aston and C. H. E. Philpin (eds), *The Brenner Debate. Agrarian Class Structure and Economic Development in Pre-Industrial Europe* (Cambridge, 1985).

The wave of works critical of Postan's approach is represented by B. M. S. Campbell (ed.), *Before the Black Death. Studies in the 'Crisis' of the Early Fourteenth Century* (Manchester, 1991); R. H. Britnell and B. M. S. Campbell (eds), *A Commercialising Economy. England 1086 to c.1300* (Manchester, 1995); G. Astill and J. Langdon (eds), *Medieval Farming and Technology. The Impact of Agricultural Change in Northwest Europe* (Leiden, 1997); B. M. S. Campbell, *English Seigniorial Agriculture, 1250–1450* (Cambridge, 2000). Campbell in particular has been inspired by E. Boserup, *The Conditions of Agricultural Growth* (1965) and E. Boserup, *Population and Technology* (1981).

On commercial and urban growth the most important recent works have been S. Reynolds, *An Introduction to the History of English Medieval Towns* (Oxford, 1977); R. H. Britnell, *The Commercialisation of English Society 1000–1500* (Cambridge, 1993); E. Miller and J. Hatcher, *Medieval England.*

Towns, Commerce and Crafts (1995) and H. Swanson, *Medieval British Towns* (Basingstoke, 1999).

Medieval archaeology is summarized in D. M. Wilson (ed.), *The Archaeology of Anglo-Saxon England* (Cambridge, 1976); J. Hunter and I. Ralston (eds), *The Archaeology of Britain* (1999); G. Astill and A. Grant (eds), *The Countryside of Medieval England* (Oxford, 1988); and D. Hinton, *Archaeology, Economy and Society* (1990).

Another approach is represented by C. Dyer, *Standards of Living in the Later Middle Ages. Social Change in England, c.1200–1520* (revised edition, Cambridge, 1998); C. Dyer, *Everyday Life in Medieval England* (1994).

Scottish economic and social history of the period is covered by chapters in more general surveys: A. A. M. Duncan, *Scotland: The Making of the Kingdom* (Edinburgh, 1975); G. W. S. Barrow, *Kingship and Unity. Scotland 1000–1306* (Edinburgh, 1989); A. Grant, *Independence and Nationhood – Scotland 1306–1469* (1984).

The most useful recent book which is focused on the economy is I. Whyte *Scotland before the Industrial Revolution. An Economic and Social History, c.1050–c.1750* (1995). For archaeological evidence there is a popular survey of recent research: P. Yeoman, *Medieval Scotland. An Archaeological Perspective* (1995). For Wales, again useful surveys of the economy appear in general histories: W. Davies, *Wales in the Early Middle Ages* (Leicester, 1982); R. R. Davies, *Conquest, Coexistence and Change. Wales 1063–1415* (Oxford, 1987); G. Williams, *Recovery, Reorientation and Reformation. Wales c.1415–1642* (Oxford, 1987).

On the social history of the period, there are two surveys, M. Keen, *English Society in the Later Middle Ages* (Harmondsworth, 1990), and S. Rigby, *English Society in the Later Middle Ages. Class, Status and Gender* (Basingstoke, 1995).

On controversial terminology, 'feudal' is treated sceptically in S. Reynolds, *Fiefs and Vassals. The Medieval Evidence Reinterpreted* (Oxford, 1994). For the broad view of feudalism as a social formation, see M. Bloch, *Feudal Society* (1965).

'Aristocracy' and 'nobility' are discussed in M. Bush (ed.), *Social Orders and Social Classes in Europe since 1500* (1992).

The best definition of 'peasant' in an English context is to be found in Hilton, *English Peasantry*; the denial of a peasantry is to be found in A. Macfarlane, *The Origins of English Individualism* (Oxford, 1978).

For a clear definition of 'town' and 'urban', see R. Holt and G. Rosser (eds), *The Medieval Town. A Reader in English Urban History* (1990).

PART ONE: ORIGINS OF THE MEDIEVAL ECONOMY, *c.*850–*c.*1100

Chapter 1: Living on the land, c.850–c.1050

On the natural environment, for which most of the evidence is scientific, from animal bones and surviving traces of pollen and vegetation, see P. Dark, *The Environment of Britain in the First Millennium* AD (2000); O. Rackham, *Ancient*

Woodland (1980); O. Rackham, *The History of the Countryside* (1986); J. Rackham (ed.), *Environment and Economy in Anglo-Saxon England* (CBA Research Report, 89, 1994).

Sustainable agriculture is discussed in J. N. Pretty, 'Sustainable Agriculture in the Middle Ages: the English Manor', *AgHR*, 38 (1990); M. K. Jones, 'Agricultural Productivity in the Pre-Documentary Past', in B. M. S. Campbell and M. Overton (eds), *Land, Labour and Livestock. Historical Studies in European Agricultural Productivity* (Manchester, 1991). On the landscape, T. Williamson and L. Bellamy, *Property and Landscape. A Social History of Landownership and the English Countryside* (1987); D. Hooke, *The Landscape of Anglo-Saxon England* (1997); S. Rippon, *The Severn Estuary. Landscape Evolution and Wetland Reclamation* (Leicester, 1997); T. Williamson, *The Origins of Norfolk* (Manchester, 1993); R. Silvester, 'The Fenland Project in Retrospective', *East Anglian Archaeology*, 50 (1993); D. Hooke (ed.), *Anglo-Saxon Settlements* (Oxford, 1988); K. P. Witney, *The Jutish Forest* (1976); A. King, 'Gauber High Pasture, Ribblehead – an Interim Report', in R. A. Hall (ed.), *Viking Age York and the North* (CBA Research Report, 27, 1978); H. S. A. Fox (ed.), *Seasonal Settlements* (Leicester, 1996); J. Blair, *Anglo-Saxon Oxfordshire* (Stroud, 1994); R. Dodgshon, *Land and Society in Early Scotland* (Oxford, 1981); S. Foster and T. C. Smout (eds), *The History of Soils and Field Systems* (Aberdeen, 1994); A. Everitt, *Continuity and Colonisation: the Evolution of Kentish Settlement* (Leicester, 1986); J. Thirsk (ed.), *The English Rural Landscape* (Oxford, 2000).

On the protection of deer and their habitat, D. Hooke, 'Pre-Conquest Woodland: its Distribution and Usage', *AgHR*, 37 (1989); for Shotover, S. P. Day, 'Post-glacial Vegetational History of the Oxford Region', *New Phytologist*, 119 (1991); on venison consumption, U. Albarella and S. J. M. Davis, 'Mammals and Birds from Launceston Castle, Cornwall: Decline in Status and Rise of Agriculture', *Circaea*, 12 (1996).

The rise of the village and settlement history in general are addressed in C. C. Taylor, *Village and Farmstead. A History of Rural Settlement in England* (1983); C. Lewis, P. Mitchell-Fox and C. Dyer, *Village, Hamlet and Field. Changing Medieval Settlements in Central England* (Manchester, 1997; Macclesfield, 2001); R. Dodgshon, *The Origin of British Field Systems: An Interpretation* (1980); T. Rowley (ed.), *The Origins of Open Field Agriculture* (1981); D. Hall, 'Field Systems and Township Structure', in M. Aston, D. Austin and C. Dyer (eds), *The Rural Settlements of Medieval England* (Oxford, 1989); J. Blair, *Early Medieval Surrey: Landholding, Church and Settlement before 1300* (1991); A. Brown and G. Foard, 'The Saxon Landscape: a Regional Perspective', in P. Everson and T. Williamson (eds), *The Archaeology of Landscape* (Manchester, 1998).

On changes in technology, R. A. Hall, *Viking Age York* (1994); on woodland management, G. Milne, *Timber Building Techniques in London, c.900–1400* (London and Middlesex Archaeological Society, Special Paper 15, 1992). Norfolk turf-cutting is surveyed in T. Williamson, *The Norfolk Broads. A Landscape History* (Manchester, 1997). Drainage is discussed in Rippon, *The*

Severn Estuary. For milling, see R. Holt, *The Mills of Medieval England* (Oxford, 1988).

The 'great estate' or 'multiple estate' idea was developed by G. R. J. Jones, for example, in 'Multiple Estates and Early Settlement', in P. H. Sawyer (ed.), *Medieval Settlement* (1976); it is discussed in G. W. S. Barrow, *The Kingdom of the Scots* (1973) and in D. Hadley, 'Multiple Estates and the Origins of the Manorial Structure of the Northern Danelaw', *JHG*, 22 (1996). The Howden Charter and Hickling food rent are summarized in C. Hart (ed.), *The Early Charters of Northern England and the North Midlands* (Leicester, 1975) and Llandybie in *AgHEW*, vol. I, part 2, 43–1042.

Bampton is analysed in Blair, *Anglo-Saxon Oxfordshire*. The lease of Luddington will be found in A. J. Robertson, *Anglo-Saxon Charters* (Cambridge, 1956); and Pendock is discussed in C. Dyer, 'Dispersed Settlements in Medieval England: a Case Study of Pendock, Worcestershire', *Med. Arch.*, 34 (1990).

On the origins of the manor there is a huge literature. Its modern study began with an article by T. H. Aston, 'The Origins of the Manor', *TRHS*, 5th ser., 8 (1958); the most recent work is D. Hadley, *The Northern Danelaw. Its Social Structure, c.800–1100* (Leicester, 2000) which contains a comprehensive bibliography. The key documents for the early manor are discussed by P. D. A. Harvey in *EHR*, 108 (1993) and C. Dyer in C. Cubitt and N. P. Brooks (eds), *St. Oswald of Worcester. Life and Influence* (Leicester, 1996). Slavery and its decline have been thoroughly documented in D. Pelteret, *Slavery in Early Mediaeval England from the Reign of Alfred to the Twelfth Century* (Woodbridge, 1995). Pelteret has also edited the Hatfield list, in 'Two Old English Lists of Serfs', *Mediaeval Studies*, 48 (1986). Place names are discussed in M. Gelling, *Place-Names in the Landscape* (1984) and churches in R. Morris, *Churches in the Landscape* (1989).

The reports of bad harvests come from D. Whitelock, D. C. Douglas and S. Tucker (eds), *The Anglo-Saxon Chronicle* (1965).

Chapter 2: Crisis and new directions, c.850–c.1050

There are numerous books and articles about the Vikings; this account is influenced by P. Sawyer, *Kings and Vikings* (1982); H. R. Loyn, *The Vikings in Britain* (1977); J. Richards, *Viking Age England* (1991); B. Crawford, *Scandinavian Scotland* (Leicester, 1987); C. E. Batey and others (eds), *The Viking Age in Caithness, Orkney and the North Atlantic* (Edinburgh, 1995); J. Graham-Campbell and C. E. Batey, *The Vikings in Scotland* (Edinburgh, 1998); D. Hadley, ' "Cockle Among the Wheat": The Scandinavian Settlement of England', in W. O. Frazer and A. Tyrrell (eds), *Social Identity in Early Medieval Britain* (Leicester, 2000); A. Richie, 'Excavations of Pictish and Viking-Age Farmsteads at Buckquoy, Orkney', *Proceedings of the Society of Antiquaries of Scotland*, 108 (1976–7); J. R. Hunter, 'Rescue Excavations on the Brough of Birsay, 1974–82', *Society of Antiquaries of Scotland, Monograph* 4 (1986). On the English reaction, N. P. Brooks, 'England in the Ninth Century: The Crucible of Defeat', *TRHS*, 5th ser., 29 (1979).

For the Anglo-Saxon state, H. R. Loyn, *The Governance of Anglo-Saxon England 500–1087* (1984); J. Campbell, 'The Late Anglo-Saxon State: A Maximum View', *Proceedings of the British Academy*, 87 (1995).

On the burh system, J. Haslam, *Anglo-Saxon Towns in Southern England* (Chichester, 1984); D. Hill and A. Rumble (eds), *The Defence of Wessex* (Manchester, 1996). On the relationship between burh and town, see R. Hodges, *The Anglo-Saxon Achievement: Archaeology and the Beginning of English Society* (1989); and S. R. H. Jones, 'Transaction Costs, Institutional Change, and the Emergence of a Market Economy in Late Anglo-Saxon England', *EcHR*, 46 (1993).

On the 'feudal revolution' see T. N. Bisson, 'The "Feudal Revolution"', *P & P*, 142 (1994), and the 'Debate' in *P & P*, 152 (1996), and 155 (1997); The system of coinage is discussed in R. H. M. Dolley (ed.), *Anglo-Saxon Coins* (1961); M. A. S. Blackburn (ed.), *Anglo-Saxon Monetary History* (Leicester, 1986); P. Spufford, *Money and its Use in Medieval Europe* (Oxford, 1988).

On town origins, J. H. Williams, 'A Review of late Saxon Urban Origins and Developments', in M. L. Faull (ed.), *Studies in Late Anglo-Saxon Settlement* (Oxford, 1984); R. Hodges and B. Hobley (eds), *The Rebirth of Towns in the West AD 700–1050* (CBA Research Report, 68, 1988); G. G. Astill, 'Towns and Town Hierarchies in Saxon England', *Oxford Journal of Archaeology*, 10 (1991); R. Fleming, 'Rural Elites and Urban Communities in Late Saxon England', *P & P*, 141 (1993); N. J. Baker and R. A. Holt, 'The City of Worcester in the Tenth Century', in N. P. Brooks and C. Cubitt (eds), *St. Oswald of Worcester: Life and Influence* (1996); A. Vince, *Saxon London: An Archaeological Investigation* (1990); Blair, *Anglo-Saxon Oxfordshire*.

Domesday's towns are conveniently listed in H. C. Darby, *Domesday England* (Cambridge, 1977). They are discussed in G. H. Martin, 'Domesday Book and the Boroughs', in P. Sawyer (ed.), *Domesday Book: a Reassessment* (1985) and S. Reynolds, 'Towns in Domesday Book', in J. C. Holt (ed.), *Domesday Studies* (Woodbridge, 1987). See also C. Dyer, 'Towns and Cottages in Eleventh Century England', in H. Mayr-Harting and R. I. Moore (eds), *Studies in Medieval History Presented to R. H. C. Davis* (1985).

The archaeological evidence for early York is summed up in R. A. Hall, *Viking Age York* (1994). For excavations in other towns see M. O. H. Carver, 'Three Saxon-Norman Tenements in Durham City', *Med. Arch.*, 23 (1979) and P. Ottaway, *Archaeology in British Towns* (1992).

On the towns in general, D. Palliser (ed.), *The Cambridge Urban History of Britain*, vol. 1, *600–1540* (Cambridge, 2000). For proto-urban settlements, P. Hill, *Whithorn and St. Ninian* (Stroud, 1997); P. Courtney, *Medieval and Later Usk* (Cardiff, 1994).

For the debate on the supposed wealth of England, see P. H. Sawyer, 'The Wealth of England in the Eleventh Century', *TRHS*, 5th ser., 15 (1965); M. K. Lawson, 'The Collection of Danegeld and Heregeld in the Reigns of Aethelred II and Cnut', *EHR*, 99 (1984), and the subsequent exchange of views between J. Gillingham and M. Lawson in *EHR*, 104 (1989) and 105 (1990). On trade

M. Gardiner, 'Shipping and Trade between England and the Continent during the Eleventh Century', *Anglo-Norman Studies*, 22 (1999).

Chapter 3: Conquest c.1050–c.1100

On the pre-Conquest aristocracy the best study is P. A. Clarke, *The English Nobility under Edward the Confessor* (Oxford, 1994); on military institutions see R. Abel, *Lordship and Military Obligation in Anglo-Saxon England* (Berkeley, 1988); N. P. Brooks, *Communities and Warfare, 700–1400* (2000). Local studies include A. Wareham, 'Saint Oswald's Family and Kin', and V. King, 'St. Oswald's Tenants', in Brooks and Cubitt (eds), *St. Oswald of Worcester*. On the three orders see T. E. Powell, 'The "Three Orders" of Society in Anglo-Saxon England', *Anglo-Saxon England*, 23 (1994). Studies of aristocratic residences include G. Beresford, *Goltho. The Development of an Early Medieval Manor, c.850–1150* (English Heritage, Archaeological Report, 4, 1987); J. Fairbrother, *Faccombe Netherton: Excavations of a Saxon and Medieval Manorial Complex* (1990).

On changes in the church, F. Barlow, *The English Church 1066–1154* (1979); J. Burton, *Monastic and Religious Orders in Britain 1000–1300* (Cambridge, 1994). The huge literature on the Norman Conquest includes A. Williams, *The English and the Norman Conquest* (Woodbridge, 1995) and B. Golding, *Conquest and Colonisation: the Normans in Britain 1066–1100* (1994). R. Fleming, *Kings and Lords in Conquest England* (Cambridge, 1991) disagrees on the land settlement with P. Sawyer, '1066–1086: a Tenural Revolution?', in P. Sawyer (ed.), *Domesday Book. A Reassessment* (1985). On the aristocracy see C. P. Lewis, 'The Early Earls of Norman England', *Anglo-Norman Studies*, 13 (1970); S. Harvey, 'The Knight and the Knight's Fee in England', *P & P*, 49 (1970).

On Domesday see Sawyer (ed.), *Domesday Book. A Reassessment*; J. C. Holt (ed.), *Domesday Studies* (Woodbridge, 1987); D. Roffe, *Domesday. The Inquest and the Book* (Oxford, 2000); J. J. N. Palmer, 'The Wealth of the Secular Aristocracy in 1086', *Anglo-Norman Studies*, 22 (1999). The text of Domesday is available in translation in the Phillimore series, edited by J. Morris; for many counties there is an authoritative translation and commentary in the *VCH*.

The economic consequences in terms of destruction are discussed in R. Welldon Finn, *The Norman Conquest and its Effects on the Economy* (1971). A more rounded picture comes from W. E. Kapelle, *The Norman Conquest of the North: The Region and its Transformation, 1000–1135* (1979); D. Palliser, 'Domesday Book and the "Harrying of the North"', *Northern History*, 29 (1993); M. Chibnall, *Anglo-Norman England 1066–1166* (Oxford, 1986). On the rural scene, see S. Harvey, 'Domesday England', in *AgHEW*, vol. II; for the towns in Domesday, see the titles given above for Chapter 2.

The Pinbury survey is in M. Chibnall (ed.), *Charters and Custumals of the Abbey of Holy Trinity Caen* (British Academy, Records of Economic and Social History, new ser., 5, 1982).

For Domesday population, see J. Moore, ' "Quot homines?" The Population of Domesday England', *Anglo-Norman Studies*, 19 (1996). The monumental series of volumes on the Domesday geography of each region is summed up in H. C. Darby, *Domesday England* (Cambridge, 1977).

PART TWO: EXPANSION AND CRISIS, *c.*1100–*c.*1350

The estimates of population vary: R. Smith, 'Human Resources', in Astill and Grant (eds), *Countryside*; Campbell, *English Seigniorial Agriculture*. The Scottish and Welsh estimates come from Whyte, *Scotland before the Industrial Revolution* and Davies, *Conquest, Coexistence and Change*.

On money see N. J. Mayhew, 'Modelling Medieval Monetisation', in R. H. Britnell and B. M. S. Campbell (eds), *A Commercialising Economy. England 1086 to c.1300* (Manchester, 1995); D. M. Metcalfe (ed.), *Coinage in Medieval Scotland* (British Archaeological Reports, 45, 1977).

The economic effects of Stephen's reign are discussed in E. King (ed.), *The Anarchy of King Stephen's Reign* (Oxford, 1994); E. Amt, *The Accession of Henry II in England. Royal Government Restored, 1149–59* (Woodbridge, 1993); G. White, *Restoration and Reform, 1153–1165. Recovery from Civil War in England* (Cambridge, 2000).

On the growth in documents, M. T. Clanchy, *From Memory to Written Record* (1979).

Chapter 4: Lords, c.1100–c.1315

The importance of the honour was argued in F. M. Stenton, *The First Century of English Feudalism, 1066–1166* (2nd edn, Oxford, 1961). This has since been modified by J. Green, *The Aristocracy of Norman England* (Cambridge, 1997); S. F. C. Milsom, *The Legal Framework of English Feudalism* (Cambridge, 1976); J. Hudson, *The Formation of the English Common Law* (1996); J. C. Holt, 'Feudal Society and the Family in Early Medieval England', *TRHS*, 5th ser., 32–5 (1982–5). J. M. W. Bean, *The Decline of English Feudalism* (Manchester, 1968); H. M. Thomas, *Vassals, Heiresses, Crusaders and Thugs: The Gentry of Angevin Yorkshire, 1154–1216* (Philadelphia, 1993); D. A. Carpenter, 'The Second Century of English Feudalism', *P & P*, 168 (2000).

On the Scottish and Welsh aristocracy, see K. J. Stringer (ed.), *Essays on the Nobility of Medieval Scotland* (Edinburgh, 1985); R. A. McDonald, *The Kingdom of the Isles, Scotland's Western Seaboard, c.1100–c.1336* (East Linton, 1997); T. Brotherstone and D. Ditchburn (eds), *Freedom and Authority. Scotland c.1050–c.1650* (East Linton, 2000); R. R. Davies, *The First English Empire. Power and Identities in the British Isles 1093–1343* (Oxford, 2000). Much of the generalization in this chapter derives from studies of individuals, families and institutions. On the lay aristocracy these include M. Altschul, *A Baronial Family in Medieval England. The Clares, 1217–1314* (Baltimore, 1965); W. E.

Wightman, *The Lacy Family in England and Normandy 1066–1194* (Oxford, 1966); D. Crouch, *The Beaumont Twins. The Roots and Branches of Power in the Twelfth Century* (Cambridge, 1986); D. Crouch, *William the Marshal. Court, Career and Chivalry in the Angevin Empire, 1147–1219* (1990); B. English *The Lords of Holderness 1086–1260* (Oxford, 1979); K. Stringer, *Earl David of Huntingdon 1152–1219* (Edinburgh, 1986); P. Dalton, *Conquest, Anarchy and Lordship. Yorkshire 1066–1154* (Cambridge, 1994); R. R. Davies, *Lordship and Society in the March of Wales* (Oxford, 1978).

For church estates, historians have been able to say more about estate management and agricultural production. Some of the most substantial works which emphasize the period up to 1315 are R. A. L. Smith, *Canterbury Cathedral Priory* (Cambridge, 1943); E. Miller, *The Abbey and Bishopric of Ely* (Cambridge, 1951); J. A. Raftis, *The Estates of Ramsey Abbey* (Toronto, 1957); F. R. H. Du Boulay, *The Lordship of Canterbury* (1966); E. King, *Peterborough Abbey 1086–1310* (Cambridge, 1973); C. Dyer, *Lords and Peasants in a Changing Society. The Estates of the Bishopric of Worcester, 680–1540* (Cambridge, 1980); J. I. Catto (ed.), *The History of the University of Oxford* (Oxford, 1984). Studies specifically of the administration of estates and of the methods of agriculture include N. Denholm-Young, *Seigniorial Administration in England* (Oxford, 1937); P. D. A. Harvey, *Manorial Records* (British Records Association, 2nd edn, 2000), D. Oschinsky (ed.), *Walter of Henley and Other Treatises on Estate Management and Accounting* (Oxford, 1971); B. M. S. Campbell, *English Seigniorial Agriculture 1250–1450* (Cambridge, 2000); B. M. S. Campbell and M. Overton (eds), *Land, Labour and Livestock: Historical Studies in European Agricultural Productivity* (Manchester, 1991); J. Langdon, *Horses, Oxen and Technological Innovation: The Use of Draught Animals* in *English Farming from 1066–1500* (Cambridge, 1986); G. Astill and J. Langdon (eds), *Medieval Farming and Technology: The Impact of Agricultural Change in North-West Europe in the Middle Ages* (Leiden, 1997); R. Holt, 'Whose Were the Profits of Corn Milling?', *P & P*, 116 (1987); J. Langdon, 'Lordship and Peasant Consumerism in the Milling Industry of Early Fourteenth-Century England', *P & P*, 145 (1994); M. A. Atkin, 'Land Use and Management in the Upland Demesne of the De Lacy Estate of Blackburnshire', *AgHR*, 42 (1994).

On the leasing of demesnes, P. D. A. Harvey, 'The English Inflation of 1180–1220', in R. H. Hilton (ed.), *Peasants, Knights and Heretics* (Cambridge, 1976). The lease of Kensworth is in W. H. Hale (ed.), *The Domesday of St. Paul's* (Camden Society, 1858).

For the new monastic lords, see R. A. Donkin, *The Cistercians. Studies in the Geography of Medieval England and Wales* (Toronto, 1978); C. Platt, *The Monastic Grange in Medieval England* (1969); D. H. Williams, *The Welsh Cistercians* (Pontypool, 1969); B. Golding, *Gilbert of Sempringham and the Gilbertine Order c.1130 to c.1300* (Oxford, 1995); J. Burton, *The Monastic Order in Yorkshire, 1069–1215* (Cambridge, 1999); the special character of Cistercian lordship is doubted in I. Alfonso, 'Cistercians and Feudalism', *P & P*, 133 (1991).

For lords' relations with peasants some important works include R. H. Hilton, 'Freedom and Villeinage in England', in Hilton (ed.), *Peasants, Knights and Heretics*; P. R. Hyams, *Kings, Lords, and Peasants in Medieval England: The Common Law of Villeinage in the Twelfth and Thirteenth Centuries* (Oxford, 1980); J. Hatcher, 'English Serfdom and Villeinage: Towards a Reassessment', in T. H. Aston (ed.), *Landlords, Peasants and Politics in Medieval England* (Cambridge, 1987); C. Dyer, 'Memories of Freedom: Attitudes towards Serfdom in England, 1200–1350', in M. L. Bush (ed.), *Serfdom and Slavery. Studies in Legal Bondage* (1996).

On knights and small landowners see P. R. Coss, *The Knight in Medieval England 1000–1400* (Stroud, 1993); P. R. Coss, *Lordship, Knighthood and Locality. A Study in English Society c.1180–c.1280* (Cambridge, 1991); P. R. Coss, 'Sir Geoffrey de Langley and the Crisis of the Knightly Class in Thirteenth Century England', *P & P*, 68 (1975); D. A. Carpenter, 'Was There a Crisis of the Knightly Class in the Thirteenth Century? The Oxfordshire Evidence', *EHR*, 95 (1980); P. R. Coss, 'Bastard Feudalism Revised', *P & P*, 125 (1989), and the 'Debate' that followed in *P & P*, 131 (1991); P. R. Coss, 'The Formation of the English Gentry', *P & P*, 147 (1995); K. Faulkner, 'The Transformation of Knighthood in Early Thirteenth Century England', *EHR*, 111 (1996); P. Brand, *The Origins of the English Legal Profession* (Oxford, 1992); on military roles, M. Prestwich, *Armies and Warfare in the Middle Ages* (New Haven and London, 1996); The documents used are from H. E. Salter (ed.), *Eynsham Cartulary* (Oxford Historical Society, 1907), and John Rylands Library (Manchester), Phillipps Ch. 17.

Other sources of information about peasants' relationship with lords (apart from the estate histories listed above) are P. D. A. Harvey (ed.), *The Peasant Land Market in Medieval England* (Oxford, 1984); P. D. A. Harvey, *A Medieval Oxfordshire Village. Cuxham 1240–1400* (Oxford, 1965); J. Hatcher, *Rural Economy and Society in the Duchy of Cornwall 1300–1500* (Cambridge, 1970); Z. Razi and R. Smith (eds), *Medieval Society and the Manor Court* (Oxford, 1996); R. H. Hilton, 'Gloucester Abbey Leases of the Late Thirteenth Century', in Hilton, *English Peasantry in the Later Middle Ages*; T. Jones Pierce, *Medieval Welsh Society* (Cardiff, 1972).

The documents quoted are (for Navestock), Hale (ed.), *The Domesday of St. Paul's*; (for Street) C. J. Elton (ed.), *Rentalia et Custumaria* (Somerset Record Society, 5, 1891); (for Weedon), F. W. Maitland (ed.), *Select Pleas in Manorial and other Seignorial Courts* (Selden Society, 2, 1888).

For lords' relations with towns, see the reading for Chapter 6.

Chapter 5: Peasants, c.1100–c.1315

This is informed by a number of the histories of estates listed for Chapter 4. A great deal of information is embedded in *AgHEW*, vol. II. On population, there are R. M. Smith's essays in Astill and Grant (eds), *Countryside*, and B. M. S. Campbell (ed.), *Before the Black Death* (Manchester, 1991). On marriage and families, see J. Hajnal, 'European Marriage Patterns in Perspective', in

D. V. Glass and D. E. C. Eversley (eds), *Population in History* (1965); R. Helmholz, *Marriage Litigation in Medieval England* (Cambridge, 1974); M. Sheehan, 'Marriage Theory and Practice. The Diocesan Legislation of Medieval England', *Mediaeval Studies*, 40 (1978); E. Clark, 'The Decision to Marry in Thirteenth and Early Fourteenth Century Norfolk', *Mediaeval Studies*, 49 (1987); P. Biller, 'Birth Control in the West in the Thirteenth and Early Fourteenth Centuries', *P & P*, 94 (1982); Z. Razi, 'The Myth of the Immutable English Family', *P & P*, 140 (1993).

On the relationship between population and landholding, see Z. Razi, *Life, Marriage and Death in a Medieval Parish. Economy, Society and Demography in Halesowen, 1270–1400* (Cambridge, 1980); R. M. Smith (ed.), *Land, Kinship and Lifecycle* (Cambridge, 1984); C. Clarke, 'Peasant Society and Land Transactions in Chesterton, Cambridgeshire, 1277–1325' (University of Oxford DPhil. thesis, 1985).

The idea of 'cottage economy' is used in D. Levine, *Reproducing Families* (Cambridge, 1987). The record of Elyas de Bretendon is from J. A. Raftis, *Tenure and Mobility. Studies in the Social History of the Mediaeval English Village* (Toronto, 1964).

On expansion there are many studies, such as H. E. Hallam, *Settlement and Society: A Study of the Early Agrarian History of South Lincolnshire* (Cambridge, 1965); J. McDonnell, 'Medieval Assarting Hamlets in Bilsdale, North-East Yorkshire', *Northern History*, 22 (1986); J. Kissock, '"God Made Nature and Men Made Towns": Post-Conquest and Pre-Conquest Villages in Pembrokeshire', in N. Edwards (ed.), *Landscape and Settlement in Medieval Wales* (Oxford, 1997); Rippon, *Severn Estuary*; M. Parry, *Climatic Change, Agriculture and Settlement* (Folkestone, 1978).

For contrasts between woodland settlement and a 'champion' village C. Dyer, *Hanbury, Settlement and Society in a Woodland Landscape* (Leicester University Department of English Local History, 1991) and C. Dyer, 'Compton Verney: Landscape and People in the Middle Ages', in R. Bearman (ed.), *Compton Verney. A History of the House and its Owners* (Stratford-upon-Avon, 2000). The record of assarting comes from J. Birrell (ed.), *The Forests of Cannock and Kinver: Select Documents 1235–1372* (Staffordshire Record Society, 4th ser., 18, 1999). The Halesowen preservation of the common pasture comes from R. A. Wilson (ed.), *Court Rolls of the Manor of Hales*, part 3 (Worcestershire Historical Society, 1933). For size of holdings E. A. Kosminsky, *Studies in the Agrarian History of England in the Thirteenth Century* (Oxford, 1956), and *AgHEW*, vol. II. For the peasant budget, C. Dyer, *Standards of Living in the Later Middle Ages* (revised edn, Cambridge, 1998).

On the pastoral dimension, K. Williams-Jones (ed.), *The Merioneth Lay Subsidy Roll, 1292–3* (Cardiff, 1976); M. Page (ed.), *The Pipe Roll of the Bishopric of Winchester 1301–2* (Hampshire Record Series, 14, 1996); on the general commitment of peasants to the sale of produce, Britnell, *Commercialisation of English Society*.

Land management and technical changes are discussed in A. R. H. Baker and R. A. Butlin (eds), *Studies of Field Systems in the British Isles* (Cambridge, 1973); H. S. A. Fox, 'The Alleged Transformation from Two-Field to Three-Field Systems in Medieval England', *EcHR*, 2nd ser., 39 (1986); Langdon, *Horses, Oxen and Technological Innovation*; B. M. S. Campbell and M. Overton, 'A New Perspective on Medieval and Early Modern Agriculture: Six Centuries of Norfolk Farming, *c.*1250–*c.*1850', *P & P*, 141 (1993); Astill and Langdon, *Medieval Farming and Technology*.

For rural industries see J. R. Birrell, 'Peasant Craftsmen in the Medieval Forest', *AgHR*, 17 (1969); H. E. J. Le Patourel, 'Documentary Evidence and the Medieval Pottery Industry', *Med. Arch.*, 12 (1968), and for women's brewing J. M. Bennett, *Women in the Medieval English Countryside. Gender and Household in Brigstock before the Plague* (New York, 1987); J. M. Bennett, *Ale, Beer and Brewsters in England: Women's Work in a Changing World, 1300–1600* (New York and Oxford, 1996).

For revised views on peasant houses, C. Dyer, 'English Peasant Buildings in the Later Middle Ages', *Med. Arch.*, 30 (1986); J. Grenville, *Medieval Housing* (Leicester, 1997); M. Gardiner, 'Vernacular Buildings and the Development of the Late Medieval Domestic Plan in England', *Med. Arch.*, 44 (2000). For dates of buildings, and much else, the journal *Vernacular Architecture*.

William Lene's inventory is published in R. Lock (ed.), *The Court Rolls of Walsham le Willows 1303–1350* (Suffolk Records Society, 41, 1998); for Sturminster Newton, Elton (ed.), *Rentalia et Custumaria*. For other peasant purchases, R. S. Kelly, 'The Excavation of a Medieval Farmstead at Cefn Graeanog, Clynnog, Gwynedd', *Bulletin of the Board of Celtic Studies*, 29 (1982); P. A. Rahtz, 'Upton, Gloucestershire, 1964–8', *Transactions of the Bristol and Gloucestershire Archaeological Society*, 88 (1969).

The examples of land transfers are from G. J. Turner and H. E. Salter (eds), *The Register of St. Augustine's Abbey, Canterbury* (1924); Maitland (ed.), *Select Pleas in Manorial Courts*. On various aspects of the peasant land market, see Harvey (ed.), *Peasant Land Market* and Smith (ed.), *Land, Kinship and Life-cycle*. Specific examples given here come from M. K. McIntosh, *Autonomy and Community. The Royal Manor of Havering, 1200–1500* (Cambridge, 1986); King, *Peterborough Abbey*; D. W. Ko, 'Society and Conflict in Barnet, Hertfordshire, 1337–1450', (University of Birmingham PhD thesis, 1994); Razi, *Life, Marriage and Death*; A. Jones, 'Caddington, Kensworth and Dunstable in 1297', *EcHR*, 2nd ser., 32 (1979); P. Schofield, 'Dearth, Debt and the Local Land Market in Late Thirteenth-Century Village Community', *AgHR*, 45 (1997); L. B. Smith, 'The Gage and the Land Market in Late Medieval Wales', *EcHR*, 2nd ser., 29 (1976); L. B. Smith, 'Deeds of Gage of Land in Late Medieval Wales', *Bulletin of the Board of Celtic Studies*, 27 (1977).

The various cases of unrest and rebellion come from B. F. Harvey, *Westminster Abbey and its Estates in the Middle Ages* (Oxford, 1977); A. D. Carr, 'The Bondsmen of Penrhosllugwy: A Community's Complaint', *Transactions of the Anglesey Antiquarian Society and Field Club* (1988); E. Searle, *Lordship and Community. Battle Abbey and its Banlieu 1066–1538* (Toronto, 1974);

J. R. Birrell, 'Common Rights in the Medieval Forest: Disputes and Conflicts in the Thirteenth Century', *P & P*, 117 (1987); J. H. Bettey, *Wessex from* AD *1000* (1986).

On strains within communities, H. S. A. Fox, 'Exploitation of the Landless by Lords and Tenants in Early Medieval England', in Razi and Smith (eds), *Medieval Society and the Manor Court*; W. O. Ault, *Open-Field Farming in Medieval England* (1972); L. Poos, 'Population Turnover in Medieval Essex: The Evidence of Some Early Fourteenth Century Tithing Lists', in L. Bonfield, R. M. Smith and K. Wrightson (eds), *The World We Have Gained* (Oxford, 1986); C. Dyer, 'The English Village Community and its Decline', *Journal of British Studies*, 33 (1994); R. M. Smith, 'Kin and Neighbours in a Thirteenth-Century Suffolk Community', *Journal of Family History*, 4 (1979).

Chapter 6: Towns and commerce, c.1100–c.1315

On towns in general in this period, D. Palliser (ed.), *The Cambridge Urban History of Britain*, vol. 1, *600–1540* (Cambridge, 2000) surveys every aspect of the subject. Other overviews include S. Reynolds, *An Introduction to the History of English Medieval Towns* (Oxford, 1977); E. Miller and J. Hatcher, *Medieval England. Town, Commerce and Crafts* (1995) and H. Swanson, *Medieval British Towns* (Basingstoke, 1999). A remarkable work which locates towns in society as a whole is R. H. Hilton, *English and French Towns in Feudal Society. A Comparative Study* (Cambridge, 1992). Another book which views towns in their rural surroundings is J. Masschaele, *Peasants, Merchants and Markets. Inland Trade in Medieval England, 1150–1350* (New York, 1997). On Scotland and Wales, I. Adams, *The Making of Urban Scotland* (1978); M. Lynch (ed.), *The Scottish Medieval Town* (Edinburgh, 1988); E. Ewen, *Townlife in Fourteenth-Century Scotland* (Edinburgh, 1990); R. A. Griffiths (ed.), *Boroughs of Mediaeval Wales* (Cardiff, 1978), and I. Soulsby, *The Towns of Medieval Wales* (Chichester, 1983). On the new towns M. W. Beresford, *New Towns of the Middle Ages. Town Plantations of England, Wales and Gascony* (London, 1967).

The section on the urban hierarchy is based on numerous detailed studies. For example, on markets see R. H. Britnell, 'The Proliferation of Markets in England, 1200–1349', *EcHR*, 2nd ser., 34 (1981); T. Unwin, 'Rural Marketing in Medieval Nottinghamshire', *JHG*, 7 (1981), D. Postles, 'Markets for Rural Produce in Oxfordshire, 1086–1350', *Midland History*, 12 (1987).

For fairs, E. W. Moore, *The Fairs of Medieval England* (Toronto, 1985). On small and large towns R. H. Hilton, 'Small Town Society in England before the Black Death', *P & P*, 97 (1982); R. H. Hilton, 'Medieval Market Towns and Simple Commodity Production', *P & P*, 109 (1985); J. Laughton and C. Dyer, 'Small Towns in the East and West Midlands in the Later Middle Ages: A Comparison', *Midland History*, 24 (1999); M. Kowaleski, *Local Markets and Regional Trade in Medieval Exeter* (Cambridge, 1995); H. Summerson, *Medieval Carlisle: The City and the Borders from the Late Eleventh to the mid-Sixteenth Century* (Cumberland and Westmorland Antiquarian and

Archaeological Society, extra ser., 25, 1993). For the country people attached to towns, J. Masschaele, 'Urban Trade in Medieval England: The Evidence of Foreign Gild Membership Lists', *Thirteenth Century England*, 5 (1994); I. J. Sanders, 'Trade and Industry in Some Cardiganshire Towns in the Middle Ages', *Ceredigion*, 3 (1959).

On London's influence, B. M. S. Campbell, J. A. Galloway, D. Keene and M. Murphy, *A Medieval Capital and its Grain Supply* (Historical Geography Research 30, 1993); C. Barron, 'Centres of Conspicuous Consumption: The Aristocratic Town House in London, 1200–1550', *London Journal*, 20 (1995); D. Keene, 'Wardrobes in the City: Houses of Consumption, Finance and Power', *Thirteenth-Century England*, 7 (1999); D. Keene, 'Small Towns and the Metropolis: The Experience of Medieval England', in J. M. Duvosquel and E. Thoen (eds), *Peasants and Townsmen in Medieval Europe. Studies in Honorem Adriaan Verhulst* (Ghent, 1995). Bishop Swinfield's purchases are recorded in J. Webb (ed.), *A Roll of the Household Expenses of Richard de Swinfield* (Camden Society, 56, 62, 1854–5).

On migration, the sudden death of an immigrant was recorded in R. R. Sharpe (ed.), *Calendar of Coroners' Rolls of the City of London* AD *1300–1378* (1913). Historical comments include P. McClure, 'Patterns of Migration in the Late Middle Ages: The Evidence of English Place-Name Surnames', *EcHR*, 2nd ser., 32 (1979); E. D. Jones, 'Some Spalding Priory Vagabonds of the Twelve-Sixties', *Historical Research*, 73 (2000); C. Dyer, 'Stratford-upon-Avon: A Successful Small Town', in R. Bearman (ed.), *The History of an English Borough. Stratford-upon-Avon 1196–1996* (Stroud and Stratford, 1997); E. Miller, 'Medieval York', *VCH Yorkshire, City of York* (1961); T. James, 'Medieval Carmarthen and its Burgesses. A Study of Town Growth and Burgess Families in the Later Thirteenth Century', *Carmarthenshire Antiquary*, 25 (1989); A. J. L. Winchester, *Landscape and Society in Medieval Cumbria* (Edinburgh, 1987).

On urban topography, T. R. Slater, 'Ideal and Reality in English Episcopal Medieval Town Planning', *Transactions of the Institute of British Geographers*, new ser., 12 (1987); T. R. Slater, 'Understanding the Landscape of Towns', in D. Hooke (ed.), *Landscape. The Richest Historical Record* (Society for Landscape Studies supplementary ser., 1, 2001). On urban property and the environment, S. Penn, 'Social and Economic Aspects of Fourteenth Century Bristol' (University of Birmingham PhD thesis, 1989); W. Urry, *Canterbury under the Angevin Kings* (1967); R. Goddard, 'Bullish Markets: the Property Market in Thirteenth-Century Coventry', *Midland History*, 23 (1998); D. Keene, 'Shops and Shopping in Medieval London', in L. Grant (ed.), *Medieval Art, Architecture and Archaeology in London* (British Archaeological Association, 1990); Grenville, *Medieval Housing*; P. Holdsworth (ed.), *Excavations in the Medieval Burgh of Perth, 1979–81* (Society of Antiquaries of Scotland, Monograph ser. 5, 1987); C. Moloney and R. Coleman, 'The Development of a Medieval Street Frontage: The Evidence from Excavations at 80–86, High Street, Perth', *Proceedings of the Society of Antiquaries of Scotland*, 127 (1997). The leaking cesspit is recorded in H. M. Chew and W. Kellaway (eds), *London Assize of Nuisance 1301–1431* (London Record Society, 10, 1973). For London's fuel crisis, J. A. Galloway,

D. Keene and M. Murphy, 'Fuelling the City: Production and Distribution of Firewood and Fuel in London's Region, 1290–1400', *EcHR*, 49 (1996).

On the variety of urban occupations, R. Karras, *Common Women: Prostitution and Sexuality in Medieval England* (New York and Oxford, 1996); R. H. Hilton, 'Towns in English Feudal Society', in his *Class Conflict and the Crisis of Feudalism* (1985); D. and R. Cromarty (eds), *The Wealth of Shrewsbury in the Early Fourteenth Century* (Shrewsbury Archaeological and Historical Society, 1997), D. Keene, *Survey of Medieval Winchester* (Oxford, 1985), P. J. P. Goldberg, 'Urban Identity and the Poll Taxes of 1377, 1379 and 1381', *EcHR*, 2nd ser., 43 (1990), J. H. Munro, *Textiles, Towns and Trade* (Aldershot, 1994); G. Egan and F. Pritchard (eds), *Dress Accessories, c.1150–c.1450* (1991); G. Egan (ed.), *The Medieval Household. Daily Living c.1150–c.1450* (1988) (these are two in a series of publications entitled *Medieval Finds from Excavations in London*). The thirteenth-century lists of towns' specialisms is printed in H. Rothwell (ed.), *English Historical Documents, 1189–1327* (1975). The herring fishery is described in A. R. Saul, 'Great Yarmouth in the Fourteenth Century. A Study in Trade, Politics and Society' (University of Oxford DPhil. thesis, 1975).

My main sources for trade have been E. Ashtor, *Levant Trade in the Later Middle Ages* (Princeton, NJ, 1983); T. H. Lloyd, *The English Wool Trade in the Middle Ages* (1977); W. R. Childs, *Anglo-Castilian Trade in the Later Middle Ages* (Manchester, 1978); P. Nightingale, *A Medieval Mercantile Community. The Grocers' Company and the Politics and Trade of London, 1000–1485* (New Haven and London, 1995); C. Platt, *Medieval Southampton. The Port and Trading Community, 1000–1600* (1973); J. Donnelly, 'Thomas of Coldingham, Merchant and Burgess of Berwick upon Tweed', *Scottish Historical Review*, 59 (1980); J. Donnelly, 'An Open Port: The Berwick Export Trade, 1311–1373', *Scottish Historical Review*, 78 (1999); M. K. James, *Studies in the Medieval Wine Trade* (Oxford, 1971); E. M. Carus-Wilson, *Medieval Merchant Venturers* (1954); T. H. Lloyd, *Alien Merchants in England in the High Middle Ages* (Brighton, 1982); J. W. F. Hill, *Medieval Lincoln* (1948).

On credit, important articles by M. M. Postan are reprinted in his *Medieval Trade and Finance* (Cambridge, 1973). See also H. Jenkinson, 'William Cade, a Financier of the Twelfth Century', *EHR*, 28 (1913); H. G. Richardson, *The English Jewry under Angevin Kings* (1960); R. Stacey, 'Jewish Lending and the Medieval English Economy', in Britnell and Campbell (eds), *A Commercialising Economy*; R. R. Mundill, *English Jewish Solution. Experiment and Expulsion, 1262–1290* (Cambridge, 1998); R. Kaeuper, *Bankers to the Crown: The Riccardi of Lucca and Edward I* (Princeton, 1973). For industry see J. Blair and N. Ramsay (eds), *English Medieval Industries* (1991); D. Crossley (ed.), *Medieval Industry* (CBA Research Report, 40, 1981); R. Holt, *The Mills of Medieval England* (Oxford, 1988). The controversy over fulling mills is raised in A. R. Bridbury, *Medieval English Clothmaking* (1982). On other aspects of technology, G. G. Astill, *A Medieval Industrial Complex and its Landscape* (CBA Research Report 92, 1993); M. K. McCarthy and C. M. Brooks, *Medieval Pottery in Britain AD 900–1600* (Leicester, 1988).

For transport F. M. Stenton, 'The Road System of Medieval England', *EcHR*, 7 (1936–8); C. C. Taylor, *Roads and Tracks of Britain* (1979); B. P. Hindle, *Medieval Roads* (Princes Risborough, 1982); J. Langdon, 'Horse Hauling: A Revolution in Vehicle Transport in Twelfth and Thirteenth Century England', in T. H. Aston (ed.), *Landlords, Peasants and Politics in Medieval England* (Cambridge, 1987); D. Harrison, 'Bridges and Economic Development, 1300–1800', *EcHR*, 45 (1992); J. Masschaele, 'Transport Costs in Medieval England', *EcHR*, 46 (1993). A debate on inland water transport between B. P. Hindle, J. Edwards, E. Jones and J. Langdon will be found in *JHG*, 17 (1991); 19 (1993), and 25 (1999). For shipping see G. Hutchinson, *Medieval Ships and Shipping* (Leicester, 1994) and I. Friel, *The Good Ship* (1995).

On trading techniques an essay on partnerships by J. Masschaele and on the Exeter grain trade by M. Kowaleski will be found in E. B. Dewindt (ed.), *The Salt of Common Life. Individuality and Choice in the Medieval Town, Countryside and Church* (Kalamazoo, Mich., 1995). For the shopping technology of Chester, A. Brown (ed.), *The Rows of Chester* (English Heritage Archaeological Report, 16, 1999). Coinage and currency are discussed in N. J. Mayhew, 'Modelling Medieval Monetization', in Britnell and Campbell (eds), *Commercialising Economy*; N. Mayhew, 'Alexander III – a Silver Age? An Essay in Scottish Medieval Economic History', in N. H. Reid (ed.), *Scotland in the Reign of Alexander III, 1249–1286* (Edinburgh, 1988); D. Metcalf (ed.), *Coinage in Medieval Scotland (1100–1600)* (British Archaeological Report, 45, 1977).

On boroughs the classic work is J. Tait, *The Medieval English Borough* (Manchester, 1936), together with C. Gross, *The Gild Merchant* (Oxford, 1890). Additional works include M. McKisack, *The Parliamentary Representation of the English Borough during the Middle Ages* (Oxford, 1932). The most thorough study of a struggle between a monastery and its town is M. D. Lobel, *The Borough of Bury St. Edmunds* (Oxford, 1935).

A self-governing town has been revealed in R. B. Peberdy, 'The Economy, Society and Government of a Small Town in Late Medieval England: A Study of Henley-on-Thames from c.1300–c.1540' (University of Leicester PhD thesis, 1994). For the monopolies of Welsh and Scottish towns see Griffiths (ed.), *Boroughs of Mediaeval Wales*; J. M. Houston, 'The Scottish Burgh', *Town Planning Review*, 25 (1954–5); A. Gibb and R. Paddison, 'The Rise and Fall of Burghal Monopolies in Scotland: The Case of the North-East', *Scottish Geographical Magazine*, 99 (1983).

Trade restrictions are recorded in R. W. Greaves (ed.), *The First Ledger Book of High Wycombe* (Buckinghamshire Record Society, 2, 1947); M. Bateson (ed.), *Records of the Borough of Leicester* (Cambridge, 1899).

Chapter 7: Crisis, c.1290–c.1350

W. C. Jordan, *The Great Famine. Northern Europe in the Early Fourteenth Century* (Princeton, 1996) deals with northern Europe as a whole, and plays down the events. Many aspects of the crisis of the first half of the fourteenth century appear in Campbell (ed.), *Before the Black Death*.

For the famine in England, I. Kershaw, 'The Great Famine and Agrarian Crisis in England 1315–1322', *P & P*, 59 (1973); I. Kershaw, *Bolton Priory: The Economy of a Northern Monastery 1286–1325* (Oxford, 1973); Smith (ed.), *Land, Kinship and Lifecycle*; M. Stinson, 'Assarting and Poverty in Early Fourteenth Century West Yorkshire', *Landscape History*, 5 (1983); B. Hanawalt, 'Economic Influence on the Pattern of Crime in England, 1300–1348', *American Journal of Legal History*, 18 (1974); J. Lister (ed.), *Court Rolls of the Manor of Wakefield*, vol. 4 (Yorkshire Archaeological Society Record Ser., 78, 1930); Dyer, 'English Village Community'; Catto (ed.), *University of Oxford*.

The mortality estimates are reviewed in Smith's essay in Campbell, *Before the Black Death*; but see also M. Eccleston, 'Mortality of Rural Landless Men before the Black Death: The Glastonbury Head-Tax Lists', *Local Population Studies*, 63 (1999). For mortality after the famine, M. C. Coleman, *Downham-in-the Isle. A Study of an Ecclesiastical Manor in the Thirteenth and Fourteenth Centuries* (Woodbridge, 1984).

On the decline in cultivation, J. Birrell, 'Agrarian History', *VCH Staffordshire*, 6 (1979); A. R. H. Baker, 'Evidence in the *Nonarum Inquisitiones* of Contracting Arable Lands in England during the Early Fourteenth Century', *EcHR*, 2nd ser., 19 (1966); C. Dyer, 'The Rise and Fall of a Medieval Village: Little Aston (in Aston Blank), Gloucestershire', *Transactions of the Bristol and Gloucestershire Archaeological Society*, 105 (1987); D. Austin and M. J. C. Walker, 'A New Landscape Context for Houndtor, Devon', *Med. Arch.*, 29 (1985); Kelly, 'Excavation of a Medieval Farmstead'; L. A. Toft, 'A Study of Coastal Village Abandonment in the Swansea Bay Region, 1270–1540', *Morgannwg*, 32 (1988).

On yields, D. L. Farmer, 'Grain Yields on the Winchester Manors in the Later Middle Ages', *EcHR*, 2nd ser., 30 (1977); E. I. Newman and P. D. A. Harvey, 'Did Soil Fertility Decline in Medieval English Farms? Evidence from Cuxham, Oxfordshire, 1320–1340', *AgHR*, 45 (1997).

The information on prices and wages, calculated by D. L. Farmer, is from *AgHEW*, vol. II; on the meals of harvest workers, C. Dyer, 'Changes in Diet in the Late Middle Ages: The Case of Harvest Workers', *AgHR*, 36 (1988).

On land purchases, S. F. Hockey, *Quarr Abbey and its Lands, 1132–1632* (Leicester, 1970); S. Raban, *The Estates of Thorney and Crowland: A Study in Medieval Monastic Land Tenure* (Cambridge, 1977); G. A. Holmes, *The Estates of the Higher Nobility in Fourteenth Century England* (Cambridge, 1957).

Information on entry fines and variable rents comes from Raftis, *Ramsey Abbey*; J. Z. Titow, *English Rural Society, 1200–1349* (1969); J. Hatcher, *Rural Economy and Society in the Duchy of Cornwall 1300–1500* (Cambridge, 1970); M. Mate, 'The Estates of Canterbury Cathedral Priory before the Black Death', *Studies in Medieval and Renaissance History*, 8 (1987).

The problems of aristocratic expenditure are highlighted in Dyer, *Standards of Living*. On repercussions in towns, Beresford, *New Towns*; G. Rosser,

Medieval Westminster 1200–1540 (Oxford, 1989); M. Carlin, *Medieval Southwark* (1996); R. H. Britnell, *Growth and Decline in Colchester, 1300–1525* (Cambridge, 1986); P. Short, 'The Medieval Rows of York', *Archaeological Journal*, 137 (1980).

The statistics of overseas trade given here, and in subsequent chapters, come from E. M. Carus-Wilson and O. Coleman, *England's Export Trade, 1275–1547* (Oxford, 1963); J. Hatcher, *English Tin Production and Trade before 1550* (Oxford, 1973); James, *Wine Trade*. For major churches see R. Morris, *Cathedrals and Abbeys of England and Wales* (1979). The comments on cloth are based on J. H. Munro, 'The "Industrial Crisis" of the English TextileTown, *c.*1290–*c.*1330', *Thirteenth-Century England*, 7 (1997).

On the debate, the key works have been indicated in the books listed for the Introduction, above. Continental approaches can be seen in W. Abel, *Agricultural Fluctuations in Europe* (1980). The most thorough investigation of 'marginal' land is in M. Bailey, *A Marginal Economy? East Anglian Breckland in the Later Middle Ages* (Cambridge, 1989).

For Scotland in this period, Whyte, *Scotland before the Industrial Revolution*; E. Gemmill and N. Mayhew, *Changing Values in Medieval Scotland. A Study of Prices, Money and Weights and Measures* (Cambridge, 1995); Duncan, *Scotland: The Making of a Kingdom*; Grant, *Independence and Nationhood*; P. Dixon, 'A Rural Medieval Settlement in Roxburghshire: Excavations at Springwood Park, Kelso, 1985–6', *Proceedings of the Society of Antiquaries of Scotland*, 128 (1998); Moloney and Coleman, 'Development of a Medieval Street Frontage'.

For climate, the best survey is M. L. Parry, *Climatic Change, Agriculture and Settlement* (Folkestone, 1978); on money N. J. Mayhew (ed.), *Edwardian Monetary Affairs (1279–1344)* (British Archaeological Reports, 36, 1977); N. J. Mayhew, 'Money and Prices in England from Henry II to Edward III', *AgHR*, 35 (1987). For arbitrary lordship in the Welsh marches, Davies, *Lordship and Society*; W. Rees, *South Wales and the March, 1284–1415* (Oxford, 1924); L. B. Smith, 'The Arundel Charters to the Lordship of Chirk in the Fourteenth Century', *Bulletin of the Board of Celtic Studies*, 23 (1968).

On war in general, M. Prestwich, *War, Politics and Finance under Edward I* (1972); H. J. Hewitt, *The Organisation of War under Edward III 1338–62* (Manchester, 1966); Prestwich, *Armies and Warfare*; C. McNamee, *The Wars of the Bruces. Scotland, England and Ireland, 1306–1328* (East Linton, 1997); R. Lomas, 'The Impact of Border Warfare: The Scots and South Tweedside, *c.*1290–*c.*1520', *Scottish Historical Review*, 75 (1996); A. J. Taylor, 'Scorched Earth and Flint in 1294', *Flintshire Historical Society Journal*, 30 (1981–2).

On the total tax burden, M. Ormrod, 'England in the Middle Ages', in R. Bonney (ed.), *The Rise of the Fiscal State in Europe c.1200–1815* (Oxford, 1999); for the experience of the taxpayers, J. R. Maddicott, *The English Peasantry and the Demands of the Crown, 1294–1341)* (*P & P* supplement, 1, 1975). E. B. Fryde, *William de la Pole* (1988), deals with the wool monopoly, as does Lloyd, *Wool Trade*.

PART THREE: MAKING A NEW WORLD *c.*1350–*c.*1520

The primary sources in this introductory section include W. Nelson (ed.), *A Fifteenth Century School Book* (Oxford, 1956); J. Gower, *Confessio Amantis* (Harmondsworth, 1966); N. Davis (ed.), *Paston Letters and Papers of the Fifteenth Century* (2 vols, Oxford, 1971, 1976).

On money, J. Day, 'The Great Bullion Famine of the Fifteenth Century', *P & P*, 79 (1978); N. J. Mayhew, 'Population, Money Supply, and the Velocity of Circulation in England, 1300–1700', *EcHR*, 48 (1995); Spufford, *Money and its Use*; Gemmill and Mayhew, *Changing Values in Medieval Scotland*; W. W. Scott, 'Sterling and the Usual Money of Scotland, 1370–1495', *Scottish Economic and Social History*, 5 (1985).

The best sources of information on prices and wages in England and Wales are the chapters by D. Farmer in *AgHEW*, vols II and III, and Bowden's chapter in *AgHEW*, vol. IV.

Chapter 8: The Black Death and its aftermath, c.1348–c.1520

On plague and its effects see J. Hatcher, *Plague, Population and the English Economy 1348–1530* (1977); C. Platt, *King Death. The Black Death and its Aftermath in Late Medieval England* (1996); M. Ormrod and P. Lindley (eds), *The Black Death in England* (Stamford, 1996). The primary sources used are R. H. Hilton (ed.), *The Stoneleigh Leger Book* (Dugdale Society, 24, 1960); Westminster Abbey Muniments, 21037–9; J. Toomey (ed.), *Records of Hanley Castle Worcestershire*, c.1147–1547 (Worcestershire Historical Society, 18, 2001). R. Horrox (ed.), *The Black Death* (Manchester, 1994) conveniently gathers together chroniclers' descriptions. For the archaeological evidence, D. Hawkins, 'The Black Death and the New London Cemeteries of 1348', *Antiquity*, 64 (1990). On ruined houses in the countryside, P. Hargreaves, 'Seigniorial Reaction and Peasant Responses: Worcester Priory and its Peasants after the Black Death', *Midland History*, 24 (1999).

For mortality after 1350 see A.-B. Fitch, 'Assumptions about Plague in Late Medieval Scotland', *Scotia*, 11 (1987); R. Gottfried, *Epidemic Disease in Fifteenth-Century England* (Leicester, 1978); J. Hatcher, 'Mortality in the Fifteenth Century: Some New Evidence', *EcHR*, 2nd ser., 39 (1986); B. Harvey, *Living and Dying in England 1100–1540. The Monastic Experience* (Oxford, 1993); L. R. Poos, *A Rural Society after the Black Death. Essex 1350–1520* (Cambridge, 1991); Razi, *Life, Marriage and Death*; A. J. F. Dulley, 'Four Kent Towns at the End of the Middle Ages', in M. Roake and J. Whyman (eds), *Essays in Kentish History* (1973).

Delayed marriage and the shortage of children are highlighted in P. J. P. Goldberg, *Women, Work and Life Cycle in a Medieval Economy: York and Yorkshire, c.1300–1520* (Oxford, 1992); on families, Z. Razi, 'The Myth of the Immutable English Family', *P & P*, 140 (1993).

On the liberation of the lower orders, R. H. Hilton, *The Decline of Serfdom in England* (1968); S. A. C. Penn and C. Dyer, 'Wages and Earnings in Late Medieval England: Evidence from the Enforcement of the Labour Laws', *EcHR*, 2nd ser., 43 (1990); M. Rubin, *Charity and Community in Medieval Cambridge* (Cambridge, 1987); C. Dyer, 'The English Medieval Village Community and its Decline', *Journal of British Studies*, 33 (1994); Z. Razi, 'Family, Land and the Village Community in Later Medieval England', *P & P*, 93 (1982); Hilton, *English Peasantry*; C. Barron, 'The Golden Age of Women in Medieval London', *Reading Medieval Studies*, 15 (1989); C. Barron and A. Sutton (eds), *Medieval London Widows 1300–1500* (1994); M. E. Mate, *Women in Medieval English Society* (Cambridge, 1999); R. M. Smith, 'Coping with Uncertainty: Women's Tenure of Customary Land in England 1370–1430', in J. Kermode (ed.), *Enterprise and Individuals*.

The primary sources quoted in this section are from Raftis, *Tenure and Mobility*; R. Sillem (ed.), *Records of Some Sessions of the Peace in Lincolnshire 1360–1375* (Lincoln Record Society, 30, 1937); C. Gross (ed.), *Select Cases from the Coroners' Rolls 1265–1413* (Selden Society, 9, 1895); A. V. C. Schmidt (ed.), *William Langland. Piers Plowman* (Oxford, 1992); E. C. Furber (ed.), *Essex Sessions of the Peace 1351, 1377–1379* (Essex Archaeological Society, 1953).

For the origins and course of the 1381 rising, R. H. Hilton, *Bondmen Made Free: Medieval Peasant Movements and the English Rising of 1381* (1973); W. M. Ormrod, 'The Peasants' Revolt and the Government of England', *Journal of British Studies*, 29 (1990); R. H. Hilton and T. H. Aston (eds), *The English Rising of 1381* (Cambridge, 1984); C. Dyer, 'The Rising of 1381 in Suffolk: Its Origins and Participants', in Dyer, *Everyday Life*; R. B. Dobson (ed.), *The Peasants' Revolt of 1381* (2nd edn, 1983); S. Justice, *Writing and Rebellion: England in 1381* (Berkeley, Cal., 1994); H. Eiden, 'Joint Action against "Bad" Lordship: The Peasants' Revolt in Essex and Norfolk', *History*, 83 (1998).

William Smith's story is in Wadham College, Oxford, 44 B/1. On the Welsh revolt, R. R. Davies, *The Revolt of Owain Glyn Dŵr* (Oxford, 1997); L. B. Smith, 'Seignorial Income in the Fourteenth Century: The Arundels in Chirk', *Bulletin of the Board of Celtic Studies*, 28 (1979).

On the economy in the late fourteenth century, see A. R. Bridbury, 'The Black Death', *EcHR*, 2nd ser., 26 (1973); J. Hatcher, 'England in the Aftermath of the Black Death', *P & P*, 144 (1994); L. R. Poos, *A Rural Society after the Black Death: Essex 1350–1525* (Cambridge, 1990); Grant, *Independence and Nationhood*; Bailey, *A Marginal Economy?*; Hatcher, *Rural Economy and Society*; H. Grieve, *The Sleepers and the Shadows. Chelmsford: A Town, its People, and its Past* (Chelmsford, 1988).

Chapter 9: Towns, trade and industry, c.1350–c.1520

See Chapter 6 for a list of books on towns, many of which cover this period. On urban decline, A. D. Dyer, *Decline and Growth in English Towns 1400–1640* (Cambridge, 1995); S. Rigby, *Medieval Grimsby. Growth and Decline* (Hull,

1993); R. Holt, 'Gloucester in the Century after the Black Death', in Holt and Rosser (eds), *Medieval Town*; J. M. Bartlett, 'The Expansion and Decline of York in the Later Middle Ages', *EcHR*, 2nd ser., 12 (1959–60); A. F. Butcher, 'Rents and the Urban Economy: Oxford and Canterbury in the Later Middle Ages', *Southern History*, 1 (1979); A. F. Butcher, 'Rent, Population and Economic Change in Late-Medieval Newcastle', *Northern History*, 14 (1978). On buildings, Griffiths (ed.), *Boroughs of Mediaeval Wales*; Keene, *Medieval Winchester*. On civic duties, J. I. Kermode, 'Urban Decline? The Flight from Office in Late Medieval York', *EcHR*, 2nd ser., 35 (1982).

On town populations and failed towns, A. Dyer, ' "Urban Decline" in England, 1377–1525', in T. R. Slater (ed.), *Towns in Decline AD 100–1600* (Aldershot, 2000); I. Adams, *The Making of Urban Scotland* (1978). On the ups and downs of trade, T. H. Lloyd, *England and the German Hansa, 1157–1611* (Cambridge, 1991); J. Kermode, *Medieval Merchants. York, Beverley and Hull in the Later Middle Ages* (Cambridge, 1998).

On London, C. Barron, 'Richard Whittington: The Man Behind the Myth', in A. E. J. Hollaender and W. Kellaway (eds), *Studies in London History* (1969); P. Nightingale, *A Medieval Mercantile Community. The Grocers' Company and the Politics and Trade of London, 1000–1485* (New Haven and London, 1995); Blair and Ramsay (eds), *English Medieval Industries*; M. Norris, *Monumental Brasses, the Memorials* (1977); J. Galloway (ed.), *Trade, Urban Hinterlands and Market Integration c.1300–1600* (2000).

On individual towns, Courtney, *Medieval Usk*; C. Phythian-Adams, *Desolation of a City. Coventry and the Urban Crisis of the Later Middle Ages* (Cambridge, 1979); R. H. Britnell, *Growth and Decline in Colchester, 1300–1525* (Cambridge, 1986); E. M. Carus-Wilson, *The Expansion of Exeter at the Close of the Middle Ages* (Exeter, 1963). There are also regional studies: H. S. A. Fox, 'Medieval Urban Development', in Kain and Ravenhill (eds), *Historical Atlas of South-West England*; G. Sheeran, *Medieval Yorkshire Towns. People, Buildings and Space* (Edinburgh, 1998); Laughton and Dyer, 'Small Towns in the East and West Midlands'; A. J. L. Winchester, *Landscape and Society in Medieval Cumbria* (Edinburgh, 1987).

On merchants S. Thrupp, *The Merchant Class of Medieval London* (Chicago, 1948); A. Hanham, *The Celys and Their World. An English Merchant Family of the Fifteenth Century* (Cambridge, 1985); H. W. Booton, 'Sir John Rutherford: A Fifteenth-Century Aberdeen Burgess', *Scottish Economic and Social History*, 10 (1990).

For artisans, Swanson, *Medieval Artisans*; H. Booton, 'The Craftsmen of Aberdeen between 1400 and 1550', *Northern Scotland*, 13 (1993); Grenville, *Medieval Housing*; J. Schofield, *Medieval London Houses* (New Haven, 1994); J. Schofield, 'Urban Housing in England, 1400–1600', in D. Gaimster and P. Stamper (eds), *The Age of Transition. The Archaeology of English Culture, 1400–1600* (Oxford, 1997).

John Symond's will is in Suffolk Record Office, Ipswich branch, J 421/3. fo. 5.

For hospitals and almshouses, N. Orme and M. Webster, *The English Hospital, 1070–1570* (New Haven and London, 1995).

On civic pride and urban regulation, L. Toulmin Smith (ed.), *The Maire of Bristowe is Kalendar by Robert Ricart* (Camden Society, new ser., 5, 1872); J. R. Green, *Town Life in the Fifteenth Century* (1894); Gemmill and Mayhew, *Changing Values*; W. B. Bickley (ed.), *The Little Red Book of Bristol* (Bristol, 1900); H. Swanson, 'The Illusion of Economic Structure: Craft Guilds in Late Medieval Towns', *P & P*, 121 (1988); G. Rosser, 'Crafts, Guilds and the Negotiation of Work in the Medieval Town', *P & P*, 154 (1997); R. H. Hilton, *English and French Towns in Feudal Society. A Comparative Study* (Cambridge, 1992); A. H. Thomas and P. E. Jones, *Calendar of Plea and Memoranda Rolls of the City of London* (6 vols, Cambridge, 1926–61); *VCH Cambridgeshire*, vol. 4; G. Rosser, 'Communities of Parish and Guild in the Late Middle Ages', in S. J. Wright (ed.), *Parish, Church and People* (1988); D. G. Shaw, *The Creation of a Community. The City of Wells in the Middle Ages* (Oxford, 1993); J. A. F. Thomson (ed.), *Towns and Townspeople in the Fifteenth Century* (Gloucester, 1988) contains essays by Rigby, Kermode and Horrox on elites.

On the informalities of small towns and trading places, M. Bailey, 'A Tale of Two Towns: Buntingford and Standon in the Later Middle Ages', *Journal of Medieval History*, 19 (1993); C. Dyer, 'The Hidden Trade of the Middle Ages: Evidence from the West Midlands of England', *JHG*, 18 (1992); P. J. P. Goldberg, 'Urban Identity and the Poll Taxes of 1377, 1379, and 1381', *EcHR*, 2nd ser., 43 (1990).

For consumption, H. S. Cobb, 'Textile Imports in the Fifteenth Century: The Evidence of Customs Accounts', *Costume*, 29 (1995); Bennett, *Ale, Beer and Brewsters*; A. Sutton, 'Mercery through Four Centuries, 1130–1500', *Nottingham Medieval Studies*, 41 (1997). M. Mellor, 'A Synthesis of Middle and Late Saxon, Medieval and Early Post-Medieval Pottery in the Oxford Region', *Oxoniensia*, 59 (1994); M. Threlfall-Holmes, 'Late Medieval Iron Production and Trade in the North-East', *Archaeologia Aeliana*, 27 (1999); R. I. Jack, 'The Cloth Industry in Medieval Wales', *Welsh History Review*, 10 (1981); E. Power, *The Paycockes of Coggeshall* (1920); J. Hatcher, *History of the British Coal Industry vol. 1: Before 1700* (Oxford, 1993).

Capitalism and credit are discussed in a number of essays in Kermode (ed.), *Enterprise and Individuals*; J. Kermode, 'Money and Credit in the Fifteenth Century: Some Lessons from Yorkshire', *Business History Review*, 65 (1991). On a new outlook, M. K. McIntosh, *Controlling Misbehavior in England, 1370–1600* (Cambridge, 1998); C. Dyer, 'Work Ethics in the Fourteenth Century', in J. Bothwell, P. J. P. Goldberg and W. M. Ormrod (eds), *The Problem of Labour in Fourteenth Century England* (Woodbridge, 2000).

Chapter 10: The countryside, c.1350–c.1520

AgHEW, vol. III is a very important source for this period. On the policies of lords while they kept their demesnes in cultivation Campbell, *English Seigniorial*

Agriculture; H. P. R. Finberg, *Tavistock Abbey. A Study in the Social and Economic History of Devon* (Newton Abbot, 1969); R. H. Hilton, *The Economic Development of Some Leicestershire Estates in the Fourteenth and Fifteenth Centuries* (Oxford, 1947); Harvey, *Westminster Abbey*; Hilton, *English Peasantry*; M. Carlin, 'Christ Church, Canterbury and its Lands . . . 1391–1540' (Oxford University B.Litt. thesis, 1970); Du Boulay, *Lordship of Canterbury*; Dyer, *Lords and Peasants*; T. H. Lloyd, *The Movement of Wool Prices in Medieval England* (EcHR Supplement 6, 1973).

For the administration of the leased estate, K. B. McFarlane, *England in the Fifteenth Century* (1981); K. B. McFarlane, *The Nobility of Later Medieval England* (Oxford, 1973); R. Britnell, 'The Pastons and Their Norfolk', *AgHR*, 36 (1988); T. B. Pugh (ed.), *The Marcher Lordships of South Wales, 1415–1536* (Cardiff, 1963); J. C. Hodgson (ed.), *Percy Bailiff's Rolls of the Fifteenth Century* (Surtees Society, 134, 1921).

On revenues, Carlin, 'Canterbury and its Lands'; Hatcher, *Earldom of Cornwall*; A. J. Pollard, *North Eastern England during the Wars of the Roses. Lay Society, War and Politics 1450–1500* (Oxford, 1990); C. Rawcliffe, *The Staffords, Earls of Stafford and Dukes of Buckingham 1394–1521* (Cambridge, 1978); J. M. Gilbert, *Hunting and Hunting Reserves in Medieval Scotland* (Edinburgh, 1979); I. S. W. Blanchard, *The Duchy of Lancaster's Estates in Derbyshire 1485–1540* (Derbyshire Archaeological Society Record Series, 3, 1971).

For the gentry C. Dyer, *Warwickshire Farming, 1349–c.1520* (Dugdale Society Occasional Paper, 27, 1981); C. Carpenter, *Locality and Polity. A Study of Warwickshire Landed Society, 1401–1499* (Cambridge, 1992); E. W. Ives, *The Common Lawyers of Pre-Reformation England* (Cambridge, 1983); A. D. Carr, *Medieval Anglesey* (Llangefni, 1982); C. E. Moreton, *The Townshends and their World: Gentry, Law and Land in Norfolk, c.1450–1551* (Oxford, 1992); H. Thorpe, 'The Lord and the Landscape', *Transactions of the Birmingham and Warwickshire Archaeological Society* 80 (1962); S. M. Wright, *The Derbyshire Gentry in the Fifteenth Century* (Derbyshire Record Society, 8, 1983); the documents cited include Public Record Office, E101/691/41; Cumbria Record Office D/Penn/200 (Pennington); Dorset County Record Office, D10/M231 (Giffard); W. W. Skeat (ed.), *The Boke of Husbandry by Master Fitzherbert* (English Dialect Society, 1882); I. S. Leadam (ed.), *The Domesday of Inclosures, 1517–1518* (Royal Historical Society, 1897).

For gentry creating new manors and units of production F. C. Taylor, 'Thomas Tropenell, Esquire: A Local Lawyer, the Gentry and Estate Creation' (University of Birmingham MPhil thesis, 1997); McIntosh, *Autonomy and Community*; C. Welch, 'Glassmaking in Wolseley, Staffordshire', *Post-Medieval Archaeology*, 31 (1997); D. Youngs, 'Estate Management, Investment and the Gentleman Landlord in Later Medieval England', *Historical Research*, 73 (2000).

There are many local studies of farmers, for example J. N. Hare, 'The Demesne Lessees of Fifteenth-Century Wiltshire', *AgHR*, 29 (1981), which cites earlier writings on the subject; see also J. N. Hare, 'Durrington, a Chalkland

Village in the Later Middle Ages', *Wiltshire Archaeological Magazine*, 74/5 (1979–80); E. Roberts, 'Overton Court Farm and the Late-Medieval Farmhouses of Demesne Lessees in Hampshire', *Proceedings of the Hampshire Field Club*, 51 (1995), C. Dyer, 'Were There Any Capitalists in Fifteenth-Century England?', in Kermode (ed.), *Enterprise and Individuals*. Documents cited include D. J. H. Michelmore (ed.), *The Fountains Abbey Lease Book* (Yorkshire Archaeological Society Record Series, 140, 1981); C. Rogers (ed.), *Rental Book of the Cistercian Abbey of Coupar-Angus* (Grampian Club, 1879); J. Raine (ed.), *Testamenta Eboracensia*, vol. 3 (Surtees Society, 45, 1864).

The most recent view of the importance of expropriation is R. Brenner, whose views provoked a debate: T. H. Aston and C. H. E. Philpin (eds), *The Brenner Debate* (Cambridge, 1985). The view here is expounded in C. Dyer, 'Deserted Medieval Villages in the West Midlands', *EcHR*, 2nd ser., 35 (1982); C. Dyer, 'Peasants and Farmers: Rural Settlements in an Age of Transition', in D. Gaimster and P. Stamper (eds), *The Age of Transition. The Archaeology of English Culture, 1400–1600* (Oxford, 1997).

For peasants, in addition to the reading recommended for Chapters 5, 7 and 8, J. Whittle, *The Development of Agrarian Capitalism. Land and Labour in Norfolk 1440–1580* (Oxford, 2000); R. K. Field, 'Migration in the Later Middle Ages: The Case of the Hampton Lovett Villeins', *Midland History*, 8 (1983); P. D. A. Harvey (ed.), *The Peasant Land Market in Medieval England* (Oxford, 1984); A. Watkins, 'Cattle Grazing in the Forest of Arden in the Later Middle Ages', *AgHR*, 37 (1989); M. Yates, 'Change and Continuities in Rural Society from the Later Middle Ages to the Sixteenth Century: The Contribution of West Berkshire', *EcHR*, 52 (1999); I. Harvey, *Jack Cade's Rebellion of 1450* (Oxford, 1991).

John Mell of Bramfield: Suffolk Record Office (Ipswich branch), J421/3, fo. 117r; HB26, 371: 41, 71, 110; for enclosure of Lydd, S. Dimmock, 'English Small Towns and the Emergence of Capitalist Relations, c.1450–1550', *Urban History*, 28 (2001).

Index

HOW THE WORLD WORKS

WORLD WORKS

THE STORY OF HUMAN LABOR
FROM PREHISTORY TO THE MODERN DAY

PAUL COCKSHOTT

MONTHLY REVIEW PRESS

New York

Library of Congress Cataloging-in-Publication Data available
from the publisher

MONTHLY REVIEW PRESS, NEW YORK
monthlyreview.org

Typeset in Minion Pro and Brown
5 4 3 2 1

Contents

Preface for
the General Reader

This book has an ambitious scope, ranging as it does from pre-history to a future post–fossil fuel era.

I wrote it because there is a lack, as far as I am aware, of a recent introduction to the materialist theory of history. Although it is not a history book, it is about the successive economic and social forms within which our history has taken place. I follow the approach pioneered by Adam Smith and Karl Marx of seeing history as being structured by the successive forms of economy within which people have worked to win their survival. I draw on the work of generations of historians, economists, and social theorists who have contributed to this materialist view of history, and I attempt to summarize their results for the non-specialist reader.

There are certain broad themes in my account: the interaction of human reproduction with technology, social domination, and the division of labor. In chapter 2 I look at the biggest change human society ever went through as we developed from being hunters to becoming farmers. We will see how, according to modern research, this transition was neither easy nor immediately beneficial, so the problem is to understand why it took place at all. But, once the transition took place, the additional food resources that became available allowed a dramatic rise in population density and to a process of migration and colonization that have left their marks in the languages we still speak.

While archaeology shows that the first agricultural societies retained an egalitarian structure, this had by the era of classical civilization thoroughly broken down. In area after area, freedom gave way to slavery. Slaves were forced to produce surplus goods for sale giving rise to international trade, money, and banking. I explain in chapter 3 the internal structure of slave economies, their markets and processes of reproduction and how their limited markets and their squandering of human resources led them to stagnate.

Since it was slave economies that invented money chapter 3 explains the classical theory of price, according to which the prices of commodities tend to be proportional to the amount of labor expended making them. In the process I explain how the classical theory is more scientific than the supply and demand theory that most social science students have been taught.

Slave economies have arisen at different times in various parts of the world, but in the end they have given way to peasant economies. In these, relatively self-sufficient family farms are subject to the exploitation a landlord or military class. In chapter 4 I look at the basic reproduction process of such economies, the degree of exploitation to which the peasants were subjected, and the efficiency of the overall economic model. In particular I am concerned to counter the modern prejudice that assumes feudal society to have been inefficient and irrational compared to modern capitalism.

Most of the world now lives in the capitalist economic system. Chapter 5, the longest in the book, explains how capitalism works. I show that the classical theory of price still applies under capitalism, and that this, combined with the existence of private firms, necessarily implies that goods will be sold at a markup or profit over the wage cost of their production. I show that it was ultimately the development of technology, particularly powered machinery, that enabled the owners of such machines to become the new dominant class. A large part of the chapter is devoted to the interaction between technology, profits, and real wages. I show that a freer and better paid workforce led to a more rapid rate of technical progress.

The next big theme of chapter 5 is how capitalism has interacted with population growth and family structure. Early and late capitalist societies have radically different demographics. An exploding population in the nineteenth century fueled European settler colonialism. Now, in contrast, developed capitalist states are scarcely able to reproduce their workforces. This shift has led to chronically depressed profit rates and stagnant levels of investment. It presages an existential crisis for capitalism.

One of the more controversial points I make is that far from the early twenty-first century being a period of very rapid technical change, such advances are now much slower than they were in the twentieth century. This slowdown in technical progress is a mark of capitalism having passed its heyday.

For a century now, socialist economies have existed as an alternative to capitalism. Chapter 6 examines the basic structure of socialism. I start with technology. Electricity, and lots of it, was seen as one leg of socialist transformation. The other leg was people and the number of people depended on birth rates, death rates, and family structures, all of which are covered in section 6.3.

In capitalist economies the surplus available for investment depends on private profits; in a socialist system it depends on the planned division of output between consumer goods and investment goods. In classical Marxist terms, socialist economies have a historically unique mechanism for the extraction of a surplus product. This mechanism underlay the very fast growth rates achieved by the USSR before the 1970s and by China right up until to the present. Section 6.5 presents the basic theory of socialist growth developed by Feldman in the 1920s and shows that his theory gives a good explanation of what was achieved over the next fifty years. What is not widely appreciated in the West was just how successful the USSR was in the production of mass consumption goods. Why, if it was producing so much, was there an impression of continuous shortages?

It comes down in the end to how the Soviets managed the consumer market, and, more fundamentally, to why there still was a market in consumer goods. The later parts of the chapter deal with why the socialist economies still retained money, and why it was impossible for them to escape what Marxists term "the law of value." The chapter finishes with an examination of the processes that led to the final disintegration of the European socialist countries.

I finish with a chapter on future economies. I look at the constraints that will be imposed by a shift to carbon-neutral economics. I ask whether future economies will be communist and whether communism has some specific technical basis on which it must rest. This chapter is inevitably slightly speculative!

COMMENTS FOR MORE TECHNICAL READERS

Although this book is written from a perspective strongly influenced by Marx, there are a number of points on which my presentation will differ significantly from what has become common in Marxism.

The first difference is on the role assigned to technology. Back in the mid-nineteenth century Marx put forward a bold, technologically determinist view of society. But this view came to be seen as something of an embarrassment by the late twentieth century, particularly by European and American theorists. Western Marxist theory was dominated by people with a training in the humanities or social studies. Exceptions like Bernal, Bordiga, Pannekoek, or Machover were so few that their very existence was noteworthy. The specialized educational background of Western Marxists had a number of effects: slow adoption of new concepts from the sciences, hostility to what is seen as technical determinism and reluctance to use mathematical and quantitative methods.

From the mid-1980s a new type of Marxism has gradually developed that has been more sympathetic to the hard sciences and to quantitative analysis. Here I apply this approach to the general history of modes of production. In the process I give the term "mode of production" a much more literal, technological interpretation than most recent Marxists have done. For each historical form of economy, I focus first on its underlying technology and then its demography. In my view, technology and population constrain everything else.

I have long been critical of the "value form" school of economists [Heinrich and Locascio, 2012] who, in my opinion [Cockshott, 2013a], unduly restrict the idea of value and abstract labor to modern capitalist society. I think that the idea of abstract labor is critical to the analysis of all forms of economy, not just to capitalism. Abstract labor denotes an attribute of the human species being, our plasticity and adaptability. I lay out this approach right at the start of chapter 1. Along with a misapprehension about labor, the value form school has tended to see value as a concept that only applies to capitalist economies. I think this view gets the history all wrong. I thus chose, with some deliberation, to introduce my analysis of value in chapter 3.5 where I am examining classical slave civilizations. I am also concerned to correct the illusion that value relations, seen as something specifically capitalist, have no relevance to socialist economies. In section 6.8 I show why, even in socialist economies, value relations still operated. Officially, the Soviets accepted that the "law of value" still applied to them. Despite the theoretical acceptance, political pressures were such as to make socialist governments act as if value relations could be simply ignored. The consequences were unfortunate. It would be an even worse misfortune were a future socialist government, influenced perhaps by value form theory, to repeat that mistake.

Althusser et al. [2006] criticized the use of unilinear models in traditional Marxism. In response to this critique, when I look at transitions between forms of economy I discard the old unilinear succession of forms of economy for an approach based on Markov models. The Markov approach allows you to conceptualize history as having both a statistical trend and at the same time the possibility of "backward" transitions [Cockshott, 2013b].

Readers familiar with the work of Farjoun and Machover will notice that my presentation of price theory is derived from those authors. I have, however, gone beyond them in applying the same forms of argument to analyzing the rise of patriarchy (section 2.4), and to a reformulation of the classical law of wages (section 5.7). I try to show that one can still apply the classical idea of the wage minimum as being set by the lowest wage on which people can still feed themselves. Empirical work since Farjoun and Machover [1983] has shown that, contra Marx, the rate of profit does not equalize between industries. Marxist economists have taken some persuading that this is the case. Mere real-world data does not seem to carry that much weight in economics. In the hope that more formal methods will be found convincing, Appendix B introduces a novel mathematical approach based on random matrices to show why profits do not equilibrate.

In sections 4.4 and 5.4.8 I develop a critique of the Weber-Brenner thesis about the superior rationality of capitalist relations of production. In this view, the need to perform calculations in terms of money, forces capitalists to be more economically rational than previous ruling classes had been. In section 5.4.8 I show that this idea is based on a misunderstanding of the cost structures driving innovation under capitalism, and that in fact capitalist costing systematically biases against innovation. On theoretical grounds, precapitalist social relations are actually more conducive to labor-saving rationalization. In section 4.4 I use the recent work of McDonald to show that this was the case: feudal agriculture was as efficient as, if not more efficient than, capitalism.

Capitalism is inefficient because of the misleading signals that come from monetary calculation. Low wages mean that it constantly underestimates the true cost of labor. This does not just apply to capitalism. It happens wherever costs are estimated in terms of money wages not hours of labor. In section 6.8.1 I show that the system of monetary calculation used in the USSR also generated the wrong signals when it came to a rational use of labor. Only by a transition to a fully communist system of economic calculation could the USSR have escaped its terminal stagnation.

CHAPTER 1

Introduction

Human society has to work to survive.[1] Our food, clothing, and shelter are won by work and, as every parent knows, the next generation is raised by work. Society is, before all else, a collective effort to ensure its own physical continuity.

We are all born into and formed by a society already structured around collective tasks of physical production, of human reproduction, and the reproduction of the social relations that achieve it all.

Societies distribute their members into different social roles, and divide up their waking hours between activities. Some activities, like feeding or dressing oneself, are purely personal. Some, like childcare, family cooking, farming, or industry, benefit others. Different kinds of activity produce their own useful effects: sex—babies, baking—bread, bricklaying—walls. For each effect we need to carry out particular sequences of body movements that interact with the environment, implements, and other people. These are the concrete aspects of activity.

But from the standpoint of society as a whole, each activity has another more abstract aspect, since each is part of the division of labor. The bodies and time of its members are society's fundamental resource. They are both limited. There are only a given number of people alive on any given day, and there are only 24 hours in the day, for some of which our bodies must sleep. The social division of labor has to partition the available time of all these bodies between the tasks required for survival. What is being divided up here are all the millions of person hours that go to make up the social working day. This is the abstract social aspect of activity: activity as part of the social organism.

The division of labor combines a concrete achieved result, particular bodies performing specific actions, with the abstract possibility of a different result. The allocation of bodies to tasks would have to be different. You or I could be doing a different job in six months' time. Had circumstances been other, we could have been doing something different right now.

For a division of labor to exist bodies must be flexible, able to perform more than one task. We can do this. We can switch, we can learn.

We humans are neither the only, nor the first social animals on Earth. Before our towns, there were the castles of the termites, the apartment blocks of the bees, and mazes of the mole rats. Termites are, in terms of sheer biomass and food consumption, the dominant social organism. Our biomass totals some 350 million tons [Walpole et al., 2012], that of termites, 450 million tons [Sanderson, 1996].

These societies too have their division of labor. Termite workers build towers every bit as tall in relation to their bodies as our skyscrapers. They gather wood, they tend underground mushroom gardens and look after young ones. This is a fluctuating division of labor. The proportions of workers performing different tasks vary according to the needs of the colony.

They have a limited repertoire of tasks and their technology changes only over evolutionary time scales, but this is still a division of labor. Individual termite workers do not learn. As species they learn, but any technology they use, and once, millions of years ago, each of their technologies must have been new, was acquired by the slow process of genetic adaptation.

Alongside the workers, their mounds contain others. They are polymorphic species.

There are soldier termites with huge heads and mandibles, huge mothers, and medium-sized fathers. The soldiers cannot work. Their sole task is to defend the home from ants. They block the passages with their huge heads, biting intruders, or squirting noxious glue at them. Aside from this, they are unproductive, unable to gather wood or raise crops, dependent on the workers for their food.

The huge mother or "queen," a sort of yellowish pulsating striped sausage as big as a man's finger, can't work either. She lies in her secure chamber, panting, being fed fungus as she lays eggs. The activities of the mother and the soldiers are always concrete: the mother lays eggs, the soldiers defend. They cannot take up tasks as the need arises the way the workers do.

Faced with insect societies people find it hard not to make analogies to our own. The terms *worker, soldier, queen* are obvious analogies: a projection of the class systems of our society onto a very alien one. People use the term *castes* to describe the different termite body forms, an obvious analogy with the ancient social system of India. But this analogy is limited. The bodies of people in different Indian castes are the same, it is social pressure, not physique, that forces people into the types of work associated with castes. Indian

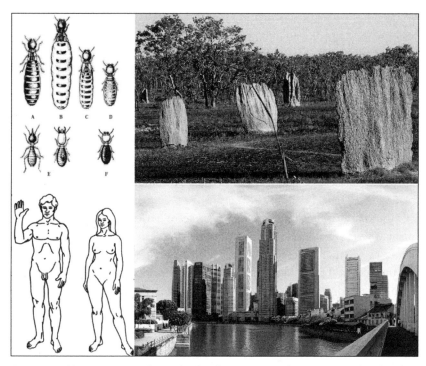

Figure 1.1. Termites are, in biomass, the dominant social organism on Earth. Their workers build towers every bit as tall in relation to their bodies as our skyscrapers. They are polymorphic animals with multiple different body forms within a colony. A: Primary king, B: Primary queen, C: Secondary queen, D: Tertiary queen, E: Soldiers, F: Worker. Because of this polymorphism they do not have a fully developed division of labor. The other main social animal on Earth is dimorphic and can have a more general division of labor. Source: NASA and Wikimedia.

castes, moreover, are hereditary, whereas the members of different "castes" in a termite nest, workers or soldiers all share the same parents.

The point that is validly made when talking of termite castes though, is that like the castes of the Hindus; the different body forms of the termites impede a flexible division of labor [Ambedkar, 1982].

Although termite soldiers cannot transfer to building work or vice-versa, there has to be some mechanism regulating the proportions of these two body forms. Too few soldiers in an environment with a lot of hostile ants could be fatal for the colony, but too many means a lot of idle mouths for the workers to feed. In principle the caste ratios could be regulated genetically with different queens laying eggs whose soldier ratio varied. There is some evidence that this is the case [Long et al., 2003]. Here, although a given termite society could not fully regulate its division of labor, natural selection would mean that over a series of generations of colonies, the soldier ratio would adapt to the average needs of these colonies.

Another possibility is that pheromones are used to adjust the development of individuals into different body forms as the need arises [Long et al., 2003]. If this is the mechanism, then even though a mature termite cannot change caste, the caste into which a young one matures is decided quite late in life, so that the colony can adjust the composition of its workforce quite rapidly. This would imply that there was actually more occupational mobility among the termites than in human caste societies.

Why pay attention to these odd little creatures with their grotesquely differentiated bodies?

Because it is easier to recognize features of the familiar when contemplating the strange.

The termites and other social insects seem perfect examples of communism. The individuals act primarily in the interests of the community as a whole rather than themselves. Termite soldiers willingly sacrifice their lives for the sake of their colony. If there is a hole formed in the nest, the soldiers rush out to confront any ants that attempt to break in, while behind them the workers wall up the hole. There is no retreat for them. When the workers finish the wall, the soldiers are marooned outside. Worker bees will fearlessly mob hornets. Many die from the hornet's sting, but by surrounding the hornet and buzzing they cause it to die of heat exhaustion.

The superiority of this communist lifestyle is testified by the ecologically dominant position that the social insects, particularly the termites and ants, occupy. Anyone who has seen these creatures cannot but be impressed by the complete domination that an army of carnivorous African driver ants exerts over the territory it marches through, the fearful network of miniature tracks, trunk, and major roads with multilane traffic and the panic of other insects in the locality. and their fruitless attempts to escape before being torn limb from limb by tiny tormentors who form up into teams to pull a beetle or cockroach apart. Their distant relatives, the peaceful termites, exert a hidden, more subtle but even greater domination, venturing out only in their temporary vaulted paths. Secure from predation behind these walls they gather so much dead wood for their mushroom caves that they dominate their ecosystems. No land animal, other than our domestic cattle, has more biomass.

The literally fraternal solidarity of social insects arises because they are all members of the same family with the same parents. When a soldier termite sacrifices itself, it is protecting its direct kin, and indirectly maximizing the survival of its own genes. But look at it another way and we see in these communities the very image of monarchical despotism and exploitation, with workers perpetually on the verge of rebellion.

Think of the poor worker bees. Genetically female but deprived of the power to bear their own offspring, they toil all their lives for a queen who alone is allowed to lay eggs. They are kept in this subordination by the pheromones released by the queen. Take these pheromones away and they rebel. Nieh [2012] writes that:

> After their queen has left with a swarm, orphaned larvae exhibiting rebel traits emerge in honeybee colonies. As adults, these orphans have reduced food glands to feed the colony's larvae and more developed ovaries to selfishly reproduce their own offspring.

Until exo-planets were discovered we had imagined that all planetary systems would be like ours. Now, with a knowledge of their vast diversity, the masked peculiarity of the solar system becomes apparent, and hence a problem for science.

Contemporary academic economics eternalizes the institutions not just of human society, but of contemporary Western capitalism.[2] Anthropologists, archaeologists, and biologists studying social organisms all bring home to us the variety of forms that the production and reproduction of social life can have. They help us to question features that economics takes for granted.

Termite polymorphism (fig. 1.1) might seem irrelevant unless it reminds that we are no more monomorphic than them. We are dimorphic, with male and female body forms. Externally the differences between human females and males do not strike us as grotesque, the way those between termite queens and termite workers do. But in reality we are acutely aware of these slighter differences that impinge profoundly on our social division of labor.[3]

All termite castes are to some degree disabled: only soldiers can defend themselves, only alates[4] can fly, only queens lay eggs, only workers build. Their forms mean that among them the abstract potential of the division of labor is only realized between generations. But this is not true of humans: half have bodies that allow full participation in all social tasks. Women have a flexibility no termite has. They can do any human work.[5] But unlike insects we each learn our tasks within one lifetime. The great development of human technology owes itself both to this ability to learn and to the ability to transmit learned skills between generations.

There is technological evolution by other animals. Spider webs are a technology that has developed from orb webs, which seem to be the primitive form, to sheet webs or cobwebs (fig. 1.2). The oldest orb webs known from fossils date from the Cretaceous, but we have fossils of the orb web spiders themselves dating from the Jurassic. There appear to have been several subsequent independent inventions of the sheet web since then [Blackledge et al., 2009]. Dimitrov et al. [2012] argue that sheet webs do not have to obey

Figure 1.2. Technological development by animals. The primitive orb web (left) was developed into the sheet web (right) which can be placed in positions that are unusable by orb webs. Source: Wikimedia.

the same strict architectural constraints that govern orb webs. This allows spiders to use spaces where orbs cannot be constructed or are very inefficient in catching prey. This is an example of technological development, but one that took tens of millions of years to achieve. Knowledge of how to build a new type of web can only be passed on from a mother spider to her offspring if it is encoded in her genes, and it has been acquired by natural selection.[6] But when women started to develop weaving and textile technology—perhaps around 7000 BC [Barber, 1991] they were able to pass on improvements to their daughters by word and example leading to a rapid development of forms and types of cloth: linen, woolen, different weaves and knits.

This kind of transmission of cultural information is not unique to us. It has been known since Darwin's day that other primates can use tools.[7] Since Goodall's studies at Gombe we have known that tool use can be a local culture [Whiten et al., 1999] rather than a universal trait. The ability to form distinct technical cultures is a primitive primate trait, just more developed among humans. Our greater ability in this stems from our being able to use language rather than mere example to educate our infants.

Our dynamic development of technology has allowed our species to completely transform the way it lives. This is not just a matter of changes in the way we obtain our food: going from hunting to herding, from gathering wild plants to raising crops. It is also a matter of changing divisions of labor, changing the social relations that organize labor, and the growth of ever more complex relations of domination, subordination, and rebellion.

We will be looking at the way technologies have structured the allocation of human time, the social relations under which this has been regulated, and the forms of exploitation and struggles for freedom that this has given rise to. We will deal relatively briefly with the period before the Industrial

Revolution, but look at social relations in increasing detail as we explain the dominant structures of today's world economy.

The precondition of any society is the reproduction of people. This is the most basic, in the sense of fundamental, branch of the division of labor. But it is something that in contemporary society appears as not part of the economy. Instead it appears as just "family life," something that is private rather than social. Capitalist market society does not think of an activity as economic unless it involves money. But activities done for payment have been only a very small part of economic life until recently. Even now, they constitute barely half of economic life. If we cast aside the historically narrow perspective that only paid work is work, it becomes clear that sex and the bearing, feeding, and socialization of children are the foundation of economic life.

It is trivially true that without people there would be no economy, but in asserting that human reproduction is the foundation of the economy we are saying more than this.

- The production of the next generation takes time and bodily effort, and the availability of time and energy are the fundamental constraints that any economy has to obey.
- Reproduction determines population. Population changes can drive economic change and changes in power relations. This applies as much today as it ever did.
- The perspective that orthodox economics has is individualist. It defines the "economic problem" in terms of individuals maximizsing their satisfaction. When we take reproduction as our starting point we focus instead on society as an organism. This organism has to reproduce its own conditions of existence: the people, the resources they use, and the social relations they live in. The matter making up a living organism constantly changes, cells die, new ones are generated, but the structure remains. The same applies to a society. Its cells, individuals, change. Its matter, the buildings and tools, change. They both change by being reproduced and replaced.

To produce and wean a baby a mother must consume enough energy for two. The amount of food available determines the extent to which this is possible. If food is in permanently short supply, she may not have enough energy to supply milk to twins, or to feed both a new infant and an unweaned two-year-old. So under these circumstances mothers must regulate their fertility and at times practice infanticide [Diamond, 2012, chap. 5]. The carrying of children also consumes energy, and until very recently babies always had to be carried. Unless cloth has been invented, allowing the baby to be strapped to her back, the baby must be carried on one arm. This means that a mother loses half her ability to produce food while carrying the child. The survival of the child is then likely to depend on the mother's ability to call on the assistance of others: grandmothers, older siblings, male relatives or partners to provide food or care for the infant [Hawkes et al., 1997]. Here, in reproduction, we have the basis for social cooperation and a division of labor.

Once weaned, children have to eat solid food. Where is this to come from?

The age at which the child can be weaned depends on the technological level of society and how it produces food. In an agricultural society the milk of animals and gruels made from grains can be fed to infants before their teeth have developed. In a pre-agricultural society this is not possible, so breastfeeding has to go on for longer. In modern society the availability of formula milk and bottles means that breastfeeding can be eliminated entirely: the modern labor market is unforgiving toward mothers who want to breastfeed or carry their baby around during paid work.

Children, once they can run around, immediately start to be able to gather some food for themselves. In most societies children make up a significant part of the labor force [Minge-Klevana et al., 1980], but it is not until they are teenagers that the food they produce is sufficient to feed themselves. They remain a net energy drain on their adult relatives until then. The removal of children from productive work, which has happened progressively since the nineteenth century, has a huge impact on the allocation of time in society as a whole and on the labor of other family members.

Fertility is the first constraint on the reproduction of the population. The next is mortality, particularly infant mortality. To reproduce a society needs a level of female fertility sufficient to ensure that on average at least one daughter survives until child-bearing age. The number of surviving male children is less of a constraint. In humans about 21 boys are born for every 20 girls. It might at first sight appear that the reproductive potential of the population might be best served by mothers selectively killing off a portion of their male offspring, but this never seems to happen. There are recent instances of societies in which baby girls are killed off [Hughes, 1981; George et al., 1992]. There are also cases where babies of both sexes are killed off [Eng and Smith, 1976]. But selectively killing off female children is only possible in a society with a relatively long life expectancy. Engels [1980] showed that in a society with a life expectancy at birth of between twenty and thirty, which was typical of the world until recent times, any significant level of female infanticide will result in population decline since there will not be enough

TABLE 1.1: Division of Workforce by Age and Gender

Demographic	Part of the Workforce?
Grandmothers	Yes
Mothers	Yes
Men	Yes
Children	Partially
Infants	No

women surviving to become mothers. Others argue that Engels made unrealistic assumptions about other causes of death, and that the very stability of population in the ancient world should be explained by female infanticide [Harris, 1982]. Although more boys are born than girls, this can be offset by a higher rate of mortality. The type of work they do is more likely to result in fatal accidents, and they are more likely to die in wars.

Leaving aside deliberate killing of babies or dying in conflict, the main constraints on people surviving until they can have children of their own have been hunger and disease. Disease itself is a social phenomenon. Diseases have to pass from person to person, so their existence depends on a certain density of population and the degree of connectedness of the population. Isolated small populations do not allow disease germs to survive [McNeill, 2010; Diamond and Ordunio, 1997]. As population density rises and as trade and travel grows, epidemic plagues become a huge danger. They have to spread initially from some sort of animal in which the germ or virus lives naturally. For example, the germ causing the Black Death spread to humans from marmots on the Mongolian Plains and variants of influenza spread to us from domesticated pigs and ducks. So for this to be a danger society needs to have advanced to the stage of domesticating animals and have a sufficiently dense population for the disease to spread. The animal hosts able to spread diseases to us seem to have been concentrated in Africa and Eurasia. In previously isolated populations in the Americas that had never been exposed to Old World germs, the effect of contact with Europeans carrying viruses for colds and smallpox were catastrophic [Diamond and Ordunio, 1997]. Whole populations collapsed in the face of the new disease pressure.

But collapses due to plagues are episodic catastrophes. The more pressing and permanent barrier to population growth is food. The human ability to expand its population in the absence of food constraints is huge. Dickeman examined different estimates of this from populations that settled on previously uninhabited islands and came up with the figure that population numbers could triple every thirty years [Dickeman, 1975]. These were agricultural subsistence populations settling on islands with already developed agricultural techniques and crop varieties, but they indicate just how fast population growth can be. If populations generally do not grow at that rate it is often because they have in some way reached the carrying capacity of the environment, given the technology they have at the time. Lower food availability increases mortality and induces people to take steps to limit their population. So the production of food is the most urgent, and thus in the short term the most important production process.

(In the following chapter we will be looking at the main historical developments in food production and the implications this has had for the general economic structure of society.)

After food our primary need is clothing. We are a tropical species that has migrated across all the climatic zones on the planet. Lacking normal mammalian fur, our penetration of these zones has been dependent on an ability to manufacture a substitute in the form of clothes. The importance of keeping warm is so great that humans have been willing to devote huge effort to it. The manufacture of thread and cloth were, for millennia, the single most labor-intensive activity carried out by human economies [Barber, 1991]. Transformations in cloth-making technique—the invention of power spinning and weaving—were fundamental to the establishment of modern capitalist society.

There is no activity, no transformation of nature without an energy source. Muscles provided our first motors, and food our first energy supply. But next came fire. The use of tools is not specifically human, nor even the learned use of tools. Other primates and even birds can do this. But the manipulation and use of fire is unique to our species. For warmth, for cooking, for light and for defense it has been with us for at least 400,000 years [James et al., 1989; Roebroeks and Villa, 2011], with some suggestions that it could be even earlier than that. Whatever the date of its earliest use, fire allows access to food resources that would otherwise be indigestible. It allows people to live in climates that are below freezing for part of the year. It allows materials to be processed: initially just hardening of wooden tools, but later ceramics, metals, glass, and other chemical processes driven by heat.

Thus the acquisition of fuel has, for hundreds of thousands of years, been a significant absorber of human effort. Firewood or animal dung had to be collected at first. Later it became possible to mine fossil fuel resources. This continues to be a major part of our own economic activity.

After fire came the harnessing of energy in general: the muscles of draft animals, wind in sails and then windmills, the power of falling water, and now energy from atoms or the sun. The quantity of energy under human control determines the scale of our transformation of nature and the productivity of our daily efforts. By monopolizing energy sources individuals, companies, and states have been able to dominate others.

We have kept warm using fire and clothing, but to stay dry and shaded we needed shelter. This involved construction and maintenance of houses and the hard work which goes along with that. Once people have permanent houses, housework in the sense of day-to-day cleaning and maintenance follows. If you live on the move this is not necessary, but settled accommodation forces you to tidy things, remove and dispose of waste, and transport fuel and water into the house. Houses can take several person years of work to build. If these are built up over one or more generations, then the existence of houses must be supported by appropriate social relations. These can involve communal effort like the longhouses of the Iroquois or the Iban of Borneo, which implies a social system based on clans [Loeb and Broek, 1947]. If houses are smaller and settlements are organized on a territorial rather than a lineage basis, every family has its own house, which it maintains. Once cities arise, the time cost of building houses, which are often multistory, means that ownership passes out of the hands of families. Instead a landlord class or later the banks or the state effectively own the dwellings. The mass of the population is then subjected to the need to pay rent to the ultimate owners of their houses.

Housing is one way of modifying the environment: locally. But as human society has advanced it has changed much more of the environment. It has restructured the ecosystems within which people live, replacing wild animals with domestic ones, forests with fields, redirecting water flows, and changing the composition of the atmosphere. These changes in their turn have an impact on the social system we live in.

Any economy depends on information. Information is required for physical production and for the coordination of the economy. At the level of production, information is required about how to make things. Once a new skill or invention is known, the information can pass rapidly, changing the whole way people do things. This is information that is passed between people by example, word of mouth, and later in written texts. Information is also required to *in-form*, that is, give form to things. The information for a building can preexist as an architect's diagram. The information for a book can preexist as an original manuscript. The information for a car can preexist in the shapes of the dies, and the tapes of the machine tools on the production line. To such different stages of the embodiment of information there correspond different stages in the division and subordination of labor. At the economy-wide level, information is required to coordinate production: quipu records of the Inca, tax records written on clay, commercial correspondence on paper, information encoded in prices and in purses. All these will feature in our analysis of different social forms of production.

The problem of how processes come to take on a stable recurrent form is widespread in science. It has been of particular concern to biologists and biochemists working on the origins of life. They have to explain how, contra the apparent preference of thermodynamic laws for maximal disorder, we see highly ordered structures, including ourselves. Both Dawkins [2004] and Kauffman [1993] have made useful contributions to how we can conceptualize the stability of orderly processes. The basic argument they develop is that features stabilize if their existence at one time increases their probability of existence at a future moment. But this probability is a conditional probability, conditional on the features being situated in what Kauffman calls "autocatalytic networks." These are networks initially conceptualized in terms of polymer synthesis [Farmer et al., 1986], each of whose components, when present, increases the probability of the whole network persisting. A flame or a cell is such an autocatalytic network. A cell is a polymer collection: enzymes, lipids, and nucleic acids which, in the presence of an external energy source, will maintain itself and perhaps grow. The different enzymes work together to synthesize one another. Current cells depend on DNA, but at a much earlier epoch more primitive self-sustaining networks must have existed from which cells evolved. These networks, in the absence of the directing influence of DNA, would have relied purely on enzymatic feedback.

These concepts are applicable to modes of production and in particular to those, like capitalism, that develop without a definite directing influence. We will use these concepts either implicitly or explicitly in our analysis of the different historical modes of production and the social forms to which these give rise.

CHAPTER 2

Pre-Class Economy

The founder of Enlightenment political economy, Adam Smith, said that human social development went through the states of Nations of Hunters, Nations of Herdsmen, and Nations of Farmers [Meek et al., 1978]. This last category represents the civilized world of the eighteenth century when all civilized nations were still, in the majority of their population, farmers.

Although presented as an ascending sequence, and thus a series of stages, these social forms could, and indeed did, coexist in different areas of the world. The key thing about this materialist method in history was to seek the explanation for social institutions in the methods by which societies produced their needs.

This view of economic history was given an initial short summary by Marx[8] and was refined by him and Engels [Marx and Engels, 1976; Marx and Engels, 1977; Engels and Hunt, 2010] into a more elaborate set of forms of society: savagery (Smith's Nations of Hunters), barbarism, slave society, feudalism, simple commodity production, and capitalism, which were presented as a historical sequence.

The approach we take here broadly follows those of Smith and Engels updated in the light of historical experience and historical work published since their days.

It is important to note that though these forms of society have an order in terms of their earliest historical appearance, at any given time there can be several of these different forms coexisting. These forms will be interacting on a world scale, and at times even within one country. For example, the United States in the 1850s combined slavery, small-scale commodity production, and capitalist industry within a single country, something that turned out to be a highly explosive combination.

We will in this and the next few chapters give a short run-through of the characteristic combinations of technology and social relations of production in the main hitherto existing types of society: hunting-gathering bands, nomad tribes, early agricultural communities, slave economies, landlord economies, capitalist economies, and industrial socialist economies. We will look in much more detail at the economic structure of capitalist and socialist economies as these are most relevant to the twenty-first century. The earlier forms provide a degree of historical perspective on the more recent ones.

2.1 AGRICULTURE

The biggest revolutionary step in human development is the one that separates hunting and gathering from all subsequent forms, since the development of agriculture and animal husbandry involves humanity descending to a lower trophic level. For any ecosystem on the surface of the world, the primary energy source is sunlight. Primary producers—plants and algae—capture sunlight and use it to fix CO_2 to produce sugars and other carbohydrates. Living organisms also require fixed nitrogen to manufacture the proteins from which all enzymes and most animal tissues are made. This fixed nitrogen comes, in natural environments, primarily from specialized bacteria, some of which are symbiotic with plants. Carbohydrates and proteins made by plants constitute the base of the ecosystem, the lowest trophic level. It is at this base level that the greatest flow of organic material takes place. The organisms at this level are termed autotrophs or self-feeding.

Above this level come the heterotrophs, organisms that feed on others. Animals, fungi, and decomposition bacteria are heterotrophs. Feeding is an inefficient process. Only about a tenth of the chemical energy in food is converted into building up an animal's own body. So if plants are trophic level 1, herbivorous animals are trophic level 2, and carnivores that eat these herbivores are trophic level 3. In marine environments there may be several more trophic levels: zooplankton eating phytoplankton, being eaten by fish, being eaten by seals, which in turn are eaten by bears and people.

A hunting-gathering population lives in upper trophic levels: 3 or above. They may gather some plant food where climate permits, but the human digestive system restricts what plants they can eat. In a natural ecosystem only a small part of the plant biomass can be eaten: primarily fruit and tubers. Many tubers are indigestible unless cooked, so the harnessing of fire must have been a key technological step in expanding food resources. A population of hunters also has to compete with other apex predators like wolves and bears for the available game, so only a portion of the biological resources at the apex is captured by humans.

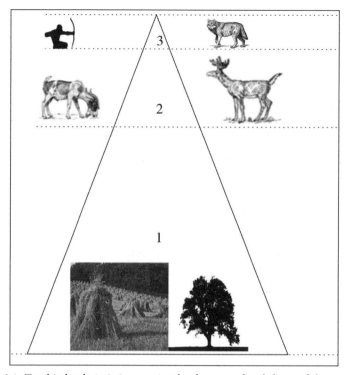

Figure 2.1. Trophic levels 1, 2, 3 as a triangle; the area of each layer of the triangle is proportional to the biomass that trophic level can support.

The penalty for living at a high trophic level is that only a low population density can be supported. This in turn constrains the size and complexity of social groups. Hunting populations can settle down and build small settlements if they happen to live somewhere abundant in fishing resources or at the edge of lakes to which game must come to drink. But the settlement sizes cannot be as big as can be supported by agricultural societies.

We are not in a position to say much about the social relations of Stone Age hunting societies but more recent hunting and gathering societies in Africa have been studied in detail by anthropologists. Woodburn [1982] argues that while hunting and gathering societies are not all egalitarian, all egalitarian societies studied have been hunting and gathering ones.

For a hunting and gathering society to be egalitarian, he argues, nomadism is essential. They must be what he calls "immediate return societies" in which people go out hunting and gathering and eat the food they produce the same day. There is an absence of non-portable products of labor that produce a return only after a significant delay, such as boats, weirs, stockades, pit-traps. There is an absence of stores of food in buildings. There is no dependence on edible wild plants that have been tended by selectively removing competitors. There are are no assets in the form of women held by men and exchanged by marriage systems. In egalitarian hunting and gathering societies people can and do move between different nomadic groups at will, undermining the establishment of authority structures. But this happens more for men than women. In general, the principle of matrilocality holds for women. They stay with their mothers. Genetic study of hunting-gathering societies bear this out showing that the Y chromosome linked variations are much more geographically dispersed than mitochondrial ones [Destro-Bisol et al., 2004]. Since the former are inherited in the male line and the latter in the female line, this indicates a long prehistory of matrilocality. The evolutionary advantages of the matrilocal family are clear—the mother is likely to have the help of a grandmother in bringing up children [O'Connell et al., 1999]. Given the very long time it takes humans to grow up, this is likely to have been a decisive advantage.

Hunting societies also have a universal access to means of violence. Weapons for hunting animals can easily kill people. Any man attempting to dominate another can reasonably fear secret ambush and murder in return.

There is also a universal access to food—up to the effects of a sexual division of labor. Any man can go off and hunt by themself and feed himself if he wishes. Of course in practice people share food, but they are not constrained to do so. A man will expect to be able to feed himself off berries and game when out hunting. A woman will eat most of what she gathers on the spot, only food surplus to personal need is exchanged between the sexes. This personal independence prevents the buildup of authority—including intergenerational authority. As soon as they are physically able, young persons can hunt or gather by themselves. Fathers have no control over stored food, cattle, etc., with which to exert authority over their children.

Sharing is widespread. When an animal too big for one person to eat is killed, it is divided among the band. There may be protocols in which somebody other than the hunter dismembers the carcass and distributes the pieces. These protocols mean that a particularly good hunter will end up contributing more meat than he himself gets from others. Further distribution of goods occurs via gambling. Woodburn notes that among the Hadza he studied men spent far more time gambling than they did hunting. Certain basic goods were excluded from gambling, such as bows and wooden arrows. These are enough for a person to survive. But slightly rarer tools like poison arrows were gambled in games of chance. This prevents any substantial and lasting buildup of possessions.

Combined, these characteristics prevent the formation of relationships of private property as a means of exerting social domination.

Modern authorities are of the opinion that the number of hours a day

TABLE 2.1: Time Allocation among Hadza Hunters and Gatherers (hours per week)

	Food Aquisition ex-Domus	Food Processing Domestic	Domestic Maintenance	Domestic Mfg. and Repair	Total
Female (weaned–5)	3.01	12.01	2.35	0.87	18.24
Female (6–13)	18.26	10.46	5.80	1.97	36.49
Female (14–marriageable)	27.76	6.96	7.17	4.05	42.49
Childbearing aged Women	27.58	8.16	2.91	6.23	44.88
Post-menopausal Women	36.80	6.91	2.47	3.53	49.71
Male (weaned–5)	9.05	10.17	2.94	1.44	23.60
Male (6–13)	29.91	8.37	2.60	2.09	42.97
Male (14–marriageable)	44.41	4.05	2.86	2.33	53.65
Adult Men	28.94	4.19	3.22	7.99	44.34

Source: Hawkes et al., 1997..

TABLE 2.2: Time Spent by Nepalese Women (hours per day)

	Conventional Economic Activity	Subsistance Domestic Tasks	Other Domestic	Child Care	Total
Bargsonle	3.64	1.38	3.22	0.56	8.80
Lohuorung Rei	4.99	3.20	4.05	0.14	12.38
Xham Magar	4.93	1.73	1.59	0.78	9.03
Tamang	5.80	1.17	1.46	0.03	8.46
Parbatiya	5.51	1.71	4.37	0.91	12.50
Wewar	2.42	2.50	3.14	1.27	9.33
Tharu	3.39	2.51	2.83	1.88	10.61
Maithili	2.39	2.02	4.35	1.25	9.98
Average	4.13	2.0275	3.12	0.8525	10.13

If comparing with table 2.1, note that these figures need to be multiplied by 7. Source: Levine, 1988.

that hunters and gatherers had to work was less than in the agricultural society that followed.

A good case can be made that hunters and gatherers work less than we do; and, rather than continuous travail, the food quest is intermittent, leisure abundant, and there is a greater amount of sleep in the day-time per capita per year. The average length of time per person per day put into the appropriation and preparation of food was four or five hours. Moreover, they do not work continuously. The subsistence quest was highly intermittent. It would stop for the time being when the people had procured enough food, which left them plenty of time to spare. [Sahlins, 1998]

Among the Dobe bushmen Sahlins reports that the average working day was even shorter: between two and three hours obtaining food. A woman would gather enough food for three days with one day of foraging. On non-foraging days, food preparation routines took between one and three hours. So given that people in hunting and gathering society could easily survive on a short working day, the problem is to explain why agriculture was ever adopted.

Considering that cultivation techniques are time-costly, meaning that hunters and gatherers, contrary to common belief, worked less than early farmers, and that the transition to agriculture involved little or no increase in standards of living, the reluctance to take up farming is hardly surprising. [Weisdorf, 2003]

The figures given by Hawkes et al. for the Hadza are rather more than Sahlins estimates for the Dobe. These would imply a maximum of 42 hours work a week, with the implication that the average was substantially less. Table 2.1 shows that the minimum spent by any over-14 group was 42 hours a week, and that for young men and grandmothers the total was around 50. Nonetheless this is still less than women in some agricultural societies expend (table 2.2). Reviewing a wide range of sources Cohen [1977] concludes that in terms of calorie output per labor hour expended, hunting and agriculture are broadly comparable.

The last hunting and gathering period in Eurasia is referred to as the Mesolithic or Middle Stone Age. The process of transition to agricultural society has been referred to as the Neolithic Revolution.

PERIOD	ECONOMY	WHEN
Paleolithic	Nomadic hunting	*from* 2.5 million BC
Mesolithic	Sedentary hunting, fishing	*from* 12,000 BC
Neolithic	Agriculture and herding	*from* 8,000 BC

The technology complex available to Mesolithic people can be character-ized by:

- Wood, bone, stone tools
- Fire
- Cords, nets
- Needles, leather implements and garments
- Building of small temporary and permanent shelters of wood, skin, or wattle and daub
- Log and other boats

This technology complex induced the division of labor shown in table 2.3. The Mesolithic appears to have been a transition stage between a nomadic hunting and gathering society and a settled agricultural one, During the Mesolithic fixed communities established themselves in areas particularly rich in game or fish. Long-lived means of production like boats came to be built. According to Woodburn this type of hunting and gathering society is no longer as egalitarian as the purely nomadic type. We do not yet get the formation of social classes but we do get inequalities between men and women and between parents and offspring. The habit of living in settled communities may well have aided the process of transition to agriculture. People living in one place could repeatedly harvest the same wild grains and learn to improve their yield by selectively removing competing plants. Dried grain will keep, so the habit of keeping seeds instead of eating them immediately would prepare people for the discipline that farmers need in order to refrain from eating their seed grain.

For grain to be harvestable it must have ears that remain intact after the seeds have ripened. Wild grasses tend to drop their seeds as soon as they mature. If this happens they will fall to the ground when one tries to cut them, making gathering appreciably more difficult. Once people sow seeds

TABLE 2.3: Division of Labor in Mesolithic Levant and Anatolia

Reproductive Work	Bearing babies, feeding infants, feeding post weaning, language instruction, etc.
Production of Tools	Bone working, cord making, net making, flint, obsidian work, wood working.
Shelter	Building wood-and-daub or wood-and-skin shelters, leather working for clothes.
Transport	Carrying flint/obsidian, water carrying in skins, transporting gathered vegetable foods and meat, gathering fuel, by hand or in leather bags or nets.
Obtaining Food	Hunting, fishing, collecting nuts, tubers, wild grains, wild olives.
Food Preparation	Grinding seeds and tubers, roasting.

Source: Düring, 2010.

deliberately, keeping seeds on the ear actually becomes a survival trait in grain. Humans would selectively harvest the whole ears and keep seeds safe until they were re-sown. What had once been a harmful mutation was now favored.

But since the work of an agricultural population seems harder than that of hunters, we have to ask, why did people go to the trouble?

It is not a matter of discovery. Cohen argues that the principles of domestication were well understood.[9] All hunter-gatherer people seem to know that plants come from seeds. The problem is providing a motivation to bother with seeds.

One theory is that of Weisdorf [2003], who argued that it was the rise of non–food-producing specialists that made it worth shifting to agriculture. His argument was that it takes time to learn new skills. It might not be worth working longer to get food when food may be more easily had by hunting, but it may be worth working longer to get clothes, shoes, or tools made by skilled workers. This, he argued, provided the incentive to shift to an agricultural economy in which a farming majority could support a minority of skilled craftspeople. But this sort of argument is in danger of of assuming what it wants to prove. The population of specialized workers depended on an agricultural surplus to support them. But if these did not already exist, then how would people gain a taste for the things that workers were to make?

It also assumes that hunting and gathering people would see having more durable goods as more important than the loss of freedom associated with settling down, but observation of such peoples does not seem to bear this out.

If these specialists already existed in the Mesolithic, that would allow a taste for their goods to be acquired, but it would imply that it had been possible for a hunting and gathering population to support them. If hunting and gathering enabled food to be obtained at less effort, then it would actually have been easier to support the specialists by sticking to hunting rather than swapping to agriculture. If hunting and gathering had worked for a million years, why suddenly change to an entirely different mode of life?

Until 10,000 years ago everyone lived off wild foods. By 2,000 years ago the majority of the world population lived off agriculture. In 8,000 years, on four continental landmasses, people switched to crops. Only in Australia, which arguably lacked appropriate wild precursors of grains,[10] did agriculture not develop.

The remarkable thing is not only that agriculture developed so quickly, but that it developed independently, with different crop plants in so many different places. The transition started a short time, in geological terms at least, after

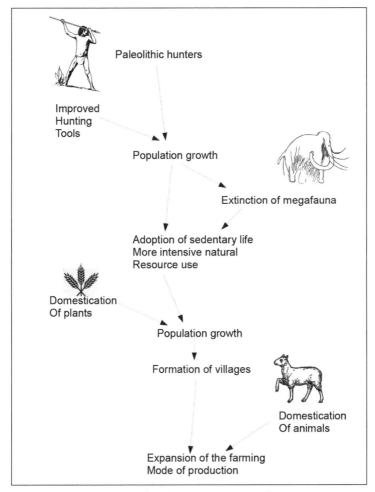

Figure 2.2. Transition from hunting economy to farming economy.

the end of the last Ice Age. That naturally leads people to suspect that climate change may have had something to do with it. But there have been several Ice Ages and interglacials since humans evolved. Why did this last one trigger agriculture around the world, whereas previous ones did not?

An alternative theory puts the change down to population pressure [Cohen, 1977]. The argument is that the key thing about agriculture is that it allows more people to be supported per square kilometer, a consequence of moving down a trophic level, and also a consequence of ensuring that the food crops dominate all other plant life in the cultivated area. The argument is that due to improvements in hunting technology the population had grown to the point where it was beyond the carrying capacity of the ecosystem in terms of game available. The resulting food shortages gave people the incentive to take advantage of the opportunity to deliberately grow previously wild plants. In the process they set themselves on the path to a mode of production that was on the one hand more labor intensive than hunting, but on the other more productive in terms of output per square kilometer. This step to agriculture allowed further population growth that blocked forever the possibility of a generalized reversion to a hunting mode of life. There is considerable evidence that hunting and gathering populations were responsible for the extinction of large prey animals in many parts of the world, especially where hunters entered new areas that until then had been unpopulated by humans [Mosimann and Martin, 1975; Burney and Flannery, 2005]. This seems to have occurred first in Australia about 45,000 years ago and then in the Americas 12,000 years ago. After the Clovis people arrived in North America from Siberia with their advanced stone spears, they seem to have swept through the Americas like a blitzkrieg wiping out the large prey animals as they went [Harris, 1991]. Northern Eurasian extinction of megafauna took longer but ended about the same time as in the Americas. The extinction of these, outside of Australia, may have prompted the move to a more sedentary Mesolithic mode of life based on a more intensive harvesting of the remaining wild resources. The removal of the possibility to relieve population pressure by migrating into as yet unoccupied territory could further intensify the incentive to develop new food sources. In this view it is the overexploitation of existing resources relative to the size of population that drove change in the mode of production.

Once the transition to raising crops and later to domesticating animals had taken place the population density rose enough to allow the formation of large villages or small towns, though the design of such early settlements as Askl Hồyuk (8500 BC) or Çatalhồyuk(7500 BC–6000 BC) in what is now Turkey was very unlike towns and villages we are now familiar with. Neighborhoods consisted of buildings packed so close together that there were no passageways or roads between them and the houses had no doors, access to them apparently being via flat roofs with ladders down into the rooms [Düring, 2010], as shown in figure 2.3. The settlements appear to have been egalitarian with no obvious distinction between sizes of dwellings and no evidence of temples. The settlements were also unfortified.

The people still used stone tools, and at the earlier stages lacked pottery, though this was acquired in the later Neolithic Period. Subsistence was based on a mixture of domesticated and collected wild plants. Wild sheep were initially herded but by the time of Çatalhồyuk they appear to be domesticated. In addition, cattle and horses were eaten, though these still seem to be wild varieties. Although fewer cattle than sheep were eaten, each cow provides as much meat as thirty sheep, so cattle probably provided more of the meat.

Figure 2.3. Reconstruction of the interior of a house at Çatalhöyuk.

The primitive division of labor is a sexual one, with women gathering plants and preparing vegetable foods, which probably provided the majority of the calories [Mies, 1981] and men catching animals. Artistic evidence indicates that Çatalhöyuk had a similar division of labor.

It is not clear whether in the transition to agriculture Neolithic communities became matriarchies, though they may well have been. This idea was lent credence by some of the artwork excavated at Çatalhöyuk (figure 2.4). These, and the Paleolithic predecessors, are normally referred to as goddess figures, but one should be careful about interpreting them in a language drawn from a much later date. The excavations at Çatalhöyuk have also yielded a plethora of phallic sculptures, so representations of both sexes are present. It is a moot point whether to call archaeological finds like these religious images, erotic images, or sex toys. It is even more risky to come

Figure 2.4. Paleolithic (left) and Neolithic (right) female figures The example on the right was excavated at Çatalhöyuk.

to conclusions about the dominance of one sex or the other on the basis of them. More recent excavations have been interpreted as showing that in Çatalhöyuk there was rough equality between the sexes—equal prominence to both sexes in ceremonial burials, similar diet,[11] and patterns of bone wear and tear are cited as evidence for this. Deposits of soot, inhaled during life, are found equally in male and female skeletons implying that both sexes did similar amounts of work in house and outside. In light of the data overall, Hodder [2004] concludes that there is no evidence for either patriarchy or matriarchy. However, as Ryan and Jethá [2010] point out, anthropologists and archaeologists are not necessarily that good at recognizing matriarchies, being wont to see them as simple inversions of patriarchies. There also seems to have been no judicial system. The burials show no evidence of anyone having died from violence, and there are no depictions of tribunals, executions, or punishments in the art of the town.

The Neolithic Revolution led to a long period of comparatively egalitarian social development. If we date the start of agriculture to about 11,000 years ago, then around half the time since then was taken up by the expansion of classless agrarian societies. According to the influential archaeologist Lord Renfrew, the invention of agriculture in Anatolia had a profound effect on languages now spoken across Europe, Australasia, and the Americas [Renfrew, 1989]. The main European, Iranian, and North Indian languages have long been known to have a common ancestor—referred to as Proto Indo-European. This was established by studies of the similarities in vocabularies between current and historical versions of the languages spoken in these areas (figure 2.5).

Renfrew realized that this pattern of languages was consistent with a spread of population out of Anatolia following the invention of farming. Farming can support a larger population per unit area than hunting can, so a farming people will tend to expand at the expense of their hunting neighbors. Not only do they have more food, but having settled down their birth rate rises. A nomadic woman who has to carry her children will not have another until the last one can walk and keep up. A settled life removes this problem while making available animal milk and gruels as baby food, shortening lactation and the return of fertility.

As farming populations grew and spread beyond their original homeland they took their languages with them. The current distribution of languages is the result of thousands of years of migrations that have partially erased the original Neolithic focus of the language spread. Anatolia, within recent history, was settled by Turkic speakers who displaced the original population. But detailed study of how the various languages have changed over time indicates that they started to diverge 8,700 years ago, which is consistent

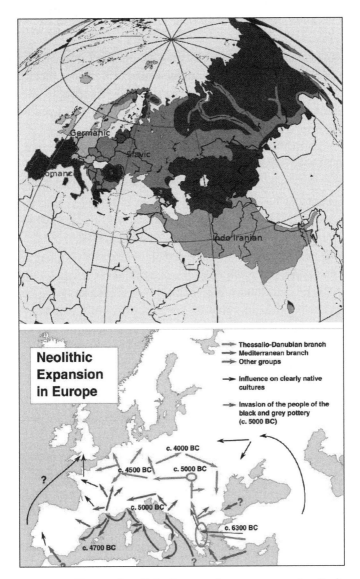

Figure 2.5. Areas in Eurasia where Indo-European languages are spoken (top); suggested population expansion from Anatolia (bottom).

with the idea that the spread of the languages coincided with the Neolithic Revolution in Anatolia [Gray and Atkinson, 2003; Bouckaert et al., 2012].

According to Renfrew, this was not an isolated occurrence. Similar population expansion and associated language spreads happened at other places where agriculture was invented [Renfrew, 1994]: in China and with the spread of the Bantu languages from a locus of plant domestication in West Africa.

2.2 REPRODUCTION

A classless agricultural society can be divided into three groups: adults who are direct producers, children who in due course will replace them, and the elders and infirm unable to do the hard work of growing food. In this section we shall derive a simple economic model of production and reproduction in such a society.[12]

We will use the symbol A to stand for the fraction of the population in their years of adult working life, C the fraction of years spent as a dependent child, and E the fraction of years a person spends as an elder. Suppose a person is able to do heavy agricultural work from 18 and at 60 is too old to continue, and that if they reach 60 they are likely to die at 65. This would imply C = [18/65] = 27.7%, A = [42/65] = 64.6%, E= [5/65] =7.7%.

This is shown as the first estimate in table 2.4, but that ignores the effect of infant mortality. A large part of those born never reached adulthood. Suppose half the babies born die in childhood at an average age of 5, but afterward childhood death rates are low. The effect of this is that at birth a child has the prospect of only 11.5 years of childhood, 21 years of adult life, and 2.5 years as an elder, to give a life expectancy of 35 years (figure 2.4). The net effect of high infant mortality is that the fraction of the whole population who are productive is lower than would otherwise be the case.[13]

Suppose that in a year an adult consumes α calories and a child consumes β, then the annual food consumption F by a community of n people will be: $F = n((A+E)\alpha+ C\beta)$.

Now let us assume that an adult worker can produce p calories per year in the form of crops. So the community food output will be nAp. Clearly, in order for the community to survive the amount of food grown must on average exceed what is eaten. It must exceed it since they will have to set aside stores to make allowance for bad harvests. A community that ate its entire harvest each year will run short and experience high mortality with the first bad harvest that arrives. But storage of grain is unreliable. Pests eat part of what is stored, so the granaries have to be constantly replenished. If we assume that the community keeps 1/f a year of grain in reserve and that a fraction of this w is wasted each year the food requirement will be $F((1+[w/f])$.

The base productivity condition that has to be met for a community to simply survive is pb $\geq ((A+E)\alpha+ C\beta)(1+w/f)/A$.

Let us take some figures for this. As a basis we take UN figures [Tontisirin and de Haen, 2004] for food requirements of people doing moderately strenuous work. These are given separately for men and women and depend on their weights. If we take average weights of men as 68kg and women as 60kg

TABLE 2.4: Effect of High Infant Mortality on Average Productive Life

Category	Children (C)	Working Adults (A)	Elders (E)	Life
Start Year	0	18	60	-
Finish Year	18	60	65	-
First Estimate Years	18	42	5	65
Births	100%	-	-	-
Child Death Rate	50%	-	-	-
Average Child Death Rate	5.0	-	-	-
Survivors	50%	50%	50%	-
Average Years in Category	11.5	21	2.5	35
Population Fraction	32.9%	60%	7.1%	-

[Igiri et al., 2009], we get an average α = 922,000kcal per year for adults, and for children an average of β = 600,000kcal per year.

Using the values of A, C, E from table 2.4, and the assumption that the famine reserve is half a year's harvest, a quarter of which spoils each year, implies that an adult peasant in subsistence farming had to have a calorie production of around 1.5 million kcals per year.[14]

In addition to having a minimum food production rate per adult worker, simple social reproduction required a minimum effective fertility rate. The example so far has assumed a replacement level fertility rate of 4 children per woman and a 50 percent rate of child mortality. If the level of child mortality was higher, say 55 percent, then a fertility level of 4.4 would be needed. The rule is that the replacement fertility FR is defined by $FR=2/(1-DC)$ where DC is the child death rate.

For the population to expand the actual level of fertility must be above the replacement rate. This can come about either by the number of births per woman rising or by child mortality declining. Deaths in childhood are very sensitive to the supply of food, so an improvement in agricultural productivity can allow better-fed, healthier children more likely to survive to adulthood. But from the standpoint of simple survival, any increase in production beyond the basic reproduction threshold constitutes a surplus. The obverse of this is that any system of class exploitation that confiscates this surplus tends to raise infant mortality and prevent population growth.

Agriculture introduces, for the first time, a dependence of present labor on past labor. Hunters cannot long preserve their catch, so production is directed at immediate needs. Agriculture is, in most places, tied to an annual cycle. Over and above the need to maintain a buffer stock of grain to cover a bad harvest, even normal production depends on storage. Autumn grain must be stored for next year's seed and to feed next year's workers. Those working on planting in the spring are fed by grain harvested the previous year. This creates a dependence of those now working on those who worked before. This temporal dependence first appears as a dependence on the elders, those who came before and harvested before. It later becomes the basis for exploitation by employers or lenders. The elders control the grain that feeds the young and in turn take possession of this year's harvest.

Social relations of production overlap with, and are perceived as, relations of descent and later of patronage. In terms of ritual we can observe, with Neolithic agriculture, the rise of ancestor cults. Elaborate burial mounds are constructed and become lasting memorials. The dependence of the present generation on the past one, a real relation of production, gets projected into the world of myth. The annual real honoring of the father and mother, the handing over the harvest, becomes the basis for sacrificial offerings, first to the ancestors, and later to more abstract divine parents. Relations of filiation become the organizing principle of clan society, of nested circles of relationship out of which hierarchies of clan leadership and ultimately of kingship can grow.

2.3 CLASS FORMATION

Termite society, like all insect societies of which we are aware, is classless. On an evolutionary timescale class society does seem to be selected against. But on the shorter timescale of human civilization it is prevalent. As far as we can make out, the early Neolithic towns like Çatalhöyuk were also egalitarian. There seems to have been a delay of thousands of years between the development of farming 11,000 years ago and the rise of class-based states about 5,000 years ago. This period saw the expansion of agricultural populations from the original centers of domestication across Europe, India, China, et al. By our previous argument that expansion would have been dependent on an appreciable food surplus devoted to extra children. The consumption of a food surplus by an exploiting class would have inhibited the population spread.

Though a precondition for class is a food surplus, this is not enough. A food surplus could go to simply extend the division of labor, allowing some people to specialize in non-agricultural work: potters or smiths. A society with farmers, smiths, and potters is not, as such, a class society, even if the trades become hereditary, since the relationship among the trades is one of equals. There would be no exploitation involved.

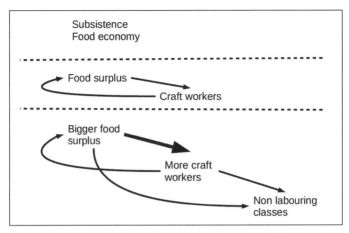

Figure 2.6. Precondition stages for the formation of classes.

Class formation requires that at least part of the food surplus goes to support a group of people that no longer engages in physical production. And this non-productive status has to extend over generations. In any society, infants are non-productive, but that does not make babies a class. For a non-productive class to exist there must be people who spend the greater part of their life as non-producers, and their children in turn must be likely to have the same status.

But of course the upper class in society tends to consume more than food. They typically have a disproportionate share of other goods, clothes, jewelry, utensils, ornaments, etc. So the surplus they depend on cannot simply be a food surplus. A food surplus is the precondition. Without it there would be no food for the craftspeople producing the items of display and ostentation. An upper class implies a more general surplus. If only enough cloth is produced to clothe the working population rulers go naked. Emperors with clothes imply a cloth surplus, and shodden kings a leather surplus.

A surplus of food is initially required for population growth, next for a specialized division of labor. If smiths are to spend most of their time making bronze tools, they have little time left for growing their own food. But this surplus need not come about by an actual increase in food production. If in a community of 50 one person becomes a smith and another his assistant, no more food is required than if all 50 were engaged in farming. But it does require the 48 who remain farming to either work a bit harder or to become more productive. In the case of bronze or later iron smithing, the products include agricultural tools, initially axes and later digging tools, so a smaller group of agricultural workers equipped with metal tools would have been able to produce as much as a larger group with stone tools.

Gilman et al. [1981] argued that relatively few bronze agricultural tools have been found in European bronze age sites. But Wells [ibid.] argues that this is due to differential preservation, that bronze tools, unlike ornaments, are too useful to be buried in the grave sites that are the focus of excavations, and would have been melted back down if damaged. So there is some dispute among archaeologists as to whether the production of bronze agricultural tools actually contributed much to production.

Why is this relevant?

Because social stratification first becomes evident in the European archaeological record during the Bronze Age. Neolithic Europe, like Neolithic Anatolia, seems to have been relatively egalitarian. Relatively communal dwelling is indicated by longhouses, such as those excavated at Balbridie, similar to those used within recent history by communities known to be classless. In addition, during the Neolithic the custom was to have communal burials in barrows [Barclay, 1998]. Bodies were probably exposed to birds of prey [Hedges, 1984] in order to have the flesh removed before bones were transferred to the barrow. In the Bronze Age this shifts to individual burials with some large burial mounds having only one body. Associated with the bodies we now find ornaments, pottery, and weapons. Over the same period ceremonial sites of increasing complexity, including the famous stone rings, start to be built.

However, we have a problem with explaining the rise of class stratification as a direct result of rising productivity—whether bronze tools contributed or not. If bronze tools made it easier, why should the farmers have not simply worked less, or perhaps supported bronze smiths to make them bronze cooking pots, etc.?

The topic is more general than one specifically relating to the Bronze

Figure 2.7. Hoe agriculture today (left); Bronze Age hoe heads (right).
Source: Creative Commons, Cristian Chirita

Age, since we know that outside of Europe societies without bronze or iron became class societies. Why should a surplus have led to a class structure?

A class society requires a surplus, but the converse does not hold. A food surplus does not necessitate an exploiting class. Establishing that seems to have required other misfortunes: war, patriarchy, and religion.

2.4 WAR, PATRIARCHY, RELIGION, AND THE LAWS OF STATISTICS

For warfare to exist you need something to fight over. Whereas warfare in pure hunter-gatherer societies seems rare [Fry, 2007; Ryan and Jethá, 2012] it has been common in societies with either herding or at least some form of agriculture. It is clear that once cattle or other beasts are herded they can be stolen, and can be the object of a war party. But fighting is not limited to what Smith called Nations of Shepherds, formidable as these have been.[15] Nations and tribes that combine some hoe horticulture with hunting have been warlike. Why?

According to Meillassoux [1981] the motive for the conflict was the capture not of cattle but young women. Pure hunter-gatherer societies are nomadic, with no fixed villages, and mobility of people between wandering small bands. Agriculture ties people down. He argues that the initial form of family in the transition to agriculture is the matrilocal, which means a society in which adult women stay in their mother's home or community. Insofar as there is mobility between communities, it is the men who move, seeking wives in other communities.

In principle either sex can move. You can have a matrilocal system where women stay in their birthplace and the men move, or patrilocal communities where the reverse happens. Although these seem logically to be no more than mirror images, their economic effects are actually very different. The reproductive potential of a community is set by how many young women, rather than young men, it has. This has serious implications for relatively small communities, ones that are not yet able to fully support themselves through the whole year by agriculture. Such communities have to be small relative to their hinterland to prevent the exhaustion of the available game.[16] Within such small groups the laws of chance mean that the numbers of each sex coming of age will fluctuate.

Suppose that we have a small community in which each generation coming of age has on average 40 people. We would expect about half of these to be young women, but as figure 2.8 shows, the number of women could vary between 0 and 40. There is about a 30 percent percent chance that in a given generation there would be fewer than 18 women, a shortfall

of 4 women relative to men in their age group. This would presage a 10 percent fall in the population over the next generation. In smaller communities
the effect is more marked. A community of 8 families would end up with
fewer than 6 young women about 22 percent of the time. But a shortfall of 4
women in this small community implies a shrinkage of the population by a
quarter, which would threaten the future survival of the community, bearing
in mind that not all of these may be fertile, some may die young, etc.

In principle some of the young men could leave and try to join another
community with a surplus of women, but what often seems to have
happened, according to Meillassoux, is that the men raid neighboring communities and abduct young women. Given that the community still depends
partly on hunting, the men are skilled in the use of bows and arrows, and
these skills transfer readily from hunting to raiding.

This leads to endemic hostility and suspicion between communities.
Men acquire the social role of warrior both to abduct women from other
groups and to protect their own women. Such societies may remain matrilineal, with children being brought up in a relatively communal household
with their uncles playing what we would regard as a paternal role. There
may be no system of strict monogamy. But the beginnings of the collective
dominance of men over women exist. Men as hunters and warriors develop
ideologies that represent them as protectors and heroes and which justify
relegating women to what are presented as menial horticultural tasks. In
particular the abducted women, cut off from their own community, are
likely to be in a very subordinate position.

The combination of hunting with horticulture limits the size of settled
communities. Meillassoux claims that the precariousness of reproduction
leads to abductions and raiding. Hunters develop warrior attributes and
male dominance begins to develop. But this is collective rather than individual. There is not yet the figure of the patriarch, exercising exclusive control
over the sexuality of "his" women. The society may still approve of considerable sexual license, with various orgiastic rituals and very blurred ideas of
paternity [Beckerman and Valentine, 2002; Ryan and Jethá, 2010].

The basic contradiction associated with small matrilineal communities
could be solved

• by becoming more exclusively agricultural and piscatorial. While growing in size it is possible to form big matrilineal or even matriarchal
  communities that do not suffer from frequent random shortages of
  women of childbearing age.
• by moving toward a patrilineal and subsequently patriarchal form of
  family and clan.

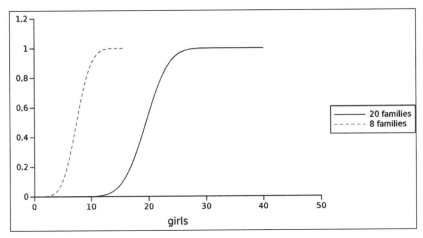

Figure 2.8. Expected number of women in the next generation of small communities where there are 8 or 20 families and each woman has two children surviving to adulthood. The form is a cumulative binomial distribution: $\Sigma_{k=0}^{n}\,[n!/(k!(n-k)!)]$.

The probability that a community with several hundred people will suffer serious random swings in its sex ratio is very low. Communities like the Neolithic towns of Anatolia would have been big enough, and sufficiently dependent on agriculture, to avoid the raiding and warrior culture that Meillassoux observed in the more recent tribes that combined hoe agriculture with hunting. Such societies would still have had potential problems within individual matrilineal households if there were no daughters. But this is not such a problem for a peaceful community. It could be dealt with by adoption of daughters from other families, as occurs among the modern matriarchal Mosuo [Stacey, 2009]. While we can only speculate as to whether this took place in Anatolia, it could account for what seems to have been a long period of peaceful development of these communities, without evidence of either stratification or gender inequality in the archaeological record.

What we do know is that later historical cultures with grain agriculture seem to have been predominantly patrilineal and patriarchal. Meillassoux gives a theoretical account of why this happens: The higher output of settled grain agriculture allows a denser population and at the same time makes the diversion of effort from growing things into fighting less attractive. Peaceful relations between adjacent small domestic communities allow the nonviolent exchange of young women to make up the deficits that would always occur by chance. Women moving to another community, where they lack maternal support, are likely to be assimilated to the status that was formerly held by female captives: subordinate to their mother-in-law and husband.

Once such transfers become more common, an increasing number of women are in a subordinate status which then generalizes to all brides being subject to the authority of the existing matriarch and the new husband. In the process the general authority of men over women rises.

> It is the procreative powers of a woman that are the subject of negotiation when she is taken into another group for a period generally held a priori to last as long as her fertility. An agreement is reached which decides the devolution of the woman's offspring since, due to the circumstances cited above, a woman does not procreate for her community of origin (the identity of the family which will benefit from her procreation must be made public while the claims of the other community are restricted) and also because, since the woman does not procreate for her own benefit, jurally constituted patrilineal filiation must replace self-evident maternal filiation. [Meillassoux, 1981, 43]

The exchanges between communities can become quite complex, involving debts over time: if 2 women go from community A to community B this year, then it is agreed that at some time in the future 2 other brides will come back in return. This makes daughters valuable in an exchange process that has some similarities with trade. The head of the family, perhaps initially a woman, more probably a man, views them as a resource that gives them power and influence. As such, the default assumption becomes that all daughters will take partners outside the community, and exogamy becomes general.

> Since marriage and social reproduction are the main reason for these external relations, marriage, in order to maintain the elder's authority, must be prohibited within the group so that nubile girls remain available as subjects of these transactions. Paradoxically, this restriction on marriage becomes increasingly necessary and rigorous in that the group, by expanding, could grow through endogamous intermarriage. When reproduction becomes statistically possible through the mating of members of the community, the power of the elders, rebuilt on matrimonial management, is threatened by the very effects of this management which makes expansion of the community possible. Thus political authority depends on a circumstance which it tends to abolish when it reinforces itself.
>
> The authority must, to be preserved, devise and develop a coercive and authoritarian ideology. Religion, magic ritual, and a terrorism

based on superstition is inflicted upon dependants, young people and above all on pubescent women; sexual prohibitions become absolute and punishments for transgression increase. Endogamy becomes incest, and sexual prohibition a taboo. [Meillassoux, 1981, 45]

Religion, magic, ritual, and terrorism based on superstition justified both patriarchy and class hierarchy. Watts et al. [2016] present convincing evidence that religion, specifically in the form of human sacrifice, was deeply implicated in the formation of stratified societies. The Watts study used as their data a large sample of 93 different Austronesian societies, which being island cultures were comparatively isolated.

Evidence of human sacrifice was observed in 40 of the 93 cultures sampled (43 percent). Human sacrifice was practiced in 5 of the 20 egalitarian societies (25 percent), 17 of the 46 moderately stratified societies (37 percent), and 18 of the 27 highly stratified societies (67 percent) sampled.

They then performed a Markov model simulation of the evolution of high stratification and human sacrifice superimposed on the phylogentic tree of the language evolution of the cultures, tracing the origins of stratification and the origins of human sacrifice. They concluded that human sacrifice enhances the probability of transition to a highly stratified state, and stabilizes such a state once it exists.

They conclude:

Human sacrifice legitimizes class-based power distinctions by combining displays of ultimate authority—the taking of a life— with supernatural justifications that sanctify authority as divinely ordained. . . .

Our results provide strong evidence for the claim that human sacrifice played a powerful role in the construction and maintenance of stratified societies. Though human sacrifice was practiced in the majority of highly stratified societies in our sample, it was scarce in egalitarian societies, and we find that its effect depended on the level of stratification. Specifically, human sacrifice substantially increased the chances of high social stratification arising and prevented the loss of social stratification once it had arisen, yet was not found to increase social stratification in egalitarian societies. This is consistent with historical accounts that speculate that in order for human sacrifice to be exploited by social elites, there must first be social elites to exploit it.

Ingham [1984] makes a similar argument using data from Aztec society. With war, patriarchy, religion and hierarchy in place, the scene was set for the emergence of slavery.

CHAPTER 3

Slave Economy

Among hunting and fishing societies slavery is little developed. Nieboer [1971] listed 88 examples of tribes of hunters and found that only 18 of these had slaves.[17] Slavery arises in clan society through war. Captives can be killed, ransomed, or put to work. But in clan societies without developed commodity production, the potential scale of the institution is limited by the consumption needs of the household holding the slave. This kind of tribal domestic slavery existed until recently in parts of Africa [Evans-Pritchard, 1940] and was in the past widespread. For slaves to be used on a large scale, for it to become the determining element of an economic system, the crops they produce must be sold and that in turn depends on several other things:

1. There must be a market of consumers[18] who are not able to grow their own food. Typically this implies an urban population.
2. There must be the means of transport to move the product from the farms to distant consumers.
3. There must be a market for slaves themselves.

Thus the establishment of a slave economy depends on a certain density of population, without which there are no towns; and a certain level of technology, particularly the technology of transport, without which there are no commodity markets.

3.1 TECHNOLOGY COMPLEX

Unaided human labor cannot transport large loads economically for long distances. For that you need non-human sources of power. Modern globalized capitalism rests on the power of the marine diesel and the high bandpass turbine [Smil, 2010]. Classical slavery depended on the Mediterranean square rig [Whitewright, 2007] and the ox cart.

The precondition of this distinctive feature of classical civilization was its coastal character. Graeco-Roman antiquity was quintessentially Mediterranean in its innermost structure [Anderson, 1996, 20].

Long-distance transport always depends on the sea. Overland, now as in the past, costs far more in energy to move heavy cargoes than water transport. Land transport by pack animals was limited to high-value products: salt, cloth, etc. Wheeled transport depends in turn on roads and is heavily constrained by the efficiency of the harnesses available. Ancient horse harnesses only allowed limited weights to be pulled without exerting a choking pressure on the horse's neck [Singer and Holmyard, 1956], so the yoked ox cart was the preferred goods vehicle in the classical Mediterranean civilizations. A person can only sustain a power output of between 50W and 90W when working, where a pair of oxen drawing a cart can deliver around 1000W [Smil, 2004].

High slave civilization had the wheel for transport; it also harnessed rotation for other purposes: the potter's wheel, the lathe, mechanical computers,[19] the screw press for olive oil production and, with the water

Figure 3.1. Hero's turbine, or *aeolipile*. Source: Jude, 1910.

Figure 3.2. Model of a Roman merchant vessel. The square rig may have been capable of adopting a lateen-style configuration by selective reefing. Photo:Wolfgang Sauber, Creative Commons.

wheel harnessed for the first time, an artificial source of rotary mechanical motion [Singer and Holmyard, 1956]. It knew the crank, contra claims by White [1964], and could build reciprocating machinery of a sophistication not achieved again until the nineteenth century. Although the Romans knew of a steam turbine or *aeolipile* and could make reciprocating pistons that were almost homomorphic to those in steam engines,[20] they had no powered land transport. Even on good roads the cart was only economically effective for shorter journeys. Longer heavier transport relied on water. Carts can transfer from farm to shore, but the overall viability of slave-based export industries, whether in the ancient economy or during the early modern renaissance of slave civilization around the Atlantic, depended on sea and sail.

Human energy, via oars, can propel a small ship at a cruising speed of 2 to 3 knots. But to achieve this the ship must be narrow and thus ill suited to carrying heavy cargo. A beamy, seaworthy cargo ship needs sail or engine power.

Sails were the first technology that could be used to harness inanimate power. The classical Mediterranean sailing vessels had single masts and were square-rigged. It was believed until recently that this would have limited them to sailing more or less directly before the wind. More recently it has been concluded that sailing to the windward was possible using the rig then available.[21] But the speeds attained beating to windward would be much slower. Casson [1951] provides tables of probable sailing times based on a combination of ancient textual accounts and modern data on prevailing winds. He suggests that while a voyage from Rome to Alexandria, with favorable westerlies, could be made in about 12 days, the return voyage, going against the wind, would have taken between 50 and 70 days.

By modern standards the ships would have been small. While ships of over 350 tons certainly existed, the great bulk would have been under 100 tons. Overall the size range would not have been dissimilar to those used in early modern Europe [Houston, 1988]. Sail continued to be the prime mover during the period of transatlantic slavery, though the ships used in the transatlantic trade up to the late 1700s tended to be twice as large as Houston estimates classical vessels to have been [Garland and Klein, 1985; North, 1968].

The slave economy of the Indian Ocean littoral between 1000 and 1900 also used sea transport, with fore-aft rigging. In this case, the seasonal shifts in the prevailing winds of the monsoon made sailing to windward less essential than in the Mediterranean [Heuman and Burnard, 2010]. The principal technical advances in shipping between the Mediterranean and Atlantic slave economies were:

- Improved navigational instruments, compass, astrolabe and later the sextant.
- Adoption of stouter keel and frame internal construction.
- Internal decks—particularly important for slave transport.
- Better rig, multiple masts, and more fore and aft sails, improved sailing to windward.

The slave economy of Arabia and the Indian Ocean is thought by some to have pioneered the fore and aft rig with what was called the lateen rig. The English term "mizzen," as in mizzenmast, arguably derives from the Arabic *mizan* meaning a balance. A lateen sail is triangular but hangs from a yard that looks like a balance, low at one end [Hourani and Carswell, 1995]. But Casson [1956] and Whitewright [2009] argue that there is evidence that the lateen sail was in use during the late Roman period. If that is the case, then a key technical step facilitating the long- distance trade required for the slave form of economy may, via the fifteenth-century Portuguese, have been transmitted from the classical to the early modern slave economies.

These advances were a precondition for the establishment of a slave economy of oceanic rather than Mediterranean scale.

Figure 3.3. The lateen rig. Source: Pearson Scott Foresman archive, released to public domain.

The operation of sailing ships necessarily tended to take a capitalist form. Not only were the ships expensive, necessitating partnership forms that presaged the joint stock company [Banaji, 2016], shipping was, in the pre-capitalist economies, the main instance of production by means of powered machines. The sailing ship used wind power to replace what would otherwise have required a large number of galley slaves. In this it shared one of the archetypal traits of capitalist industry—the replacement of human labor with powered devices. The anomaly of merchant capital existing in antiquity and the Middle Ages should be understood as arising from shipping being the first field to which such machines were applied. The profit of merchant capital should then be understood as a special early and precocious case of the production of relative surplus value (see section 5.4.9).

By using sail-power shippers in, say, first-century Italy could convert grapes for wine into Egyptian corn for sale in Italy such that the labor that would go into growing the grapes, plus the labor of shipping, was less than the labor that would be required to grow the same amount of corn in Italy. To the extent that the corn imported from Alexandria entered into the subsistence of slaves exploited in Italy, the cheapening of corn would have decreased the fraction of time that slaves had to work to produce their subsistence, increasing the number of hours a week that yielded an income for the slave owners. A portion of this increased surplus was then appropriated by the sea captains and shippers as monetary profit.

3.2 SCHEME OF REPRODUCTION

Slavery can dominate an economy even if slaves make up only a minority of the population. According to Finley [1980] slaves made up around a third of the population in the U.S. South, and similar proportions in Brazil, ancient Rome, and ancient Athens.[22] These were slave societies because slavery was the main source of exploitation and hence the main source of the economic surplus upon which the prosperity and political power of the ruling classes depended. Each great economic system is characterized by a distinct mechanism by which an economic surplus is extracted. This mechanism then structures the whole system of social reproduction. From it arise characteristic political struggles and forms of state.[23] From this standpoint, the crucial feature of slavery is that the slave is a person who is bought and sold and who is forced to perform labor for another.

This element of being bought on the market means that slave economies have, like capitalist ones, a relatively well-developed set of markets. Figure 3.4 outlines the essential market flows associated with the basic unit of slave production: the agricultural estate. The estate owner must lay out money for the purchase of slaves. Once bought the slaves are set to work. Some of the crops they raise are retained on the estate to feed the workforce. This portion of the crop does not enter the market. The surplus product of the estate does. Hence the viability of a slave estate depends on the surplus product being worth significantly more than the slaves bought to produce it. The existence of slaves on a market, whose value can be compared to the value of the crop they can be forced to grow, means that it is at times rational for the slave owner to work them to death.

While countries depended for the supply of servile labor on the natural increase of their own slave population, there existed an obvious limit to the range of the system and the hardships it was capable of inflicting. Where the character of the climate, or the nature of the work to be done, was such as to be seriously prejudicial to human life, slavery, if recruited from within, could only exist through giving attention to the physical requirement of slaves. Without this slavery would become extinct by the destruction of its victims. But, once a commerce in slaves is established, restraints upon the fullest development of slavery are effectually removed [Cairnes and Smith, 2003, IV.iii].

Unlike a modern capitalist system, slaves do not constitute a large market for commodities. They themselves are commodities, and are not[24] buyers of commodities. The agricultural slaves subsist largely on the food they grow on the estate. Such clothes as they are provided can be produced by other slaves on the estate. So though a slave society does develop a market, its extent is

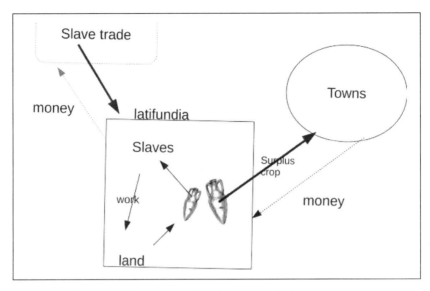

Figure 3.4. Main pattern of purchases and sales by slave estates.

much more limited than in a modern economy. The surplus product of the slaves is marketable, but not the product necessary for their subsistence, nor the product of what is often a very large subsistence agriculture sector alongside and between the slave estates.

The surplus product of the countryside, predominantly from slave agriculture, had to be sold to urban markets. This presupposed technical means of transport, as I have discussed, are roads, carts, ships, and harbors. But it also implied that the urban population had to have the money to buy the crops.

The basic balance of the political economy has to be:

1. Sales by latifundia – purchases of slaves = Owners' profits
2. Food purchases by urban economy = Owners' profits + sales
   to slave importers

The urban sector gets the money to buy the products of the latifundia because the slave-owning aristocracy live in town and spend their profits there. They maintain their *familia urbana* there. This is made up not only of the *paterfamilias*, his wife, and children, but also a retinue of domestic slaves. Food and supplies for these families are bought on the urban market and indirectly support a whole middle class of professionals and traders, many of whom would themselves own one or two slaves. This entire mass is directly or indirectly supported by the revenues of the slaveowners.

There remains the cost of the slaves purchased by the latifundia. The money for these goes from the latifundia to slave merchants. How does that money circulate back to the towns to enable them to purchase food?

Without it, the towns would not have sufficient cash to buy the entire surplus product of the latifundia. Although one possibility would be for the slave merchants to purchase export goods from the towns which they then exchange for slaves on the barbarian frontier. This is an oversimplification for classical slavery but a fair model of the relation between the metropolitan British economy and its slave plantations in the West Indies. So the closing and balancing equation of the slave political economy is:

Sales of slaves = Purchases by slave merchants

3.3 CONTRADICTIONS AND DEVELOPMENT

In reality the reproduction scheme outlined so far is a considerable oversimplification. There would be some sales to the towns by free peasant farmers, and some exports of manufactures to these peasants. But we can think of this exchange as being independent of the monetary circuit generated by the slave economy. Remove the slave sector, and the volume of commodity exchange between town and country would be much lower. Conversely, should the market shrink, so would the viability of large-scale slave agriculture. Indeed, with the collapse of the classical slave economy in the West by

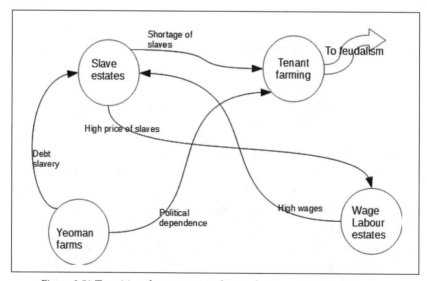

Figure 3.51 Transitions between agriculture subsystems in a slave economy.

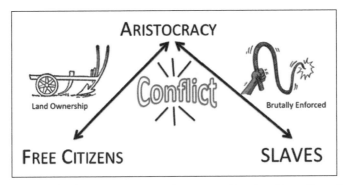

Figure 3.6. Class antagonisms in slave society. Drawing: Karen Renaud.

the sixth century there was a huge relapse in the level of commodity circulation and shrinkage of the monetary economy.

Rostovtzeff [1927] attributed this to the progressive spread of classical civilization undermining the market conditions necessary for its own
existence.

> The time was past when Greece and then Italy supplied the whole
> world with wine and oil. Under the Roman Empire nearly all the
> provinces grew enough of both commodities to satisfy their own
> requirements and even export the excess. This was a serious blow
> to the agricultural prosperity of Greece and Italy. Having nothing to
> export in return for the imported grain they were forced to revert to
> a more primitive form of agriculture and once more to grow corn for
> their own needs [Rostovtzeff, 1927, 258]

In addition there was, at various times, exports of specialized manufactures: cloth, pottery, metal, and glasswares, etc., from one area to another.
Much of this too was made by slaves. According to Rostovtzeff the spread
of the technology of mass production of pottery from Greece to Italy, to
Southern and then Northern Gaul, had the effect of suppressing the original
industrial prosperity of Italy.

At the same time a shift to an increasing employment of wage labor and
sharecropping took place on the land. This was a rational response to the
increasing difficulty in obtaining slaves. Finley [1980], Harper [2011], and
Rostovtzeff all argue that the choice by the estate owners between employing
slaves and other forms of exploitation—wage labor, sharecropping, tenant
farming—was rational and dependent on the relative availability of these
types of workers (Figure 3.5). The free yeomanry, from the period of the
Republic on, were subjected to the pressure of competition from the slave

estates and were constantly threatened with being forced into debt slavery themselves or into the statuses of tenants or urban proletarians.

A slave economy is unstable unless it has a political superstructure that uses a substantial free population as a counterpoise to the slaves.[25]

> The slave lives in a society that regards him as a slave; slavery cannot exist where there is not a society of freemen. Therefore the despot, however great his power, is not, as such, a master of slaves. The slave owner has the community on his side. [Nieboer, 1971, 32]

We know from the United States that in the traditional slaveholding territories the armed free citizenry formed a solid block against the slaves, with their militias being readily available to suppress slave rebellions.[26] The same principle held in the ancient slave republics, which also rested on an armed free citizenry. But while the distinction between slaves and freemen and the pride of the latter prevented any solidarity between free peasant and slave, it was not enough to suppress class conflict within the free. As described by Parenti [2004] and Rostovtzeff [1927], the resulting class conflicts between the free peasants and proletarians on the one hand and the slave-owning aristocracy dominated the late Roman Republic. Similar conflict in Athens had led to a revolution (508 BC) which inaugurated the Athenian democracy (figure 3.7). This was recognized by contemporaries to be the rule of the poor as opposed to the "rich," which we can interpret to mean the political dominance among the free of the peasants and artisans as opposed to wealthier slave owners.[27] In the Roman constitution political power was pretty securely in the hands of the slave-owning aristocracy, a factor that doubtless encouraged the American slaveholding aristocracy to adopt it as a model.

The existence of a large slave sector in both agriculture and manufacturing made it impossible for the Roman proletariat to combine in unions to achieve better conditions. Slavery degraded the condition of all labor. Real wages for free laborers in the late Roman Empire (300 AD) were about a third of those in London or Amsterdam during the early period of capitalism. They were even below wages in India during the seventeenth century, though they probably compared well with wages in India during the nineteenth century [Allen, 2009] after the native Indian handicraft industry had been ruined by British industrial competition. Very little of the great material wealth of the slave society, evident in its monuments and archaeological remains, filtered down to those working at the base. Competition with slaves means that wages of the free cannot rise much above the level of the slaves themselves. This is true wherever and whenever slavery exists and recognition of this was behind the solidarity shown by the British workers

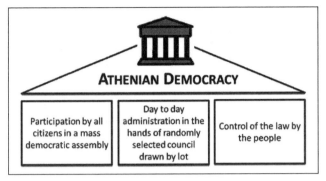

Figure 3.7. The Athenian constitution represented the most extreme form of the political influence of the free peasants and artisans. Drawing: Karen Renaud.

movement to the Union cause in the U.S. Civil War. The depression of wages produced by the institution of slavery meant that there could be only a restricted market supplying wage earners either in the town or the country.

3.4 HUMAN REPRODUCTION

Unlike the feudal economy that succeeded it, the slave mode of production of antiquity possessed no natural, internal mechanism of self-reproduction, because its labor force could never be homeostatically stabilized within the system [Anderson, 1996, 76].

The preservation of the slave system depended on a steady stream of new chained captives. In the view of Weber [2013], slave economy creates a permanent deficit of slaves that can only be made up from outside sources. Initially, during the centuries in which first the Republic and then the Empire spread over Italy, North Africa, Greece, and then Asia Minor and much of Europe, this source of slaves were as war captives. This process supplied slaves to man the latifundia and at the same time, by war taxes, impoverished the free peasantry, enabling slavery to become the dominating economic form.

As captives, slaves suffered high levels of mortality through overwork and had few opportunities to form families. Weber argued that the Roman slaves tended to be sexually segregated with men kept in barracks on farms, and women kept as domestic servants. Coupled with a high rate of mortality through overwork and ill treatment this meant that there would be a perpetual deficit, which in turn motivated the ruling class in its centuries-long spree of war and conquest. Caesar was reputed to have sold off literally hundreds of thousands of captives from his conquests [Finley, 1980, 71]. With the end of conquests, Dacia (modern Romania) in the second century being the last sizeable one, the supply dried up. In consequence the ruling

TABLE 3.1: Excess Mortality among Slaves in Ante-Bellum U.S. (figures per 1,000)

Age	Slaves	Entire United States
0	350	179
1–4	201	93
5–9	54	28
10–14	37	19
15–19	35	28
20–24	40	39

Source: Steckel, 1986.

class found it economic to shift to a system of landlord-based exploitation—either sharecropping or a form of proto-feudalism called the *colonate*. Tenants were still tied to their patron, and their families could be relied on as a source of labor from generation to generation.

Slavery was associated with a patriarchal family structure in the ruling class. Strict control was exercised over the sexual activity of free women. In Roman law any sex with a free woman outside of marriage was a criminal offense: criminal adultery in the case of a married woman; *stuporum,* or violation, in the case of an unmarried one. Because the Roman state had no standing police, such crimes would only be prosecuted if the family or husband of the woman brought criminal charges. The sexual powers of a woman were regarded as the property of her family or husband, who were, consequently, the ones who had to seek redress.

Although formally the system was one of monogamy, for the slave-owning men it was one of polygyny. Only children of a man's free-born wife could count as family heirs, but over and above that there were socially sanctioned forms of extramarital sex:

1. *Concubinage* relationships were openly acknowledged with women of inferior social class, either slaves or at best freed slaves. The aim of these non-marital relationships was sex without offspring.
2. *Prostitution* as an institution arose with the slave system. The necessary conditions for its existence were, and remain:
    a. Patriarchal dominance of men over women.
    b. A trade in enslaved or impoverished women to fill the brothels. Heuman and Burnard [2010] report that, even today, the flow of sexually trafficked women in South Asia is on the order of 300,000 a year.
    c. A class of relatively wealthy men.
    d. A well-developed system of monetary economy, in order that sex could be converted into a paying business.
3. *Sexual exploitation* of domestic slaves.

In all class societies employing servants,[28] domestic servants have fallen victims to the lusts of their masters. While this was deplored by the *mater familia* the servants were at once powerless in the face of their masters and liable to whipping by their mistresses if their having yielded was discovered. The *dominus* on the other hand obtained not only sexual gratification but saleable slave children.

The prostitutes were, in the main, slaves, and the slave-owning class felt no particular shame in exploiting them. The hypocritical double standards of Roman sexual policy were summarized by the Christian moralist Salvian in his aphorism *adulteria vetantes, lupanaria aedificantes*, "prohibition of adultery, building of brothels."

It is worth noting here that sexual and economic exploitation are distinct. Economic exploitation involves the appropriation of the physical product of a laboring class by an exploiting class. Sexual exploitation is any practice in which persons achieve sexual gratification or offspring through the abuse of another person's sexuality [Defeis, 2000]. This remains an issue in post-slave societies.[29]

Weber's analysis has been criticized more recently by Harper [2011], who says that Weber underestimates the significance of natural reproduction among the slaves. Even if female and male slaves were kept apart, slave women were objects of sexual exploitation by their masters, and any resulting children could be sold off at a profit at the slave market. Harper argues that it is unsafe to generalize from the generally high slave mortality of the United States to older slave economies. Mortality in early slavery may have been somewhat lower, though in the absence of reliable data there is an inevitable uncertainty about estimates of mortality so long ago. We do, however, know that slavery survived in the United States for some time after the termination of the slave trade, and it certainly survived, though not necessarily on the same scale, in the Roman Empire after conquests ceased. This indicates that a substantial proportion of the labor force in the latter period of both slave systems may have been born slaves.

On the other hand Harper himself documents the extent of the long-distance slave trade, importing slaves from sub-Saharan Africa, from the Gothic frontier, and as far away as the Caucasus. Such large-scale imports indicate that natural reproduction was insufficient to maintain the slave economy, and that it remained to a significant extent parasitic on the population surplus of the surrounding tribal and clan societies. It is therefore possible that Weber was right, that as the external supply of slaves slackened, whether from conquest or trade, their price rose and motivated a shift to the colonate. This in turn would have changed the basic relation of exploitation from one that presupposed commodity production to one in which commodity production was ancillary. This change in production relations would then produce as an effect the general collapse of markets observed alongside the collapse of the Western Empire.

The Weber account, in which slavery collapses into a system of landlord dominance over sharecroppers and tied peasants, also fits in with what happened in the United States and Brazil after slavery. If the possibility of slave exploitation is shut off, but land is still held by the old slave owners, this is probably the inevitable consequence.

Why, then, did importing slaves over the frontiers not continue indefinitely?

Technological development of weapons is one possible answer. The greater availability of iron enabled the development of the cataphract, or armored knight. With the invention of the stirrup (fifth century) an armored horseman could use a lance without being thrown from his horse by impact. These technical changes produced a decisive shift in the balance of military power from infantry to the shock power of cavalry [Wintringham and Blashford-Snell, 1943; Ferrill, 1986; White, 1964]. The slave state had relied on the superior fighting ability of its professional infantry to maintain strategic dominance over the barbarian societies around it. Whether this military technology was a factor in the collapse of empire, it does explain why, feudalism having been established, citizen infantry were unable to challenge the dominance of the horse-riding aristocracy until the late Middle Ages. The undermining of heavy cavalry, and thus the military aristocracy, had to await musketry.

The progressive social transformation of barbarian society into class society [Heather, 2009] also removed the organizational superiority that the Roman state had over its neighbors and may have undermined its ability to exploit them in slave raids.

The precise historical contingencies by which the Roman slave state fell are not, however, central to a theory of the overall dynamics of the slave form of economy, since that is just one slave society. Slavery continued to exist, even if as a minor component of the system of exploitation well into the Middle Ages. Perhaps 10 percent of the English population were slaves in 1066, and in the Byzantine, Arab, and Ottoman empires that succeeded Rome slavery also continued [Heuman and Burnard, 2010]. Slaves never stopped being captured in sub-Saharan Africa and traded across the desert to the North. The slave mode of production became firmly established in the Sahel empires like Bornu and Sokoto. Heuman and Burnard report that by the mid-nineteenth century there were as many slaves in Sokoto as in the United States. From the 1500s on the slave trade, which had previously been directed North and East, was diverted to the South, to the Bight of Benin and the transatlantic trade. Between 1500 and 1900, about 12 million slaves were shipped from the coasts of Africa to the plantations of Brazil, the Caribbean, and North America. Over the same period about 5 million African slaves were sold to the Islamic world. The total number of slaves traded in the Indian Ocean area over this period was much larger, but most were traded from other areas: within India, from Central Asia and China (ibid., chap. 3).

The effect of two thousand years of slave trade on Africa was a chronic demographic drain, slowing down social and economic development. This is the essential parasitism of the slave system. Slave labor is profitable because the reproduction costs of the slaves are met by the societies from which they are taken. Overall they transfer the work of human reproduction from one territory to another. And by reducing the price of slave labor below the level that would allow their reproduction, it encourages the most reckless over-working of the wretched captives.

The important things to take away about the slave economy are:

- It is a system of production that generates a well-developed commodity exchange. This is something it has in common with capitalism.
- Its dominance over other forms of exploitation rests on an ability to draw on external sources of slave labor. This dependence on external supplies of labor is something we will meet in capitalist economy.

3.5 COMMODITIES AND PRICES

In the preceding discussion of slavery I said that one of the distinguishing features of slave economies is that they have well-developed markets. But so far I have treated the idea of markets and commodities in an informal, commonsense fashion. We need to go into the issue more deeply and present a theory of commodities. In this book I will use the classical theory of commodity circulation and price.

By the classical theory, I mean the theory that labor is the source of value. This was generally accepted from the time of Ibn Kaldun[30] through Petty[31] and Adam Smith down to that of Karl Marx.[32, 33]

3.5.1 Neoclassical Prices

If you had an economics course at school or college, classical theory is unlikely to be the theory you were taught. Instead you would have been taught the neoclassical theory that was developed in the late nineteenth century by writers like Jevons or Marshall. It is arguable that neoclassical theory gained its popularity because the classical theory, having by then been adopted by socialist writers, had a rather disreputable image in polite society. The neoclassical theory appeared considerably more sophisticated. It was more mathematical and had a scientific feel.[34] Its plausibility for young students is enhanced by a beguiling use of diagrams. For those of you who did not take an economics course, figure 3.8 is what millions of students have been given as the theory of price.

There are two lines, sometimes drawn slightly curved: one is called the supply function, the other the demand function. The demand function rests on the commonsense notion that if something is cheap, people will buy more of it, so it slopes down. Teachers have little difficulty getting this idea accross to their class.

The other line, the supply function, is shown sloping the other way. What it purports to show is that as more is supplied, the cost of each item goes up. Teachers have more difficulty with this, as common knowledge and experience will have taught students that the reverse is the case: as industries ramp up production they find they can produce more efficiently and supply the output at a lower cost. Such objections provoke some hand waving at the blackboard as well as excuses.[35]

The great thing about a classic diagram is that it is both memorable and intuitively understandable. If you can present math this way you leverage the processing ability of our visual cortex to understand it. That is why Venn diagrams are so much easier for students to grasp than axiomatic set theory [Lakoff and Nunez, 2001]. Our brains tell us that if it looks right, it not only is right, but it is real. So having seen the diagrams, students come out thinking that supply and demand functions are real things—after all, they have seen them. Not only that, one can see that the intersection of these functions exactly predicts both the quantity of the commodity sold q, and its price p.

Had the theory been presented entirely in algebraic form it would be more confusing, less appealing, and more subject to critical analysis. I will demonstrate that once you convert it to algebraic notation it is evident that the theory violates two cardinal principles of the scientific method. Its science feel is faked.

"Occam's razor" is the principle widely credited to the monk William of Ockham in the Middle Ages. He is supposed to have said that in an explanation "*frustra fit per plura quod potest fieri per pauciora*" [Adams, 1987], "it is futile to explain with many things what can be done with fewer." His dictum has been widely adopted by scientists who interpret it to mean that when constructing a hypothesis you should keep it simple.[36]

Why is this a good principle for science?

Beyond philosophical beliefs that the laws of nature are simple and elegant, there are pragmatic reasons why sticking to Occam's razor is good

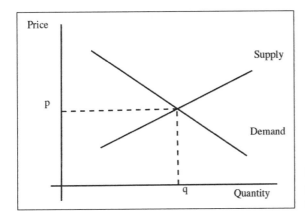

Figure 3.8. The theory of price taught to millions of students.

scientific practice. The main one is that if you make your theory complicated enough you can make it fit any particular set of observations, but this is at a cost of loss of generality of predictive ability. A famous example is the way that the Greek geocentric theory of astronomy was extended by adding epicycles to account for the retrograde apparent movement of Mars.[37] Ptolemy was able to get good predictions, something that classical economists signally fail to do, but he got them at the cost of a theory with little inner logic, and one that we now know was totally inside out.

The neoclassical supply and demand theory does multiply entities without cause. Each of the functions has at least two parameters specifying its slope and position.[38] But the real observed data only has two parameters: a price and quantity on a particular day. So the theory attempts to explain two numbers and in the process introduces four new numbers—entities lacking necessity.

For Ptolemy the epicyclic complexity brought precision in predicting planetary motion, and in the sense that there were no more epicycles than was necessary to achieve that precision, Ptolemy's theory obeyed Occam's razor. But the profligacy with which the economists strew free variables around, brings the opposite effect. Their price theory is underdetermined and makes no testable predictions at all.

Testability is another cornerstone of the scientific method. A causal theory should be testable to see if it is true. For that to work, the entities you use have to be measurable. But what testable predictions does the neoclassical theory make about the structure of industrial prices in, for example, the U.S. economy?

It can make none, since the supply and demand functions for the various commodities are not only contingently unknown, but are in principle unknowable. The theory says that the two functions uniquely define the

price and quantity that will be sold on a particular day, but there are infi-
nitely many pairs of lines that could be drawn so as to intersect at the point
(q, p) in figure 3.8. It is no good trying to look at how the prices and quantities sold vary from day to day, since the theory itself holds than any changes
in price or quantity must be brought about by "shifts" in the functions. What
this means is that the economics teacher goes to the board with a ruler
and draws two more lines intersecting at the new price and quantity. This,
the teacher tells the class, is what happens in a real market: prices change
because the supply and demand functions move about.

But splatter any arbitrary set of points on the price-quantity graph, and
you can draw intersecting lines through each and every one of them. Let
these points be prices on successive days, there could never be a sequence
of these price value measurements that could not be explained by suitably
shifting a ruler about and drawing pairs of intersecting lines. So the theory
is unfalsifiable. It makes no specific operational predictions about prices and
quantities. It is true by definition and vacuous by definition. It is not even
wrong [Woit, 2002].

3.5.2 The Classical Theory of Prices

The classical theory of prices, was simple, testable, has been tested, and has
been shown to be correct. It said that the prices at which commodities sell
tend to be in proportion to the labor required to make them. Things are
valuable if they are hard to make, they are cheap if they are easy to make. A
pithy summary of the theory was Marx's statement:

> The value of one commodity is to the value of another commodity as
> the quantity of labor fixed in the one is to the quantity of labor fixed
> in the other. [Marx, 1910, sec. 6]

The classical economists hedged this position with various qualifications
but these do not prevent the theory from giving rise to meaningful, testable
predictions. The qualifications are mostly of the form that such and such will
cause some degree of random fluctuation between relative prices and relative labor ratios.[39] For example, if one woman is an unusually fast worker an
hour of her work will create more value than average. If one factory uses an
unusually efficient system of production that enables it to use less labor than
usual, then one hour of its workers' time will create more value than average.
In addition classical economists expected relative market prices to fluctuate slightly above and below the ratios of labor the goods contained. The
theorists were working prior to the development of statistics as a modern

discipline, but it is easy to translate what they were saying into modern terms.

Two mathematicians in the 1980s, Farjoun and Machover [1983], formulated the classical claims roughly as follows: price ratios between pairs of commodities are random variables whose expected value is the ratio of the labor contents of the two commodities.

So if we take two commodities: a particular model of size 8 men's boots, and a particular model of a Volkswagen Golf car, and we knew the ratio of how much work went into each of them, then we would have a reasonable prediction of what their relative prices would be. More precisely, the price ratio will be normally distributed (figure 5.21) around the labor content ratio with a relatively small standard deviation.

3.5.3 Evidence for the Theory

In this form the prediction of classical price theory is eminently testable, provided that we make some stipulation about how small this standard deviation will be. It has been argued that at least one of the classical economists, Ricardo, estimated that 93 percent of the differences in relative prices would be explicable by differences in labor content [Petrovic, 1987]. Farjoun and Machover argue on very general statistical grounds that the standard deviation of the price/labor ratio would be about 1/6 of the mean of the distribution. Thus if the average ratio of money to time was $18 per hour, the spread of this ratio for different goods would be about $3.

Since the 1980s it has been possible to use computer calculations to obtain estimates of just how closely the selling prices of industrial outputs correlate with the direct and indirect labor used by these industries. There have been a large number of studies done[40] that tend to confirm these hypotheses. In general the studies find the correlation between industrial output prices and labor contents to be greater than the 93 percent anticipated by Ricardo. Generally the correlations are in the range of 95 to 97 percent. Cockshott and Cottrell [1997a] tested the standard deviation of the price to value distribution and found that the standard error was actually smaller than that predicted in Farjoun and Machover [1983], closer to 1/10 than 1/6.

The classical theory of price has been tested and found to be correct. The neoclassical theory is untestable, and will be ignored in what follows.

3.6 LABOR AND PRICE UNDER SLAVERY

But this evidence that labor content determines price all comes from the modern economy. The first historical writing linking labor time to value is in the work of Ibn Kaldun in the fourteenth century. If he at that date was stating as a fact that value originated in labor, we can safely assume that he observed this relationship in practice. Of course, it would be a rough and ready empirical observation, not a precise econometric study, but it does indicate that this relationship was apparent in the fourteenth century.

We do not have any written sources making a similar causal observation from the time of classical slave society. North Africa in the fourteenth century did have a fairly extensive use of slaves, but they were predominantly in domestic contexts and in small-scale agriculture. A series of slave revolts between the seventh and ninth centuries had led to a reduction in large-scale plantation slavery [Heuman and Burnard, 2010]. Large groups of slaves were more likely to rebel. So Kaldun's observations cannot have been based on observing prices in a full slave economy.

We do not know that prices were governed by labor content in these periods, but the idea is plausible because slave plantations appear to have made rational use of the labor available to them. Consider the following discussion of how to organize slave labor by Cato.

> When the master arrives at the farmstead, after paying his respects to the god of the household, let him go over the whole farm, if possible, on the same day; if not, at least on the next. When he has learned the condition of the farm, what work has been accomplished and what remains to be done, let him call in his overseer the next day and inquire of him what part of the work has been completed, what has been left undone; whether what has been finished was done betimes, and whether it is possible to complete the rest; and what was the yield of wine, grain, and all other products. Having gone into this, he should make a calculation of the laborers and the time consumed. If the amount of work does not seem satisfactory, the overseer claims that he has done his best, but that the slaves have not been well, the weather has been bad, slaves have run away, he has had public work to do; when he has given these and many other excuses, call the overseer back to your estimate of the work done and the hands employed. If it has been a rainy season, remind him of the work that could have been done on rainy days: scrubbing and pitching wine vats, cleaning the farmstead, shifting grain, hauling out manure, making a manure pit, cleaning seed, mending old harness and making new; and that the hands ought to have mended their smocks and hoods. Remind him, also, that on feast days old ditches might have been cleaned, road work done, brambles cut, the garden spaded, a meadow cleared, faggots bundled, thorns rooted out, spelt ground, and general cleaning

done. When the slaves were sick, such large rations should not have been issued. After this has been gone into calmly, give orders for the completion of what work remains; run over the cash accounts, grain accounts, and purchases of fodder; run over the wine accounts, the oil accounts—what has been sold, what collected, balance due, and what is left that is saleable; where security for an account should be taken, let it be taken; and let the supplies on hand be checked over. Give orders that whatever may be lacking for the current year be supplied; that what is superfluous be sold; that whatever work should be let out be let. Give directions as to what work you want done on the place, and what you want let out, and leave the directions in writing. Look over the livestock and hold a sale. Sell your oil, if the price is satisfactory, and sell the surplus of your wine and grain. [Hooper and Ash, 1935, 9]

Note the reference to the need to calculate the amount of labor time expended to produce particular yields of wine, grain etc. It is assumed that there are "cash accounts, grain accounts, wine accounts, oil accounts," everything that is required for a rational computation of the labor devoted to each branch of agricultural production and the yields it produces. The instructions end up with the instruction to sell if the price is satisfactory. We have here all that is necessary for labor time to regulate prices in a slave economy.

The *dominus* knows what each product has cost in terms of labor, knows the prevailing market price and will only sell if the price is "satisfactory." But what can this mean? The standard of what is satisfactory is provided by the "calculation of the laborers and the time consumed" along with the oil, grain, and wine accounts. He knows the relative costs in terms of slave labor of the different products, and can thus judge when the relative prices are satisfactory enough to justify selling. If the price falls below a satisfactory level, the estates will withdraw from selling that product until the price rises.

It is not necessary to do what Smith did, and project back the regulation of price by labor to an imagined past when individualized hunters exchanged beavers for deer. A past that could only be imagined, since the individualization required for regular trade does not exist in hunter-gatherer society. Smith imagines specialized deer and beaver hunters prior to the private property and general commodity exchange in order to give a mythical account for something that he observed to be actually occurring in the combined slavery and capitalist systems of the eighteenth-century Atlantic economy. But if we read the classical writers on agriculture we can grasp the process better. The latifundia produced multiple commodities, their relative labor costs were known to the owners and this provided the basis for labor to regulate price.

The slave-owning class did not only own farms, they also ran other forms of business. If slave labor yielded a higher return in cash terms in some other branch of activity, they would either set up rural production on their estates, or invest in urban slave workshops. We do not know that prices were actually regulated by labor in Rome, but it is a reasonable hypothesis. It is also one that could be tested.

In principle, research could be done to see if prices in slave economies followed a law of labor value. The relative prices given for example in the edict of Diocletian [Bolin, 1958] in 301 A.D. could be compared with estimates of the time taken to make things under the technical conditions of that era. For agricultural products, techniques of production remained similar until recent history, so data on labor use from more recent periods could be exploited. For the slave economies of the Americas there is of course much more extensive data available. This would make a similar investigation much easier.

3.7 MONEY

Money in the form of coinage arises in societies with markets, and indeed it is arguable that it is a major factor forcing such markets into existence. Developed slave economy presupposes money and monetary exchanges. In this section I will look at the general properties of money that first arose under slavery. These are properties that persist right down to the present.

Purchases with money allow the establishment of a set of consistent market values. Suppose, as in Diocletian's price edict, an egg sold for 1 denarius, and a measure of wine for 8 denarii, and a measure of olive oil for 40. We can set this out as a table A (page 73).

Then we can easily see that a measure of wine has the value of 8 eggs.

This is obvious with two commodities and with money, but if you consider a hypothetical barter economy without money then the whole business is much more complicated. You now have a matrix of pairwise swap ratios as in table B (page 73).

Read this as saying, for example, that a measure of olive oil will swap for 40 eggs or for 5 measures of wine.

But consider the complexity that can arise with these three commodities without money prices. Instead of 3 prices, we have 9 exchange ratios. If we had 4 commodities we would have a 4×4 table with 16 ratios. In general the size of your exchange rate table grows as the square of the number of commodities being bartered. Diocletian set the prices of around 1,000 of them.

Commodity	Denarius Price	
Eggs	1	
Measure of Wine	8	(A)
Measure of Oil	40	

Commodity	Eggs	Measure of Wine	Measure of Oil	
Eggs	1	1/8	1/40	
Measure of Wine	8	1	1/5	(B)
Measure of Oil	40	5	1	

Commodity	Eggs	Measure of Wine	Measure of Oil	
Eggs	1	1/8	**1/20**	
Measure of Wine	8	1	1/5	(C)
Measure of Oil	**20**	5	1	

If, instead of specifying money prices he had fixed a collection of barter rates, the table would have had a million numbers. Given that the Romans had to do all their calculations using the abacus it would have been quite impossible to do the calculations for such a table, let alone distribute copies of it.

One effect of money is therefore data compression.

Instead of specifying a million ratios it was enough to give a thousand prices in denarii.

But this compression only works for what I have called consistent swap tables. In a sense this definition is circular, since the consistent swap rate tables are the ones you can create from a single set of money prices. But the logic of private agents engaging in exchanges means that any other sort of swap table is unstable. Suppose we took table B and changed just one number, the swap ratio between olive oil and eggs to give table C (above) with the changed entries is shown bold.

Suppose I start out with 20 eggs. By the exchange ratio in table C I can get 1 measure of oil. Then, by the last row, I swap that for 5 measures of wine. Then by the middle row, I can swap each of these for 8 eggs each, giving me $5 \times 8 = 40$ eggs, twice as many as I started with.

A consistent swap table does not let you do this. It is consistent because any circular sequence of barters takes you back to what you initially had. It does not allow trading for profit. In reality, you never get elaborate systems of barter, the number of exchange ratios that would be needed are simply intractable to manage. But even supposing you could have such a barter economy, inconsistent swap tables would be unstable. Consider table C again. Nobody who had olive oil would be willing to swap it directly for only 20 eggs, since they would know that by swapping first for wine and then for eggs they could get 40 eggs. So, subject to a certain amount of random noise, you would only get consistent sets of swap ratios.

Pairwise barter gives an intractable number of ratios: a thousand goods imply a million swap ratios. They also involve hard calculations, and lots of divisions, which were hard to do in the past.[41]

Consistent swap ratios are reducible, in information terms, to a single column of numbers as in table A.[42] Such a column gives us the relative values of the goods. Any society in which exchange occurs is thus enabled by the logic of exchange, and forced by reasons of computational complexity to use something equivalent to a column of prices. The information content in this column, associating a number with each type and unit of a good, is a value system. The units used to express the values are the standard of value. It does not matter if we use one of the goods on the market as the standard of value: cattle, silver, volumes of barley, or instead use a state-issued unit like the denarius. Any of these are capable of acting as the standard of value. We are dealing with an abstract computational imperative that is indifferent to the material used.

You do not need physical coins to have a standard of value. Polanyi et al. [1957] argued that in ancient Mesopotamia there was a standard of value, the shekel, which was either a measure of barley or the amount of silver that weighed the same as a barley corn. The existence of this standard did not imply that transactions were actually carried out by handing over measures of barley to buy things. Instead accounts were kept by scribes on clay tablets, recording physical movements of goods and their equivalent value in shek-els. But for this kind of transaction to work you depend on written records and a class of numerate scribes. The Mesopotamian system, which relied on scribes, did not allow illiterate people to engage in distributed transactions as easily as coinage does.[43]

Standards of value have not just been used for buying and selling. They were also used in the Sumerian civilization to measure tax liabilities. By expressing these in measures of barley, but allowing tax debts to be settled in different goods: oil, salt, dates etc., barley as the standard of value allowed the state to accept different goods in kind without having to specify exactly which goods each farmer would supply. Law codes therefore specified the barley equivalent of a wide range of goods [Postgate, 1992]. As I said, the idea of a system-generalized barter is a fantasy for computational reasons, but one could still hypothesize that the logic of consistent exchange along with computational simplicity drove commodity producers to adopt a universal equivalent like the

Sumerian *gur* of barley. But it is not even clear that this arose out of commodity exchange rather than the demands of tax collection.[44]

What distinguishes circulating money from an abstract measure of value or unit of account is that money is made up of distinct physical objects that can be carried about, counted, and passed from hand to hand. These take two distinct forms:

1. Relatively rare privately produced objects like the cowrie shell, widely used in the urbanized semi-slave economy of West Africa, or the bronze bracelet manillas they used for higher denominations.[45] This is referred to as "primitive money."
2. State-issued coins that originated in China and later in the slave economies of the Mediterranean.

The physical properties of the money are important. The money has to be made up of durable discrete units rather than being a continuous quantity. Cowries could serve as money but palm wine cannot. There is a link between discreteness and calculation. The term "calculation" derives from the Latin for pebble, because calculations were done with pebbles or counters. Coins are a self-recording and self-calculating system. If you have a collection of coins in your purse, they, by their physical presence, act as a record of your claim upon social labor. You do not have to make a separate symbolic record of it in a ledger or on a computer.

Banking systems of recorded credits have existed since Babylon [Davies, 2010] at least. They were widespread in the Roman period [Banaji, 2016] and have reached full fruition now. Systems of giro transfer were already well developed in Hellenistic Egypt, with the unit of account in this case being grain rather than coin. But banking requires the permanent recording of transactions and balances. This demands time, resources, and a class of literate and numerate laborers that was, until the modern age, in short supply. These costs meant that while merchants and the wealthy could resort to banks to facilitate transactions, the vast bulk of the population stood outside the banking system until the invention of computerized records,. They might have local debit accounts with individual traders, buying on the slate, but that was all. Credit accounts, or debit accounts of the sort run by Visa, could not extend to the whole population until electronic record keeping became general in the late twentieth century.

In contrast, coins or cowries provide a distributed system of record that requires no more than a simple ability to count. You do not even need to know how to add or subtract. Take the coins out of your purse and hand them over and the relevant sum is automatically deducted from your account. Similarly, the sellers' accounts are credited as soon as they pocket the coins without them needing to know how to do long addition.

In addition to these practical advantages, money has to be logically distinguished from banking. This is no longer obvious to us today since so much of modern commodity exchange uses banking operations rather than money. This leads people to identify bank accounts with money. But there is a big logical difference. Money only comes in positive quantities. Bank accounts may hold positive or negative values, credits or debits. Money therefore is a model for the positive whole numbers whereas bank accounts are a model for the signed whole numbers [Badiou et al., 2007]. This difference is obscured in modern discourse about the "money supply" and public finance. Arguments that are logically valid when applied to money are no longer valid when applied to bank credit.

Records that embody social power need to be proof against forgery. Today we use elaborate electronic ciphers for the most mundane purchase, ciphers that were beyond the ken of the most sophisticated intelligence services in the mid-twentieth century. Other ages have relied on signatures and seals on records or on the matching ends of broken tally sticks [Wray, 2004]. Whatever the technique, money relies on its units being hard to forge. Cowrie shells were used as currency far from where the mollusks were found, and as natural products could not be handmade.

Coins have relied on two techniques. The exact replication of the dies from which they are stamped is hard, so counterfeit coins were visibly different from originals when closely examined. Second, for high-denomination coins, the material from which they are made may itself be expensive: either a pure precious metal or an alloy that has expensive components. Many European coinage systems for the past 2,600 years worked this way.

In contrast, Chinese money was exclusively base metal for three thousand years until they issued silver coin in 1890. Initially the coins were shaped like cowries or agricultural implements: hoes, knives, etc. [Davies, 2010]. By the third century BC the standard form of round coin with a central hole had been arrived at.[46] Western economists, ignoring this long history of base metal money in China, tended to assume that the precious metal content of a currency was essential. The Chinese had to rely on the power of the state rather than the composition of the coins to suppress forgery. Incentives to forge were also diminished by the low value of the individual coins. For larger transactions paper money has been in use in China for over a thousand years. Paper notes obviously have the same discrete self-recording character that cowries and coins had.

Why are coins and, leaping ahead, paper notes able to measure value and record claims on social labor?

The answers given by the classical economists differed somewhat. According to Marx, money had value because the coins were made of gold or silver and the value of a gold coin was simply the value of the gold it contained.[47] Gold required a lot of labor to mine, so a small weight would exchange against many hours spent on other activities. In this view, coins were just state-standardized weights of gold. The state simply steps in to provide convenient portable chunks of the metal. The royal stamp on them was a certificate to say that the gold was pure and the weight accurate.

Ricardo started out from a similar assumption, but then said that the actual prices of goods would be affected not just by the labor required to mine gold, but by the quantity of money circulating in a country [Ricardo, 1811]. If there was an outflow of gold to pay for imports, the stock of gold circulating as coin would be curtailed. With less money being available to purchase commodities, there would be a general fall in prices. Lower prices of that nation's goods would then promote exports, while at the same time the shortage of bullion would hamper imports. In the end the imbalance in trade would be compensated for by price shifts brought about by the change in the quantity of money. This was the initial form of the famous quantity theory of monetary value.

Marx disputed this mechanism. He held that only a small portion of the bullion in a country was at any time actually in circulation. A larger part was held as hoards so that these would buffer the effect of changes in quantity. An increase in the gold stock in a nation would simply cause more bullion to be hoarded as reserves in private strongboxes or banks.

These views reflect the range of debate taking place in early nineteenth-century Europe, and are posed in the context of a specifically European history of gold and silver coinage. But the perspective fails to generalie to the long history of money in China or to the monetary systems that exist in the contemporary world, neither of which rely on gold or silver. Ricardo's concern with bullion outflows actually related to a persistent feature of the trade between Europe and China. While Europe had, since the opening up of sea routes to the East, craved high-quality Chinese manufactures, it had little of equivalent quality that it was able to export in return. The West had to resort to exporting bullion to purchase its imports from China. A large part of the silver from European colonies in the New World went across the Pacific to pay for imports of tea, ceramics, silks, and the like from China. Ricardo's purported equilibrating mechanism was ineffective given the poor quality, as seen from the Chinese perspective, of European exports. A fall in the price of substandard European potteries would not induce the Chinese to buy from these rather than their own fine porcelain manufacturers. The recourse of the East India Company was instead to go into the drug trade and export addictive opium to China via their Hong Kong trading post. Once in China, of course, the bullion did not have the inflationary effect predicted by Ricardo because the currency was not bullion based; it vanished into hoards as predicted by Marx's monetary theory.

However, neither Ricardo's nor Marx's theory adequately explained the Chinese situation. Since China's money was either paper or copper why did it have any value at all?

If we look at the historical origin of coinage in the West, the earliest coins were issued by Lydia, home of the legendary King Midas, at the start of the seventh century BC [Bolin, 1958]. These certainly seemed to fit in with the idea that they were state-standardized weights of precious metal. They were shaped like coffee beans and had an emblem of a lion on one side. They were made to an accurate standard weight. Within a short period of less than a century these evolved into round coins.

The classical account of the origin of coins falls down on one crucial detail. The Lydian coins were not made of gold but of electrum, a gold-silver alloy that naturally occurs in the area. This means that people accepting the coins as a standard weight in gold would have been deceived. Not only that, but the gold content of these coins was lower than in naturally occurring electrum, indicating that the kingdom of Lydia was adding silver to the mix before stamping the coins [Cowell and Hyne, 2000]. Bolin [1958] points out that from the earliest days the issue of coins could be a profitable activity. He recounts that during the Roman Empire there was a process of reducing the precious metal content of the currency, with the denarius moving from a silver coin to a predominantly copper coin with a thin silver coat for appearance's sake. The process is mirrored in more recent monetary history with the English penny moving from a silver coin, up to the eighteenth century, and then switching to copper, then to bronze, and shrinking as it did so. The contemporary penny is not even solid copper; it has an iron core coated with copper.[48] This reinforces the Chinese experience that commercial activity can be carried out for prolonged periods with token currencies—much of the third century in the Roman case, since 1947 in the British case.

Coins found in hoards are one of the most common relics of past ages, and there has been a temptation on the part of some[49] to equate periods of fine silver and gold coins with particularly well-developed commodity production. Were this a safe assumption, then London must have been more prosperous and commercial under George I than under George VI in whose reign the coinage became entirely base metal.[50]

An alternative theory of money, whose recent exponents include Wray [2004] and Ingham [2004], attributes its value to the ability of the state to impose obligations like taxes and fines on its subjects. The state lays claim to part of the social surplus product. If the state specifies that the tax obligation is to be met in labor or grain, then money does not arise. But if it is willing to accept coins of its own issue, then these acquire value. They do this not because of labor that went into the coin, but because the coins stand in for the labor that would otherwise have been directly performed. So long as there is within an area a unified state with effective tax or tribute-raising powers, and it is willing to accept its own coin in settlement of tax debts, then these coins will have an effective circulation. This theory explains:

1. Why there is usually a distinct monetary or coinage system for each state.
2. Why societies have been able to operate for long periods with purely token monies.
3. Why the issue of money is not only a source of revenue for the state but has been protected by ferocious penalties.
4. Why and how states can change the monetary system. For example, British colonial authorities demonetized the cowrie by specifying that tax debts now had to be met in British-issued coin [Forstater, 2003].

Prior to the invention of coins or paper money the state's appropriation of surplus labor was in the form of labor obligations or it was specified in the physical form of grain or crops. We call this the real appropriation of the surplus product. Monetary taxes are, in contrast, a merely formal or symbolic appropriation of wealth.

But the state needs to appropriate a real surplus. It needs actual labor to build roads, actual food for its soldiers, real iron for its weapons. Such real wealth is purchaseds with coin.

Coin divorces real from formal appropriation. The two become separate in time, space, and person. They can be separate in time because the state can purchase resources, appropriating the real surplus, prior to money taxes being paid. Indeed, unless the state has issued the coins by buying things, there is no money available to pay taxes. It is separated in space since taxes raised in one part of the state can be used to purchase labor and resources in another part. This frees a regional state administration in an empire from a dependence on purely local resources. Finally, the invention of coinage allowed the separation of the taxpayer from the physical surplus provider. Taxes levied on peasants can pay the wages of a professional standing army without the peasants themselves having to serve. Without the ability to pay a mercenary professional army, the conquests of an Alexander or Trajan would have been impossible [Davies, 2010].

For all this to happen, society had to reorganize itself on mercantile lines. The peasants, to pay their taxes in money, must produce cash crops.

Merchants, sea captains and crew must link the provinces where taxes are raised to the metropolis where they were spent, and whose population partly depended on the imperial expenditure.

Whether in the Macedonian, Roman, or British empires, imperial coins and imperial taxes transformed self-sufficient communities into commodity producers [Forstater, 2003]. Monetization transformed limited domestic slavery into the ruthless exploitation of the latifundia, boosting the surplus that supported an urban ruling class. Cash linked state and aristocracy, via a chain of commodity production and handling to free or enslaved primary producers. From the moment the state issued money and compelled its return in tax, people saw the world in its silver mirror, and in a mirror everything is reversed. Forced to give unto Caesar that which was Caesar's, the very instrument of their subjection, coin, came to appear as the truest of true wealth. Their actually useful crops and artifacts now appeared as mere instruments to acquire money, which alone now counted as real value. In the epoch of the transition to what Aristotle called chrematistics, or the striving for money, its absurdity could still be seen by poets or philosophers. The parable of Midas, king from the land where coins were invented, demystified the image in money's mirror, but heedless of fable or moralist, humanity were yet forced to live the illusion.[51]

Figure 3.9. Image from Trajan's Column. Without coins to pay a mercenary professional army, the conquests of Trajan would have been impossible. Source: Cichorius, 1900.

CHAPTER 4

Peasant Economy

The power of enclosing land and owning property was brought into the creation by your ancestors by the sword; which first did murder their fellow creatures, men, and after plunder or steal away their land, and left this land successively to you, their children. And therefore, though you did not kill or thieve, yet you hold that cursed thing in your hand by the power of the sword; and so you justify the wicked deeds of your fathers, and that sin of your fathers shall be visited upon the head of you and your children to the third and fourth generation, and longer too, till your bloody and thieving power be rooted out of the land.

—GERRARD WINSTANLEY

The pre-class economy discussed in chapter 2 was a world system, or to put it another way, a universal state in social development. The capitalist economy that I examine in chapter 5 likewise has become a world system, a near universal state of economic development. The slave economy of Chapter 3 contrasts with these in that it became dominant only in certain portions of the world, at widely spread intervals. The worlds of slavery were seas and their littorals. In this chapter I return to a near global form of economy, peasant economy, with its accompanying forms of exploitation. Some parts of the world did skip peasant economy or, at least, never experienced it from autochthonous development: boreal regions, steppes, and semi-deserts. But it has been, for most of settled humanity, the most widespread and longest-lasting sort of economy. In the traditional Marxist schema peasant economy was subsumed variously under feudalism or Asiatic production, with the latter being a dangling branch from the otherwise nice historical sequence in Figure 4.1.

In contrast, I will present a model in which there is a peasant mode of production in the context of which more than one type of class structure

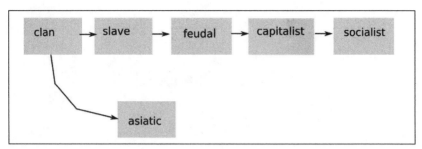

Figure 4.1. Marxist model of sequence of modes of production.

is possible. For now just consider all peasant economies as a group and replace the sequential model in figure 4.1 with something more like figure 4.2. This kind of picture (see also figure 3.5) is what would now be called a Markov process or state transition diagram. Markov processes[52] are a way of conceptualizing the time evolution of systems with a finite number of distinguishable states. The ellipses in the diagram are states and the labeled arrows, often called arcs, between them represent possible transitions. For a proper Markov model the labeled arcs would each have a probability associated with them, giving the likelihood that a transition would occur along one of those arcs in a given period of time. For historical processes one would probably want to have transition probabilities per century. In principle, given enough historical data, one could assign rough values to the transitions I have labeled a to i in the diagram.[53]

The labeled arcs in figure 4.2 are those for which clear instances are easy to find. Looking at either of the two diagrams the impression is given of entirely self-sufficient development in which an individual society either goes through a sequence of stages or jumps between states. That indeed is what simple Markov models describe. But real societies interact with one another in different places: trade and invasions; and the diffusion of information allows one society to affect others, so a simple Markov process is inadequate as a representation. Some of the transitions, (b) for example, the transition to feudalism in Germany, came about as a long-term consequence of the confrontation between German clan society and the adjacent slave empire of Rome [Anderson, 1996].[54]

The overall picture is one of a directed graph of historical states. There may be loops in the system, but despite this there is an overall directionality. The directionality arises from the absence of certain transitions—no back transition to peasant economy from capitalism, for example—and from differences in the probabilities of transitions. In the graph given, it is an open question what mix of socialist and capitalist economies will prevail in the long run, depending as it does on the relative transition probabilities (i) and (f).

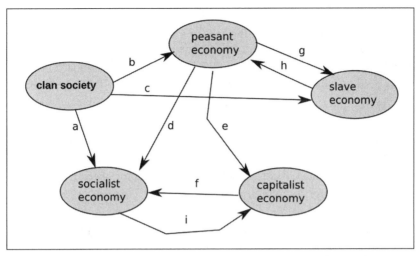

Figure 4.2. Markov model representation of transitions between forms of economy. Examples of the labeled transitions: (a) Mongolia; (b) Germany transition to feudalism; (c) slave economy West Africa; (d) Chinese Revolution; (e) Britain; (f) East Germany; (g) Roman Republic; (h) Late West Roman Empire; (i) Russia.

The nodes in Figure 4.2 should be understood as macroscopic descriptions of the states of societies. Within the macro description "peasant economy" there would be a variety of different possible property relations and class relations, just as the node labeled "slave economy" contains a nested Markov model (figure 3.5) that describes its internal dynamics.

4.1 NATURAL AND TECHNICAL CONDITIONS

Peasant economies, as the name implies, are primarily agricultural. The greater part of the population live in families whose main activity is the growing of crops. Secondary activities of the families are food preparation, textile preparation or production, building, and some ancillary crafts.

The only available mechanical energy source for agriculture is muscle power, though wind and water may be used for milling. The only available thermal energy sources are biological waste such as wood, dung, or straw.

What general implications do these conditions of existence have for peasant economies?

What restrictions do they pose on life and the social relations operating in these economies?

The technological restrictions are pretty broad, since peasant economies have existed in so many climatic zones, with such a broad range of crops. One has to ask what the common properties of this mode of production are that reach across all the incidental differences in types of farming. North Indian peasant economy of the Middle Ages depended on advances in the lifting of water: the Persian wheel, lined wells and tanks. But from the standpoint of European feudalism other technologies: moldboard ploughs, three-field rotation have been seen as crucial [White, 1964]. The varieties of technology and the existence of rather different forms of surplus extraction have been used to argue [Mukhia, 1981] that it is pointless to use the single concept of feudal to designate such different systems. Others have argued that the existence either of *extra-economic* coercion [Hirst and Hindess, 1975], or very detailed features such as serfdom, manorial economy, restriction of commodity circulation were quite general [Sharma, 1985; Sharma, 1958] and allow us to use the same basic concept right across continents. The applicability of the term *feudal* is a controversial question.[55] Instead I will look at general constraints of peasant economy and how these shape the variations in the types of exploitation they have supported.

The first point is that peasant economy is distinct from nomadism: recall Smith's distinction between nations of farmers, shepherds, and hunters. A stationary population is the precondition for the establishment of exploitation. Nomads can simply remove themselves.

What fixes a peasantry in place?

One may say that they were serfs tied to the land, but that kind of legal binding to the land only becomes necessary if there is some alternative, if the peasants have the option of moving. This either involves them moving to unclaimed land or emigrating to towns.

If there is plentiful unclaimed land this certainly acts as a potential constraint on feudal exploitation. Any servile workforce given the opportunity will try to escape, and the prevention of such escape depends on multiple factors. One is that there must be an effective state structure that can be relied on to return escapees. Another is that the distance to the virgin soil must not be too far. Finally, the type of natural vegetation plays a role. Clearing hardwood forests for fields is much harder work than plowing steppe-land, and this work acts as a practical disincentive to migration. So the strategic position of a peasant population in an area with a weak state on the edge of steppe is rather different from a peasant in the middle of a densely settled and long cleared river valley. In the first circumstance, whatever the law says, there will tend to be a drift to free settlements, in the latter the legal proscription on movement only takes effect as a way of restricting migration to cities, and that is only effective where the same state power prevails in town and country. Where you have free towns, as in Europe during the feudal period, once in the town the serfs were safe. Where state power operates as effectively in town as in country, for instance in the Ottoman Empire or the antebellum U.S. South, servile flight was much harder.

Frontier territory between agriculturalists and hunter gatherers, as in the original Neolithic expansion or European colonies, is not conducive to feudalism, whereas the edge of steppes inhabited by nomads, as in sixteenth-century Russia, allows a feudal military caste to justify its existence. Domar [1970] argued that in a peasant economy there are three elements that can never coexist: a class of exploiting landlords, free unoccupied land, and free peasants. Two of the three can exist but not all three. If there is unoccupied land free peasants will migrate to it rather than submit to paying rents, so a landlord class cannot stabilize. If there is no free land, then a free peasantry can be forced to pay rent to gain access to privately held land. But if an exploiting landlord class exists, and there yet remain untilled forests or steppes, then the peasants must be reduced to serfdom to prevent their movement.

> Assume that labor and land are the only factors of production (no capital or management), and that land of uniform quality and location is ubiquitous. No diminishing returns in the application of labor to land appear; both the average and the marginal productivities of labor are constant and equal, and if competition among employers raises wages to that level (as would be expected), no rent from land can arise, as Ricardo demonstrated some time past. In the absence of specific governmental action to the contrary . . . the country will consist of family-size farms because hired labor, in any form, will be either unavailable or unprofitable: the wage of a hired man or the income of a tenant will have to be at least equal to what he can make on his own farm; if he receives that much, no surplus (rent) will be left for his employer. A non-working class of servitors or others could be supported by the government out of taxes levied (directly or indirectly) on the peasants, but it could not support itself from land rents. [Domar, 1970]

The Domar/Neiboer theory of the fundamental economic origins of serfdom predicts the dynamical transition system shown in figure 4.3. It is not difficult to find historical examples of these transitions.

4.2 FORMS OF SURPLUS

One should avoid the anachronism of projecting back the trinity of land, labor, and capital of modern political economy onto precapitalist society.

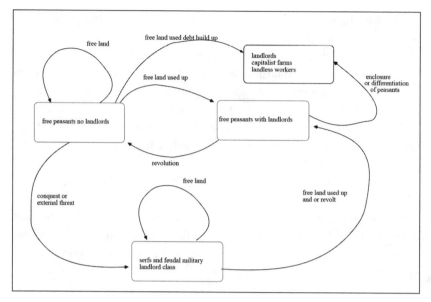

Figure 4.3. Transitions between property relations in peasant agriculture.

There is a temptation to see slavery as being based on property in persons, feudalism on property in land, and capitalism on property in capital goods. This may be formulated as a landed aristocracy having either a class monopoly over land or individual private ownership of land. The surplus they live off is then seen as the consequence of that ownership or monopoly. While this concept makes sense in the modern period and in countries where there is a well-developed market in the rent of land and a multiplicity of farmers wanting to rent it, projecting this back onto earlier peasant economies is questionable. The very existence of serfdom, or the restrictions that Indian feudal law placed on village communities moving [Sharma, 1985], shows that it was not the land that was key, but the workers on the land. Only when labor productivity and the population rises to the point where all the land can be productively worked using only part of the population, can ownership of the land itself act as a monopoly source of revenue [Domar, 1970]. Otherwise, feudal exploitation, like slavery, was about the direct or indirect control over the labor of the working population.

Titles to ownership, which passed mainly by royal assignment, inheritance, or marriage rather than purchase, were titles against other members of the feudal class. They were not property titles against serfs, but over them. They entitled one family and their descendants to the revenues accruing from the population of a territory, to the exclusion of other families from the same class. Whether these revenues are called by historians rents or taxes is not terribly significant to us now, nor was it important to the peasants. The distinction between these relates at most to which part of the military feudal class it went to. In all cases the revenues are local and arise from the labor of a peasant population that directly or indirectly gives up part of its working year to generate the revenues. This giving up of work time can come in three basic forms:

1. Direct labor service on manorial estates.
2. Giving up part of the crop they had grown on the plot they were allotted for their own cultivation.
3. Paying a rent in money.

Which of these dominate at a particular time and place will be history sensitive. The first form is only going to occur if the land is divided between peasant plots and manorial estates, which in turn may be dependent on the prior history of a country. In Western European lands where feudalism succeeded the prior Roman system of slave labor on villas, manorial lands were more likely than in places where feudal subjugation occurred by the conquest of a free peasantry. The standard Marxian account of this is to treat all of these as varying forms of extra-economic coercion, contrasted with the purely economic labor contract under capitalism. This extra-economic coercion is then used to explain why the state form under feudalism devolves judicial powers to the local aristocracy, who as a military caste have the means to directly coerce their subordinates. Relations thus appear as those of personal dependence and subjugation, unlike the apparently impartial anonymity of capitalist law.

Figure 4.4. The castle of the contemporary Duke of Buccleuch in Scotland. Feudal concentration of land ownership and land revenue continued well into the modern era.

One may wonder whether this notion of extra-economic coercion really gets to the heart of things.

Consider the position of a farmer in contemporary Scotland, where the feudal concentration of land holding has scarcely changed. Half of the country is owned by 432 aristocratic families [Hunter et al., 2013]. Suppose the farmer, renting from, say, the Duke of Buccleuch, fails to pay his rent. The Duke can apply to the Dumfries Sheriff's court for an eviction order and, if the tenant does not comply, the sheriff officers, or Queen's Messengers at Arms, will be dispatched to enforce the eviction order. The Duke is no longer, since the abolition of feudal tenure in 2000 [Parliament, 2000], the personal feudal superior of the farmer, but he can still apply for coercion to be used. He no longer sends his own men-at-arms to enforce his will, but the authority royal still enforces it.

In Scotland, one may say that this is just a residual trait of feudalism and monarchy. But consider a farmer in Oklahoma who, having got into debt to a bank, having the loan foreclosed, has the Oklahoma County Sheriff conduct a forced sale of the farm. Here we have the State of Oklahoma, which has never known feudalism or monarchy, applying the same extra-economic coercion to a farmer, not to enforce subservience to a lord, but to a bank. The same coercion applies to any homeowner who defaults on their mortgage. Is this coercion economic or extra-economic?

The payment of interest and rent in today's society is presented, by law and economic theory, as something reciprocal. You pay a price for capital you borrow or land you rent. As such it is a market exchange, something purely economic, a voluntary transaction with a fair price. But this is no more than a convenient fiction. The Duke provides nothing to the farmer. He is just entitled, no longer by the title *duke*, but still as a landowner, to collect a rent to which he has not contributed. Behind right still stands coercion.

Equivalence and reciprocity likewise masked relations of feudal dependence. The superior offered armed protection to the subordinate, and, perhaps, aid in time of want:

> To that magnificent lord so and so, I, so and so. Since it is known familiarly to all how little I have whence to feed and clothe myself, I have therefore petitioned your piety, and your good-will has decreed to me that I should hand myself over or commend myself to your guardianship, which I have thereupon done; that is to say in this way, that you should aid and succour me as well with food as with clothing, according as I shall be able to serve you and deserve it.
>
> And so long as I shall live I ought to provide service and honour to you, suitably to my free condition; and I shall not during the time

of my life have the ability to withdraw from your power or guardian-ship; but must remain during the days of my life under your power or defence. Wherefore it is proper that if either of us shall wish to with-draw himself from these agreements, he shall pay so many shillings to the other party (pari suo), and this agreement shall remain unbroken. [A Frankish Formula of Commendation, Whitcomb, 1899]

To label contemporary interest payments by a farmer to a bank eco-nomic but corvée, extra-economic, is to remain within the viewpoint of modern law. From the standpoint of feudal law, a modern mortgage agree-ment might seem impersonal, naked, and un-Christian exploitation. Class societies have their own specific ways of justifying exploitation. There is, however, something that is being pointed out when historians talk of extra-economic coercion. The term is mystification, but it hints at a real contrast between two modes of production: small-scale agriculture—the mode of production of feudalism versus machine industry—and the mode of pro-duction of capitalism.

As Table 4.1 brings out, the basic unit of production under feudalism was small.[56] The median workforce on an estate listed in the Domesday Book was only five. Since the peasants' wives and children may have worked part of the year this is a bit of an underestimate, but this is still a pretty small enterprise, with the median estate having access to only 3 plows. If these are 2 ox teams

Table 4.1: Average Properties of Essex Estates in the Domesday Book		
Variable	Mean	Median
Annual Value	£108	£65
EQUIPMENT: Demesne Plow Teams	1.9	2.0
Peasant Plow Teams	2.3	1.0
Livestock	542	388
LABOR: Freemen	0.6	0
Serfs	12.1	4.0
Slaves	2.2	1.0
LAND: Plow Land Acres	504	360
Woods Pigs	105	30
Meadow Acres	12	6
Pasture Sheep	28	0

then the medieval land measurement system would imply that they could plow 2 oxgangs of 15 acres for a total of 30 acres. If the teams were of 4 oxen then the amount would be twice as much, if 8 ox teams 4 times as much. If we assume that the demesne teams exclusively plowed the manorial land, and were 8 ox teams the maximum estimate of median demesne would have been around 240 acres. Alongside this there may be another 120 acres of land directly farmed by the peasants for their own benefit. When cultivating their own plots the peasants were in control of the production of the crop and took direct possession of the crop they harvested. In parallel with this, the same kind work process goes on each year to cultivate the lord's land.[57]

Because the production is small-scale, with only a limited division of labor, the peasants see the whole process through from sowing to harvest, and literally see the results going to their granary or the lord's granary. The end result is something with which they could potentially feed their own family. The diversion is clear and unmasked. If we contrast this to a capitalist firm there are at least the following differences:

1. The employees are not replicating what they do at home; they are making something quite different.
2. The scale of production is much larger; each employee is a small fragmented part of a complex workforce.
3. The final product may well never be seen by many employees, given the fragmented character of the process. No one person sees the whole process through.
4. In only exceptional cases, such as bakeries, breweries, etc., is the end product something that the workers could potentially live off directly. Instead it is destined to be invisibly sold for prices that are obscure.
5. The worker appears to be directly paid for the work put in—it is not free labor like a corvée obligation.

The technical structure of capitalist production means that there is no real possibility of the product being individually appropriated by the employees of the firm. Even the value of the product is obscure, immensely so nowadays when the sale of the product may go through so many shell companies that even highly trained government tax inspectors have difficulty finding out what is really happening. The only alternative to the appropriation of the product's value by the firm would be some form of takeover by the state or workers' cooperatives. An attempt to do this would be directly political, the equivalent of a peasant revolt. Workers who unofficially take over factories are stymied by legal proceedings that block supplies, confiscate products, etc. They meet extra-economic legal coercion.

The product in a peasant economy can, in contrast, be directly appropriated. An individual peasant family gathers its harvest and would retain all of it did they not have to pay rent. It is not only feudal exploitation that is backed by coercion. That is a property of all exploitation. It is that the exploitation is more transparent and the state power that backs it takes on the character of personal authority.

This personal character of state authority in feudal economies is a necessary outgrowth of circumstances in which it is difficult for the state to maintain a salaried bureaucracy and a salaried standing army. If the state lacks a regular monetary income it is forced to allocate land for the maintenance of its officials and troops. The exact legal form in which this occurs, whether it is the delegated right to raise local taxes from the peasantry or an explicit grant of estates in return for raising troops, is a secondary issue. It is the absence of a well-developed monetary revenue that is the underlying cause. That absence may have immediate reasons associated with the inability to establish a reliable tax base, but the overriding long term cause will be a poorly developed commodity circulation. A poor commodity circulation is itself the result of either or both of two economic causes: a small surplus product or an undeveloped transport technology that impedes the consumption of commodities far from where they were produced. From thence comes the contrast between slave economies with developed commodity circulation, good road and sea transport, and early feudal economies with neither. With the redevelopment of transport and monetary economy, more impersonal forms of state authority again became possible.

4.3 REPRODUCTION STRUCTURE

Figure 4.5 illustrates the flow of labor and goods under a manorial system such as existed in classic European feudalism. Contrast this with the flows under the villa/latifundia economy of the high Roman Empire, illustrated in Figure 3.4.

In both cases the direct producers get only a portion of the food they produce. Another portion is appropriated by the *dominus* or lord. Only a portion of the product enters into trade. But whereas the villa system was obliged to run at least a partial monetary surplus on current account to pay for replacement slaves, a manor can survive with a much lower portion of the product being traded. At its minimum, trade can be limited to luxuries and weapons purchased by the lord. Early feudal economies therefore supported a smaller urban sector than slave economy had. In Essex in 1086 less than 5 percent of the population was urban (Table 4.2). One can use population breakdowns like this to set some broad limits on the rate

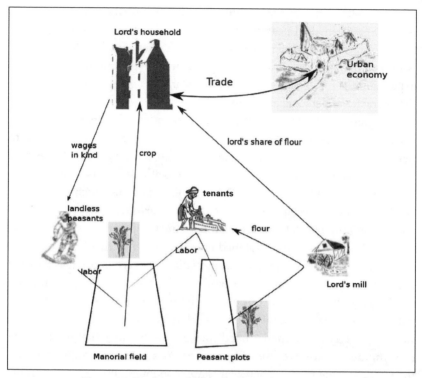

Figure 4.5. Product and labor flows in manorial system.

of exploitation in the economy. To get an upper limit, assume that all of the urban sector was supported by the expenditures of the lords, that the slaves were all domestic servants, and that the others—who are variously described as "men" and priests—were all unproductive. We then get the calculation shown in Table 4.3.

To get a lower bound on the rate of exploitation assume that none of the slaves were domestic servants, all being field laborers, and that half of the output of the towns was sold to peasants in return for part of their crop. If we apply the same method as above, that gives an exploitation rate of only 3 percent, which seems implausibly low, so the assumption has to be that a significant proportion of those listed as *servi* were actually servants in the modern sense. But note that even the upper bound for the rate of exploitation is very low by modern standards.

The next important distinction between slave and feudal economies is that on the manorial estate; the majority of the direct producers formed family households which either fed themselves on their own plots or were fed by wages. In either case the laboring population reproduced itself without recourse to imported forced labor.

TABLE 4.2: Breakdown of Population of Essex, 1086

Category	Percent of Population
Rural	95.5%
Urban	4.5%
Bordars	47.9%
Villains	27.6%
Slaves	12.3%
Freemen	7.1%
Others	0.7%

Source: McDonald, 2002.

TABLE 4.3: Calculation of a Feudal Rate of Exploitation

Urban	4.5%	-
Slaves	12.3%	+
Others	0.7%	+
Maintained out of Surplus	17.5%	(s)
Productive Population	82.5%	(p)
Rural Exploitation Rate	21.2%	(s/p)

Feudal estates in China and Europe made extensive use of artificial power—primarily water, but also in places wind power. There are over 6,000 mills listed in the Domesday Book, about one mill for every three manors, and this is for the eleventh century. The mills provided an additional means by which the lords could exploit their tenants, since the estate would take a share of all grain milled. In a sense this was analogous to a form of capitalist exploitation, since it gave the lords a revenue by virtue of owning machinery rather than land. But it differed from later capitalism in that the people being exploited did not operate the machinery. There was obviously a limit to the cut that the lords could take, since in the last resort the peasants could go back to grinding the corn the old way, using querns at home. But the lords could appropriate part of the productivity gain that came from water power.

The most critical feature that differentiates peasant agriculture from commercial slave economies and capitalist agriculture is that a large part of the working population has access to land on which they can feed themselves. This access may be in the form of secure ownership of plots, communal access rights, or rented plots. The crucial thing is that they are able at least to survive, and that there is often a sufficient reproductive surplus to allow gradual population growth. The Domar theory predicts that population growth in a serf economy should lead to a transition out of serfdom once the unoccupied, unappropriated land no longer exists. But this is at most a necessary condition. It is not sufficient since the landowners are likely to try to hold onto serfdom for some time. An actual shift from free tenants paying money/rent to one where farming is carried out mainly by capitalist tenant farmers, as occurred in Britain, requires that a significant part of the rural population be deprived both of security of tenure and of access to communal lands. The persistence of communal lands was a key feature of much traditional peasant economy.

4.4 COMPARISON WITH CAPITALISM

We should neither accept the view that suggests that traditional agriculture with substantial resources held in common is inefficient, nor concede that feudal agriculture, a sub-species of traditional peasant farming, is economically irrational. The Hardin [1968] thesis that communal lands will inevitably be degraded by overuse has been systematically refuted by Ostrom et al. [1999]. We know that communities tended to have elaborate procedures and rules to prevent the overuse of common land and to regulate fair access.

There is a certain retrospective complacency that holds that capitalist ways of organizing are uniquely rational, and that only monetary economy, with universal private property in land and wage labor, can be efficient. That this view is prevalent in Anglo-Saxon liberal economics is not surprising, given that in Britain the old landowning classes remain secure not only in their traditional estates, but also in their position within the social hierarchy. Similarly, the Austrian school of economics, formed under an aristocratic Habsburg monarchy, has long emphasized the impossibility of rational economic organization without private ownership and money [von Mises, 1935; von Mises, 1951; Hayek, 1935]. But this arguably Weberian notion of unique capitalist rationalism is influential even among Marxist economists Heinrich and Locascio [2012]. In this conception, unless you have wage labor there can be no rational calculation of comparative costs. The argument goes that rational calculation requires the value form, and that this form only comes into dominance once labor becomes abstract labor, which is treated as being equivalent to waged labor. In section 3.6 I argued that not only were prices well developed in slave economy, but that there was, at least in the manuals of agriculture of the day, a clear attempt to make rational use of the slave labor available. The weakness of my earlier argument is that it lacked statistical support, relying as it did on literary sources. For feudal economy much better statistical sources have survived, and it is possible to make a strong case for the economic rationality of the system.

Contra the claims of the Austrian school, techniques have been known since the 1930s [Kantorovich, 1960; Panne and Rahnama, 1985] that allow efficiency calculations independent of prices. The branch of math used, linear optimization, was pioneered in the USSR as a means of maximizing industrial output in the planned economy. If a factory had a particular set of machinery—say three types of lathes—and was tasked with maximizing output of two goods in fixed proportions, what was the best way to schedule the use of the machines?

Linear optimization provided an answer.[58]

The key idea here is that a unit of production, whether it is a feudal manor, a Soviet factory, or an American open-cast coal mine, will have several types of resources that have to be combined to produce outputs. The nature of the productive resources along with contemporary knowledge will determine what are called "techniques" which combine inputs in fixed proportions. For example, when plowing in the Middle Ages, plowmen, plows, and oxen could be combined as two, four, or eight ox teams. Each of these would comprise a technique. If one has enough data on inputs and outputs from enough farms one can use linear optimization algorithms to deduce what the best underlying techniques are.

McDonald [2002] applied linear optimization analysis to large databases of estates in Essex and Wiltshire [McDonald, 2010] described in the Domesday record. For each of over 500 individual estates he had the data summarized (see Table 4.1), along with information on the output of each estate. From this it was possible to rate the efficiency of each of the estates against what was contemporary best practice. For each estate he calculated the maximum it could have produced given its acreage, labor force, plow teams, mills, etc. He compared this with what it actually produced. The ratio gives the efficiency of that particular estate. He found that on average the feudal estates ran at 64 percent efficiency.

Was 64 percent good or bad as an efficiency rating? One can only make a judgment if one has efficiency ratings for large groups of production units from other historical periods. These ratings, to be comparable, must have been computed by the same linear optimization technique used for the Domesday sample. McDonald compared Domesday estates with other examples in the linear programming literature where similar methods had been used. His results are summarized in Table 4.4.

It has to be admitted that, from this data, Saxon feudal economy looks pretty good. It was a lot more efficient than nineteenth- or twentieth-century U.S. farms and comparable to the efficiency of mechanized U.S. open-cast coal mines. Only in the highly engineered technology of steam power stations did a population of units of production show better efficiency.

Remember, what is being measured is not the absolute labor productivities of farms or mines. This would be impossible since the crops produced in England in 1086—wheat, barley , wool—are not the same as the cotton, corn, and beans grown in the U.S. South, or the Mediterranean-style crops of California. Nor can we conclude that wheat production per worker year in Essex was as big as it was on the same Essex land in the nineteenth or twentieth centuries. No, what is being compared is how efficiently the enterprises were being run given the technology available at the time. Table 4.4 shows that even in the absence of competitive-factor markets, at a time

TABLE 4.4: Comparing the Efficiency of Feudal Production with Modern Production

Historical Sample	Dates	Mean of Efficiency
Domesday Manors	1086	64.3%
U.S. Southern Farms	1880	12.0%
U.S. California Farms	1977	28.0%
U.S. Midwest Mines	1975	60.8%
U.S. West Mines	1975	61.1%
U.S. Steam Power Stations	1947–63	80.0%

Source: McDonald, 2002, chapter 6.

when manors never needed fear bankruptcy, with the labor of serfs and slaves, feudal demesnes were at least as efficient as their modern equivalent. McDonald's work has to be counted as strong evidence against claims of superior capitalist rationality.

The productivity of modern farms owes, I think, more to tractors and to Haber[59] than to any inherent capitalist efficiency.

4.5   THE SMITHIAN CRITIQUE OF FEUDALISM

An economy can be partitioned into two aggregate sectors: the productive or basic sector [Sraffa, 1960], the output of which enters directly or indirectly into the consumption of the working people and their dependants, and the "unproductive sector" that comprises the remaining economic activities.[60] I used this distinction in section 4.3 to get ballpark figures for the rate of exploitation in mid-feudal England.

The conceptual distinction between these two types of labor goes all the way back to Adam Smith. He criticized the extent to which the landlord classes and "great merchants" wasted resources in employing unproductive personal servants:

> The rent of land and the profits of stock are everywhere; therefore, the principal sources from which unproductive hands derive their subsistence. These are the two sorts of revenue of which the owners have generally most to spare. They might both maintain indifferently either productive or unproductive hands. They seem, however, to have some predilection for the latter. The expense of a great lord feeds generally more idle than industrious people. The rich merchant, though with his capital he maintains industrious people only, yet by his expence, that is, by the employment of his revenue, he feeds commonly the very same sort as the great lord. [Smith, 1974, II.3.7]

He goes on to argue that with the transition out of feudalism the proportion of the national revenue that goes to the support of productive workers rises.

> Thus, at present, in the opulent countries of Europe, a very large, frequently the largest portion of the produce of the land is destined for replacing the capital of the rich and independent farmer; the other for paying his profits and the rent of the landlord. But anciently, during the prevalency of the feudal government, a very small portion of the produce was sufficient to replace the capital employed in cultivation. It consisted commonly in a few wretched cattle, maintained altogether by the spontaneous produce of uncultivated land, and which might, therefore, be considered as a part of that spontaneous produce. It generally, too, belonged to the landlord, and was by him advanced to the occupiers of the land. All the rest of the produce properly belonged to him too, either as rent for his land, or as profit upon this paltry capital. The occupiers of land were generally bondmen, whose persons and effects were equally his property. [Smith, 1974, II.3.9]

Smith alternates in his argument between an individualistic and a social approach to the question. From the standpoint of the individual rich man he says that spending on servants depletes his capital whereas spending on productive workers returns the capital with a profit. He also looks at the effect that this has on the overall division of labor.[61] In progressive bourgeois states like England and Holland the cities were manufacturing centers, whereas under the ancien regime at Rome or Versailles they were full of idle, dissolute, and poor servants of the court. So his basic argument was that under feudalism the surplus product was overwhelmingly spent unproductively, whereas in the modern (eighteenth-century) countries, the greater part of funds were spent employing productive laborers creating a more industrious, prosperous, and sober society.

To see the implications of Smith's argument look first at the physical and monetary accounts of a feudal style economy about the size of sixteenth-century Scotland's economy in Table 4.5. The population division is designed to resemble that shown in Table 4.1 as part of the earlier discussion of feudalism. We neglect the food consumption of the lords themselves and of the urban masters. The peasants are assumed to deliver rent in kind of 1,752,000 qts corn to the lords who use 1,314,000 qts to feed their servants and themselves and the remainder, 438,000 qts, is sold on the town markets for £657,000. With the money they get from selling the corn, the lords buy

TABLE 4.5: Feudal Economic Consumption

	People (in thousands)	Corn Consumed (1,000 qt.)	Corn Produced (1,000 qt.)	Rent & Profit	Urban Goods
Peasants	400	7,008	8,759	£2,628,000	-
Servants	75	1,314	0	-	-
Townsfolk	25	438	0	£164,000	£657,000
Total	500	8,759	8,759	-	-
Value	-	£13,139,000	£13,139,000	£2,792,000	-

Feudal economy of the type criticized by Adam Smith as being unproductive, prices taken to be in ballpark for 1500 at 30/- per quarter. Consumption of food is estimated on the basis of 2,200 calories per person per day, which is then converted to corn on the basis that 1lb of corn provides 1,637 calories. Source: Compiled by the author.

an equivalent £657,000 of urban goods. We can assume that these will be a mix of agricultural implements, arms, and luxuries. On the assumption that in both town and country the rate of exploitation is 25 percent, the masters in the towns must make a profit of £164,000 that they are assumed to spend on urban goods.

Although the table shows the value of corn produced and consumed in money terms, this is just an attributed value, since in a feudal economy most of the crop is never marketed. The total sum of "vendible" commodities, to use Smith's terminology, can be calculated as follows:

Sales of urban goods to lords	£657,000
Sales of urban goods within towns	£164,000
Sales of corn to towns	£657,000
Total	£1,478,000

Now suppose that there is a social transformation and the servant class is transformed into wage workers in urban manufactories as Smith advocated. The output of the urban sector would grow by 300 percent as there would now be four times as many urban workers. Similarly, grain sales to the urban sector would grow, since while servants were fed in their master's hall, wage workers had to buy bread on the market. The overall effect would be to grow the market economy to £5,192,000. Is this just an illusion, though, brought about by commodifying what was previously an element of natural economy?

No, not entirely, since the real output in kind of the urban economy would be three times what it was before the erstwhile retainers were proletarianized, though the increased sale of grain to the towns does not involve any more actually being grown than before. The growth of commodity circulation exaggerates the real increase in production; but there is a real increase all the same.

But this does not get to the heart of Smith's distinction between the unproductive economy generated by feudalism and the productive one generated by the manufacturing bourgeoisie. For in the example I have given almost the entire market for the urban product is still provided by the rural aristocracy. Their marketization of the grain they collect as rent gives them the revenue to consume the greater part of the augmented urban production. Smith contrasts the situation of Edinburgh in the seventeenth century and earlier with its position after 1707 as follows:

> There was little trade or industry in Edinburgh before the union. When the Scotch Parliament was no longer to be assembled in it, when it ceased to be the necessary residence of the principal nobility and gentry of Scotland, it became a city of some trade and industry. It still continues, however, to be the residence of the principal courts of justice in Scotland, of the Boards of Customs and Excise, etc. A considerable revenue, therefore, still continues to be spent in it. In trade and industry it is much inferior to Glasgow, of which the inhabitants are chiefly maintained by the employment of capital. The inhabitants of a large village, it has sometimes been observed, after having made considerable progress in manufactures, have become idle and poor in consequence of a great lord having taken up his residence in their neighbourhood. [Smith, 1974, II.3.12]

The observations that Smith makes about the two cities remained valid at least until the late twentieth century. He considered cities like Glasgow "as trading cities . . . as cities which trade not only for their own consumption, but for that of other cities and countries." In contrast to cities like Paris or Rome or seventeenth-century Edinburgh that traded only for the consumption of the royal courts and nobility in residence. One could make similar observations today, contrasting Washington to New York, Brasilia to Rio, Canberra to Sydney. The key issue is the ratio between capital and revenue, and thus between productive and unproductive employment.

> The proportion between capital and revenue, therefore, seems everywhere to regulate the proportion between industry and idleness. Wherever capital predominates, industry prevails: wherever revenue, idleness. Every increase or diminution of capital, therefore, naturally tends to increase or diminish the real quantity of industry, the

number of productive hands, and consequently the exchangeable value of the annual produce of the land and labor of the country, the real wealth and revenue of all its inhabitants. [Smith, 1974, II.3.13]

The issue is not just the sort of static comparison I calculated above, a one-time transfer of retainers to wage laborers, but the process of continuously accumulating capital, continuously converting revenue into capital, which increases physical productivity. Smith's fundamental objection to unproductive expenditure is that it impedes the accumulation of capital. It is only by converting revenue into capital that the productive capacity of society in real terms can increase:

As the capital of an individual can be increased only by what he saves from his annual revenue or his annual gains, so the capital of a society, which is the same with that of all the individuals who compose it, can be increased only in the same manner. [Smith, 1974, II.3.15]

He realizes that with the accumulation of capital an increased part of the workforce is engaged in simply replacing and maintaining the capital, and that in consequence the rate of return on capital will fall as the proportion between capital and revenue rises.[62] This, he believed, was a necessary accompaniment to economic progress. We will examine this in more detail in the next chapter.

His concern with the accumulation of capital is why he makes a sharp distinction between productive activities, which actually produce a persisting physical product, and unproductive services that "perish in the very instant of their performance." The objection to feudalism as a social order was not inefficiency, but profligacy and waste. It was the way that the nobility wasted labor in prodigal displays of luxury that held back progress. We will see in a subsequent chapter that this same objection comes to apply to the rentier classes of modern capitalism.[63]

CHAPTER 5

Capitalist Economy

The hand mill gives you society with the feudal lord; the steam mill,
society with the industrial capitalist.

—KARL MARX, 1847

The capitalist mode of production *is* machine production. Capitalist
societies feature:

- Energy mainly from artificial not human sources
- High-yield agriculture supporting large urban populations.
- Widespread use of machinery and applied science.
- Lots of waged workers making commodities in private enterprises.
- The surplus product appearing as monetary profit.

The components listed above constitute an auto-catalytic system [Kauffman,
1993]. Given external sources of energy, the composed system reproduces
itself and grows. Obviously these components do not spring full-formed.
There were earlier auto-catalytic social systems. Some of the elements that
make up capitalism must be generated by these prior systems before capitalist
dominance.[64] As Althusser et al. [2006] argue,[65] partial combinations of capitalist elements have come together before without leading to full capitalism.
If Russo [2013] is to be believed almost all the elements came together in
Ptolemaic Egypt. Althusser cites Renaissance Italy as another capitalism that
might have been. The eventual formation of a new system was a stochastic
sputtering process before it finally caught fire.

Each historical type of economy involves a characteristic technical way
of making things—Marx's mode of production—which is combined with
social forms or relations of production. The most critical of the latter is the

form of extraction of the surplus product. In later sections of this chapter I will examine how this surplus is produced and how that interacts with the typical technology complex of capitalism: high-yield agriculture, machinery, applied science, and artificial power. Since all of these are tied together by production for the market, that is what I look at first.

5.1 THE CAPITALIST PRICE MECHANISM

In section 3.6 I discussed how the regulation of prices by expended labor worked in slave economies. And in section 3.5.3 I referred to the extensive empirical literature showing that labor time regulates contemporary prices. But in modern capitalist economies the mechanisms by which this happens are not as self-evident as they were under slavery. A similar process to that I described for latifundia would work for companies that also made several product lines. They can compare the labor required by different lines of products—different models of cars, for example—and set their selling prices to be roughly proportional to the labor used. The situation of a car company, though, is different in two important respects from a slave estate:

1. A car firm has to buy many of the components that make up the final car. The cost of these components can be a significant part of the final selling price, whereas the latifundia was much more self-sufficient. They may have brought in some supplies, but not many.[66]
2. A *dominus*, or feudal lord, already claims the laboring capacity of his slaves and serfs. He can therefore directly calculate labor time expended on different crops without resorting to calculations in money terms. Thus precapitalist economy should be more directly rational in terms of social labor. A firm has to buy the labor force by the week or month, and so is faced with a more immediate monetary cost, not just a cost in terms of labor. The wage cost is then homogeneous with component costs. Both are in terms of money.

The first point, that firms buy in components, is not a serious problem. If the firms simply pass on the component costs in the final product, and make their markup on components proportional to the labor they employ, and if all firms follow this practice, all prices including those of the components will, by recursion, end up being determined by the ultimate labor used.

Although firms do have to hire labor power, and are thus presented with it as a monetary cost, this does not prevent them from doing internal estimates of what a project will cost in terms of person months. Indeed they are obliged to do this first, otherwise they do not know many workers they must hire. Even in a capitalist monetary economy direct calculations of labor time are logically prior to calculations in cash.

But by itself this is not a watertight argument. Why should different firms in different industries use the same markup for labor?

Why indeed should it be labor that they base their markup on, rather than other costs?

In my argument I will repeatedly rely on what is called either the law of averages or the law of large numbers. An example of the law of averages is: individual women vary in heights, but it you take 100 women at random and work out the average height of these 100, it will be very close to the average height of all women. The tall women in the sample will cancel out the short women. I will use this kind of argument repeatedly.

Returning to firms: we do not have to assume that all firms have the same markup We only have to demonstrate that there must in practice be a narrow range of markups used. If most markups are pretty close to the average, then labor ends up determining the price structure.

First, consider that the labor content of any product is made up of two parts:

$$\begin{array}{r} \text{Labor content of components} \\ + \text{ Direct labor used to make it} \\ \hline = \text{Labor content of the product} \end{array}$$

The term "components" here should be understood to include not only things that physically pass into the product like tires on a car, but also the things like the electricity used and the fractional wear-and-tear on the productionline machinery.

Now consider the ratio of selling price to labor content. We can expect this to vary randomly among products, but the scale of this random variation will be small. The price will also have two components:

$$\begin{array}{r} \text{Money cost of components} \\ + \text{ Wages} \times \text{Markup} \\ \hline = \text{Total price of the product} \end{array}$$

Since many different components will be used in any given product, and since the price-to-labor ratios of these will vary in different directions, some above the average, some below the average, these variations will tend to cancel out. The total price-to-labor ratio of any large bundle of components will, by the law of large numbers, be very close to the average ratio prevailing in the economy. So to a good approximation, we have:

$$\text{Components' labor content} \approx \frac{\text{Money cost of components}}{\text{Average markup} \times \text{Average wage}}$$

The expression *Average markup* × *Average wage* gives the Average Value Added by Labor (AVAL). It measures how many £, $, or € are added to the output by an hour's work. What do we know about the *markup* in individual firms?

Well we know that the *average mark-up* must be greater than 100 percent. Were it not, there would be no profits and the economy would not be capitalist. If the markup was 150 percent it would mean that firms made a gross surplus of 50p on every £1 they paid in wages. How this gross surplus is divided up into profit, rent, interest, and tax does not concern us here. What is important is that it exists.

We also know that very few firms will be operating at a loss. Some firms may be loss making for a short while, but the process is self-limiting. They either return to profit or close. So very few individual firms will have a mark-up that is below 100 percent. Let us say that at most 1 percent of firms have a markup that means they make a loss. If the average markup is 150 percent we can use a table of the normal distribution to work out what the standard error of the markup must be to ensure that only 1 percent of firms make a loss. It has to be 21.5 percent. This means that 95 percent of firms would end up with a markup of between 107 percent and 193 percent.

One measures the spread of data by its coefficient of variation given by the rule

$$\text{Coefficient of variation} \approx \frac{\text{Standard error}}{\text{Average}}$$

In the example we have so far the coefficient of variation (CV) in the markup would be 21.5/150 = 14 percent. The laws governing the markup's variance are:

- The smaller the fraction of firms that are loss making, the smaller the spread of the markup
- The higher the average markup, the higher the spread of the markup. A normal distribution is symmetrical so if the average markup is 200 percent then the spread of markups would be between 114 percent and 286 percent, which is twice what you get with a 150 percent markup.

The average markup for the whole economy is given by:

$$\text{Average markup} = \frac{\text{Total wages} + \text{Total surplus}}{\text{Total wages}}$$

The data needed can easily be obtained from published National Income statistics allowing us to estimate the spread of markups used by firms. It is obvious that the variation of the £/hour ratio of the final output is bound to be smaller than the spread of markups. Selling prices are determined by firm markups plus the passed on cost of components. By the law of averages, the spread in the £/hour ratio in a bundle of components is smaller than the spread for individual commodities. So passing on the component cost will dampen the £/hour spread of final selling prices.

If the component costs were to make up, say, 1/3 of the selling price then this would reduce a CV of 14 percent in mark-ups to something more like a CV of 10 percent for selling prices [Cockshott and Cottrell, 1998b].[67]

In conclusion, I have shown[68] why the classical economists were right in assuming that prices are determined by labor. The classical theory has the simplicity prescribed by William of Ockham, is testable as the scientific method demands, and its operation is enforced by simple statistics. So we see in table 5.1 that the correlation between the monetary value of output in different U.S. industries stands at the 97 percent level with the direct and indirect labor required to produce these outputs. Note that the variation in industry monetary outputs is almost completely due to the differences in direct and indirect labor used to produce their outputs [Cockshott and Cottrell, 1997d].

Another testable consequence of this classical theory of prices is that profit rates will be higher where the labor-to-capital ratio is higher and vice versa. We will see later that this is an important historical effect shaping the long-term future of capitalism, but it also operates in real time to cause those industries with a high capital-to-labor ratio to have a lower rate of profit.

TABLE 5.1: Correlation of Matrix of Logs of Estimates of Total Industry Output for 47 Sectors of U.S. Industry as Predicted by Sraffian (Sraffa, 1960) Prices

	P	E_1	E_2
P	1	-	-
E_1	0.971	1	-
E_3	0.968	0.998	1

P = observed monetary value of output; E1 = labor content;
E2 = monetary value of output. Source: Cockshott and Cottrell, 1997d.

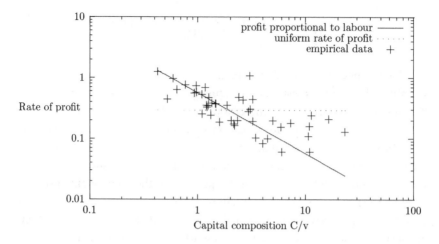

Figure 5.1. Relationship between profit rates and capital composition for U.S. industries, Bureau of Economic Affairs fixed capital plus one month's circulatingconstant capital as estimate of capital stock (log scales). Source: Cockshott and Cottrell, 1997d.

This is shown in Figure 5.1 and Table 5.2. The table displays the correlation coefficient between the rate of profit and organic composition, and also between the profit rate and the inverse of organic composition, across 47 U.S. industries. The former coefficient—at .454—is statistically significant at the 1 percent level.[69] Figure 5.1 shows very clearly that those U.S. industries with high capital-to-labor ratios have low rates of profit.

5.2 RECURRENCE RELATIONS

The arguments for why labor regulates prices have so far been pragmatic and detailed. They rely on firms not going bankrupt, and on contingent information about the distribution of national value added between labor and capital. These factors are real and immediate, but they are themselves consequences of deeper structures.

Any economic system is a process, one that undergoes constant change at the fine level, but shows relative stability at the coarse level. There is change at the level of all the individual products that are being transformed by labor and are then consumed or emplaced. The population is made up of mortal members, so its membership constantly turns over. But there are certain stabilities. From year to year the number of people changes only slightly. Towns grow and shrink, but they can endure with the same basic street plan for centuries. Industries and family lines grow and die over periods from decades to centuries. Firms and households do the same over shorter periods.

But what are these things that grow, persist, and die?

TABLE 5.2: Profit Rates, Markup, and Capital Composition, Bureau Economic Affairs Fixed Capital Plus One Month's Circulating Constant Capital as Estimate of Capital Stock for 47 U.S. Industries

	s/C	C/v	s/v
Mean	0.29	1.95	0.57
Standard Deviation	0.22	3.04	0.50
Coefficient of Variation	0.76	1.56	0.88
	s/C and C/v (weighted by C)	s/C and v/C (weighted by C)	
Correlation Coefficient	−0.45	0.78	

Profits = s, wages = v, capital stock = C. Source: Cockshott and Cottrell, 1997d.

They are all processes, and their apparent "thingness" rests on repetition, which enmeshes a homeostasis that preserves a certain basic structure. Production is often directly recurrent, as in the annual agricultural cycle, or the three-minute repetition cycle of the original Ford production line. In other industries, like shipbuilding, the repetition is more approximate. The individual ships differ in size, shape, and construction time, but still retain a structural cycle, from laying the keel, through assembly, to launch and fitting out.

The fleeting stability of units of production rests on their slowly changing workforces and long-lasting production facilities. For the domestic economy, the slowly changing workforce was one or more generations of family members, who gradually replace one another. The long-lasting facilities were the buildings, granaries, and farmland which, having been originally cleared from forest, had by generations of effort been developed. For a car firm you have employees who, as a collectivity, have the knowledge and skill to cooperate in making cars. The long-lasting facilities are the buildings and equipment, which, like the farm, gradually develop over time.

These stable components combine, at any one instant, with material in flux. There is material waiting to be transformed: seed, car parts. There is material undergoing transformation: growing oats, partially assembled cars on the line. At times, there are transformed products: a full granary, finished cars in the lot. The whole process is impelled by external sources of energy.

Traditional farms are solely solar. Industry has two energy sources. First is the primary motive power, electricity today, but once coal or flowing water. Second is human labor power, energized by food. The domestic farm generated human energy internally, but for a factory it comes from outside. Workers walk in fed, energized for the day's work. Whereas the farm regenerated its own inputs, its seed corn, the factory's components and raw inputs come in the gate. The transport and sale of commodities fits within these (almost) repetitive cycles.

The fact that the factory exists and produces things constrains the rest of society to be so organized that each day a cohort of workers are ready to cross its threshold; that there is a flow of its primary energy source; that there is a stream of components and raw materials being delivered regularly; and that there is a regular uplift and transport away of the products it makes.

When I say that the factory constrains the rest of the society to have certain features I mean:

1. That a particular combination of embodied technologies and social forms together form an auto-catalytic net that tends to persist.
2. That the actual existence of factories implies that there must exist one of the possible auto-catalysis systems that boost the probability of factories.
3. In this sense the factory, which we know to exist, constrains the rest of society.

In all, the factory implies a much more stringent set of constraints on the rest of society than is implied in the existence of a subsistence farm. The interface between the factory and society is complex. It implies that the society in which it is embedded must be able to generate and sustain the workers who come in each day. It is not enough that the people exist and have the relevant skills. They must be generated as factory workers, not as some other kind of person. They must be free to work in the factory rather than tilling their own farms or being tied up in some different activity.

The delivery of primary energy implies a whole organized supply network. At one time this might be something local, an enchanneling of a river by weirs and millraces. Later it is more encompassing: canals to deliver coal, mines to extract it. Now it implies electricity grids, with networks of generators synched to a 50Hz cycle.

The supply of raw materials and components implies a transport network and a supply chain. It implies other factories. The complexity of the supply network grows, literally exponentially with the the number of inputs to the factory.[70] This complex of recurrence constraints is the determining role of the productive forces. Recurrence relations select out only certain sets of social forms and relations as compatible.

There is not just a single set of reproductively competent social relations for industrial production. Theory and history teach us that there are at least two, possibly more, characteristic social forms of industrial society. Which set of social relations the factory is embedded within depends on real history. In modern terminology it is path-sensitive, dependent on whether the society has undergone capitalist or socialist industrialization.

We are in this chapter only concerned with the former. So we have to assume that there is no overarching social planning mechanism that will deliver the components that the factory needs, no system of general labor allocation that will ensure that fed and clothed workers turn up each day. Instead, all of these preconditions must be arrived at by the exercise of private contract. Nothing arrives without a prior promise to pay a monetary equivalent.

In the absence of a public direction of labor and resources, the social power of the state symbolized in money is co-opted by private firms to command[71] both the living and embodied labor their survival demands. They can demand labor and components, so long as they have the cash. Behind these transactions, admittedly, stands the state power, ready to enforce the law of contract, ready to enforce debts in its currency, but the contracts themselves are private. Hence the arguments I used earlier to explain the enforcement of another law, what Marxist economists called the "law of value,"[72] express the real dependence of firms' reproduction on the laws of contract. These are constructed so as to be neutral with respect to the distribution of the social power of money. The state treats both firms in a contract equally and is concerned only that stipulated monetary equivalents are paid for goods delivered. The law of contracts is neutral with respect to the distribution of money between legal personalities.[73] The survival of the firm as a technical and labor cooperative unit then depends on its survival as a contractual unit, as a legal person, an owner of property.

In order to reproduce themselves in the absence of a social plan, factories have to be able to command the delivery of labor and components. The latter implies that they must, albeit indirectly, be able order the allocation of social labor into the making of those components. The statistical laws regulating price, which I explained in section 5.1, act to make sure that command over money becomes, on average, command over an equivalent amount of labor, thus allowing a decentralized planning of the economy to take place.

Finley [1980] argues that whereas ancient authors were quite open about the exploitative nature of their society, modern ideology strives to suppress talking about it. The power of command, domination of the slave lord or *dominus* was open, unashamed and enforced with whips and branding irons. That of the capitalist is presented in the guise of equality on the market and fraternity as citizen. The worker and Ford, the farmer and chain supermarket Walmart, meet and contract as legal equals. The fact is, of course, that behind the legal facade, they are far from equal. Ford or Walmart have financial resources that are perhaps a million times as great as an individual worker or farmer. The £-millions in the accounts of the firms put them in a position of vastly greater bargaining strength than a worker who would be

Figure 5.2. The labor certificates issued by the labor exchanges of
the socialist pioneer Robert Owen.

hard put to survive a month without pay, or a farmer who, by harvest time,
has run down his assets to almost nothing.

The classical economists had unmasked what was happening in this process. They wrote in a still aristocratic Britain, in which the common people
could neither vote nor, in the main, read. You find in Smith an openness
about class and command that came to those with a classical education. He
saw that money was the power to command the labor of the lower classes.
In his day the coinage was still gold; open fiat money in Europe was yet to
come, though the Chinese had long known it. But by the early nineteenth
century, having experienced the suspension of banknote redemption during
the French wars, socialist writers started to propose that instead of gold,
money should be openly denominated in terms of labor. Instead of having
the motto "I promise to pay the bearer on demand the sum of One Pound"
they would promise goods to the value of one hour (Figure 5.2).

There are two reasons why this idea has never been implemented. One
of these is minor. Although prices are regulated by labor, it is approximate,
so there is around a 10 percent margin of error above and below, thus
there would never be an exact equality between the labor performed and
the price obtained. But that pales to insignificance compared to the much
bigger political obstacle. Were such notes to be introduced they would highlight that behind the apparent equality of employer and employee there is
in reality a deeply unequal relationship. Such notes would be little short of
revolutionary pamphlets. They only made sense, in the context of socialist
pioneer Robert Owen's exchanges, if they were to be part of a process of
moving the whole economy over to communist operation.

5.3 CAPITALIST SURPLUS

Under slavery, the profits of the slave owners were no mystery. The slaves worked for free, and everything they produced belonged to their master. He had to give them part of the crop as food, but anything that remained he sold as a profit. In modern society it appears, according to orthodox economics, that workers are not only paid, they are paid the full marginal product resulting from their efforts. The slave was nakedly exploited, whipped to work, with no standing before the law. An employee enters into a voluntary contract that, in law at least, is one between equal parties, and if economic theory is to be believed, the wage he/she gets actually expresses a relationship of equal exchange. She gets paid the value of her labor, and that value is defined by the marginal or extra product that the company gets by taking her on as an employee. The argument goes that were she paid less, then it would be worth the company taking on more workers until the point was reached at which the last worker taken on yielded no additional profit.

The theory on which this account of remuneration rests is the one that gave us the supply and demand functions shown in Figure 3.8. We explained in section 3.5 just how vacuous this theory was from a scientific viewpoint, but even if we accept the counterfactual assumption of diminishing returns to scale, then all workers but the last one taken on must be exploited. All others are paid less than the value of the product that their labor produces. Clearly if Owenite principles applied and each worker was paid the average value added by labor there would be no profit; the entire value product would go to labor. That would imply a cooperative rather than a capitalist economy. If the ownership structure remained capitalist, and if in each industry the average wage was equal to the average value added by labor in that industry, then clearly around half the firms, those with below average labor usage, would make a profit, and half, those with above-average labor usage, would make a loss. This would be an unsustainable situation. Half of the firms would soon be bankrupt. So we have to assume that in a capitalist economy there will be a markup on wages. Clearly, if real wages can be reduced, or people can be made to work longer and harder, the markup will be bigger. We will look at what governs this markup in more detail in sections 5.4 and 5.7 but a typical example of what average markup prevails in a capitalist economy is given in Table 5.3 (page 116).

One could envisage that an economic reform, say analogous to the abolition of slavery in the nineteenth century, could similarly abolish wage labor and capitalist profit. Legislation specifying that the employees of a company are the owners of residual value added would abolish the need for a markup over wage income. In a cooperative economy like that which used to

TABLE 5.3: Calculating the Markup on Wages in the UK

	£M
Total Consumption of Intermediates	£1,526,425
Taxes Less Subsidies on Production	£23,303
Compensation of Employees	£873,202
Operating Surplus	£650,409
Value Added	£1,546,914
Output	£3,073,339
Markup on Wages	£1.77
Rate of surplus value	£0.77

Data from *2013 Summary Supply and Use Tables* for the United Kingdom, Office of National Statistics.

operate in Yugoslavia, with workers the final owners of residual value added, markup is unnecessary because there will be differences in take-home pay between more and less productive cooperatives. Workers in this case bear both the risks of market variations and pocket its benefits.[74]

In terms of its current reproduction, the capitalist form of economy stands directly on property relations and property law. It is sustained by an edifice of company law that defines shareholders not employees as the appropriators of value. Its replacement, like the replacement of the slave system in the Americas, will ultimately be the result of political and legal changes. But that does not explain how, within the system of private commodity exchange, the specifically capitalist mode of making things, with its accompanying social relations, became dominant. To understand this we have to examine in more detail why the technological complex specific to capitalism reinforces capitalist social forms.

5.4 TECHNOLOGY AND SURPLUS

We said earlier that capitalist societies have high-yield agriculture able to support a large urban population; a significant part of social labor time devoted to the production of commodities by private producers; widespread use of machinery and science; artificial sources of energy; and a significant part of their surplus product represented as private profit obtained from wage slavery. It should be clear that taken individually, several of these features have existed in precapitalist societies. Any urban civilization needs an agriculture that delivers a surplus product. The slave economies had many private producers of commodities, and a significant part of their surplus, since it was sold, was represented as money profits. Both antiquity and the

Middle Ages knew of wage labor. Where slave and feudal economies differed significantly from capitalism is in a much more limited use of artificial energy and their failure to carry out ongoing scientific research that could be applied to improving the economy.

5.4.1 Vital Energy

The Neolithic Revolution had such a big impact because it enabled humanity to access much more energy by moving down a trophic level. But between the Neolithic Revolution and the development of capitalist economy, societies remained in a sense natural economies. They were natural in that their energy source was still biological, and as such was limited by the inherent losses that are incurred as solar energy goes through photosynthesis, metabolic loss in plants, and then metabolic inefficiencies in human and animal bodies before being converted into mechanical energy in muscles. There were two exceptions to this, first and most important the harnessing of zephyrs for navigation, and second, enslaving naiads to turn wheels.[75] Though the key inventions required for water power, undershoot and overshoot mills, were there, industrial use seems to have been relatively limited. We know of only one industrial scale application of water power in the ancient world, the 16-wheel mill at Barbegal [Leveau, 1996], though smaller mills were apparently widespread. The famous Barbegal mill, even at 100 percent mechanical efficiency would have had a maximum output of only 0.044MW from the estimated flow of 250L/s over an 18M drop [Lorenz et al., 2012]. A more realistic estimate at a typical 60 percent efficiency would be 0.026MW.

As table 5.5 shows, even at the earliest stage of capitalist industrialization Britain had a thousand times as much installed water power as that behemoth of antiquity, the Barbegal mill. At the same time we should avoid a tendency to prettify capitalism in comparison to prior forms of social relations, and claim that prior forms of economy had little incentive to minimize labor input. If you read the passage I quoted from Cato on the management of latifundia he is anything but sloppy about the use of labor. Labor time is an expensive resource to the slave owner as well as for the capitalist; slaves were only intermittently cheap. It makes sense to minimize the number of slaves you set to do a task.

Any set of social relations has some incentive to reduce expended labor. Every free peasant or artisan wants to reduce their effort, and will use any technique available to them to do so. Feudal lords or slave owners likewise wish to maximize the output their slaves or serfs produce. If anything, Marx argues that capitalism, because of the wage labor relation that involves paying for labor at a fraction of its true value, is irrational in its tendency to undervalue living labor relative to dead labor. We should therefore expect capitalism's progressiveness in terms of implementing labor-saving machinery to be inversely proportional to the level of real wages. The more that workers are impoverished and have their wages driven down by the flood of dispossessed peasantry, the slower capitalism will mechanize. In contrast, where proletarians had the opportunity to emigrate to virgin lands, as to the America of the nineteenth century, the greater was the incentive to use machinery.

There are about sixty known Romano British water wheels, but we must assume that only a small proportion of sites have been discovered. It is also unclear how many of the 6,000 or more English mills in 1086 had been in use continuously since Roman times. The presence of many horizontal Saxon or Norse mills probably indicates most had been built in the subsequent 600 years. What we do not know is the total installed power, but allowing say 1.5kw to 2kw per mill, which seems reasonable for small undershoot or Saxon horizontal ones, we get a total installed power in mid-feudal England of about 12MW, or 460 times what the largest known Roman industrial establishment used. Lynne White [1964] argued that the diffusion of watermills was a characteristic superiority of the feudal as opposed to the slave economy.

Peak usage of water mills in the feudal period in England in the 1300s would have been about twice that. Given that in the period from 1086 to the mid-fourteenth century the population more than doubled, it would indicate that there was a stable ratio of artificial to human energy available during the period. We have a ratio of only around 7 watts of water power per head of population. By this point almost all villages would have had a mill or been within easy reach of one. Langdon [1991] indicates that up to 90 percent of feudal manors in England had mills, in which case control over these vital means of production would have been a critical factor in the dominance of the upper class.

None of this indicates that the feudal ruling class was slack in its adoption of such labor-saving machinery as was known at the time. If we assume that the sustained output of an adult manual worker in peasant agriculture is no more than 75 watts and that in 1086 the peak output of human labor would have been around 70MW, then in mid-feudalism artificial energy supplied about 17 percent of the peak human energy. If we look at the mid-1700s we have an installed base of artificial power of about 63MW, mostly water, but some wind and steam. A population of around six and a half million gives a human labor output of at most 285MW, so that by this phase artificial power was providing around 22 percent of the human effort. A bit better than feudalism, but not much.

By 1870 we have a British population of 21 million, which doing heavy manual work could have delivered about 945 MW, but had an installed capacity of artificial power of 1700 MW or almost twice the manual output of physical power. This is a phase change in the mode of production brought about by steam power and reinforces Marx's argument that it is the steam mill that gives rise to the industrial capitalist.

5.4.2 Hero's Turbine Not Enough

The ancient Romans already had a working steam turbine in Hero's aeolipile. Why were they not able to turn this to use in industry, pumping water or turning millstones?

Why no Industrial Revolution in antiquity?

There are well-known arguments about the social relations of slavery impeding the development of labor-saving technology, but is this enough of an explanation?

We know that the ancients harnessed the power of water for grinding corn and other industrial uses, so they were not completely indifferent to artificial sources of power.

Could they not have used steam turbines instead of water wheels to grind corn?

After all, steam turbines are used in current nuclear and coal power plants, surely they would have been ideal?

I think not. There are inherent limitations to the usefulness of Hero's device, basically its low torque and inefficiency. Steam turbines are now the preferred prime mover, but their superiority has depended on the ability to produce high-pressure steam and high-rotational velocity. The actual technology that started the Industrial Revolution—the Watt steam engine—had the virtue that it could develop very high torques at low velocity using very low steam pressures.

In order to get a functioning fossil fuel economy you had to have a prime mover and a way of providing fuel for it. The main fuel available was coal, which was obtained from mines, which were prone to flooding. It is almost a chicken and egg situation. You need coal for steam engines, but to drain coal mines you needed steam power. The Watt engine was originally developed for pumping out mines, an application that required a lot of force but tolerated a relatively slow engine. The torque T supplied by a Hero-style turbine is given by the rule: $T = p \times 2a \times r$, where wheel p is the steam pressure, a the area of each exhaust nozzle, and r the radius of the turbine.

The torque provided by a Watt beam engine was given by a similar rule: $T = p \times a \times l$.

Here p is now the pressure difference between the boiler and the condenser, a the area of the cylinder and l is the beam length.

The early Watt engines were huge, with beam lengths of over 3 meters compared to the few centimeters for the length of hero turbines. This is a factor of 100 difference. In terms of diameter of bore a practical Hero turbine would not have exceeded 1 cm against half a meter for a Watt engine. This is a factor of about 2,500 greater area for the Watt machine. Let us assume both operate at the same steam pressure, since the technology of boiler construction was initially the limiting factor. That means that the torque of an early Watt engine was about a *quarter of a million* times greater than an aeolipile.

Could you build an aeolipile that generated comparable torque?

Well yes, if you had arms a couple of meters long on the turbine and nozzles a half a meter in diameter, then the torque would be comparable. But the nozzles of the aeolipile are open to the air, so a nozzle half a meter across would use up an entirely impractical quantity of steam.

5.4.3 Practical Turbines

An aeolipile is only practical as a power-generating device if the revolutions per second are very high. A small torque multiplied by a very high number of revs per second can generate a useful amount of power.

The aeolipile had to go through a series of steps before it could be converted, in the 1880s into practical turbines by Laval and Parson. The first

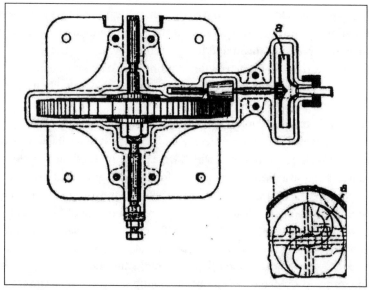

Figure 5.3. Laval's first turbine used to power a cream centrifuge in 1884. It used a simple modification of Hero's turbine in concept, but relied on precision engineering and high-pressure steam. The part marked *a* is the modified aeolipile. Steam enters from the right. Source: Jude, 1910.

TABLE 5.4: Performance of Production of Laval Turbines

Horsepower	Radius	Revs per minute of turbine	Revs per minute of geared output
5	5cm	30,000	3,000
30	11cm	20,000	2,000
300	35cm	10,000	750

Source: Data from Jude, 1910.

practical use of a reaction turbine was for Laval's cream separator. This required very rapid rotation, around 1000rpm, to centrifugally separate cream from milk, so a high-speed device was desirable. Laval's first prototype was based on the aeolipile but heavily geared down, using friction gear to get it to 1000rpm. His second prototype switched to the impulse principle—directing a jet of high-pressure steam against a rotating set of turbine blades.

Rotation speeds were very high. The 300hp turbine in table 5.4 had a peripheral velocity of 366M/s or 1317Kmph—supersonic velocity. Such huge velocities needed high-tensile steel.

Between the start of steam power and the first practical use of a reaction turbine over a hundred years elapsed, during which many engineers came up with suggestions for turbines. But it was not until the 1880s that Parson and Laval designs actually got into use. They depended on having high-pressure steam, precision engineering, and high-strength steels to work. None of these were available to the Romans. They had neither the blast furnaces and forges to make the wrought-iron boilers, nor Bessemer converters to produce turbine steel. Steam turbines only became practical as a source of power once industrial society was in full swing.

Well, even if turbines were not practical, what stopped the Romans building something like one of Watt's engines?

Basically a lack of scientific knowledge. The Watt engine depended for its power stroke on atmospheric pressure. Steam was supplied at near atmospheric pressure, and then condensed to create a vacuum. That depended in turn on key prior concepts—the discovery of atmospheric pressure by Torricelli, the demonstration of Guericke, and the concept of heat as a quantity to be conserved developed by Watt's supervisor at Glasgow, Professor Black.

Technologies have an order of dependence to them that cannot be arbitrarily skipped over. Without the knowledge and skills associated with a particular stage of technology, you cannot simply go on to develop the next.

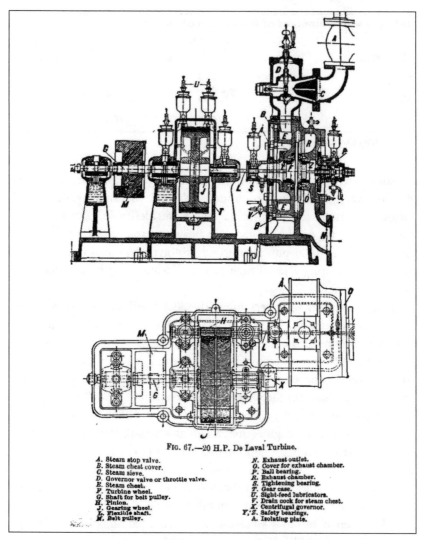

FIG. 67.—20 H.P. De Laval Turbine.

A. Steam stop valve.	*N.* Exhaust outlet.
B. Steam chest cover.	*O.* Cover for exhaust chamber.
C. Steam sieve.	*P.* Ball bearing.
D. Governor valve or throttle valve.	*R.* Exhaust chamber.
E. Steam chest.	*S.* Tightening bearing.
F. Turbine wheel.	*T.* Gear case.
G. Shaft for belt pulley.	*U.* Sight-feed lubricators.
H. Pinion.	*V.* Drain cock for steam chest.
J. Gearing wheel.	*X.* Centrifugal governor.
L. Flexible shaft.	*Y.*'*Z.* Safety bearings.
M. Belt pulley.	*A.* Isolating plate.

Figure 5.4. Laval's second turbine switched to the impulse principle and went into production. With this the principle of the turbine was turned into a practical device. The electricity you use today is produced by a machine derived from the turbines of Laval and Parson. Source: Jude, 1910.

5.4.4 Why Power Was Essential

Why was energy so vital to the development of capitalism?

Fundamentally it is because by substituting inanimate energy for human muscle, the amount of human time and effort required to make things was reduced. A powered machine replaced the work of human hands and arms. This produced gains in speed, mass, and parallelism.

The natural resonant frequency of human limbs sets a maximum number of strokes per minute with which a hammer, saw, or needle can be moved. A powered reciprocating mechanism can operate considerably faster. Contrast the number of stitches per second on an electric sewing machine with what can be done with a hand-held needle. When the completely rotary motion of a circular saw replaces the back and forth of a handsaw the acceleration is even more marked.

The weight that can be moved with each stroke or motion can be hugely increased by applying power. Trip hammers turned by water wheels were vastly heavier than any blacksmith could wield, steam hammers and hydraulic presses increased the mass of the hammer by further orders of magnitude. The same magnification applies in a comparison between spades and steam excavators.

Alongside gigantism went parallelism. Instead of one woman turning one spindle, a water wheel or steam engine could turn 100 spindles for each horsepower it produced. A megawatt is 1341 horsepower, so the 90 megawatts or so of installed British water power in 1800 could have turned about 12 million spindles. Of course some of these were powering other machines, but this gives some indication of the equivalent number of workers who would have been needed to produce the same result. But it underestimates the gain in productivity from external power, since the speed of the power spindles is so much faster.

In table 5.6 note the phase change brought about by steam power between 1760 and 1871. Assume that the sustained energy output of a worker doing manual work averages 75 watts, and that 58 percent of the population was able to do manual work. We assume that mills in the Middle Ages had an output of the order of 2Kw.

A hand spinner could attain a productivity of between 2.5lb and 6lb of yarn per week [Humphries et al., 2016]. A water-powered spinning mule, the standard device used in the British textile industry, would have hundreds of spindles per worker and each of these spindles could produce between 25lb and 120lb of yarn per week [Leunig, 2003].[76] In consequence,

TABLE 5.5: Installed Artificial Power in Britain, in MegaWatts

	1760	1800	1830	1870	1907
Steam	3.75	26	123	1,535	7,181
Water	52	89.4	123	186	132
Wind	7	11.2	14.9	7.4	3.7
Total	63	126	260	1,713	7,332

Source: Figures computed from Crafts, 2004.

TABLE 5.6: Comparison of Human and Artificial Energy Output in England

Year	Mills (in thousands)	Megawatts (artificial)	People (in millions)	Megawatts (human)	Artificial as a % of human
1086	6	12	1.6	70	17
1348	13	26	4.5	198	13
1750	-	63	6.45	285	22
1870	-	1,713	21.4	942	181

Source: Population for 1086 and 1348 from Broadberry et al., 2010, tables 1 and 2. Population for 1750 and 1870 from Chandler, 2014. Mill numbers from Langdon, 1991.

each water-powered spindle was of the order of 10 or 20 times faster than the human-powered one. This means that 90 megawatts of water power devoted to spinning would produce more like the output of 200 million hand spinners. By comparision, prior to the application of powered spinning female labor working on spinning had grown exponentially (see Figure 5.5). By 1770 it had required about three-quarters of a million women, or 62 percent of English women in the 25–59 age group. Only a few decades later machine power equivalent to over a hundred million workers had been installed, which gives some impression of the leap in productivity involved.

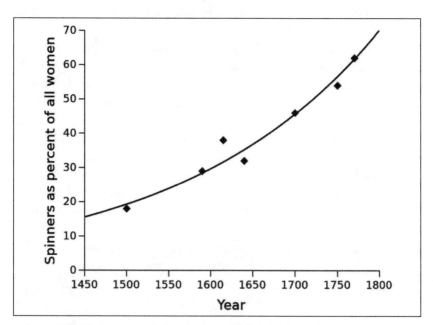

Figure 5.5. The proportion of the female population required to work as spinners to support the textile industry grew exponentially in the leadup to industrial capitalism in England. Prior to the adoption of the mules shown in figure 5.6 the number of spinners was already near its practical limit. Source: Graph drawn from data in Allen, 2015.

Figure 5.6. Water-powered mules such as this one at Robert Owen's old mill at New Lanark applied artificial energy to a huge number of spindles while an automatic sequencing mechanism replicated on a much larger scale the motions of a human spinner's arms.

Capitalist production first took root using the water power technologies available from antiquity; its novelty in this respect was not the power source but the scale on which it was used and its application to highly parallel machinery. The real novelty, steam power, was at first relatively specialized in its application—used exclusively for pumping water, particularly from mines. It was not until the 1830s that steam power overtook water in installed capacity in Britain, even later in the United States. It has been suggested [Malm, 2013] that the reason steam eventually replaced water in the cotton industry was more a matter of class conflict than technical rationality. Water mills were in isolated rural spots where it was easier for the mill workers to organize strikes than in big cities with their abundant potential scabs among the unemployed. Steam power enabled masters to move from where labor was scarce and strong to where it was abundant and weak.

Could capitalism have developed differently, in a way that did not rely on fossil fuel?

Was it just a contingent accident that Faraday's dynamo and electric motor were invented decades after Watt's engine?

Had electro-magnetism been investigated earlier, power could have been transmitted from fast-flowing rivers to power factories in cities, thus giving the masters the edge over their workers that steam provided. This transformation, though, had to await Edison, Tesla, and Kelvin in the late nineteenth century. But even then water power would not have been sufficient to rival steam. In the year 2000 the installed hydropower of the UK was 1400 MW, which is less than the installed steam power was in 1870, and only about a quarter of the total installed power of all types by the end of the nineteenth century.

TABLE 5.7: Average Output of Thermal Energy Equivalent in UK Coal Mines (25GJ per ton)

Years	MW Thermal
1760–1765	4,122
1800–1805	11,019
1830–1835	25,367
1853–1862	56,690
1873–1882	111,219
1883–1892	136,860
1893–1902	163,762
1903–1912	204,565

Source: Figures from Pollard, 1980; and from 1873 in *Historical Coal Data: Coal Production, 1853–2014*, UK Dept of Energy and Climate Change.

I speculated above about a counterfactual situation in which Faraday's generator had been invented before Watt's engine. There might be conceivable circumstances in which electromagnetism was developed before steam power, but there are real logical dependencies existing between scientific and technological advances. Heilbroner [1967] argues that it is just this set of dependencies that lie behind Marx's insistence on the primacy of the productive forces in giving direction to economic and historical development. Knowledge is cumulative. You need prior knowledge of one technology before you can think of improving it. Without the Newcomen engine as a starting point Watt would not have hit on his separate condenser. The possibility of him thinking that it would be worth using a separate condenser, however, depended on his having a prior concept that heat was a quantifiable "substance" that could be saved by not repeatedly cooling the cylinder the way Newcomen did. That in turn was only possible because of Watt's scientific training in Black's laboratory in Glasgow University [Cardwell, 1971], then the leading center for thermodynamic research.

Newcomen and Savery's pioneering engines in turn depended on the prior dissemination of Torricelli's work on atmospheric pressure, since these devices were, in the language of the day, "atmospheric engines." The power stroke of the engine was driven by atmospheric pressure. The fact that improvements to machines often came not from professional scientists but from technicians like Watt and Cugnot should not be taken to indicate either that the technicians were ignorant of the underlying scientific principles of the machines or that the discoveries were not dependent on these principles. For example, the conversion of rectilinear motion into rotary motion was a considerable engineering problem.[77] This was solved by cranks or planetary gears, but that left another problem. With a beam engine you

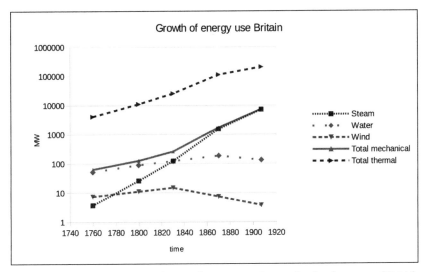

Figure 5.7. Growth of different forms of energy use during the development of British capitalism. Given the log scale of the Y axis, a straight line represents an exponential growth rate. Source: From Tables 5.5 and, 5.7.

had to combine vertical motion of the piston rod with rocking motion of the beam that would tend to bend and unseat the piston rod. Watt solved this with his parallelogram linkage [Koetsier, 1983; Ferguson, 1962]. The ability to come up with this requires at least a deep grasp of classical geometry and probably also of Cartesian techniques [Dennis, 1997] in order to prove its validity.[78] Something which, when we see it in a museum now, looks literally clunky and crude, actually involved math that would severely tax most contemporary students.

A condition therefore of capitalist civilization, and the technical advances on which it depends, has been the continuing development of science and the educational and research base on which science relies. These are not something generated internally by capitalist enterprise. They depended initially on royal and later republican state patronage which well preceded the growth of actual capitalist machine industry. Russo [2013] shows to what extent the science of the seventeenth and eighteenth centuries still rested on royally funded research of the Hellenistic period in Syracuse or Alexandria. From the seventeenth century royal patronage of research resumed and the universities in Europe became centers of science rather than just religion.

Scientific knowledge, once published, is not property. There is no profit to be made from it, so it has in the main to be produced by social rather than private research. However great the incentive for capitalists to innovate may have been, the mere existence of commodity relations and wage labor would not have been sufficient to generate the capitalist mode of

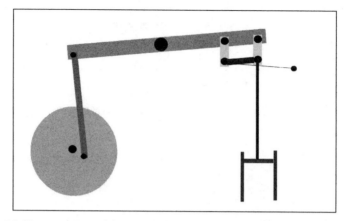

Figure 5.8. The conversion of the straight-line motion of the piston rod into the rocking motion of the beam was a difficult geometry problem solved by Watt's parallelogram linkage. Solving the problem requires a good level of geometrical education.

production. Innovations driven just by trial and error, without theory, are slow and limited. They only become rapid when coupled with socially produced and accumulated, non-commodified, theory. Patents and intellectual property rights allow certain innovations to be made profitable to firms by giving them a temporary monopoly—usually around twenty-five years. But scientific advances usually bring their benefit well into the future so that were basic research to be done for a profit it would be necessary to make scientific knowledge itself patentable, and also make these patents last for much longer—of the order of a century or more.

But a rational capitalist firm will discount future returns from patents by a guess at what the long -term rate of interest will be. Let us make the conservative estimate that they would use a 5 percent discount rate. This means that the present value of future revenue from the long-term patents you would need to take out on scientific theories becomes negligible (see page 129).

So capitalist profit seeking will itself never generate the science needed for substantial technical change. This basic property of capitalist accounting further undermines the Brenner [2001] thesis about the existence of commodity–wage labor relations themselves being a sufficient explanatory factor for the rise of the capitalist mode of production. McDonald's data on the economic efficiency of classic feudalism casts additional doubt on the Brenner thesis.

5.4.5 An Iron Subjugation

If we take into account that motive power was only one use of fossil energy,

Life of Patent	Present Value of Revenue Stream for Last Year of Patent
1	95%
10	60%
25	28%
50	8%
100	1%
200	0.01%

and for a long time only a subsidiary use, it becomes even clearer how much capitalist industry had to depend on fossil fuel. Coal was obviously used domestically for cooking and heating, but that is not a capitalist use of energy. But the iron industry, the brick industry, cement production, pottery, baking, brewing, etc., were all huge consumers of coal. This was either to provide heat or to provide direct chemical energy. You cannot convert iron oxide to metallic iron without the chemical energy of carbon as a reducing agent. The rapid expansion of all of these industries in the nineteenth century was only possible because coal mining provided far more carbon than coppicing and charcoal burning did.

With the transition from biological to fossil fuel in iron production we definitely have a resource depletion-driven transition, analogous to the megafauna extinction hypothesis, which was discussed in an earlier chapter. From the start of the iron age until the eighteenth century, iron production had relied on charcoal for fuel and to provide chemical energy. For the greater part of that period the consumption of wood was limited by the small size of the hearths and the fact that their airflow came from manually operated bellows.[79]

The first furnaces were of the "bloomery" type. They produced a solid bloom containing a mix of iron and slag. This then had to be hammered to expel the slag and form wrought iron. The early small furnaces, operating by manual bellows, did not produce high enough temperatures to actually melt the iron. Now, consider that the heat loss of a furnace is proportionate to its surface area, whereas the heat-generating capacity is proportionate to the volume of burning fuel. Heat loss is consequently proportional to the square of the linear dimension of the furnace, and heat produced to the cube of its dimension. So if you build a larger furnace the temperature it can attain will rise.

But a larger furnace requires more air to be driven through it, more than a man can drive. Water-powered bellows allowed these larger furnaces. Initially the aim was to provide larger blooms, from which bigger objects could be forged. But a side effect was that, with sufficient blowing, it became possible to heat them to the point at which they obtained liquid iron that could then be cooled as cast iron.

When operated as bloomery furnaces, the blooms were too big to be

Figure 5.9. Water-powered trip hammers could strike much heavier blows than a person. Modern hydraulic ones (right) are even more powerful. Source: Wikimedia, license Creative Commons, attribution Rainer Halama.

hand forged, requiring instead the trip hammers shown in figure 5.9. This stage had been reached by the end of the fifteenth century in Italy and by the sixteenth century in central Europe [Williams, 2003].[80]

The larger scale of production, made possible by water power, meant that iron works moved over to a specifically capitalist mode of production at this quite early date. The scale of production was beyond what the individual smith working on his own could achieve, needing both substantial fixed capital and a larger employed workforce. As the physical mode of production developed, its social form had to change, but it still remained embedded in the natural feudal economy. The iron works used three energy sources in descending order: the chemical energy of charcoal, gravitational energy of flowing water, and metabolic energy of its workers. But the chemical energy was still provided from an organic source: wood that was burned in low-oxygen conditions to produce charcoal. As such, the iron works had to be situated where there were both woodlands and flowing water and thus have a semi-agricultural dependence on woodlands owned by the aristocracy. This process was integrated into feudalism in a second sense in that a major product of the iron industry in the fifteenth and sixteenth centuries was the armor worn in battle by the upper class. In addition, although water power was used to drive bellows and trip hammers, forging of much of the final product—swords, mail, helmets, etc.—was still done manually by smiths. In the early stages of powered iron works they were often owned by the aristocracy or by church institutions—the superstructure of feudalism. Later they were rented out to capitalist masters, with rent being due on the woodlands used for fuel, etc. In formal terms the iron masters and their workers might have to acknowledge the lord who owned the land as their feudal superior—swearing the appropriate fealty oaths, but in practice the relationship was one of renting.

It has been a point of controversy as to whether blast furnaces and foundries of the Middle Ages should be considered industry or manufacture [Myska, 1979]. Nowadays we do not tend to conceptually differentiate between the two, but Marx claimed that there was an important historical distinction. What he termed manufacture was a process in which manual labor with hand-operated tools predominated.[81] In his conception, industry required the use of powered machinery instead. Manufacture might group together many workers in a single site, and they might be wage laborers, but they were still working by hand. As such their subordination to the capitalists was "formal," that is to say, only existing in the social *form* of wage labor. Manufacturing in this sense also existed in classical antiquity using slaves. What Marx considered the capitalist mode of production proper, where workers were subjected to a "real" subordination to the capitalists, came with modern powered industry. Prior to that the workers could in principle have set themselves up as independent producers—the tools they used still being cheap and simple. Indeed, one typically had a coexistence of self-employed workers and manufacturing, since the technical advantages of manufacturing were not yet sufficient to force the independent worker out of production.

On this account, the iron foundries of the Middle Ages involved real subordination of laborers to their employers. They were free wage laborers rather than serfs, but they had no real possibility to compete with the iron masters unless they could acquire sufficient capital to buy a blow-furnace, water wheel, dam, mill-race, etc. These means of production were inherently too big to be operated by one smith and his family. Local blacksmiths were, as a result, displaced from the initial production of iron, instead working up small ingots or chunks originally produced by large blow furnaces into final products. It is thus better to see both water-powered ironworks and sailing ships as pockets of capitalist industry within a predominantly feudal agricultural economy. Capitalist shipping merchants and capitalist iron masters both depended on the harnessing of an artificial source of power: wind or water. In both cases the scale of the investment, and the rise in productivity it allowed, secured their real class position.

The sequential development, first of water-blown bloomery furnaces and then of the actual blast furnaces producing liquid iron, caused a reduction in the labor input needed. A bloomery furnace had an intermittent operation. It was loaded, blown, the bloom extracted, and then a new load and batch had to be started. Blast furnaces worked nonstop, being periodically tapped. This reduced the labor required to produce 100kg of iron from 4 working days in the fifteenth century to 2.7 working days in the eighteenth. In addition the availability of liquid iron meant that objects could be cast from it. Casting is much less labor-intensive than forging, and allows the easy production of more elaborate standardized products: cooking pots, stoves, railings, and later machine parts. It had long been possible to make such objects out of cast bronze, but iron is much cheaper. This widening of the market and cheapening of the product meant a greater demand for fuel. So long as furnaces were hand-blown and used hand-forging, one could have an equilibrium between two bio-energetic processes. The human energy to operate the forges depended on photosynthesis in cornfields, whereas the chemical energy to provide heat depended on photosynthesis in forests. The limited human energy to drive bellows constrained the oxygen supply to the furnaces which in turn constrained the demand for charcoal. Water power, however, could supply so much more oxygen that the forests could no longer keep up with the demand for charcoal. Deforestation threatened the iron industry's continued operation unless an alternative source of carbon was found. The answer of course was coke, independently invented in China and England. Pyrolysis of coal produced almost pure carbon, suitable for furnace operation.

Freed from the bounds set by biological carbon production and, by using steam blowing, freed from the vagaries of erratic river flows, the capitalist iron and steel industry was able to embark on exponential growth.

I have given iron production as an example of capitalist development for several reasons. It was a pioneer capitalist industry, one of the first to apply artificial energy and one of the first to rely on fossil fuel. It illustrates the process by which employees came to be, in a real and inescapable sense, under the subordination of capitalists. It shows how technical advances improved the productivity of labor: expanding scale, improving thermal and labor efficiency, and, via casting, allowed new and less labor-intensive production processes. It was also a strategic industry, one on which a whole mass of others came to depend, since almost all of them came to depend on iron machines and fitments. But all of these features could, in varying degrees, be replicated in examinations of other industries: transport, power, food processing. In all of them the application of powered machines and fossil fuels allowed rising labor productivity that closed off whole branches of production from the self-employed artisan.

5.4.6 Automation or Self-Action

The sailing ship or the water mill harness a non-biological power to produce continuous motion. As animals we can only do the same by performing a repeated sequence of movements by our limbs. Before the invention of the water mill, grain was processed by rubbing a grinding stone backwards and forwards in a kneeling position, an action that produced premature degeneration of the knee [Hedges, 1984]. The next advance was the hand-operated rotary quern, two circular stones with flat surfaces and a central axis, one on top of the other. The upper stone is turned by a cranking motion of one hand using a stick poked into a hole in the upper stone. This greatly reduced the effort needed and allowed work to be done from a sitting position. The water-powered mill was a direct development of this sort of hand-operated small grinding device. But the hand miller had to repeatedly carry out the same rhythmic motions of his arm to achieve the continuous rotation. Similarly, with spinning, continuous motion of the wheel comes from reciprocation of the limbs, onto which is superimposed the arm motions necessary to first draw out, twist, and then wind on the yarn.

So much, so obvious. But this ability to perform a sequence of actions, even if it is repetitious, is something that was initially unique to humans and other animals. The sails of a ship simply transmit a continuous force, there is no sequencing required. A model sailing boat, with its sails appropriately set, will glide autonomously across a pond.

A labor process, in contrast, is not simply an expenditure of energy, it is a structured sequential pattern of, typically repetitive, motion. The key invention enabling the mechanization of repetitive motion is the pinned cylinder, such as that shown in figure 5.10.

The earliest known representation of this device dates from 1201 in a musical automaton, described by Al Jazari Meneghetti and Maggiore [2011]. It came to be extensively used in musical automata, barrel organs, musical boxes, etc., during the early modern period, and from the eighteenth century started to be applied to industrial automata. The automation of the spinning industry with the mule, as much as Charles Babbage's early computer called the "difference engine" depended on variants of this device. Another device following the same principle would be the Jacquard loom. These devices allow the automation of any labor process that, in modern computing terms, is a "do forever" loop made up of multiple *parallel* steps. What these cannot do is make decisions; they have nothing equivalent to the "if . . . then . . . else . . . " construct in modern programming languages. Because of this they could only be used by capital to replace routinized labor, work that involved repetitively performing exactly the same actions all day long. Any kind of work that requires sensory interaction and decisions on this basis remained outside its scope. That obviously included the great mass of clerical work, accounting work, or activities like those of Hayek's famous shipping agents. But many other tasks, which in social terms are still seen as menial or low status: fruit picking, sorting potatoes, cleaning, etc., also require the workers to make continual decisions and judgments.

The pinned cylinder model of automation is the one satirized by Kurt Vonnegut [1952] in his dystopian *Player Piano* dating from the early 1950s. He portrayed an image of a late twentieth-century American capitalism in which skilled workers have their every action copied to magnetic wire and replicated on automatic machines like the piano of the title. The late date of this novel indicates just how long capitalism had relied on this type of automation—170 years after the invention of the spinning mule.

The principle of a machine able to make decisions, and thus able to replace a large part of clerical, computational, and accounting work, had already been arrived at by the first third of the nineteenth century [Lardner, 1834], but its practical application was delayed until the availability of electronic switching devices [Turing, 2004] and appropriate electronic memory technology [Williams, 1948]. Vonnegut's owl of Minerva flew just before the dawn of computer capitalism.

Decision making in a much more primitive form had been available in the form of Watt's governor, a device based on centrifugal force that regulated the speed of stationary steam engines used in mills. But until the development of the electronic computer it was not possible to build machines that could deploy complex and varying behaviors in response to external conditions. This meant that the first wave of capitalist automation was restricted to the replacement of tasks that were either of inherent simplicity or those upon which the division of labor had already enforced a simplicity. The electronic computer, however, had the potential to replace any decision-making or guidance task that had previously been performed by humans [Turing, 1950]. Initially the effect was in clerical occupations, insurance, banking, etc. But the productivity gains from automation in these areas were slow, not enough to stop these sectors using up a growing part of social labor.

A key point about the electronic computer is that it is a universal machine, a very general-purpose technology. The standard design of a PC can be applied to a whole range of computational or industrial control tasks. The first-generation sequencing technologies tended to be machine specific. You could not take a barrel organ mechanism and incorporate it, unmodified, into a weaving machine. The generality of the computer means that it begins to approximate to the generality of human work. Standard, mass-produced IBM 360 computers were able to replace a wide range of different clerical and accounting tasks during the 1960s and '70s, and various generations of derivatives of IBM 5150 type machines continued the process from the 1980s. This process of using general-purpose computing machines was

Figure 5.10. Pinned cylinder mechanism used in the ancient clock tower in Bruges. This basic sequencer device was the key to the first generation of capitalist automation. Photograph: Beverley Armstrong.

the second wave of capitalist automation—roughly covering the second half of the twentieth century. A third phase opens up with the development of multipurpose robots. Typically these had one arm, though two-arm versions are also available. They differed from first-generation automation in being multipurpose, and from second-generation automation in being applied to physical production rather than information processing. They are, however, still not the universal workers of fiction, since they are in the main screwed to the floor. Those that can move around have so far very limited mobility, endurance, and situational awareness. They are, as yet, quite unable to act as a general purpose replacement for human workers.

This is not to imply that such universal robots will be impossible to build some time in the future.

5.4.7 Profit of First Use

Technology boosts profits in two distinct ways. The first affects the individual business introducing the innovation, the second affects all capitalist businesses collectively.

The first mechanism is easy to understand. Recall that commodity prices are closely correlated with the labor required to make things. It is evident therefore that the adoption of labor-saving technology in a branch of business will tend to reduce the relative price of its product.

But technology adoption is typically not even. One or two businesses will be early adopters. The first adopter is able to slightly drop their price and increase market share. This is illustrated in table 5.8. The initial situation is that the product requires a total of 10 hours' labor, which, with the average value of an hour's labor being £20 means a selling price of £200. After the innovation the labor content falls by half. Before the innovation the per-unit profit was £50, after the new technique becomes general it falls to £20.

We assume that a firm selling 1,000 units originally may now be able to sell 1,200, so their total profit does not fall as much as the per unit profit.

However, during the actual period of innovation, the first user of the technology has a big competitive advantage. Suppose that while everyone else is selling a £200 unit, they sell at £150 per unit on a cost base of £80. They increase their profit per unit, while undercutting their competitors. We assume that they double their sales during this transition period to 2,000 per year. So their profit goes up on two accounts, the margin rises, and the throughput rises. Unless the first adopter can prevent access to the new technology it will become general and the advantage will be short term. Both the adopter and other firms will end up in a position similar to that in the second column of the table.

The existence of patent laws may allow the first user a relatively extended period of advantage, promoting concentration and monopolization of the industry. But there are often multiple ways of improving a production process. Patenting one of them increases the incentive for other firms to devise alternatives not yet patented. In the absence of patent protection, the incentive for competitors to adopt the new technique will be even stronger.

5.4.8 Wage Levels and Innovation

A capitalist economy thus has a mechanism that stimulates the adoption of labor-saving technology that was not present in previous systems. Dependent as they are on the sale of commodities for existence, the very survival of the productive units comes to depend on keeping up with the prevailing rate of technical improvement. This mechanism is argued by Brenner [2001] to have been a key factor in generating the improvements in agricultural activity that provided the surplus labor supply for the subsequent growth of capitalist industry.

But one should be cautious not to overstress capitalism's ability to innovate. For one thing, agriculture of the early modern period was relatively small-scale, competitive, and did not make extensive use of machinery. For another, pressure to innovate does not work reliably, it can be stifled either by very low wage rates or by monopoly.

Robert Allen [2011, 2015] has convincingly argued that the initial conditions for the profitability of powered industrial machinery first occurred in Britain in the late eighteenth century. In other countries, the level of wages was so low that it just did not pay to use such machines. Figure 5.11 provides selected information from the databases Allen has compiled of real wages over time in different countries.

While for England, France, and Italy the real wage rose sharply after the labor shortages of the Black Death, it can be seen that it was only in England that it stayed high. Thus when the scientific knowledge and arts necessary for powered industry had been developed in the Renaissance, only in England did it pay to use them.

In table 5.8 the improved technology involved a reduction in both direct and indirect labor. Suppose instead that we consider an innovation that reduces direct labor at the cost of using more indirect labor in the form of machines, as occurred during the early Industrial Revolution.

Table 5.9 gives an example of a technical change that, unlike the previous example, saves direct labor by using some additional indirect labor in the form of machines. The innovation saves 10 percent of the total labor, but there is no profit to be gained from its use. The capitalist must pay in full for the indirect labor that they buy in from other capitalists, but he only has to pay for half of the labor that he gets from his employees. Thus there is no additional profit to be had from making the switch to the new technique.

But if wages rose from £10 an hour to £15 an hour, as shown in the High Wages columns of the table, then the relative profitability changes. The innovation now becomes profitable.

It should be noted that this implies that free peasants, with access to enough land, should have a greater incentive to use labor-saving machinery than capitalist farmers. The free farmer will value his own labor at full value since all the marginal produce returns to him, so any machinery that brings an overall improvement in labor productivity is worth adopting. Capitalist farmers in contrast have the perverse incentives shown in Table 5.9. This may have relevance to the idea that it was the spread of wage labor that

TABLE 5.8: Profit of First Use

Value added per hour: £20
Wage per hour: £10

	Old Technology as Standard	New Technology as Standard	First User
Indirect Labor Content	5	3	3
Direct Labor	5	2	2
Total Labor	10	5	5
Components Price	£100	£60	£60
Wages	£50	£20	£20
Profit	£50	£20	£70
Unit Price	£200	£100	£150
Volume Sold by Firm	1000	1,200	2,000
Total Profit	£50,000	£24,000	£140,000

TABLE 5.9: How the Motivation of Capitalists To Use Labor Saving Inventions Depends on the Level of Wages

	LOW WAGES		HIGH WAGES	
	Old Tech	New Tech	Old Tech	New Tech
Indirect Labor	5	6	5	6
Direct Labor	5	3	5	3
Total Labor	10	9	10	9
Wage	£10		£15	
Indirect Cost	£100	£120	£100	£120
Wage Cost	£50	£30	£75	£45
Total Cost	£150	£150	£175	£165
Unit Price	£200			
Profit	£50	£50	£25	£35
Adopt?	No		Yes	

encouraged innovation in what is, in retrospect, seen as the runup to capitalism in Britain.

Whether this is plausible depends on what one's standard of comparison is. Are we comparing the incentives to use machinery or the incentives to invest in agricultural fixed investment?

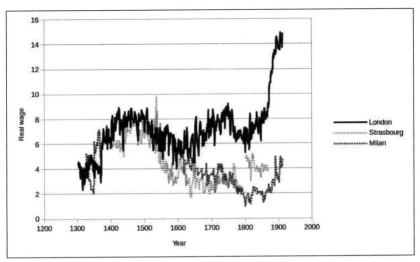

Figure 5.11. The higher rate of pay in England compared to other European countries in the 1700s provided the incentive for industrialization. Source: R. C. Allen database.

Are we comparing capitalist farmers to free peasants, to a manorial economy with serfs, or to slave latifundia?

Vis-à-vis yeoman farmers, the argument from Table 5.9 implies that a transition to wage labor would delay the use of machinery.

If we examine other forms of "capital investment" in farming—clearing, draining, manuring, planting windbreaks, building dykes, etc.—the situation is quite different. A feudal lord or slave owner has the same relative incentive to make these improvements as a free farmer since these are not really capital investments. They are not bought in as commodities. Instead the lord sets his already enserfed or enslaved workforce to the task. The calculation is again one in which labor is compared with labor, and the investment that maximizes increased output will be chosen. So the slave owners of the U.S. South were quite willing to set their slaves tasks of clearing forest and bringing land into cultivation. A large capitalist farmer in early nineteenth-century England would have the same rationale with respect to land improvements. Again the "fixed capital" is valued the same way as current labor; both are paid the same weekly wage. Indeed, it is arguable that the incentive for a slave owner to engage in fixed investment may be greater than that of a capitalist. If the capitalist employs labor by the week, each additional week costs him. Hiring labor to clear forest or put in drains is expensive.

For the *dominus*, his slaves are a sunk cost. He also has to feed them all year-round. The number of slaves he must own is set by the labor requirements at the busiest times of the year—plowing and harvesting. During the slack periods, there is surplus labor available, which effectively costs nothing if it is set to improving the land. This would imply that, if anything, the advent of wage labor would slow down the rate of fixed agricultural improvement.

The superiority of capitalist production in terms of fixed agricultural improvements should not be assumed. In this domain both capitalist agriculture and servile agriculture are on at least the same footing with respect to the comparative costs of immediate versus longer-term use of the labor they control. The superiority of capitalism over servile relations could only exist in the context of bought-in means of production: machinery or chemical fertilizers. We can illustrate this with a concrete historical example. Suppose a nineteenth-century slave owner had to choose between two ways of maintaining output:

1. Buying in Chile saltpeter to maintain fertility.
2. Allowing the soil to become exhausted, but using his slaves to clear virgin forest to replace it.

Option 2 would be the rational course to follow. Saltpeter costs money; the spare labor time of the slaves was free. This had consequences. The slave plantations had an incentive to constantly expand onto virgin soil as Cairnes and Smith [2003, pp. 52–54] recounted. This process brought them into fatal conflict with a free peasantry also migrating to the same territories.

The superiority of wage labor over servile labor exists only with respect to bought-in capital goods. Before powered machinery and agricultural chemicals had been invented, the mere institution of wage labor would not tend to bring a big boost in efficiency. Indeed, allowing for the technology then available, McDonald [2010] showed that feudal economy could be very efficient.

Returning to machinery and extending this argument to cooperatives, these again have a higher motivation to use modern machinery than capitalist firms. In general the higher the level of wages and the lower the degree of exploitation, the greater will be the incentive for the employers to introduce labor-saving inventions. Conversely, low wages and servile conditions act as a huge deterrent to the use of modern machinery.

This is brought out by contrasting two parts of the former British Empire, India and the United States. Modes of production, ways of making things, do not exist in isolation. Slaveholding and landlordism were discussed in chapters 3 and 4 but historically capitalist production has coexisted with both of these, and in some parts of the world like India, still does.[82] It is easy to think of the United States as always having been a capitalist society, and to consider the American Revolution as an archetypal bourgeois one. That is not the standpoint I argue here. I have presented the antebellum U.S. South as a classic slave mode of production.

The class structure after independence was unlike anything in early capitalist Europe. You had to go back more than 2,000 years to find something similar: the slave republic Rome on which the Americans consciously and deliberately modeled themselves. At the top was the slave-owning aristocracy that did no direct productive work, but lived off the labor of the slaves. Below the aristocracy was a class of free citizens who worked for a living. These would be small farmers or artisans. At the bottom were slaves with no political or civil rights, the private property of aristocrats. The main class conflicts were between the slave owners and the slaves on the one hand, and between the slave owners and the free citizens on the other. Since the slaves had no political rights either in Rome or the United States the conflict between them and the slave owners was brutally physical, with the owners' dominance enforced by whips and chains. Free citizens on the other hand had civil rights, and the fact that they outnumbered the richer slave owners meant that the political power of the slave owners was potentially threatened by the free peasants and artisans. The main conflict between the slave owners and free peasants was typically over land ownership. The progress of slavery meant that more and more land tended to fall under the control of the big slave estates, threatening to proletarianize the free citizens. In both Rome and the United States, the free-citizen farmers and artisans were allies of the slave owners. As with expansionist Rome, the external contradiction was between the propertied classes of the Republic and the surrounding free peoples. The expansionary imperialism of both states was driven by both the desire of the senatorial classes to acquire further estates and, more significantly, to promote colonies in which a potentially threatening proletariat could be settled as independent farmers. As Weber [2013] argued, the parallels between Roman and American peasantry were exact right down to the geometry of landholding. In both cases the land was divided up on a square grid of farm plots with long straight roads—something that only a conquering empire could achieve.

The ending of slavery did not mean a direct transition of the U.S. economy to capitalist production. The mode of material production across much of the economy remained firmly pre-capitalist, reliant on manual work without powered machinery. Social relations were characterized by a mix of semi-feudal and semi-servile relations in the South, free peasants in the West, and capitalist industry in the Northeast. The twentieth century saw the United States undergo a transition from a predominantly rural economy of semi-feudal black peasants and independent white ones to a predominantly urban waged population. The agricultural depression from the 1930s allowed banks to foreclose on farms driving farmers into cities. In the South, the landlords made use of mechanization to dispense with and evict their black sharecroppers who also moved into the cities.

By the end of the nineteenth century in India mechanization had made little inroads into agriculture, and even in textile production, which is normally the first industry to be automated, the transition from manufacturing to machine industry was far from complete (see Table 5.10).[83]

Why was this?

Important factors seem to have been a combination of very low wages with the persistence of semi-servile relations of production in India. Although slavery had been formally abolished in India in 1843, in practice it continued in 1900 and still exists, with estimates that there are around 40 million bonded laborers in modern India [Narula, 1999]. Scheduled caste tribes made up 24 percent of the Indian population in 1991. But the government itself accepts that more than 86 percent of bonded laborers are from these groups. This occurs despite the prohibition of all forms of forced labor under article 23 of the Constitution and the 1976 Bonded Labor System Abolition Act.

Bonded labor by members of the lower castes is rife in agriculture, even in more developed regions like the Punjab [Srivastava, 2005]. In the brick kiln industry some three million workers are employed in conditions amounting to bonded labor. Brick kilns are heavily guarded and severe restrictions placed on workers' movements. Workers are typically in debt to their employers and the debt relation persists from season to season [Gupta, 2003].[84]

Similar conditions of near slavery exist in other sectors where heavy manual labor is done in quarries, mines, hand loom weaving, salt pan work. and construction. In Tamil Nadu of 750,000 workers in the quarries two-thirds are bonded laborers, with, in many cases, whole families being enslaved.

Given the close link that exists between slavery and caste oppression it is worth considering the United States. Slavery had remained legal there even after it was formally prohibited in India. Dilip Menon [2006] recounts how in the nineteenth century, novelists of the Indian lower castes saw the similarity between their own condition and that of the Negro in America. Even after the Civil War and Lincoln's abolition of slavery, a social upheaval far greater than anything India went through in its path to independence, the Negroes in America remained a caste apart. Deprived of civil rights until the 1960s, segregated from the white population, denied entry into many jobs and professions—prohibited even from fighting for their country.

TABLE 5.10: Cloth Production in India by Sector

Year	Mill Production	Decentralized Powerloom Production	Decentralized Handloom Production
1900–03	483	0	793
1936–39	3,630	0	1,420
1980–81	4,533	4,802	3,109
1997–98	1,948	20,951	7,603

Sources: Clark and Wolcott, 2003, 7; Mazumdar, 1984, 36.

Ex-slaves or descendants of ex-slaves faced many of the same prejudices as untouchable slaves and ex-slaves. What was it but a fear of pollution that forced them to use separate water supplies—Dalits being prohibited from using the tanks supplying Hindus and Negroes having to use separate drinking water fountains?

The whole edifice of segregation was a series of pollution taboos meant to enforce a subhuman status.

One system was called *caste* and the other *race*, but what is a name?

Both are imaginary justifications for real exploitation. Given the fundamental mixing of the human gene pool, and the fact that we are all of African descent, race was as much an imaginary social construct as caste. Its functional meaning was the same, to demarcate a servile section of the population. Both categories drew on religion for their support—with Negroes being labeled as children of Cain by white Christian sects.

The notion of caste and the notion of race are part of what Althusser [1971] termed the ideological state apparatus of exploitative society. By this he means the set of ideas and institutions by which human agents are socialized, whose function is to ensure the continued reproduction of the existing relations of domination and servitude.

In the context of what I have said about the role of economic backwardness in sustaining caste in India, the economic background to the struggles of the Negroes in mid-twentieth century United States are relevant. There was nearly a century of delay between the abolition of slavery and the winning of civil rights by the Negroes in the 1960s. Why did it happen then and not in the 1890s, for example?

A theory put forward by Marxists among the black proletariat of the United States who lived through this change is that during the 1950s and '60s a crucial economic change had occurred. When the slaves were freed, they had remained a semi-servile class of sharecroppers. They continued to carry out the same agricultural labor as their erstwhile masters transformed into landlords. The former slave owners continued to profit from the labor of the freed slaves, but now it was done with a semi-feudal relation. The crucial fact was that the mode of material production had not changed. Cotton production still depended on manual labor to tend the fields and harvest the crop. The Negroes were formally free, but they were still doing the same sort of physical labor as the slaves had done. It was not until the 1940s that the federal government stepped in to enforce legislation against bonded labor.[85] Alongside semi-feudal sharecropping and peonage, slave production continued on a large scale in the United States using prison labor. By the 1870s it had already started to be the case for Southern states to pass vagrancy laws whose main purpose was to allow poor, predominantly black, men to be rounded up and hired out as slave labor [Blackmon, 2009].

With the enforcement of legislation against debt slavery, and with the migration of sharecroppers to the industrial North there arose for the first time an incentive to mechanize Southern agriculture. In the 1950s machines were introduced that could harvest cotton, weeding came to be done by spraying chemical weed killers, and the whole process of agricultural production shifted from manufacture to machineofacture. The mode of material production became specifically capitalist. Consequent upon a change in the mode of material production, the social relations of production had to change too. The semi-feudal sharecropping system gave way to capital-intensive agriculture. The class of sharecroppers was freed from the land to become a proletariat who migrated to the great urban manufacturing centers. The physical movement away from the rural South, and the social movement from the personal dependence of sharecropping, laid the grounds for a political struggle for equal civil rights. Blacks were now participants in the labor market, working side by side with white workers on the assembly lines of Detroit. Under these circumstances the clash between their caste status and the formal equality of labor presupposed by the capitalist market became intolerable. But the process of gaining civil liberty was not automatic. It was only through a prolonged and bitter struggle that legal rights could be enforced. Like any state apparatus the ideological apparatus of race could only be broken by struggle. This struggle in the United States is clearly not complete:

- blacks are disproportionately found in the less skilled and worse paid sections of the proletariat
- and as proletarians they are still very much exploited, now by capitalists, where previous generations were exploited by landowners and slaveholders.

But their struggle has progressed further than that against untouchability in India.

In this process there have been feedbacks between social relations and technology. The class of white farmers and landowners introduced machinery to their farms in the mid-twentieth century not with the view to its social effects but in order to make more profit. The social consequences that followed the black struggle for equal political rights were unforeseen. A new form of technology changed economic relations; this in turn brought political conflict which changed society. But one should not assume from this that technological change was inevitable. If slavery had persisted in the Southern states, had, for example, the Confederates won the Civil War, it is doubtful that there would have been the motive to mechanize.

The points of similarity between the United States and India during the twentieth century are:

1. The existence of a depressed caste subjected to at first openly servile and later semi-servile relations;
2. The predominance of manual labor in the semi-servile sector;
3. The use of violence and terror to maintain the depressed caste in its place;
4. Severe social segregation.

The significant differences are:

1. The somewhat more advanced level of capitalist industrialization in the United States during the 1960s relative to India now (see Figure 5.12, p. 142);
2. Historically the United States suffered from chronic shortages of labor relative to capital.

Eventually, Indian agriculture will mechanize, and the peasantry disperse. The mines, quarries, brickworks, etc., within which Dalits are enslaved will use Leibherr and Komatsu mass excavators rather than human labor.

This is what one can expect from capitalism, but how long will it take?

One of the basic points I made earlier is that the rate of technological advance in a society tends to be inversely proportional to the rate of exploitation. Where labor is cheap, it will be wasted. Marx and Cairnes Smith [2003] made this point with respect to slavery, that it was inimical to mechanical progress. Marx emphasizes that under capitalism, where wages are low, the most backward techniques of production will be used. From this standpoint, the very intensive exploitation of Dalit labor must be a major cause of technical backwardness in the Indian rural economy. Why else should the full mechanization of some industries have been so long delayed?

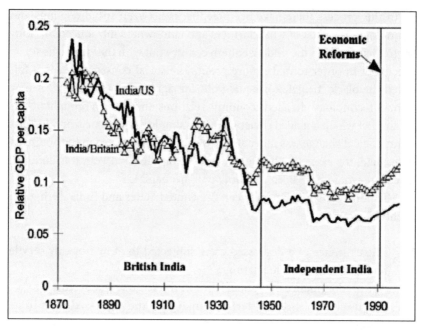

Figure 5.12. Indian GDP per capita relative to the United States 1873 to 1998. Source: Clark, 2003.

Until labor becomes expensive there is little incentive to replace it with machinery. This is a crucial difference between India and the United States, which, from its founding, had a relative shortage of labor, both compared to available agricultural land and, later, compared to capital stocks. The shortage of labor had both been the drive behind the initial capture and transportation of slaves from Africa and the nineteenth-century flow of European immigrants. When this was cut off by the 1921 Quota Act, the demand for industrial workers in the North allowed the rapid absorption of former sharecroppers into the industrial working class. The labor shortage was a necessary consequence of colonial economy. Land from which the natives had been dispersed became available for settlement, acting as a constant drawdown on the pool of employable workers in urban areas. Capitalism demands a working class deprived of the means of production— but if land was to be had for free from the federal authorities, that condition was not met. Retaining workers depended on U.S. wages being substantially higher than in contemporary Europe, where land had long been monopolized by the aristocracy. This in turn led to intensive use of machinery and high productivity of labor in the United States. As Figure 5.12 shows, the result was a long-term tendency for India's productivity to fall further and further behind that of the United States.

5.4.9 Relative exploitation

Marx distinguished two forms of exploitation: absolute and relative. In absolute exploitation, which he called absolute surplus value, the workers are forced to work longer hours. He described working 12 or 14 hours a day in British factories in the early nineteenth century.[86] In relative exploitation, although the working day stays the same, the proportion of it going to the employer rises because of technical advances.

The mechanism here is not the same as the profit of first use described earlier. That is a transitory phenomenon and involved a redistribution of profit between competing firms. A general increase in exploitation requires that the proportion of total social labor making goods consumed by workers falls while the proportion making goods that go to the employing class rises. Clearly, if the average labor cost markup, in the sense of Section 5.1, is 200 percent, and if there is a general proportionality between prices and labor content, then half of social labor would be devoted to supplying the needs of the workforce and would be surplus.

This change in proportion could come about by simply reducing the living standards of employees so that their total consumption fell, or it could happen because the labor required to produce wage goods had fallen. So labor productivity must rise in the industries producing articles of mass consumption. Not all rises in productivity increase relative exploitation. Higher productivity in factories making Rolls-Royce cars would not contribute to an overall increase in exploitation. It would not reduce the proportion of the labor force necessary to support the working classes. The rate of exploitation would remain the same, even if it meant the rich could now buy more—slightly cheaper—luxury cars.

In contrast, higher productivity in agriculture or oil extraction tends to increase relative exploitation. If food and heating can be had with less labor, fewer millions will be working to grow food for the laboring population. Some of those redeployed from farming may end up making mass-produced consumer goods, but some of them will end up producing luxuries or being employed as personal servants of the rich. The net effect is a shift from labor that supported the direct producers to labor that supports the propertied classes. This was very evident in the big rise in the number of personal servants during the nineteenth century in England. Something like oil enters directly into working-class consumption, but also, as a source of energy, enters into almost every item of mass consumption. Thus shifts to cheap energy sources have been, along with improvements in agriculture, one of the main sources for the growth of relative surplus value.

It is important to recognize that the relative exploitation mechanism does

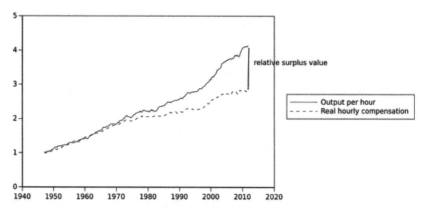

Figure 5.13. Production of relative surplus value in the United States using 1947 as index year. Source: Dataset from Fleck et al., 2011.

not depend on the mechanical advances occurring within a capital-labor relation. The big improvement in productivity in French peasant agriculture from the 1950s to the 1970s contributed to relative exploitation there even though the improvements took place on non-capitalist family farms. Any technical advance reducing the labor that goes to sustain the working population counts.

Clearly for this mechanism to work, the rate of growth of the real wage must be slower than the rate of technical innovation in the industries producing the real wage. But this consideration lies beyond the development of technology or productive forces. It depends on the relative rates of growth of capital and labor, on demographics and accumulation. However, if we look at Figure 5.13 the conditions in the United States from the late 1960s allowed lots of relative surplus value to be produced. Although productivity rose, very little of that gain went into wages. More and more of the value produced ended up in the hands of the top 1 percent of the population and less in the hands of the lower classes. Indeed if we look at the pretax incomes of the bottom 50 percent of the population of the United States, the bulk of the working classes, we can see that they have remained almost static for half a century (Figure 5.14).

Innovation in the production of consumption goods will thus tend to increase relative exploitation and as a result the total profit per worker will increase. Whether or not the annual rate of profit per £1 of capital advanced will rise is a more complex question that, again, can only be properly understood in the context of the dynamic analysis of accumulation in Section 5.9, which will show that developments in labor productivity do tend to raise the rate of profit.

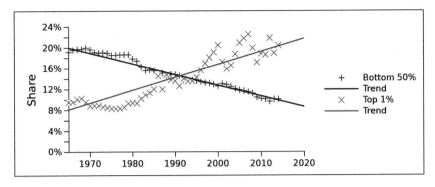

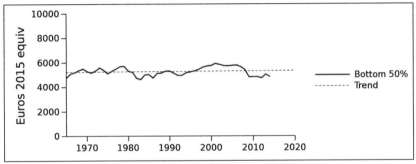

Figure 5.14. Income share and real per capita of the bottom 50 percent of U.S. adults. Source: http://wid.world/data/.

5.4.10 Summary

The argument in Section 5.4 is that powered machinery is essential to capitalism.

- The higher productivity of capitalist machine industry drove independent producers to ruin, and subjected them to the domination of capital.
- This has historically depended on the harnessing of artificial power along with automatic control mechanisms.
- Competition and the potential profits from innovation encourage technical change.
- But the drive for innovation varies inversely with the existing level of exploitation. The stronger the position of the working classes, the more capital seeks machinery to replace them.

5.5 CAPITALISM AND POPULATION

The first phases of capitalist development are characterized, except in colonies like the United States or Australia, by an abundance of labor relative to capital. If the capitalist system is to fully take hold in the form of machine industry, the growth of capital stock must outrun the growth of the labor supply. It was for this reason that Adam Smith was so keen to emphasize the distinction between productive and unproductive labor. If a man employed a multitude of menial servants, Smith said, he dissipated his capital. If on the other hand he employed workers in manufacture, his capital returned with a profit. Smith emphasized the importance of accumulating and not wasting what Marx would later call surplus value. Smith's polemic was directed at waste occasioned by an idle and profligate aristocracy. Though society was, by modern standards, poor, with relatively primitive technology and a more limited social surplus, productive accumulation and thrift were essential.

This, too, emphasizes the importance of thoroughgoing agrarian revolutions of the French, Russian, or Chinese types. The forcible suppression of unproductive classes of landowners and priests freed resources for industrialization. China in 2006 was reinvesting 50 percent of its total national product in new capital goods. It could never have reached this level of accumulation were it not for an agrarian revolution in the 1940s that stopped the landlords from unproductively consuming the peasants' surplus.

5.5.1 Population, food, and empire

Capitalism is a hyper-urban civilization. The urbanization implies a rise in the labor productivity in agriculture to support the urban population. The historical problem of achieving this was made harder by the fact that in its early phase capitalist societies show a rapid exponential growth in total population. Indeed I will show in Section 5.9 that rapid exponential growth of population is a precondition for the very profitability of capitalism. Simple urbanization, the move of a given population from country to town, only requires a growth in labor productivity on the land, so that each peasant can support several townsfolk. When urbanization is combined with rapid population growth, there must also be an increase in absolute farm production alongside an increase in production per farmer.

How can this increase in total production come about?

Obviously there either has to be an extension of the area of cultivated land or the output per square meter of ground has to go up. With pre-industrial agriculture, that is, agriculture that does not depend extensively on industrial inputs, increases in production from a fixed area of land are dependent on biological processes. Fertility can be raised by more sophisticated crop rotation regimes, and the recycling of human and animal waste. The first process, however, requires that part of the land be set aside for clover, beans, etc., to restore soil nitrogen. The nitrogen fixation is ultimately dependent

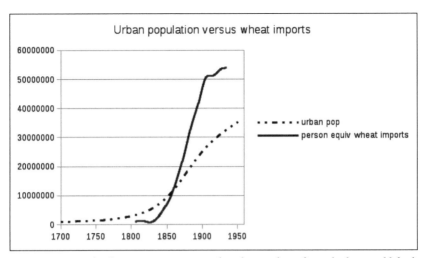

Figure 5.15. British wheat imports, expressed as the number of people they could feed, compared with English urban population. Assumption is that wheat consumption per head would be 100kg per year. Source: Mathias, 2013; and Thompson, 1993, chapter 1.

on a rather indirect energy path: photosynthesis in legume leaves, transport of surplus glucose to the roots where some of it is made available to nitrogen-fixing bacteria, which then use a portion of that energy for their own reproduction and another portion for fixing nitrogen. As such the process of nitrogen fixation requires on the order of one-quarter of the total solar energy being captured on the arable land. Some of this may be recaptured as subsidiary protein foods: pulses or milk from cattle grazed on clover. White [1964] argues that the improved availability of proteins from these sources under feudalism contributed to a healthier and denser population than that achieved under classical agriculture. However, the point remains that natural nitrogen fixation competed for land with grain production.

Chinese pre-capitalist agriculture achieved significantly higher outputs per acre than contemporary European systems, thanks to intensive reuse of human and animal fertilizers, but as Braudel [1992] points out this was achieved at the cost of a great deal of labor; and as a consequence of the high population density, the availability of meat protein was much poorer than in Europe. The lower population density in pre-capitalist Europe allowed more land to be set aside for grazing. This meant both more meat as food, and more animal muscle power to supplement human labor in the fields.

Prior to the tractor, raising labor productivity on the land depended on harnessing horses and oxen. Nineteenth-century agricultural machinery was designed to be horse-drawn, but horses compete for land. They need grazing and, when working intensively, require forage grains like oats. So pre-industrial agriculture depended on using part of the photosynthetic energy for nitrogen fixation, and part to provide animal motive power. The greater the labor efficiency of the system, the greater the proportion of the captured solar energy that was diverted from human food. The combination of an exponential population growth and a mode of production in agriculture that combined high labor productivity with animal power could only be achieved by:

- Territorial expansion into previously uncultivated lands.
- The development of improved means of transport to bring grain from these marches to the great cities.

Thus the nascent capitalist mode of production was inevitably imperialist. It evaded the Malthusian dilemma by extirpating the native inhabitants of the North American prairies and the Argentine pampas to feed the burgeoning cities of England and New England. As Figure 5.15 shows, by the 1850s Britain was already importing sufficient wheat to feed the entire urban population of England. In the next 75 years the urban population grew threefold, but wheat imports outstripped this. Canals, railways, and clipper ships became vital means of food production. By 1900 other growing capitalist powers were justifiably convinced that industrial development depended on the acquisition of colonies [Fischer, 1967; Fischer and Fletcher, 1986]. The future seemed to lie with those great empires that dominated temperate agricultural plains: Britain, the United States, and Russia. Without empires of their own to supply food imports and, by colonial emigration, to relieve the population pressures of early capitalism, industrial developments in Germany and Japan were, it seemed, bound to falter. So began a period of inter-imperialist rivalry that tore the world for half a century and gave birth to a German project to replicate on the steppes the extirpation and colonization already achieved on the prairies.

It is a mistake to see this colonial rivalry as just arising from the relations of production, from the need to export capital, as presented in the classical Marxian critique of imperialism [Lenin, 1999; Bukharin, 1976]. This played a part, but colonialism had deeper roots. Its roots extended down to the actual mode of material production out in the fields; roots in bio-energetics; and in the specific demography of capitalist industrialization.

After 1945 the drive for agricultural colonies died out. Capitalism in Germany and Japan could now, apparently, prosper without them. Why this change?

Three things are the answer: birth control, the Haber process for ammonia production, and tractors. The first slowed population growth. Artificial nitrogen fertilizer freed agriculture from the constraints of crop rotations.

Tractors meant that labor productivity on the land no longer depended on setting aside land to feed horses. Agricultural productivity in Europe rose to levels at which grain colonies became redundant. By the late twentieth century even England grew enough wheat to feed itself. A major change in geopolitics was driven by changes in the underlying mode of production and population dynamics.

5.5.2 Family and population

In all countries capitalism coexists with, or better articulates with, the domestic or household economy. Sahlins [1972] developed the concept of the domestic mode of production to describe early economies, and Delphy [1980; Delphy and Leonard, 1984] develops the concept of the coexistence of the domestic way of making things with capitalism in her studies of French patriarchal families, particularly peasant families. The idea of the domestic mode of production or domestic economy is examined in greater depth by the Marxist anthropologist Claude Meillassoux [1981] who says:

> Neither feudalism, nor slavery, even less capitalism, know such regulating and correcting built-in mechanisms governing the process of reproduction. On the contrary, in the last analysis, we find that all modern modes of production, all classes of societies depend, for the supply of labor-power, on the domestic community. As for capitalism, it depends both on the domestic communities of the colonized countries and on its modem transformation, the family, which still maintains its reproductive functions although deprived of its productive ones. From this point of view, the domestic relations of production can be considered as the organic basis of feudalism, slavery as well as capitalism or bureaucratic socialism. None of these forms of social organization can be said to represent an integrated mode of production to the extent that they are not based on homogeneous relations of production and of reproduction. (xiii)

Domestic production in the feudal period was the real base of the economy. Peasant households grew food, milled grain, cooked it, spun wool, wove it, and out of this fed themselves, clothed themselves, and raised the next generation. Since this could typically be done in, say, three days' labor a week, that left three other days during which they could work, unpaid, in the manorial economy. With the liberation of the peasantry in France from feudal dues, the surplus time could be devoted to producing cash crops to sell on the market.

Inside the domestic economy there is, Delphy argues, a class antagonism between patriarchs on the one side and on the other side wives and to an extent older children. The patriarchs exploit their wives and children. The wives and children provide labor that yields goods that are partly consumed on the farms, and partly sold on the market. The property relations ensure that the product from the sales of these commodities belong to the male head of household. In addition, the patriarchs typically did fewer hours' work a week than their wives. This is not from a historical materialist standpoint of *women's oppression*, which is too liberal and vague. It is an exploitative class relationship built into the production and property relations.

In the stage of patriarchal commodity production, the patriarchs have a direct interest in their wives bearing children. Children, in a period before compulsory schooling, are an additional labor force to be exploited on the farm from an early age. The pro-natalist ideology of Catholicism, with its accompanying emphasis on premarital chastity for girls, is a pretty direct ideological expression of these production relations.

As capitalist industry developed the number of use values produced within the domestic economy started to decline. First to go was milling as water and windmills replaced querns. This was well underway in the late feudal period. Next, spinning and weaving as factory production of cloth took over by the mid-nineteenth century. Home manufacture of clothes, extended by home sewing machines, lasted until the mid-twentieth century. But production of people continued unabated. So much so that the domestic economy characteristically produced a surplus population that migrated to towns to become wage workers. This stage constituted Lenin's second economic form: petty commodity–producing peasant farms. It was also the dominant economic form over much of the U.S. countryside at the same period.

Expanding capitalist industry required an ever greater labor force, and got it cheap. The wage rate paid did not have to be sufficient to fully recompense the cost of reproducing the next generation, since the patriarchal domestic economy was the main source of supply of labor. This is still the case in India, for example.

Marx termed the supply of workers from the countryside the latent reserve army of labor. Latent, because the reserve population was hidden but present, to be called to the colors when the industrial cycle goes through an expansionary phase. But this latent reserve army eventually dries up. Once the latent reserve starts to be exhausted real wages have to rise to fully cover the cost of reproducing labor power. Kuczynski [1946] argued that it was not until almost a century after the start of the Industrial Revolution in Britain that this stage was reached in the 1870s.

5.6 DOMESTIC AND CAPITALIST ECONOMY

Working-class families are a partial transformation of the old domestic economy. They still produce people, but they no longer produce any other commodities, and the children they produce have a quite different economic significance to the family. In the rural patriarchal family the children were, within a few years, useful workers who contributed to the family income. In the first phase of industrialization, families would hire out their children as young factory workers. But soon capitalist industry required an educated workforce. Compulsory schooling followed. Children now became a cost not an asset. The work of child-rearing lasts longer, without the income in kind or cash that kids once brought.

Children remain necessary to society, and as a future source of labor power they are an obvious necessity for employers, but the family now raises them in what amounts more to a social duty conditioned by ideological expectations rather than an internal economic necessity. The inevitable consequence of this has been a decline in family size, a falling birth rate. As Figure 5.16, shows, the tendency is for birth rate to fall below reproduction

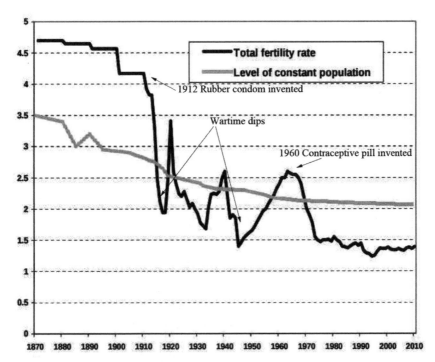

Figure 5.16. Characteristic capitalist law of population. Developed capitalism suppresses fertility below reproduction requirements as shown in this historical trend of German birth rate. Source: Michael J. Kendzia, 2012.

levels. Similar trends exist for other developed countries. Capitalist countries like the United States, with substantial immigration from predominantly agricultural countries, show higher fertility due to the delayed transformation of family forms.

In patriarchal domestic economy the labor of wives and children are directly exploited by the husband. Their labor contributed directly to his property. The development of capitalist society gives women equal rights to property and eliminates most of the productive activity in the household. Both sexes are now forced to sell their labor power, something that neither did in the old patriarchal family. For both sexes the working day is divided into working hours they sell to an employer, and hours they continue to work in the domestic economy. If we take Canada as an example—it publishes excellent statistics on time use—we can see in Table 5.11 that while total working hours for men and women are almost exactly the same, the way these hours divide between work in the domestic and market economies are in reciprocal proportions for men and women. For men it divides 3:2 in favor of the market economy, whereas for women the ratio market/domestic is only 2:3. The important thing to note, however, is that while we would conventionally say that Canada is a capitalist economy, the time-use statistics show that it is only at most 50 percent capitalist. Half the work done each day is still done in the home, and a significant part of the paid work, particularly that done by women [Morissette et al., 2013], is done for the state not for private firms, and as such generates no profit.

5.6.1 Gender pay inequality

Now let us look at how the interaction of the domestic and capitalist modes of production affects the position of women in paid employment.

In 2005, the year that Table 5.11 covers, average male hourly pay was $23.41 and average female pay was $19.96 [Morissette et al., 2013].Taking into account the difference in hours worked that means that on average a Canadian woman earned only a little over half as much money per day as men (Table 5.12).

It is obvious that the biggest factor affecting daily earnings of women was the shorter number of hours for which they sold their labor power. But that left a gap in pay rates to explain. Let us take what a prominent organization speaking for women says. The Canadian Womens' Association[87] gave the following reasons for the gap:

1. First, traditional "women's work" pays less than traditional "men's work." As one researcher notes: "Female-dominated job

TABLE 5.11: Time Use of Canadians, Calculated by Sex

	Males hours per day	Females hours per day
Total	24	24
Total Work	7.8	7.9
Paid Work and Related Activities	4.7	3.1
Paid Work for Employer	4.2	2.8
Commuting	0.4	0.3
Unpaid Work in Domestic Economy	2.7	4.2
Household and Related Activities	2.3	3.8
Childcare	0.3	0.5
Civic and Voluntary Activities	0.3	0.4
Education and Related Activities	0.5	0.6
Personal Care	10.4	10.8
Night Sleep	8.2	8.4
Meals (excl. Restaurant Meals)	1	1
Other Personal Activities	1.2	1.4
Free Time	5.7	5.3

Figures averaged over a seven day week, for population age 15 and older. Source: Statistics Canada, *General Social Survey, 2005*, Catalogue no. 12F0080XWE. Last modified: 9/8/2009.

TABLE 5.12: Median Wages in Canada, 2005

	Paid Hours per Day	Pay Rate	Daily Earning
Female	2.8	19.96	55.89
Male	4.2	23.41	98.32

classes are often seen as not being skilled because the tasks are related to domestic jobs that women were expected to carry out for free in the home."

2. Second, most women workers are employed in lower-wage occupations and lower-paid industries. Women work in a narrower range of occupations than men and have high representation in the 20 lowest-paid occupations. About two-thirds of the female workforce are concentrated in teaching, nursing, and health care, office and administrative work, and sales and service industries. Women aged 25 to 54 accounted for 22 percent of Canada's minimum-wage workers in 2009, more than double the proportion of men in the same age group.

3. Another reason for the wage gap is that more women than men work part-time. About 70 percent of part-time workers in 2013 were women, a proportion that has remained steady for three decades. Women working part-time or temporary jobs are much less likely to receive promotions and training than those in full-time jobs. Women work part-time for several reasons, including lack of affordable child care and family leave policies, along with social pressure to carry the bulk of domestic responsibilities. These factors make it more likely for women to have interruptions in employment, which has a negative effect on income.

4. A large portion of the wage gap remains unexplained and is partly due to discrimination. An estimated 10–15 percent of the wage gap is attributed to gender-based wage discrimination.

This appears as a good surface account of the difference but it begs some questions. Why does traditional women's work pay less? Surely that is just using the gender wage gap to explain the gender wage gap?

The same circular reasoning is present in point 2. If there is a gender wage gap, it follows that any industry with a high proportion of women will have relatively low wages compared to an industry with a high proportion of men. So this is again circular and cannot get to the cause of the gap.

Point 3 is the only real causal explanation, related to the role of women in the domestic economy and a reason why they have difficulty getting out of that economy. Point 4 is merely saying that there is some unexplained difference and that by this definition must be discrimination. But what causes this discrimination? Employers would like to reduce the wages of all employees. The question is why they are more successful in holding down women's wages.

In Figure 5.17 it is clear that the historical trend has been for the wage gap to decline. There was a 20-year period from the mid-1980s during which men's wages were static and during which women's wages rose. We need to explain first why a gap exists at all, and then why the gap has changed with time.

Morissette et al. [2013] examine the change in the gap by doing multi-factorial analysis against union membership, marital status, tenure of job, education, and occupation. Taking all factors into account they could explain about 38 percent of the decline in the wage gap. The three most significant explanatory variables were union membership, educational status, and occupation. Changes in union membership by men and women accounted for 11 percent of the decline in the wage gap (see Table 5.14).

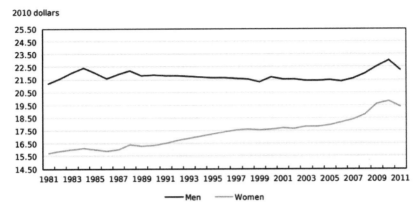

Figure 5.17. Canadian real wages for men and women. Source: Morissette et al., 2013.

Women in Canada are now more unionized and better educated than men, reversing the previous situation. Women typically have been in their job slightly longer than men, again reversing the situation that used to hold. Both men and women are more likely to be employed in health or government services, which have been growth sectors of the economy (Table 5.13).

Morissette et al. [2013] have as summary conclusion:

> Although women today still earn relatively less than men on average, the gender hourly wage gap decreased significantly over the last three decades. Relative to men, women increased their productivity-enhancing characteristics at a faster pace than men did.

This account depends on the idea that wages are determined by productivity. That is to say it follows the textbook neoclassical idea that wages are

TABLE 5.13: Change in Statuses for Men and Women in Canada

Workers Aged 17–64	Men 1998	2011	Change	Women 1998	2011	Change
Average Tenure (mos.)	102.2	99.9	–2.3	94.2	101.3	7.1
% with Univ. Degree	19.4	24.6	5.5	20.4	29.9	9.5
% Unionized	33	29.7	–3.3	31.3	33.1	1.8
% in Health Occupations	1.5	1.9	0.3	8.9	11.7	2.8
% in Occupations in Social Science, Education and Gov't Service	5.2	5.3	0.1	11.2	14.5	3.3

Source: Morissette et al., 2013, table 3.

TABLE 5.14: Explanation of Change in Wage Gap

	Change	Percent of Gap Explained
Age	0.002	–2.8
Education	–0.006	10.5
Province	0.003	–4.6
Union Status	–0.006	11.4
Marital Status	–0.001	1.3
Tenure	–0.004	7.3
Occupation	–0.010	18
Industry	0.002	–2.8
Total Portion Explained	–0.021	38.4
Portion Unexplained	–0.035	61.6

Source: Morissette et al., 2013.

set by the marginal product of labor and that the wage contract is an equal non-exploitative one. But even if we accept this, which obviously Marxian economists do not, they are only able to account for 38 percent of the change. They are left with 62 percent unexplained.

The statistical analysis in Table 5.14 focuses on things where there are only minor differences between men and women and leaves out the one big thing that differentiates them: women's greater participation in the domestic economy.

Now look at Figure 5.18 and compare it with Figure 5.17, and you can see that they look pretty similar. As the women's share of the workforce rises their wage rate as a percentage of men's wages rises. In fact, the correlation between the two series is 90.9 percent. That means that only 9.1 percent of the change in the wage gap needs to be explained by other factors: for instance union membership.

This strongly suggests that should men and women end up working an equal number of hours in Canada the wage gap will either be eliminated or slightly reversed; taking into account women's higher unionization and better education.

6.2 Narrowing the wage gap

But what are the obstacles to a higher rate of women participating in the workforce?

The key point is that a set of activities are still performed within the domestic economy, and of these women do more than men (Table 5.11). The domestic economy still organizes a part of the work necessary for social reproduction. This work still needs to get done. Basically there are

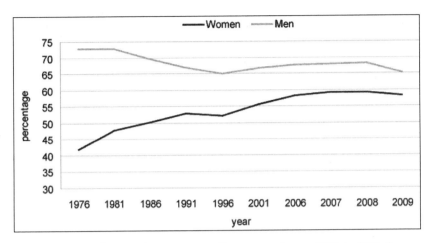

Figure 5.18. Canadian employment rates of women and men, 1976 to 2009. Source: Statistics Canada, Labor Force Survey.

three ways that women's workload in the home can be reduced: (1) a larger share of housework has to be done by men; (2) the productivity of labor in these tasks has to rise; (3) the same tasks have to move out of the domestic economy.

5.6.3 Division of domestic labor

We have been using Canada as an example. Canada and the United States have almost identical figures for the share of housework done by women and both countries are near the top of the world ranking for having the comparatively equal divisions of domestic work between the sexes (Table 5.16). Bianchi et al. [2000] use data from the United States to show that there was a significant fall both in women's share of housework and their absolute hours from 1965 to 1995. Starting at 30 hours a week, unpaid housework by women fell to 17.5 hours, while that of men rose from 4.9 hours to 10 hours. However, it is unclear if this shift is continuing. There was a previous edition of *Time Use of Canadians* in 1998. By comparing it with the 2008 edition we can see if, over a decade, there was a change in the housework done by men and women. As Table 5.15 shows the share of housework done by men did rise modestly over the ten years, but this did not reduce women's housework, since both men and women did more of it.

If women were actually doing more housework in 2008 than in 1998, how did their participation in paid work rise?

Because they worked longer paid hours too! In general, as Figure 5.19 shows, the higher the total amount of unpaid domestic labor shared between the two sexes the more equal the male share of it is likely to be.

TABLE 5.15: Comparison of Hours of Housework in Canada, 1998 and 2008

Year	Men's hours Housework Per Day	Women's Hours Housework Panama	Ratio m/f
	m/f	-	-
1998	2.4	4.1	0.58
2008	2.7	4.2	0.64

So men doing more housework only frees women of it if the total amount of housework remains constant.

5.6.4 Reducing overall housework

At first sight it might seem that an answer to reducing domestic work would be more machinery in the home: washing machines, dishwashers, vacuum cleaners, mowers etc. However, it is questionable that these are effective in reducing overall hours spent in housework. Vanek [1974], using U.S. data, reported that over the period during which these sorts of machines became available there was no significant decline in the housework done by women. Subsequent detailed time use study of Australian households has backed this conclusion. The Australian time use surveys collected data not only on time spent on tasks but also what appliances were available in each household. In a multiple regression study drawing on this data Bittman et al. [2004] conclude:

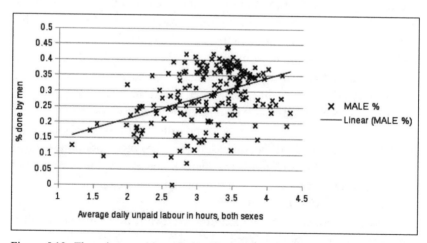

Figure 5.19. There is a positive relationship between the average number of hours spent by both sexes in the domestic economy, and the share of unpaid labor done by men. Source: UN Gender Statistics, Time Use database, showing 188 country/year combinations.

**TABLE 5.16: Share of Unpaid Domestic Work
Done by Men in Some Countries**

	Male Percent of Unpaid Work
HIGHER	
Sweden	44.17%
Canada	39.81%
Estonia	39.30%
Bulgaria	34.28%
MEDIUM	
Lesotho	28.43%
China	28.00%
Peru	27.43%
Israel	26.80%
LOWER	
Tunisia	11.27%
India	9.38%
Cambodia	9.09%
Pakistan	8.89%
Mali	7.02%

Despite its capacity to cook food in a fraction of the time needed by conventional stoves, owning a microwave has no significant effect on the time use patterns of women, even when the number of meals out is held constant. Nor does the deep freezer's ability to harvest the economies of scale in meal production significantly reduce the average time that women devote to meal preparation or to housework overall. While the data does not separate the process of food and drink preparation and the associated meal cleanup, it would seem reasonable to expect that a dishwasher, by reducing the time required for meal cleanup, might lower the overall time spent in the kitchen. Contrary to expectations, however, dishwashers appear to

**TABLE 5.17: Relative Rates of Exploitation of Men and Women
in Canada, 2011**

	(1)	(2)	(3)	(4)	(5)	(6)	(7)
	Wages	Surplus	(2)/(1) s/v	Av. Wage Male	Av. Wage Female	Av. Both	Av. Value Created
s/v	$766B	$497B	0.65	25.03 0.55	$21.85 0.77	$23.48 0.65	$38.72

Note: s/v indicates rate of surplus value. Source: Statistics Canada, income and expenditure tables; Statistics Canada, *Labour Force Survey*; and figure 5.17.

have no significant effect on the time Australian women spend in food or drink preparation and cleanup or in the daily hours devoted to housework.

Possible explanations are that the growing availability of machine washing coincided with people owning more clothes, and perhaps greater social pressures toward keeping them spotless. Time saving need not be the motive for buying machines. Dishwashers may be more pleasant than sink washing even if they give little speed-up. The overall conclusion would seem to be that short of general-purpose domestic robots becoming available, domestic machinery will have little further impact on women's labor in the home.

5.6.5 Moving tasks out of the domestic economy

Improvements in labor productivity in industry have in the past depended not only on the use of machinery but also on economies of scale. Greater scale allows greater division of labor and rationalized economical steps. Less labor is used to prepare a burger and fries at McDonald's than if it is made at home, not just because McDonald's has bigger fries fryers and racks to hold burgers, but because the higher throughput allows the intensive use of the equipment. It is the small scale of domestic production that ultimately limits its productivity.

But of course in a market economy people can buy services. They can go out to fast-food joints instead of eating at home. They can send their infants to preschool instead of looking after them all day themselves. If they are rich enough in the UK, they send older children off to boarding schools as soon as the kids turn seven. The rich hire housekeepers to clean, send clothes out to laundry, etc.

These services are available as commodities but who can afford them?

For a task to move out of the domestic economy, the hourly wage earned by the lowest-paid family member must be enough to purchase goods or services that could otherwise have been done within the household in one hour. Thus if a family has one child under school age, they can only afford to buy childcare if one hour of childcare costs less than the lowest-paid person in the house, usually a woman, earns in an hour.

But the childcare, if provided by a profit-making business, will sell at the full value of the service. That is, the childcare fee will include wages, profits, rent on the building, heating, etc. Suppose that the salary of the childcare worker is $16 an hour, that a further $12 goes in profit and rent, and $4 in other overheads. Then if each childcare worker can look after three children the overall cost per hour will be on the order of $11. At this level it would not be worthwhile for a worker who was herself on $16 an hour to put a child into care since, allowing for tax deductions, travel costs, she would have almost nothing left over. If two children had to be put into care, it would be impossible.

It is no surprise then that private childcare has initially been only affordable by households on higher wage rates. But this is clearly irrational from the standpoint of economizing on social labor. A single child at home ties up one adult. A single child in a kindergarten ties up only one-third of an adult. But since workers only get part of the value they create back in wages, something that would be socially efficient becomes privately unaffordable.

There is a feedback mechanism here. So long as women are disproportionately tied to home childcare, their participation in the labor force is lower, and we have seen that this results in lower average wages for women. But this lower pay rate makes childcare unaffordable and ensures that it is women, not men, who are likely to stay at home. The elimination of a gender pay gap thus depends, at a minimum, on the socialization of childcare. The socialization of infant care, its move out of the household, is thus dependent on the provision of either free state nurseries or highly subsidized private ones.

We will return to this topic in chapter 7.

5.7 DISTRIBUTION OF WAGE RATES

But behind the question of gender differences in wages is a bigger question. What determines the distribution of wages in general? For there is not just a single male and female wage. For men and women there are spreads of pay rates. Figure 5.17 shows a line for men's wages and a line for women's. But these are the median lines, as many men's wages fall below the male median line as lie above it.

In Figure 5.20 there are two lines, one for male and one for female wages, but these represent cumulative distribution. The horizontal axis is wage levels and the vertical axis measures the fraction of people earning less than a given wage. The horizontal lines represent 10 percent, 25 percent, and 50 percent of the respective gender. The circles and triangles represent raw data from the U.S. Bureau of Labor Statistics for the first quarter of 2016.

The shape of the curve fitted to the data is what is called a log normal cumulative distribution. What does this mean? Well, readers will be familiar with the bell curve–shaped normal distribution. A normal distribution is one of the most commonly occurring in statistics. You get it where a measurement is the result of a collection of randomly operating causes that add together.

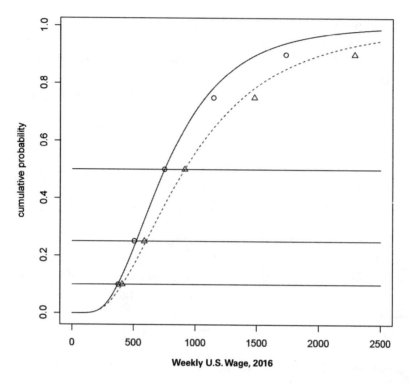

Figure 5.20. Distribution of weekly wage rates for the United States, 2016, fits for the bottom half of the distribution a log-normal curve. The solid line is a log-normal distribution fitted to the median and lowest decile of female wages, the dotted line is a log-normal curve fitted to the median and lowest decile of male wages. Note that for the third quartile and ninth decile the empirical distribution is shifted to the right compared to a log-normal form. Source: Bureau of Labor Statistics, Usual Weekly Earnings of Wage and Salary Earners, April 19, 2016.

If we consider the wages of every person in the United States during a particular week, these wages will be affected by all sorts of factors, which, if we select someone at random that person will seem random. The gender, the job they do, how long they have done it, their age, the region of the country they live in, whether they had days sick that week—the list of factors is vast. Should we therefore expect wage rates to be normally distributed?

A little thought tells us that wage rates cannot be distributed this way. The normal distribution is symmetrical about the average. The average value occurs in the middle as the most frequently occurring value. It then spreads out on either side. Suppose the average weekly wage is $900. We know that there are plenty of people who earn more than twice the average wage, more than $1,800 in this case. Suppose 10 percent of people earn more than $1,800, or $900 above the average. If wages were normally distributed, the same number of people would have to earn less than $900

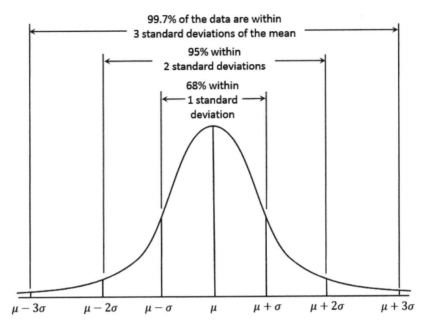

Figure 5.21. Classical normal distribution in which μ is the mean of the distribution. Source: Dan Kernler.

below the average, that is to say less than 0 dollars. There would have to be significant fraction of people earning *negative* wages. But we know this does not happen.

It is not logically impossible for wages to have a normal distribution. If the distribution of wage rates was very narrow, so that with a mean of $900 the standard deviation was, say, only $100, then the probability of anyone earning either twice the mean wage, or less than nothing, would be vanishingly small. It is an empirical fact that wage dispersions are much bigger than this in the upward direction, which precludes the distribution being normal.

While a normal distribution is generated by random processes that are additive, processes in which random factors are multiplied together have a log normal distribution. That is, if you plot the factor you are measuring on a logarithmic scale, the frequency curve you get is the familiar bell shape. The point is that multiplication on normal numbers becomes addition of their logarithms and so gives a bell curve when we plot it on a log scale. Suppose that some of the factors I described as working on wages actually work in a multiplicative way. If mean wages are multiplied by 0.8 if you are a woman and by a further 0.85 if you are black, 1.2 if you have a degree etc., etc., then you would expect the distribution to be log normal.

Mandelbrot [1962], whose research into fractals later won him fame, observed that the lower part of income distributions is well described by a log normal function while the upper part has what is termed a power law distribution, that is, there are more people on higher incomes than a log normal distribution would predict. We will not discuss the problems of the upper income distribution, which includes property and managerial income here, but it is examined in some detail in Cottrell et al. [2009].[88] Figure 5.20 bears out Mandelbrot's observation. All of the first decile, first quartile, and the median for male and female wages fall nicely on log normal curves, but the third quartile and the ninth decile indicate that the right tail of the distribution is flatter than log normal.

The key things we need to determine for wages are:

- What is the mean wage
- What is the median wage
- What is the spread or standard deviation of the distribution
- Can these arguments be used to account for the difference in male and female workers' wages

Given the standard deviation of the distribution and its mean, the median will be determined, so in essence we have to understand what drives these two parameters. For a log normal distribution the mean wage should be somewhat above the median wage, which is what we always observe.

In a fundamentally chaotic system like a market economy we should expect random processes to spread out the wage distribution until some constraint sets a bound on its spread. It has long been known that there is a lower limit to the wage distribution: a subsistence minimum.[89] That this is not some outdated nineteenth-century concept is borne out by the statistics that show that at the tail end of the income distribution even in a rich country like the United States many families go hungry. Coleman-Jensen et al. [2015] state that 8.4 percent of American households have low food security and 5.6 percent very low food security. Overall 48 million people in the United States were food insecure in 2014. People on wages that put them in the low food security category have a wage that is not enough to survive on without federal or charitable food aid.

Households classified as having low food security have reported multiple indications of food acquisition problems and reduced diet quality, but typically have reported few, if any, indications of reduced food intake. Those classified as having very low food security have reported multiple indications of reduced food intake and disrupted eating patterns due to inadequate resources for food. In most, but not all, households with very low food security, the survey respondent reported that he or she was hungry at some time during the year but did not eat because there was not enough money for food.

- 96 percent reported that they had eaten less than they felt they should because there was not enough money for food.
- 69 percent reported that they had been hungry but did not eat because they could not afford enough food.
- 45 percent reported having lost weight because they did not have enough money for food.
- 30 percent reported that an adult did not eat for a whole day because there was not enough money for food. [Ibid.]

The category that is now called very low food security used to be simply described in the statistics as "hunger," but the U.S. government now uses a euphemism for the same thing. But as Table 5.18 shows, hunger, far from declining as the United States gets richer, has been increasing.

Bear in mind that the wage in dollars necessary to feed oneself will vary between countries and in terms of mode of life. If a person is still in a position to grow some food of his own, that obviously makes a difference. If a person can collect firewood or other fuel, he needs less cash to live on than a city dweller who can only cook with electricity. In addition, part of the wage goes to housing costs, which vary enormously between high-rent cities and poor rural areas. A wage that allows people to feed themselves in the countryside can leave them hungry in a city. The subsistence minimum sets the lowest wage, but what then sets the average wage?

Any chaotic system will tend to increase in entropy until it hits some constraint. For distributions like the normal or log normal ones, an increase

TABLE 5.18: Trends in Prevalence Rates of Food Insecurity and Very Low Food Security (Hunger) in U.S. Households, 1995–2014

	Food Insecurity % of Households	Very Low Food Security % of Households
1995	11.94	4.14
2000	10.47	3.13
2005	11.00	3.87
2010	14.51	5.35
2011	14.94	5.72
2012	14.51	5.72
2013	14.28	5.58
2014	14.05	5.59

Source: Coleman–Jensen, et al., 2015.

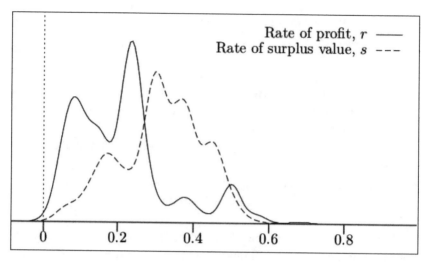

Figure 5.22. Probability density functions for the rates of profit and surplus value in Britain, 1984. Source: Cockshott and Cottrell, 1998a.

in entropy involves a rise in the variance, a spreading out of the curve. But if the left-hand lower limit of the curve is fixed by the minimum subsistence wage, a spreading out necessarily increases the average wage. What stops this entropic pressure?

Clearly the process must ultimately be bound by the added value produced by labor. The mean wage cannot be higher than the mean value added by labor; indeed, so long as capitalism persists it must fall some way short of that. We know that across the economy as a whole labor adds surplus value that feeds into property incomes. The question we should ask is what stops the average wage from rising so high that surplus value is reduced to a minimal level? Why does surplus value typically make up something between a third and a half of national revenue, rather than only 2 or 3 percent of revenue?

To answer this you have to realize that there is not just a single rate of surplus value in an economy. Like all economic variables it has a distribution. There are different rates of surplus value from firm to firm and from industry to industry. As an example, Figure 5.22 gives the dispersion of rates of surplus value between British industries in 1984. Some producers within an industry are less efficient and use more labor than average. Wages paid also vary by industry and by firm, but the effect of a general upward shift of the wage rate distribution will particularly affect industries and firms with low rates of surplus value.

If you look at the distribution in Figure 5.22 you can see that its lower edge just touches a zero rate of surplus value. A rise in wages will tend to tip the lower tail of firms into the red. We know that only a small portion of

firms can be in the red at any one time. Firms making a loss either shut down
or lay off staff to end the losses. A shift in the wage distribution of the type
shown in Figure 5.20 to the right shifts a surplus value distribution like that
in Figure 5.22 to the left.

If we look at a snapshot picture, it seems that any tendency of the wage
distribution to spread out is being prevented by the dispersion of the rate of
surplus value. An increase in the variance of the wage rate pushes firms on
the lower edge of the surplus value rate distribution into crisis. They lay off

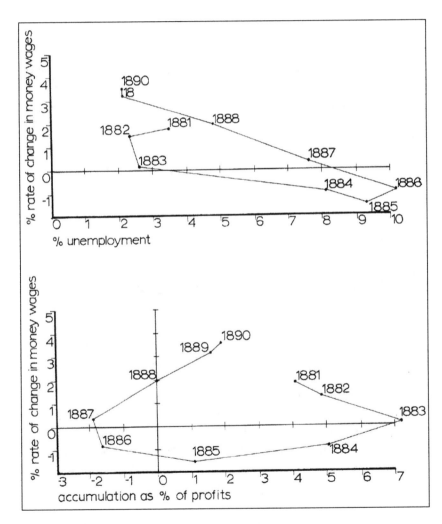

Figure 5.23. The British busiensss cycle, 1881–1890. The above figures show the process
for a classical nineteenth-century business cycle, one in a period when the basic
mechanism was not obscured by government counter-cyclical policies. These basic cycles
took on the order of 7 to 10 years.

workers and the resulting unemployment and competition for jobs forces down wages again.

Snapshot pictures suggest a nice stochastic equilibrium with the dispersion pressure of the rate of surplus value distribution acting to limit the entropic spread of the wage distribution. But that is misleading. The feedback relations are not instantaneous. There is no equilibrium; instead what happens is a cyclical process. Figure 5.23 shows the process for a classical nineteenth-century business cycle, one in a period when the basic mechanism was not obscured by government counter-cyclical policies. These basic cycles took on the order of 7 to 10 years.

Rising wages lead to layoffs, which lead to unemployment, and wages start to fall. Later firms take workers on again at lower wage rates and unemployment falls. With falling unemployment firms have to bid up the price of newly hired labor allowing the wage dispersion to rise. Then the cycle repeats.

There is, however, no reason to suppose that it repeats exactly, so over time the rate of surplus value may wander. Capitalism is an anarchic, disorderly system. State regulation may reduce disorder, but in the absence of such intervention we should assume that the system will show maximal disorder. Is there a rate of surplus value in the economy that corresponds to maximal disorder?

Surprising as it may seem, the most disorderly state of the economy occurs when there is no surplus value. Disorder is measured using the concept of entropy [Shannon, 1948]. The higher the disorder of something the higher its entropy. The idea originated in the study of heat, thermodynamics, but has subsequently been extended to information theory, statistics, and many other areas of science. There is an entropy or disorder involved with statistical distributions like the normal or the log normal

As median wages rise, the entropy of the wage distribution rises. But wage rises reduce the rate of surplus value. For the economy to remain viable, with only a tiny fraction of firms being in the condition of having a negative rate of surplus value, a smaller mean s/v requires the surplus value distribution to become more compressed—to have a smaller variance. A compression of the surplus value distribution makes the conditions of firms more orderly. The firms become more alike in their ratio of wages to profits. Firms in a given industry come to use a more standardized technology. If firms become more alike their entropy must fall. A spread of the wage distribution means that wage disorder rises. Does the disorder of the wages rise faster than the consequential fall in firm disorder?

The answer is yes. Table 5.19 shows that as the mean wage rises, the disorder of the whole system is maximized. So even if we assume that capitalism is in the long run governed by a principle of maximal disorder this would not preclude a long-term rise in the proportion of income going as wages. One could have a sequence of business cycles, each of which resulted in the least competitive firms being forced out of business. When expansion took place again the dispersion of rates of surplus value could be lower allowing a lower overall rate of surplus value. But for this optimistic process to occur it would have to be the case

- That the fall in wages during the downswing was less than the rise in the upswing.
- That no other factors, such as increasing reserve army of labor, forced down wages in the long term.
- That the internal disorder of the firms was not so increased by technical advances as to offset the culling of less productive firms in the crisis.

Since technical change occurs all the time, and occurs unevenly in a competitive capitalist economy, this will set a lower limit on the dispersion of rates of surplus value, and thus on the wage share. The theoretical possibility of wages rising until they consume the entire social product could only happen if there was no disorder among firms—in effect, it demands a comprehensively planned economy not a capitalist one.

In Table 5.19 the minimum, mean, and median wages are given as labor-value fractions of the working day. H(w) is the entropy of the wage distribution, H(s) the entropy of the surplus value distribution. Rising median wages correspond to rising disorder in the whole system, and thus are not prohibited on thermodynamic grounds. Wage distribution assumed to be log normal and surplus value distribution to be normal.

5.8 THE NEXT GENERATION

Let us now return to the issue of the differences in male and female wage distributions. A working hypothesis for what causes this is as follows:

- Male and female wage distributions are both constrained to be log normal.
- Lower bounds of each distribution are almost the same and are set by the survival wage of a single person.
- Slightly higher up is the subsistence minimum wage for a family.
- Since a larger number of men than women are the sole earners in a household, a smaller number of men can be employed at levels below the family subsistence level.

TABLE 5.19: As the Median Wage Rises, the Mean Wage Rises More Rapidly

Minimum Wage	Median Wage	Mean Wage	H(w)	H(s)	H(w)+H(s)
0.1	0.43	0.50	1.63	1.05	2.68
0.1	0.44	0.54	1.77	0.97	2.74
0.1	0.45	0.58	1.91	0.88	2.79
0.1	0.46	0.63	2.06	0.78	2.85
0.1	0.47	0.68	2.23	0.68	2.91
0.1	0.48	0.73	2.39	0.58	2.97
0.1	0.49	0.78	2.57	0.46	3.04
0.1	0.50	0.84	2.76	0.35	3.10
0.1	0.51	0.90	2.95	0.22	3.18
0.1	0.52	0.96	3.16	0.09	3.25

In the table, the minimum, mean, and median wages are given as labor value fractions of the working day. H(w) is the entropy of the wage distribution; H(s) is the entropy of the surplus value distribution. Rising median wages correspond to rising disorder in the whole system and thus are not prohibited on thermodynamic grounds. Wage distribution assumed to be log-normal and surplus value distribution to be normal.

- Thus the standard deviation of the male wage distribution function must be greater.
- Thus the median of the male wage distribution must also be greater.

This is explained slightly more formally in a note.[90] It follows that the male-female wage gap will persist until it is equally probable that either sex is the sole earner of a family. This is compatible with the observation that the wage gap declines in proportion to the decline in the male-female participation rate gap. (See Figures 5.17, 5.18.)

In the past this basic mechanism has been cast in terms of the need of the male wage to be enough to ensure the reproduction of the next generation of workers.[91] But this is a rather teleological argument. The next generation is twenty years in the future, so how is their existence or nonexistence supposed to affect wages today?

The Ricardian law of wages provided a feedback mechanism. It is when it:

> exceeds its natural price that the condition of the laborer is flourishing and happy, that he has it in his power to command a greater proportion of the necessaries and enjoyments of life, and therefore to rear a healthy and numerous family. When, however, by the encouragement that high wages give to the increase of population, the number

of laborers is increased, wages again fall to their natural price, and indeed from a reaction sometimes fall below it.

When the market price of labor is below its natural price, the condition of the laborers is most wretched: then poverty deprives them of those comforts which custom renders absolute necessaries. It is only after their privations have reduced their number, or the demand for labor has increased, that the market price of labor will rise to its natural price, and that the laborer will have the moderate comforts which the natural rate of wages will afford. [Ricardo, 1951, chap. 5]

But my formulation, derived from Marx, is not presuming that. I, like Marx, expect the mean wage to be significantly above the subsistence level, and I do not assume that a capitalist society is necessarily able to successfully reproduce its working population. Indeed, the evidence is to the contrary.

All I am assuming is that if the lower limit of wages crosses the narrow boundary between hunger wages and starvation wages, mortality among the workers rises rapidly. Well before wages fall to starvation levels undernutrition results in increased mortality from disease [Harris, 2004]. Capitalist firms and governments have not been stopped by moral scruples from working people to death on starvation wages. In famine relief projects the government of British India worked literally millions to death on public works projects [Davis, 2002], and in the 1940s German firms notoriously did the same with forced foreign labor. It is not morals, but the very rapid death rate of such practices, that makes them unsustainable.

In concluding that this reality forces the lower boundary of the adult male wage up a bit to be above family starvation levels, the only other assumptions necessary are: (a) that families exist, (b) that more men than women are sole breadwinners, and (c) that a great many poor parents will go hungry themselves to put food on their children's plates.

As a larger portion of the population becomes economically active, that is, employed in the capitalist sector, the share of the surplus product tends to rise. The same population has to be supported, but more workers are there to do it. At the same time, tasks essential to life, like the preparation and cooking of food, move out of the home. Food is semi-prepared before it appears in the supermarkets, clothes are ready-made. As food preparation and clothes preparation moves out of the house, it is done with less labor. The total time necessary for the day-to-day reproduction of the population shrinks while the number of workers grows. In order to get by a mode of life is established that becomes dependent on all adults in the household engaging in waged work. The result is to intensify the perception of child-raising as a burden. Children become seen as a lifestyle choice to be avoided if you cannot afford them. The birth rate falls below reproduction levels, the working population shrinks, and the economy goes into a long-term crisis expressed in declining profitability.

Teleology aside, capitalist economies have relied on coexisting patriarchal and subsistence communities to supply at least part of the next generation of workers. Migrants from the countryside within their boundaries, or colonies without, fed the industrial growth of the great powers. The same process clearly continues. Single migrant labor has the advantage that it can be employed at below a family wage. The cost of bringing up the worker was met by the distant household into which they were born. So capitalism, like slave economy, has long relied on importing labor. In some cases like the coolies imported from China to the Americas in the nineteenth century the social form was only marginally advanced from slavery. But the principle of increasing exploitation by offloading the reproduction costs of labor to surrounding societies remains in force in the metropolitan countries to this day. If this avenue is restricted the form economy goes into structural crisis.

5.9 LONG-TERM TREND OF PROFITABILITY

Capitalism is production for profit. It is run with the aim of monetary gain. This drive may seem far removed from issues of population, but, from the standpoint of political economy, they are closely related. Ultimately, monetary gain is a demographic question. Monetary quantities are determined by labor. They are the abstract symbolic representation of labor relations.[92]

Population growth is the fundamental constraint on profit because population growth constrains labor. Profits are measured in money, but this is only a nominal measure since the value of money changes over time. The real measure of profit, or any other sum of money, is the amount of labor embodied in commodities that it will exchange against. It is of no advantage to a firm if their money profit goes up, but the amount of embodied labor that this commands actually falls.

If we want to ask what, in the long run, and at the level of society as a whole, determines the possibility of making a profit, we concern ourselves with the amount of labor society has, not the amount of money.[93]

We can express the process informally with the following argument. Suppose initially that profits make up 50 percent of net national income and that the capital stock is equal to 200 percent of national income. Now suppose half the profits are reinvested, then the capital stock grows and profit rate will fall, as show in the table on page 173.

This simple process is behind the tendency of the profit rate to fall over time. Understanding the process in more detail requires that we look at how

	Year 1	Year 2	Year 3	Year 4
Profit % of National Income	50	50	50	50
Capital Stock as a % of National Income	200	225	250	275
Profit Rate %	25	22	20	18

population growth and productivity will affect things. To do this we have to move from an argument in terms of money national income, which is affected by inflation, to one in terms of person years. The total profit in the economy will then be given by

$$\text{Profit} = (1 - \text{wage share}) \times \text{Number of workers}$$

Here the wage share is expressed as the fraction of a full-time equivalent working year required to produce the goods consumed by the average laborer. The dimension of Profit is millions of full-time person years per annum, which is obviously the same as millions of full-time equivalent persons. We can view this as the population that produces those goods purchased out of profits. The reality of profit, behind the screen of money, is the millions of people it commands: the producers of luxury goods, tax advisers, servants plus the people working to produce new capital goods whose wages are paid out of reinvested profit. Capital stock is the accumulation of past labor; it can be accounted for in terms of the working years it took to produce. The rate of profit per annum is then given by the capital stock measured in millions of person years:

$$\text{Profit rate} = \frac{\text{Profit}}{\text{Capital stock}}$$

The dimension of Profit Rate, persons/person-years, is Time^{-1} as we would expect. The profit rate will fall if the rate of growth of capital exceeds the rate of growth of profits, that is to say, if the capital stock grows faster than the population available to produce profit goods.

The main determinant of the rate of growth of the mass of profit will be the growth of the working population. A secondary influence will be any change in the wage share over time. Why is movement of the wage share secondary?

Suppose the working population grows by 5 percent a year. If the wage share remains constant then total profit will also grow by 5 percent. Consider the effect of a reduction in the wage share: if the wage share is initially 0.6 then a 5 percent reduction in the labor content of the real wage will produce

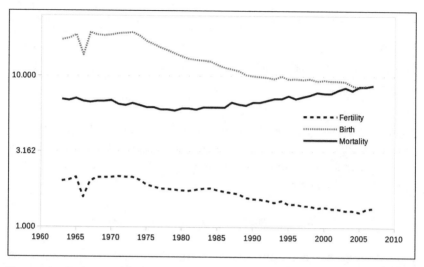

Figure 5.24. Evolution of the birth rate and death rates in Japan. Source: Extended Penn World Tables (EPWT) Marquetti, 2003.

a 3 percent increase in the profit rate; but if the initial wage share is merely 40 percent, the same 5 percent reduction in the labor content of the wage will raise the rate of profit by 2 percent. The lower the wage share falls the less significant is the impact a given percent reduction in the wage share.

In the long term the rate of change of profit is strongly affected by the rate of growth of the working population:

n = rate of working population growth ≈ rate of profit growth

In the early stages of capitalist development it grows very rapidly. In nineteenth-century Europe this was as a result of improved food supply after the Agricultural Revolution. In the twentieth century the same process was experienced in many third world countries, as a result partly of the Green Revolution, and also as a result of medical advances limiting infant mortality. This phase of rapid population growth is the first demographic transition as societies moved from patriarchal agriculture to capitalist or socialist industrializations.

Later, with the elevation of the social status of women, the abolition of child labor, and with education becoming more costly, family sizes shrink. In highly developed capitalist countries the population stabilizes or even starts to decline, in a second demographic transition. What is the implication of this?

So long as population was expanding there existed the possibility of a

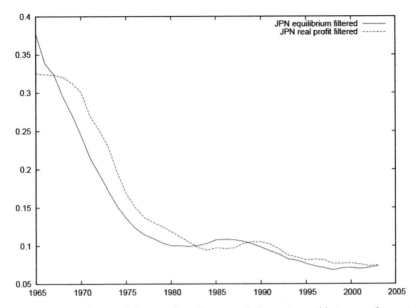

Figure 5.25. Evolution of the actual profit rate and dynamic equilibrium profit rate in Japan. Source: Image produced by software written by T. Tadjadinov.

positive equilibrium rate of profit so long as capital stock grew no faster than the working population.

The growth rate of capital stock is given by:

$$\frac{\text{accumulation share} \times \text{profit rate}}{\text{growth of labor productivity } - } \\ \text{depreciation rate } - \\ \overline{\text{growth rate of capital stock} = }$$

where the accumulation share is share of profit going as accumulation. The growth of labor productivity(g) has a negative effect since it accelerates the obsolescence of existing capital, as does the rate of depreciation (δ). It follows that the dynamic attractor for the rate of profit, the equilibrium rate of profit is:

$$\text{equilibrium rate of profit} \quad = \quad \frac{n + g + \delta}{\text{accumulation share}}$$

The second most important determinant of the rate of profit is the share of profit that is accumulated.

When a large portion of profit is accumulated this will depress the percent rate of profit. Conversely, if most of profit is consumed unproductively, then the effect is, paradoxically, to raise the rate of profit.

If population stabilizes, n = 0 and the rate of profit falls to a level only sufficient to cover depreciation plus a boost term due to improvement in labor productivity. It is not widely recognized in the media, but the general trend is for technical improvements to slow down over the course of the development of a capitalist economy [Eichengreen et al., 2012; Marquetti, 2003; Edgerton, 2011b]. Economies with stable or falling populations like Japan end up with very low rates of profit as shown in Figure 5.24. The equilibrium profit rate in that graph is r* given above. Note how closely the actual rate tracks the rate predicted on first principles from the labor theory of value. The actual rate of profit tracks the dynamic equilibrium rate after a couple of years delay.

Because of the tendency of the rate of profit to fall, capitalist economic growth does not correlate positively with a high rate of return on capital. A country like Japan with a high investment rate can grow fast, but the effect of the high investment rate is a low rate of return on capital as shown in Figure 5.26. Contrary to expectations high rates of capital return do not correlate with fast growth.

A tendency for the rate of profit to move to zero after the second demographic transition lies behind the ever lower rates of interest in Japan. If the rate of population growth falls to zero, the dynamic equilibrium rate of profit is also zero. If population growth is negative, the attractor for the rate of profit is negative.

A key factor in the stagnation of the Japanese working population is that a declining birth rate—common to many capitalist countries—combines with a policy of strict immigration restriction.

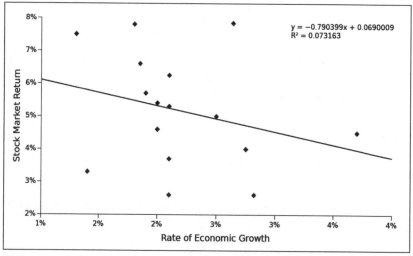

Figure 5.26. Relationship between return on stocks and economic growth for 16 developed nations between 1900 and 2006. Source: Siegel, 2002.

Countries that allow immigration can offset the tendency of the rate of profit to fall to zero. Immigration boosts the working population in three ways:

1.   It directly and immediately compensates for a low birth rate.
2.   The activity rate of immigrants is high because they are disproportionately of working age.
3.   Immigrants' families tend to have higher birth rates than the settled population of developed capitalist countries, so that they indirectly compensate for the low birth rate of the former.

The net result of rapid immigration is to raise the rate of exploitation (Figure 5.28). For the UK between 1970 and 2008 there was a 75 percent correlation between the rate of exploitation and the level of inward migration. Statistically this means that 75 percent of changes in exploitation can be explained by changes in immigration. A high rate of immigration tends to produce a higher rate of exploitation. When we say that 75 percent of changes in exploitation can be explained by changes in immigration, this is in a statistical sense if you correlate one against the other. In practice there are temporal trends in both immigration and exploitation. Both rose from a low in the 1970s. This corresponded to a move toward a general neoliberal policy of freer movement of both labor and capital and restrictions on the rights of trade unions. Figure 5.27, upper panel, shows the growth in immigration from 1976 with a short dip in the early 1980s. The lower panel shows that the equilibrium rate of profit r* starts to rise steadily from 1976 onward, with no interruption. Since changes in the equilibrium profit rate r* are driven mainly by changes in the growth of the workforce and by the accumulation share, we can conclude that the rapid rise in r* from 1978 was due to a slower rate of accumulation combined with the more rapid growth of the labor pool.

The actual rate of profit generally lags the equilibrium rate for the UK as for Japan. It lags because it takes time for the capital stock to adjust in response to changes in accumulation. It also has some independence, in that over the short term changes in the rate of surplus value affect the rate of profit. Changes in the rate of growth of the labor force—the slowdown from 1965 to 1975 and the gradual acceleration from then on, are the single biggest factor explaining the long-term shape of the profit rate curve, with fluctuations in accumulation during the trade cycle explaining the decadal oscillations imposed on that.

Variations in the rate of accumulation affect the equilibrium rate of profit because a fall in accumulation reduces the capital stock over which the rate of

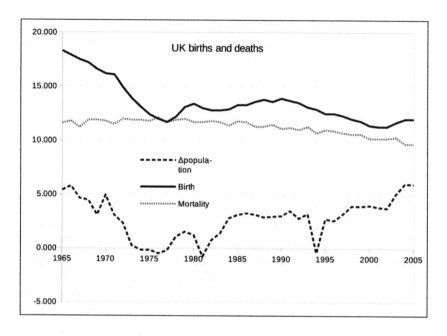

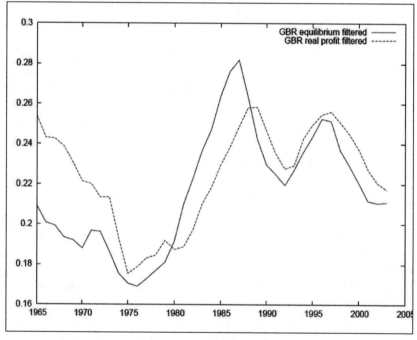

Figure 5.27. Evolution of the population growth (top), actual profit rate and dynamic equilibrium profit rate (bottom) in UK. Source: T. Tadjadinov; Extended Penn World Tables (EPWT), Marquetti and Foley, 2002,ver 4.0.

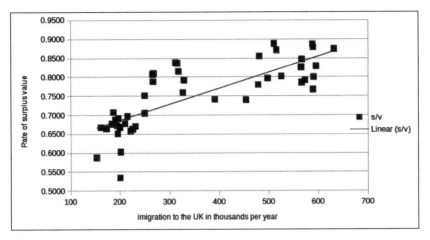

Figure 5.28. UK rate of surplus value as function of immigration levels.

profit is calculated. In addition, the real rate of profit can be affected by slower accumulation tending to increase exploitation, as shown in Table 5.20.

The connection between population growth and real wages was a key component of the classical theory of wages. In this, wages were the sum necessary to reproduce labor. The regulation of wages was seen as occurring via population growth. If wages rose substantially above what was needed to reproduce the existing population, then more children would survive to adulthood and the population would grow. Competition between workers would then work to drive down wages toward the subsistence level.

This classical theory does appear to be a good fit to the long-term movement of wages over many centuries in the pre-industrial era. In Figure 5.29 we can see that real wages move in an almost mirror image to the movements

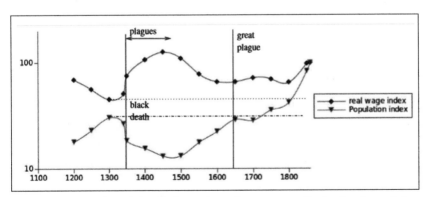

Figure 5.29. The effect of the Black Death on farm wages in England, subsampled at 50-year intervals. Vertical axis shows indices of population and real agricultural wages, with 1860 being the base year. Source: Data from Clark, 2007.

of population for the period 1200 to 1750. An extra data point is inserted for 1340, just before the Black Death, to show that the rise in real wages coincides with the fall in population.

The Black Death produced a sharp fall in population and an equally sharp rise in wages. Successive outbreaks of the plague continued to drive population down for one hundred years, with corresponding wage rises.

From 1500 a combination of better wages with some degree of immunity to *Yersinia pestis* allowed population to recover. With the growth in population the levels of wages fell again. They did not, however, fall right back to pre-plague levels (upper horizontal line) even though the pre-plague population was regained by the early eighteenth century. The great plague of the late seventeenth century again reduced population, by as much as 20 percent in some areas of the country. This is associated with a late seventeenth-century rise in wages. Even in the late eighteenth century the time when the classical theory of wages was developed, some inverse relation between population growth and wages still held, though less strongly than before. It was not until the takeoff of the specifically capitalist mode of production in the nineteenth century that the strong inverse relationship partially broke down. The higher rate of relative surplus value made possible by machine industry allowed real wages to rise even while population grew. But if you look at the vertical scale, you can see that even by 1860 real wages had not regained the peak attained during the labor shortage of the late Middle Ages. Farm laborers were better off in 1450 than in 1850.

More rapid population growth boosts the rate of profit by two distinct mechanisms. On the one hand a more rapid expansion of the labor force increases competition for jobs and allows the rate of exploitation to be increased. The rate of surplus value tends to be higher in years when the rate of population growth is higher,[94] Secondly, a growing population absorbs accumulated capital preventing, or at least slowing down, a rise in the capital-to-labor ratio.

Table 5.20 shows that the exploitation rate tends to be high when the birth rate is high and the workforce expands rapidly and tends to be low if the rate of accumulation is high. These reflect the relative competitive positions in the market of labor and capital.

TABLE 5.20: Correlation of the Exploitation Rate

Variables	Correlation
(b, s/v)	35%
(dN, s/v)	13%
α, s/v	−56%

Note: Correlations were performed accross vectors of 1220 individual year samples drawn from 30 countries; "b" is the birthrate, "dN" is the annual percentage change of the employed workforce, α is the share of investment in surplus. Source: Extended Penn World Tables.

The effect of a rapidly growing population is most strikingly seen if we contrast an emerging capitalist economy like South Africa with a mature one like Japan. As Figure 5.30 shows, instead of falling the South African profit rate rose rapidly from the 1970s. A similar pattern is seen in other African countries like Egypt [Zachariah, 2008]. Note how the acceleration of employed population growth allows a rising rate of profit. Compared to Figure 5.27 the absolute rate of profit on capital stock in South Africa is about 4 times as high as in the UK.

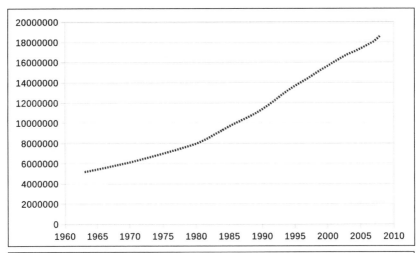

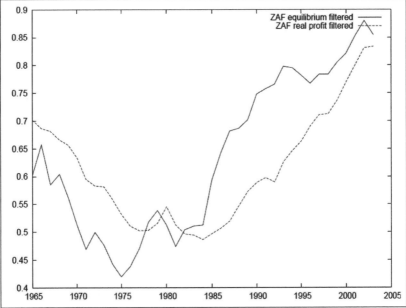

Figure 5.30. South African employed population (top), profit rate (bottom).
Source: Extended Penn World Table, Marquetti and Foley, 2002,ver 4.0.

In such nations the capital accumulated each year is insufficient to keep up with the rising population, so the capital-to-labor ratio falls. A lower capital-to-labor ratio then gives rise to a higher rate of profit. Ultimately it is sex that drives capitalism. The soaring profit rate in South African capitalism is driven by the much greater sexual productivity of South African women. South African fertility was still 2.5 in 2008 against only 1.3 in Japan. But South Africa is already on the path toward capitalist maturity. In 2008 the fertility rate was only half what it was forty years earlier. In other African countries the demographic transition is barely starting. In Nigeria, fertility in 2008 was a huge 5.7 children per woman, in Zambia 5.8, in Tanzania 5.6. Equatorial Africa is, in the early twenty-first century, capitalism's last best hope of profitability. But across most of the world, fertility is falling (Figure 5.31). It is barely at reproduction levels. This poses a long-term threat to capitalism since the essence of the accumulation of capital is the growth of the proletariat.[95]

What are the implications of this for profitability worldwide?

If world population growth halts, the dynamic equilibrium gross rate of profit worldwide will end up just being sufficient to replace depreciation of existing capital stock. Data by Maito et al. [2014], given in Figure 5.32, indicate that the core capitalist countries have leveled out at a profit rate of 10 to 15 percent. Since Marquetti and Foley [2002] give figures in the same range for the depreciation of stock in the core countries it seems probable that capitalism is already reaching a stationary state in these countries. Zachariah [2008] found in his study that in the core countries "gross investments are increasingly going to cover depreciation, i.e. the part of the capital stock used up in production."

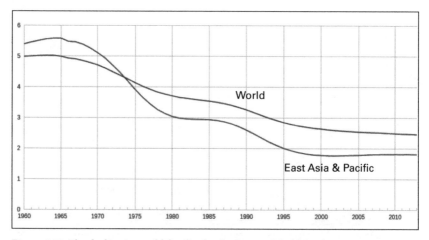

Figure 5.31. The decline in world fertility levels. Source: World Bank., 2014.

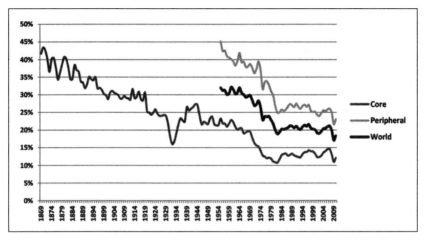

Figure 5.32. World rate of profit and average rate in core and peripheral countries (1869–2010). Source: Maito et al., 2014.

Due to the continuing availability of labor from the countryside, the peripheral countries show a higher rate of return, but if data in Figure 5.31 is taken into account the trend for the world as a whole will be toward what has already happened in the core.

At this point the value of the world capital stock in billions of person years would be stationary. Investment would only be sufficient to compensate for depreciation and the gradual cheapening of the capital stock in value terms due to productivity improvements. But accumulation of value will have ceased. This amounts to an existential crisis for capitalist civilization.

5.10 PRODUCTIVE AND UNPRODUCTIVE ACTIVITIES

In Section 4.5 we recounted Adam Smith's critique of the feudal profligacy. It was a critique that focused on the distinction between productive and unproductive workers. With this distinction Smith was expressing the viewpoint of a social group—the urban manufacturing capitalists—who had scarcely existed in the feudal period. As critic of the great lords' profligate waste he stood on the ramparts of modernity, from whence to glower with disdain on previously *honorable* professions. From such heights, ministers of the church and army officers were down on the same level with Punch and Judy shows and menial servants.

The wheel of history turned and there came a day when the manufacturers themselves aspired to great lordship. They bought titles and ordered mansions to rival the old aristocracy. That of engineering magnate William George Armstrong, Cragside (Figure 5.33), epitomizes this fusion of aristocratic and manufacturing values. Built in a grand Tudor revival style, looking like a castle, it contained the latest inventions of the Victorian era: electric lights, hydraulic lifts, powered washing machines; and it was staffed by dozens of servants. With manufacturers now aping aristocrats, Smith's radicalism passed into a decent obscurity. Only Marx, theoretical spokesman of the International Working Men's Association, still thought Smith's idea worth remembering. Manufacturing workers, it seems, were not blind to the profligacy of their masters.[96]

Recall that Smith proposed two conditions for paid work in order to be considered productive:

1. The workers must be employed out of capital not revenue.
2. The work must result in the physical production of lasting vendible commodities.

In his notes on Smith, Marx [1999] initially weakened the definition so that only the first criterion was needed. Any work that was employed out of capital should, he said, be counted as productive. However, he later seemed to have realized the inadequacy of this simple criterion, when he argued that labor employed by merchants could not count as productive, since buying and selling was not itself a productive activity [Marx 1971, chap. 27). In effect he shifted back to accepting Smith's rule that to count as productive labor had to be both physically productive and employed out of capital. Marx's followers use a broad definition of "unproductive," where all work that is devoted either to the distribution of income (accountancy, banking, advertising, etc.) or to the maintenance of the social order (police, army, church etc.) counts as unproductive, and productive activity is defined similarly to the way Smith did, but with the proviso that transport is also productive [Deepankar, 2015]. That is, productive work must either produce or move a physical and vendible commodity. The opera singers or prostitutes of Smith's time produced no persisting commodity and were unproductive. But if today Placido Domingo is recorded singing, and CDs are pressed and sold of the recording, or if today an actress performs for a sexually explicit film that is then sold as a DVD, the same physical acts become capitalistically productive. [97]

The unproductive sector exists by the support of the surplus product of the productive sectors. The expansion of the former reduces amount of surplus available for reinvestment in the latter, and thus affects long-run capital accumulation. As argued in section 5.4.9, it is only in the productive sector that technical advance reduces the necessary labor of society [Cockshott and Zachariah, 2006]. Any critique of unproductive activity is comparative. It

Figure 5.33. Cragside House, constructed for the Newcastle armaments manufacturer William George Armstrong, later Lord Armstrong. Photo: Dave Sumpner, English Wikipedia.

says that if society were organized differently, production would increase. So Smith was saying that once great feudal lords no longer maintained retinues, the retainers could be put to profitable and productive work. Marxians say that if society were communistically organized, then many of those currently working for the banks would be redeployed to making things or providing other social services. Neo-Smithians argue that if those currently employed by the state to provide public services were redeployed to the private sector, production would rise [Bacon and Eltis, 1978].

It is worth looking at a number of sectors of the economy to see what is meant by designating them as unproductive. We will soon discover that there can be a marked contrast between how things appear from private and social perspectives.

5.10.1 Violence

First let's return to the Gothic splendor of Cragside and its owner, Lord Armstrong, who employed hundreds of workers in his engineering works in the north of England. These, surely, were the very archetype of the productive laborer. But what were they making?

In the main they were making cannons. Armstrong's greatest invention had been a breech-loading gun that fired explosive shells rather than the old solid cannon balls (Figure 5.34). With these, the Royal Navy equipped a new fleet of "ironclads." But was this productive?[98]

There is no doubt that the guns were physical and vendible commodities, meeting one of Smith's criteria. And the workers who made them were paid out of Lord Armstrong's capital, not his revenue. Indeed, he grew rich enough as a result to retire in baronial style. From his private standpoint the answer was surely yes. He had followed Smith's advice and employed workers in manufacture to great profit. But from the standpoint of society how could this activity count as productive?

The whole point of the original distinction by Smith was to show how labor could be deployed to increase the wealth of nations. The manufacture of instruments of destruction can never do this. Once, in 1914, when the accumulated engines of Armstrong, Schneider, and Krupp were set to work, they wrought a destruction that took decades to recover from. Table 5.21 shows that in the period Smith was writing, wars were frequent. Between 1702 and 1815, Britain was at war almost half the time. The absorption of labor and resources in war, from an as yet largely unmechanized economy, must, by absorbing so much of the surplus product, have significantly slowed the accumulation of capital. With the advent of a full war economy in the twentieth century, with up to 70 percent of output being wasted on weapons, the destructive effect on the economy was huge.

From the early days of industrial capitalism until the late twentieth century armaments production in the UK was carried out both in Royal

Figure 5.34. A 7-inch-caliber rifled breech-loading gun manufactured in the works of William George Armstrong. Photo: public domain.

TABLE 5.21: Additional Expenditures in Time of War for Britain 1702–1918

Year	War	Peak Percent of GDP Devoted to War
1702–1713	Spanish Succession	5.1
1740–1748	Austrian Succession	5.7
1756–1763	Seven Years	16.1
1775–1783	American Independence	9.8
1793–1815	French and Napoleonic	9.4
1854–1856	Crimean	0.7
1899–1902	Boer	2.7
1914–1918	First World	49.3

These are expenditures over and above normal state expenditure which averaged 6.7% of GDP over the period. From Barro, 1987.

Arsenals and Royal Dockyards, and by private firms like Armstrong's Elswick works. It is clear that if the work was done in a Royal Dockyard, the laborers there could no more count as productive laborers than could the sailors who manned the British navy's ships.

For a ship built in the Royal Dockyard, the cost to the government would simply be the wages of the workers plus the costs of machinery and steel that the dockyards could not make. For a ship built by a private firm it would include these costs plus a profit margin. If the private yard was to make a profit it could do so in either of two ways:

1. It levied a markup over and above the cost of building the same ship in a Royal Dockyard. But for this to occur we have to assume some degree of collusion by the state, with the government being deliberately willing to subsidize the private company when it could have the work done more cheaply using its own facilities.

TABLE 5.22: Percent of GDP of the Great Powers Going to War Expenditure, 1939–1944

	1939	1940	1941	1942	1943	1944
U.S.	1.00	2.00	11.00	31.00	42.00	42.00
UK	15.00	44.00	53.00	52.00	55.00	53.00
Germany	23.00	40.00	52.00	64.00	70.00	-
Italy	8.00	12.00	23.00	22.00	21.00	-
Japan	22.00	22.00	27.00	33.00	43.00	76.00
USSR	-	17.00	28.00	61.00	61.00	53.00

Source: Harrison, 2000.

2. It sold the ship at about the same price as the cost of construction in a Royal Dockyard but either used better machinery to reduce labor costs or paid lower wage rates, and as a result could still skim a profit. This would only operate if the management or the capital equipment of the private works was substantially better than the government facility.

Clearly the same costing argument applies to any activity that can be provided directly by the state or put out to tender by the state.

Buxton and Johnston [2013] examined the costs of comparable work done in the private and public shipyards. Their work indicates that the costs of ships to the government in terms of pounds sterling per ton were the same for both. The efficiency of the Royal Dockyards was no different from that of the private yards.

The third column of Table 5.23 indicates if a sister ship was ordered from a publicly owned shipyard. The means are given for all ships in the second column and for only those ships with publicly built sisters in the third column. Table 5.23 shows that the average markup on ships where private yards were in direct competition with publicly owned shipyards was very low at only 1.8 percent. Given the spread of markups on ships, with many selling at a loss, it means that private yards had to quote the Navy break-even prices.

Figure 5.35. Heavy cannons, probably 13.5-inch rifled breech loaders, being constructed at the state-owned Royal Arsenal in the 1880s. Private arms firms like Armstrong and Vickers were in competition with these and similar state works. Photo: public domain.

TABLE 5.23: Markup on Prime Costs on Sample of Privately Built Royal Navy Capital Ships

Ship	Mark-up %	Royal Dockyard Sister Ship
Vengeance	−4.2	Y
Dominion	21	Y
Agamemnon	−6	-
Invincible	2.9	-
Inflexible	11.1	-
Superb	−15.3	Y
Vanguard	4.9	Y
Colossus	4	Y
Australia	2.4	Y
Ajax	5	Y
Audacious	−5.1	Y
Conqueror	5.3	Y
New Zealand	6	Y
Princess Royal	11.2	Y
Benbow	−5.7	Y
Emperor of India	1.4	Y
Tiger	4.8	-
Valiant	−5.6	Y
Mean	2.1	1.8
95% CI for the Mean, FROM	−1.9	−3.3
TO	6.2	6.9

The third column indicates if a sister ship was ordered from a publicly owned shipyard. The means are given for all ships in the second column and for only those ships with publicly built sisters in the third column. Source: Buxton and Johnston, 2013, chapter 11.

Armaments firms like Armstrong and Vickers seem to have made most of their profits from selling to foreign navies who lacked their own shipyards.

The data for naval construction seems to indicate that for an activity where the state directly competed with private contractors, it was very hard for them to make a profit (Figure 5.36). If, however, the state loses its ability to compete directly—as has happened as a result of privatizations in the late twentieth century, the opportunity for private firms to mark up costs at the taxpayer's expense is bound to be much higher.

Armstrong's ships and guns exchanged against tax revenue. Every £ of profit his firm earned had been taken in tax from someone else, whether in

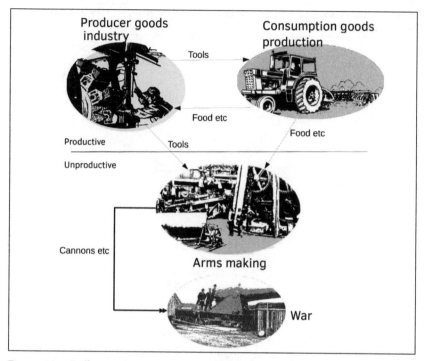

Figure 5.36. Difference between the unproductive war industry and the productive economy when outputs of industries are examined. There is a mutually supportive feedback between the productive sectors, whereas war production acts as resource sink.

England or overseas. The classical economists had argued that taxes had to fall on the surplus revenue of the landowners and capitalists—the workers being too poor to be worth levying an income tax on. So Armstrong's profit was a direct deduction from the profits of other capitalists. The resistance of the manufacturers' party, the Liberals led by Gladstone, to expensive naval budgets stemmed from this fact [Friedman, 2012].[99] So by the argument used by Marx against the productivity of shop workers[100] we must rule the Armstrong cannon works and all they employed as unproductive.

More generally, no activity which is itself unproductive becomes productive by a mere change in the social form under which it takes place. Privatization does not make an unproductive activity productive.

5.10.2 Vice

The existence of money and monetary payments gives rise to the illusion that anything that garners money must itself be productive, an illusion actively fostered by those who derive their incomes form activities thus sanctified. A contemporary example is how, since the ideological dominance of neo-liberalism in the 1980s, there has been a move to re-label prostitution as "sex-work" [Jeffreys, 2008] and gambling as an "industry." Since in capitalist society a major component of work is waged labor, where it appears that labor is being exchanged for money, any transaction in which money changes hands is made to seem like labor. Again, since in commercial societies most industry is run for a profit, then anything run for a profit, including casinos and brothels, looks like an industry. This is what Marx termed commodity fetishism, and Schumpeter called the "veil of money" [Klausinger, 1990]. It blinds us to the actual social relations behind cash transactions. A moment's thought is enough to see that gambling merely redistributes existing money, and produces nothing new of value. It makes as little sense to talk of a gambling industry as of a pickpocket industry. Indeed, prior to 1960 the law in Britain regarded the one as criminal as the other.

We saw with warship building how an ultimately destructive activity can be presented as a productive industry. If one compares the BAE Systems yard in Govan that is building aircraft carriers, with the Daewoo shipbuilding yard in Korea building container ships there are obvious similarities: the employment of waged workers, the use of similar skills, the production of a physical ship. It is only by looking at what the resulting ships do, that we can see that the first is destructive and the second productive. Brothel-keeping sits at an intermediate level of veiling: not as obviously unproductive as casinos nor so obscurely unproductive as BAE Govan. Brothels are not in business to turn out a physical product, they are one of Smith's unproductive services vanishing at the moment of their performance, but the sex work advocates ask, Do they not employ waged workers; what is special about the work of prostitutes that makes it different? Should they not be treated like any other job and given the security that comes with a recognized form of employment?

One response is to point out that as an institution, brothels originated in slave society and, internationally, are still to a substantial degree dependent on what was called the "white slave trade" and is now termed human trafficking. Another response is to pull away the money veil and point to what would ultimately be criminal actions. Just as warship building hides a conspiracy to commit piracy and murder, procuring veils conspiracy to rape [Jeffreys, 2008]. Kollontai [1921], speaking well before the cant about sex work had been invented, and in an early socialist, rather than capitalist, economy, understood very clearly why it exists in capitalist countries and why it was unproductive in a socialist economy:

> The trade in women's flesh is conducted quite openly, which is not surprising when you consider that the whole bourgeois way of life is based on buying and selling. There is an undeniable element of

material and economic [*sic*] considerations even the most legal of marriages. Prostitution is the way out for the woman who fails to find herself a permanent breadwinner. Prostitution, under capitalism, provides men with the opportunity of having sexual relationships without having to take upon themselves the responsibility of caring materially for the women until the grave.

And what, after all, is the professional prostitute? She is a person whose energy is not used for the collective; a person who lives off others, by taking from the rations of others. Can this sort of thing be allowed in a workers' republic? No, it cannot. It cannot be allowed, because it reduces the reserves of energy and the number of working hands that are creating the national wealth and the general welfare, [and] from the point of view of the national economy the professional prostitute is a labor deserter. For this reason we must ruthlessly oppose prostitution. In the interests of the economy we must start an immediate fight to reduce the number of prostitutes and eliminate prostitution in all its forms.

There is a commonsense obviousness under the changed social conditions about why prostitution is unproductive. In a society where goods were allocated on ration, a prostitute was seen to be taking the rations of others and not contributing to national wealth and general welfare. When economic relations were no longer disguised by money but seen in physical terms, this was a commonsense practical observation, and if it was obviously true in an unveiled economy, it must already have been true behind the money veil in the previous capitalist economy. Gilded by money, unproductive activities in a commercial economy appear productive, intercourse becomes "sex work."

In one sense of course, sex is work, and productive. Both parties involved expend metabolic energy in the act, and the productive issue causes the mother to expend far more energy in the gestation and birthing. Such labor is, in reality, the foundation of all other production. But this is not what apologists for brothels mean. To them, work is where money changes hands. Never mind that since Roman times the aim of commercial sex has been for men to avoid any responsibility for the children who result. They could expect neither inheritance nor sustenance from the fathers. Exposure, abandonment or the dubious mercy of the foundling hospital was often their fate:

The figures for this traffic, available for many cities, are truly shocking. In all of France fully 127,507 children were abandoned in the year

1833. Anywhere from 20 to 30 percent of all children born were left
to their fate. The figures for Paris suggest that in the years 1817–1820
the "foundlings" comprised fully 36 percent of all births. In some of
the Italian hospitals the mortality (under one year of age) ran to 80
or 90 percent. In, Paris, the Maison de la Couche reported that of
4,779 babies admitted in 1818, 2,370 died in the first three months
and another 956 within the first year. [Langer, 1963, p. 9]

So notorious was the mortality rate of these institutions that Malthus
[1872] remarked:

> Considering the extraordinary mortality which occurs in these insti-
> tutions, and the habits of licentiousness which they have an evident
> tendency to create, it may perhaps be truly said that, if a person
> wished to check population, and were not solicitous about the means,
> he could not propose a more effective measure than the establish-
> ment of a sufficient number of foundling hospitals, unlimited as to
> their reception of children. [152]

As an institution prostitution was doubly destructive of labor power; not
only did it condemn to an early death the prostitutes' infants but the money
that patrons spent in the brothels was taken from the mouths of their legitimate offspring.

5.10.3 Finance

What is now called the finance industry is another big unproductive sector.
Apologists for the banks say this Smithian classification is misleading. The real
criterion of whether the banks are productive is to be found in their balance
sheets. It was, they would say, an archaic Calvinist prejudice on Smith's part to
tie productiveness to physical production. But do banks produce anything of
value? Do they produce "financial services," and if so what are these services?

One instance of a financial service is charging for clearing checks or for
making payments into other accounts. However, what one sees when one
looks at the UK banking sector is that such charges are insufficient even
to meet the wage bills of the banks. For the general public, this is the main
use of banks, but it is not their main source of revenue. That comes instead
from profits on financial contracts. Over time the banks and other financial
institutions have come to make a part of their revenue by trading in financial
contracts of ever greater complexity and abstraction.

The orthodox justification for the banks playing a productive role is that they provide the finance that the economy needs.[101] Money, according to Adam Smith, is the ability to command the labor of others.[102] The provision of credit gives a capitalist the authority or permission to commandeer part of the pool of social labor to his project.

The provision of a line of credit by a bank is simply an act of giving permission. What makes it seem different from, for example, a building permit, is that the permit is allocated by a private body. If you want to extend your house you need two permits, one from an office of the city who checks the soundness of the design, and one from the bank who checks the soundness of your credit. The fact that somebody can hand out permissions does not make them productive.

If we look at what actually happens, it is builders, plasterers, and plumbers who actually make houses. The city or bank official who signs a permit no more makes the house than did Hadrian in building the wall that bears his name. Society projects onto the powerful a creative genius that really pertains to those they command. When permits are in demand, those handing them out can take their cut. If a city official does this we call it a bribe, when a bank does it we call it interest. At one time the charging of interest (usury) was regarded as the moral equivalent of an official taking a bribe. With the rise of bankers to political dominance, their very wealth, obtained in this way, comes to be seen as a token of social respectability.[103]

It may seem that a loan, unlike a permit from the town hall, gives access to the real resources to build the house. But this is an illusion. Workers build houses using bricks and timber, the loan gives the homeowner command over these resources. If the building industry was under state control, or even when, as in the 1940s in the UK, bricks were simply rationed by the state, access to the bricks and labor would also depend on an official permit. It is an artifact of the current legal order that private citizens cannot print their own money or issue generally acceptable authorization for work. Banks, on the other hand, are in the special position that they can issue money without legal constraint. Section 3.5 explained how monetary relations arose from the action of states in commuting taxes in kind into money taxes. This forced everyone subject to tax to acquire money and to enter the commodity economy. The power of money to command labor is a delegated power, derived from a prior direct command that the state has over the persons of its citizens. Nowadays, such direct command it limited to military conscription, and usually only young men are subject to it. For the rest, the state accepts money in settlement of citizens' debts.

Debts to the state are the original sins. They exist independent of our volition or actions. The innovation of the modern age is the way that absolution is offered: by check or credit card.

The state accepts private checks for tax payments because the clearing banks have deposit accounts with the state bank. When people sent the exchequer checks drawn on bank X, the account of bank X with the state bank is debited correspondingly. The combination of state banks with private banks gives rise to the specifically capitalist monetary system. The volume of commercial transactions required by the capitalist economy long outgrew the possibility of cash settlements in precious metal coins.[104] The replacement of money by credit has been essential to the growth of capitalism, but it has in the process given immense power to private financial institutions.

Deposits with private clearing banks holding accounts with the Bank of England, European Central Bank, etc., are in general as acceptable as cash, but the banks themselves can create them at will. The banks do not, as is naively supposed, channel capital from savings to investment.[105] Instead, when a bank gives a line of credit to a firm for investment, this in effect authorizes the firm to draw on and mobilize social labor for its private purposes. The creation of credit in the account of the firm is an instantaneous bookkeeping operation and does not depend on any prior saving of real resources. Conversely, the advance of credit need not fund any current social labor. If a bank advances credit to a firm to employ staff that obviously does use labor, but if credit is advanced as mortgages for already existing houses, or the acquisition of speculative financial assets there is no corresponding allocation of labor. The former is productive in a very limited sense—in that it authorizes real production—the latter is unproductive in every sense. It is an illusion to see the banks as acting as intermediaries, lending out the deposits of the rentier classes to industry. It is not a two-step operation: first take deposit; then make loan. Instead the two operations occur simultaneously, and it is at least as realistic to say that the lending creates the deposits as vice versa.

Suppose Deutsche Bank advances an overdraft facility to BMW. BMW then orders steel plate for its plants from ThyssenKrupp AG. A month after delivery BMW pays ThyssenKrupp 5,000,000 euros, drawing on its overdraft facility. What happens next is that in a single *atomic transaction* the Deutsche Bank computers debit the account of BMW and credit that of ThyssenKrupp. The software operation is designed to be indivisible, and its effect is to create a deposit that exactly counterbalances the loan to BMW.

As a consequence of the falling rate of profit described in Section 5.9 opportunities for profitable investment shrink, and the share of financing provided for productive purposes becomes less. The financial sector now directs most of its loans to financing the government debt, real estate, or speculation in paper or electronic assets. These purely symbolic operations, operations on computer records, can still effect an indirect claim on real resources since, in addition to clearing transactions and taking deposits, banks act as fund managers. In the latter role they levy a management fee of perhaps 1 percent of the value of the funds they actively manage. The ongoing extension of credit means that all assets tend to appreciate over time so the total fees become huge. Between 2009 and 2014 the portion of management fees paid out to individual bankers in London amounted to more than £100 billion [Kollewe, 2015].

5.10.4 Modern rents

Even when banks operated as they are theoretically supposed to, extending credit for real productive investment, the work that went into granting the loans remained unproductive—and administrative overhead was analogous to issuing building permits. But at least it enabled productive activity. Finance today, as in the early years of capitalism, operates more as a rent collection agency. Since so little finance goes to increasing real production, these rents can only be sustained by depressing the real living standards of much of the population.

This process is particularly evident in housing. The price of houses breaks down into two components, one being the actual cost of building a house, and the other being the capitalized rent of the underlying ground. As feudal rents gradually converted into money rent, farming land acquired a price that was set by the rule:

$$\text{Price} = \frac{\text{Rent}}{\text{Interest rate}}$$

Suppose that in 1800 an estate in Ireland yielded £1000 a year in rent from the peasantry and the interest rate was 5 percent.[106] The price of the estate would then be £ [1000/0.05]=£20,000 as this is the sum that an investor would have to lend to the government to obtain the same revenue as from the land. From the earliest stage of industrial capitalism there has been a close unity between rent collection, debt, and violence. The great bulk of the interest-bearing securities in the early nineteenth century were ones issued by the state to finance the purchase of ships and cannons. The biggest source of funding for these loans were grand aristocratic families whose incomes came initially from ground rent. The banking system, and the markets in land and government bonds, then allowed this class to balance its revenues between direct exploitation of their tenants and indirect exploitation of the taxpayers.

But what determines the rent that can be obtained?

Ricardo [1951] argued that rent levels depended on the differential fertility between the worst land in use and the land on which the rent was paid. [107] If the worst land yielded no rent, then the landlord could charge almost the entire differential fertility of the better land as rent. Were he to charge more than the difference in fertility the peasants would shift to the worse, rent-free land. Whether this is realistic is questionable, since even on the worst land in a province, the landlords were unlikely to allow peasants to till scot-free.[108, 109] But whatever the zero-point rent on the worst land, Ricardo's principle will still apply. Landlords, free to alter rent, will charge rents that cancel out any gains from differences in soil fertility. The mere threat to withhold land from production is sufficient to allow the landlord class to appropriate part of the surplus produced in capitalist economy [Campbell, 2002], since all economic activities other than shipping take place on land and as such are dependent on access to it.

In agriculture the landlord is able to appropriate not only natural differences in fertility—due to differences in aridity, rockiness, and slope of the soil—but the accumulated result of past improvements carried out over centuries. A constant struggle exists between the landlord and the capitalist farmer over these improvements. The interest of the landlord is to rack up rents as a consequence of any improvement made by the tenant. The tenants as a class, in contrast, have an interest in long leases during which rents are fixed to allow them to benefit from capital invested in improvements. The threat that any investment by the tenant will end up in the landlord's pocket inevitably acts as a disincentive to investment and improvement.

This dependence of rent on past capital investment is even more pronounced with urban rents. These are rents on a built environment that is entirely an effect of past labor. On the surface, the rent that an urban tenant pays appears as a payment for an artifact—the house. As such, it seems to the landlord too that house rent is a return on the capital he invested in buying the property. The actual causal relation, that the property price is capitalized rent, is thereby inverted. The rent that can be obtained for two similar flats, one in the center of a big city and one a 50km commute from that city, will be very different. The city-center flat will rent for more, because the city-center tenant saves the travel cost in money and time of the 50km commute. Private property in land then imposes on all tenants a financial loss equivalent to the travel cost met by the distant commuter. As capitalism concentrates jobs in huge cities, workers are either forced to spend hours traveling, and to buy the cars needed to do this, or to forfeit an equivalent cost in rent to the landlord class. In economically developing cities rents trend up, as the commuting circle expands. The price of a house bought to rent is determined by the capitalized rent, so property prices similarly

Rent per Year	Return on Capital	Price Floor of Flat
£5,000	6.0%	£83,333.33
£5,000	4.0%	£125,000.00

escalate. Expectations of capital gains on rented houses make such investment doubly profitable—there is the rent return, plus the speculative profit to be had from selling the house at a higher price later.

The rent-driven appreciation of property prices then becomes coupled with another process: the generally declining rate of profit in productive investment. Suppose the rate of return on productive investment falls from 6 to 4 percent, then, quite apart from any change in general rent levels, the price of a flat returning a rent of £5,000 a year will appreciate as shown above.

Figure 5.37 illustrates how these two processes have operated in the London area. It shows prices for flats in London and in East Anglia, the latter area being effectively on the margin of the London commute distance. London flats are consistently more expensive due to differential rent effects. Landlords in London can charge higher rents than landlords in, say, Norwich, because the cost of working in London and commuting from Norwich is so prohibitive. Flat prices, which are dominated by the buy-to-let market, are in consequence much higher in London. But in both areas the long-run trend, in units of the median annual wage, has been up. It is plausible that this is a consequence of the long-term fall in the rate interest, which itself is an enforced result of the falling rate of profit. As the rate of return on capital generally falls, the central banks of leading countries are motivated to drive interest rates down to try and encourage investment despite the generally low rate of return on industrial capital. The availability of cheap mortgage finance then allows landlords to bid up the price of flats and still turn a profit on the rent they earn. Since private buyers must compete with landlords in the housing market, they too have to pay a higher price.

Home ownership was promoted in Britain in the twentieth century as the path to a property-owning democracy. Even if the mass of the population could no longer hope to be economically self-sufficient, owning their own house would at least make them independent of landlords. This dream was used to justify the selling of publicly owned low-rent housing to sitting tenants. As the original sitting tenants died and their homes were sold, these flats, originally built by the cities to provide cheap housing, fell into the hands of a new landlord class, which had either the ready capital or the access to credit that allowed them to outbid young working-class families for flats coming on the market. Those who are able to buy flats or houses are, in big cities, faced with prices so high that the bank debts they assume

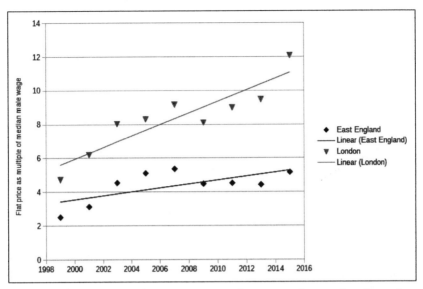

Figure 5.37. Movement in flat prices, measured in terms of years of median salary needed to purchase the flat, for London and an area at the outer limit of the London commute zone.

leave them little better off than tenants once were. As Figure 5.37 shows, by 2016 a London flat, let us not speak of houses, cost the equivalent of twelve years' wages. Home ownership is more apparent than real, since legally the banks have first call on any proceeds of the sale, and the payments in interest to the bank will be almost as much as a landlord would have charged. The banks become indirect landlords, and their revenues, although taking the form of interest, are, in effect, rent. Ground rent in capitalist society is always a payment for inefficiency. Classical differential rent tended to rise, according to Ricardo, as less efficient land was brought into cultivation. Urban rents rise as cities become more inefficient; unplanned development forces workers to bear either higher transport costs or higher rents. The banks and the landlord classes are then the beneficiaries of such inefficiency.

What governs the relative value of landed property versus productive capital?

The value of landed property is an imputed capitalization of the revenue that flows as rent. If the average rate of return on capital is used for calculating its value, then the share of wealth represented by landed property will stand in the same ratio as the ratio of total rents to total profits on capital. Under conditions of falling profit rates, however, the apparent rate of return on land will be greater than that on capital, since landed property steadily appreciates in market value.

TABLE 5.24: Structure of U.S. Bank Loans Just before the Onset of the Credit Crisis

Financial Instrument	1 October 2008	
Residential Mortgages	$2,103	
Commercial Real Estate	$1,721	
Consumer Loans	$860	
Non-Producer Loans	$4,684	75%
Commercial and Industrial	$1,586	25%

Figures in $billions. Source: U.S. Federal Reserve.

Assume that the working population of a nation is fixed at 20 million and that half the working year goes as surplus. The value of the surplus is then fixed at 10 million person years. Suppose that the initial capital stock is 40 million person years, and the rent revenue is 2 million. This rent has to be deducted from the surplus to give the profit to capital. The rate of return on capital is then $[(10-2)/40]=20\%$, and the market value of the landed property will be 10 million.

Now suppose that of the surplus of 10 million, 5 million goes in investment. Next year the capital stock will be 45 million and the rate of return will have fallen to $[(10-2)/45]=17.8\%$.

At this new rate of return the capitalized value of 2 million in rent is now 11.25 million. The landlords have thus had a return of 2 million in rent, plus capital gains of 1.25 million, so the market profitability of landed property will be $[(2+1.25)/10]=32.5\%$, which is much better than the return to be had on productive capital. So long as the capital stock grows faster than the population this will go on. Investing at the same rate of 5 million per year the effect after twenty years is that the capital stock has reached 140 million and the rate of return is down to 5.7 percent. Landed property now has a capitalized value of 35 million, and the market profitability of landed property, including appreciation, is 9.6 percent. Landed property will, in late capitalism, seem to be consistently more profitable than productive investment. As a result the funding provided by the banks goes disproportionately to real estate.

Where does this inflow of cash end up?

Some of it goes to build new properties. Higher land prices justify higher buildings, so city centers are continually in the process of being destroyed and reconstructed to pack the maximum square meters of residential and commercial property onto each square meter of land. Another part of the loans simply go to finance purchase of existing properties or to remortgage properties at inflated prices. Since the flow of funds into the sector must balance the flow of funds out, and only part of the inflow goes to meet real new building costs, where does the rest end up?

In the main it gets diverted into consumption expenditure. Upper-middle-class home owners sell houses in the cities, move elsewhere to consume the profits. Commercial real estate firms distribute, in dividends, profits gained by selling properties at higher prices. This too ends up funding the consumption of the rentier classes. A similar phenomenon applies to any property title that promises to bring a stable future income. A declining general rate of profit means that shares in companies that do not expand their capital base appreciate. Holders of these shares, whether individual rentiers or fund managers, can then appropriate a portion of the capital appreciation as revenue. In the process the capitalist class as a whole takes on more and more the aspect of former ruling classes: rent seeking and revenue consuming. Periodic banking crises reveal how the capital base of the system has vanished in an orgy of luxury consumption. Now, all free market objections to state intervention vanish overnight; the taxpayer is called in to make up the loss.

CHAPTER 6

Socialist Economies

6.1 WHAT DOES SOCIALISM MEAN?

Mises [1951] noted that socialists have no uniform idea of what socialism is. Each socialist, or at least each group of socialists, proclaims that only its view of socialism is right and that all others are misleaders, enemies of the people, etc. Each socialist, he claims, implicitly assumes that the future socialist state will be headed by himself. True socialism is what that socialist will decree. All other views are dangerous heresies best dealt with by the firing squad.

This seems to be a fairly accurate caricature of a substantial fraction of the socialist movement. While the communist parties tended to have a fairly clear idea of what they wanted to achieve, based for the most part on an emulation of the USSR, other socialist parties have been loath to give a concrete view of how socialism should be organized. On all sides there has been a reluctance to examine the practical problems of organizing a socialist economy.

Socialism arose first as philosophical movement by thinkers like Owen and Fourier in the early nineteenth century. At that stage socialist thinkers were willing to advance quite detailed utopian plans for the reorganization of society. Later it became a political movement of the working classes seeking a just society. Marx and Engels, the thinkers with the most lasting influence in the workers' movement, applauded the work of the early utopians in establishing the socialist movement. They were in particular full of praise for Owen. But they were severely critical of the utopias of later philosophers like Proudhon and Dühring. They claimed that the later utopians were pale reflections of the earlier pioneers and that their utopias were for the most part internally inconsistent.

Marx took the view that as a scientist he could not put forward detailed theories about socialism, a form of society that did not yet exist. Economic and social research had to base itself upon the data provided by real society. He was ready to identify features of contemporary capitalism that revealed the potential for a future socialized production system but not to construct a detailed theory of socialism in the absence of data. He was willing to say that capitalism had generated a class struggle that would lead ineluctably to the dictatorship of the proletariat and thence to a classless society. As to what this society would be like, he was only willing to give sketchy predictions— that it would be based on planned production rather than the market, that it would not use money, etc.

After the Russian Revolution, and in particular after the mid-1930s, the Communists held that Marx's views had been amply born out in practice. The dictatorship of the proletariat held sway, the economy was operated under a single plan and classes were being abolished. They had had to invent things as they went along. They had had to improvise and much of what they did could not have been predicted in detail from Marx's writings. But this was to be expected, socialism was something born out of real life and history not the crystallization of philosophers' dreams. For the Communists, from the '30s to the '60s, if you wanted to know what socialism was you just had to look at Russia.

For other, non-communist socialists the issue was more problematic.[110] Although the great majority of socialists during the period from the '30s to the '50s took things at face value and accepted that Russia was socialist, there was always a minority who did not, and in Western Europe during the last fifty years such views have probably come to represent a majority of socialist opinion.

From the early days of the communist revolution in Russia the Social Democratic parties in Europe argued that socialism could not be established by the methods of dictatorship that the Bolsheviks were using. They argued that the workers' movement had during the previous decades struggled hard to win the franchise, for freedom of association and the press. To establish a one-party dictatorship, impose censorship, and to imprison and execute political opponents went against everything the movement had stood for.

Socialism, they argued, could only be established on the basis of a free press, free political parties, and open parliamentary elections. A socialism that denied this was either not socialism or not worth having. This is a clear and principled argument and the Social Democrats stuck to it for decades. Its weakness was that the communists could simply retort: "Who says you can't build socialism using a dictatorship? That's just parliamentary cretinism. We have tried dictatorship and it works. You tried parliament and where is your socialism?"

On economic grounds, the Social Democrats had less to say against communism. Social democracy has a liberal definition of socialism both in the sense of looseness and in the Manchester sense. A mixed economy with social welfare legislation and some elements of industrial planning would certainly qualify, so their economic criticism of Soviet Communism was that *it is not necessary to go so far so fast.* The economic direction was not in question, rather, it was the counsel of moderation. Public ownership of the means of production, planning, welfare rights, and an egalitarian income distribution were accepted as socialist objectives by both Communists and Social Democrats. The latter presented themselves as the democratic socialists without challenging the socialism of the latter, only their totalitarianism.

Although there has been considerable overlap between Trotskyism and social democracy, with all Social Democratic parties worth their salt having Trotskyist fractions, their founder had been a prominent Communist politician, and in consequence their arguments as to why the Soviet Union was not socialist started from different premises. The two key arguments were:

1. Socialism in one country:
    a. It is in principle impossible to build socialism in a single country.
    b. The USSR is one country.
    c. It follows that the USSR could not be socialist.
2. The argument from plenty [Mandel, 1985]:
    a. Socialism is only possible in conditions of abundance when mankind passes from the realm of necessity to freedom.
    b. The USSR was plagued by shortages, which in turn stem from it being an isolated country.
    c. Hence the USSR could not be socialist.

There seems to be not one but several possible questions relating to socialism in one country.

1. Is socialism possible in one country?
2. Is socialism possible in more than one country?
3. In the long term is socialism more stable in:
    a. A single country.
    b. Many countries.

In short, my answers to this would be 1) Yes, 2) Yes, 3) a. This may seem a bit paradoxical but my meaning will become clearer as the argument progresses.

From my perspective questions 1 and 2 are partly empirical. Only partly, because the meaning of the question still relies upon the interpretation one makes of the word *country*. This is commonly used to refer to a nation-state, but nations and states are not coterminous. The USSR was an international organization not a nation-state in the old sense. If by country we mean explicitly a nation then it must be said that we lack empirical evidence to decide if socialism is possible in a single country. If by a country then we mean a single state power, then we have historical experience of the existence of a single socialist state from the early '30s to the late '40s. The time period given is determined by the point at which the distinguishing characteristics of a socialist economy came into being.

On either definition of a country, nation or unitary state power, then since the late 1950s it has been clear that a plurality of socialist countries can coexist. I give the late '50s as the crucial period here, since until then the People's Democracies of Eastern Europe were only nominally independent state powers. Communist parties there were the effective agents of state power and the parties remained so tightly coordinated that it was doubtful that the states could really be considered as independent. China, where the Communist Party was independent of Moscow, had not established a socialist economy in the early 1950s.

On the question of whether socialism is more stable in one country or several, it appears that it is more stable in one, provided that by "country" one means a unitary state power.

A unitary state power was better placed to present a united front to the hostile capitalist world, and best placed to coordinate the economic development of nations at different levels of development. One only has to consider what the chances of socialism's survival would have been had the USSR not been formed, and had there existed instead a multiplicity of sovereign nation-states on its historic territory. The great imperial powers of 1919 would likely have subordinated them one by one. In the post–WWII period, splits between socialist states, USSR/Yugoslavia or USSR/China or China/Vietnam, were exploited to strategic effect by opponents like the United States and hamstrung by their economic development. In a paradoxical sense, it can be said that the abandonment of the policy of socialism in one country *in* the sense of a monolithic state by the communist movement in the late '40s to early '50s contributed to their collapse in 1990.

The argument from plenty against socialism is convincingly dealt with by Nove [1983b, 15–20], but we can give a brief summary of its problems here. Consider the standards of life of the working classes of Europe when Marx or even Lenin were writing. Now consider what the conception of abundance would have been then: adequate and nutritious food, warm clothing and good dry shoes, houses with good heating and sanitation, access to education, culture, literature, and leisure, an 8-hour workday, free medical treatment. Given the conditions of life of the nineteenth-century British proletariat, or the workers in czarist Russia, this would have seemed abundance. It would still be abundance to most of the world's population. It is easy to forget, living in Western Europe, that the norm for the world capitalist economy is Mexico City rather than Berlin, Lagos rather than Stockholm. Cars, televisions, home video cameras, computers would not have featured in the agenda of nineteenth-century socialists. By the standards that the workers movement originally had in mind, the workers of East Germany, Czechoslovakia, and to large extent the USSR were already entering into an age of abundance by the '80s, while for significant sections of the population even a rich free market economy like the United States in the '80s failed to provide abundance of such necessities. Despite this, these economies were still clearly in the thrall of scarcity.

This was true whether the measure of scarcity was the presence of queues, the budgetary constraints faced by the government, or the aspirations of the population for oriental luxuries. The advance of technology had given rise to new aspirations that had yet to be met. In any technically advancing world this is bound to be the case. Newly developed technologies open up possibilities that cannot immediately be met in unlimited quantities. It may well be the case that in market economies advertising artificially stimulates these needs (which is a case against advertising), but even in the absence of ads there was no lack of black market demand for Sony products in the USSR. Beyond this, it is an open question as to whether the current consumption pattern of, for example, France could be extended to the whole world population given ultimately limited resources.

It is, moreover, doubtful that the establishment of a socialist world economy would have been helpful in alleviating scarcity in the USSR. Although its national income per head was below that of the leading capitalist countries, it was still well above average by world standards. As such, it would have had to make substantial aid contributions to socialist countries in the Third World. It had to do this for China in the '50s. The contributions it made to Vietnam, Cuba, Angola, etc., were already a subject of some popular resentment.

Another school of socialist thought was the Communist left. Their most articulate theorist was Amadeo Bordiga, the founder of the Italian Communist Party, who actually remained politically active down to the 1960s. In 1952 Stalin published a short book, *Economic Problems of Socialism*, which set the terms of communist orthodox debate about the Soviet economy. Shortly thereafter a publication by Bordiga appeared under the imprimatur of the International Communist Party, called *Dialogue with Stalin* [1954]. In this Bordiga argued against the idea that the USSR was socialist, holding instead that its economy was a form of state capitalism. Some of his arguments parallel those of the Trotskyists, that socialism was not possible in one country and that it demanded abundance. To this he added the argument that the USSR continued to be a commodity-producing society. The Marxist vision of socialism had always been one in which commodity production was abolished, he argued. But in the USSR workers still worked for money wages and payed rubles for goods in the shops.

At a formal level he was correct—money did exist. But the difficulties involved in establishing a genuine market economy in Eastern Europe after the counterrevolution of 1990 indicate that the social reality behind money and prices in these countries was somewhat different from that in the West. In the consumer goods markets, prices bore only a weak relation to the amount of social labor required to produce them or to demand. In producer goods there was not really a market at all, since money alone was not enough for an enterprise to ensure supply of a good, if this good had not been allocated to it in the plan. Bordiga was right in raising the existence of money and the commodity form as a potential problem, but like most other leftist writers he was none too specific as to what alternative form of economic calculation to use.

During the 1960s the leaders of the Communist Party of China started to argue that the USSR had reverted to capitalism. It was claimed that Khrushchev, and then Kosygin, had taken the road to capitalism and that the USSR had passed from being a socialist state to being a social-imperialist one.

Given that the economic changes introduced by Khrushchev were fairly minimal this argument was hard to sustain. If, however, one views them as allegorical comments on an internal Chinese political debate about the appropriate way forward, then they make a lot more sense. Within China there was a fierce struggle between the Maoists and the followers of Liu Shaoqi and Deng. Liu was stigmatized as China's Khrushchev. Alternatively this can be seen as labeling Khrushchev as Russia's Liu.

If the economic policies followed by Deng after he came to power are indicative of what was being proposed in secret party debates during the '60s then the charges of "capitalist roadism" seem to have had some reality in the Chinese context. But until Gorbachov, those advocating similar measures in Russia were far from the centers of political power.

It is now a century and a half since Marx was writing, and today we have much more historical evidence to go on than he had. We have had extensive opportunities to observe societies that were by common understanding called socialist. We say "by common understanding" being well aware that some people dissent from this, but whether one takes account of the constitutions of these societies, which proclaimed them to be socialist, the common view of their citizens who believed them to be socialist, or the common view of the international press which declared them to be socialist that appears to have been the consensus view.

Many currents of thought in the socialist movement have dissented from this consensus, on the grounds that the conditions in countries of "hitherto existing" socialism violated numerous socialist ideals.

This may well be true, but as social scientists we cannot judge the real world by the standards of an ideal one. It is not the job of reality to materialize our ideals. Reality just *is* in all its glories, horrors, and contradictions. When judging the reality of socialism in comparison with ideals advanced by its early advocates, we adopt an unusual criterion. We do not judge feudalism or capitalism by the standards of an ideal, and were we to do that we would soon find that no real capitalist society corresponded in whole to this ideal. One may note that it was a common argument by opponents of socialism to say that since welfare-state Britain differed in many respects from the ideal type of nineteenth-century capitalism, it was no longer really capitalist.

If a thinker advances a theory about a kind of society before it ever comes into existence, the scientific status of the theory is weak. If the predictions of the theory come to conflict with later observation one can either decide that the theory needs modification or that reality has been misbehaving. If one adopts the latter policy and says that socialism has never existed anywhere in the world, one may hope (perhaps vainly) to escape some current political unpopularity, but one has hardly advanced one's ability to deal practically with the problems that led to this unpopularity. An ideal can be kept pristine but its very distance from reality vitiates its practical political force and the left is in precisely the predicament that Marx criticized in Utopianism.

We therefore take an empirical approach to determining what the distinguishing characteristics of socialist society have been.

- Widespread use of electrical energy.
- Agricultural productivity sufficient for a large urban populations.
- The absence of a class of wealthy private proprietors in agriculture or industry.
- Widespread use of machinery and applied science.
- Public or cooperative ownership of most of the economy.
- A system of state planning that determines the scale of the surplus product by the relative priorities it assigns to consumption versus other goods, with allocation of instruments of production by means of a system of state directives.

- A consequent absence of capital goods or raw materials markets. (Indeed one may question the meaning of the term "capital goods" in these societies.)
- The continuation of household economy as a site for the preparation and consumption of food and the raising of children, which gives rise to:
  - The formal existence of a consumer goods market subject to the constraints that:
  - A significant portion of consumer goods were distributed by means other than purchase or sale.
  - The price mechanism in the consumer goods market was generally non-operative.
  - The absence of a market in land, and the absence of rent as an economic category.
  - A lower variance of incomes from the mean than was the case in capitalist countries at an equivalent stage of industrial development.
  - A distinct mode of extraction of the surplus product, that is, the politically determined division of the concrete forms of the social product between the categories of current consumption, accumulation, and unproductive consumption.
  - Formal appropriation of the surplus product as tax but the relegation of taxation from a means of extraction of a surplus to means of securing monetary stability.
  - The existence of money and wage labor.
  - The absence of a reserve army of unemployed, often associated with chronic labor shortages.

These are the significant structural features that marked off the socialist world from the capitalist. These are also the features that the advocates of capitalism in these countries wish to abolish.

Those socialists to the left of social democracy who deny that socialism has ever existed do not generally specify which of them are incompatible with socialism. One has to assume that the socialist systems they advocate would share most of these features. [111]

Socialist economies have the same basic mode of production as capitalism: machine industry and agriculture. What distinguishes them are the forms of property and the way in which the surplus product is determined.

Actual countries have shown mixtures of socialist and other production relations. Socialism may exist as a subsystem within countries that are predominantly capitalist, and capitalism or domestic peasant economy may exist as subsystems in predominantly socialist economies. Though political revolutions may permit changes in property relations, they are, at least in the short term, powerless to effect a change in the mode of production. The 1917 Revolution was no more able to establish the socialist mode of production than the revolutions of 1776 or 1789 were able to establish the capitalist mode of production. The establishment of socialism in Russia, as with the establishment of capitalism in North America and France, came later with a sequence of changes in production technologies and economic relations. It took France until 1900, over a century after the revolution, to achieve the degree of urban industrial development that Russia achieved in less than a quarter-century after 1917. [112] Arguably the transition to capitalism in France and that to socialism in Russia was not complete until the 1960s. That these changes in the mode of production took place much faster in the Russian case does not obscure the fact that changes in the mode of production take time. If capitalism and socialism's shared mode of production already largely exists, as in Germany or Czechoslovakia post-1945, the change to socialism can occur much faster.

Socialism was born from political successes by working-class and peasant movements, not spontaneous economic development.

It was produced by movements that had socialism as an objective. But this is not so different from capitalism in most of the world. The socialist movement had its economic theorists, whose ideas in their turn influenced socialist governments. But this is not so different from capitalist governments. They too have been influenced by economists advocating an ideal type of capitalist society. The theory of free-market capitalism developed well before capitalism was established as an international system. Its spread, by British bayonets and gunships, showed the Chinese in the generations before Mao where the political power needed for social transformation came from.

6.2 POWER

Communism is Soviet power plus the electrification of the whole country.
—LENIN 1965B, VOL. 34

Political power grew from the barrels of guns, but what about real power?

Capitalism progressed from water and wind power to steam for motive power, but communists, from the outset, plumped for electricity. German author Liebknecht [1901], writing in the 1890s, described having met Karl Marx in the 1850s after he had seen a model electric train. Marx enthused that just as steam had created capitalism, electric power would create a new economic and social order. Liebknecht remarked sardonically that in the ensuing forty-five years there had been no signs of electricity taking over yet. The trains were still steam, and the few electric tramcars were of no significance.

Looking back from the twenty-first century, Marx appears to have had the more acute sense of the promise of electric power. You have to take the long view when looking at the development of technology.

> Revolutions are not accomplished in a sleight-of-hand fashion. Only the sensational shows in politics are called revolutions by the wonder-working rustic faith. And whoever prophesizes revolutions is always mistaken in the date. [Liebknecht, 1901]

We know that electricity has turned out to be quite important, as Marx suspected, but why was it seen as so crucial that Lenin should have singled it out as the very key to Soviet industrialization?

Human labor is a universal, abstract productive capacity. Our energy output may be modest at under 100 watts, but it can be applied in any trade or profession. The first available alternative to human effort was that of our brute servants the ox and horse. Strong as these companions are, their skills are limited. They helped us draw vehicles or pull plows, but they could not help crew ships, lay bricks, or spin wool. Steam went to sea with us, supplanting half a crew, replaced our beasts in traction, turned spinning mills and cut stone for our cities. But the steam engine was heavy, inflexible, and produced only motive force. It could not sing, wash, or see for us. With electricity we harnessed for the first time a power that rivaled that of human labor in flexibility, while vastly surpassing it in magnitude. Electricity wrote for us, then spoke for us then saw for us in telegraphs, telephones, and televisions. Its motors range in size and power from our little fingers to that of 50,000 horses. It lights our darkness, heats our homes, stores our records, reasons and calculates. It becomes power in the abstract, the General Watt.

We have become so accustomed to electric power that we have difficulty relating it to real effort so it is worth relating it to human power. A trained human cyclist, peddling hard, generates only enough power for one incandescent light (see Figure 6.1).

To become abstract general power, electricity requires networks of supply, initially urban, then national, continental, and in the future, world girdling. In the construction of these networks, competition of multiple private firms was counterproductive. Initially, with competing suppliers, there was no standardization of voltages or connectors, which slowed the uptake of anything more complicated than simple electric lighting. Providing power

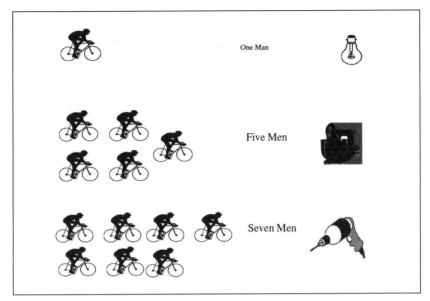

Figure 6.1. Comparison between human power output and the electricity used in common appliances.

mains to a city or region is expensive, making it uneconomic for multiple competing companies to lay their own wires down every street. Electricity trends to monopolies. Even in capitalist countries the state had to take on a directing or ownership role in its supply. Thus the state either built the national grids and power stations or at the very least set technical standards and regulated prices for private suppliers. Because of its integrated character and because of the forward investment it required, electricity became one of the first industries for which long-term national plans were made. Even after the Thatcher government in Britain privatized electricity, it proved impossible for the state to relinquish its directive role in regulating price and enforcing the development of wind and nuclear generation. When the British state required new nuclear power stations it had to turn to the state-owned French electricity monopoly to supply them.

It is no surprise then that the leaders of Soviet Russia saw electricity not only as an enabling technology for industrialization and the development of the countryside, but also as the paradigmatic example of where central state planning could steal a march on competitive capitalism. When a socialist government was elected in Britain in 1945, it too immediately set about the establishment of a nationalized system of electricity supply, including a state Hyroelectric Board.

As a general rule internationally, the state was needed to embark on huge capital-intensive electricity projects like building dams across major rivers.

Figure 6.2. Socialist economies have embraced hydropower despite the high initial costs of this technology in dams over the Dnieper and Yangtze rivers.

Figure B.1 shows that, in a capitalist country, the rate of profit is widely divergent between different industries. The industries in which labor costs are a small fraction of the advanced capital tend to have a lower rate of profit, which is what one would expect from the labor theory of value. Private industry is reluctant to embark on capital-intensive projects like hydropower or tidal and are even reluctant to use nuclear energy unless given state financial incentives. The U.S. electricity industry was a partial exception to the general trend for highly capitalized industries to have a lower rate of return. The combination of a natural monopoly and public regulation ensured that it earned a rate of profit somewhat above what its capital composition would predict [Cockshott and Cottrell, 2003b], though still well below the average rate of return in the United States. So even there, the large-scale development of hydropower was undertaken by the government owned Tennessee Valley Authority in the 1930s.

The Soviet government's first economic planning body was GOELRO, responsible for drawing up the comprehensive electrification program. Construction of three large hydropower plants rapidly took place from the mid-1920s, and by 1932 the Dnieper hydro-station was producing 560MW, for its day the biggest electric generator in the world. The Communist government in China showed similar enthusiasm for hydroelectricity. The Three Gorges Dam across the Yangtze becoming in its turn the world's largest power plant, but at a vastly greater scale, 22,000MW in this case. By the end of the Soviet period in 1990, hydropower made up 18 percent of electric generation, nuclear 12 percent, with the remainder being from fossil fuel sources [Rudenko, 1993].

To get some sense of the scale of the electric energy available to economies like the mature USSR, China and other countries around the time of writing, see Tables 6.1 and 6.2.

The first thing to note is that contemporary China has access to almost the same order of magnitude of energy per head as the USSR had twenty-five years earlier, and that both of these were similar to the per capita energy

TABLE 6.1: Comparison of Power Available to Different Economies

Country	Year	Average GW
China	2014	663.3
U.S.	2014	494.6
EU	2014	361.4
USSR	1990	197.3
GB	2014	38.6
GB	1907	7.0

For all but the GB 1907 figure, which comes from Table 5.5, these are figures for average electrical power use computed from the annual number of billion KW hours produced. The figures, except for GB 1907, are for average power delivered for each hour in the year, and will be somewhat below the installed capacity. The figure for the UK in 1907 is given for continuity with Figure 5.7. Source: For recent data, *Global Energy Statistical Yearbook 2016*; Soviet data from Rudenko, see bibliography, 1993.

TABLE 6.2: Comparison of Power Available to Different Economies Converted into Human Labor Effort Equivalents per Head of Population

Country	Year	GWh	Human Labor Equivalent per Head
China	2014	5,665,000	19.2
U.S.	2014	4,331,000	63.1
EU	2014	3,166,000	19.7
USSR	1990	1,728,000	27.3
USSR	1940	48,000	1.2
USSR	1931	8,000	0.3
Russia	1913	1,900	0.0
GB	2014	338,000	24.8
GB	1907	61,320	7.3

Assumption is that a manual worker could do 216 KWh per year of work.

use of Europe in 2014. The tables also reproduce the data for energy use for Britain in 1907 (from Table 5.5) for comparison. This shows what a huge increase in energy use took place during the electrical revolution of the twentieth century. Britain in 1907 was one of the three richest and most highly mechanized countries in the world. For each man, woman, or child within its coastline it had steam power equivalent to the efforts of seven human workers. By 2014 that had risen to the equivalent of 24 people. But a quarter of a century earlier, the USSR was already using the electrical equivalent of 27 humans for each citizen. [113]

Production of electricity from heat inevitably involves energy losses in the form of waste heat, both in the flue gases and in the warm water that has been used to condense steam from the turbines. Efficiency is measured in amount of heat used to produce a kilowatt hour of electricity. In these terms the USSR had overtaken the UK by 1963, using 12,200 BTU/KWh against 12,400 in the UK [Anon., 1965], but was still some way behind the United States, which used only 10,500. A significant difference between the power plants in the socialist and capitalist countries was the widespread use of combined heat and power in the former [Diskant, 1979]. In these systems the waste heat from thermal power plants was taken in pipes to heat whole city districts. Moscow had 1,800 miles of such piping. The overall efficiency of energy use was thus considerably higher than the simple BTU/KWh figures would imply.

The Soviet practice was to heat new housing developments using local thermal heating plants, whose heat output was thermostatically determined by the outside air temperature. Once the development had reached a sufficient size, heat would be piped into the main hot water network from thermal power plants. After this, the original local thermal plant was kept as a backup. The USSR achieved economies of scale by using standardized modular thermal power plants, though such standardization may have slightly slowed down the improvement in thermal efficiency.

That this district heating was supplied unmetered was held up by the American press as a terrible example of inefficiency [Paddock, 1997]. Russians would, it was said, simply open their windows rather than turn down a thermostat if their room got too hot. This ignored the fact that in New York City the heat that would, in Moscow, have heated flats, was simply dumped into the Hudson River by the power company.

Electricity is not a primary energy source. It depends on other primary sources such as the flow of rivers, burning oil, or splitting atoms. In Section 5.4.4 I argue that water power alone could not have provided sufficient energy to sustain even late-Victorian capitalism. With much bigger rivers than Britain, the USSR made more extensive use of hydropower. If, however, they had only used this source of energy, the amount of mechanical power available per head would have been less than was used in late-Victorian England. Instead the economy relied heavily on fossil fuels, in the late USSR mainly gas and oil. According to Allen [2003], one reason for the slowdown in Soviet economic growth from the 1970s was that the continued expansion of energy use could only be achieved by accessing oil and gas from Siberia, a much more costly task than getting it from the Caspian Basin.

The hitherto existing industrial mode of production, variants of which both historical capitalism and socialism have shared, depends on sunlight long sequestered in fossil form. Any such mode of production is self-limiting, destroying its own conditions of existence. This limitation lies, in a sense, below even the demographic constraints we already analyzed for capitalism. Their dependence on resources which, by the scale of human

TABLE 6.3: Chinese Electricity Sources in 2015 and as Projected in the 13th 5-Year Plan

Source	GW 2015	GW 2020	Percent 2015	Percent 2020
Fossil	990	1,210	66%	63%
Hydro	319	340	21%	18%
Wind	129	210	9%	11%
Solar	43	110	3%	6%
Nuclear	26	58	2%	3%
Total	1,507	1928	100%	100%

history, will quickly be exhausted, marks out their mode of production as transitory. It will not be the first mode of production to exhaust its resources. Mesolithic hunting seems to have done the same, precipitating the Neolithic Revolution in agriculture. Peasant feudal economy, in contrast, was relatively self-sustaining, if stagnant. If necessity again proves the mother of invention, a similar revolution to a more sustainable mode of production will take place. A key element of this will be the shift from fossil fuels to other modes of energy production.

China, which up to now has relied preponderantly on coal to fuel its power stations, uses far less nuclear than the USSR did. Benefiting though from a quarter-century of technical development it was by 2015 using much more recyclable sources of energy. But even allowing for a very rapid growth in solar, wind, and nuclear energy in the 5-year plan to 2020, fossil fuel generation is so big that it will still produce over 60 percent of electricity.

Chinese nuclear power, like that of the USSR, has been based on water-cooled designs. It is arguable that such reactors are inherently more dangerous than gas-cooled ones, since there are inherent explosion risks on overheating with water cooling. The serious accidents at Chernobyl and Fukushima were with different variants of water-cooled reactors. Development of safer high-temperature gas reactors has been set as a high-priority technical goal in China.

Fast neutron reactor technology, which makes far more efficient use of nuclear fuel, is also being developed [News, 2010].[114] Ambitious plans to install hundreds of GW of these exist, but whether the Chinese economy in the twenty-first century is any more successful with them than the aborted plans that the UK, France, and Japan had for fast reactors in the past, remains to be seen. The technology has in the past proven very difficult to master, but China may have the resources of scale and population needed to make it work.

6.3 REPRODUCTION AND DIVISION OF LABOR

We are now approaching a social revolution in which the economic foundations of monogamy as they have existed hitherto will disappear just as surely as those of its complement prostitution. Monogamy arose from the concentration of considerable wealth in the hands of a single individual man—and from the need to bequeath this wealth to the children of that man and of no other. For this purpose, the monogamy of the woman was required, not that of the man, so this monogamy of the woman did not in any way interfere with open or concealed polygamy on the part of the man. But by transforming by far the greater portion, at any rate, of permanent, heritable wealth—the means of production—into social property, the coming social revolution will reduce to a minimum all this anxiety about bequeathing and inheriting. Having arisen from economic causes, will monogamy then disappear when these causes disappear?

One might answer, not without reason: far from disappearing, it will, on the contrary, be realized completely. For with the transformation of the means of production into social property there will disappear also wage-labor, the proletariat, and therefore the necessity for a certain—statistically calculable—number of women to surrender themselves for money. Prostitution disappears; monogamy, instead of collapsing, at last becomes a reality—also for men.

—ENGELS AND HUNT, 2010

Societies have characteristic family ideologies and family laws structured by their economies. This was a basic thesis of Engels and Hunt [2010], who used this premise to try to predict how the family would change in a post-capitalist society. The nice point is that this theory of the history of the family then itself became part of the ideological foundation of socialist family relations.

The professed aim of the Communists was to reform the relations between the sexes along the lines advocated by Engels. The universal participation of women in public industry would have as a consequence the abolition of the monogamous family as the basic economic unit of society. Private household work would be transformed into a social industry and society as a whole would take responsibility for the care and education of all children whether born in or out of marriage.

With considerations of property removed, marriage would be based on mutual love alone. Arranged marriage would vanish. We tend to think of arranged marriages as something oriental, but the underlying principle, of the marriage being a matter of passing down and accumulating property, was widespread. Even in nineteenth-century England, marriages among the upper class centered on the property motive: "It is a truth universally acknowledged, that a single man in possession of a good fortune, must be in want of a wife" [Austen, 1994].

Only the poor, Engels maintained, could afford to marry for love. But in the socialist future, love would become the sole basis for marriage.

Under the influence of radical legal theorists [Pashukanis, 1989], the Soviets at first envisaged that marriage law, like other contractual law, would be phased out in socialist society. The only interest the state would have in people's cohabitation would be to register it for statistical purposes along with births and deaths [Berman, 1946]; so the RSFSR 1926 Family Code treated sex, marriage, and divorce as a private matter in which the state did not interfere. This liberal attitude extended to not prohibiting incest, bigamy, homosexuality, or marriage with post-puberty minors. Bigamy or polygamy, though not prohibited in marriage law, insofar as these involved economic exploitation of women, could be criminally prosecuted under the heading of exploitation. While contemporary Western commentators largely approve of the liberal attitude of the early Soviet state to homosexuality, they are more silent on its liberalism toward incest, bigamy, and other practices that would now be frowned on.

In 1920 free abortion had been introduced, which produced a rapid decline in the birth rate in urban areas. During the 1920s the Moscow birth rate fell from 30.6/1000 to 21.7/1000, while abortions rose from 5.7/1000 to 35.2/1000 [Berman, 1946]. Given that the overall death rate in the mid-1920s for the RSFSR was 21/1000 this appeared to represent a potential fall to below replacement birth rates [Engelman, 1932]. The birth rate in Moscow was unrepresentative. In rural areas where state hospitals providing abortion did not exist, that is, for the majority of Russians, the birth rate was much higher at 44/1000 for the greater Russian population. Clearly there was no general threat to reproduction in the 1920s, but projecting forward for a rapidly urban population in the mid-1930s, or a population vastly depleted by war in the mid-1940s, the outlook may have seemed different. Such a projection failed to take into account the fall in the death rate that could be anticipated to follow rising living standards. On the other hand, given the international environment, a sharp rise in deaths due to enemy action may have been anticipated. The subsequent 1936 law severely restricted abortion to cases of danger to maternal health or genetic disorder, and at the same time introduced substantial subsidies to women with large families. For the sixth and each subsequent child a stipend of 2,000 rubles a year, equivalent at the official exchange rate to $2,300, was introduced. Given that the average annual wage at that time was 2,700 rubles [Petroff, 1938], this was a large benefit. Paid maternity leave of 112 days was introduced along with birth benefits. One could either see these measures as natalist, or alternatively as being to protect mothers and children. They introduced, albeit partially, the principle that Engels had advocated: that the cost of raising children should be borne by society as a whole. If it is a social obligation then it applies to all members of society. Those who have no children have to support the costs of those with children, and by paying a penalty, be encouraged to have kids themselves.

A 1941 law [Nakachi, 2006] sought to make this economic obligation explicit by introducing a tax on bachelors, single, and childless citizens of the USSR. The socialization of childcare costs was still partial because even as late as 1960 the regular child benefit was paid only to unmarried mothers or mothers with large families [Lantsev, 1962]. The principle that children were to be supported by the joint earnings of the parents for smaller families was thus not questioned, and marriage continued to have an economic role even before the division of domestic labor between husband and wife was taken into account.

The German-Soviet war of 1941 to 1945 caused a huge demographic shortfall—initially of the order of 40 million, rising to around 70 million by the end of the Soviet period, as can be seen in Figure 6.3, which projects what the Soviet population would have been on prewar growth trends. But throughout the Soviet period the population continued to grow, probably as a result of social policy. The effect of the war on the sex ratio was drastic, with the ratio of men to women of reproductive age falling as far as 19:100 in rural areas [Nakachi, 2006]. This led to changes in family policy oriented toward: encouraging families with only two children to have at least one

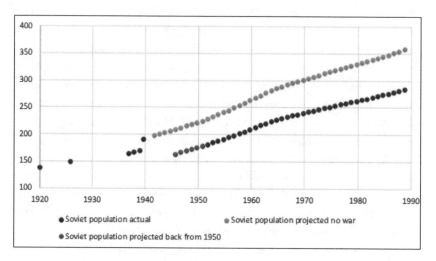

Figure 6.3. Soviet population suffered a huge demographic setback due to the German-Soviet war of 1941–45. Source: Pockney, 1991.

more, legitimizing single motherhood, and making benefits available to those women.

These goals were encoded in the 1944 Family Law. The bachelor tax was increased and also levied at a rate of 1/3 on couples with only one child. [115] Child support benefits were also made available to those single mothers who were not claiming child support from the father. Single mothers included both millions of war widows and unmarried mothers. Given a shortage of young men brought about by the war, single mothers were expected to be a significant fraction of all mothers.

The USSR underwent its primary demographic transition between the late 1930s and late '50s. The main component of this was a shift from the high infant mortality rate of around 200 per 1,000 live births at the end of the '30s to around 50 in the late 1950s and down to 25 in the mid-1960s [Shkolnikov and Meslé, 1996]. The decline was largely due to reductions in infectious diseases, particularly food and water-borne infections. As a result life expectancy at birth rose by 24 years in males and 27 years in females between the end of the 1930s to the mid-1960s. Overall birth rates and death rates declined sharply during the transition, reaching a minimum for death rate in the mid-1960s, and for birth rate around 1970 (Figure 6.4). After that both rates increased. Allen [2003] argues that the fall in the birth rate was critical to ensuring that food production per head rose, and that the growth in population was significantly slower than would normally have been expected in an industrializing country.

The increase in death rate from the 1970s was most marked in men. It

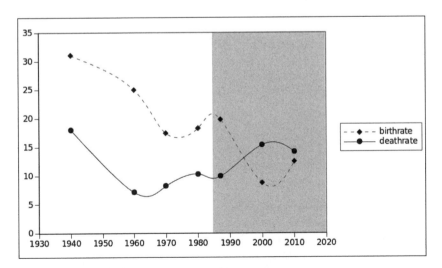

Figure 6.4. Evolution of Russian birth and death rates in Soviet and post-Glasnost periods. Source: Pockney, 1991; and UN Demographic Yearbooks.

was largely due to a rise in heart disease, accidents, suicide, and interpersonal violence. A factor producing the minimum in male death rate in the late 1960s was that during the '50s and '60s the age structure of the population was skewed toward younger men. So many who reached maturity in the '30s and early '40s had been war casualties, that the number reaching the age when heart diseases strike was unusually low.

The birth rate remained well in excess of peacetime deaths throughout the first demographic transition giving a steady increase in population.

The transition from socialism to capitalism in the USSR in the late 1980s early 1990s induced a second, far more drastic demographic transition. The birth rate fell sharply into the range typical for developed capitalist countries. But, whereas in many capitalist countries the birth rate falls below the death rate, both are normally on a downward trend. In Russia the death rate rose sharply (Figure 6.4 and Table 6.7). A rise of this scale in peace was at the time unprecedented in a developed country. Those without university education, that is to say the manual workers and farmers, suffered increased mortality [Shkolnikov et al., 2006]. The intelligentsia experienced no decline in mortality. Subsequently Case and Deaton [2015] have pointed out that the same has been happening to white working-class men in the United States with similar causes: mass unemployment and de-industrialization [Stuckler et al., 2009]. As Figure 6.5 shows, this demographic crisis was a general phenomenon affecting the ex-socialist countries. The onset of capitalism and the deterioration of social conditions that followed meant that the region as a whole went into demographic decline.

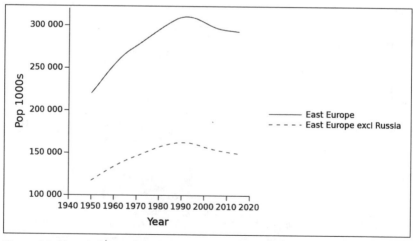

Figure 6.5. The whole socialist area of Europe experienced steady population growth until the transition to capitalism, after which population declined sharply. Source: UN World Population Spreadsheet, 2015.

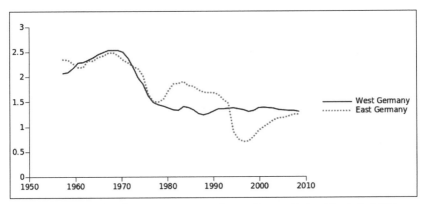

Figure 6.6. German fertility rate per woman. Souce: German Federal Statistical Office.

The contrast between capitalist and socialist family policy is best illustrated by a comparison of East and West Germany. Both Germanys experienced declines in fertility following the availability of modern contraceptive technology in the 1960s. By the early 1970s fertility had fallen below replacement levels in both East and West (Figure 6.6). But the birth rate in East Germany recovered to around replacement level by the late 1970s following the 1976 introduction of policies to socialize a considerable part of the burden of child raising [Salles, 2006]. Single mothers had priority access to kindergarten places. If no place was available they could go on sick leave at half pay, with the return of their job guaranteed as soon as a place became available. One year of paid parental leave was available for single women on the birth of their first child. For married women this was available only for subsequent children. Along with free nursery schools, birth bonuses, workplace childcare and workplace canteens all helped parents.

These policies clearly worked (Figure 6.6). The overall effect was to increase the birth rate in the East above the contemporary rate in the West. The availability of maternal benefits to single mothers increased the proportion of babies born to them, and led to greater social acceptance of their situation. Rents were low, but waiting lists for flats gave priority to single mothers and married couples. A common family pattern emerged of women having their first child before marrying and a second one after marriage [Salles, 2006].

With the union with West Germany, this benefit system was withdrawn and the consequent demographic shock led to East German fertility rates falling as low as 0.7 before converging on the all-Germany average of 1.4. This is still well below replacement level.

It was argued in Sections 5.6 and 5.8 that the combination of capitalist and domestic economies is antagonistic. Capitalist mass production replaces one economic function of the household after another: spinning, weaving, growing food, sewing clothes, baking, etc. The demand for skilled and educated adult workers converted children from being part of the domestic labor force to economic dependents, creating an incentive to limit family size. The development, by the chemical industry, of contraceptive technology then made this possible. The continuing demand for more labor then drew an increasing fraction of women into capitalist employment, which for a few decades allowed the workforce to go on growing. It then became necessary for both parents to work and the cost of private childcare becomes more of a disincentive to have large families or even have families at all.

Socialist states have had the aim of improving the status of women through their participation in the social economy. As such they could have been faced with the same spontaneous tendency toward below-replacement fertility. They avoided this because women's participation in the socialist sector went alongside a deliberate policy of socialization on childcare.

A socialist economy does not face the same problem of a demographically induced falling rate of profit that affects capitalism. The state can choose to continue to invest even if the rate of return falls to levels at which capitalists would stop investing. But the rising share of old people in a rapidly shrinking population, as implied by very low birth rates, is a problem whatever the economic system.

Turning from Europe to Asia we see an inverse problem. Socialist governments, instead of trying to hold the birth rate up, tried to reduce it. Across the continent, the 1950s and '60s launched a process of two demographic transitions:

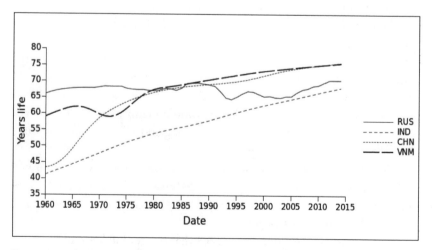

Figure 6.7. Life expectancy in India, China, Russia, and Vietnam. Source: World Bank.

1. From a high birth rate high-mortality society to a high birth rate low-mortality one.
2. From a high birth rate low-mortality society to one where both birth rates and mortality were low.

If we look at big developing Asian countries, we see that the socialist ones were the most successful in bringing about the demographic transitions. On life expectancy (Figure 6.7), Asian socialist countries have been very successful, overtaking the USSR just before that state collapse, and being well ahead of non-socialist India. The decline in life expectancy in Vietnam from the late 1960s coincided with the most intense period of the Vietnamese-American war. In China the most rapid improvement in life expectancy was during the Maoist period when initiatives like the mass training of medical auxiliaries to improve rural health care were rolled out.

A consequence of the rising life expectancy was to create a danger that there would be more people than could be fed on China's limited arable land, so from the 1970s the government had an active birth control program [Banister, 1984]. This was remarkably effective. The rapid rise in life expectancy in the 1960s was followed by an equally dramatic fall in fertility during the 1970s (Figure 6.8). The government population policy culminated in restricting most families to have only one child, with the restriction lasting thirty-five years from the end of the 1970s. As Figure 6.8 shows, current fertility falls below the reproduction level. By 2010 the fertility rate was down to 1.5.[116]

The effective female fertility rate, the number of daughters per woman, is what determines long-term population dynamics. It must be at least 1 for

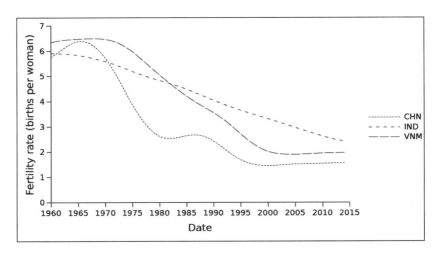

Figure 6.8. Fertility in India, China, and Vietnam. Source: World Bank database.

steady reproduction. In China, preference for boys has skewed the population by several mechanisms: selective abortion of female infants, higher mortality of girls due to neglect [Banister, 2004], and a lower likelihood of having a second child if the first is a boy. As a result the male/female ratio in China is 117/100. So each woman in China was, by 2010 giving birth to on average only $1.5 \times [100/217] = 0.69$girls.

The official abandonment of the one-child policy indicates that the government considers that the birth rate has fallen too far.

Between the 1980s and the 2010s China enjoyed what some economists call a demographic dividend [Fang, 2010]. The birth rate had fallen so the number of children supported by each adult was lower while there were still plenty of young adult workers born during the baby boom and low infant mortality of the 1960s. This accelerated the expansion of an industrial urban economy [Cockshott, 2006a]. The productive workforce grew disproportionately fast compared to the overall growth of population.

By the middle of the 2010s the productive share of the Chinese population startsed to decline [Banister et al., 2012]. Some growth of the urban population will continue as a result of the continued mechanization of agriculture, but overall the dependency rate will rise. Given that China has a high ratio of population to agricultural land, there may be some justification for a slow and managed decline in its population. In the long term a somewhat lower population density should make a sustainable form of economy easier to achieve. But that sort of managed decline would imply an effective female fertility rate closer to 0.9 than 0.7. If population is to

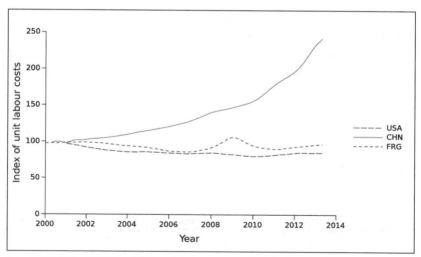

Figure 6.9. Movement in relative unit labor costs in Germany, United States, and China. National labor cost in year 2000 is taken as 100.

be either stabilized or allowed to shrink more gradually China will have to adopt mother-friendly reforms similar to those introduced by the DDR in 1976 and to carry out a big cultural campaign to raise the perceived worth of baby girls.

China in the 1980s developed a mixed economy that combined state-owned industry alongside semi-private agriculture and private capitalist firms. The position of workers, whether in state firms or private capitalist firms, was similar. They were employed for a wage and lacked long-term security of employment. The level of wages was determined by supply and demand on the labor market. In these circumstances the one-child family policy acted to favor the labor interest. It reduced the number of young workers entering the labor market and, by the 2010s, was strengthening the bargaining position of workers. When combined with the rapid rate of investment in China this allowed wages to rise very fast (Figures 6.9 and 6.10). A policy introduced when the socialist economy was dominant operated a generation and a half after its introduction to strengthen the position of workers at a time when the private sector was just becoming the dominant element of the economy. The long lags associated with any demographic feedback means that social relations may change considerably before the feedback takes effect. [117]

The social relations of any economic system have to ensure the reproduction of the society from year to year. I have written in the last part about the most fundamental function of any economy: human reproduction. Let us now look at the reproduction of the non-human aspect of the economy.

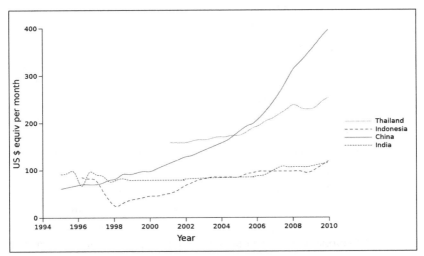

Figure 6.10. Movement in monthly wages in India, Indonesia, Thailand, and China. Money wages in equivalent $USD.

Any economy must schedule regular productive activities and ensure that the non-human environment is prepared for these activities. Some of this preparation is carried out by nature, by the cycle of the seasons, and the flow of elements and life through the ecosystem. Some of it is prepared by human activity itself, plowing and weeding land, setting aside seed corn, preparing stocks of fuel, raw materials, and tools for future production.

Even a relatively simple peasant economy needs to have a specialized branch of the division of labor responsible for organizing such scheduling. The rise of calendar priesthoods in the Neolithic is an example of such a temporal coordination branch of the division of labor. With rises in the density of population in places like Egypt, the functions of such priesthoods went beyond saying when crops should be sown and land plowed to maintaining and distributing buffer stocks of grain.[118]

With the development of more advanced industrial production, the preparation of the portable conditions of production won importance. The land stays there to be plowed each year, but the raw materials and tools of industry must be delivered to where they are used. Delivery depended in turn on the harnessing of beasts, the conquest of the wind, and the taming of steam. The masters of these forces, the classes first of merchants, then merchant capitalists, and finally industrial capitalists, then assumed control of the conditions of production. The industrial capitalist had to organize both the human and the inanimate resources needed for his factory. He had to order in and schedule the delivery of the machinery, buildings, and raw materials for the workers he hired. Unlike the priest who had only to adapt to the regular movement of Apollo and the helical rising of Venus, the capitalist had to attend more numerous and capricious gods. The manager of the Riihimaki-Saint Petersburg Railway had to order his locomotives from Neilson and Company in Springburn, Scotland, his steam coal from the mines of Wales, sleepers cut from local timber, etc. In all cases he had to be sure that the goods met his technical specification and that they would be available on time, delivered to the right place. This presupposes a developed commercial correspondence. The suppliers and users have to exchange letters, telegrams, and later emails that inform one another about technical specifications, likely delivery times, quantities, prices offered and prices agreed. I will call all the information about the physical properties of the goods the "use-value channel" in this information flow, and the information about prices the "exchange-value channel." The use-value channel is needed in any industrial system, whether it is a mass of independent firms, a big multinational with component parts spread around the world, a state organizing in wartime production, or a socialist planned economy. The comparative importance of an exchange-value channel has been disputed.

Hayek [1945 and 1955] laid great store on the importance of the exchange-value channel, scarcely acknowledging the existence of the other channel. [119] His fellow countryman Neurath [1919, 1917, and 2004; Uebel, 2005] claimed that real industrial coordination depended overwhelmingly on the use-value channel. Basing himself on his practical experience of wartime industrial planning, he emphasized that wars were not won by calculations about bond prices, but by the logistics of food, munitions, and supplies. Efficiency in war economy depended on calculations in physical terms along with controls and rationing of physical products and labor. By applying these methods, it was possible for the Central Powers to overcome shortages and obstacles such as the British blockade that would otherwise have proven fatal at an early period of the war. Neurath believed that after the war the organizational structure used by the war economy would be readily adapted for a peacetime socialist economy. Neurath briefly attempted to put these principles into practice in the short-lived Bavarian socialist republic of 1919, before being imprisoned on its suppression. Similar sentiments about the peaceful application of wartime planning, which Neurath termed state capitalism, were expressed by Lenin [1965a], [120]

War was key to the transitions to socialism, whether the revolutionary civil wars in Cuba, China, Vietnam or the great world wars of the twentieth century. The world wars disrupted many capitalist states through invasion or mutiny and fostered war economies which were halfway to socialism.

6.4 DETERMINATION OF THE SURPLUS PRODUCT

In capitalist war economies, production, by and large, still took place in privately owned firms. There were state munitions factories like the Royal Arsenal (Figure 5.35) or the Oak Ridge and Los Alamos atomic weapons plants, but these were exceptions. The state directed labor by conscripting it into the army, and by conscripting women and men in key trades into essential war work. It also rationed the supply of key materials, fuels, and foodstuffs. Firms were subject to negotiated direction to produce only munitions, or restricted ranges of utility products [Edgerton, 2011a]. Money was still used to pay for the munitions delivered, and to pay workers. Buying food required both money and ration cards. Money alone was not enough, either for the consumer or for firms. In peace, money as the universal ration constrains everything. Shortage of it constrains the working-class consumers and uncertainty about future revenue constrains even those firms who have good cash reserves. Because the constraint on production comes via the exchange-value channel, not the use-value one, peacetime capitalist economies typically operate somewhat below full capacity. In war, national survival dictates that every available resource be put to use. The economy operates at the limits of its physical resources in materials, people, and machines.

The state as primary purchaser has to look not just at the projected costs of ships, aircraft, etc. it is ordering, but at all sorts of material constraints. In deciding what type of destroyers to order the navy first takes into account the requirements of their admirals for the ships to carry guns of different types, torpedoes, and anti-submarine weapons—all technical not financial issues. They then had to take into account the number of shipyards in the country able to build ships of different sizes, the delivery schedules for different kinds of projected weapons and ship machinery, the availability of metals and alloys of different weights and strengths. They then have to ask whether the demands on skilled labor would require the cancellation or postponement of other orders.[121] Money was a relatively secondary concern. The availability of state credit, at least within the domestic economy, that was effectively unlimited removed money as a constraining resource [Keynes, 2010]. The same point about money applied *a fortiori* to the socialist economies.

Keynes's [2010] essay on war economy is extraordinarily important for giving English-language readers an insight into the common problems facing both war economies and socialist ones. He starts by posing the basic question:

> We shall, I assume, raise our output to the highest figure which our resources and our organization permit. We shall export all we can spare. We shall import all we can afford, having regard to the shipping tonnage available and the maximum rate at which it is prudent to use up our reserves of foreign assets. From the sum of our own output and our imports we have to take away our exports and the requirements of war. Civilian consumption at home will be equal to what is left. Clearly its amount will depend on our policy in the other respects. It can only be increased if we diminish our war effort, or if we use up our foreign reserves.
>
> It is extraordinarily difficult to secure the right outcome for this resultant of many separate policies. It depends on weighing one advantage against another. There is hardly a conceivable decision within the range of the supply services which does not affect it. Is it better that the War Office should have a large reserve of uniforms in stock or that the cloth should be exported to increase the Treasury's reserve of foreign currency? Is it better to employ our shipyards to build war ships or merchant-men ? Is it better that a 20-year-old agricultural worker should be left on the farm or taken into the army? How great an expansion of the Army should we contemplate? What

reduction in working hours and efficiency is justified in the interests of A.R.P.? One could ask a hundred thousand such questions, and the answer to each would have a significant bearing on time amount left over for civilian consumption.

Keynes argued that under wartime conditions there was a permanent shortfall of supply of consumption goods. While the normal effect of this was to induce inflation, the effects of wartime legislation such as Excess Profits Taxes were to suppress the inflation in the short term. In wartime the size of the civilian cake was fixed. Working harder increased the surplus for war production but not for consumption "If we work harder, we can fight better. But we must not consume more."

Assuming people worked longer hours, there would be more going out in wages. In the long term inflationary pressures would break through. In the absence of a common plan by the government, the effect would be that prices would rise to absorb the additional wages. So all the extra money paid out for the longer hours worked would end up in the accounts of the capitalist class and workers would experience no rise in real wages. The capitalists would then lend their increased profits to the government to finance the war, or perhaps spend some of them on personal consumption, further reducing the share available to workers. If they lent the money to the government, they would end up owning even more of the national debt, giving them thereby a claim on postwar resources.

But of course not only goods were in short supply. So was labor. This put trade unions in a position to bargain for higher wartime wage rates. But given the actual fixed output of consumer goods, no increase in real wages would result, simply more inflation. To avoid inflation it was therefore necessary to remove from circulation and transfer back to the government the extra money that it was spending on the war. Were this done simply by increasing income taxes and indirect tax, the money would be removed, but workers would see no benefit from their extra work. Instead Keynes proposed a scheme of deferred pay. A graduated scale of enforced savings, analogous to progressive income tax, would be imposed. Workers would get war bonds that could be redeemed for cash after the war.

Keynes notes that in war, in the face of rising costs, there was strong pressure both to subsidize essential foodstuffs and to introduce to the UK family benefits of the sort discussed earlier in the context of the USSR and the DDR. He warns that such policies, aimed at greater equality, would only be viable in the context of the deferred wages scheme, since otherwise they would have led to further inflationary pressures.

6.5 SOCIALIST ECONOMIC GROWTH

Peacetime socialist economy shares many of the attributes of a war economy: tight resource and labor constraints, money no longer a constraint,
suppressed inflation, controls over the allocation of physical resources. The
suppression of inflation was more effective in socialist economies, since the
large bulk of the consumer goods market was served by state enterprises
whose output was sold at planned prices. The Keynesian solution to suppressed inflation was not really available. People ran up balances in their
savings accounts, but the idea of forced saving into bonds that would be
redeemed for consumption at a later date was not feasible in the long term. It
only works if the period of increased labor output and restricted consumption is going to be relatively short. There has to be a reasonable prospect
that at a later date circumstances will be more relaxed. The socialist growth
theory of Feldman [1964] had something of this character. It proposed that
there would be a period of sacrifice while a larger share of national income
went into the production of means of production. This would lead to a larger
possible output of consumer goods since the expanded machine producing
sector could supply the consumer goods sector with the means to increase
its output.

> The rate of growth of income increases as a function of the indus-
> trialization of the country at every stage of its development, for the
> ratioKu/Kp is undoubtedly one of the primary indicators of the level
> of industrialization of the country, by virtue of the constantly increas-
> ing significance of industry in the contemporary economy. Thus an
> increase in the rate of growth demands considerable industrializa-
> tion. In order to raise the constant increment of income from 10
> percent to 15.7 percent it is necessary to almost double Ku/K – p.
>
> Thus an increase in the rate of growth of income demands indus-
> trialization, heavy industry, machine building, electrification. [194]

In the quote above, Ku/Kp refers to the ratio of capital in Sector I producing means of production to Sector II producing consumer goods.

The basic equation of the Feldman growth model is

$$D'S_f = D_u/D$$

where: D' is the overal rate of economic growth; S_f is the index of capital
effectiveness or the output to capital ratio (using the subscript f to distinguish it from Marx's variable S); D is the overall output in the current period

of the economy; Du is the net output of the capital goods sector, analogous to Marx's sector I, but net also of the capital consumption in sector II. [122]

Given Marx's labeling of reproduction as

$$O_1 = C_1 + V_1 + S_1$$

$$O_2 = C_2 + V_2 + S_2$$

Where suffix 1 indicates producer goods and suffix 2 consumption goods, Ci is capital goods consumed in sector i and Vi wage goods consumed in sector i.

We can obtain Feldman's Du as $D_u = O_1 - (C_1 + C_2) = S_1 + V_1 - C_2$.

Although Marx's reproduction schemes only deal with flows of wage goods and producer goods, the Feldman model uses a variable S which is the annual output, in rubles, produced per each ruble of producer goods in use. It thus has dimension time^{-1} as is required of any rate of growth (see also discusssion in Section 5.9).

Marx's variable C refers to *flows* of producer goods, but it is common to use another variable K to stand for the stock of capital goods when discussing capital composition and the rate of profit. The organic composition of capital which Marx showed to be inversely related to the rate of profit is then $[K/V]$; Feldman's capital effectiveness can then be defined as $S_f[(S + V + C)/K]$.

If we assume that in a socialist economy there is no luxury consumption by capitalists, then the entire surplus is directed into building up the stock of means of production. Further, since this is a socialist economy in expansion, Marx's basic static equilibrium condition that $C_2 = V_1 + S_1$ does not hold. First because of the accumulation, and second because the two sectors are not financially independent properties balancing their trade with one another. They are instead seen as both parts of the same unified property. Transfers between them therefore do not have to take the form of equivalent exchange.

In Marx's analysis there is an assumption that the same variable symbol can stand for different things as a consequence of commodity trade. So his symbol V stands initially for a sum of money advanced to buy labor power. But later it stands for the labor time required to make the wage goods bought by the workers under the assumption that the value of the wage goods will be the same as the value of the money paid for them. [123]

But how are we to relate this to the Feldman model, which historically appears to have been the original guiding theory behind Soviet industrial policy [Clark, 1984]? What are the units in which the growth is expressed? The simple answer is that the units are monetary, but how do these money quantities relate to physical output and to labor hours?

By its nature a growth theory is talking about development over time. For a snapshot view, as in Marx's reproduction theory, we can abstract from changes in the value of money; over periods of several years this is no longer safe. We would expect that in an industrializing economy the productivity of labor will rise, so that either or both of the ratios:

$$\frac{\text{money}}{\text{use values}}$$

or

$$\frac{\text{money}}{\text{labor time}}$$

will change. But for the moment let us assume that we are looking at a sufficiently small interval for these changes to be insignificant. It would then be valid to treat all of the quantities in the Feldman model as measures in terms of labor time. Let us see what this implies.

1. The variable D' is rate of growth of money national income. National income is in millions of rubles (₽) per year so its units would be [₽/yr], and the growth of national income ΔD would be in $[((₽/yr))/yr] = [₽/(yr^2)]$. The proportionate rate of growth is then obtained by dividing through by national income $D \in [₽/yr]$.

    Assume for the sake of argument that in those days a ruble was the product of one person hour of labor, what the growth of national income converts to is a measure of [(Persons × hrs)/(yr2)]. But since years and hours are both time, they cancel out, and the final measure is equivalent to $\Delta D \in [\text{Persons/yr}]$.

    What does this tell us?

    It says that if we assume that over the short term labor values do not change, the Feldman equation is actually giving us a measure of the number of new people added to the economy each year, that is, the growth of the industrial labor force. The growth Feldman is concerned with is the proportionate growth of the labor force since he divides ΔD through by existing national income, D which is a flow of value, and in dimensional terms a flow of value is equal to a number of persons—more strictly it is equal to a number of people working average full-time hours.[124] So dividing through by national income is dimensionally equivalent to saying the D expresses the rate of growth of the workforce. We can check the rationality of this by looking at the other terms of his formula.

2. The term $[(D_u)/D]$, by the rule that a flow of value is a number of

persons, expresses the fraction of the workforce devoted to the net production of means of production.

3. The "effectiveness of capital" index S measures the flow of output value
    made possible by a unit investment in means of production. If our unit
    of means of production is one person year, and the units of value flow
    are persons as before, this expresses how many years a worker would
    have to work to produce the means of production needed for one more
    worker.

4. I leave it to the reader to check that after translation into the language
    of the labor theory of value, both sides still have dimension [1/yr].

So Feldman's formula, once you strip it of its monetary form, is relating
the rate of growth of the productive labor force to the share of the labor
force making means of production, via a constant of proportionality. One
can view Feldman's as a master equation governing the dynamics of socialist economy for the dynamics of capitalism. Let us next look at some of its
implications in the short, medium, and longer term.

The equation above indicates that the larger the proportion of output
devoted to new means of production the faster will be the rate of growth.
To move to a high growth mode a socialist economy had to raise the relative
size of Sector I compared to Sector II. Once this shift had been achieved,
both sectors could grow more rapidly.

Allen [2005, 2003] presents evidence that the early years of the Soviet
planned economy fitted this Feldman pattern rather well. As Figure 6.11
shows, over the first 5-year plan (which ran 1928 to 1932) real consumption
per capita fell. This is consistent with overwhelming emphasis being devoted
to the machine-building industries, and little investment going into consumer goods industries. This produced a shift in the relative proportions of
Sectors I and II. But in the subsequent plan, where the output of the machine
building could be directed into increasing the capital stock of consumption
industries, there was a rapid rise in real per capita consumption.[125] It can
be seen that in the period of overlap the two trends are very similar, which
validates Allen's data. The underlying point is that the rate at which children
grow will be closely dependent upon living standards, particularly the available diet.

This did not necessarily mean that urban real wage rates rose rapidly;
rather, a larger portion of the population moved from the countryside to
the cities, and urban living standards were substantially above the primitive
levels of peasant life. Thus, averaged across the whole population, real consumption rose, and the corollary of this is that production of consumer goods
rose rapidly. The critical point is that without first raising the relative size of

Sector I it would be impossible to have ever achieved a rapid growth rate, since it is the net product of Sector I (D_u) that constrains the whole process.

What is the precondition for the Feldman model working?

Since, at least instantaneously as a derivative, it is an equation that, once translated to the labor theory, is about the growth of the workforce, it must depend on such growth being possible. It is, more specifically, a theory about the growth of the industrial economy—the two-sector model on which it is based assumes an industrialized structure with capital goods and consumer goods industries.

The industrial economy can grow its workforce in several ways: through

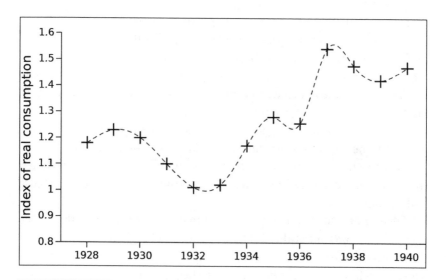

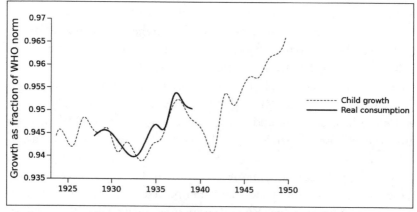

Figure 6.11. (top): Movement in real consumption per capita in the USSR during first phase of planned industrialization, as of 1928. Source: Allen, 2005. (bottom): Data from above are superimposed on time series of Soviet child growth rates. Source: Pelkonen and Cockshott, 2017.

natural population growth, through immigration from other nations, or by internal migration from the countryside. All of these occurred during capitalist industrializations, only the first and the last during socialist ones. A previous section discussed the measures taken by European socialist countries to ensure that they continued to have a growing population. But natural population growth was relatively slow—of the order of 2 percent a year in the USSR. This would only support a modest rate of economic growth.

Figure 6.12 shows a Feldman growth path for an economy like the USSR starting out with an industrial population of 18 percent. Initially I assume that 90 percent of all investment was channeled into Sector I, which is not enough to compensate for depreciation in Sector II, so consumption per capita falls during the first plan period—as it actually did. In subsequent plans I assumed that 60 percent of investment went to sector I. Assumptions about initial population distribution are realistic. The relative size of sector I grows to a peak at the end of the first plan and then falls and levels off during the subsequent ones. Clearly this would have been a very rapidly growing economy. Equally clearly, this growth path could not have continued, since urbanization would have approached 100 percent by the end of the 1940s. In the model, it is assumed that migration into the cities stops once urbanization reaches 80 percent. This has the effect of sharply slowing the rate of growth of per-capita consumption. In reality the slowdown did not occur that sharply, but slid in gradually at the practical limit of urbanization was gradually reached.

We know that the real economic history of the USSR was much like this, modified by the effects of urbanization being more gradual, and with an almost ten-year delay produced by the war. As time went on, and as the

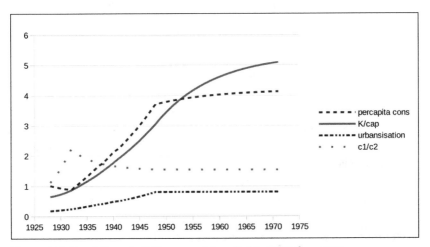

Figure 6.12. Simulation of a Feldman model applied to USSR from 1928.

stock of means of production measured in person years per capita rose, then even the possibility of further investment became blocked off. If plant and machinery has a fixed life, say twenty years, then more and more of the output of Sector I has to be devoted to simply replacing existing machinery. If Sector I makes up half the economy, then it would be impossible to sustain a long-term K/cap of more than ten person years. At that level, even when working flat out, sector I could only make good the annual wearing out of plant. All the measurements in Figure 6.12 are in terms of labor value—person years.

It is evident that the law of the declining rate of profit is just a particular capitalist social form of a more general law that affects the industrial mode of production, whether socialist or capitalist, as the ratio of embodied to living labor rises over time. Socialist economy, however, avoids certain of the worst effects of this process while being susceptible to others. It avoided the recessions, unemployment, and pressure to drive down real wages that affected the capitalist world on and off since the 1970s when the high organic composition of capital became a general problem. On the other hand, the slowdown in the rate of economic growth in the socialist world produced a much more severe ideological and political crisis than that which hit the West in the economic crises of the 1970s and post-2008.

Calculations in terms of labor values are the same basis that one uses to arrive at the law of the falling rate of profit. The leveling off in value terms may still be compatible with an increase in use-value terms, but it does enable you to show that the end state must be one in which simple reproduction occurs in value terms.

In contrast to labor value calculations, measurement in use-value terms is difficult. You are comparing incommensurables—quantities of different use-values at different times. While growth in terms of labor values uses a unit—time expended by a human body—that does not vary from year to year, the physical mix of outputs produced by the USSR in 1930 and 1980 was very different. There were no jet airliners, no TVs, no nuclear power plants, no computers in 1930, no horse-drawn reapers in 1980. Output in each year can be represented by a list of how much of each type of good was produced: 60×2 engined jets, 8×4 engine jets, 1,600,000 GHhrs electricity, 1,506,000 Lada cars, etc. The problem is not just that there will be items produced in later years that were never thought of in the earlier years; even over shorter periods like five years comparison is hard. Suppose that over a 5-year plan there is a predefined categorization of products, which we could set up as a column of labels in a spreadsheet. In 1975 we list how much of each product was produced in the USSR as a column of figures, and do the same for 1979. How much did the USSR then grow between 1975 and 1979?

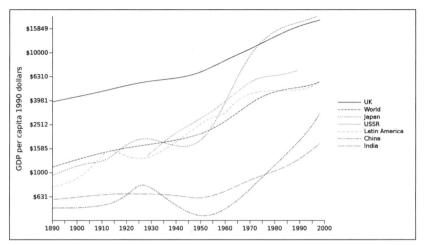

Figure 6.13. GDP per capita figures for some world regions over lifetime of USSR. Source: Maddison, 2001.

There is no definite answer unless all industries grew at the same rate. If for every product code, output in 1979 was 24 percent greater than in 1975 then the economy unambiguously grew at 24 percent. But what if car production grew 50 percent, aircraft production 20 percent, and electricity by 17 percent?

All you can definitely say is that growth was between 17 and 50 percent.

You can try to attach a more precise figure to it by giving all outputs a nominal ruble value and adding these up, but the resulting growth rate will depend heavily on the relative prices you use, and the change in the value of the ruble between 1975 and 1979. [126]

If, instead of inconstant monetary units, you value the output in each year in terms of labor values, you avoid the problem of price inflation, but you are back to the situation of the overall economic growth rate being equal to the growth rate of the hours worked that we have in the simple Feldman model. If technology improves over time, this means that hours worked might fall while the physical output of most industries rose. In terms of labor values the economy would be shrinking even if, in physical terms, it was growing. From the standpoint of state propaganda aimed at showing economic growth, this might be unwelcome.

GDP growth figures combine three processes. First is the movement of labor between the domestic and industrial modes of production. Second, there is the effect of absolute population growth. Third, new technology increases the physical production by each person. If one measures output in terms of GDP per head, this at least compensates for population increase but it still conflates technological innovation with shifts between modes of production.

It is widely believed that at the time the USSR broke up, its GDP per capita was substantially below that of the UK. The contrast between the living standards of the Soviet professional classes compared to their British and other Western counterparts is thought to have discredited the socialist economy. Although Western Europe was an immediate geographical neighbor, in terms of economic history, Latin America or Japan would have been better reference points. Figure 6.13 shows, using data published by the OECD [Maddison, 2001], that in the late nineteenth-century Japan, Latin America, and the then Russian Empire were clustered around the world average in terms of income per head. They fell into a middle-income group, well ahead of China and India, but were far poorer than the UK. Compared to the world average, the Soviet planned system did pretty well. Planning started at the end of the 1920s and finished at the end of the 1980s. The USSR started the period of planned economy with 4/5 the world average income per head, level with Latin America. It ended it 1 1/3 world average. Latin America had tracked the world average. Soviet income per head was 25 percent of the UK level in 1928 but had climbed to 45 percent by 1960. In the next thirty years Soviet incomes roughly tracked UK growth ending at 43 percent of UK levels.

According to the OECD, Soviet long-run rates of income growth were better than those of the UK for most of the USSR's life, slipping back slightly in the 1980s. Internationally the really big success stories were Japan and China. Japan moved from being a middle-income country to overtake the UK by the 1970s despite the severe setback caused by wartime bombing that had razed most of its cities [O'Brien, 2015].

Estimates of the long-term growth of the USSR or estimates of the comparative sizes of the U.S. and Soviet economies in, say, the 1980s are inevitably controversial, with proponents of different political views giving divergent estimates depending on the pricing models that they choose to adopt. Thus the Bezier curves in Figure 6.13 should be interpreted as giving the rough shape of what happened. There are no totally objective answers to these questions. The very idea of precise comparisons between the overall national products of different countries, or different periods, is a monetary illusion.

If instead of looking at monetary estimates of output per head we look at statistics for physical production and consumption we get a rather different picture. Let us look first at food production. Figure 6.14 (top) shows the growth in Soviet production of four big food categories for benchmark years in successive decades. From 1950 to 1970 all categories expanded rapidly. Grain and milk production then leveled off while meat and egg production continued to grow rapidly. The leveling off of grain production appears initially to be a failing, but if we compare the Soviet performance with the

United States the long-term trend of grain production is very similar (Figure 6.14, bottom). As countries become richer they tend to shift their agriculture from starch production to higher-quality protein foods. We see that Soviet output high-quality foods continued to grow after 1970.

But hold on. Figure 6.14 gives only the proportionate growth of output. A rapid growth from a very low base could still leave the USSR with a relatively poor supply of food. How did Soviet food production per person stack up by international standards?

Figure 6.13 shows that monetary estimates of output per head put the early USSR level with South America rather than the UK or the United States. How did things compare in real terms by the end of the USSR?

If we look at production of protein foods per head in Brazil and the USSR in 1988 (Table 6.4) we see that the USSR was substantially ahead for meat, milk, and eggs. That is not surprising. What is surprising, given the poor image that Soviet agriculture had in the West, is that Soviet supplies of these foods had also overtaken the UK and the United States.

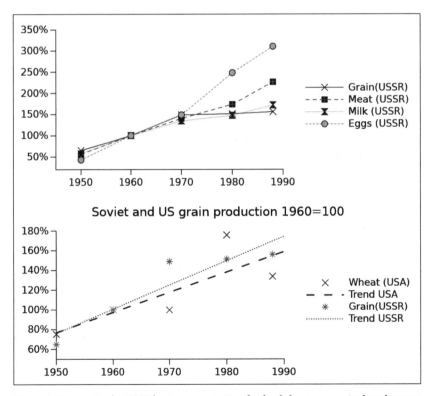

Figure 6.14. Despite the USSR having a reputation for food shortages, agricultural output actually grew rapidly. The growth trend for grain was similar to that of the United States. Source: Pockney, 1991; and USDA database.

TABLE 6.4: Comparison of Late Soviet with UK, Brazil, and U.S. Annual per Capita Output of Major Protein Foods

Country	Year	Meat (Kg)	Milk (Kg)	Eggs (units)
USSR	1988	69	375	299
Brazil	1988	49	96	163
UK	1988	55	265	201
U.S.	1988	58	-	-
U.S.	1990	-	-	236
U.S.	1995	-	259	-

Note that for all categories, the late USSR had better figures. Sources: Pockney, 1991; FAOSTAT and USDA databases.

The Soviets were also relatively successful in the production of consumer durables. Production of TVs, washing machines, and refrigerators increased exponentially in the 1950s and '60s, expanding hundredfold or thousand-fold. Then from the late '60s durables stabilized at levels of several millions a year. But that is not surprising with new products. They start out from a base of zero, and stabilize at a level sufficient to replace wear and tear. Soviet production levels of a range of products stabilized at levels that would allow the majority of households to have a TV, a radio, a washing machine, etc. Compared to the West, the biggest shortfall was in the production of cars. This leveled off at a production level of 1.3 million a year, which was far too low to allow car ownership to be general. At the end of the Soviet period they were producing only about 1 car per 200 inhabitants.

The relative underdevelopment of the car industry in the 1960s can be ascribed to ideological imperatives—the view that private cars were a bour-geois form of transport and that the only acceptable socialist form of car was the public taxi. In the age of global warming, an opposition to widespread car use may again come to seem rational, but in the 1970s with fossil fuels still plentiful, the decision was taken to mass-produce cars. With the ideo-logical objection gone, the default assumption became that in due course every family would have one. The long waiting lists for cars then became a source of discontent, evidence that socialism could not mass-produce cars the way capitalism could.

The failure of the USSR to provide general car ownership was real, and if you accept that car ownership is praiseworthy then the failure was a legiti-mate ground for complaint. But that does not explain why loaves, not Ladas, loomed large as a grievance. The Soviets actually produced more food per head than in the West, so why the discontent?

It comes down to money, and prices. Food was systematically under-priced, with consequences we will describe below.

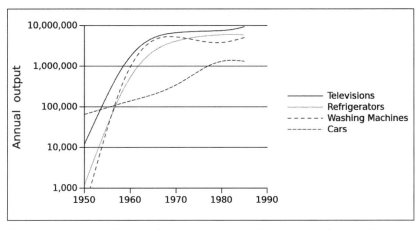

Figure 6.15. Soviet production of major consumer goods. Source: Pockney, 1991.

6.6 WHY THE SOCIALIST ECONOMIES STILL USED MONEY

This leads us on to the question of why socialist economies like the USSR still used money. Money was a

- way of integrating national accounts.
- a means of preparing the accounts of individual factories.
- a means of distributing income to workers.

The official doctrine from Preobrazhenski [1973] to Stalin [1952] was that money was due to be abolished and that it remained only as an auxiliary mechanism of use in state budgeting and trade with the as yet unsocialized sections of the economy.[127] It is easy to see that the overall state budget required some sort of scalar unit of calculation. If you want to make decisions about the overall proportions in which resources are to be distributed between consumption and investment, between civilian and military production, between health and education, you need some unit in which these proportions could be expressed. Money provided that. In principle a socialist economy might have followed Marx's suggestion [1970] and used labor directly as its unit of account, but Preobrazhenskii [1973] was dismissive of this possibility: "Under the mixed system of economy money had a great advantage, and could not be replaced by any 'labor-units' or other artificially conceived methods of calculation."

This is not entirely convincing, since it is hard to see why labor units would have been more artificial than printed paper sheets with numbers of rubles written on them. The state could equally well have issued notes with hours of labor written on them (see Figure 5.20).

Marx had made the slightly enigmatic statement that such notes were no more money than a theater ticket:

The question: Why does not money directly represent labor-time, so that a piece of paper may represent, for instance, x hours' labor, is at bottom the same as the question why, given the production of commodities, must products take the form of commodities? This is evident, since their taking the form of commodities implies their differentiation into commodities and money. Or, why cannot private labor—labor for the account of private individuals—be treated as its opposite, immediate social labor? I have elsewhere examined thoroughly the Utopian idea of "labor-money" in a society founded on the production of commodities [1847]. On this point I will only say further, that Owen's "labor-money," for instance, is no more "money" than a ticket for the theater. Owen presupposes directly associated labor, a form of production that is entirely inconsistent with the production of commodities. The certificate of labor is merely evidence of the part taken by the individual in the common labor, and of his right to a certain portion of the common produce destined for consumption. But it never enters into Owen's head to presuppose the production of commodities, and at the same time, by juggling with money, to try to evade the necessary conditions of that production. [1954, chap. 3]

The implication of this passage from Marx was that he thought that labor notes were practical in the situations where production was "directly associated," which in the Soviet context would mean once the whole economy was nationalized: once private firms and collectives had been replaced by state farms and private handicraft no longer existed. The argument of Preobrazhenskii, and later Stalin, was that these conditions did not exist in either the 1920s or the 1950s, though that does not dispose of the issue. We need to ask why the existence of commodity trade with private or semi-private producers excludes the use of labor units.

Marx's answer [1847] in his polemic against Proudhon had been to argue that in a commodity-producing society without overall direction and planning there was no reason to suppose that overall supply and demand for each commodity will balance. Hence even if a tailor expended 4 hours on a pair of trousers, there is no guarantee that it will sell for 4 hours. If demand is slack he may have to accept a lower price.[128]

This is fair enough as an argument as to why fluctuations in supply and demand must lead to prices oscillating around their labor values, but it does not say why labor units could not have been used in the USSR by the 1970s or somewhat earlier in, for example, East Germany. Nor, more interestingly, does Marx's argument explain why the paper notes issued by the East German and Soviet states were labeled marks and rubles, not hours. At one level the signs on the pieces of paper are arbitrary. With an appropriate monetary and price policy it would have been possible to reissue new currency marked in hours such that, taken on average across the economy, goods sold in the shops for one hour of notes actually had, again on average, required one hour to make.

This would still be money, it would have circulated and could have supported a private or black market. There would have been nothing to prevent it passing from hand to hand like any other paper money. It would thus not have fully met Marx's criterion of being certificates issued to individuals certifying their part in common labor, but the unit of account would at least have ceased to be arbitrary, and the social relations of the economy would have become a bit clearer. But clarity would have been unwelcome to Preobrazhenskii and Stalin. The former developed the policy of "primitive socialist accumulation" under which the the rapid growth of heavy industry was to be funded by forcing the agricultural sector to sell its output at below value. Industrial products were to be sold back above value. If the currency had been denoted in hours it would have been blatantly clear to collective farmers that the state was cheating them. They were being paid for only a fraction of the time expended growing grain.

Marx's objection to Proudhon showed that even were you to denominate the currency in hours, you would still have to leave some leeway for prices oscillating. But that was only part of what the Soviet theorists were alluding to when they said that the prevalence of a collective farm or peasant sector forced them to use money. The real problem was that labor units would have exposed the exploitation of collectives.

There were other more technical problems with the idea of labor certificates. Marx clearly envisaged them being used in an economy in which private trade had been totally eliminated, but if the certificates had just been transferable sheets of paper, they could still have been used for private transactions. Marx seems to have been thinking in terms of some sort of individual nontransferable labor certificate. With modern information technologies it is not hard to see how to do this. Smart cards, terminals, databases keeping the records and software that prohibits transfers between private accounts would do it. But it is quite a lot harder to see how such a system could have been made to work with paper and pencil technologies and a population that was not yet 100 percent numerate.

Something similar to checking accounts would have worked, with people being issued labor checkbooks and writing checks to public stores against their purchases while having their accounts credited by the hours work they had done. But the labor associated with maintaining such a system with paper ledgers and paper reconciliation of accounts each week would have been massive. Paper checks only worked in the capitalist world so long as a) they were used for large purchases, small ones being in cash; b) only a minority of the population had bank accounts. It took computers and databases before it became practical for everyone to have accounts and to pay even for a cup of coffee with an electronic bank payment.

Social relations are always constrained by technology. In the historical socialist economies, possible social relations were constrained by the then existing state of information technology. Coins and banknotes were a much simpler low-tech solution.

It is easy to forget how important it is to have systems of accounting that prevent fraudulent diversion of resources. Socialist economies had to operate what Lenin termed the strictest accounting and control to try to prevent public resources being diverted into private pockets. Take the horrendously complicated payment system in large Soviet shops: the customer picked items they wanted, and the sales assistant gave them a chit, which they took to a cashier's booth elsewhere in the shop. Here they paid for the goods and in return got a receipt which they took to the pickup point and exchanged the receipt for the actual goods. Compared to the way business was done in British or American shops by the 1980s, the USSR seemed to use a system of Byzantine complexity. Not only did you have to interact with staff three times, but the calculations often seemed to use an abacus. Why have such a system?

Such systems were not unknown in the West; some high-class butchers in the UK used it, and the motive in that case was clear. It was for hygiene, since it prevented the counter staff from handling both meat and money. In the USSR, though, it was to provide a paper trail whereby the honesty of the cashier could be checked. At the end of the day the chits and receipts could be reconciled with the cash in the cashier's drawer. The low technology of the abacus and the complicated paperwork were related.

Prior to the development and mass production of cash registers, checking on the honesty of cashiers was a universal problem. In smaller shops, the owner would make sure that he or a close family member worked the till. Large capitalist department stores used the Moscow system. In more advanced ones, the customers did not have to walk up to the till; instead the chit and the cash were dispatched to cashiers in the basement using pneumatic tubes. It was the invention of cash registers that allowed firms to trust their cashiers, since the machine automatically accumulated all transactions, and only opened the till drawer at the end of the transaction. Any dishonesty was revealed at the end of the day by comparing the total on the machine's register with what was in the till.

If they made too few cash registers, then the Soviets had to keep the old paper system. This is partly a reflection of the low priority assigned commercial activity, and thus to its technology. There was a pre-revolutionary history of disdain for trade in Russia, an association of trade with the despised Jews, and an almost complete breakdown of retail organization during the 1920s. Although an attempt was made to modernize and mechanize it in the second 5-year plan, it remained a low priority sector [Randall, 2008]. But the lack of mechanization in trade was symptomatic of a more general slowness in adopting labor-saving techniques.

Labor was not used as efficiently in Soviet industry as it was in the United States or West Germany. In one sense, of course, the USSR used labor very effectively: it had no unemployment and the proportion of women in full-time employment was higher than in any other country. But a developed industrial economy has to be able to transfer labor to where it can be most efficiently used. Under capitalism this is achieved by the existence of a reserve of unemployment, which, though it is inefficient at a macroeconomic level, does allow rapid expansion of new industries.

The Soviet enterprise tended to hoard workers, keeping people on its books just in case they were needed to meet future demands from the planning authorities. This was made possible both by the relatively low level of money wages and because the state bank readily extended credit to cover such costs. The low level of money wages was in turn a consequence of the way the state raised its revenue from the profits of state enterprises rather than from income taxes.

6.7 SOCIALISM OR STATE-OWNED CAPITALISM

This relates to what has long been a controversial issue: Was the Soviet economy a new socialist form of organization or simply a state-owned capitalist one? In Marxist discussions this has been posed in terms of whether the USSR had a new mode of production or not.

Scholars like Hillel Ticktin [2011] hold that socialism is, in principle, a new mode of production but that the existing socialist economies did not have this mode of production and the USSR had no mode of production:

> In socialist and Marxist theory this is both theoretically and technically impossible, as socialism is a global system, a mode of production succeeding capitalism, which can only be implemented on a world

scale. Hence any statement that the USSR, China, Venezuela or Cuba were building socialism does not make sense, unless the building of socialism is implicitly or explicitly re-defined away from Marxism and practically any socialism within the Marxist tradition.

I think that there are many problems with this. First, there is a highly selective narrowing of the Marxist tradition. Ticktin may think that no Marxist would ever have seen the Soviet bloc or China as socialist. But he can only hold that by defining out of existence all those millions who have been members of Communist parties in these countries and who considered themselves to be Marxist. These people were apparently "not part of the Marxist tradition." In effect he is saying nobody who agrees with me could possibly disagree with me.

Well, yes.

At best it is no more than an appeal to authority, and a dubious one at that. It is questionable that Marx even proposed such a thing as a socialist mode of production.[129] He certainly never published any theory of such a mode of production, far less any argument that it could only exist globally. Even if he had argued that, how would he have known that socialism could only exist globally?

There could have been no empirical backing for this alleged theory in the nineteenth century. What is the empirical evidence now to back up such a theory?

This comes down, in part, to what people mean by mode of production. How could any society exist without a mode of production?

If we ask the question "What mode of production did the USSR have?" in the sense of a mode of material production, then it is clear that the mode was electrified machine industry. But we know that this was also the mode of material production in the United States at the same time. So the mode of material production is either not enough to distinguish capitalism from socialism, or socialism must have required some radically different technologies. Ticktin could be arguing the latter—that some as yet unknown technology which can only operate at a global scale is required for socialism. Any claims about technologies yet to be thought of must be rather speculative and would not sit with Ticktin's claim that the USSR had no mode of production at all. Instead, what he means is that a mode of production was something self-sustaining and stable with a unique mode of extracting a surplus product.

I argue that Tictin is fundamentally wrong, the USSR did have a distinct mode of surplus extraction. All societies beyond subsistence level need to produce a surplus and socialist societies are no exception. If we accept Marx's argument that the different economic forms of society are distinguished by the means by which the surplus is produced, then socialist society must have its own form of surplus extraction. It is by looking at actual socialist societies like the USSR that we can grasp what this is.

Socialist planned economy does indeed have a distinct form of surplus extraction. The magnitude of the surplus is determined by the planned allocation of labor between that for the reproduction of the working population versus other activities. This is the inverse of the mechanism that operates under capitalism where the monetary division of the value added between wages and profits comes first. In a capitalist economy the allocation of labor between reproduction and other activities occurs as a second-order effect when the wages and profits are spent. In a socialist economy it is the allocation of labor that comes first. Keynes [2010] was focusing on just this issue with respect to war economy in the passage I cited earlier. He makes it even more clear in another passage from his essay:

> This leads up to our fundamental proposition. There will be a certain definite amount left over for civilian consumption. This amount may be larger or smaller than what perfect wisdom and foresight would provide. The point is that its amount will depend only to a minor extent on the amount of money in the pockets of the public and on their readiness to spend it.

A socialist economy, because a determining part of its economic calculation and control is performed in physical rather than monetary units, has something in common with other economies that were either non-monetary or had limited use of money. The easiest comparison is with classical European feudalism where the labor performed for the lord was distinct in time and space from the work the peasants did for themselves. Money had no influence over it. The peasants' obligations were specified in terms of time or material products. Given the dwarf scale of the feudal division of labor this appears as a direct interpersonal relation between the peasant and the lord. For the socialist economy the determination was impersonal and vast, operating at the scale of a whole continental economy, via the allocation of millions of workers to tens of thousands of branches of production.

Once the amount of labor allocated in the plan to making consumption goods is fixed, no changes in wages, etc., can alter the overall ratio of surplus to necessary labor. If money wages rise without the labor allocation going to consumer goods rising, then the effect is the accumulation of money in people's bank accounts that will ensure a "tight" market in consumer goods. Goods would fly off the shelves but there would be no overall rise in real wages.

The existence of planning introduces a disconnect between monetary relations and value relations, understood as quantities of embodied labor. Money ceases to be a general form of command over labor. For a start, socialist economies have often explicitly prohibited the private employment of workers. In addition, a rise in monetary demand for consumer goods versus means of production will not cause a shift in labor toward consumer goods production. Wages and prices policies then become a matter of controlling monetary demand to make it fit the real product of the consumer goods industries.

6.8 WHY THE LAW OF VALUE APPLIES IN SOCIALIST ECONOMIES

The issue of the role of commodities and money in socialist economies was debated by the Communists in terms of what they called the Law of Value [Stalin, 1952]. The term had exoteric and esoteric meanings. The exoteric, or superficial, meaning is that in a capitalist-type economy, relative labor values will act as attractors for relative prices. The esoteric meaning is that the distribution relations in all societies are constrained by the distribution of labor.[130]

In a capitalist economy the great branches of production subsist by trade and their respective revenues must at least be roughly proportional to the populations they support.

Although in a socialist economy the great bulk of the economy is publicly run, the distribution of the population accross sectors of the economy continues to exert an influence as does the fact that the population still lives in households. This may seem an unexceptional observation, but communist organizations that grew up within previous class societies dispensed with the household as an institution. Think of a monastic community or Owen's New Harmony. In such householdless communities there would be no personal property, as opposed to community property. Food preparation was communal, and childcare was either abolished as in monastic orders or carried out communally. But if you have households then private property of the household is distinct from community property. Since the composition and consumption needs of households differ, it is impractical to give all households a uniform ration of goods. An old couple would have little need for children's shoes or toys, for example. So a socialist economy with households has to allow some flexibility in consumption, which they achieve by distributing a portion of people's income in money. In principle they could have used something other than coins and notes. They could have kept social credit accounts or labor accounts for people, but in all cases many goods for household consumption would have something very like a price.

Figure 6.16. The New Harmony utopian community in Indiana, designed by Robert Owen in 1825.

In a socialist society, then, with households, how does the esoteric aspect of the law of value, the underlying constraint posed by the social division of labor, express itself?

6.8.1 Intersectoral relations

I shall divide the socialist economy into three sectors:

1. The production of means of production.
2. The production of articles of personal consumption that are distributed for sale or charge to individual workers' families. At this point it makes no difference whether the articles are sold for actual money or against the debit of a labor account.
3. The provision of uncharged services such as education, health care, defense, and public infrastructure. This is not to say that being conscripted into the army is not a charge on the conscript, but that they do not individually have to pay in cash or labor credits for their military service. Similarly, education costs adult society time and resources, and costs the pupils a keenly felt loss of playtime, but it is assumed that there are no school fees.

I will use the numbers 1, 2, 3 to denote these sectors. Sectors 1 and 2 produce physical outputs, that is to say, they are materially productive in the sense of Adam Smith's use of the term productive. I will call the output of sector 1 machines, though it also includes all other means of production, and will use the symbol m, in lowercase, to indicate a flow, for the gross output of machines and the stock of machinery and equipment used in the sectors as M_1, M_2, M_3.

Machines wear out. I assume that a fraction (δ) of them wear out each year. So for the sectors the flow of new machines needed to simply stand still is given as $\delta M_1, \delta M_2, \delta M_3$. If the economy is growing there will be some surplus flow of machinery over wear and tear, set aside for growth, which I will call m_g:

$$m_g = m - (\delta M_1 + \delta M_2 + \delta M_3)$$

I will assume that the working population is P divided into P_1, P_2, P_3 working in the three sectors, and that for each year of work the government credits a person with a wage of w, either by paying them cash or by recording some units into their personal consumption account in a database. The state also, for budgetary purposes, has to account for the usage of machinery and equipment in different sectors right down to the individual factories, hospitals, etc. The accounting unit for such charging is assumed to be the same, either money, labor hours, or concievably energy, as is used for personal consumption accounts. I will use c for the charging rate for a machine. This then gives the current accounting costs C_i of each sector, assuming that the government does not charge itself interest, of

$$C_1 = c\delta M_1 + wP_1$$

$$C_2 = c\delta M_2 + w P_2$$

$$C_3 = c\delta M_3 + w P_3$$

The accounting costs of each sector are made up of the charge for the use of publicly owned machinery, and the payments to the people working there. The first is a charge internal to the public sector, but the government has to carry out such sectoral charging if it is to make overall budgetary decisions about the scale of the sectors. The only point at which an actual sale happens, with change of ownership, is when the output of the consumer goods industry is sold to the working population. I will call this the bread or baking industry and label the total output of the industry b and the price of bread p. If we assume for the moment that there is no mechanism by which the working population can save, then we have

$$pb = w(P_1 + P_2 + P_3)\,(1-t)$$

where t is the income tax rate. That is to say, the price of bread times the bread output equals the after-tax income that the working population gets. This is their money wage, but in addition they consume a social wage of education, health care, etc., provided by public sector 3. The equation above gives the price of bread as a function of the money wage.

It is not so obvious how the government should set the charge for machinery used by the public sector, but one simple way is to charge machines at their imputed cost of production:

$$c = C_1 / m$$

The tax revenue plus any profit on sales of consumer goods is then used to cover the cost of the free public services and the net accumulation of new machinery:

$$cm_g + C_3 = tw(P_1 + P_2 + P_3) + pb - C_2$$

We now have 7 equations with 8 unbound variables m_g, c, w, t, p, C_1, C_2, C_3. I assume that m, b, M_1, M_2, M_3, P_1, P_2, P_3, δ are fixed by the actual structure of activity, so in principle the government could fix either the tax rate or the wage rate, but having done that, all the other variables are constrained. Let us look at options. If the socialist country retains money, but delivers many services free, it has to balance the monetary demand in the hands of workers from their wages with the amount of social labor going into consumer commodities. Since a part of the socialist working day had been allocated to producing free goods and services, and another part to the accumulation of new buildings, infrastructure and machinery, the disposable income of the working class had to be limited to the money equivalent of the number of hours spent making consumer commodities. There are, in principle, a number of ways this could be done:

1. By levying an income tax or poll tax on employees [Marx and Engels, 1977; Marx, 1970; Marx and Guesde, 1880].
2. By levying a sales tax, that is, one that is raised as a percentage of the selling price like VAT. [131] Both this and the turnover tax are indirect taxation; they differ in where they are collected: at production or at sale.
3. By pricing all goods at a markup or profit. This profit, since it accrues to state factories, can then become government revenue and be used to fund free services, accumulation, etc. In the USSR this was formalized as a turnover tax levied on all government factories.

There are strong arguments to favor the first option [Cockshott and Cottrell, 1992]. It may initially have been politically popular to claim that under socialism there was no need for income tax, but that is dishonest, since indirect taxation remained. Wages were still held down to a level that would allow the turnover tax to fund government services, so in terms of take-home pay people were no better off. A direct deduction of income tax is more visible, but the converse is that something visible is easier to understand, and as a result easier to make open democratic decisions about.

I will present a simple example and compare the effect of different wage and tax policies.

The technical structure of the economy is assumed to be as given in Table 6.5. We assume machines are depreciated over ten years, so that the current cost of using a machine is machine price ÷ 10.

1. The wage is fixed at 1, this ends up equivalent to valuing things at labor values, no profit is made on the sale of consumer goods, and income taxes are adjusted to meet the cost of the public services and accumulation.

    Solving the equations gives us:

p	c	t	income tax revenue
0.0073	53.3	51%	₱7,666,570

2. In this scenario income tax is abolished and the price of the consumer goods have to rise to cover the shortfall in government revenue. Given that the physical output of consumer goods stays the same, the only effect of reducing income tax is to increase prices. The net effect is that the government raises most of its income from what can either be viewed as a tax on consumer goods or on the profits of nationalized industry. Wages turn out to be the same, as does the charge for means of production, but consumer goods cost almost twice as much.

    Solving the equations gives us:

p	c	t	sales tax revenue
0.015	53.3	0%	₱7,666,570

    The relative prices of machinery and bread now diverge significantly from labor values, with bread being sold at a premium due to the tax being levied on it.

3. In the turnover tax variant—which the USSR used—the tax is levied in both sectors 1 and 2. The tax is determined by the equations:

TABLE 6.5: The Technology Structure Used in the Worked Example of Socialist Reproduction

Sector	People [P]	Machines [M]	Output
1	4,000,000	250,000	100,000 machines
2	6,000,000	250,000	1,000,000,000
3	5,000,000	250,000	no physical output

$$c = (1 + r) \, C_1/m$$

$$p = (1 + r) \, C_2/b$$

The key point is that the tax is levied on both sectors rather than just at the point of sale of consumer goods. This means that the accounting price of means of production is raised by the turnover tax.

Solving the equations gives us:

p	c	t	turnover tax revenue
0.015	117	0%	₱1,086,640

Note that the price of machinery has more than doubled here. The final selling price of bread remains what it would have been under the sales tax variant. Thus the revenue collected from workers remains the same in all cases, but now the government also collects revenue from its factories in sector 1. The revenue collected internally in sector 1 is then all spent internally on the higher costs that sector 3 has to charge for the machines it uses and higher cost of the new investment goods. Because machinery is now more expensive at book prices, the total apparent cost to the government of providing free public services and new investment is substantially higher than before, and needs a correspondingly higher tax revenue.

In all three scenarios the same flows of goods exist, but there are three different sets of relative prices. The extent to which a socialist government can disregard labor values is constrained by the level of tax it levies. If they rely on income tax for public revenue, then sector prices will be proportional to labor values. If they attempt to curtail income tax to a level too low to support public services, then the price of consumer goods has to be raised in what amounts to a sales tax to prevent the accumulation of purchasing power in the hands of the public, and thus suppress inflation. The use of a turnover tax has a generally inflationary effect, which, as we shall see later, holds back the development of labor-saving technology.

But more serious than this, the policy of holding down wages and funding public services out of what can either be considered a turnover tax, or a rate of profit in public factories, had adverse effects on economic efficiency.

In scenario 1 above, where accounting prices are proportional to labor content, the investment charge for a machine was 53 units of labor. If machinery was priced at full value, a rational factory management would cost 5.3 units of labor, the same as one machine, whereas in the turnover tax case a machine is costed at 117 units of labor and a rational manager would treat the use of one machine for a year as equivalent to 11.7 units of labor.

In sector 1, a factory with a technology that uses 960 people and 60 machines to produce 24 new machines. With the income tax the total cost of that technique is booked as 1278, with the turnover tax the booked cost is higher at 1662. For full details, look in Table 6.6.

Suppose a new technology comes along that can make 24 new machines using 140 machines and 200 people. If we cost this out according to the income tax scenario, that is, in terms of labor values, the new technique gives a 26 percent saving. Total booked cost falls from 1,278 to 942, so it is clearly advantageous to switch to the new way of making machines. But with the turnover tax, machines are more than twice as expensive. The cost of additional machines outweighs the big laborsaving the machines bring about.

Note in Table 6.6 that under the income tax scenario the new and highly mechanized technique is cheaper, but under the turnover tax scenario it would appear to be more expensive. Under the turnover tax scheme, a more manual process, of greater social cost will be preferred to the mechanized one. Use of direct labor time calculation would of course have revealed the right answer.

The Soviet solution of a turnover tax was short-term populism that hampered efficiency. In the long run it encouraged the wasteful hoarding of labor by factories since the combination of low wages and subsidization of services and essentials meant that the true cost of labor was hidden. As more free social services were provided, funded by the turnover tax, the

TABLE 6.6: Relative Cost of Two Techniques under the Income Tax and Turnover Tax Scenarios

Machine Cost	Machines	People	With Income Tax 5.3% Total Cost	With Turnover Tax 11.7% Total Cost
Table 6.5 Technique	60	960	1,278	1,662
New Technique	140	200	942	1,838
Saving			26%	−11%

Note that under the income tax scenario, the new and highly mechanized technique is cheaper, but under the turnover tax scenario, it would appear to be more expensive.

wage came to represent a smaller and smaller part of the necessary labor time—the rest being provided free. But this made labor appear cheap and new machinery appear expensive. Rational managers would not replace labor-intensive processes with machines, because using lots of workers seemed more cost effective. Hence chronic overstaffing and poor uptake of more efficient techniques.

The combination of labor value calculation and income tax would have been a much sounder basis for rational economic calculation.

6.8.2 Intra-sectional constraints

Even if you assume that the number of people allocated to make consumption goods does not change, that still leaves considerable flexibility in which consumer goods are made. Asume the intention is to adjust output to consumer wants as expressed by the goods they choose to spend their social credits on. What does this imply for the relative prices of goods?

Should these relative prices correspond to relative labor values?

Yes, they must, for it is only under this condition that the attempted adjustments people make in their consumption will be compatible with the predetermined number of people working making consumer goods. Suppose that one group of goods—say furniture—is systematically undervalued compared to another group of goods, let us say clothes. Suppose clothes are priced at par for labor values and furniture is sold at a 50 percent discount with respect to its labor value. Note that it does not matter if the social credits are measured in hours or in some arbitrary currency units, there will always be some quantity of the currency that, averaged across all prices, represents an hour of embodied labor. Consumers then attempt to shift part of their clothes consumption to furniture. Suppose they cut clothes consumption by the equivalent of 100 million hours of credits, and switch these credits to furniture. Since the furniture is being marked at a 50 percent discount, these 100 million hours of credits switched from clothing appear to be enough to buy furniture that took 200 million hours to make. Even if the workers who in the past worked the 100 million hours in the clothing industry were shifted to make furniture, that would not provide enough additional labor to make 200 million hours' worth of chairs, tables, etc.

More generally, if prices are not proportional to labor values, then shifts in purchases from one good to another will lead either to patterns of demand that are too big to be met with the existing workforce, or if the demand shift goes from undervalued to overvalued goods, to unemployment and part-time working in the consumer goods industry. Some of the socialist states in twentieth-century Europe had chronic problems associated with serious

Figure 6.17. Workers demonstrate with the demand for cheap bread in Poland 1956.

divergences between relative prices and relative labor values. This was particularly prevalent with agricultural products. The great political influence of the urban working classes in socialist societies made it very hard for governments to raise the prices of basic foodstuffs. The Polish protests of 1956, 1970, and 1976 all focused on this issue and in all cases the government backed down and resorted to holding food prices down, in 1976 this was combined with the reintroduction of rationing. In general we can say that if prices do not correspond to values, the excess demand for undervalued items will be greater than what it is possible to produce with the available labor force, technology, etc. In consequence there will be evident shortages that can only be curtailed by rationing.

The Polish case was complicated by the particularly backward state of agriculture there, which right into the 1980s continued to be based on small peasant farms with the low levels of mechanization and high labor intensity that goes with that mode of production. The labor required to produce food was thus relatively high, and a large portion of the population was still tied up in growing it. Look at Figure 6.18 and see the discrepancy between labor used and value added in Polish agriculture. Note that the monetary value added by agriculture is disproportionately low compared to the workforce

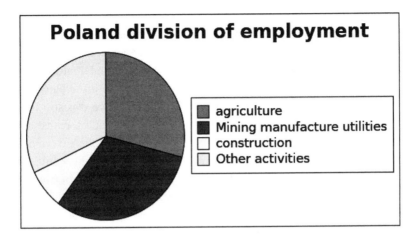

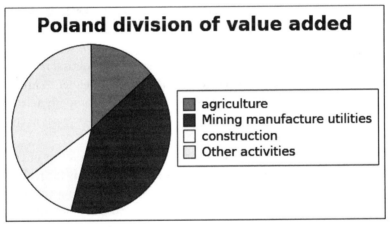

Figure 6.18. Comparison of the distribution of the labor force in Poland in 1981 with the distribution of value added. Source: UN statistical databases.

engaged in it. It is clear that agricultural products were sold well below their values in terms of domestic labor. One can interpret this in two ways:

1. Political pressure from the urban working class held food prices down below what they should have been, given the labor used.
2. The efficiency of Polish agriculture was low by international standards, hence the low value added per unit of labor used. This would presuppose that the international prices of food imports also entered into the calculations made by the government when it set domestic prices.

Whatever the mix of these two causes, the agricultural sector in Poland was selling its output at only 47 percent of its real value in 1981. Poland was a particularly critical example of a socialist country where prices diverged drastically from values. If we compare it with Bulgaria (Figure 6.19), we see that Bulgaria had a much smaller disparity between agricultural prices and agricultural values. Bulgarian agriculture was still undervalued, since its products sold at 74 percent of their true value, but the discrepancy was far lower than in Poland. Unlike Poland, where agriculture was still based on the peasant mode of production, Bulgaria had large-scale socialist agriculture, which was markedly more efficient in its use of labor. I traveled in both countries during the early 1980s and it was very evident that while food appeared to be in very short supply in Poland, it was plentiful in Bulgaria. The food shops in Poland were relatively bare, whereas those in Bulgaria seemed loaded with produce. Political discontent about food was a repeated occurrence in Poland, and absent in Bulgaria.

It is the development of the productive forces and forms of cooperation that determine the values of goods. The available technology determines the minimum amount of labor that society has to use to make something and this will hold true even if property relations change. If a political revolution occurs in a country, there is no corresponding change in either technology or in cooperation. That can only come later as the new property relations shape the introduction of technology or cause the rise of new types of cooperative work—like collective farms or People's Communes.

So we are talking about the long term, over which new forms of cooperation and technology are introduced. In a socialist economy the really big decisions about this are political not economic. Collectivizing agriculture and introducing tractors, combine harvesters and so on in Bulgaria was a political decision. Forming People's Communes in China and engaging in large-scale irrigation and land reclamation was a political decision. These decisions led to improvements in productivity but it was not the discipline of the market that brought it about. The actual labor productivity in a sector will be a random variable. If the minimum labor required shifts due to new technology then, unless the dispersion of the random variable increases over time, the mean also goes down. I emphasize minimum as the leading edge of technical change shifts the minimum requirement. But on accounting grounds you have to charge goods at the average labor content, not the minimum content.

On the other hand, in countries where a reverse political decision was made, as in Poland in 1956 where Gomulka decided to abandon collectivization, as a result agriculture remained peasant farms. I recall flying over the country in 1980 and saw two types of fields from the air. In areas that prior to 1945 had been part of Prussia, there were large square fields of the former aristocratic estates, but over most of the country one saw strip field

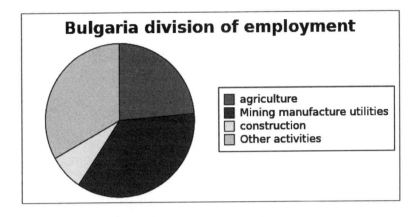

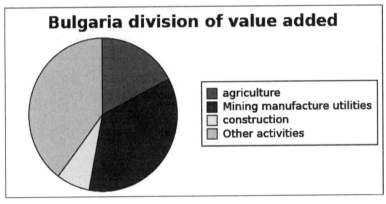

Figure 6.19. Comparison of the distribution of the labor force in Bulgaria in 1981 with the distribution of value added. Source: UN statistical databases.

systems characteristic of agriculture from the Middle Ages. This form of property relations could not develop the productivity of labor effectively. In consequence a large part of the overall social working day was devoted to growing food (see Figure 6.18). Roughly a third of the total working day went on that.

On the other hand political pressure from the working class meant that food had to be sold cheaply—I remember that in 1980 the prices were ridiculously low by our standards. This meant that in terms of the selling prices, the farming sector—one-third of the economy—sold its output at well below its value. In selling price, the apparent value added by agriculture was around 12 percent of the GDP. So there was a big discrepancy between price and true labor value. If the population attempted to devote 20 percent of total income to food, which was easily affordable at the prices prevailing, then peasant agriculture could not have supported that. An expenditure of 20 percent of income would be a rise in demand by two-thirds and would have required two-thirds more labor on the land to produce it—quite impossible.

I give Poland as an example because it is the most striking instance of a socialist government attempting to ignore value in setting prices in the state shops. That was a political decision, and the effects it produced were also political—chronic shortages as shops were quickly sold out of meat. This in turn produced discontent that could be harnessed by those arguing for the return of a full capitalist system. The irony was that the consumption of meat per capita in Poland was actually greater than in Scotland at the time, and there were no complaints about meat shortages in Scotland. The point I am making is that the temptation to say you can ignore labor value in a socialist economy should never be given way to. Its results are politically disastrous.

How can you plan with the Law of Value?

The answer depends on whether you are talking about the exoteric or esoteric interpretation of the term. The esoteric interpretation is that the law of value is an expression of something deeper—the proportions in which the social workforce is distributed between different concrete activities. Planning with the law of value is in this sense planning the distribution of social labor, and ensuring that the social labor is used effectively. [132] As compared to the traditional Soviet techniques this would have involved several important differences:

1. Accounting for all products in terms of embodied social labor and ensuring that the selling prices of consumer goods is proportional to the labor embodied. It is only under these circumstances that shifts in consumer demand between products is labor conserving.
2. Using labor time as the general unit of account, with some form of nontransferable personal labor accounts.
3. Charging factories for the total labor used by abolishing the distinction between labor and labor power. If money wages are paid then labor appears undervalued since labor power has a lower value than the labor itself. This biases the choice of techniques toward inefficient labor-intensive ones.
4. Setting goals for output of consumer goods modulated by the shifts in spending of labor tokens.
5. Giving factory collectives hard labor budgets. They would have a budget in hours to achieve a given physical output, but they would be free to select between using living labor or machinery evaluated at its labor content to do so. If they overused their budget they would face staffing transfers, with individuals being transferred to other collectives where their labor was more socially necessary.

Labor time accounting demystifies or de-fetishizes social relations. Rather than relations appearing to be between people and an objective thing called money, they make it evident that what is involved are people's lives. If I get one hour of social credit for each hour I work, and can for this credit acquire goods that took an hour to make, then it is clear that I am participating as an equal in social exchange. If I am only credited with 40 minutes' time for working an hour, it is clear that there is something odd going on. If the difference is made of a 33 percent income tax that I had a chance to vote on, that is one thing. If instead I see that someone else is getting credited with more than an hour for each hour that they work, I am going to be asking some hard questions.

Labor time accounting has a presumption of equality and equity. If one person gets credited more than they actually work, the *a priori* implication is that there is something dodgy about it. Its adoption would thus involve a big pressure toward leveling: between different categories of work and leveling between men and women. It of course eliminates completely the possibility of unearned capital income. It makes the moral presumption that labor is the only legitimate source of income. Any other income, to the old, the sick, to families with children, has to be an explicit voluntary deduction from the incomes of those who work.

The significance of labor tokens is that they establish the obligation on all to work by abolishing unearned incomes; they make the economic relations between people transparently obvious; and they are egalitarian, ensuring that all labor is counted as equal. It is the last point that ensured labor tokens were never adopted under the bureaucratic state socialisms of the twentieth century. What ruler or manager was willing to see his work as equal to that of a mere laborer?

There is nothing terribly original in this scheme, which is set out briefly here, but in much more detail elsewhere. It is simply a detailed and literal elaboration of the proposals Marx [1970] made in his comments on the draft of the 1875 program of the German Socialists.

The assumption is that people would have electronic labor credit cards whose credits could only be cancelled out, not circulated. You could not pay credits into somebody else's account but you could get things from communal stores. This completely eliminates the possibility of a black market.

It is absolutely essential that distribution labor values of goods be realistic. A socialist government must avoid the temptation to undervalue necessities in the communal stores. If they are undervalued, there will be excess purchasing power in terms of labor credits. If bread used 300 million person hours to make but was sold for 100 million hours, an excess of 200 million credits would have been issued to the bakers, millers, farmers, etc.

Such undervaluation, we know from bitter experience, just leads to queues and apparent shortages.

If prices are equal to labor content, then deviations of sales from actual production can be used to adjust plan targets on a real-time basis, reallocating labor from products whose demand falls short of production to those that are selling out.

Deviations of distribution price from labor content would, however, still occur in a planned economy for environmental reasons. If the planning system had a constraint that total production of fossil fuel had to decline by 2 percent a year, then the planning authorities would be forced either to raise the distribution price of fuel above its labor content or to ration petrol. If petrol was distributed at a premium, goods that did not contain fossil fuels would have to be distributed to consumers at a discount. There might be a case for the environmental premiums or discounts being displayed on the label.

Free distribution of goods and services is only viable for those goods or services for which certain special conditions are met. The actual allocation can be rationed by deliberate decisions or by queues—this is how the NHS is able to function. You can get free treatment but only if a doctor decides you need it and you are willing to wait your turn. This rules out, for example, resources being wasted on penis or breast enlargement surgery, where the actual usage is easily calculable. We know that demand for primary schooling is set by the number of children reaching school age. Making schools free increased demand up to this limit and no further. The resources being used would otherwise go to waste. Examples are the free district heating provided in the USSR from waste heat of power stations; providing free travel to pensioners outside of rush hours; free use of Internet once the basic infrastructure has been installed.

6.9 CRISIS OF SOCIALISM AND EFFECTS OF CAPITALIST RESTORATION

The main criticism leveled at the socialist economies was that a planned economy was inherently less efficient than a market one, due to the sheer scale of the bureaucratic task involved with planning a major economy. If there are hundreds of thousands, or perhaps millions, of distinct products, no central planning authority could hope to keep track of them all. Instead they were forced to set gross targets for the outputs of different industries. For some industries like gas or electric power, this was not a problem. Electricity and gas are undifferentiated, a kilowatt is a kilowatt—no argument. But even for another bulk industry like steel, there was a wide variety of different rolled plates and bars, different grades of steel with different tensile strength, etc. If the planners could not keep track of all these different varieties and just set rolling mills targets in tons, the mills would maximize their tonnage of whatever variety was easiest to produce.

The steel example is a little forced, since this degree of differentiation was still fairly readily handled by conventional administrative means. Tonnage targets could still be set in terms of distinct types of steel. But when you turn to consumer goods—clothes, crockery etc., the range of products was too big and targets were started set in terms of monetary output.

The plan would specify a growth in the value of output of clothing, furniture, etc. What this translated to then depended on the price structure. In order to prevent other forms of gaming the plan by enterprises it was important that the prices were economically realistic. If the price for chairs is set too high compared to tables, it becomes rational for factories to concentrate on chair production.

By resorting to monetary targets, the socialist economies were already conceding part of Mises's argument. They were resorting to the monetary calculation that he had declared to be vital to any economic rationality. Liberal economists argue that it was impossible for planners to come up with a rational set of prices, as only the competitive market could do so. Planning required aggregation. Aggregation implied monetary targets. Monetary targets required rational prices. Rational prices required the market. But if you had the market you could dispense with planning. Planning dialectically implied the supersession of planning.

It is worth noting that this is a largely theoretical argument. It was, in late Soviet days, backed up with lots of anecdotal evidence, but empirical evidence for the greater macroeconomic efficiency of markets even when compared to classical Soviet planning is on much thinner ground. As Allen [2003] shows, the only capitalist economy whose long-term growth rate exceeded that of the USSR was Japan, whose own model was some way from unplanned capitalism. Compared to other countries starting out at the same economic level in the 1920s, the USSR grew considerably faster. One could argue that this was due to marcroeconomic advantages of planning, that is, by removing uncertainty about future market demand it encouraged a higher level of investment. It is possible that this macroeconomic advantage outweighed any microeconomic inefficiency associated with plans.

The strongest evidence that markets may perform better than plans would come from China, and that certainly is the orthodox Chinese view. Their claim is that a socialist market economy avoids the macroeconomic instability of capitalism while harnessing the microeconomic efficiency of the market. As evidence they cite a higher rate of growth after Deng's restructuring. But China since Deng has followed a mercantilist road. It has the effect of beggaring the workers of China whose products are exported to the United States in return for U.S. paper. The latter is of no benefit for the Chinese workers, though it does enable private Chinese companies to buy up assets in the United States. From the standpoint of the Chinese state it is a more nuanced issue. On the one hand Chinese state companies can buy up overseas firms, but whether this is a long-term advantage is a moot point since real goods which could have been used to improve the Chinese economy and living standards have been sacrificed.

Historically the process of having an export-led economy allowed China to avoid the technology bans that the West imposed on the USSR, allowing rapid catch-up in manufacturing techniques. Now that China is overtaking the United States in some areas of mass production, that advantage is less clear, and a shift toward higher domestic consumption and higher wages makes sense, and is indeed being followed in China, unlike Germany. It could be that the growth advantage that China experienced post-Deng owed a lot to a new ability to import the latest productive techniques instead of microeconomic efficiency. But what is abundantly clear is that the pro-market restructuring had the effect of drastically widening economic inequalities and giving rise to a new domestic billionaire class. This in turn produces political pressure to extend private ownership and undermine the still dominant position of state industry.

So the question arises, could a planning system work in a modern economy with a highly diversified product range, and how would it overcome the socialist calculation argument of Mises? I and others have since the late 1980s been arguing that the answer is yes.

The Mises critique of socialism focused on the need to compare the costs of alternative ways of making things. Unless you can do that you cannot choose the most efficient. Our response has been not only that labor time in principle is an alternative, which Mises conceded, but that with modern computer technology it is perfectly possible to maintain up-to-date figures for the labor cost of each input to the production process. Using these, workplaces will have data that are as good as prices for choosing between techniques.

There are limitations to labor values as there are to any scalar measure like price, since the constraints on production are multifactorial. Not only labor power, but also natural resources and ecological considerations constrain what we can make. No single scalar measure can handle this. But the problem of how to deal with multiple constraints like this was already solved by socialist economics way back in the 1930s. Kantorovich came up with a completely general technique for how to meet a socialist plan subject to constraints additional to labor time.[133] Kantorovich's method is a form of in-kind calculation, that is, non-monetary. It was not practical to use it at the level of the whole Soviet economy during his lifetime as the computing resources were too poor, but by the 1990s computers were up to the job. [134]

So the basic problem of socialist economic calculation without money had been solved since Mises wrote. It was impractical in the USSR for two reasons: 1) the computer technology was not there; 2) it would have involved replacing money calculation and payment with nontransferable labor accounts. This would have been a radical step toward greater social equality.

The collapse of the Soviet and later the Russian economy under Gorbachev and then Yeltsin was an economic disaster that was otherwise unprecedented in time of peace. The world's second superpower was reduced to the status of a minor bankrupt economy with a huge decline in industrial production and in living standards. Nothing brings out the scale of the catastrophe better than the demographic data that show a huge rise in the mortality rate brought about by the poverty, hunger, homelessness, and alcoholism that these brought in their wake (Table 6.7).

In determining what caused this one has to look at long-term, medium-term and short-term factors that led to relative stagnation, crisis, and then collapse. The long-term factors were structural problems in the Soviet economy and required reforms to address them. The actual policies introduced by the Gorbachev and Yeltsin governments, far from dealing with these problems, actually made the situation catastrophically worse.

6.9.1 Long term

During the period from 1930 to 1970, and excluding the war years, the USSR experienced rapid economic growth. There is considerable dispute about just how fast the economy grew, but it is generally agreed to have grown significantly faster than the UK between 1928 and 1975, with the growth rate slowing down to the UK level after that. This growth took the USSR from a peasant country whose level of development had been comparable to Brazil in 1922 to becoming the world's second industrial and technological and military power by the mid-1960s.

A number of reasons contributed to this relative slowdown in growth in the latter period.

It is easier for an economy to grow rapidly during the initial phase of industrialization when labor is being switched from agriculture to industry. Afterward growth has to rely upon improvements in labor productivity in an already industrialized economy, which are typically less than the difference in productivity between agriculture and industry. I discussed this earlier in the context of the Feldman theory.

A relatively large portion of Soviet industrial output was devoted to defense, particularly in the latter stages of the Cold War, when they were in competition with Reagan's "Star Wars" programs. The skilled manpower used up for defense restricted the number of scientists and engineers who could be allocated to inventing new and more productive industrial equipment.

The United States and other capitalist countries imposed embargoes on the supply of advanced technological equipment to the USSR. This meant that the USSR had to rely to an unusually high degree on domestic designs of equipment. In the West there were no comparable barriers to the export of technology so that the industrial development of the Western capitalist countries was synergistic.

Although Soviet industrial growth in the 1980s slowed down to U.S. levels, this by itself was not a disaster; after all the United States had experienced this sort of growth rate (2.5 percent a year) for decades without crisis. Indeed, while working-class incomes in the United States actually stagnated over the 1980s, in the USSR they continued to rise. The difference was in the position of the intelligentsia and the managerial strata in the two countries. In the United States income differentials became progressively greater, so that the rise in national income nearly all went to the top 10 percent of the population. The bulk of the working class in the United States has seen its income stagnate for half a century (Figure 5.14). In the USSR income differentials were relatively narrow, and while all groups continued to experience a rise in incomes, this was much smaller than had been the case in the 1950s and 1960s. This 2.5 percent growth was experienced by some of the Soviet intelligentsia as intolerable stagnation—perhaps because they compared themselves with managers and professionals in the United States or Germany. A perception thus took root among this class that the socialist system was failing when compared to the United States.

Again, this would not have been critical to the future survival of the system were it not for the fact that these strata were disproportionately influential within the USSR. Although the ruling Communist Party was notionally a workers' party, a disproportionately high proportion of its members were drawn from the most skilled technical and professional employees, and manual workers were proportionally underrepresented.

The slowdown in Soviet growth was in large measure the inevitable result of economic maturity, a movement toward the rate of growth typical of mature industrial countries. A modest program of measures to improve the efficiency of economic management would probably have produced some recovery in the growth rate, but it would have been unrealistic to expect the rapid growth of the 1950s and 1960s to return. What the USSR got, however, was not a modest program of reform, but a radical demolition job on its basic economic structures. This demolition job was motivated by neoliberal ideology. Neoliberal economists, both with the USSR and visiting from the United States, promised that once the planning system was removed and once enterprises were left free to compete in the market, then economic efficiency would be radically improved.

TABLE 6.7: Excess Deaths as a Consequence of the Introduction of Capitalism in Russia

Year	Thousands Deaths	Excess Relative to 1986
1986	1,498	0
1987	1,531	33
1988	1,569	71
1989	1,583	85
1990	1,656	158
1991	1,690	192
1992	1,807	309
1993	2,129	631
1994	2,301	803
1995	2,203	705
1996	2,082	584
1997	2,105	607
1998	1,988	490
1999	2,144	646
2000	2,225	727
2001	2,251	753
2002	2,332	834
2003	2,365	867
2004	2,295	797
2005	2,303	805
2006	2,166	668
2007	2,080	582
2008	2,075	577
2009	2,010	512
Total	48,388	12,436

Figures amount to some 12 million deaths over 20 years.
Source: Successive *UN Demographic Yearbook(s)*, Table 18.

6.9.2 Medium term

The medium-term causes of Soviet economic collapse lay in the policies that the Gorbachev government embarked on in its attempts to improve the economy. The combined effect of these policies was to bankrupt the state and debauch the currency.

One has to realize that the financial basis of the Soviet state lay mainly in the taxes that it levied on turnover by enterprises and on sales taxes.

In an effort to stamp out the heavy drinking that led to absenteeism from work and to poor health, the Gorbachev government banned alcohol. This and the general tightening up of work discipline led, in the first couple of years of his government, to some improvement in economic growth. It had, however, unforeseen side effects. Since sales of vodka could no longer take place in government shops, a black market of illegally distilled vodka sprang up, controlled by the criminal underworld. The criminal class that gained money and strength from this later turned out to be a most dangerous enemy.

While money from the illegal drinks trade went into the hands of criminals, the state lost a significant source of tax revenue, which, because it was not made up by other taxes, touched off an inflationary process.

Were the loss of the taxes on drinks the only problem for state finance, it could have been solved by raising the prices of some other commodities to compensate. But the situation was made worse when, influenced by the arguments of neoliberal economists, Gorbachev allowed enterprises to keep a large part of the turnover tax revenue that they owed the state. The neoliberals argued that if managers were allowed to keep this revenue, they would make more efficient use of it than the government.

What actually ensued was a catastrophic revenue crisis for the state, which was forced to rely on the issue of credit by the central bank to finance their current expenditure. The expansion of the money stock led to rapid inflation and the erosion of public confidence in the economy. Meanwhile, the additional unaudited funds in the hands of enterprise managers opened up huge opportunities for corruption. The Gorbachev government had recently legalized worker cooperatives, allowing them to trade independently. This legal form was then used by a new stratum of corrupt officials, gangsters, and petty businessmen to launder corruptly obtained funds.

6.9.3 Results

Liberal theory held that once enterprises were free from the state, the "magic of the market" would ensure that they would interact productively and efficiently for the public good. But this vision of the economy greatly overstated the role of markets. Even in so-called market economies, markets of the sort described in economics textbooks are the exception restricted to specialist areas like the world oil and currency markets. The main industrial structure of an economy depends on a complex interlinked system of regular producer-consumer relationships in which the same suppliers make regular deliveries to the same customers week in, week out.

In the USSR this interlinked system stretched across two continents, and drew into its network other economies: East Europe, Cuba, North Vietnam. Enterprises depended on regular state orders, the contents of which might be dispatched to other enterprises thousands of miles away. Whole towns and communities across the wilds of Siberia relied on these regular orders for their economic survival. Once the state was too bankrupt to continue making these orders, once it could no longer afford to pay wages, and once the planning network that had coordinated these orders was removed, what occurred was not the spontaneous self-organization of the economy promised by liberal theory, but a domino process of collapse.

Without any orders, factories engaged in primary industries closed down. Without deliveries of components and supplies secondary industries could no longer continue production, so they too closed. In a rapid and destructive cascade, industry after industry closed down. The process was made far worse by the way the USSR split into a dozen different countries all with their own separate economies. The industrial system had been designed to work as an integrated whole; split up by national barriers it lay in ruins.

TABLE 6.8: Output of Selected Branches of Industry in Russia in 2003 Compared to 1998 (1990=100)

Industry	Output
Total Industry	66
Electric Power	77
Gas	97
Oil extraction	94
Oil Refining	70
Ferrous Mettallurgy	79
Non-Ferrous Metallurgy	80
Chemicals and Petrochemicals	67
Machine Building	54
Wood and Paper	48
Building Materials	42
Light Industry	15
Food	67

Source: Goskomstat, 2004, Table 14.3.

The figures in Table 6.8 show how far the economy had regressed in 2003. These figures show how little recovery there had been, even after 13 years of operation of the free market.

If the economy had continued to grow even at the modest rate of the later Brezhnev years, say 2.5 percent, then industrial production would, on this scale, have stood at 140 percent of 1990 levels. The net effect of thirteen years of capitalism was to leave Russia with half the industrial capacity that could have been expected even from the poorest performing years of the socialist economy.

CHAPTER 7

Future Economies

In the social production of their existence, men inevitably enter into definite relations, which are independent of their will, namely relations of production appropriate to a given stage in the development of their material forces of production. The totality of these relations of production constitutes the economic structure of society, the real foundation, on which arises a legal and political superstructure and to which correspond definite forms of social consciousness. The mode of production of material life conditions the general process of social, political and intellectual life. It is not the consciousness of men that determines their existence, but their social existence that determines their consciousness. At a certain stage of development, the material productive forces of society come into conflict with the existing relations of production or this merely expresses the same thing in legal terms with the property relations within the framework of which they have operated hitherto. From forms of development of the productive forces these relations turn into their fetters. Then begins an era of social revolution. The changes in the economic foundation lead sooner or later to the transformation of the whole immense superstructure.—MARX ET AL., 1978, PREFACE

What distinguishes a utopian approach to social transformation from a materialist one is that the latter must start with the real contradictions that exist between technological imperatives and the social forms that currently exist. These specify not a future that might be desired, but what may be required.

One therefore has to start with technology complexes and demographics since all social formations combine a particular set of technologies with a particular density of human population. Only some technology complexes are compatible with a given population density. Our current population could not survive on the basis of pastoralism; so much is obvious. Nor can the present population long survive on the basis of an extractive fossil-fuel economy.

The consequences of the existing economy for climate change, food security, and health are so severe that even with the existing social relations, something historically unprecedented is happening. International organizations, particularly the IPCC (International Panel on Climate Change) are embarked on a coordinated scientific investigation of how, at a broad level, the technology complex of the world would have to be shaped to allow a world economy that is sustainable in terms of climate, health, and food security. This involves a huge effort to build complex, in natura, models of the world economy,[135] the sort of thing that Neurath [1919] speculated about one hundred years ago.

Several scenarios, called Representative Concentration Pathways (RCP), have been modeled, depending on the radiative forcing per square meter[136] involved with different concentrations of greenhouse gases. So, for example, the hottest model is RCP8.5 involving an 8.5 watt per square meter forcing by 2100. The model that would, it is hoped, keep temperature rises under 2 degrees is RCP2.6, which requires significant emission reductions, essentially ending all net fossil fuel emissions by the end of the century, with an immediate start to reductions this decade. Van Vuuren et al. [2011] claim that there is sufficient technical potential to achieve these emission reductions. CO_2 emissions could, they suggest, be reduced by a combination of energy efficiency, use of renewables, a lot more nuclear power, and most critically, bioenergy with carbon capture and storage. In principle, bioenergy with carbon capture could actually start reducing atmospheric CO_2.

I will take the targets of RCP2.6 as a starting point for discussion, before examining the plausibility of actually achieving them with the proposed technical means and policy mechanisms.

7.1 TECHNOLOGY COMPLEX

Contemporary capitalism is heavily dependent on fossil fuels. Almost 90 percent of world primary energy comes from these sources, and the percentage coming from nuclear and renewable sources has if anything tended to fall slightly in recent years. Industry and commerce use about 60 percent of all primary energy; transport and residential use around 20 percent each.

The current mature alternatives to fossil fuels are nuclear energy and hydropower. The latter has severe geographical limitations. The limitations to the use of nuclear power are on the one hand political opposition, and on

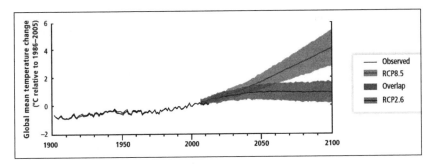

Figure 7.1. High and low RCP projections. Lower projection is necessary to keep anthropogenic climate rise below 2 degrees. Source: Field et al., 2014, Fig. SPM.4.

the other the small number of countries and firms that have the ability to commission nuclear plants. In terms of cost it is already competitive with coal power for electricity.[137]

The the two rapidly maturing alternative energy sources are solar and wind power. Prices of both of these have been falling rapidly and in the United States are already competitive with coal for electricity generation when measured as levelized costs. Both of these depend for their yield on the local wind and sunshine, and so will vary from place to place.

Although Van Vuuren et al. [2011] put great emphasis on carbon capture and storage as a mechanism that will allow green house gas emission targets to be met, this is one of the least developed techniques so far. Although there is experience of injecting CO_2 into oil reservoirs for enhanced recovery, there is as yet little practical experience in operating full-scale coal-fired power stations far from oil reservoirs, extracting the CO_2, and then piping it to appropriate injection sites. The components are plausible, but the working experience that, for example, nuclear power has, is absent. There are clearly hazards associated with the subsequent escape of carbon dioxide from subterranean reservoirs, as shown by the Lake Nyos disaster [Baxter et al., 1989] where 1,700 people were killed by a sudden escape of the gas.

However, given the good progress being made in other areas, it seems plausible that, at least for electricity generation, a combination of nuclear, solar, and wind power could replace a large part of current dependence on coal.

Marx claimed that the stage of development of technology is what ultimately determines the bounds on social relations. He believed that communism was the likely future of industrial society and that coal-powered steam engines were the foundation of capitalist economy. Is there anything about the transition to a post-fossil fuel economy that would favor communism over capitalism?

The USSR depended heavily on large-scale integrated production both of energy and other products. The economic regression that followed the establishment of capitalism made it clear that capitalist property relations were incapable of sustaining this form of the productive forces. The one industry that did relatively well in the new capitalist Russia was fossil fuel extraction.

The USSR did have long-term plans for non-fossil energy sources: nuclear, thermonuclear, and orbiting solar power stations. All of these are post-capitalist forms of energy production in the sense that their development has depended on socialist economy in the East or in the West on state-sponsored development: AEC in the United States or the AEA in the UK for nuclear power. Thermonuclear power research has been overwhelmingly state-funded, and the most promising reactor design, the Tokamak, was invented in the USSR and forms the basis for the international ITER experimental power reactor [Azizov, 2012]. Orbiting solar power stations [Glaser et al., 1974] were a futuristic technology much talked about in the 1970s and 1980s. They would overcome the limitations of day and night and bad weather by being bathed in permanent sunlight, and would beam energy to Earth as microwaves. The ultimate Soviet space launcher, Energiya, was seen as the tool to build such orbiting stations [Hendrickx and Vis, 2007].

So we could hypothesize that the energetic basis of Communist economy would be orbiting solar power stations and huge Tokamaks able to supply essentially limitless energy from the deuterium in sea water. This is a pair of technologies that private capital has been unable to develop because of the huge initial investment, over many decades, before any possible profit could be returned. It would

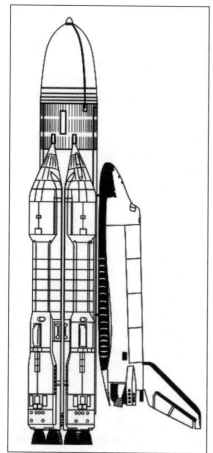

Figure 7.2. The Soviet Energiya launcher, designed to release orbiting solar power plants. The *Buran* shuttle is shown attached.

moreover, be a highly capital-intensive path and, as I have established in Section 5.9, high-capital intensity is associated with low profitability, which deters private firms.

The development costs of the scale associated with thermonuclear power are so large that they are beyond even what individual nations can afford. The only practical project to build a thermonuclear reactor, ITER, is being constructed by a consortium of 35 states. ITER was started at the initiative of the USSR at the Geneva Superpower Summit in November 1985.

Figure 7.3. Model of the ITER reactor. Note tiny human figure for scale. Photo: Stephan Mosel, Creative Commons.

Design work took from 1988 to 2001. In 2005 it was agreed that the site of the reactor would be in France. In 2010 construction started near Aix-en-Provence. It will be the largest and most complex machine ever constructed. The first plasma is scheduled to be generated in 2025 but it is not anticipated to use actual deuterium/tritium plasma to generate useful power until 2035. The whole project will thus have taken fifty years to yield power. But prior to ITER being formed there had already been a 35-year Soviet history of development of the technology since Sakharov and Tamm initially proposed the design in 1950.

The development of thermonuclear plasma reactors is something that private capitalism could not have done. It required foresight based on an appreciation of future human needs that only public bodies, indeed a world public body, could undertake.

Solar and wind power can, in contrast, be developed piecemeal with relatively modest capital costs. A such, private firms are quite willing to invest, given modest initial government incentives. We do not know yet whether these lower-tech approaches to alternative energy will be enough to power future civilization. If they are enough, then other than international political sanctions restricting fossil fuels, there will be nothing in the energy base that militates against the perpetuation of private ownership. If it turns out that the supply of energy from wind and sun is too intermittent, too dependent on the seasons, or too deficient at night, then fusion power will be the most plausible way of providing base load power. If energy storage technologies, either batteries, pumped storage, compressed air storage, or even flywheel storage, develop fast enough, fusion may not be needed.

This possibility gives rise to fantasies about self-sufficiency and a society of people who are economically self-sufficient, living off-grid. The idea breaks down as soon as it is examined in detail. Solar power only brings an element of self-sufficiency to those with enough capital to buy the panels, and enough roof area or free land to install it on. It is not an option for urban dwellers in rented flats or for those who cannot afford the initial capital. While owners of houses with big roofs will be able to reduce their electricity purchases, electric grids will still be needed for industry, telecoms, offices, electric railways, and the like.

7.1.1 Materials

Industrial society is heavily dependent on materials whose production either uses fossil fuel or unavoidably emits carbon dioxide. In the nineteenth-century industrial buildings and housing in industrialized nations were largely built from brick. Brick production involved the mixing of clays with ground coal which was then dried and sintered in kilns, with the coal in the mixture providing a large part of the fuel.

In the twentieth century concrete became the main building material. But this too involves a lot of energy in its construction. Concrete is a mixture of sand, stones, and cement powder. Cement powder is the biggest energy consumer here. The process involves heating limestone to disassociate the $CaCO_3$ it contains to produce $CaO + CO_2$. This obviously involves a direct release of carbon dioxide. The process requires between 4GJ/ton and 7GJ/ton of energy [Worrell et al., 2001]. This energy is currently supplied by fossil fuels with on the order of 5 percent of world industrial energy involved in the process. Worrell estimated that in 1994 around 5 percent of total carbon dioxide emissions worldwide came from cement production. For China something between 7 percent and 9 percent of all emissions are from cement making. [Liu et al., 2015]

It is in principle possible to produce cement without carbon dioxide by a combination of solar heating to melt limestone and then electrolysis by the Solar Thermal Electrochemical Process (STEP) [Licht et al., 2012]. By choice of temperature one can obtain the electrolytic transformation $Ca\,CO_3 \rightarrow CaO + C + O_2$ with elemental carbon and oxygen being released. Assuming that the carbon produced was buried, the overall process would be carbon neutral. [138] If operated in a strictly carbon-neutral fashion the cost of cement produced this way would be two to three times as great as with current methods.

Steel has been the fundamental metal of industrial society, used in making machinery, ships, bridges, cars, and in the construction industry. Today steel production comes from the basic oxygen process and the electric arc process. The basic oxygen process refines pig iron produced in blast furnaces into structural steel, though a portion of the feedstock is recycled scrap steel. Electric arc furnaces work entirely with recycled scrap. In the United States around 70 percent of all steel output is from recycled sources. The remaining 30 percent comes from the processing of iron ore. The iron oxide in the ore is reduced to metallic iron using carbon, currently in the form of coke, though charcoal was used in the past. As such the process inevitably emits carbon dioxide: the coke provides the fuel to heat the furnace, and because carbon monoxide, produced by burning the coke, is the reducing agent.

If we assume that the world will require drastic reductions in CO_2 emissions, this implies:

- That the steel industry will have to become overwhelmingly based on recycling, supplemented with only such small amounts of basic steel as can be produced from charcoal.
- That other metals, most likely aluminum, will have to substitute for steel in many uses. Aluminum is produced by an entirely electrolytic process, with a relatively small carbon dioxide emission from the erosion of the carbon electrodes.

Per ton, in 2017, aluminum cost about five times as much as steel. It is also weaker than steel so aluminium structural members have to be thicker than the corresponding steel ones. But given its lower density these effects partially cancel out, and corresponding aluminum parts will weigh only about 60 percent of steel parts. Overall, then, the use of aluminum instead of steel is about three times as expensive.

So it is likely that the two fundamental construction materials of industrial civilization, concrete and steel, will have to be replaced by alternatives that are around three times as expensive. Cheap concrete has been the foundation of world urbanization [Edgerton, 2011b], and cheap steel of mechanization.

Stone will remain available as a low-carbon building material when carbon emissions restrict brick and concrete. Smout [1986] attributes the greater overcrowding and worse slum housing conditions in industrial Scotland to the statutory requirement, up to the 1930s, to use expensive stone in residential accommodations in Scotland whereas cheap brick could be used in England.

The old stone tenements of Glasgow are appreciated for their aesthetics, in comparison to the brick and concrete housing that went up in the 1950s. But if the billions of new urban dwellers accross the world will have to depend on the building of stone housing, then overcrowding will persist. Overcrowding brings exploitative landlords and reinforces the dominance of the propertied classes. On the other hand, once population growth slows down, the durability of stone construction is an advantage. Over time, with a static population, relatively high standards of housing could be achieved using stone. In the shorter term it may be necessary for mass-produced aluminum units to stand in for the poured concrete flats of twentieth-century urbanization.

7.1.2 Transport

As Smil [2010] says, the two engines of globalization are the high bypass turbine and the high compression diesel. One powers aircraft, the other ships, trains, trucks, and buses. MAN and Wärtsilä diesel engines drive the vast ships linking Asia, Europe, and America. Diesel trains carry more than half of America's goods. Turbines power all air freight. All run on oil; without oil, most world transport stops.

Oil is not going to run out or be banned overnight, but it will become progressively less available over a few decades, either due to resource exhaustion or international restrictions of fossil fuel use. How then is a transport system, and behind that, a whole global capitalist division of labor, going to respond?

Looking first at shipping, it is clear that costs will rise. Today we have diesel-powered steel ships. At the end of this century what will ships be built of and powered by?

Before steel ships we had wooden ones, and sail power hung on into the early twentieth century, so international trade would still be possible by a reversion to earlier technologies. But this would mean both a severe reduction in trade volume and a rise in carrying costs. Vessels of modern size cannot be built of wood. Wooden construction implies ships of at most a couple of thousand tons, about a hundredth of the size of the largest contemporary container ships and a tenth the size of the most common bulk carrier. Costs would be much higher because of the large crews needed to handle sails.

But there are obvious alternatives. Aluminum has been extensively used in warship construction, and could be used for merchant shipping were owners forced to pay the higher construction cost. But nobody has yet built large aluminum ships. The largest have been around 100 meters whereas current freighters run up to four times that length.

Figure 7.4. The Flettner rotor ship. The original ship is on the left with the modern experimental Eship1 on the right.

Aluminum ships have been plagued by corrosion problems. As a highly electo-positive metal, any contact with other metals like bronze or steel sets up a battery on contact with water. The consequence is electrolytic corrosion that eats away at the aluminum. In principle this can be avoided by using only aluminum in the hull. Designs have existed for bulk cargo ships of this type for decades, but have been uneconomic [Altenburg, 1971]. Overall, and over decades, however, there seems little doubt that the technology of building such ships can be mastered. Propulsion is the bigger problem.

Batteries and solar power are ruled out. Batteries, which have long been used in submarines, do not last long enough for ocean voyages, and solar power provides too little energy for a large heavy vessel. Wind remains the most likely alternative. Designs do exist for cargo ships with conventional masts and sails, but the crew required to handle sails, even with some form of power assist, is likely to be more than would be needed for a motor vessel. A promising alternative is the Flettner rotor. [139] This relies on wind that will exert a perpendicular force on a spinning cylinder. It requires a modest power to rotate the cylinder but, by harnessing the wind, yields much more propulsive power than is put in. Such ships do not need big crews. A couple of cargo ships using this were built in the 1920s (Figure 7.4), but at that time they proved uneconomic in comparison to diesel. Given that diesel ships have improved a lot since then, they remain uneconomic in the absence of controls on the use of fossil fuels. [140]

Another possibility is that nuclear energy, long used in warships, might be applied to cargo vessels. There is no doubt that it works, and can drive ships very fast. But there is a big difference between operating nuclear energy in an environment where cost is no object, with highly trained crews, and using it in a commercial ship. Of the four experimental atomic cargo ships, *Savannah* (US), *Otto Hahn* (German), *Mutsu* (Japanese), and *Sevmorput* (Soviet) only the last was a success. Cost, reliability, and safety considerations have prevented a general uptake of the technology.

So the conclusion to take from this is that the end of the fossil fuel era is likely to lead to a significant increase in shipping costs. Ships will cost more to build, more to operate, and probably be slower.

This will substantially undermine the current model of globalization. Higher shipping costs will favor local producers compared to global ones, and land links rather than sea links. Rail freight is still heavily dependent on diesel in many countries, but electric railways are an old and well-tried technology. It is expensive to put in the wires and to buy new locomotives, but running costs subsequently are similar. Even with the current structure of electricity generation electric trains release less carbon than diesel [Givoni et al., 2009]. As the electricity generation system moves toward renewables and nuclear, this advantage will become more pronounced. Electrification tends to be high in countries like China where the railways are state owned and planned and low in countries like the United States where the infrastructure is private.

China's rail transport volume is one of the highest in the world, having a 93,000km network of which 46,000km is electrified [Ministry of Railways, China, 2012]. The rate of electrification increased gradually: in 1975 it was only 5 percent , by now it is about 40 percent as a result of a conscious central planning [Juhász et al., 2013].

In contrast, only 1 percent of the U.S. network is electrified. We discussed earlier how, in capitalist economies, high capital-intensive industries have a low rate of profit, which discourages investment in them. The contrast between U.S. and Chinese railways is a particularly stark example. The electrification of the railways in large countries like the United States is technically feasible as China shows, but it is held back by private ownership. Thus, the need to convert to electric trains will tend to favor the replacement of private with public railways.

The percentage of freight carried by trains may well rise, because in the absence of diesel engine trucks, long-distance trucking is likely to be unviable. The best electric heavy trucks have a range of only 100km and take several hours to charge. The goods transport system is likely to have electric trucks being used only for final delivery within cities. [141]

For urban transport, electric cars with lithium batteries are certainly a viable replacement for fossil fuel ones. There are questions associated with the long-term availability of lithium for the batteries [Kushnir and Sandén, 2012]. If the whole world were to attain the current European levels of car ownership, and these all used lithium batteries, it is questionable whether world lithium resources are sufficient, though that is a relatively extreme projection of future use. Gaines et al. [2009], using more modest projections of future car use, conclude that lithium resources are unlikely to be a big constraint.

Lithium is geographically concentrated with the top four producing countries having 90 percent of world reserves. In the event of it being used in all cars, these countries would be in a position to gain rent revenues analogous to the leading oil producers today. On the whole, though, these are likely to be smaller than the oil rents in the current world economy, because lithium can be recycled, but unlike oil it will not be a primary energy source.

There are no serious engineering problems with converting the aviation industry to use non-fossil fuels. Liquid hydrogen is a viable alternative [Koroneos et al., 2005; Contreras et al., 1997] and has a much better energy-to-weight ratio than existing fuels. Its main drawback is that it is much less dense, so that a substantial part of the fuselage volume would have to be given over to fuel tanks. Designs exist for modified Airbus and Boeing jumbo jets powered by hydrogen [Price, 1991]. The Boeing design had the upper deck extended to the length of the fuselage and entirely filled with liquid hydrogen tanks. In 1988 Tupolev actually built a modified Tu155 that flew on hydrogen [Pohl and Malychev, 1997], the back part of the passenger cabin having to be occupied by the fuel tank.

Although the conversion is possible, it will come at the cost of more expensive flights. Because the fuel is so bulky, the aircraft will be able to carry fewer passengers than a conventional one of the same size. The fuel is also more expensive. Although photovoltaic electricity is begining to rival fossil fuel electricity in lifetime costs, this does not imply that hydrogen produced by electrolysis from solar power is as cheap as kerosene.

Producing electricity from oil proceeds thus:

(a) *oil (40 percent efficient)→ electricity*
Producing hydrogen by electrolysis starting with oil fuel progresses thus:

(b) *oil (40 percent efficient)→ electricity (70 percent efficient)→ hydrogen*
Because of the thermodynamic loss in electrolysis. If we substitute this with photovoltaic we have:

(c) *photovoltaic electricity (70 percent efficient)→ hydrogen*
The hydrogen or kerosene aviation fuel then has to be turned into motive power:

(d) *aviation fuel (40 percent efficient)→ motive power for flights*
Suppose photovoltaic electricity costs the same as process (a). Thus photovoltaic electricity is of the same cost as flight motive power in process (d) where the aviation fuel is kerosene. But if we have to generate hydrogen and then burn it in a turbine, the overall subsequent efficiency is 70 percent × 40 percent = 28 percent. So even if

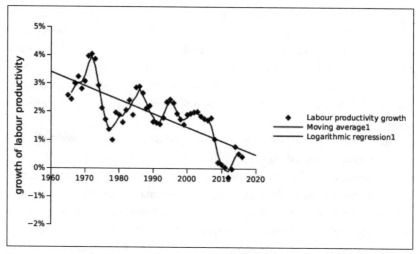

Figure 7.5. Growth of labor productivity over the last half-century in the UK. Growth rates computed as moving average over last 5 years for output per worker for the whole economy. Source: ONS data.

photovoltaic electricity is as cheap as fossil fuel electricity, as a source of aviation fuel it will still be more than three times as expensive as kerosene.

Lower passenger capacity and lower thermodynamic efficiency mean that cost per passenger mile will rise substantially.

The change to a non–fossil fuel economy involves big increases in costs in a number of areas: materials, transport, process heating. In air and sea transport this could amount to a doubling or more of costs assuming current labor productivity.

Throughout the Industrial Age labor productivity has risen, so one might hope that once human ingenuity is devoted to increasing the productivity of wind-powered aluminum ships or hydrogen planes the initial loss will soon be recovered. The changeover will take decades. Will this not leave plenty of time for productivity rises to offset the loss?

There are several problems with such an optimistic view. The first is that labor productivity growth has been declining over the last half-century (Figures 7.5, 7.6). We should expect late industrializing economies that are importing the most advanced techniques to have more rapid productivity growth than those that are already industrialized. That labor productivity growth should decline in countries like Japan and Italy, which had not completed industrialization in 1960, is not surprising, but even economies like the UK, fully industrialized in 1960, show the same trend. Even before

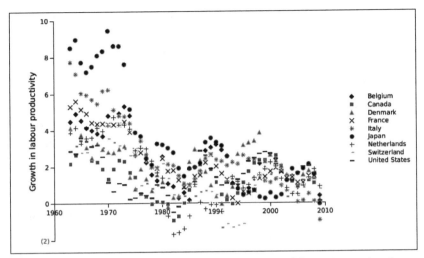

Figure 7.6. Decline in productivity growth, up to the start of the 2008 recession. Sourc: Extended Penn World Tables.

the 2008 recession, the bulk of industrial economies were improving their productivity at under 2 percent a year, and, if current trends continue, productivity growth will stop generally in the next decades.

If productivity grows at 2 percent a year, it would take 35 years to offset a doubling of costs of air and sea transport. If growth shrinks to 1 percent it would take 70 years. This, however, may not be enough to save globalization. The figures of 1 percent or 2 percent are average increases in productivity across the whole economy.

It currently pays to fly prawns caught off the cost of Britain to Thailand to be shelled and then fly them back to supermarkets here. This is only viable with cheap air freight. Suppose air freight charges doubled and the business became unprofitable. Suppose that in 2067, the general improvement in UK labor productivity is such that the initially doubled air freight charges have now fallen, in terms of labor time, to the same number of worker days as now. Would we expect the flying of prawns to Thailand to resume?

No. For one thing the cheap labor to be had in Thailand today is unlikely to be available after half a century of development there. For another, labor productivity in the UK prawn-shelling business can be expected to have increased as well. If it grows the same way as the rest of the economy, it too will have doubled. So the comparative advantage of shelling in Thailand would not reappear.

People are being overconfident about the rate of technical change. I am old enough to have seen the rate of technical change slow down a lot within my own lifetime. I remember that it was in the late 1970s that Greg Michaelson and I first noticed this slowdown happening and started to discuss it. Technical change is nothing like as rapid as it was in the 1950s or 1960s, let alone between 1890 and 1914. The tendency is for labor productivity to slow down.

Perhaps our grandchildren will be using magnetic levitation trains, but in the 1960s we expected linear induction monorail trains to be in use by 1980. After all, they were building a prototype in East Anglia. High-speed tilting trains were being developed by British Rail in the late 1960s and were scheduled for use in the '70s along with 125 mph diesels for other lines. [142] Current Virgin Train diesels are no faster than those HSTs. In 1975 I could go from Edinburgh to London in 4 hrs 20 mins; it is no faster today, forty years later. Where are the flying cars, personal jetpacks, and 15-hour working weeks we were promised?

In some areas transport and technology have regressed considerably. Nineteenth-century-style bicycle delivery boys are back on the streets, "badge engineered" by Deliveroo. In the '70s Britain could, build supersonic airliners, the Americans could land people on the moon. Neither of those technologies are available now. In the 1950s the UK could from a complete standing start, build a whole series of nuclear power stations, with each one taking about five years. Now we have to import the technology at vast expense from China and France, and it takes over a decade.

During my grandfather's lifetime, travel went from horse transport in towns and the only form of flight being by balloon to generalized use of cars and mass jet transport. Entertainment went from magic lantern shows to cinema, and then television. There was no telephone system when he was born, let alone computers, but in his old age he came and saw the workstation I was using (an ICL PERQ) and was immediately able to understand the Unix filing system.

Is this because of some inherent property of the development of technology, or is it evidence that Marx was right about social forms eventually becoming a fetter on the development of new technologies?

We know that many individual technologies develop with a logistic or S curve like that shown in Figure 7.7. For example, the diffusion of steam engine technology in Britain developed this way [Nuvolari et al., 2011]. But, as Modis [2013] showed, the overall development of productivity in leading industrial economies also has this shape. Japanese GDP growth almost exactly fits a logistic curve, with GDP per capita having leveled off and been stagnant since 1990. In the early stages of logistic growth, it looks exponential, then it slows down and eventually tends toward an upper bound. So for countries like India or China we cannot tell if the growth is logistic or exponential. If we concentrate on the countries that do show a logistic pattern, what is happening?

There are two possible answers. It may be that the basic technology complex of industrial society is drawing close to its limit. Alternatively, capitalist social relations have become an absolute fetter on productive forces. If that is the case, we could attribute the leveling off of growth to the fall in the rate of profit, shown for example in Figure 5.25. This fall in profit rates would, in this interpretation, curtail investment. Because of the decline in investment, then, the rate of technical progress would have slowed down.

This is a plausible explanation as there does appear to be a decline in net investment per worker over the period shown in Figure 7.8. Here data is computed as (i–d)/x for net investment and i/x for gross investment, where d is estimated depreciation per worker in 2005 purchasing power parity, i is investment per worker-year in 2005 purchasing power parity, and x is GDP per worker in 2005 purchasing power parity.

It is noticeable that gross investment is not declining. A rise in the capital stock per worker implies that depreciation eats up more and more of gross investment [Zachariah, 2008]. The decline in net investment is thus expected whatever the property relations prevailing.

Whether it is the whole story is another matter. Even when net accumulation of value declines, there is still a process of replacement of old machinery with new as it wears out. Even if the new machinery is of the same value as what it replaced, since it was more modern it should be more effective. It should, as a result, still raise the productivity of labor.

Stagnation in that case is compatible with a continued modest growth in productivity.[143] The productivity gains would then be eaten up by the aging of the Japanese population. A shrinking workforce, getting slowly

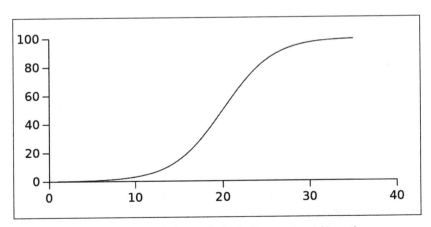

Figure 7.7. The logistic curve, which initially looks like exponential growth.

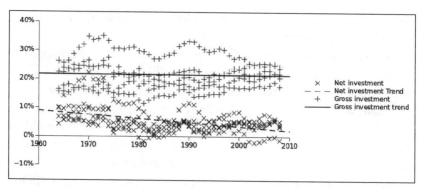

Figure 7.8. Long-term trend of net investment per worker as a share of output per worker is declining in this data for UK, United States, Italy, France, Japan. Source: Extended Penn World Tables.

more productive, might just be enough to hold GDP per capita constant. The logistic in GDP per capita would then be the combined effect of zero net accumulation and changing demography.

But we should still be cautious about saying that the decline in labor productivity is simply an artifact of capitalist property relations. Even if these are a proximate cause, my analysis of Feldman growth theory showed that there were analogous, ultimately demographic, constraints on socialist growth. As society raises the stock of means of production, an increasing portion of the labor force has to work replacing and updating this stock. So net accumulation also slows down under socialism, as the history of the USSR showed.

This implies that the industrial mode of production that underlies both capitalism and socialism has its own inherent limitation. Producing by means of machinery that must wear out, along with a demographic transition that slows population growth, means that the value of machinery built up per worker hits limits. This holds whatever the property relations.

A capitalist economy will be more seriously affected. The consequence of a falling rate of profit is a slackening of accumulation, which leads to unemployment, unused capacity, over indebted firms, and a generalized slump. A socialist economy, where investment is not carried out for private gain, can go on investing even when the growth rate slows down. Capitalist economies also go through additional cycles driven by the expansion and contraction of credit. In Figure 7.5 these cycles are clearly visible, overlaid on a secular declining trend.

So I have given an explanation relating to the capitalist social relations plus an explanation relating to the industrial mode of production. There are other possible explanations relating to innovation, the relationship between society and nature, or to inherent thermodynamic limits of technology. Perhaps the problem is the exhaustion of the innovations on which twentieth-century growth was powered, without sufficiently radical new ones coming onstream. Maybe the last thirty years have just not seen any innovations as radical as the steam engine, electricity, the railway, or powered flight. We have had cellphones and smartphones, but do these compare in significance to the initial development of the telephone and wireless?

A smartphone combines telephony, computing, wireless, and a screen with moving pictures, but these are all classic twentieth-century technologies. The innovation was to shrink them and mass-produce them. The iPhones may seem like bright stars in our sky, but they are nothing like the constellations of innovation that transformed life in the nineteenth and twentieth centuries. The modern world has nothing like the dizzying speed of technical and social change that Wells conveyed with such immediacy [2005a; 2005b; 1930; 1914; Wells and Parrinder, 2005]. The rapid growth of the twentieth century combined, or superposed, the exponential stage of the S-curves of many different technologies. As these curves shift into their asymptotic phases, growth slows down unless a large number of entirely new technologies start on their own S-curves. The individual S-curves have that shape for two reasons:

1. *The diffusion process of a technology is S-shaped.*
    Initially a few people had handmade cars. Ford's production line allowed their mass production. Then all manufacturers switched to production lines, and car use grew exponentially. Eventually the majority of families had cars and growth slowed down to replacement levels.

2. *Technologies hit limits set by natural law.*
    Steam-engine efficiency grew exponentially from the late eighteenth to the mid-nineteenth century. Double then triple expansion engines were introduced. Then came the Parson's turbine. But there is an ultimate limit to the efficiency of all these Rankine cycle engines. In theory their maximum efficiency is in the 60 percent range, but in practice the best power stations hit only 42 percent. To get higher efficiency they would need hotter steam. Higher steam temperatures would weaken the steel used in their turbines, so the efficiency has plateaued.[144]

We have already touched on the relationship between society and nature in identifying the end of fossil fuel as a looming issue, saying that it implies a rise in real costs, that is to say labor costs, across all energy dependent branches of production. But the effects are already being experienced. Shifts to non–fossil fuel sources of power are already having impacts on power costs. The production of biofuels withdraws land from food production and raises food prices. Even without the Kyoto Protocol and Paris Agreement, the growth in demand for oil had enabled the price to be raised in two great waves, in the 1970s and again the 2000s (Figure 7.9). This represented an increase in the amount of labor that had to be exchanged for a kilowatt hour of power. These waves of high prices coincided with clear slowdowns in the rate of labor productivity growth internationally (Figure 7.6).

Improvements in productivity had been dependent on substituting energy for labor. When the amount of labor required to acquire a given amount of energy rose, that made it much harder to increase the productiveness of labor. What made things worse was that the increase in costs was largely in the form of rents to the oil states, which were then spent unproductively.

Green lobbyists talk enthusiastically about the number of future jobs to be had from alternative energy. This is a tacit admission that alternative energy will cost more labor. With green energy, the extra cost translates into revenue for labor and capital rather than ground rent as at present, but overall it is still a real economic cost.

The argument that I have been making about the slow rate of modern technical advance is intended, in part, as a counter to the idea that automation and robotics are advancing at unprecedented speed threatening a

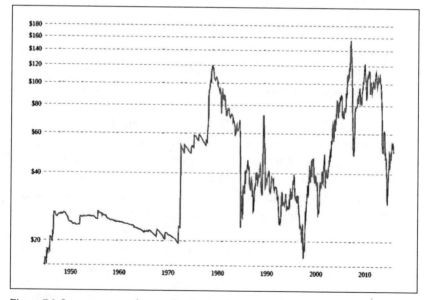

Figure 7.9. Long-term trend in crude oil prices. Source: www.macrotrends.net

jobless future [Martin, 2015]. In fact, the labor productivity figures show a slowdown, at the same time as changing demographics threaten a labor shortage. But the figures are for *real* productivity, where real productivity in the national statistics is this monetary productivity divided by a deflater for the rate of inflation. It only measures the productivity of labor in producing commodities. What if the *real* change brought on by automation is in something not measured in these statistics?

7.1.3 Information

The biggest impact of automation has been on the dissemination of information rather than on the production of physical objects. When you interact with the Internet, your computer communicates with a plethora of other computers: an ADSL modem and wireless router, routers in the local telephone exchange building, switches at major hubs, and server farms owned by big companies like Google, Apple, or Microsoft. These all respond automatically and without any human intervention to deliver the information you request. People worked to build the equipment, to set it up, to write the software it uses, and to generate the electricity on which it depends. That is all in the background, prior to and independent of your particular interaction. The actual information that the web delivers to you is not foreseen by or dependent on the enabling work that people did. It is hard, even in principle, to associate any quantum of human labor to the quanta of information you get back. All we can be sure of is that the fraction of an hour of labor per bit delivered will be tiny.

In consequence, the bits are not commodities.

GDP measured in monetary transaction hardly grasps this activity. All that appears in the accounts are the fees paid to access the Net, and the fees that advertisers pay Google.

From an accounting standpoint, Google is in business to sell ads, and its labor productivity can only be measured in terms of the dollars of advertising sold in comparision to the number of people it employs. But this misses the real utility of the Web, the rapid discovery of information, and substitutes an adventitious measure, one born out of the funding model used to support it. In principle, governments could put out tenders to supply ad-free Web indexing and social media services. The productivity in terms of service delivered to end users would probably be higher. Much of the software development effort by Google and Facebook goes into identifying better leads for advertisers rather than improving services to end users.

The capitalist Web develops via a curious mutual parasitism, in which the value form abolishes itself. The end users parasitize the free services offered.

But the providers of these free services in turn parasitize the end users by selling information about their activity and interests to third parties. But the very possibility of Google being able to offer a useful indexing service depends on there being lots of free information. It depends on people being willing to write blogs, post news about themselves, take and upload videos, make their own audio recordings, etc. It depends on scientists being willing to post their research on free archive sites, on public bodies making statistics and reports freely available. Free information on this scale is something qualitatively new. Some free knowledge has always existed. That taught in schools belonged to nobody. Scientific results have been the common property of scholars. Folksong belonged to the community of musicians. But their encoded distribution, as books, sheet music, phonograph records, etc., took commodity form.

The work individual people do posting stuff on the web is communism in action: work done for self-realization, unalienated labor, uncommodified labor. Even the means of web production escape, in the main, value relations. Much of the edifice rests on free open-source software. Some open-source software is written during paid working hours by employees of firms that, for their own business reasons, choose to release the software open-source. But another large part is written by people in their free time, or by people at educational or research institutes, with no commercial motive. The existence of these new productive forces gives rise to a new form of communist ethic among those who work them, summarized in the slogan: *information wants to be free* [Brand, 1987].[145]

This nascent non-commodity distribution is restricted to information goods rather than physical ones, and further restricted by intellectual property rights. Personal computers are the means by which multiple copies of software, music, books and so on can be produced by minimal labor. But if people engage in such production they are labelled *pirates*. Thus a label originally applied to violent criminals who seized ships and killed their crews is attached to people engaged peacefully in production. Here we have a clear example of property relations holding back production. If pirates grab the cargo of a ship, they deprive others of it. If a hacker distributes copies of a song, nobody is deprived of it. Indeed more people get to hear it. The only deprivation is that of the copyright holders who forgo some of their monopoly profit.

A whole series of technical and legal measures are enacted to prevent copying. Digital Rights Management (DRM) watermarking is used to try to make copies of e-books unreadable. Laws are passed to ban the circumvention of these provisions. In the end the technical attempts to protect digital property rights are all circumvented. The monopolists are forced to rely on

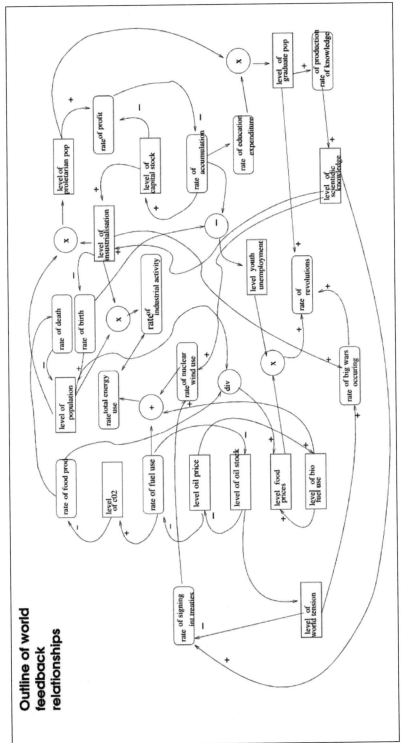

Figure 7.10. Environmentally driven feedbacks in the world sociopolitical system.

the courts to imprison those who create the indexing tools and sites that allow free file sharing.

PREDICTION IS A RISKY AFFAIR, especially, one might add, when applied to the future. The best one can do is make rational extrapolations from apparent causal processes. We know that technological change and labor productivity have been slowing down for fifty years. The transition to a post–fossil fuel economy will put further pressure on labor productivity and particularly on transport costs. It may be that this portends the inherent limits of industrial civilization and its mode of production. Alternatively, maybe it is the capitalist structure of the world economy that is to blame. I have identified several areas of technology, in energy production and information distribution, where capitalism appears to hold things back.

A social compromise in which the income of all classes continues to rise becomes harder to establish. Political economy becomes more of zero sum game that pressages an intensified class struggle over the distribution of income.

7.2 POPULATION

From the 1980s, alongside a slowing in the growth of labor productivity, there was an increase in exploitation across the industrialized capitalist countries. The productivity growth that did occur went disproportionately to the upper classes. There were immediate political reasons for this. The pioneering of neoliberal policies in Chile during the 1970s, after the military coup, heralded their spread to other countries via Thatcher and Reagan and their generalization following the fall of the USSR. But these are secondary phenomena. The driving forces were demography and technology. Vast reserves of labor power were being thrown onto the world market in Asia at a time when improvements in transport, large diesel container ships, were driving down shipping costs.

The economic and political weakness of labor relative to capital was due to there being a glut of labor in a more unified world market. All the other measures of trade liberalization were predicated on this basic fact.

As I write in 2017, we are passing the inflection point of the S-curve that governs this process. World fertility levels are approaching simple reproduction (Figure 5.31), with the decline in Asia being even more rapid. Already in China this is leading to fast rises in wages (Figure 6.10). India and Africa remain as reserves of labor but, with East Asia, Europe, and North America now industrialized, the ratio of labor reserves to capital generation is shifting to favor labor.

Absent the disruption that would be caused by another world war, a tightening labor market and a slowdown in technical change will lead to a more intense struggle over the distribution of income. The first response of the business class to this labor shortage is to encourage immigration, an effective means of increasing exploitation (see Figure 5.28). Eventually the pool of cheap labor will be exhausted, but well before that, working-class support for anti-immigrant populism is likely to block the process.

Developed economies will increasingly face the constraint of a shrinking working population. I showed earlier that under these circumstances capital accumulation becomes impossible. The equilibrium rate of profit tends to zero with a stable population. If the working population shrinks, then accumulation must become negative, and if you take into account losses on capital account, then the whole economy ends up running at a loss.

At this point the issue of how the economy itself is organized will become more and more an issue of politics. The questions of how economic decline and population decline can be halted will be increasingly asked.

These issues will be raised in a society that is already highly polarized between a wealthy elite and a majority whose standards of living are falling. The elite response will be to raise profitability by attacking the living standard of the majority. But, with a stagnant population, there are insufficient opportunities for profitable investment. The elites boost their share of national income but increasingly spend it on unproductive luxuries. Insulated by their burgeoning share of national wealth, the elites continue to live in the illusion that all is well, until social pressures become insufferable.

7.3 POLITICS

The coming era of social conflict could well result in nothing more than the mutual ruin of contending parties. None can predict the final outcome of these contests. But it is certain that socialist ideas will return from their post-Soviet exile to the center of national debate. Premonitions have already been seen in the Americas and Europe. For socialist ideas to succeed not only in winning government but in guiding the economy once in power, they will have to coalesce around a set of answers to the problems of this century. Socialist ideas will become practical common sense for the mid-twenty-first century just as they were sixty years ago.

Unless rapid and drastic steps are taken to limit fossil fuel use contemporary civilization faces a terrible crisis. Earth is not threatened by climate change; it has survived all sorts of vicissitudes of climate in the past. But for species, including our own, it is a real threat. Humanity is faced with famine and climate strains of an entirely new scale. Studies using a variety of climate and economic models all predict falls in food output and rises in world food prices [Nelson et al., 2014a; 2014b]. Averaging across many models, the mean projected effects on key grain crops are for drastic falls in output in hot countries, whereas cold countries, particularly Canada and Russia, will see marked improvements in yields [Rosenzweig et al., 2014]. Since the hot countries are poor and the cool countries tend to be relatively rich, those who are already struggling to survive would be the hardest hit if CO_2 goes on rising. Estimates of food price increases range from 20 to 100 percent depending on the climate model and economic model chosen. Such price rises would be enough to threaten the survival of hundreds of millions. The effects can only be worsened if biofuels become widely used, since these divert crops from feeding people to feeding cars. It follows that a central goal of a socialist politics today has to be to bring about rapid reduction in fossil fuel use, provided that food crops are not sacrificed in the process.

Rather than ideas like carbon taxes or emissions trading, a socialist policy would be expressed in terms of quantitative limits to the amount of coal being mined, and oil being pumped. Carbon taxes tend to be regressive and uncertain in their effect. It is not known in advance what level of carbon tax would be needed to produce, for example, a 20 percent reduction in emissions. Emissions trading schemes, as used by the EU, reward existing polluters by giving them property rights in emissions. The greater the pollution a firm starts off with, the more rights it gets. They act, therefore, to transfer rent income to big firms.

A socialist planned economy always has to set various constraints on its overall plan, such as the length of the working day, number of people available, and attempts to maximize some measure of social welfare subject to these constraints. If the planning process uses mathematical methods for this optimization, as developed by Kantorovich [1960, 1965], it is straightforward to add environmental constraints to those being set by population, existing stocks of machinery, etc. [Cockshott, 2006b]. Society could make a 20 percent reduction in carbon use an explicit plan objective. This would constrain the plan algorithm to select technologies for development that would fall within that goal. But that only becomes possible in an economy that is already subject to directive planning. In mixed economies, like the Chinese one, or in purely capitalist ones, direct quantitative control of carbon emissions is still possible by explicit rationing. Something similar to the U.S. Standby Rationing Plan for Gasoline, developed in the 1970s, could be used:

> The Department of Energy will establish different allotments for different types of vehicles. Allotments will be based on an average annual fuel consumption of vehicles in various categories and will be

made for each type of vehicle. All vehicles within a given category (for example, all passenger cars) will receive the same ration allotment in a given state regardless of fuel efficiency. This will give a significant advantage to fuel-efficient vehicles and should provide an incentive for their use during a period of rationing. . . .

Under the standby plan, ration coupons that have not been redeemed will be freely transferable on a white market. There will be no regulation of the price at which they are transferred. Hence, those who wish to exceed their allocated ration may do so by purchasing coupons from willing sellers. [Crompron and Gitelson, 1981, 28]

This U.S. legislation, which is only put into effect in time of emergency, is surprisingly egalitarian. The effect of distributing tradeable rations to all car users, thus to a large portion of the whole population, is leveling. If the wealthy want to drive big gas-guzzling SUVs they have to purchase tokens from those with smaller cars, producing net transfer of income.

A similar mechanism could be applied to carbon rationing. All citizens would get ration books which they could use when they buy fuel for cars, oil and gas for heating, etc. Government inspectors at the refineries and coal mines would ensure that coupons handed over by the oil companies matched the deliveries from the refineries. Haulage companies, airlines, and other industrial users of fossil fuel would have to purchase coupons on the open market from citizens. The net effect would be to ensure that the environmental target was met without regressive effects on income.

If, as seems likely, climate change leads to general shortages of food, some similar form of food rationing may be necessary. In general a socialist government should avoid rationing. It is better to meet egalitarian goals by means of full employment and narrowing of pay differentials. But rationing is the least worse option if the economy is not yet fully socialized and if big income differentials still exist. The U.S. principle, that ration cards be transferable, is essential if the full egalitarian potential of rationing is to be achieved.

Insofar as private ownership of industry had a historically progressive role it rested on the process of capital accumulation. It was this that allowed Western societies to industrialize. This was not the only possible route to industrialization, as the history of the twentieth century showed. The process of accumulation itself is fundamentally a disequilibrium phenomenon. Steady accumulation is dependent on a steady growth of the population or, as Marx put it, accumulation of capital is growth of the proletariat.

With that process coming to an end, the sustainability of private ownership is undermined. It no longer has an objective economic justification, relying instead on politically supported monopoly power. But the growing imperative of climate control amounts to an implicit undermining of property rights. Restricting carbon emissions implies the abolition of the ground rent of the oil states—one of the most important single rivers of surplus revenue. The vituperative opposition of much of the property-owning classes to climate control measures, extending to funding climate change denial, is based on a recognition that the whole process is a threat to property rights. It posits the general interest of humanity as a whole overriding private rights. A thorough program of curtailing fossil fuel use requires the political defeat of fossil fuel interests. The implementation of a transition to a non–fossil fuel economy progresses most rapidly where the entire energy economy is publicly owned, as in China. From the standpoint of the Chinese state it makes no pecuinary difference whether it generates fossil fuel electricity or uses solar, nuclear, or wind power.

Let us set aside for the moment whether the twenty-first-century crisis will progress toward a socialist outcome or instead a victory of existing propertied interests that leads to general climate catastrophe. Let us look at what type of property relations a future socialist economy might have. Allin Cottrell and I set out a model for this twenty-five years ago [Cockshott and Cottrell, 1995]. Developments since then have confirmed our conviction that the basic model we outlined remains valid. It is a view of an economy that is publicly owned and planned using modern computer technology to handle the sheer volume of data—on which the old Soviet planning system foundered. Within this model, the labor theory of value occupies a crucial position. It provides an answer to the old objection of Mises [1935] that without money there was no practical way of comparing the costs of different alternatives. Empirical research since then has strongly validated the labor theory of value, confirming the soundness of the basic proposal. [Petrovic, 1987; Shaikh, 1998; Cockshott and Cottrell, 1997e, 2005; Zachariah, 2006; Fröhlich, 2013]

There have been big advances in computerization since the end of the 1980s, which make the task of operating a cybernetic moneyless economy even more practical. Google solves everyday systems of linear equations far bigger than those required for continental-scale economic planning [Widdows, 2004]. The huge bandwidth Internet now makes the modified 1980s broadcast technology that we proposed to use for disseminating planning information redundant.

In our proposal people would be paid not in money but with nontransferable electronic work accounts. Purchases would be made with smart cards as they are today, but with the difference that the only way people could accumulate work credits would be by actually working. The more hours you work the more credits you get. Goods in the shops would then be priced in hours, and the exchange principle is basically one for one. For one hour of work you get goods that took one hour to make.

Contrary to the dreams of futurists, human labor remains essential to the economy.[146] It is humanity's fundamental resource limit. Calculation in terms of human time allows public finance to be divested of the fetishism that money engenders. It becomes clear that decisions about public spending are in reality decisions to allocate a finite working population to different tasks. In combination with modern communications technology, the unfetishized nature of time decisions allows broad democratic participation. The broad headings of public expenditure can be settled by a process of participatory consensus.[147]

In Section 6.4 I explained how the system of surplus production operates in a planned economy and argued that one of the big failings of the twentieth-century socialist systems was that they relied on various forms of indirect taxes to fund free public services. I showed how this system systematically biases economic decision-making against socially rational technologies. It is important that the twenty-first-century socialist movement not repeat this mistake. By far the most rational and equitable approach to public finance is to rely on income taxes.

I argued in Section 5.9 that the fundamental constraint on capitalist profitability is the falling birth rate. Across much of the developed world this has sunk well below reproduction levels. In the short run, this may be favorable to the labor interest, since labor shortages could allow the price of labor power to be bid up. In the long term it poses a serious problem in whatever form of economy. A rapidly declining population bears a heavier burden of caring for the old, and will have difficulty sustaining the basic infrastructure of the economy in the face of wear and tear. So socialist family policy aims for a population that is roughly stable. I recounted how socialist economies in the past sought to reduce the burden of having children by providing free education, free childcare, and substantial financial allowances to mothers. This included full benefits to single mothers, who contemporary Western society tends to stigmatize as "welfare queens," etc. Whether such measures will be enough in the future is an open question. For my part I suspect that once the bonds of patriarchy are loosened, and the constant destabilizing effect of men and women having to move long distances to find insecure jobs has been removed, we may revert to long forgotten, but more natural, forms of matriarchal extended families.

APPENDIX A

Showing Which Sectors Are Productive

A useful way to understand which employees can produce surplus value is to use the reproduction schemes that Marx developed in volume 2 of *Capital*.

He divides the whole economy into three sectors. Sector I produces means of production, that is, machinery, industrial fuel, and raw materials. Sector II produces actual consumer goods. He further breaks down Sector II into Iia, which produces goods consumed by the working class, and sector IIb, which meets the consumption needs of the capitalist class. He then constructs what amounts to notional tables of national accounts based on these sectors (Table A.1).

We can assume the numbers in this table are £billion per year. The important thing is that the output of Sector I has to equal the total constant capital (c) used in all sectors, the output of Sector IIa has to equal the total wages (v) used in all sectors, and the output of Sector IIb has to equal the total profits (s) over all three sectors.

Table A.1 was produced using a spreadsheet that incorporates all of the constraints that Marx assumes for his reproduction schemes. The spreadsheet contains the formulae shown in Table A.2.

Marx assumes a steady state or simply reproducing economy at first, so that there is no surplus being accumulated. The important point is that the reproduction schemes, and with them the actual reproduction of a real economy, is

TABLE A1: Starting Reproduction Table

Sector	c	v	s	Living Labor	Total Output
I	100	50	50	100	200
IIa	50	100	100	200	250
IIb	50	100	100	200	250
Total Used	200	250	250	500	
				Wage Rate:	0.5
				Rate of s/v:	1.0

TABLE A.2: Spreadsheet Used for Reproduction Tables

	A	B	C	D	E	F
1	Sector	c	v	s	Labor	Output
2	I	**100**	F6xE2	E2–C2	**100**	B2+E2
3	IIa	C2	F6xE3	E2–C3	**200**	B3+E3
4	IIb	D2	F6xE4	#r–C4	**200**	B4+E4
5	Total	F2	F4	F4	Σ(E2:E4)	
6					Wage:	[F2/E5]
7					s/v:	[D5/C5]

a highly constrained process. You cannot simply write down a reproduction scheme willy nilly; the equational constraints have to be observed. If you look at Table A.2 there are actually only four degrees of freedom to it: the cells with numbers in them. All other cells have formulae in them.

The particular way you choose to enforce this four-degrees-of-freedom constraint is arbitrary. By a series of algebraic manipulations you could choose a different set of 4 cells to contain data and have the remaining ones filled with formulae.

In the examples that follow the formulae are unchanged, and only data cells are altered. The formulae then enforce changes in the remaining cells. This property of reproduction as a constrained system is further developed in Appendix B.

The theory of relative surplus value is that a larger share of surplus value can only come about by reducing the labor time required to reproduce the real wage. Now assume that there is an improvement in labor productivity in Sector IIa so that the same physical output can be produced with half the living labor. Let us assume that the redundant workers emigrate and wages for them no longer appear in the accounts. We then arrive at Table A.3.

The effect is that the rate of surplus value doubles, so clearly Sector IIa can produce relative surplus value.

Now suppose we do the same experiment with Sector IIb and reduce the amount of living labor required to produce its output by half; we now get Table A.4.

The effect of this is to actually lower the rate of surplus value to half. It is relatively easy to see why, since a saving in labor in Sector IIb means that less labor is being spent to support the upper classes, so both the total mass of surplus value and the rate of surplus value fall. Sector IIb includes luxury goods production, advertising, commercial law, armaments production, banking, etc.

TABLE A3: Less Labor Used in Sector IIa

Sector	c	v	s	Living Labor	Total Output
I	100	33.3	66.7	100	200
IIa	33.3	33.3	66.7	100	133.3
IIb	66.7	66.7	133.3	200	266.7
Total Used	200	133.3	266.7	400	
			Wage Rate:	0.333	
			Rate of s/v:	2.0	

TABLE A4: Less Labor Used in Sector IIb

Sector	c	v	s	Living Labor	Total Output
I	100	66.7	33.3	100	200
IIa	66.7	133.3	66.7	200	266.7
IIb	33.3	66.7	33.3	100	133.3
Total Used	200	266.7	133.3	400	
			Wage Rate:	0.66	
			Rate of s/v:	0.5	

If for all these activities the amount of living labor used fell by half, this is what would happen. The rate of surplus value would have to be lower since less social labor was now being expended on the consumption of the upper classes.

Consequently, the effect of improvements in labor productivity in Sector IIb is to reduce the rate of surplus value, hence no relative surplus value can be produced here, which means the whole sector is unproductive. Changes in labor productivity in this sector have the opposite effect to changes in Sector IIa.

You cannot tell whether a given group of employees are productive just by looking at the formal legal contract of employment they have with their employers. It depends on their position within the structure of social reproduction. The production of relative surplus value, the characteristic surplus under capitalism, is a process that takes place at the level of social reproduction as a whole.

Modern capitalism with its huge unproductive sectors looks more and more like the feudalism that Smith critiqued.

APPENDIX B

Illusions Engendered by Averages

In this appendix I examine the problem of how to reconcile the determination of prices by labor with the existence of an average rate of profit. In previous chapters I have used a simple labor theory of value to analyze commodity exchange. I have ignored what is called the "transformation problem" between labor values and actual prices. This has long been a controversial topic and the position I have taken, that one can simply ignore it, needs some justification. My case inevitably involves a certain amount of mathematical argument. As such it is better in an appendix that you can read at will, rather than being in the main text of the book.

Although Smith, Ricardo, and Marx all hewed to a labor theory of value, they all seem to have thought that this theory was too simple. They introduced amendments to their initial bold statements to account for what they took to be a self-evident truth about capitalism, that capitals in all branches of production would tend to earn an average rate of profit. This led them to formulate modified theories of prices to take profit into account. Smith called these natural prices and Marx termed them production prices.

They were all writing before the science of statistics had been developed, and it can now be seen that their misgivings about the simple labor theory of value rested on a couple of statistical misunderstandings. But before I explain these, let us first try to understand why the classical economists thought that there was a problem.

In Table B.1 we see the accounts of two firms. Firm A splits its advanced capital equally between component costs and wages, but for Firm B components make up 2/3 of its expenditure. If they both compute their selling price with the same markup on labor costs, then Firm A earns a higher rate of profit on its advanced capital. Since the classical economists assumed that this kind of variation in component cost ratios would be common, the implication for prices appeared to contradict the commonsense wisdom that there was a prevailing average rate of profit. Surely a situation with the two firms earning a different rate of profit could not be stable?

TABLE B.1: Capital of Different Compositions Earns Different Profit Rates

Firm	Components	Wages	Markup	Selling Price	Capital Advanced	Profit Rate
A	$2,000	$2,000	150%	$5,000	$4,000	28%
B	$8,000	$4,000	150%	$14,000	$12,000	16.7%
Average	$10,000	$6,000	150%	$19,000	$16,000	18.7%

Firm B must either raise its markup to make the same rate of return as Firm A, or diversify and start producing a product that competes with that of A in the hope of earning more. The only stable situation would be one where the markups on wages were adjusted to allow each firm the same rate of profit.

What is wrong with this argument?

1. The existence of an average profit rate does not imply that every firm will have this average rate. There is an average height for men in the European Union, but that does not mean that all men are of average height.
2. The idea that there should be an almost uniform rate of profit on capital is fostered by the operation of the stock market. If we go back to Table B.1, shares in Firm A would sell at a premium and those of Firm B at a discount. If $1 shares in A sold for $1.33 and those of B sold at $0.89 then the rate of return on shareholders' capital would be equalized. This feature of profitable company shares selling at premium is at the heart of the stock market. Changes in share prices bring about an equal rate of return for investors but do not require that firms alter their final selling prices.
3. The idea that firms can diversify their capital out of less profitable lines of business is often false. Consider Eurotunnel Ltd. It was floated to build a railway tunnel from France to England. It raised capital to build the tunnel which cost £9 billion. However, the rate of return on the investment was very low. There was no way that Eurotunnel could decide to take its capital out and shift into running a low-cost airline between Paris and London. The capital was literally sunk under the sea. If the company's capital was fixed, the original shareholders were in no better position; their shares depreciated to a fraction of their issue price. The mobility of capital was presupposed by the classical theory of a near uniform rate of profit.
4. Finally, and most seriously, the empirical data shows that the assumption of a uniform rate of profit operating accross different industries is false. Figure B.1 shows that:

- The rate of profit is widely divergent between different industries.
- Industries in which labor costs are a small fraction of the advanced capital tend to have a lower rate of profit than those for which labor costs make up most of the advanced capital. This is consistent with the simple labor theory of value. It is inconsistent with the theory of Natural Price or Production Price.

Over the last two hundred years much ink has been devoted to debating how to construct a consistent theory combining the classical insights about labor being the source of value with an assumed equal rate of profit. The whole debate was a testimony to the dogmatism of Marxist and Ricardian economists who have preferred to construct the most elaborate mathematical models without bothering to look at empirical data. They shared with the neoclassical school a preference for beautiful math over messy reality. They succumb to the illusion that their equations are the real world. Although some commentators argued that prices of production tended to undermine the theory of labor values and exploitation [Samuelson, 1973; Steedman, 1981; Hilferding, 1951], the basic hypothesis of a law of an equal rate of profit was accepted until the publication of the pioneering econophysics work *Laws of Chaos* [Farjoun and Machover, 1983]. This argued on probabilistic grounds that the distribution of prices was more likely to follow a simple labor value model than a price of production model. More recently Greenblatt [2014] has also proposed a stochastic model in which labor values appear as an emergent property along with a spread of profit rates.

Multiple empirical studies have indicated that production prices are not systematically better at predicting actual market prices than simple labor values [Cockshott and Cottrell, 1998a, 1997b; Shaikh, 1998; Zachariah, 2006; Sánchezc and Montibeler, 2015; Fröhlich, 2013]. It has also been shown that Marx's basic assumption that the rate of profit is the same in high and low organic composition industries is not borne out empirically today [Zachariah, 2006, 2008], whatever the case had been in the nineteenth century. However, this empirical work does not help us to say whether the observed relationship between labor values/production prices and market prices is close. The studies reproduced in Table B.7 show mean absolute errors of the order of 10 percent between labor values/production prices and observed prices. But is 10 percent close or distant?

We can only say that if we have some *a priori* estimate of just how close we should expect the market price vector to be to labor values/production

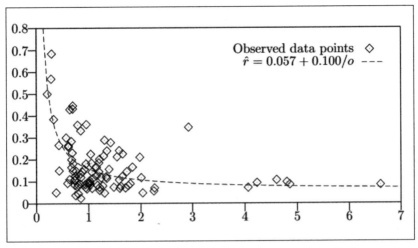

Figure B.1. The rate of return on capital tends to vary inversely with the capital-to-labor ratio. Each diamond represents a whole UK industry. Horizontal axis measures Component Cost/Wage Cost, denoted by the variable o; vertical axis measures the rate of profit r; dotted line represents the best-fitting equation for the data. Source: Cockshott and Cottrell, 1998b.

prices in the absence of the operation of a law of value, or Marx's law of the equalization of profit rates.

Although Marx is conventionally taken to have formulated two different theories of price in the three volumes of *Capital*, labor values in volume 1 and prices of production in volume 3, there is actually a third theory, hidden inside the reproduction schemes of volume 2. This theory is not explicit, but can be logically deduced from the constraints he presents on simple reproduction. It is not a theory of individual prices, but a theory of relative sectoral prices.

This theory of sectoral prices allows us to make probabilistic arguments about the relative likelihood that either production prices or labor values will operate at the level of reproduction schemes. In chapter 20 of the second volume of *Capital* Marx introduced reproduction schemes, matrices of intersectional flows of commodities that had to occur if the economy was to reproduce itself.

The matrices have four column vectors:

C: constant capital, his term for expenditure on
capital goods and raw materials.
V: variable capital, his term for expenditure on wages.
S: surplus or profit.
O: output

TABLE B.2: A Stationary State Specified in Money

	C	V	S	O
I	£100	£50	£5	£200
II	£100	£150	£150	£400

We give an example in Table B.2 of a 2 x 4 matrix, with the row labeled I representing the production of capital goods and raw materials, and row II the production of consumer goods. In Marx's tables all quantities are in terms of money rather than in terms of use values.[148]

For accounting reasons the relation $O = C + V + S$ must hold.

Further $\Sigma C = O_1$, that is to say, consumption of capital goods equals their production, and $\Sigma(V+S) = O_2$. Together this implies that Sector I of the economy must trade $O_1 - C_1$ in capital goods for C_2 worth of consumer goods produced in Sector II. So we have an equilibrium equation:

$$C_2 = V_1 + S_1$$

This is the equilibrium condition of an economy in a stationary state where it simply reproduces itself, neither growing nor shrinking. The basic analysis in this appendix will assume this stationary state. Real economies may grow or shrink, but the rate at which they do this is typically quite small. A developed industrial economy like that of the United States can go long periods in which the rate of growth averages only 3 percent a year or less, so analysis of price systems in a stationary state is a reasonable first approximation.

Although it is not done by Marx, one can in principle construct a dual table like Table B.3 in tons of consumer goods (corn) and tons of capital goods (coal). In this table the first column represents the coal used up productively by the two industries, and next come the consumer goods (corn) consumed by the workers and employers in the two sectors. Again we have the requirement that the total consumption and total production of each good must balance, 160 tons of corn and 20 tons of coal.

It is clear from this table that the coal industry must sell 10 tons of coal to the corn industry and get back in return 40 tons of corn, which in turn implies that the relative price of a ton of coal must be four times the price of a ton of corn. Referring back to the first table and comparing it with the second we see that indeed the price of a ton of coal was £4 but a ton of corn cost only £2.50. The important point here is that given the physical table, the relative prices necessarily follow.

The example is artificial in that in practice Sectors I and II would each

TABLE B.3: A Stationary State Specified in Tons Matter

	Coal	Corn Wage	Corn Profit	Output	
I	10	20	20	20 tons	Coal
II	10	60	60	160 tons	Corn
Total	20 tons	80 tons	80 tons		

produce a whole vector of outputs, but given the constants of proportionality between the elements of these two vectors, the exchange relation between them establishes relative sectoral prices.

Marx later extends the scheme to three sectors, by dividing consumer goods into necessities (IIa), which are assumed to be bought out of wage incomes, and luxuries (IIb), which are bought out of property incomes. If we retain the label II for necessities and use III for luxuries, we have the three-way trade between sectors in Figure B.2.

The tables are given in money terms, much as modern national accounts are, but the assumption explicitly remained that these quantities of money are proportional to quantities of labor [Marx and Engels, 1974, chap. 21, sec. 7]. But in principle other pricing structures are possible so long as they allow the trade pattern in Figure B.2. The reproduction schemes themselves imply a distinct set of price configurations and these price configurations only partially overlap with those presupposed by either labor values or prices of production.

In what follows a probabilistic technique using reproduction schemes is presented to evaluate the known empirical closeness of labor values to market prices. The basic intuition is that one can systematically count which fraction of possible reproduction schemes is consistent with prices of production or labor values. An initial example of how to estimate such proportions can be demonstrated without recourse to the reproduction schemes.

Consider independent industries A and B. These industries may be of very different sizes, but we would like to know whether it is more likely that they both will have the same s/v or whether it is more likely that they will both have the same: s/(c+v). Since the industries may have very different turnovers, let us normalize them by, in each case, expressing their v and c as percentages of their respective s.

Suppose further that we only allow c and v to take on the values either 100 percent or 200 percent of s. Clearly there are 16 possibilities shown in Table B.4.

For each possibility I list the c and v for each industry, and in the columns *lv* and *pp* indicate if this combination is compatible with the assumptions of

TABLE B.4: A Simple Two-Sector Discrete Model of the Relative Probabilities of Prices of Production and Labor Values

A		B			
c	v	c	v	lv	pp
100	100	100	100	y	y
100	100	100	200	n	n
100	100	200	100	y	n
100	100	200	200	n	n
100	200	100	100	n	n
100	200	100	200	y	y
100	200	200	100	n	y
100	200	200	200	y	n
200	100	100	100	y	n
200	100	100	200	n	y
200	100	200	100	y	y
200	100	200	200	n	n
200	200	100	100	n	n
200	200	100	200	y	n
200	200	200	100	n	n
200	200	200	200	y	y
		Total	yes	8	6

the labor theory of value or the assumptions of price of production theory. In 8 cases out of 16 the assumptions of the labor theory of value are compatible between the two industries, and in 6 cases the assumptions of prices of production are met. So this seems to indicate that prices of production are less likely in this simple case.

If we allow a greater range of discrete values for c and v this discrepancy becomes more pronounced. If we allow each to take on three possible values, we have 81 cases, of which 27 meet lv and 19 meet pp. The intuition one gets from this sort of simple two-industry model is that labor value examples make up a larger fraction of cases and are hence more likely.

But these are examples of independent industries, where we are free to vary the capital components of each industry, which is not the case once we look at the three industrial sectors in a reproduction scheme. These have constraints between capital components in different sectors that have to be met. These constraints make it unsafe to generalize from the sort of example in Table B.4. We will examine these constraints more formally below, and show that the constraints themselves tell us what market prices have to be in a system of simple reproduction.

Tables B.2 and B.3 show that from the physical flow between sectors one could work out the relative sectoral prices. The aim here is to show how one can start out from a physical flow pattern for a 3-sector economy and deduce the relative sectoral prices that must correspond to it.

We will use G, for Goods, to stand for our 3x3 matrix of flows of goods in kind, so that the first column corresponds to the in-kind flows of capital goods that Marx denotes by his C column vector; the second column to the in-kind flows of wage goods corresponding to the column vector V; and the last column to the flows of luxuries denoted by the column vector S.

We stipulate that all elements are positive non-zero and that each column of G adds up to 1, that is, the elements of each column in G are expressed as fractions of the total output of the coresponding sector. In other words we normalize the columns. A concrete example is given in Table B.5. For the purposes of studying the relation between physical flows on sectoral prices it is convenient to to express the flow elements as numbers between 0 and 1. We do this by normalizing a physical flow table, dividing each column element by the total of the column.

We denote the elements of G as $g_{i,j}$ for i, j:1..3.

If p is a 3-element price vector for capital, wage, and luxury goods, then in order to have only 3 prices when in fact each sector makes a wide variety of goods, we assume that the prices are index prices defined over bundles of capital, wage and luxury goods. Given the actual physical flows in G then the trade pattern in Figure B.2 establishes price constraints:

TABLE B.5: Physical Flow Table

	Coal	Corn	Caviar	Outputs
I	16,047	2,801	14,151	20,004 tons of coal
II	464	11,898	3,573	20,017 tons of corn
III	3,493	5,318	2,286	20,011 tons of caviar
Totals	20,004	20,017	20,010	

THE EQUIVALENT G MATRIX

0.80	0.14	0.71
0.02	0.59	0.18
0.17	0.27	0.11

For the purposes of studying the relation between physical flows on sectoral prices, it is convenient to to express the flow elements as numbers between 0 and 1. We can do this by normalizing a physical flow table, dividing each column element by the total of the column.

$$P_1 \, g_{3,1} = P_3 \, g_{1,3}$$

$$P_3 \, g_{2,3} = P_2 \, g_{3,2}$$

$$P_2 \, g_{1,2} = P_1 \, g_{2,1}$$

Where P is a 3-element price vector whose elements are written pi. For example, given the G matrix in Table B.5 we can use the above equations to solve for the relative prices deriving:

$$P = [2.123, 0.352, 0.524]$$

from which we can derive the corresponding monetary relations given in Table B.6.

Note that since the first equation fixes the ratio p1/p3 and the next fixes p2/p3 then this implies p1/p2 is also fixed, so we have to interpret the last of the three equalities as a constraint on what kind of physical flow matrix is compatible with inter-sector trade. The price constraints set by the G matrix define market-clearing prices for a system in which all sectors are self-financing, that is, there is no credit provided by one sector to another. This was an implicit assumption of Marx's analysis in volume 2 of *Capital*. But these reproduction constraints impose restrictions on the structure of the G matrix. Not all normalized G matrices are compatible with self-financed simple reproduction.

Volumes 1, 2, and 3 of *Capital* actually provide three distinct price models that partially overlap. Figure B.3 illustrates the volumes of configuration space that we are interested in. Reproduction schemes define, by equation B.1, a set of market-clearing price configurations—the large circle. Smaller circles denote the volumes of configuration space compatible with prices of production and labor values. Not all configurations that are compatible with

TABLE B.6: An Example of a Three-Sector Economy in a Stationary State

	Constant Capital C	Wages V	Profits S	O
I	£34,067	£986	£7,415	£42,468
II	£986	£4,188	£1,872	£7,046
III	£7,415	£1,872	£1,198	£10,485
Total	£42,468	£7,046	£10,485	£60,000

Sector II now produces wage goods and sector III, luxuries. This should be read in conjunction with figure B.2. Note the symmetry of the table around the diagonal corresponding to the trade pattern in the figure. This monetary table is derived from table B.5 by solving equation set B.1.

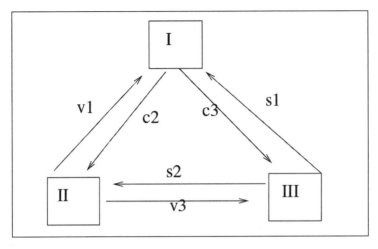

Figure B.2. Three-way inter-sector trade. Sector II sells sector I wage goods worth v1 and buys back in return means of production c2.

labor values or prices of production are compatible with simple reproduction. By being compatible with prices of production we mean that the prices derived from Equation B.1 result in rates of profit that are equal, or very nearly equal, in all sectors. By being compatible with labor values we mean that the prices from the first equation above lead to nearly equal ratios of wages to profits in each sector.

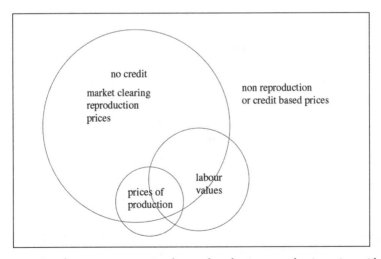

Figure B.3. Set of price systems restricted to market-clearing reproduction prices without credit.

B.1 CONSTRAINTS ON REPRODUCTION SCHEMES

Let us first examine how the structure of the G matrix is constrained by reproduction.

Given $g_{3,1}$, $g_{1,3}$, $g_{2,3}$, $g_{3,2}$, $g_{1,2}$ we can derive $g_{2,1}$ as follows:

$$p_1/p_3 = g_{1,3}/g_{3,1}$$

$$p_3/p_2 = g_{3,2}/g_{2,3}$$

$$p_1/p_2 = (p_1/p_3) \times (p_3/p_2) = (g_{1,3}/g_{3,1}) \times (g_{3,2}/g_{2,3})$$

But from the original trade relation we have:

$$p_1/p_2 = g_{1,2}/g_{2,1}$$

so

$$g_{1,2}/g_{2,1} = (g_{1,3}/g_{3,1}) \times (g_{3,2}/g_{2,3})$$

and

$$g_{1,2} = g_{2,1} /((g_{1,3}/g_{3,1}) \times (g_{3,2}/g_{2,3}))$$

Alternatively the constraint can be expressed in terms of elements of the other two columns:

$$g_{2,3} = g_{2,1} \times (g_{1,3}/g_{3,1}) \times (g_{3,2}/g_{1,2})$$

or

$$g_{1,2} = g_{2,1} \times (g_{1,3}/g_{3,1}) \times (g_{3,2}/g_{2,3})$$

Taken along with our constraint that the columns of G sum to 1, we have 4 constraints on the 9 elements of the matrix leaving only 5 degrees of freedom to the configuration space of reproduction schemes. That is, simple reproduction schemes are samples drawn from an underlying 5-dimensional vector space. Given such a space we can systematically sample it.

B.2 FIRST EXPERIMENT

A program was developed that created successive random samples of the configuration space of reproduction schemes. First the elements of G were assigned random values > 0 and < 1 such that the totals on column 2 were each 1, and the expected value of each element was 1/3. Then with equal probability one of the second to fourth equations above was used to override the previous random variable assignment to one of the elements. This constraint, however, is not guaranteed to satisfy the condition that the column must sum to 1, but that is achieved by subsequently altering the diagonal elements of the matrix to ensure that all columns sum to 1. The diagonal elements do not enter into inter-sector trade and hence can be altered without disturbing the relations established in these equations.

The mean of G over 120,000 samples to two decimal places was

$$
\begin{array}{ccc}
0.40 & 0.28 & 0.32 \\
0.25 & 0.40 & 0.28 \\
0.35 & 0.32 & 0.40
\end{array}
$$

This implies that the expected values for the organic compositions of capital, for reproduction schemes meeting the second equation, will differ between departments. This means we are not encountering a simple situation of uniform expected organic compositions. This can be seen in the distribution of relative organic compositions in Figure B.4.

For each reproduction scheme configuration the market price vector was set by constraint of the first equation above.

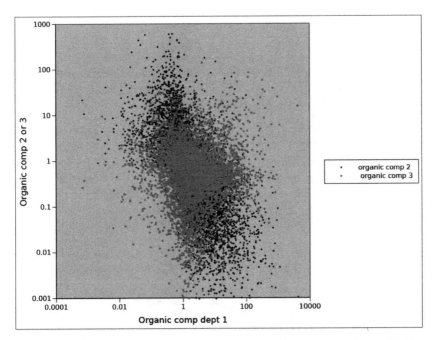

Figure B.4. Spread of relative organic compositions over the entire sample set with the sub-sampling technique.

316

APPENDIX B

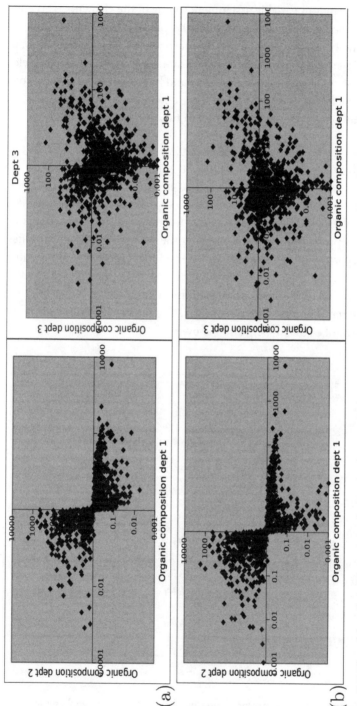

Figure B.5. Plot of the relative departmental organic compositions of reproduction schemes in which market-clearing prices were within 10 percent of (a) labor values; (b) prices of production. The characteristic "bow tie" configuration for the left plots also appears in the overall sample in Figure B.4, but though the first and third quadrants are empty here, samples were present in these quadrants in Figure B.4. This indicates that these quadrants of configuration space are incompatible with either prices of production or labor values.

Labor values were computed as follows:

$$v_1 = g_{1,2}/(1-g_{1,1})$$

That is, divide the real wage in Sector I by its net output. The assumption made is that the labor used in each sector is proportional to the flow of wage goods consumed.

$$v_2 = g_{2,2} + v_1 g_{2,1}$$

$$v_3 = g_{3,2} + v_1 g_{3,1}$$

At the end of this we have v as vertically integrated labor coefficients, derived from wages.

$$\Sigma v = 3$$

The last is a normalization condition used to ensure that under all price models the sum of prices is the same. If we do not apply this, we would have a sum of values < 3, in effect ignoring surplus value. But we are free to apply this linear rescaling to v because the assumption Marx makes is that the rate of surplus value is the same everywhere. The implicit assumption here is that the real wage is the same in all sectors.

An iterative estimation is used for prices of production. We first set all prices to 1. Then we repeatedly perform the following steps. Set r to one plus the rate of profit:

$$r \leftarrow 1 + (p_3 /(p_2 + p_1))$$

This works because the physical output of each industry is unity by virtue of using a normalized G. Next set a new estimate of the price vector np;

$$np \leftarrow (r \times (p_2 g_{\upsilon 2} + p_1 g_{\iota,1}))$$

Finally we normalize the sum of prices to be 3, the same as before.

$$p \leftarrow 3 \times np/\Sigma np$$

Runs were made with many reproduction schemes. The cumulative total number of resulting reproduction schemes was recorded along with the number of schemes that conformed either to labor values or to prices of production. Results are shown in the above equation.

Conformance of either labor values or prices of production was determined by measuring whether their mean absolute deviation (MAD) from market prices was below a specified threshold. The experiment used a 10 percent threshold since that is of the right order for the best that is observed empirically. In addition the program records the mean of the MADs between exchange-values and the two pricing theories.

B.2.1 Results

From the random sampling of reproduction schemes it appears that the mean spread of prices of production from market-clearing prices is smaller than the mean spread of labor values. This is incompatible with a number of empirical studies as shown lower in the table where the relationship is the reverse. However, the observed spreads of both values and production prices from market-clearing prices are lower than found in our *a priori* estimation. This may be a result of the empirical data typically using longer price vectors with 30 to 60 elements rather than just 3, with resultant reversion to a mean. This was essentially Farjoun's argument [1984] for why empirical dispersions of prices to market values would be smaller than those obtained in toy examples using reproduction schemes.

B.3 DISCUSSION

Sraffa [1960] showed that given

1. An assumption of an equal rate of profit
2. A technology matrix
3. A specification of the real wage

it was possible to deduce a price system that would reproduce both the material conditions of production and the class distribution of income. This appendix shows that the G matrix, a use-value dual of Marx's reproduction schemes, can also define a price system that will reproduce the material conditions of production and the class distribution of income.

The G matrix plays both the role of Sraffa's technology matrix and his real wage, but Marxian reproduction schemes do not necessitate a uniform rate of profit, nor do they require that prices are proportional to labor values. Reproduction schemes can exist with these properties, but Table B.7 shows that both labor-value conforming schemes and price of production conformant schemes make up a small portion of the possible schemes. Even with a very lax definition of *conforming*, being within 10 percent of, less than

TABLE B.7: Relative Frequencies and Spreads of Prices of Production and Labor Values

versus	Labor Value Market Price	Production Price Market Price	Production Price Labor Value
% of Schemes with MAD < 10%	0.44%	0.44%	6.84%
Mean MAD	28%	23.7%	14.8%
EMPIRICAL MAD:			
China [Sánchez and Montibeler, 2015]	14.2%	16.5%	12.0%
U.S. [Ochoa, 1989]	10.3%	12.6%	16.9%
Spain [Sánchez and Nieto Ferrandez, 2010]	12.2%	18.8%	19.0%
Germany (1978) [Zachariah, 2006]	16.0%	22.6%	-
France (1980) [Zachariah, 2006]	12.0%	18.2%	-

Figures are computed from sample of 100,000 reproduction schema and compared with empirical studies.

1/200th of all schemes meet this criterion. It would appear that labor-value conforming reproduction schemes are as common as price of production conforming ones. If one looks at Figure B.5 showing where the conforming instances occur in the planes of relative surplus value between sectors, the pattern is almost identical in both cases, with many of the same data points appearing in both rows.

From Paul Sweezy onward it has been conventional for Marxian economists to present individual example reproduction schemes that either have prices proportional to labor values or prices given by an equal rate of profit. The statistical analysis here shows that in doing so economists have been using what are, on *a priori* grounds, rare exceptions to prove rules.

Three-sector reproduction schemes, however, capture something additional that is missing in Sraffa, which is the fact that different social classes have different consumption patterns. Marx dealt with the more general case where the capitalists divide their expenditure in some fixed proportion between necessities and luxuries, what would in modern terms be called a Leontief demand function. The analysis here has taken the simpler assumption that capitalist expenditure is exclusively on luxuries. Similarly we neglect that some commodities, for instance coal, may have been a means of production, a wage good, and have been bought by capitalists to heat their houses.

The simplification is arguably valid, since one could in principle divide the coal industry into three sub-industries, one supplying factories, one supplying workers' cottages, and one supplying mansions. These sub-industries would then be statistically aggregated into Sectors I, II, or III. But the intersectoral constraints may have implications for the feasibility of attaining prices of production.

Reproduction prices represent a static macroeconomic equilibrium condition. So long as there is no growth in production and no change in technology and no movement of capital between sectors, reproduction prices will keep the economy in an equilibrium. These are market-clearing prices given the technology and income distribution. On the other hand, the alternative concept of equilibrium present in volume 3 of *Capital* and further developed in *Production of Commodities* [Sraffa, 1960] assumes capital mobility between sectors. Borkiewicz's criticism [Hilferding, 1951] of volume 3 was based on arguing that the procedure presented for transforming labor values to prices of production was statically incompatible with reproduction prices. But the dynamic question remains open. If you start off in a macroeconomic equilibrium with reproduction prices operating, but with divergent profit rates as shown in Table B.6, can capital movements produce a new equilibrium with a price structure that both achieves reproduction and profit rate equalization?

On the one hand the structure of reproduction is so finely balanced, with such intricate interdependence between the elements of the reproduction table that perhaps any movement in capital would throw the whole system into a catastrophic crisis. Alternatively, one may argue that even if one keeps technology and labor supply, and money capital constant, the system has still got some degrees of freedom left in terms of the relative sizes of three sectors.

We can see that capital movement is very likely to result in a change in the class distribution of income. A movement of capital in or out of Sector II means a bigger or smaller real wage, and in consequence reduces or increases the real quantity of luxuries being consumed by employers. So a movement into row 2 of the table must go along with balancing changes in columns 2 and 3, but whether these will be dynamically achievable is harder to say. It may depend both on the adjustment process and on the initial starting structure of the table.

B.4 SECOND EXPERIMENT

In order to investigate the dynamic process of capital movement from initial reproduction states, a second experiment was carried out. Like the first experiment it used a sample of reproduction schemes, prepared in the same way as in the previous experiment. It combined these with rules for capital mobility, for price adjustment, possible buffer stocks, and adjustment of sectoral outputs. The time evolution of the economies represented by the initial reproduction schemes was then evaluated for 150 time steps. The model is stock flow consistent both in money and in use values.

Initialization. A G matrix is prepared as in the first experiment. An initial price vector is derived and a resulting initial monetary reproduction scheme is derived. From an assumed money wage of £2 an initial vector of labor allocation λ is derived. In conjunction with the labor vector the G matrix is used to derive a linear production function for each sector. Each sector is allocated sufficient cash to pay wages and buy means of production at current prices and the current scale of production.

Simulation cycles start at the point where production has just finished, so the firms in each sector have a stock equal to what was produced, plus any unsold stock from the previous period. Stocks of goods held are recorded in the A (for available) matrix.

Capital allocation rule. Let s be the sector with the highest rate of profit. For each sector $x \neq s$ if the rate of profit in x is more than 1 percent below the rate in s, then sector x will transfer 1 percent of its money capital to sector x. Each sector divides its money capital into constant and variable capital in the same ratio as its final allocation in the previous period. We thus get new column vectors V_t, C_t for variable and constant capital for time t.

Wage and labor rule. Wage rates are then set such that

$$w_t \leftarrow \Sigma Vt/\Sigma \lambda_{t-1}$$

and the new wage rate and new V_t is used to reallocate labor so that

$$\lambda_t \leftarrow V_t/w_t$$

Prices sectors I and II. The total requirement for means of production for each sector given λ_t is then determined using the production functions. If this exceeds the total stocks of means of production held by all sectors then we have a seller's market in means of production whose prices rise to a market-clearing level.

$$p_1 \leftarrow \Sigma Ct/\Sigma_i A_{i,1}$$

Otherwise if stocks exceed requirements, we have a buyer's market and the price of means of production is reduced by 3 percent. The price of wage goods is then set as

$$p_2 \leftarrow w\Sigma\lambda/\Sigma_i {}_{i,2}$$

Sectors then pay wages and workers spend their wages on the output of Sector II at the current p_2. Each sector then purchases its requirement of means of production from Sector I at price p_1.

Demand for luxuries. For Sectors I and II we now know their total sales and their total cost of production. By subtracting purchases from sales we get their profits, which are assumed to be entirely spent on luxuries. For the capitalists of Sector III we have the odd situation where, as Marx points out, profits are self-financing. Whatever they spend on luxuries will return to them as additional profit. The simulation thus adopts the parsimonious assumption that their expenditure on luxuries will remain constant in money terms. The price of luxuries is then set to clear the market given the physical stocks available.

Production. Production takes place constrained either by the available labor in each sector or the available means of production, as per the linear production function. If labor is the limiting factor this may result in some unused stock of means of production that are carried over to the next period.

B.4.1 Results

Figure B.6 shows the results of the simulation in terms of the initial and final standard deviations of the rate of profit. A simulation run is represented as a point whose x position is given by the starting spread of its profit rate and its y position by its terminating profit rate spread. A point on the 45-degree diagonal represents a system that has undergone no profit rate convergence during the simulation. A point close to the x axis indicates a system that has undergone convergence.

One can clearly see that the simulated systems fall into two distinct clusters—one just below the 45-degree line, and one close to or below the 1 percent line. Provided that profit rates are within 1 percent they are taken to have converged, since only discrepancies bigger than this are assumed to trigger capital flows.

Detailed examination of the final sectoral output figures for the simulations run showed that many simulated economies had undergone a drastic contraction in terms of physical output. Since the amount of money circulating does not change during the simulation, rises in prices obscure this effect if one looks only at the figures for output in money terms.

We define an economy to be healthy under capital movement if the final value of output measured in the prices operating at time t0 are >98 percent of the starting value of output. We define an economy as having collapsed if output is less than 50 percent of its starting value. One can see in Figure B.6 that there is no particular relationship between the economy being healthy and its profit rate converging. Some of the economies whose profit rates equalize are healthy and some are collapsing. Conversely, some healthy economies retain dispersed profit rates even in the presence of

TABLE B.8: Geometric Mean of Initial Organic Compositions by Sector and Group for the Economies Simulated in Figure B.6

Sector	I	II	III
Collapsing	2.16	0.59	1.18
Healthy	1.23	0.65	1.88
Converging	1.60	1.31	2.21
Non-Converging	1.96	0.47	1.15

capital movements that, according to accepted theory, should result in an equalization of the rate of profit.

Table B.8 does show, however, that the collapsing economies tend to be characterized by greater sectoral disparities in organic composition, and higher organic compositions in Sector I. Systems that do not converge their rates of profit are characterized by particularly low organic compositions in Sector II.

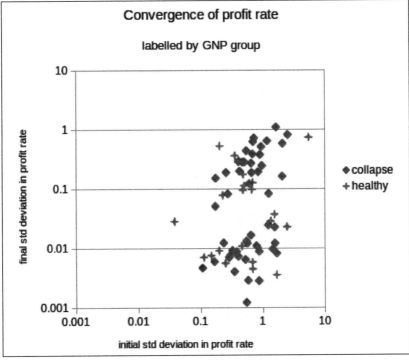

Figure B.6. When simulated over time, some reproduction schemes can converge toward an equal rate of profit. The population of schemes forms two distinct clusters, one capable of converging and one that does not converge. Schemes that show no convergence over time would lie on a line at 45 degrees going through the origin of this plot. Healthy models are those in which GNP remains constant or grows; collapse models are those whose GNP has fallen by more than 50 percent at the end of the simulation.

B.5 FURTHER DISCUSSION

The first experiment shows that only a very small fraction of possible self-reproducing capitalist economies are characterized by equal rates of profit. Similarly, only a very small fraction of possible reproduction schemes have price structures close to labor values. The existing literature on the *transformation problem* relates to either logical or temporal transition between the small subset of the value-conformant reproduction schemes and the small subset of price of production-conformant schemes.

The second experiment indicates that one cannot simply assume that the mechanism that is supposed to bring about an equal rate of profit will, in general, work. For some starting points, combinations of technology and distributions of income, the hypothesized convergence mechanism fails. In these cases the system either remains healthy with a continuing spread of profit rates, or the economy shrinks catastrophically.

The exact nature of the dynamics that produce this result are at present unclear, but it appears that in the cases of catastrophic contraction, the problem arises due to insufficient means of production being produced, which acts as a constraint on all subsequent output. If the economy moves to a labor distribution where more means of production would be used by the current distribution of the labor force than it can produce, then clearly it must undergo contracted reproduction.

In the case of simulated economies that fail to converge on a uniform rate of profit, one hypothesis is that if Sector II has a particularly low organic composition of capital, then a movement of capital into Sector II leads to a net increase in the demand for labor power. This raises wages and increases demand for Sector II, so rather than the price of necessities falling consequent on inward capital movement, wage goods may rise in price. Another possibility is that the distribution of profit rates may undergo oscillations. Further investigation into detailed trajectories of prices and profit rates of individual sectors would be required to test these hypotheses.

B.6 MODEL AND REALITY

We know that real capitalist economies do not often go into catastrophic collapse due to inadequate production of means of production, though the collapse of industrial production in the former USSR after conversion to capitalism may be an instance of this. Why is this?

It may be that some version of the Anthropic Principle is in operation. We do not see these collapses because the collapses are history sensitive, and the economies starting out in technological and income configurations that would result in collapse are eliminated. That may apply to the former

TABLE B.9: Mean Price and Value Vectors

Sector	Capital Goods	Wage Goods	Luxuries
Mean Labor Values	0.95	1.11	0.93
Mean Production Price	1.08	1.02	0.90
Mean Market-Clearing Price	1.00	0.92	1.07

socialist economies being suddenly exposed to a profit maximizing principle; they contracted until the technical structure of the economy changed. The end result would be that at any given time, the population of capitalist economies would have been purged of those with technical structures that would lead them to collapse under free capital movement.

Alternatively, the basic market-clearing price mechanism used in the model may not be realistic. The model basically assumes unit elasticity, a 1 percent fall in output, other things being equal, raises prices by 1 percent. Perhaps capitalist economies are only stable against collapse given nonlinear price responses.

Instead of looking at the problem of collapse, consider that a substantial fraction of healthy models fail to attain an equal rate of profit. This is less of a problem since it accords with what we observe in reality. We know that typical capitalist economies have a dispersion of profit rates [Fröhlich, 2013].

All reproduction schemes meeting the constraints described in Section B.1 define a set of market-clearing prices for economies with no credit operations. Real economies have credit and therefore the set of actual market prices we observe will be less constrained than is implied by reproduction schemes. However, reproduction schemes do have the virtue of allowing us to generate a large sample of simple economies and associated price structures sans any assumptions about the underlying price mechanism of the economy. They allow us to explore the space of possible self-reproducing economies and the price structures associated with them.

The input-output tables used in empirical studies are approximations to systems of simple reproduction. They are only approximations, since they depict economies that are typically growing, but the growth rate is typically small, and the conventions associated with the construction of input-output tables impose similar balance constraints to those seen in reproduction schemes. The existence of credit transfers between industries in the input-output tables will, however, introduce a complication absent in the simple Marxian schemes.

Using unbiased samples from the space of reproduction schemes we can determine the probability of different pricing theories. That is, the probability that such pricing theories would be true if real economies were distributed with equal probability over all possible positions in configuration space. We are assuming, in effect, that if economies undergo a random walk through configuration space, the probability of their transiting from one macro-state to another is proportional to the volume occupied by these macro-states.

The macro-state defined by market prices being within 10 percent of labor values has a similar volume to the macro state with market prices with 10 percent of prices of production. *A priori*, we should expect a reproducing economy to be this close to a labor value–conformant configuration as to a price of production-conformant one.

If, on the other hand, there is some bias in the random walk, so that economies end up closer to either of these pricing systems than one would expect, then this is analogous to evolution in a space with a potential defined over it. The discrepancy between observed and *a priori* probability distributions should then enable one to estimate, via some appropriate negative exponential law, the depth of potential wells. Conversely one could say how strong the potential field would have to be to produce a world in which either labor values or production prices were the operational laws. Even without a deeper analysis, though, it appears from these results that the assumption of prices of production as an operational law implies a weaker potential well favoring it than need be assumed for labor values. The expected *a priori* dispersions of labor values are wider than those for prices of production. The fact that this is not what is empirically observed implies that the potential well associated with prices of production is weaker than that associated with labor values. Possibly this is an effect of labor being more mobile than capital. It is easier for steel workers to move into catering jobs than to convert steel mills into restaurants. Alternatively, the obstacles to profit-rate equalization shown in the second experiment may act as a frustrating factor effectively reducing the potential well around prices of production.

Bibliography

Abolition of Feudal Tenure etc. (Scotland) Act, Scottish Parliament, 2000.

Adams, Marilyn M. *William Ockham*. 2 vols. Notre Dame, IN: University of Notre Dame Press, 1987.

Allen, Robert C. "Why the Industrial Revolution Was British: Commerce, Induced Invention, and the Scientific Revolution." *Economic History Review* 64, no. 2 (May 2011): 357–84.

Allen, Robert C. *Farm to Factory: A Reinterpretation of the Soviet Industrial Revolution*. Princeton, NJ: Princeton University Press, 2003.

Allen, Robert C. "How Prosperous Were the Romans? Evidence from Diocletian's Price Edict (301 AD)." In *Quantifying the Roman Economy: Methods and Problems*, edited by Alan Bowman and Andrew Wilson, 327–45. Oxford: Oxford University Press, 2009.

Allen, Robert C. "A Reassessment of the Soviet Industrial Revolution." *Comparative Economic Studies* 47, no. 2 (June 2005): 315–32.

Allen, Robert C. "The High Wage Economy and the Industrial Revolution: A Restatement." *Economic History Review*, 68, no. 1 (February 2015): 1–22.

Altenburg, Charles J., and Robert J. Scott. *Design Considerations for Aluminum Hull Structures*. Washington, D.C.: Ship Structure Committee, 1971.

Althusser, Louis. *Philosophy of the Encounter: Later Writings, 1978–1987*, edited by Oliver Corpet and François Matheron. London: Verso, 2006.

Althusser, Louis. "Ideology and Ideological State Apparatuses." In *Lenin and Philosophy*. London: New Left, 1971.

Ambedkar, B. R. *Annihilation of Caste*. Jullundar: Bheem Patrika, 1982.

Anderson, Perry. *Passages from Antiquity to Feudalism*. London: Verso, 1996.

Comparison of Power Plant Technology and Costs in the USSR and the United States. Washington, D.C.: Central Intelligence Agency, 1965.

Arena, Mark V., Hans Pung, Cynthia R. Cook, Jefferson P. Marquis, Jessie Riposo, and Gordon T. Lee. *The United Kingdom's Naval Shipbuilding Industrial Base: The Next Fifteen Years*. Santa Monica, CA: RAND Corporation, 2005.

Aristotle. *Aristotle's Physics*. Oxford: Clarendon, 1983.

Austen, Jane. *Pride and Prejudice*. Project Gutenberg, 2018 [1815]. https:// gutenberg. org/files/1342/1342-h/1342-h.htm.

Azizov, Englen A. "Tokamaks: from A. D. Sakharov to the Present (The 60-Year History of Tokamaks). *Physics-Uspekhi* 55, no. 2 (2012): 190–203.

Bacon, Robert and Walter Eltis. *Britain's Economic Problem: Too Few Producers*, vol. 2. London: Palgrave Macmillan, 1978.

Badiou, Alain. *The Concept of Model: An Introduction to the Materialist Epistemology of Mathematics*, edited by Zachary Luke Fraser and Tzuchien Tho. Melbourne: Re.press, 2007.

Baeza, Alejandro Valle. "Dimensional Analysis of Price-Value Correspondence: A Spurious Case of Spurious Correlation." *Investigación Económica* 69, no. 274 (2010): 119–30.

Bairoch, Paul, and Gary Goertz. "Factors of Urbanization in the Nineteenth Century Developed Countries: A Descriptive and Econometric Analysis." *Urban Studies* 23 (1986): 285–305.

Banaji, Jairus. *Exploring the Economy of Late Antiquity: Selected Essays*. Cambridge: Cambridge University Press, 2016.

Banister, Judith. "Population Policy and Trends in China, 1978–83." *China Quarterly* 100 (December 1984): 717–41.

Banister, Judith. "Shortage of Girls in China Today." *Journal of Population Research* 21, no. 1 (March 2004): 19–45.

Banister, Judith, David E. Bloom, and Larry Rosenberg. "Population Aging and Economic Growth in China." In *The Chinese Economy*, edited by Masahiko Aoki and Jinglian Wu, 114–49. London: Palgrave Macmillan, 2012.

Barber, Elizabeth Jane Wayland. *Prehistoric Textiles: The Development of Cloth in the Neolithic and Bronze Ages with Special Reference to the Aegean*. Princeton, NJ: Princeton University Press, 1991.

Barclay, Gordon. *Farmers, Temples and Tombs: Scotland in the Neolithic and Early Bronze Age*. Edinburgh: Canongate, 1998.

Barro, Robert J. "Government Spending, Interest Rates, Prices, and Budget Deficits in the United Kingdom, 1701–1918." *Journal of Monetary Economics* 20, no. 2 (September 1987): 221–47.

Baxter, Peter J., M. Kapila, and D. Mfonfu. "Lake Nyos Disaster, Cameroon, 1986: The Medical Effects of Large Scale Emission of Carbon Dioxide?" *BMJ* 298, no. 6685 (May 1989): 1437–41, 1989.

Beckerman, Stephen, and Paul Valentine. *Cultures of Multiple Fathers: The Theory and Practice of Partible Paternity in Lowland South America*. Gainesville, FL: University Press of Florida, 2002.

Berman, Harold J. "Soviet Family Law in the Light of Russian History and Marxist Theory." *Yale Law Journal* 56, no. 1 (1946): 26–57.

Bianchi, Suzanne M., Melissa A. Milkie, Liana C. Sayer, and John P. Robinson. "Is Anyone Doing the Housework? Trends in the Gender Division of Household Labor." *Social Forces* 79, no. 1 (September 2000): 191–228.

Bittman, Michael, James Mahmud Rice, and Judy Wajcman. "Appliances and Their Impact: The Ownership of Domestic Technology and Time Spent on Household Work." *British Journal of Sociology* 55, no. 3 (September 2004): 401–23.

Blackledge, Todd A., Nikolaj Scharff, Jonathan A. Coddington, Tamas Szüts, John W. Wenzel, Cheryl Y. Hayashi, and Ingi Agnarsson. "Reconstructing Web Evolution and Spider Diversification in the Molecular Era." *Proceedings of the National Academy of Sciences* 106, no. 13 (March 2009): 5229–34.

Blackmon, Douglas A. *Slavery by Another Name: The Re-enslavement of Black Americans from the Civil War to World War II*. New York: Anchor, 2009.

Bolin, Sture. *State and Currency in the Roman Empire to 300 A.D.* Stockholm: Almqvist and Wiksell, 1958.

Bordiga, Amadeo. *Dialogue avec Staline*. Paris: Editions Programme Communiste, 1954.

Bordiga, Amadeo. *Structure Économique et Sociale de la Russie d'Aujourdhúi: Développement des Rapports de Production après la Révolution Bolchevique*, vol. 2. Paris: Editions de l'Oubli, 1975.

Bouckaert, Remco, Philippe Lemey, Michael Dunn, Simon J. Greenhill, Alexander V. Alekseyenko, Alexei J. Drummond, Russell D. Gray, Marc A. Suchard, and Quentin D. Atkinson. "Mapping the Origins and Expansion of the Indo-European Language Family." *Science* 337, no. 6097 (August 2012): 957–60.

Brand, Stewart. *The Media Lab: Inventing the Future at MIT*. New York: Viking, 1987.

Braudel, Fernand. *Civilization and Capitalism, Fifteenth–Eighteenth Century, Vol. 1: The Structure of Everyday Life*. Berkeley, CA: University of California Press, 1992.

Brenner, Robert P. "The Low Countries in the Transition to Capitalism." *Journal of Agrarian Change* 1, no. 2 (April 2001): 169–241.

Broadberry, Stephen, Bruce M. S. Campbell, and Bas van Leeuwen. "English Medieval Population: Reconciling Time Series and Cross Sectional Evidence." Unpublished manuscript, University of Warwick, 2010.

Bukharin, Nikolai Ivanovich. *Imperialism and World Economy*. New York: Monthly Review Press, 1976.

Burney, David A., and Timothy F. Flannery. "Fifty Millennia of Catastrophic Extinctions after Human Contact." *Trends in Ecology & Evolution* 20, no. 7 (July 2005): 395–401.

Buxton, Ian, and Ian Johnston. *The Battleship Builders Constructing and Arming British Capital Ships*. Barnsley, UK: Seaforth, 2013.

Becker, Charles, S. Joshua Mendelshohn, and Kseniya Benderskaya. *Russian Urbanization in the Soviet and Post-Soviet Eras*. London: International Institute for Environment and Development, 2012.

Cairnes, John E. *The Slave Power: Its Character, Career, and Probable Designs: Being an Attempt to Explain the Real Issues Involved in the American Contest*. Columbia, SC: University of South Carolina Press, 2003.

Campbell, Martha. "Rent and Landed Property." In *The Culmination of Capital: Essays on Volume III of Marx's Capital*, edited by Martha Campbell and Geert Reuten, 228–45. London: Palgrave Macmillan, 2002.

Cardwell, Donald Stephen Lowell. *From Watt to Clausius: The Rise of Thermodynamics in the Early Industrial Age*. Ithaca, NY: Cornell University Press, 1971.

Case, Anne, and Angus Deaton. "Rising Morbidity and Mortality in Midlife among White Non-Hispanic Americans in the Twenty-First Century." *Proceedings of the National Academy of Sciences* 112, no. 49 (December 2015): 15078–83.

Casson, Lionel. "Speed under Sail of Ancient Ships." *Transactions and Proceedings of the American Philological Association* 82 (1951): 136–48.

Casson, Lionel. "Fore-and-Aft Sails in the Ancient World." *Mariner's Mirror* 42, no. 1 (1956): 3–5.

Chandler, Pat. "A Vision of Britain through Time." *School Librarian* 62, no. 2 (Summer 2014): 86–87.

Cichorius, Conrad. *Die Reliefs der Traianssäule*, vol. 3. Berlin: Reimer, 1900.

Clark, D. L. "Foundations of Growth and Planning Theory." *Journal of Contemporary Asia* 14, no. 3 (1984): 266–82.

Clark, Gregory. "The Long March of History: Farm Wages, Population, and Economic Growth, England 1209–1869." *Economic History Review* 60, no. 1 (2007): 97–135.

Clark, Gregory, and Susan Wolcott. "One Polity, Many Countries: Economic Growth in

India, 1873–2000." In *Search of Prosperity: Analytic Narratives on Economic Growth*, edited by Dani Rodrik, 53–79. Princeton, NJ: Princeton University Press, 2003.

Cockshott, Paul. "De Stora Sprången." *Clarté* 4 (2006): 12–25.

Cockshott, Paul. "Heinrich's Idea of Abstract Labor." *Critique* 41, no. 2 (2013): 287–97.

Cockshott, Paul. "On Althusser's Philosophy of the Encounter." *World Review of Political Economy* 4, no. 1 (Spring 2013): 38–62.

Cockshott, Paul. "Von Mises, Kantorovich and In-Natura Calculation." *European Journal of Economics and Economic Policies: Intervention* 7, no. 1 (2006): 167–99.

Cockshott, Paul, and Allin Cottrell. "Information and Economics: A Critique of Hayek." *Research in Political Economy* 18, no. 1 (1997): 177–202.

Cockshott, Paul, and Allin Cottrell. "Labor Time versus Alternative Value Bases: A Research Note." *Cambridge Journal of Economics* 21, no. 4 (July 1997): 545–49.

Cockshott, Paul, and Allin Cottrell. "Labor Value and Socialist Economic Calculation." *Economy and Society* 18, no. 1 (1989): 71–99.

Cockshott, Paul, and Allin Cottrell. "A Note on the Organic Composition of Capital and Profit Rates." *Cambridge Journal of Economics* 27, no. 5 (September 2003): 749–54.

Cockshott, Paul, and Allin Cottrell. "Robust Correlations between Prices and Labor Values: A Comment." *Cambridge Journal of Economics* 29, no. 2 (March 2005): 309–16.

Cockshott, Paul, and Allin Cottrell. "The Scientific Status of the Labor Theory of Value." Paper delivered at IWGVT conference at the Eastern Economic Association meeting, March 1997.

Cockshott, Paul, and Allin Cottrell. *Towards a New Socialism*. Nottingham: Bertrand Russell, 1992.

Cockshott, Paul, and Allin Cottrell. *Towards a New Socialism*. Nottingham: Spokesman, 1995.

Cockshott, Paul, Allin Cottrell, and Greg Michaelson. "Testing Marx: Some New Results from UK Data." *Capital and Class* 19, no. 1 (1995): 103–29.

Cockshott, Paul, Allin F. Cottrell, Gregory J. Michaelson, Ian P. Wright, and Victor M. Yakovenko. *Classical Econophysics*. Routledge, 2009.

Cockshott, Paul, Lewis M. Mackenzie, and Gregory Michaelson. *Computation and Its Limits*. Oxford: Oxford University Press, 2012.

Cockshott, Paul, and Karen Renaud. "Extending Handivote to Handle Digital Economic Decisions." In *Proceedings of the 2010 ACM-BCS Visions of Computer Science Conference*, 5. British Computer Society, 2010.

Cockshott, Paul, and David Zachariah. "Hunting Productive Work." *Science & Society* 70, no. 4 (October 2006): 509–27.

Cohen, Mark. *The Food Crisis in Prehistory: Overpopulation and the Origins of Agriculture*. New Haven, CT: Yale University Press, 1977.

Coleman-Jensen, Alisha, Matthew Rabbitt, Christian Gregory, and Anita Singh. *Household Food Security in the United States 2014*. Washington, D.C.: United States Department of Agriculture, 2015.

Contreras, A., S. Yigit, K. Özay, and T. N. Veziroglu. "Hydrogen as Aviation Fuel: A Comparison with Hydrocarbon Fuels." *International Journal of Hydrogen Energy* 22, nos. 10–11 (1997): 1053–60.

Cottrell, Allin, and W. Paul Cockshott. "Socialist Planning after the Collapse of the Soviet Union." *Revue Européenne des Sciences Sociales* 31, no. 96 (1993): 167–85.

Cowell, M. R., and Kingsley Hyne. "Scientific Examination of the Lydian Precious Metal

Coinages." *King Croesus' Gold: Excavations at Sardis and the History of Gold Refining.* Cambridge, MA: Harvard University Press, 2000, 169–74.

Crafts, Nicholas. "Steam as a General Purpose Technology: A Growth Accounting Perspective." *Economic Journal* 114, no. 495 (2004): 338–51.

"Criticality for Fast Reactor." *World Nuclear News.* July 22, 2010. http:// world-nuclear-news.org/NN_Criticality_for_fast_reactor_2207101.html.

Crompron, John L., and Richard J. Gitelson. "Consumer Reactions to the Standby Motor Fuel Rationing Plan." *Journal of Travel Research* 19, no. 4 (1981): 27–36.

Darwin, Charles. *The Descent of Man in Relation to Sex.* London: Murray, 1871.

David, Nicholas, Robert Heimann, David Killick, and Michael Wayman. "Between Bloomery and Blast Furnace: Mafa Iron-Smelting Technology in North Cameroon." *African Archaeological Review* 7, no. 1 (1989): 183–208.

Davies, Glyn. *History of Money.* Cardiff: University of Wales Press, 2010.

Davis, Mike. *Late Victorian Holocausts: El Niño Famines and the Making of the Third World.* London: Verso, 2000.

Dawkins, R. "Extended Phenotype—but Not too Extended. A Reply to Laland, Turner and Jablonka." *Biology and Philosophy* 19, no. 3 (2004): 377–96.

Price, D. de Solla. "An Ancient Greek Computer." *Scientific American* 201 (1959): 60–67.

Price, D. de Solla. "Gears from the Greeks. The Antikythera Mechanism: A Calendar Computer from ca. 80 BC." *Transactions of the American Philosophical Society* 64, no. 7 (1974): 1–70.

Deepankar, Basu. "A Selective Review of Recent Quantitative Empirical Research in Marxist Political Economy." Working paper, Department of Economics, University of Massachusetts, Amherst, 2015.

Defeis, E. "Draft Convention against Sexual Exploitation." *Women and International Human Rights Law* 2 (2000): 319–49.

Delphy, Christine. "The Main Enemy." *Gender Issues* 1, no. 1 (1989): 23–40.

Delphy, Christine, and Diana Leonard. *Close to Home: A Materialist Analysis of Women's Oppression.* London: Hutchinson, 1984.

Dennis, David. "Rene Descartes' Curve-Drawing Devices: Experiments in the Relations between Mechanical Motion and Symbolic Language." *Mathematics* 70, no. 3 (1997): 163–74.

Destro-Bisol, Giovanni, Francesco Donati, Valentina Coia, Ilaria Boschi, Fabio Verginelli, Alessandra Caglia, Sergio Tofanelli, Gabriella Spedini, and Cristian Capelli. "Variation of Female and Male Lineages in Sub-Saharan Populations: The Importance of Sociocultural Factors." *Molecular Biology and Evolution* 21, no. 9 (2004): 1673–82.

Diamond, Jared. *The World until Yesterday: What Can We Learn from Traditional Societies?* New York: Viking, 2012.

Diamond, Jared M., and Doug Ordunio. *Guns, Germs, and Steel.* New York: Norton, 1997.

Dickeman, Mildred. "Demographic Consequences of Infanticide in Man." *Annual Review of Ecology and Systematics* 6 (1975): 107–37.

Dimitrov, Dimitar, Lara Lopardo, Gonzalo Giribet, Miquel A. Arnedo, Fernando Álvarez-Padilla, and Gustavo Hormiga. "Tangled in a Sparse Spider Web: Single Origin of Orb Weavers and Their Spinning Work Unravelled by Denser Taxonomic Sampling." *Proceedings of the Royal Society B: Biological Sciences* 279, no. 1732 (2012): 1341–50.

Diskant, William. *USSR Practices in Heat and Power Supply.* Paper No. 84, Conference on Soviet Construction and Urban Design, Kennan Institute for Advanced

Russian Studies and U.S. Department of Housing and Urban Development, December 19, 1979.

Domar, Evsey D. "The Causes of Slavery or Serfdom: A Hypothesis." *Journal of Economic History* 30, no. 1 (March 1970): 18–32.

Dragulescu, A., and V. M. Yakovenko. "Statistical Mechanics of Money, Income and Wealth: A Short Survey." In *Modeling of Complex Systems: Seventh Granada Lectures: AIP Conference Proceedings, Volume 661*. New York: American Institute of Physics, 2002.

Dragulescu, Adrian A. *Applications of Physics to Economics and Finance: Money, Income, Wealth and the Stock Market.* PhD diss., University of Maryland, Colege Park, 2003.

Düring, Bleda S. *The Prehistory of Asia Minor: From Complex Hunter-Gatherers to Early Urban Societies.* Cambridge: Cambridge University Press, 2010.

Edgerton, David. *Britain's War Machine: Weapons, Resources, and Experts in the Second World War.* Oxford: Oxford University Press, 2011.

Edgerton, David. *Shock of the Old: Technology and Global History since 1900.* London: Profile, 2011.

Eichengreen, Barry, Donghyun Park, and Kwanho Shin. "When Fast-Growing Economies Slow Down: International Evidence and Implications for China." *Asian Economic Papers* 11, no. 1 (2012): 42–87.

Ellison, A. J., and H. Bahmanyar. "Surface-Guided Transport Systems of the Future." *Proceedings of the Institute of Electrical Engineers* 121, no. 11R (1974): 1224–48.

Eng, Robert Y., and Thomas C. Smith. "Peasant Families and Population Control in Eighteenth-Century Japan." *Journal of Interdisciplinary History* 6, no. 3 (1976): 417–45.

Engelman, Uriah Z. "Vital Statistics in the Soviet Union in 1926." *American Journal of Sociology* 38, no. 3 (November 1932): 437–40.

Engels, Donald. "The Problem of Female Infanticide in the Greco-Roman World." *Classical Philology* 75, no. 2 (1980): 112–20.

Engels, Friedrich. *The Origin of the Family, Private Property and the State.* London: Penguin, 2010.

Evans-Pritchard, Edward E. *The Nuer: A Description of the Modes of Livelihood and Political Institutions of a Nilotic People.* Oxford: Clarendon, 1940.

Falola, Toyin, and Akanmu Gafari Adebayo. *Culture, Politics and Money among the Yoruba.* New Brunswick, NJ: Transaction, 2000.

Fang, Cai. "Demographic Transition, Demographic Dividend, and Lewis Turning Point in China." *Economic Research Journal* 4 (2010): 4–13.

Farjoun, E. "Production of Commodities by Means of What?" In *Ricardo, Marx, Sraffa: The Langston Memorial Volume*, 11–43. London: Verso, 1984.

Farjoun, Emmanuel, and Moshe Machover. *Laws of Chaos: A Probabilistic Approach to Political Economy.* London: Verso, 1983.

Farmer, J. Doyne, Stuart A. Kauffman, and Norman H. Packard. "Autocatalytic Replication of Polymers." *Physica D: Nonlinear Phenomena* 22, no. 1 (1986): 50–67.

Feldman, G. A. "On the Theory of Growth Rates of National Income." In *Foundations of Soviet Strategy for Economic Growth*, edited by Nicolas Sperber. Bloomington, IN: Indiana University Press, 1964.

Ferguson, Eugene S. *Kinematics of Mechanisms from the Time of Watt.* Washington, D.C.: Smithsonian Institution, 1962.

Ferrill, Arther. *The Fall of the Roman Empire: The Military Explanation.* London: Thames and Hudson, 1986.

Field, Christopher B., Vicente R. Barros, K. Mach, and M. Mastrandrea. *Climate Change 2014: Impacts, Adaptation, and Vulnerability: Part A: Global and Sectoral Aspects.* Cambridge: Cambridge University Press, 2014.

Finley, M. I. *Ancient Slavery and Modern Ideology.* London: Penguin, 1980.

Fischer, Fritz. *Germany's Aims in the First World War.* New York: Norton, 1967.

Fischer, Fritz, and Roger Fletcher. *From Kaiserreich to Third Reich: Elements of Continuity in German History, 1871–1945.* London: Allen and Unwin, 1986.

Fleck, Susan, John Glaser, and Shawn Sprague. "The Compensation-Productivity Gap: A Visual Essay." *Monthly Labor Review* 134, no. 1 (2011): 57–69.

Földvári, Péter, Bas van Leeuwen, and Dmitry Didenko. "Capital Formation and Economic Growth under Central Planning and Transition: A Theoretical and Empirical Analysis, ca. 1920–2008." *Acta Oeconomica* 65, no. 1 (2015): 27–50.

Forstater, M. "Taxation: A Secret of Colonial Capitalist (So-Called) Primitive Accumulation." Working Paper No. 25, Center for Full Employment and Price Stability, University of Missouri, Kansas City, 2003.

Freeth, T., Y. Bitsakis, X. Moussas, JH Seiradakis, A. Tselikas, H. Mangou, M. Zafeiropoulou, R. Hadland, D. Bate, A. Ramsey, et al. "Decoding the Ancient Greek Astronomical Calculator Known as the Antikythera Mechanism." *Nature* 444, no. 7119 (2006): 587.

Friedman, Norman. *British Cruisers of the Victorian Era.* Barnsley, UK: Seaforth, 2012.

Friedman, Norman. *The British Battleship: 1906–1946.* Annapolis, MD: Naval Institute Press, 2015.

Friedman, Norman, and Arthur David Baker. *British Destroyers: From Earliest Days to the Second World War.* Barnsley, UK: Seaforth, 2009.

Fröhlich, Nils. "Labor Values, Prices of Production and the Missing Equalization Tendency of Profit Rates: Evidence from the German Economy." *Cambridge Journal of Economics* 37, no. 5 (2013): 1107–26.

Fry, Douglas P. *Beyond War: The Human Potential for Peace.* Oxford: Oxford University Press, 2007.

Gaines, Linda, Paul Nelson, et al. "Lithium-Ion Batteries: Possible Materials Issues." In *13th International Battery Materials Recycling Seminar and Exhibit, Broward County Convention Center, Fort Lauderdale, Florida, 16–18 March 2009,* 16. Red Hook, NY: Curran, 2009.

Garland, Charles, and Herbert S. Klein. "The Allotment of Space for Slaves aboard Eighteenth-Century British Slave Ships. *William and Mary Quarterly* 42, no. 2 (1985): 238–48.

George, Sabu, Rajaratnam Abel, and Barbara D. Miller. "Female Infanticide in Rural South India." *Economic and Political Weekly* 27, no. 22 (1992): 1153–56.

Gilman, Antonio, Robert McC. Adams, Anna Maria Bietti Sestieri, Alberto Cazzella, Henri J. M. Claessen, George L. Cowgill, Carole L. Crumley, et al. "The Development of Social Stratification in Bronze Age Europe [and Comments and Reply]." *Current Anthropology* 22, no. 1 (February 1981): 1–23.

Givoni, Moshe, Christian Brand, and Paul Watkiss. "Are Railways Climate Friendly?" *Built Environment* 35, no. 1 (2009): 70–86.

Glaser, Peter E., Owen E. Maynard, J. J. R. Mackovciak, and E. I. Ralph. "Feasibility Study of a Satellite Solar Power Station." Technical report, National Aeronautics and Space Administration, 1974.

Gray, Russell D., and Quentin D. Atkinson. "Language-Tree Divergence Times Support the Anatolian Theory of Indo-European Origin." *Nature* 426, no. 6965 (2003): 435–39.

Greenblatt, R. E. "A Dual Theory of Price and Value in a Meso-Scale Economic Model with Stochastic Profit Rate." *Physica A: Statistical Mechanics and Its Applications* 416 (2014): 518–31.

Gupta, J. "Informal Labor in Brick Kilns: Need for Regulation." *Economic and Political Weekly* 38, no. 31 (2003): 3282–92.

Guy, Hervé, Claude Masset, and Charles-Albert Baud. "Infant Taphonomy." *International Journal of Osteoarchaeology* 7, no. 3 (1997): 221–29.

Hardin, Garrett. "The Tragedy of the Commons." *Science* 162 (1968): 1243–48.

Harper, Kyle. *Slavery in the Late Roman World, AD 275–425.* Cambridge: Cambridge University Press, 2011.

Harris, Bernard. "Public Health, Nutrition, and the Decline of Mortality: The McKeown Thesis Revisited." *Social History of Medicine* 17, no. 3 (2004): 379–407.

Harris, Marvin. *Cannibals and Kings: Origins of Cultures.* New York: Random House, 1991.

Harris, William V. "The Theoretical Possibility of Extensive Infanticide in the Graeco-Roman World." *Classical Quarterly* 32, no. 1 (1982): 114–16.

Harrison, Mark. "The Economics of World War II: An Overview." *The Economics of World War II: Six Great Powers in International Comparison,* edited by Mark Harrison, 1–42. Cambridge: Cambridge University Press, 2000.

Hawkes, K., J. F. O'Connell, and N. G. Blurton Jones. "Hadza Women's Time Allocation, Offspring Provisioning, and the Evolution of Long Postmenopausal Life Spans." *Current Anthropology* 38, no. 4 (1997): 551–77.

Hayek, F. A. *Prices and Production.* London: Routledge, 1935.

Hayek, F. A. "The Use of Knowledge in Society." *American Economic Review* 35, no. 4 (September 1945): 519–30.

Hayek, F. A. *The Counter-Revolution of Science.* New York: Free Press, 1955.

Heather, Peter. *Empires and Barbarians.* London: Pan, 2009.

Hedges, John W. *Tomb of the Eagles: Death and Life in a Stone Age Tribe.* Lanham, MD: Rowman and Littlefield, 1984.

Heilbroner, Robert L. "Do Machines Make History?" *Technology and Culture,* 8, no. 3 (1967): 335–45.

Heinrich, Michael. *An Introduction to the Three Volumes of Karl Marx's Capital.* New York: Monthly Review Press, 2012.

Hendrickx, Bart, and Bert Vis. *Energiya-Buran: The Soviet Space Shuttle.* Berlin: Springer, 2007.

Heuman, Gad, and Trevor Burnard. *The Routledge History of Slavery.* London: Routledge, 2010.

Hilferding, Rudolf. *Karl Marx and the Close of His System by Eugen von Bohm-Bawerk and Bohm-Bawerk's Criticism of Marx by Rudolph Hilferding, together with an Appendix Consisting of an Article by Ladislaus von Bortkiewicz on the Transformation of Values into Prices of Production in the Marxian System.* Wiley-Blackwell, 1951.

Hillston, Jane. "Compositional Markovian Modelling Using a Process Algebra." In *Computations with Markov Chains,* edited by William J. Stewart, 177–96. Berlin: Springer, 1995.

Hindess, Barry. "Classes and Politics in Marxist Theory." In *Power and the State,* edited by Gary Littlejohn, Barry Smart, John Wakeford, and Nira Yuval-Davis, 72–97. London: Croom Helm, 1978.

Hirst, Paul. "Economic Classes and Politics." In *Class and Class Structure,* edited by Alan Hunt, 125–54. London: Lawrence and Wishart, 1977.

Hirst, Paul, and Barry Hindess. *Pre-Capitalist Modes of Production.* London: Routledge and Kegan Paul, 1975.

Hodder, Ian. "Women and Men at Çatalhöyük." *Scientific American* 290, no. 1 (2004): 76–83.

Hooper, W. D., and H. B. Ash, editors. *Cato and Varro on Agriculture.* Cambridge, MA: Harvard University Press, 1935.

Hourani, George Fadlo, and John Carswell. *Arab Seafaring in the Indian Ocean in Ancient and Early Medieval Times.* Princeton, NJ: Princeton University Press, 1995.

Houston, George W. "Ports in Perspective: Some Comparative Materials on Roman Merchant Ships and Ports." *American Journal of Archaeology* 92, no. 4 (October 1988): 553–64.

Hughes, Austin L. "Female Infanticide: Sex Ratio Manipulation in Humans." *Ethology and Sociobiology* 2, no. 3 (1981): 109–11.

Humphries, Jane, and Benjamin Schneider. "Spinning the Industrial Revolution." University of Oxford Discussion Papers in Economic and Social History No. 145, 2016.

Hunt, E. H., and S. J. Pam. "Essex Agriculture in the 'Golden Age,' 1850–73." *Agricultural History Review* 43, no. 2 (1995): 160–77.

Hunter, Holland, and Janusz M. Szyrmer. *Faulty Foundations: Soviet Economic Policies, 1928–1940.* Princeton, NJ: Princeton University Press, 2014.

Hunter, James, Peter Peacock, Andy Wightman, and Michael Foxley. "432:50—Towards a Comprehensive Land Reform Agenda for Scotland: A Briefing Paper for the House of Commons Scottish Affairs Committee," 2013.

Igiri, A. O., M. B. Ekong, C. A. Ogan, P. A. Odey, et al. "Body Mass Index Measure of Young Adult Nigerian Residents in the Calabar Metropolis." *Internet Journal of Biological Anthropology* 2, no. 2 (2009), http://print.ispub.com/api/0/ispub-article/12890.

Ingham, Geoffrey. *The Nature of Money.* Cambridge: Polity, 2004.

Ingham, John M. "Human Sacrifice at Tenochtitlan." *Comparative Studies in Society and History* 26, no. 3 (1984): 379–400.

Jakab, Zoltan, and Michael Kumhof. "Banks Are Not Intermediaries of Loanable Funds—and Why This Matters." Working Paper No. 529, Bank of England, 2015.

James, Steven R., R. W. Dennell, Allan S. Gilbert, Henry T. Lewis, J. A. J. Gowlett, Thomas F. Lynch, W. C. McGrew, Charles R. Peters, Geoffrey G. Pope, Ann B. Stahl, et al. "Hominid Use of Fire in the Lower and Middle Pleistocene: A Review of the Evidence [and Comments and Replies]." *Current Anthropology* 30, no. 1 (1989): 1–26.

Jeffreys, Sheila. *The Industrial Vagina: The Political Economy of the Global Sex Trade.* London: Routledge, 2008.

Jude, Alexander. *The Theory of the Steam Turbine.* London: Griffin, 1906.

Judson, Bruce. "What a Bank Is Supposed to Do?" Wall Street Pit. June 27, 2012. http://wallstreetpit.com/93320-what-a-bank-is-supposed-to-do.

Juhász, Mattias, Tibor Princz-Jakovics, and Tünde Vörös. "What Are the Real Effects of Rail Electrification in Hungary?" Paper delivered at European Transport Conference, Frankfurt, September 30–October 2, 2013.

Kaizer, Ted. "Euhemerism and Religious Life in the Roman Near East." In *Divinizzazione, Culto del Sovrano e Apoteosi tra Antichità e Medioevo Bononia,* edited by Tommaso Gnoli and Federicomaria Muccioli, 295–306. Bologna: Bononia University Press, 2014.

Kantorovich, L.V. "Mathematical Methods of Organizing and Planning Production." *Management Science* 6, no. 4 (1960): 366–422.

Kantorovich, L.V. *The Best Use of Economic Resources.* Cambridge, MA: Harvard University Press, 1965.

Kauffman, S. A. *The Origins of Order: Self-Organization and Selection in Evolution.* Oxford: Oxford University Press, 1993.

Keynes, J. M. *The General Theory of Employment, Interest, and Money.* London: Macmillan, 1936.

Keynes, John Maynard. "How to Pay for the War." In John Maynard Keynes, *Essays in Persuasion,* 367–439. London: Palgrave Macmillan, 2010.

Ibn Khaldun. *The Muqaddimah: An Introduction to History,* vol. 1, translated by Franz Rosenthal. Princeton, NJ: Princeton University Press, 1969.

Kindermann, Ross, and J. Laurie Snell. *Markov Random Fields and Their Applications.* Providence, RI: American Mathematical Society, 1980.

Hansjörg Klausinger. "The Early Use of the Term 'Veil of Money' in Schumpeter's Monetary Writings: A Comment on Patinkin and Steiger." *Scandinavian Journal of Economics* 92, no. 4 (1990): 617–21.

Klein, Judy L. "Rules of Action for War and Recursive Optimization: Massé's 'Jeu des Réservoirs' and Arrow, Harris, and Marschak's 'Optimal Inventory Policy.'" Presentation at History of Economics as History of Science Workshop, École Normale Supérieure de Cachan, 2007.

Koetsier, Teunis. "A Contribution to the History of Kinematics—I." *Mechanism and Machine Theory* 18, no. 1 (1983): 37–42.

Kofsky, Arieh. *Eusebius of Caesarea against Paganism.* Leiden: Arieh Brill, 2002.

Kollewe, Julia. "UK Finance Sector Bonuses to Top £100bn since Financial Crisis." *Guardian,* February 23, 2015.

Kollontai, Alexandra. "Prostitution and Ways of Fighting It." Speech to the third all-Russian conference of the heads of Regional Women's Departments, 1921. Available at http://marxists. org/archive/kollonta/1921/prostitution.htm.

Koroneos, C., A. Dompros, G. Roumbas, and N. Moussiopoulos. "Advantages of the Use of Hydrogen Fuel as Compared to Kerosene." *Resources, Conservation and Recycling* 44, no. 2 (2005): 99–113.

Kuczynski, Jürgen. *Labor Conditions in Great Britain, 1750 to the Present.* New York: International Publishers, 1946.

Kushnir, Duncan, and Björn A. Sandén. "The Time Dimension and Lithium Resource Constraints for Electric Vehicles." *Resources Policy* 37, no. 1 (2012): 93–103.

Lakoff, G., and R. Nunez. *Where Mathematics Comes From: How the Embodied Mind Brings Mathematics into Being.* New York: Basic, 2001.

Langdon, John. "Water-Mills and Windmills in the West Midlands, 1086–1500." *Economic History Review* 44, no. 3 (1991): 424–44.

Langer, William L. "Europe's Initial Population Explosion." *American Historical Review* 69, no. 1 (1963): 1–17.

Lantsev, M. S. "Social Security in the USSR." *International Labour Review* 86 (October 1962): 453–66.

Lardner, D. "Babbage's Calculating Engines." *Edinburgh Review* 59 (1834): 263–327.

Lenin, Vladimir Ilyich. "The Tax in Kind." In *Collected Works,* vol. 32. Moscow: Progress Publishers, 1965.

Lenin, Vladimir Ilyich. *Collected Works.* 1965.

Lenin, Vladimir Ilyich. *Imperialism: The Highest Stage of Capitalism.* Sydney: Resistance, 1999.

Leunig, Timothy. "A British Industrial Success: Productivity in the Lancashire and New England Cotton Spinning Industries a Century Ago." *Economic History Review* 56, no. 1 (February 2003): 90–117.

Leveau, Philippe. "The Barbegal Water Mill in Its Environment: Archaeology and the Economic and Social History of Antiquity." *Journal of Roman Archaeology* 9 (1996): 137–53.

Levine, Nancy E. "Women's Work and Infant Feeding: A Case from Rural Nepal." *Ethnology* 27, no. 3 (July 1988): 231–51.

Licht, Stuart, Hongjun Wu, Chaminda Hettige, Baohui Wang, Joseph Asercion, Jason Lau, and Jessica Stuart. "STEP Cement: Solar Thermal Electrochemical Production of CaO without CO_2 Emission." *Chemical Communications* 48 (2012): 6019–21.

Liebknecht, Wilhelm. *Karl Marx: Biographical Memoirs*, translated by Ernest Untermann. Chicago: Kerr, 1901.

Littlejohn, Gary. "State, Plan and Market in the Transition to Socialism: The Legacy of Bukharin." *Economy and Society* 8, no. 2 (1979): 206–39.

Littlejohn, Gary. "Class Structure and Production Relations in the U.S.S.R." PhD diss., University of Glasgow, 1981.

Liu, Zhu, Dabo Guan, Wei Wei, Steven J. Davis, Philippe Ciais, Jin Bai, Shushi Peng, Qiang Zhang, Klaus Hubacek, Gregg Marland, et al. "Reduced Carbon Emission Estimates from Fossil Fuel Combustion and Cement Production in China." *Nature* 524, no. 7565 (2015): 335–38.

Loeb, Edwin M., and Jan O. M. Broek. "Social Organization and the Long House in Southeast Asia." *American Anthropologist* 49, no. 3 (1947): 414–25.

Long, C. E., B. L. Thorne, and N. L. Breisch. "Termite Colony Ontogeny: A Long-Term Assessment of Reproductive Lifespan, Caste Ratios and Colony Size in *Reticulitermes flavipes* (Isoptera: *Rhinotermitidae*)." *Bulletin of Entomological Research* 93, no. 5 (2003): 439–45.

Lorenz, Wayne F., J. Phillip, and Phillippe Castermans. "Water Flow to the Ancient Industrial Mill of Barbegal-La Burlande Basin." Presentation at 3rd IWA Specialized Conference on Water and Wastewater Technologies in Ancient Civilizations, MN-60, Istanbul, March 2012.

Maddison, Angus. *The World Economy: A Millennial Perspective*. Paris: Organisation for Economic Co-operation and Development, 2001.

Maito, Esteban Ezequiel. "The Historical Transience of Capital: The Downward Trend in the Rate of Profit since XIX century." Munich Personal RePEc Archive, 2014.

Malm, Andreas. "The Origins of Fossil Capital: From Water to Steam in the British Cotton Industry." *Historical Materialism* 21, no. 1 (2013): 15–68.

Malthus, Thomas Robert. *An Essay on the Principle of Population; Or, a View of Its Past and Present Effects on Human Happiness; With an Inquiry into Our Prospects Respecting the Future Removal or Mitigation of the Evils which it Occasions*. London: Reeves and Turner, 1872.

Mandel, Ernest. "Marx and Engels on Commodity Production and Bureaucracy: Theoretical Bases of the Marxist Understanding of the Soviet Union." *Rethinking Marxism: Struggles in Marxist Theory: Essays for Harry Magdoff and Paul Sweezy*. New York: Autonomedia, 1985.

Mandelbrot, Benoit. "Paretian Distributions and Income Maximization." *Quarterly Journal of Economics* 76, no. 1 (February 1962): 57–85.

Markov, Andrey A. "An Example of Statistical Investigation of the Text *Eugene Onegin* Concerning the Connection of Samples in Chains." *Science in Context* 19, no. 4 (2006): 591–600.

Marquetti, Adalmir. "Extended Penn World Tables: Economic Growth Data Assembled from the Penn World Tables and Other Sources." Duncan Foley's Homepage,

New School, 2012. http://sites.google.com/a/newschool.edu/duncan-foley-homepage/home/EPWT.

Marquetti, Adalmir A. "Analyzing Historical and Regional Patterns of Technical Change from a Classical-Marxian Perspective. *Journal of Economic Behavior and Organization* 52, no. 2 (2003): 191–200.

Martin, Ford. *The Rise of the Robots: Technology and the Threat of Mass Unemployment.* New York: Basic Books, 2015.

Marx, Karl. *Capital: A Critique of Political Economy*, vol. 1. Translated by Samuel Moore and Edward Aveling and edited by Frederick Engels. Moscow: Progress Publishers. Available at http://marxists.org/archive/marx/works/1867-c1

Marx, Karl. *Capital: A Critique of Political Economy*, vol. 2, book 2: "The Process of Circulation of Capital." Edited by Frederick Engels. *Marx Engels Collected Works*, vol. 6: London, Lawrence and Wishart, 1975.

Marx, Karl. *Capital: A Critique of Political Economy*, vol. 3. Moscow: Progress Publishers, 1971.

Marx, Karl. *A Contribution to the Critique of Political Economy.* Translated by Salomea W. Ryazanskaya. Moscow: Progress Publishers, 1978.

Marx, Karl. *Marginal Notes to the Programme of the German Workers' Party [Critique of the Gotha Programme].* In *Marx and Engels Selected Works*, vol. 3. Oxford: Blackwell, 1970.

Marx, Karl. *Poverty of Philosophy.* 1847.

Marx, Karl. *Value, Price, and Profit.* Chicago: Kerr, 1910.

Marx, Karl. "Notes on Adolph Wagner." *Texts on Method*, 201, 1975.

Marx, Karl. *Theories of Surplus Value: Books I, II, and III.* Amherst, NY: Prometheus, 1999.

Marx, Karl, and Frederick Engels. *The German Ideology.* Moscow: Progress Publishers, 1976.

Karl Marx, and Friederick Engels. *Manifesto of the Communist Party.* Translated by S. Moore. Moscow: Progress, 1977.

Marx, Karl, and Jules Guesde. "The Programme of the Parti Ouvrier," 1880. Available at http://marxists.org/archive/marx/works/1880/05/parti-ouvrier.htm.

Mathias, Peter. *The First Industrial Nation: The Economic History of Britain 1700–1914.* London: Routledge, 2013.

Mazumdar, D. "The Issue of Small Versus Large in the Indian Textile Industry: An Analytical and Historical Survey." Staff Working Paper No. 645, World Bank, 1984.

McDonald, John. "Domesday Economy: Analysis of the English Economy Early in the Second Millennium." *National Institute Economic Review* 172, no. 1 (2000): 105–114.

McDonald, John. *Production Efficiency in Domesday England, 1086.* London: Routledge, 2002.

McDonald, John. "Efficiency in the Domesday Economy, 1086: Evidence from Wiltshire Estates." *Applied Economics* 42, no. 25 (2010): 3231–40.

McNeill, William. *Plagues and Peoples.* New York: Anchor, 2010.

Meikle, S. *Aristotle's Economic Thought.* Oxford: Oxford University Press, 1997.

Meillassoux, Claude. *Maidens, Meal and Money: Capitalism and the Domestic Community.* Cambridge: Cambridge University Press, 1981.

Meneghetti, U., and A. Maggiore. "Antique Applications of Cam Mechanisms." In *13th World Congress in Mechanism and Machine Science.* Red Hook, NY: Curran, 2011.

Menon, Dilip. *The Blindness of Insight.* New Delhi: Navayana, 2006.

Mies, Maria. "The Social Origins of the Sexual Division of Labor." Occasional Paper No. 85, Institute of Social Studies, The Hague, January 1981.

Minge-Klevana, Wanda, Kwame Arhin, P. T. W. Baxter, T. Carlstein, Charles J. Erasmus, Michael P. Freedman, Allen Johnson, Don Parkes, Leopold Pospisil, Robert E. Rhoades, Zoltán Tagányi, Benjamin White, and B. Whiting. "Does Labor Time Decrease with Industrialization? A Survey of Time-Allocation Studies [and Comments and Reply]." *Current Anthropology* 21, no. 3 (1980): 279–98.

Mirowski, P. *More Heat than Light: Economics as Social Physics, Physics as Nature's Economics*. Cambridge: Cambridge University Press, 1989.

Modis, Theodore. "Long-Term GDP Forecasts and the Prospects for Growth." *Technological Forecasting and Social Change* 80, no. 8 (2013): 1557–62.

Morishima, Michio. *Marx's Economics: A Dual Theory of Value and Growth*. Cambridge: Cambridge University Press, 1973.

Morissette, René, Garnett Picot, and Yuqian Lu. "The Evolution of Canadian Wages over the Last Three Decades." Statistics Canada research paper, 2013.

Mosimann, James E., and Paul S. Martin. "Simulating Overkill by Paleoindians: Did Man Hunt the Giant Mammals of the New World to Extinction? Mathematical Models Show that the Hypothesis Is Feasible." *American Scientist* 63, no. 3 (1975): 304–13.

Mukhia, Harbans. "Was there Feudalism in Indian History?" *Journal of Peasant Studies* 8, no. 3 (1981): 273–310.

Myska, Milan. "Pre-Industrial Iron-Making in the Czech Lands: The Labor Force and Production Relations circa 1350–circa 1840." *Past and Present* 82 (1979): 44–72.

Nakachi, Mie. "N. S. Khrushchev and the 1944 Soviet Family Law: Politics, Reproduction, and Language." *East European Politics and Societies* 20, no. 1 (2006): 40–68.

Narula, Smita. *Broken People: Caste Violence against India's "Untouchables."* New York: Human Rights Watch, 1999.

Nelson, Gerald C., Dominique Mensbrugghe, Helal Ahammad, Elodie Blanc, Katherine Calvin, Tomoko Hasegawa, Petr Havlik, Edwina Heyhoe, Page Kyle, Hermann Lotze-Campen, et al. "Agriculture and Climate Change in Global Scenarios: Why Don't the Models Agree." *Agricultural Economics* 45, no. 1 (2014): 85–101.

Nelson, Gerald C., Hugo Valin, Ronald D Sands, Petr Havlík, Helal Ahammad, Delphine Deryng, Joshua Elliott, Shinichiro Fujimori, Tomoko Hasegawa, Edwina Heyhoe, et al. "Climate Change Effects on Agriculture: Economic Responses to Biophysical Shocks." *Proceedings of the National Academy of Sciences* 111, no. 9 (2014): 3274–79.

Neurath, Otto. *Economic Writings: Selections 1904–1945*. Edited by Thomas E. Uebel and Robert S. Cohen. New York: Kluwer, 2004.

Newton, Isaac. *The Principia: Mathematical Principles of Natural Philosophy*. Berkeley, CA: University of California Press, 1999.

Nieboer, Herman Jeremias. *Slavery as an Industrial System*. New York: Franklin, 1971.

Nieh, James C. "Animal Behavior: The Orphan Rebellion." *Current Biology* 22, no. 8 (2012): R280–R281.

North, Douglass C. "Sources of Productivity Change in Ocean Shipping, 1600–1850." *Journal of Political Economy* 76, no. 5 (1968): 953–970.

Nove, Alec. "The Class Nature of the Soviet Union Revisited." *Soviet Studies* 35, no. 3 (1983): 298–312.

Nove, Alec. *The Economics of Feasible Socialism*. London: Allen and Unwin, 1983.

Nuvolari, Alessandro, Bart Verspagen, and Nick Von Tunzelmann. "The Early Diffusion of the Steam Engine in Britain, 1700–1800: A Reappraisal." *Cliometrica* 5, no. 3 (2011): 291–321.

O'Brien, Phillips Payson. *How the War Was Won*. Cambridge: Cambridge University Press, 2015.

Ochoa, E. M. "Values, Prices, and Wage-Profit Curves in the U.S. Economy." *Cambridge Journal of Economics* 13 (1989): 413–29.

Ostrom, Elinor, Joanna Burger, Christopher B. Field, Richard B. Norgaard, and David Policansky. "Revisiting the Commons: Local Lessons, Global Challenges." *Science* 284, no. 5412 (1999): 278–82.

O'Connell, James F. Kristen Hawkes, and N. G. Blurton Jones. "Grandmothering and the Evolution of *Homo erectus*." *Journal of Human Evolution* 36, no. 5 (1999): 461–85.

Paddock, Richard. "Central Heat Saps Moscow's Economy." *Los Angeles Times*, March 23, 1997.

Panne, C., and F. Rahnama. "The First Algorithm for Linear Programming: An Analysis of Kantorovich's Method." *Economics of Planning* 19, no. 2 (1985): 76–91.

Parenti, Michael. *The Assassination of Julius Caesar: A People's History of Ancient Rome*. New York: New Press, 2004.

Parkes, Oscar. *British Battleships, "Warrior" 1860 to "Vanguard" 1950: A History of Design, Construction and Armament*. London: Seeley Service, 1966.

Pashukanis, E. B. *Law and Marxism: A General Theory toward a Critique of the Fundamental Juridical Concepts*. Worcester, UK: Pluto, 1989.

Paulin, Alois. "Through Liquid Democracy to Sustainable Non-Bureaucratic Government." In *CeDEM14: Proceedings of the International Conference for E-Democracy and Open Government*, edited by Peter Parycek and Noella Edelmann, 205–17. Krems an der Danau, Austria: Donau-Universität Krems, 2014.

Pelkonen, Henri, and Paul Cockshott. "Use of Deconvolution to Infer Past Diet in Austria and the USSR." *Critique* 45, no. 1 (2017): 117–40.

Petroff, Peter. "The Soviet Wages System." *Labor*, February 1938, 141–42.

Petrovic, P. "The Deviation of Production Prices from Labor Values: Some Methodology and Empirical Evidence." *Cambridge Journal of Economics* 11 (1987): 197–210.

Petty, William. *A Treatise of Taxes and Contributions* [1679]. Included in Hull CH. *Economic Writings of Sir William Petty*, vol 1. New York: Augustus M. Kelley, 1899[1679].

Pockney, Bertram Patrick. *Soviet Statistics since 1950*. Aldershot, UK: Dartmouth, 1991.

Pohl, Hans W., and Valentin V. Malychev. "Hydrogen in Future Civil Aviation." *International Journal of Hydrogen Energy* 22, nos. 10–11 (1997): 1061–69.

Polanyi, K., C. Arensberg, and H. W. Pearson. *Trade and Market in the Early Empires*. New York: Free Press, 1957.

Pollard, Sidney. "A New Estimate of British Coal Production, 1750–1850." *Economic History Review* 33, no. 2 (1980): 212–35.

Postgate, J. N. *Early Mesopotamia*. London: Routledge, 1992.

Preobrazhenski, Evgeni Alekseevich. *From New Economic Policy to Socialism: A Glance into the Future of Russia and Europe*. London: New Park, 1973.

Price, Robert O. "Liquid Hydrogen—An Alternative Aviation Fuel?" *International Journal of Hydrogen Energy* 16, no. 8 (1991): 557–62.

Randall, Amy. *The Soviet Dream World of Retail Trade and Consumption in the 1930s*. Houndmills: Palgrave Macmillan, 2008.

Reifferscheidt, Michael, and Paul Cockshott. "Average and Marginal Labor Values Are: On Log (n)—A Reply to Hagendorf." *World Review of Political Economy* 5, no. 2 (2014): 258–75.

Renaud, Karen, and Paul Cockshott. "Handivote: Checks, Balances and Voiding options." *International Journal of Electronic Governance* 3, no. 3 (2010): 273–95.

Renaud, Karen, and Paul Cockshott. "HandiVote: Simple, Anonymous, and Auditable Electronic Voting." *Journal of information Technology and Politics* 6, no. 1 (2009): 60–80.

Renfrew, Colin. "The Origins of Indo-European Languages." *Scientific American* 261, no. 4 (October 1989): 106–14.

Renfrew, Colin. "World Linguistic Diversity." *Scientific American* 270, no. 1 (January 1994): 104–11.

Rey, Pierre Philippe. *Les Alliances de Classes: Sur l'Articulation des Modes de Production: Suivi de Matérialisme Historique et Luttes de Classes.* Paris: Maspero, 1973.

Ricardo, David. *The High Price of Bullion: A Proof of the Depreciation of Bank Notes.* London: Murray, 1811.

Ricardo, David. "Principles of Political Economy and Taxation." In *The Works and Correspondence of David Ricardo*, volume 1, edited by P. Sraffa. Cambridge: Cambridge University Press, 1951.

Roebroeks, Wil, and Paola Villa. "On the Earliest Evidence for Habitual Use of Fire in Europe." *Proceedings of the National Academy of Sciences* 108, no. 13 (2011): 5209–14.

Rosenberg, Nathan, and Manuel Trajtenberg. "A General-Purpose Technology at Work: The Corliss Steam Engine in the Late-Nineteenth-Century United States." *Journal of Economic History* 64, no. 1 (2004): 61–99.

Rosenzweig, Cynthia, Joshua Elliott, Delphine Deryng, Alex C. Ruane, Christoph Müller, Almut Arneth, Kenneth J. Boote, Christian Folberth, Michael Glotter, Nikolay Khabarov, et al. "Assessing Agricultural Risks of Climate Change in the Twenty-First Century in a Global Gridded Crop Model Intercomparison." *Proceedings of the National Academy of Sciences* 111, no. 9 (2014): 3268–73.

Ross, James A. "ROMAG Transportation System." *Proceedings of the IEEE* 61, no. 5 (1973): 617–20.

Rostovtzeff, Michael. *A History of the Ancient World*, vol. 2: *Rome*. New York: Biblo and Tannen, 1927.

Rudenko, Y. N. "Electric Power Development in the USSR." In *First Energy Conference Israel—Former USSR: Proceedings of a Conference Held at Ben-Gurion University of the Negev, Beer-Sheva, Israel, May 13–15, 1991*, edited by Sophie Zamkow, 2–8. Jerusalem: Ministry of Energy and Infrastructure, 1993.

Rudra, Ashok. "Pre-Capitalist Modes of Production in Non-European Societies." *Journal of Peasant Studies* 15, no. 3 (1988): 373–94.

Russo, Lucio. *The Forgotten Revolution: How Science Was Born in 300 B.C. and Why It Had to Be Reborn.* Berlin: Springer, 2013.

Ryan, Christopher, and Cacilda Jethá. *Sex at Dawn: The Prehistoric Origins of Modern Sexuality.* New York: Harper, 2010.

Sahlins, Marshall. *Stone Age Economics.* Hawthorne, NY: De Gruyter, 1972.

Sahlins, Marshall. "The Original Affluent Society." *Limited Wants, Unlimited Means: A Hunter-Gatherer Reader on Economics and the Environment*, edited by John M. Gowdy, 5-41. Washington, D.C.: Island, 1998.

Salles, Anne. "Les Effets de la Politique Familiale de l'Ex-RDA sur la Nuptialité et les Naissances hors Mariage." *Population* 61, no. 1 (2006): 141–52.

Samuelson, P. A. "Reply on Marxian Matters." *Journal of Economic Literature* 11 (1973): 64–68.

Sánchez, César, and Maximilia Nieto Ferrandez. "Valores, Precios de Producción y Precios de Mercado a partir de los Datos de la Economía Española." *Investigación Económica* 69, no. 274 (2010): 87–118.

Sánchezc, César, and Everlam Elias Montibeler. "The Labor Theory of Value and the Prices in China." *Economia e Sociedade* 24, no. 2 (2015): 329–54.

Sanderson, M. G. "Biomass of Termites and Their Emissions of Methane and Carbon Dioxide: A Global Database." *Global Biogeochemical Cycles* 10, no. 4 (1996): 543–57.

Shaikh, A. M. "The Transformation from Marx to Sraffa." In *Ricardo, Marx, Sraffa— The Langston Memorial Volume*, edited by Ernest Mandel and Alan Freeman, 43–84. London: Verso, 1984.

Shaikh, A. M. "The Empirical Strength of the Labor Theory of Value." In *Marxian Economics: A Reappraisal*, vol. 2, *Essays on Volume III of Capital: Profit, Prices and Dynamics*, edited by Riccardo Bellofiore, 225–51. Houndmills: Macmillan, 1998.

Shaikh, Anwar, Nikolaos Papanikolaou, and Noe Wiener. "Race, Gender and the Econophysics of Income Distribution in the USA." *Physica A: Statistical Mechanics and Its Applications* 415 (2014): 54–60.

Shannon, C. "A Mathematical Theory of Communication." *Bell System Technical Journal* 27, nos. 3 and 4 (1948): 379–423, 623–56.

Sharma, R. S. "The Origins of Feudalism in India (c. A.D. 400–650)." *Journal of the Economic and Social History of the Orient* 1, no. 3 (1958): 297–328.

Sharma, Ram Sharan. "How Feudal was Indian Feudalism?" *Journal of Peasant Studies* 12, no. 2–3 (1985): 19–43.

Shaw, P., and P. Cockshott. "Physical Realism and Formal Process Semantics." Unpublished paper, 1994.

Shaw, Paul, Paul Cockshott, and Peter Barrie. "Implementation of Lattice Gases Using FPGAs." *Journal of VLSI Signal Processing* 12, no. 1 (1996): 51–66.

Shkolnikov, Vladimir M., and France Meslé. "The Russian Epidemiological Crisis as Mirrored by Mortality Trends." In *Russia's Demographic "Crisis,"* edited by Julie DaVanzo with the assistance of Gwendolyn Farnsworth, 113–62. Santa Monica, CA: RAND Corporation, 1996.

Shkolnikov, Vladimir M., Evgueni M Andreev, Domantas Jasilionis, Mall Leinsalu, Olga I. Antonova, and Martin McKee. "The Changing Relation between Education and Life Expectancy in Central and Eastern Europe in the 1990s." *Journal of Epidemiology and Community Health* 60, no. 10 (2006): 875–81.

Siegel, Jeremy J. *Stocks for the Long Run: The Definitive Guide to Financial Market Returns and Long-Term Investment Strategies*, 3rd ed. New York: McGraw Hill, 2002.

Singer, Charles, E. J. Holmyard, A. R. Hall, and Trevor I. Williams, editors. *A History of Technology*, vol. 2, *The Mediterranean Civilization and the Middle Ages, C. 700 B.C. to C. 1500 A.D.* Oxford: Oxford University Press, 1956.

Smil, Vaclav. "World History and Energy." *Encyclopedia of Energy* 6 (2004): 549–61.

Smil, Vaclav. *Two Prime Movers of Globalization: The History and Impact of Diesel Engines and Gas Turbines*. Cambridge, MA: MIT Press, 2010.

Smith, Adam. *The Theory of Moral Sentiments*, 6th ed. London: Strahan and Cadell, 1790.

Smith, Adam. *The Wealth of Nations*. 1974.

Smith, Adam. *Lectures on Jurisprudence*, edited by Ronald L. Meek, D. D. Raphael, and Peter G. Stein. Oxford: Oxford University Press, 1978.

Smout, T. Christopher. *A Century of the Scottish People, 1830–1950*. London: Collins, 1986.

Spufford, Francis. *Red Plenty*. London: Faber and Faber, 2010.

Sraffa, Piero. *Production of Commodities by Means of Commodities.* Cambridge: Cambridge University Press, 1960.

Srivastava, Ravi S. "Bonded Labor in India." Working Paper No. 43, International Labour Office, 2005.

Stacey, Judith. "Unhitching the Horse from Carriage: Love and Marriage among the Mosuo." *Journal of Law and Family Studies* 11, no. 2 (2009): 239–73.

Stalin, Joseph. *Economic Problems of Socialism in the USSR.* Moscow, 1952.

Stalin, Josif Vissarionovic. *Dialectical and Historical Materialism.* London: Lawrence and Wishart, 1943.

Steckel, Richard H. "A Dreadful Childhood: The Excess Mortality of American Slaves." *Social Science History* 10, no. 4 (1986): 427–65.

Steedman, Ian. *Marx after Sraffa.* London: Verso, 1981.

Stuckler, David, Lawrence King, and Martin McKee. "Mass Privatization and the Post-Communist Mortality Crisis: A Cross-National Analysis." *Lancet* 373, no. 9661 (2009): 399–407.

Temin, Peter. "A Market Economy in the Early Roman Empire." *Journal of Roman Studies* 91 (2001): 169–81.

Thompson, Francis Michael Longstreth. *The Cambridge Social History of Britain, 1750–1950,* vol. 1. Cambridge: Cambridge University Press, 1993.

Ticktin, Hillel. "Stalinism—Its Nature and Role." *Critique* 39, no. 4 (2011): 489–523.

Tontisirin, Kraisid, and Hartwig de Haen. *Human Energy Requirements: Report of a Joint FAO/WHO/UNU Expert Consultation: Rome, 17–24 11 October 2001.* Rome: Food and Agriculture Organization, 2004.

Torres, Daniel. "Regularities in Prices of Production and the Concentration of Compositions of Capitals." Working Paper No. 1709, Economics Department, New School for Social Research, 2017.

Tsoulfidis, L., and T. Maniatis. "Values, Prices of Production and Market Prices: Some More Evidence from the Greek Economy." *Cambridge Journal of Economics* 26 (2002): 359–69.

Tsoulfidis, Lefteris, and Dimitris Paitaridis. "Monetary Expressions of Labor Time and Market Prices: Theory and Evidence from China, Japan and Korea." *Review of Political Economy* 29, no. 1 (2016): 111–32.

Turing, A. "Computing Machinery and Intelligence." *Mind* 49 (1950): 433–60.

Turing, A. "Lecture on the Automatic Computing Engine, 1947." In *The Essential Turing,* edited by B. J. Copeland, 362–94. Oxford: Oxford University Press, 2004.

Thomas Uebel. "Incommensurability, Ecology, and Planning: Neurath in the Socialist Calculation Debate, 1919–1928." *History of Political Economy* 37, no. 2 (2005): 309–42.

Van Vuuren, Detlef P., Elke Stehfest, Michel G. J. den Elzen, Tom Kram, Jasper van Vliet, Sebastiaan Deetman, Morna Isaac, Kees Klein Goldewijk, Andries Hof, Angelica Mendoza Beltran, et al. "RCP2. 6: Exploring the Possibility to Keep Global Mean Temperature Increase below 2 c." *Climatic Change* 109, nos. 1–2 (2011): 95–116.

Vanek, J. "Housework Still Takes Time." *Scientific American,* 231 (1974): 116–20.

Von Mises, Ludwig. "Economic Calculation in the Socialist Commonwealth." In *Collectivist Economic Planning,* edited by F. A. Hayek. London: Routledge and Kegan Paul, 1935.

Von Mises, Ludwig. *Human Action.* London: Hodge, 1949.

Von Mises, Ludwig. *Socialism: An Economic and Sociological Analysis.* London: Cape, 1951.

Kurt Vonnegut. *Player Piano*. New York: Scribner, 1952.

Walpole, Sarah, David Prieto-Merino, Phil Edwards, John Cleland, Gretchen Stevens, and Ian Roberts. "The Weight of Nations: An Estimation of Adult Human Biomass." *BMC Public Health* 12, no. 439 (2012): 1–6.

Watts, Joseph, Oliver Sheehan, Quentin D. Atkinson, Joseph Bulbulia, and Russell D. Gray. "Ritual Human Sacrifice Promoted and Sustained the Evolution of Stratified Societies." *Nature* 532 (April 2016): 228–34.

Weber, Max. *The Agrarian Sociology of Ancient Civilizations*. London: Verso, 2013.

Weisdorf, Jacob L. "Stone Age Economics: The Origins of Agriculture and the Emergence of Non-Food Specialists." University of Copenhagen Institute of Economics Discussion Paper No. 03-34, 2003.

Wells, Herbert George. *The World Set Free: A Story of Mankind*. New York: Dutton, 1914.

Wells, Herbert George. *The Open Conspiracy*. London: Hogarth, 1930.

Wells, Herbert George. *The Shape of Things to Come*. London: Penguin, 2005.

Wells, Herbert George. *The Sleeper Awakes*. London: Penguin, 2005.

Wells, Herbert George, and Patrick Parrinder. *The War in the Air*. London: Penguin, 2005.

Wheatcroft, Stephen G. "The First 35 Years of Soviet Living Standards: Secular Growth and Conjunctural Crises in a Time of Famines." *Explorations in Economic History* 46, no. 1 (2009): 24–52.

Whitcomb, Merrick, Herman V. Ames, John Back McMaster, Arthur C. Howland, William Fairley, and Dana Carleton Munro, editors. *Translations and Reprints from the Original Sources of European History*, volume 6. Philadelphia: University of Pennsylvania Press, 1899.

White, Lynn Townsend. *Medieval Technology and Social Change*. Oxford: Oxford University Press, 1964.

Whiten, Andrew, Jane Goodall, William C. McGrew, Toshisada Nishida, Vernon Reynolds, Yukimaru Sugiyama, Caroline E. G. Tutin, Richard W. Wrangham, and Christophe Boesch. "Cultures in Chimpanzees." *Nature* 399, no. 6737 (1999): 682–85.

Whitewright, Julian. "How Fast Is Fast? Technology, Trade and Speed under Sail in the Roman Red Sea." In *Natural Resources and Cultural Connections of the Red Sea*, edited by Janet Starkey, Paul Starkey, and Tony Wilkinson, 77–88. Oxford: Archaeopress, 2007.

Whitewright, Julian. "The Mediterranean Lateen Sail in Late Antiquity." *International Journal of Nautical Archaeology* 38, no. 1 (2009): 97–104.

Widdows, Dominic. *Geometry and Meaning*. Chicago: University of Chicago Press, 2004.

Williams, Alan R. *The Knight and the Blast Furnace: A History of the Metallurgy of Armour in the Middle Ages and the Early Modern Period*. Leiden: Brill, 2003.

Williams, F. C. "A Cathode Ray Tube Digit Store." *Proceedings of the Royal Society of London* 195A, no. 1042 (1948): 279–84.

Wintringham, Tom, and John Blashford-Snell. *Weapons and Tactics*. Harmondsworth, UK: Penguin, 1973.

Woit, Peter. "Is String Theory Even Wrong?" *American Scientist* 90, no. 2 (2002): 110–12.

Woodburn, James. "Egalitarian Societies." *Man*, n. s., 17, no. 3 (September 1982): 431–51.

Worrell, Ernst, Lynn Price, Nathan Martin, Chris Hendriks, and Leticia Ozawa Meida. "Carbon Dioxide Emissions from the Global Cement Industry 1." *Annual Review of Energy and the Environment* 26, no. 1 (2001): 303–29.

Wray, Randall. "The Credit Money and State Money Approaches." Working Paper No. 32, Center for Full Employment and Price Stability, University of Missouri, Kansas City, April 2004.

Zachariah, David. "Testing the Labor Theory of Value in Sweden." Unpublished paper, April 2004.

Zachariah, David. "Labor Value and Equalization of Profit Rates." *Indian Development Review* 4, no. 1 (2006): 1–21.

Zachariah, David. "Determinants of the Average Profit Rate and the Trajectory of Capitalist Economies." In *Bulletin of Political Economy* 3, no. 1 (2009): 13–36.

Zimmermann, Klaus F., and Michael J. Kendzia. "Celebrating 150 Years of Analyzing Fertility Trends in Germany." *Journal of Economics and Statistics* 233, no. 3 (2013): 406–42.

Notes

1. "Every child knows a nation which ceased to work, I will not say for a year, but even for a few weeks, would perish. Every child knows, too, that the masses of products corresponding to the different needs required different and quantitatively determined masses of the total labor of society. That this necessity of the distribution of social labor in definite proportions cannot possibly be done away with by a particular form of social production but can only change the mode of its appearance, is self-evident. No natural laws can be done away with. What can change in historically different circumstances is only the form in which these laws assert themselves. And the form in which this proportional distribution of labor asserts itself, in the state of society where the interconnection of social labor is manifested in the private exchange of the individual products of labor, is precisely the exchange value of these products." (Marx and Engels 1949, p. 418.)

2. The older political economy of Smith and Marx recognized that these institutional forms were just one of many that the human race has experienced.

3. "The instruments of this labor, or the bodily means of production implicitly referred to in this concept, are the hands and the head, but never the womb or the breasts of a woman. Thus, not only are men and women differently defined in their interaction with nature but the human body itself is divided into truly 'human' parts (head and hand) and 'natural' or purely 'animal' parts (genitalia, womb, etc.). This division cannot be attributed to a universal sexism of the men as such, but is a consequence of the capitalist mode of production which is only interested in those parts of the human body which can be directly used as instruments of labor or which can become an extension of the machine." (Mies 1981, p. 4.)

4. Alates are unmated winged male and female termites.

5. Men, of course, have been physically disabled from the two most important branches of social labor: producing and feeding babies, until recent years relaxed the constraint on feeding.

6. "But there is this great difference between his actions and many of those performed by the lower animals, namely, that man cannot, on his first trial, make, for instance, a stone hatchet or a canoe, through his power of imitation. He has to learn his work by practice; a beaver, on the other hand, can make its dam or canal, and a bird its nest, as well, or nearly as well, and a spider its wonderful web, quite as well, the first time it tries as when old and experienced." (Darwin 1871, chapter 2.)

7. "It has often been said that no animal uses any tool; but the chimpanzee in a state of nature cracks a native fruit, somewhat like a walnut, with a stone. (Savage and

Wyman in *Boston Journal of Natural History*, vol. iv. 1843–44, p. 383.) Rengger (*Saugethiere von Paraguay*, 1830, s. 51–56.) easily taught an American monkey thus to break open hard palm-nuts; and afterwards of its own accord, it used stones to open other kinds of nuts, as well as boxes. It thus also removed the soft rind of fruit that had a disagreeable flavour." (Darwin 1871, chapter 2.)

8. "In the social production of their existence, men inevitably enter into definite relations, which are independent of their will, namely relations of production appropriate to a given stage in the development of their material forces of production. The totality of these relations of production constitutes the economic structure of society, the real foundation, on which arises a legal and political superstructure and to which correspond definite forms of social consciousness. The mode of production of material life conditions the general process of social, political and intellectual life. It is not the consciousness of men that determines their existence, but their social existence that determines their consciousness. At a certain stage of development, the material productive forces of society come into conflict with the existing relations of production or this merely expresses the same thing in legal terms with the property relations within the framework of which they have operated hitherto. From forms of development of the productive forces these relations turn into their fetters. Then begins an era of social revolution. The changes in the economic foundation lead sooner or later to the transformation of the whole immense superstructure." (Marx et al. 1978, Preface.)

9. "The archeological evidence, such as it is, also supports the contention that agriculture is not a difficult concept to develop, that it has in fact been developed many times, and that it was not primarily ignorance which prevented human populations from becoming agricultural sooner than they did." (Cohen 1977, p. 24.)

10. Diamond and Ordunio (1997) argue that none of the wild grasses of Australia bore large enough seeds to be worth collecting.

11. "Some of our strongest scientific evidence about the relative status of men and women in the early and middle levels of Çatalhöyuk concerns diet. If women and men lived notably different lives, and if one or the other was dominant, then we might expect to uncover disparities in diet, with the dominant group having more access to certain foods, such as meat or better joints of meat. So we have searched hard for such evidence, but we have not uncovered clear differences." (Hodder, 2004.)

12. The model we present draws heavily on Meillassoux (1981).

13. The assumption we make of a 50 percent pre-adult mortality is plausible. The earliest parish registers indicate this level, as do some ancient cemeteries. Although other ancient cemeteries show lower levels of infant death this can plausibly be attributed to poorer preservation of semi-mineralized infant bones (Guy et al. 1997).

14. This is on the assumption that the work falls into the category the FAO calls an *Active Life*. They give examples of such work: "Other examples of moderately active lifestyles are associated with occupations such as masons and construction workers, or rural women in less developed traditional villages who participate in agricultural chores or walk long distances to fetch water and fuelwood" (Tontisirin and de Haen 2004, p. 39). If the work is that of farmers working entirely with hand tools, without draft animals or mechanical power, then the FAO category of *Vigorous Life* might apply. They describe this as: "non-mechanized agricultural laborers who work with a machete, hoe or axe for several hours daily and walk long distances over rugged terrains, often carrying heavy loads." In the latter case the

subsistence calorie production per adult worker would rise to around 1.75 million calories per year.

15.   "If we suppose them moving from one place to another, 4 or 5 miles every day, we can set no bounds to the number which might enter into such an expedition. If then one clan of Tartars (for instance) should, setting out on an expedition, defeat another, they would necessarily become possessed of every thing which before belonged to the vanquished; for in this state when they make any expedition of this sort wives, children, and flocks and every thing is carried along with them, so that when they are vanquished they will lose their all. The far greater part therefore will follow these and join themselves to the victor, tho some perhaps might still adhere to the vanquishd chief. If this combined army should be in the same manner successfull against a 2nd, a third, [and] a 4th tribe, they would soon become very powerfull, and might in time subdue all the nations of their country about them and become in this means immensely powerfull." (Smith 1978, p. 196.)

16.   "In a nation of hunters and fishers few people can live together, for in a short time any considerable number would destroy all the game in the country, and consequently would want a means of subsistance. Twenty or thirty families are the most that can live together, and these make up a village, but as they live together for their mutual defence and to assist one another, their villages are not far distant from each other." (Smith, 1978.)

17.   "Hunting supposes a nomadic life; and the hunter, who roams over vast tracts of land in pursuit of his game has not much opportunity to watch the movements of his slave who may be apt to run away at any moment" (Nieboer 1971, p. 194), and later: "hunting requires the utmost application of strength and skill; therefore a compulsory hunting cannot exist" (ibid., p. 197).

18.   For a survey of the evidence for the existence of a well-developed system of commodity markets in the Roman Empire, see Temin (2001).

19.   For example, the clocks of Archimedes or the Antikythera computer recovered from a shipwreck of the Roman republican era de Solla Price (1959), de Solla Price (1974), and Freeth et al. (2006).

20.   Russo (2013) gives an example of a two-cylinder pressure pump with crank and poppet valves similar to those of a Corliss steam engine (Rosenberg and Trajtenberg 2004) excavated from a Roman well.

21.   "It seems likely that all of these features would have allowed Mediterranean sailors in the first millennium AD to sail on both upwind and downwind courses…. Likewise the invention and use of a small foresail or *artemon* on the Mediterranean rig is indicative of an ability to sail on an upwind course—the *artemon* being only of limited use on other sailing courses.

      Textual evidence survives from the ancient world which provides a further indication of the ability of Roman sailing ships to make windward." (Whitewright 2007, p. 84.)

22.   Harper (2011, chapter 1) argues that Finley's estimate is too high, and that a more realistic figure for Rome is between 10 percent and 20 percent, but this range is highly sensitive to the numbers of slaves held by the richest slave-owners, since ownership was highly concentrated.

23.   "The specific economic form, in which unpaid surplus-labor is pumped out of direct producers, determines the relationship of rulers and ruled, as it grows directly out of production itself and, in turn, reacts upon it as a determining element. Upon this, however, is founded the entire formation of the economic community which grows up out of the production relations themselves, thereby

simultaneously its specific political form. It is always the direct relationship of the owners of the conditions of production to the direct producers—a relation always naturally corresponding to a definite stage in the development of the methods of labor and thereby its social productivity—which reveals the inner-most secret, the hidden basis of the entire social structure and with it the political form of the relation of sovereignty and dependence, in short, the corresponding specific form of the state. This does not prevent the same economic basis—the same from the standpoint of its main conditions—due to innumerable different empirical circumstances, natural environment, racial relations, external histori-cal influences, etc. from showing infinite variations and gradations in appear-ance, which can be ascertained only by analysis of the empirically given circum-stances." (Marx 1894.)

24. At least in the main they are not; in Rome a minority of slaves had their purse *peculium* from which some purchases could be made. New World slaves generally did not.

25. The successful slave revolt in Haiti, where black slaves outnumbered free whites by ten to one, is a striking proof of the inability of a slave state without a substantial free population to survive.

26. "In a constitutional government the fighting-men have the supreme power, and those who possess arms are the citizens." (Aristotle 1983, Book 3:7.)

27. "Whether in oligarchies or in democracies, the number of the governing body, whether the greater number, as in a democracy, or the smaller number, as in an oligarchy, is an accident due to the fact that the rich everywhere are few, and the poor numerous. But if so, there is a misapprehension of the causes of the difference between them. For the real difference between democracy and oligarchy is poverty and wealth. Wherever men rule by reason of their wealth, whether they be few or many, that is an oligarchy, and where the poor rule, that is a democracy. But as a fact the rich are few and the poor many; for few are well-to-do, whereas freedom is enjoyed by all; and wealth and freedom are the grounds on which the oligarchical and democratical parties respectively claim power in the state." (Aristotle 1983, Book 3:8.)

28. Our word servant derives from the Latin *servus* for slave, and one should read the implication of slavery into the English word servant when used in translations of old texts.

29. The UN Draft Convention against Sexual Exploitation defines sexual exploitation as follows:
   Article 1: Definition of Sexual Exploitation
      Sexual exploitation is a practice by which person(s) achieve sexual gratifica-tion, or financial gain, or advancement, through the abuse of a person's sexual-ity by abrogating that person's human right to dignity, equality, autonomy, and physical and mental well-being.
   Article 2
      Sexual exploitation takes the form of, but is not limited to:
      • The denial of life through female infanticide and the murder of women by reason of their gender, including wife and widow murder.
      • Subjection to cruel, inhuman and degrading treatment through the follow-ing: battering, pornography, prostitution, genital mutilation, female seclu-sion, dowry and bride price, forced sterilization and forced child-bearing, surrogacy, restricting the reproductive freedom of women, the use of wom-en's reproductivity for third parties (the use of women's reproductivity for

the purpose of sexual or commercial exploitation), sexual harassment, rape, incest, sexual abuse, and human trafficking.

- Subjection to sexual abuse and or torture whether perpetrated by State or non-State actors, overt or covert, including sadistic, mutilating practices.
- Temporary marriage, child marriages, or marriage of convenience for the purpose of sexual exploitation.
- Sex predetermination.

30.   "If all this has been established, it should be further known that the capital a person earns and acquires, if resulting from a craft, is the value realized from his labor. This is the meaning of 'acquired (capital).' There is nothing here (originally) except the labor, and (the labor) is not desired by itself as acquired (capital, but the value realized from it).

"Some crafts are partly associated with other (crafts). Carpentry and weaving, for instance, are associated with wood and yarn (and the respective crafts needed for their production). However, in the two crafts (first mentioned), the labor (that goes into them) is more important, and its value is greater.

"If the profit results from something other than a craft, the value of the resulting profit and acquired (capital) must (also) include the value of the labor by which it was obtained. Without labor, it would not have been acquired.

"In most such cases, the share of labor (in the profit) is obvious. A portion of the value, whether large or small, comes from (the labor). The share of labor may be concealed. This is the case, for instance, with the prices of food stuffs. The labor and expenditures that have gone into them show themselves in the price of grain, as we have stated before. But they are concealed (items) in regions where farming requires little care and few implements. Thus, only a few farmers are conscious of the (costs of labor and expenditures that have gone into their products).

"It has thus become clear that gains and profits, in their entirety or for the most part, are value realized from human labor. The meaning of the word 'Sustenance' has become clear. It is (the part of the profit) that is utilized. Thus, the meaning of the words 'profit' and 'Sustenance' has become clear. The meaning of both words has been explained." (Khaldūn et al. 1969, Book 1, chapter 5, section 1.)

31.   "If a man can bring to London an ounce of Silver out of the Earth in Peru, in the same time that he can produce a bushel of Corn, then one is the natural price of the other; now if by reason of new and more easie Mines a man can get two ounces of Silver as easily as formerly he did one, then Corn will be as cheap at ten shillings the bushel, as it was before at five shillings caeteris paribus." (Petty 1679.)

32.   "At all times and places, that is dear which it is difficult to come at, or which it costs much labor to acquire; and that cheap which is to be had easily, or with very little labor. Labor alone, therefore, never varying in its own value, is alone the ultimate and real standard by which the value of all commodities can at all times and places be estimated and compared. It is their real price; money is their nominal price only." (Smith 1974, p. 136.)

33.   "As the exchangeable values of commodities are only social functions of those things, and have nothing at all to do with the natural qualities, we must first ask: What is the common social substance of all commodities? It is labor. To produce a commodity a certain amount of labor must be bestowed upon it, or worked up in it. And I say not only labor, but social labor. A man who produces an article for his own immediate use, to consume it himself, creates a product, but not a commodity. As a self-sustaining producer he has nothing to do with society. But to produce a commodity, a man must not only produce an article satisfying some social want,

but his labor itself must form part and parcel of the total sum of labor expended by society. It must be subordinate to the division of labor within society. It is nothing without the other divisions of labor, and on its part is required to integrate them.

"If we consider commodities as values, we consider them exclusively under the single aspect of realized, fixed, or, if you like, crystallized social labor. In this respect they can differ only by representing greater or smaller quantities of labor, as, for example, a greater amount of labor may be worked up in a silken handkerchief than in a brick. But how does one measure quantities of labor? By the time the labor lasts, in measuring the labor by the hour, the day, etc. Of course, to apply this measure, all sorts of labor are reduced to average or simple labor as their unit. We arrive, therefore, at this conclusion. A commodity has a value, because it is a crystallization of social labor. The greatness of its value, or its relative value, depends upon the greater or less amount of that social substance contained in it; that is to say, on the relative mass of labor necessary for its production. The relative values of commodities are, therefore, determined by the respective quantities or amounts of labor, worked up, realized, fixed in them. The correlative quantities of commodities which can be produced in the same time of labor are equal. Or the value of one commodity is to the value of another commodity as the quantity of labor fixed in the one is to the quantity of labor fixed in the other." (Marx 1910, section 6.)

34. Mirowski (1989) argues that it deliberately borrowed from the then relatively modern Lagrangian formulations of physical field theory.

35. These tend to be to the effect that the class must distinguish between the short-term equilibrium of supply and demand shown in the diagram, and long-term processes which involve something quite different, a *shift* in the supply line to the right. This is a classic example of what historians of science call adding an *epicycle* to a theory to cover up embarrassing conflicts with evidence.

36. "We are to admit no more causes of natural things than such as are both true and sufficient to explain their appearances.

"To this purpose the philosophers say that Nature does nothing in vain, and more is in vain when less will serve; for Nature is pleased with simplicity, and affects not the pomp of superfluous causes" (Newton 1999, Rule of reasoning I).

37. Since Fourier we have known that any function can be well approximated by a sum of sine waves. We use this routinely now in things like digital TV. What adding epicycles to an astronomical model does is put in additional harmonic components. Since you can approximate any function by such harmonic components, with enough epicycles upon epicycles you can, by Fourier's theorem, get an arbitrarily good approximation of any apparent celestial motion. For a discussion of this, see Russo (2013).

38. If we assume straight-line functions then we have two equations: $p = a - dq$ for demand and $p = b + sq$ for supply, where d and s are the absolute gradients of the curves, and a and b the positions where they intercept the Y axis. Clearly these equations have 4 parameters.

39. Some of them also argued for some systematic, non-random deviations. We will discuss these later.

40. Studies showing the closeness of labor values to market prices are: Michaelson et al. (1995), Cockshott and Cottrell (1997a), Cockshott and Cottrell (1998a), Cockshott and Cottrell (1997b), Cockshott and Cottrell (2003a), Fröhlich (2013), Ochoa (1989), Petrovic (1987), Sanchez and Nieto Ferrandez (2010), Sánchez and Montibeler (2015), Tsoulfidis and Paitaridis (2016), Shaikh (1984), Shaikh (1998), Tsoulfidis and Maniatis (2002), Valle Baeza (2010), Zachariah (2004), Zachariah (2006).

41.   Division is the hardest of the four basic arithmetic operations to do. Even on a
       modern computer it is much slower than addition. The paper and pencil division
       you learned at school relies on algorithms that were not known until the Middle
       Ages; division in Babylonian times was done using complicated tables of inverses
       followed by multiplication. Fast computers still resort to this, for example the
       RCPSS-Scalar Single-Precision Floating-Point Reciprocal used by Intel computers.
42.   In maths we call a table with a single column of numbers a vector. This is slightly
       confusing if you came across the notion of vectors initially in school physics,
       where a vector is taken to mean a direction in space. But this meaning you got
       in school physics is just a special case of the mathematical vector. A direction in
       three-dimensional space—for instance, the direction of an electrostatic field—can
       be expressed as numbers in an x, y, z coordinate system. The line from the origin to
       position [x, y, z] is the direction we are interested in. So we can encode a direction
       in space as a column of three numbers. But suppose we have a fifty-dimensional
       space; how would we describe a direction?
           Clearly, by a column of fifty numbers giving a position in this fifty-dimensional
       space. If we have fifty distinct types of goods, then we have a potential fifty-dimen-
       sional space. A basket containing specific amounts of each of these goods defines a
       point in this fifty-dimensional space.
           So higher dimensional vectors are a relevant tool for the theory of value. A
       price list is a high dimensional vector. Such a list encodes values and it does not
       matter what the unit used for the encoding is. We can obviously express all prices
       in pennies as well as in pounds, all that changes is that we multiply the vector by
       100. Similarly, one can use any one of the commodities themselves as the standard
       of value, what economists call the numeraire. We could use wine or eggs in the
       example we gave. In any case, a change of numeraire just involves an appropriate
       multiplication of the vector.
           We said that a vector defines a direction in a multidimensional space. The price
       vector in Roman coins for oil, eggs, and wine that we gave in our table (A) points
       in a direction in this space, but what does that mean?
           The direction the price vector points is the direction of value. Consider the dia-
       gram below. It shows two dimensions of the value space. We know that two mea-
       sures of oil are worth ten of wine. The line joining two oil to ten wine indicates this.
       The set of lines parallel to this are the isovals. All points on these lines have the same
       value. The axis of value is at right angles to these isovals. Any point on the oil wine
       plane, i.e., any combination of wine and oil that a person owns can be projected
       onto the value axis along one of these parallel isovals. The diagram illustrates this
       for the point ten wine, five oil. The illustration is only for two dimensions, but the
       same geometric principle extends to arbitrary numbers of goods and thus arbitrary
       dimensions. The isovals are then hyperplanes and the value axis is the line through
the origin perpendicular
to the isovals. For a more
detailed discussion of the
formal properties of value,
see Cockshott et al. (2008),
chapter 11.
    What I have called a
swap table is a matrix produced by an outer divide
operation. If **S** is a swap

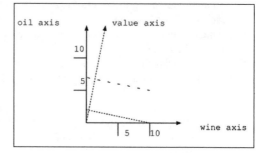

table and **p** is the price vector that is consistent with it then for all elements s_{ij} in S we have $s_{ij}= [(p_i)/(p_j)]$.

43. For a more detailed discussion of the computational techniques used by the Mesopotamians and Romans, including how the latter did economic calculations on reckoning tables, see Cockshott et al. (2012), chapter 2.

44. On the point that money did not arise from barter exchange, Davies (2010, p. 44) says: "On one thing the experts on primitive money all agree, and this vital agreement transcends their minor differences. Their common belief backed up by the overwhelming tangible evidence of actual types of primitive moneys from all over the world and from the archaeological, literary and linguistic evidence of the ancient world, is that barter was not the main factor in the origins and earliest developments of money. The contrast with Jevons, with his predecessors going back to Aristotle, and with his followers who include the mainstream of conventional economists, is clear-cut."

45. The cowries persisted in use up until the twentieth century, the British colonial authorities attempted to eliminate them as early as 1880 and officially demonetized them in 1904 (Falola and Adebayo, 2000). Attempts to demonetize the manilla were made from 1902, but remained in circulation until at least 1949. The origins of the manilla are unclear but they may date back as far as Phonecian trade with West Africa (Davies, 2010).

46. A couple of reasons are given for the Chinese having coins with holes. The hole both allowed coins to be strung together into blocks of higher value, and was an aid to manufacture. A rod was passed through a stack of coins allowing them all to be filed simultaneously to the same size. This pattern of a copper coin with a central hole was also adopted for British colonial coinage.

47. Marx develops this argument about money in the first chapters of *Capital* (Marx 1954).

48. It is easy to verify that British coinage is not what it seems. Try picking a penny up with a magnet.

49. We find this sort of tendency to explain commodity production by its numismatic relics in Hirst and Hindess (1975), who argue that the outflow of gold to the East in the late Roman period led to a shortage of currency and thus to a collapse of commodity production and monetary economy. This, they claim, led to the bureaucracy's dependence on income in kind and devolution into a sort of feudal aristocracy. In a more sophisticated form, we see it in Banaji's emphasis on the importance of gold coinage in the late empire as evidence of the opposite of what Hirst argued, that there was in fact a reflorescence of commodity production in this period.

50. The question of whether a coinage is made up of low intrinsic value tokens or fine gold coins may be better understood from the standpoint of class struggle. Creditor classes, whether the late Roman aristocracy studied by Banaji, or U.S. bankers in the late nineteenth century, are likely to favor gold coins as the only acceptable means of settling debts. This protects the real value of their debts in terms of labor. Debtors, whether indebted states in the modern period or indebted farmers throughout history, will favor a more readily available currency: silver or debased coins, or state paper. These make the paying off of debt easier, and if they depreciate, reduce the real value of debt obligations.

   The fact that a number of major ancient states, Athens, the Macedonian, Roman, or Spanish empires did rely on a silver coinage indicates both the supplementing of tax revenue by minting of coin from state-controlled silver mines, and to a persistent trade deficit in manufactures that could only be met by the export of specie.

51. The fable of Midas or the economic theory of Aristotle Meikle (1997) address the contradiction between exchange value and use value. This is to point out a confusion at a relatively mundane level of thought. There is a deeper confusion present in commercial language which speaks of value being "realized" when a commodity is sold as money. But this metaphor is even more naive and, in Marx's terms, "fetishistic" than the desires of Midas. When a state operates a system of token money, either base metal coins of paper notes, then the sale of a commodity is better seen as the idealization value. A commodity embodying real labor, and thus the real substance of exchange value, is exchanged for a mere sheet of paper bearing the symbol or idea of value. The real value has passed into the hands of the purchaser, the seller is left with state paper. If Joe in the United States sells a TV for $100 he can at least settle his U.S. tax debts with it. If TCL Corporation of Guandong sells 10,000 TV sets for $1 million, they are left with a U.S. credit that may in the long term be unrealizable in terms of anything of either use value or labor value.

52. Markov models are named after the Russian mathematician who introduced the idea in a study (Markov 2006) of the statistics of sequences of letters in text.

53. Constructing a parameterized Markov model of historical materialism would be a nice PhD thesis for someone.

54. Representation as a simple Markov model, while an advance on the standard Marxist presentation, is still a considerable oversimplification, since it abstracts from geography and the interaction between adjacent societies. There are methods by which one can extend Markov modelling to represent multiple local systems which undergo evolution as a result both of their own internal dynamics and their interaction with one another. The work of Shaw and Cockshott (1994), Shaw et al. (1996), and Hillston (1995) may well provide a starting point for this. She shows how you can compose descriptions of multiple processes evolving stochastically and in communication with one another to derive an overall Markov model of the whole ensemble. Such overall models formed by composition are defined over the tensor space of the original state spaces. The class of models required to formalize this would be the two-dimensional extension of Markov models known as Markov Random Fields (Kindermann and Snell 1980). Application of such models integrating geographical, demographic, and other constraints within historical materialism is obviously a considerable research project.

55. The position this chapter takes has a lot in common with that of Rudra (1988) in that I would class both Europe and Anatolia in the Middle Ages as instances of feudal societies, but I do not accept the definition of a mode of production that he uses. It is in essence a repetition of Hirst and Hindess's (1975) idea that a mode of production is a combination of forces and relations of production. Rudra is critical of other historians like Wickham for underplaying the role played by technology. I go even further than Rudra. I treat a mode of production as being irreducibly determined by technology, so that for me the capitalist mode of production *is* machine industry, and the feudal mode of production *is* peasant agriculture. But not all instances of peasant agriculture are feudal, since France in 1812 or China in 1955 were still peasant economies but non-feudal. So the mode of production in all societies with feudal social relations is peasant agriculture, but not all societies with peasant agriculture are feudal.

Hindess and Hirst were in turn relying on Althusser who relied on Stalin for his definition of a mode of production as being a combination of forces and relations of production:

"What, then, is the chief force in the complex of conditions of material life of society which determines the physiognomy of society, the character of the social system, the development of society from one system to another?

"This force, historical materialism holds, is the method of procuring the means of life necessary for human existence, the mode of production of material values—food, clothing, footwear, houses, fuel, instruments of production, etc.—which are indispensable for the life and development of society.

"In order to live, people must have food, clothing, footwear, shelter, fuel, etc.; in order to have these material values, people must produce them; and in order to produce them, people must have the instruments of production with which food, clothing, footwear, shelter, fuel, etc., are produced, they must be able to produce these instruments and to use them.

"The instruments of production wherewith material values are produced, the people who operate the instruments of production and carry on the production of material values thanks to a certain production experience and labor skill—all these elements jointly constitute the productive forces of society.

"But the productive forces are only one aspect of production, only one aspect of the mode of production, an aspect that expresses the relation of men to the objects and forces of nature which they make use of for the production of material values. Another aspect of production, another aspect of the mode of production, is the relation of men to each other in the process of production, men's relations of production." (Stalin 1943.)

56. The Domesday Book is a very detailed survey carried out in 1086 of all estates in England for tax purposes. It lists population, area, livestock, plow teams, mills, fish-ponds, and other resources of each manor. It is the most detailed statistical account still available of any feudal economy.

57. By way of comparison with feudal manor sizes, data from the 1870s covering the same part of England, Essex, as table 4.1, shows that by then average individual tenant farms were comparable in size to entire manorial estates. Hunt and Pam (1995) give as an example of farm sizes that: "Lord Petre's 18,000 acre Thomdon estate, for example, had 49 tenants in 1860 and 47 in 1870." Which implies that an average Victorian tenant farm in Essex was equivalent to the entire area of a median Saxon manorial estate, peasant plots included.

58. The original Soviet source for the technique of linear optimization is available in translation as Kantorovich (1960), Kantorovich (1965). Klein (2007) recount how similar techniques were independently developed by French hydraulic engineers and U.S. military logistics experts before being widely applied in U.S. industry from the 1950s. For an account of how linear optimization invalidates the claims of von Mises (1949), see Cockshott (2006b).

59. The reference is to Felix Haber, inventor of both chemical warfare and the catalytic fixation of nitrogen, originally to make explosives, later the main source of ammoniacal fertilizers.

60. "We can divide the basic activities of social reproduction into two mutually exclusive and exhaustive groups: production and non production The difference between the two is crucial: while production results in the creation of new use values (wealth), non production uses up wealth without creating new wealth. Non production activities can, in turn, be divided into three mutually exclusive and exhaustive groups: distribution, social maintenance and personal consump-

tion. Distribution involves activities that transfer use values, titles to use values or money from one set of economic agents to another. Social maintenance refers to all activities that are geared toward the maintenance and reproduction of the social order. Personal consumption includes all activities involved in the maintenance and reproduction of individuals within the social order. All schools of economic thought distinguish between production and consumption. Moreover they agree that production creates wealth and consumption uses up wealth. The difference between the neoclassical and classical Marxian traditions arises from the characterization of the activities of distribution and social maintenance. For the neoclassical (and Keynesian) tradition, these activities are understood as production as long they are marketable and some entity is willing to pay for the activity." (Deepankar 2015.)

61.   "The proportion between those different funds necessarily determines in every country the general character of the inhabitants as to industry or idleness. We are more industrious than our forefathers; because in the present times the funds destined for the maintenance of industry are much greater in proportion to those which are likely to be employed in the maintenance of idleness than they were two or three centuries ago. Our ancestors were idle for want of a sufficient encouragement to industry. It is better, says the proverb, to play for nothing than to work for nothing. In mercantile and manufacturing towns, where the inferior ranks of people are chiefly maintained by the employment of capital, they are in general industrious, sober, and thriving; as in many English, and in most Dutch towns. In those towns which are principally supported by the constant or occasional residence of a court, and in which the inferior ranks of people are chiefly maintained by the spending of revenue, they are in general idle, dissolute, and poor; as at Rome, Versailles, Compiegne, and Fontainebleau." (Smith 1974, II.3.9.)

62.   The point made by Smith that the accumulation of capital leads, via a higher capital to output ratio, to a lower rate of profit already contains the essence of Marx's later arguments about the effects of a rising *organic composition* of capital.

63.   In working notes on Adam Smith, Marx (1999) wrote that he disagreed with Smith's idea that productive labor need produce a physical output. Instead, he then thought, it was sufficient for the workers to be directly employed out of capital rather than revenue. Any worker paid out of capital would then count as productive, whatever they did.

       Elsewhere, Marx recognized that no transformation of social form can convert a previously materially unproductive activity into a productive one:
       "If by a division of labor a function, unproductive in itself although a necessary element of reproduction, is transformed from an incidental occupation of many into an exclusive occupation of a few, into their special business, the nature of this function itself is not changed.

       "One merchant (here considered a mere agent attending to the change of form of commodities, a mere buyer and seller) may by his operations shorten the time of purchase and sale for many producers. In such case he should be regarded as a machine which reduces useless expenditure of energy or helps to set production time free.

       "In order to simplify the matter (since we shall not discuss the merchant as a capitalist and merchant's capital until later) we shall assume that this buying and selling agent is a man who sells his labor. He expends his labor power and labor time in the operations C → M and M → C. And he makes his living that way, just as another does by spinning or making pills. He performs a necessary function, because the process of reproduction itself includes unproductive functions. He works as well as the next man, but intrinsically his labor creates neither value nor product. He belongs himself to the faux frais of production. His usefulness does not consist in transforming an unproductive function into a productive one, nor unproductive into productive labor. It would be a miracle if such transformation could be accomplished by the mere transfer of a function. His usefulness consists rather in the fact that a smaller part of society's labor-power and labor-time is tied up in this unproductive function." (Marx and Engels 1974, chapter 6)

I argue in section 5.10 that to determine if something is productive one has to look at the whole economy. This is closer to Smith's position and to that of Marx in *Capital*, volume 2, than it is to what Marx wrote in *Theories of Surplus Value*.

64. On the elements of capitalism arising: "I posit that the emergence of capitalist from feudal social-property relations will occur only as an unintended consequence of lords and peasants pursuing feudal type economic behaviour in order to achieve feudal goals" (Brenner 2001).

65. See also the discussion of how this relates to scientific concepts of process in Cockshott (2013b).

66. Cato advises estate owners to be sellers not purchasers, to make what they can on their own estate.

67. Measured values for the CV of prices to labor ratios in the UK economy in 1984 were in fact around 10 percent (Cockshott and Cottrell, 1998b). The argument so far has depended on the assumption that only 1 percent of firms will be making a loss at any one time, but because of the shape of the bell curve, the result would not be much different if I assumed it was either 0.5 percent or 2 percent.

68. This form of argument was pioneered by Farjoun and Machover (1983).

69. With respect to table 5.2, if prices corresponded to the simple labor theory of value, we would expect to find a positive linear relationship between profit rate and the inverse of organic composition (in other words, the relationship between profit rate and organic composition would be inverse, rather than negative linear), so the correlation coefficient between s/C and v/C is very telling: at 0.780 it has a p-value or marginal significance level <0.0001. Note also how the spread of profit rates and the spread of markups is very similar, and the narrow dispersion of capital compositions. Arguably the inverse relationship between capital intensity and profit will act to curb the spread of capital intensities. This narrow dispersion of capital intensities in the United States appears to be robust and lasting, and more recent work, Torres (2017) has confirmed it.

70. Reifferscheidt and Cockshott (2014) shows that the number of inputs to an industry grows proportionally to the logarithm of the number of industries in the economy. Inverting this relation, it follows that the number of other industries in the economy grows exponentially with the number of inputs to the average industry.

71. "Wealth, as Mr. Hobbes says, is power. But the person who either acquires, or succeeds to a great fortune, does not necessarily acquire or succeed to any political power, either civil or military. His fortune may, perhaps, afford him the means of acquiring both, but the mere possession of that fortune does not necessarily convey to him either. The power which that possession immediately and directly conveys to him, is the power of purchasing; a certain command over all the labor, or over all the produce of labor, which is then in the market. His fortune is greater or less, precisely in proportion to the extent of this power; or to the quantity either of other

men's labor, or, what is the same thing, of the produce of other men's labor, which it enables him to purchase or command." (Smith 1974.)

72. This phrase is widely used by Marxian economists. Some have taken it to simply mean contractual equality between agents in the market (Bordiga 1975; Bordiga 1954), but more generally they seem to mean the law that labor time determines price.

73. Actual inequalities, which are of course massive, arise with contractual enforcement.

74. The markup I have used in earlier discussion is similar to what Marx called rate of surplus value which he denoted by s/v where s is property income, and v is wage income. Our markup is not exactly the same but it can be derived from Marx's rate of surplus value. The markup used in section 5.1 is given by $markup = 1 + (s/v)$.

75. "Hold back your hand from the mill, you grinding girls; even if the cock crow heralds the dawn, sleep on. For Demeter has imposed the labors of your hands on the nymphs, who leaping down upon the topmost part of the wheel, rotate its axle; with encircling cogs, it turns the hollow weight of the Nisyrian millstones. If we learn to feast toil-free on the fruits of the earth, we taste again the golden age." (Anitpater of Thessalonika. *The Greek Anthology*, vol. 1. Cambridge: Cambridge University Press, 1960, p. 63.) Note that this was an overshoot mill, but these did not become the general design until the early states of capitalism.

76. Finer yarns weigh less, so productivity in pounds is lower.

77. The initial solution to generating rotary motion from steam was to use a steam engine to pump water up which was then used to turn a water wheel (Ferguson 1962).

78. A proof of the correctness of Watt's design was not long in coming. It was made in 1797 by De Prony, the French mathematician whose work on the division of mathematical labor inspired Babbage to invent the computer. Further evidence that what appears now to be a mundane improvement was actually related to the most advanced theoretical science of the day.

79. Traditional iron making reduced the ore in a solid state to produce a bloom; it was not until blast furnaces became available that the output was molten iron. A transitional technology capable of producing molten iron with a single manually operated furnace is described in David et al. (1989).

80. A description of a fifteenth-century Italian ironworks is given by a contemporary engineer known as Filarete:

> "But I will tell you how there was one which I saw, being at Rome, the which was about 12 miles from Rome at an abbey called Grottaferrata where there were monks officiating in the Greek manner. . . . the spot is wild and there are thick woods in it. . . . the place of this large hammer is a little outside the path of the water, which runs through the site, which comes [from] a little way up the mountain . . . where this water runs through the valley, adapted by a canal in such a way as to move wheels, one of which blows the bellows and the other makes the hammer beat. The manner of this is not that of the furnace where it is melted [not a blast furnace], but only a pair of bellows like those that smiths use, and there is a hearth . . . and in this the iron is remelted, and pieces thrown in such as they wish to do, and with that hammer and the water they beat it, and it comes out almost in that form as one sees it here." (Quoted in Williams 2003, p. 883.)

It is interesting to note that Althusser (2006) claims that fifteenth-century Italy was one of the occasions when nearly all the required ingredients of capitalism were present: wage labor, money capital, hydraulic powered machines, but still capitalism did not take. Was the absence of supplies of fossil fuel critical here?

81. The *man* in both manufacture and manual labor derives from the Latin *manus*, for hand.

82. The concept of the articulation of modes of production was developed and popularized in Rey (1973). Although Rey is little known to Anglophone readers, his ideas (sometimes misattributed to Althusser) are crucial and have had an influence on other thinkers.

83. "By the 1830s in England hand loom weaving of cottons was largely superseded by power looms in factories, even though the wages of hand loom workers were only about half those of factory workers. Yet 170 years later the hand loom sector in India is still very large, particularly in cottons. Indeed the output of the hand loom sector has grown steadily since 1900 when statistics were first gathered. In 1997, output of woven cloth from hand looms in India was about 10 times as great as in 1900. In 1997–8 25 percent of cloth production in India was still from hand looms." (Clark and Wolcott 2003, pp. 70–71.)

84. "At a brick kiln in Gautam Budha Nagar in Uttar Pradesh, near Delhi, 180 bonded laborers (53 men, 36 women and 91 children) were rescued in February 2000. The condition of the workers came to light when one of the women workers was raped, and her husband and a child were killed in gunfire by the employer and his henchmen when they resisted. The workers were prevented from leaving through threat and intimidation. The employer retained more than half their wages and gave them only a small sum for subsistence." (Srivastava 2005.)

85. Blackmon (2009) argues that the enforcement of legislation against peonage in the United States was made necessary for ideological reasons during the war against the Nazis.

86. Forcing people to work longer hours was not unique to capitalism. Slaves in nineteenth-century Alabama or first-century Sicily were similarly overworked.

87. "The Facts about the Gender Wage Gap in Canada," Canadian Women's Foundation, http:// canadianwomen.org/facts-about-the-gender-wage-gap-in-canada.

88. The theory of Dragulescu (2003) and Dragulescu and Yakovenko (2002), developed further in Cottrell et al. (2009) and Shaikh et al. (2014), is that the distribution of income will have a negative exponential form for labor income, and a power law form for property income. However, the arguments given for this form of distribution in the literature are not necessarily convincing when applied to an employed workforce, though they are perhaps plausible for a workforce of small traders. It is not clear that for instance Shaikh et al. (2014) have adequately excluded the possibility that the distribution may be log normal rather than strictly negative exponential.

89. "The minimum limit of the value of labor-power is determined by the value of the commodities, without the daily supply of which the laborer cannot renew his vital energy, consequently by the value of those means of subsistence that are physically indispensable. If the price of labor-power fall to this minimum, it falls below its value, since under such circumstances it can be maintained and developed only in a crippled state. But the value of every commodity is determined by the labor-time requisite to turn it out so as to be of normal quality." (Marx 1887, chapter 6.)

What is being said here is that the lower tail of the wage distribution is set by a wage so low that a person can only survive in a state crippled by ill health, a level just above that at which they will starve. But in the labor theory of value, the value of a commodity is determined not by the lower limit of its cost but by its mean cost.

So if a person is paid the subsistence limit they are paid below the mean, and thus below the value of labor power.

90.   Let m(w) and f(w) represent the male and female wage distribution probability density functions.

m(w), f(w) are both constrained to be log-normal.

    Lower bounds of each distribution are set by the survival wage of a single person

$$\int_{ws}^{\infty} m(w)dw = \int_{ws}^{\infty} f(w)dw = 1$$

Slightly higher up is the subsistence minimum wage for a family wf.

Since a larger portion of men than women are the sole earners in a household, a smaller portion of men can be employed at levels below the family subsistence level:

$$\int_{ws}^{wf} m(w)dw < \int_{ws}^{wf} f(w)dw$$

Thus the standard deviation of the male wage σm > σf.

Thus the mean of the male wage distribution must also be greater, μm > μf

91.   "The owner of labor-power is mortal. If then his appearance in the market is to be continuous, and the continuous conversion of money into capital assumes this, the seller of labor-power must perpetuate himself, in the way that every living individual perpetuates himself, by procreation. The labor-power withdrawn from the market by wear and tear and death, must be continually replaced by, at the very least, an equal amount of fresh labor-power. Hence the sum of the means of subsistence necessary for the production of labor-power must include the means necessary for the laborer's substitutes, i.e., his children, in order that this race of peculiar commodity-owners may perpetuate its appearance in the market." (Marx 1894, chapter 6.)

92.   "What is bought with money or with goods is purchased by labor, as much as what we acquire by the toil of our own body. That money or those goods indeed save us this toil. They contain the value of a certain quantity of labor which we exchange for what is supposed at the time to contain the value of an equal quantity. Labor was the first price, the original purchase-money that was paid for all things. It was not by gold or by silver, but by labor, that all the wealth of the world was originally purchased; and its value, to those who possess it, and who want to exchange it for some new productions, is precisely equal to the quantity of labor which it can enable them to purchase or command." (Smith 1974, p. 133.)

93.   This is the assumption made by Keynes that national income should be measured in employment quantities: "In dealing with the theory of employment I propose, therefore, to make use of only two fundamental units of quantity, namely, quantities of money-value and quantities of employment . . . if E is the wages (and salaries) bill, W the wage-unit, and N the quantity of employment, E=N×W." (Keynes 1936, p. 35.)

94.   The correlation between immigration levels and exploitation is stronger than that between population growth and exploitation. It is positive in both cases, but the lower correlation for population growth is probably because population changes include changes in the number of children and retired people who do not compete for jobs. The following figure (p. 361) shows the relationship between population and exploitation.

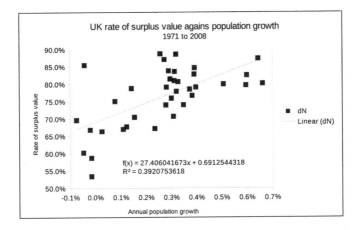

95. "The reproduction of a mass of labor power, which must incessantly re-incorporate itself with capital for that capital's self-expansion; which cannot get free from capital, and whose enslavement to capital is only concealed by the variety of individual capitalists to whom it sells itself, this reproduction of labor power forms, in fact, an essential of the reproduction of capital itself. Accumulation of capital is, therefore, increase of the proletariat." (Marx 1887, chapter 25.)

96. "The great mass of so-called 'higher grade' workers—such as state officials, military people, artists, doctors, priests, judges, lawyers, etc.—some of whom are not only not productive but in essence destructive, but who know how to appropriate to themselves a very great part of the 'material' wealth partly through the sale of their 'immaterial' commodities and partly by forcibly imposing the latter on other people—found it not at all pleasant to be relegated economically to the same class as clowns and menial servants and to appear merely as people partaking in the consumption, parasites on the actual producers (or rather agents of production). This was a peculiar profanation precisely of those functions which had hitherto been surrounded with a halo and had enjoyed superstitious veneration. Political economy in its classical period, like the bourgeoisie itself in its parvenu period, adopted a severely critical attitude to the machinery of the State, etc. At a later stage it realized and—as was shown too in practice—learnt from experience that the necessity for the inherited social combination of all these classes, which in part were totally unproductive, arose from its own organization." (Marx 1999, chapter 4.5.)

97. If we divide the economy into 3 sectors:
    1. Produces means of production.
    2. Produces workers' consumption goods.
    3. Produces articles of capitalist consumption, weapons for the army, etc.

    It is relatively easy to demonstrate that labor in department 3 is not productive of relative surplus value. By relative surplus value production is meant any increase in the surplus value brought about without altering real wages or increasing the workforce. We can model the gross product of these industries with the vector $\mathbf{v} = [v1,v2,v3]$ where vi is the mean number of person seconds of labor performed in sector i for each second of the year. The vi thus have dimension person.

    For each sector the gross value is made up of two components, direct and indirect labor, which we will denote by the vectors $\mathbf{l}$ and $\mathbf{c}$. All these have dimension person seconds per second.

    We have $\mathbf{v} = \mathbf{l} + \mathbf{c}$.

NOTES TO PAGES 186-194

Associated with each sector is a capital stock which we denote by the vector **k**. We will denote economy wide totals by the corresponding capital letters.

$$K = \Sigma k_i, \ V = \Sigma v_i, \ C = \Sigma c_i, \ L = \Sigma l_i$$

We will denote wages in each sector by the vector **w** and profits by the vector **s**, with corresponding economy-wide totals W,S.

For the economy as a whole we have it that newly created value is entirely divided between wages and profits, hence $L = W + S$. We will assume that sectoral outputs sell at their values so this scalar equation generalizes into the vector equation $l = w + s$, which says that the newly created value in each sector is divided between wages and profits in that sector. Let us for now assume that the working population is fixed as is the length of the working day, hence $dL/dt = 0$, but that accumulation of constant capital is occurring $dK/dt > 0$. We thus have that the gross output of sector 1 is equal to capital consumption plus accumulation $v_1 = C + dK/dt$.

If we further assume that workers do not save or borrow we have the total wage bill equal to the total output of sector two: $W = v_2$. Total profit is then equal to accumulation plus capitalist consumption $S = v_3 + dK/dt$.

Suppose that there is an improvement in labor productivity in sector 3. Does this have the potential to increase total surplus value? No, as v_3 is unaltered, all that changes is the quantity of use values that the capitalists get in their consumption. Thus there is no room for production of relative surplus value here.

98. For an account of the role of Armstrong in the development of naval guns, see Parkes (1966).

99. "The Royal Navy was probably the largest single item in the British national budget of the time. William Gladstone, the Liberal prime minister during much of the late nineteenth century, was an ardent anti-imperialist hostile to naval spending." (Friedman 2012.)

100. "However, we must make the same distinction between him and the wage-workers directly employed by industrial capital which exists between industrial capital and merchant's capital, and thus between the industrial capitalist and the merchant. Since the merchant, as a mere agent of circulation, produces neither value nor surplus-value (for the additional value which he adds to the commodities through his expenses resolves itself into an addition of previously existing values, although the question here poses itself, how he preserves this value of his constant capital?) it follows that the mercantile workers employed by him in these same functions cannot directly create surplus-value for him." (Marx 1971, p. 293.)

101. "Now let's turn to the purpose of banks in a capitalist economy. Finance is an intermediary good: You cannot eat it, experience it, or physically use it. The purpose of finance is to support other activities in the economy. Banks are meant to allocate capital (funds) to the best possible use. In a capitalist economy, this means allocating money to the people or entities that will create the greatest wealth for the overall society. At the same time, risk management is supposedly a primary skill for bankers. When capital is allocated well and available to wealth creating entities, societies flourish. When capital is poorly allocated, economies can collapse." (Judson 2012.)

102. "Wealth, as Mr Hobbes says, is power. But the person who either acquires, or succeeds to a great fortune, does not necessarily acquire or succeed to any political power, either civil or military. His fortune may, perhaps, afford him the means of acquiring both; but the mere possession of that fortune does not necessarily convey

to him either. The power which that possession immediately and directly conveys to him, is the power of purchasing a certain command over all the labor, or over all the produce of labor which is then in the market. His fortune is greater or less, precisely in proportion to the extent of this power, or to the quantity either of other mens labor, or, what is the same thing, of the produce of other mens labor, which it enables him to purchase or command." (Smith 1974, chapter 5.)

103. "This disposition to admire, and almost to worship, the rich and the powerful, and to despise, or, at least, to neglect persons of poor and mean condition, though necessary both to establish and to maintain the distinction of ranks and the order of society, is, at the same time, the great and most universal cause of the corruption of our moral sentiments. That wealth and greatness are often regarded with the respect and admiration which are due only to wisdom and virtue; and that the contempt, of which vice and folly are the only proper objects, is often most unjustly bestowed upon poverty and weakness, has been the complaint of moralists in all ages." (Smith 1790, p. 53.)

104. The growth of the world gold stock has been relatively slow, below 1 percent a year in the nineteenth century, and around 1.5 percent a year in the twentieth century (Cockshott et al. 2008, p. 238). This is markedly slower than the growth of the world economy.

105. "The bank therefore creates its own funding, deposits, in the act of lending, in a transaction that involves no intermediation whatsoever.... if the loan is for physical investment purposes, this new lending and money is what triggers investment and therefore, by the national accounts identity of saving and investment (for closed economies), saving. Saving is therefore a consequence, not a cause, of such lending. Saving does not finance investment, financing does. To argue otherwise confuses the respective macroeconomic roles of resources (saving) and debt-based money (financing)." (Jakab and Kumhof 2015.)

106. For nineteenth-century interest rates, see Barro (1987). Five percent for 1800 is realistic, though this was a peak brought about by high wartime borrowing.

107. "If all land had the same properties, if it were unlimited in quantity, and uniform in quality, no charge could be made for its use, unless where it possessed peculiar advantages of situation. It is only, then, because land is not unlimited in quantity and uniform in quality, and because in the progress of population, land of an inferior quality, or less advantageously situated, is called into cultivation, that rent is ever paid for the use of it. When in the progress of society, land of the second degree of fertility is taken into cultivation, rent immediately commences on that of the first quality, and the amount of that rent will depend on the difference in the quality of these two portions of land." (Ricardo 1951, chapter 2.)

108. Marx (1971, chapter 45) argued that even the worst land bears a rent as a consequence of private ownership. He called this rent which applied to the worst land "absolute rent" to distinguish it from the differential rent identified by Ricardo.

109. The term *scot-free* originally meant land held without a levy. The origin is the Scandinavian root *skat* rather than a reference to the Scottish.

110. There is obviously a vast literature discussing what type of society the USSR was, and whether it was a class society. A good overview is provided in Nove (1983a).

111. Exceptions to this are perhaps the Bordigist International Communist Party, who argue that the continued existence of money was a decisive factor in preventing the USSR, etc. from ever having been socialist.

   My view is that although it is fruitless to question whether the USSR was socialist, it does not follow that one has to accept the political and economic policies followed by its government. If one abandons the utopian viewpoint and sees socialism as a concrete form of society with its own contradictory forms of development, then one can start to ask just what economic and social policies should be followed in a socialist state. Any real society is fraught with contradictions, and is either destroyed by them or develops by resolving them.

112. We can take urbanization as a proxy for the change in the mode of production from a peasant economy to an industrial society. Russian urbanization grew from 14 percent just before the revolution to 34 percent in 1939 (Becker 2012); France was at 12 percent in 1800 and had reached 35 percent in 1900 (Bairoch 1985).

113. In 1913 Russia had generated only 1300GWh of electricity, less than one-tenth of a person power per head. This was so far behind the power usage of Great Britain and other Western industrial nations that some in the Soviet government doubted that the country could carry out an unaided socialist industrialization. The scale of Soviet power output in 1990 shows, in retrospect, that this was an overcautious estimate of what would be possible.

114. More than 99 percent of uranium is made of the U238 isotope, which cannot be used as an energy source in conventional reactors. Fast neutrons can convert this into Pu239 fuel. Fast neutron reactors use Pu239 fuel and run at such high energy fluxes that they need liquid metal cooling. In the past sodium has been used for cooling with all the attendant fire hazards associated with leaks of this metal.

115. A Soviet-type bachelor tax could potentially address the gay economic privilege.

116. Figure 6.9 drawn from data published by Economics and Statistics Administration, using data from Bureau of Labor statistics and National Bureau of Statistics China. Published at https://acetool.comerce.gov.

117. Figure 6.10 drawn from data published at Caixin Global (http://caixinglobal.com) using data from ILO Global Wage Database, U.S. Bureau of Economic Analysis, and World Bank. Published at http://acetool.comerce.gov/labor-costs.

118. Advances in technology, in particular the development of accurate calendars that could be worked by symbolic techniques, meant that priesthoods need no longer actually observe the sky. Church buildings were of little use for predicting the seasons, but the regular church festivals were. With the practical distancing of the priesthoods from astronomy could go ideological shifts which dispensed with the heavenly bodies as incarnations of deities, to a system where the gods became apotheoses of either real historical figures (the idea of Sanchuniathon [Kaizer 2014] known through Eusebius [Kofsky 2002]), or imagined emperors, Kings of the Jews, etc.

119. For a detailed critique of Hayek's conception of the price system as a communications network, see Cockshott and Cottrell (1997c).

120. Note that for orthodox communists like Lenin or Mao the term *state capitalism* refers to a situation where private capitalist firms are subjected to state control, as in the British and German war economies or in China in the 1950s. It does not refer to state-owned companies.

121. Friedman and Baker (2009) give several examples of scheduling constraints on new gun mountings, and slip sizes affecting UK destroyer construction plans in the Second World War. Friedman (2015) gives the example of construction of the Admiral class capital ships being postponed due to insufficient shipbuilding labor to build both them and destroyers in 1917. For large scale shipbuilding programs, even in peace, similar forward planning of physical constraints has to be done by the state (Arena et al. 2005).

122. I have used the notation D' for Feldman's original T and D for his ND, D–u for his ND.

123. For a general discussion of the Feldman model and its relation to reproduction scheme analysis, see Clark (1984). For worked examples of how a Feldman model is in theory optimal for growth, provided Soviet-style national accounts are used, see Földvári et al. (2015).

124. Why is a flow of money value a number of persons? Because in terms of the labor theory, a flow of money is the representation of a flow of labor, and a flow of labor is measured in [(persons×hrs)/yr], and hours and years are both time measures, so that in dimensional terms they cancel out. So the flow of value is measured in persons, the number of people having to be devoted to the production of that value flow of output.

125. Allen's data have been questioned by Wheatcroft (2009) who gives much more pessimistic estimates of consumption growth. But Allen is strongly supported by other entirely independent sources. Hunter and Szyrmer (2014) give very similar trends for consumption over the same period and Pelkonen and Cockshott (2017) show that child growth rates correlate very closely with the consumption estimates of Allen.

126 A way around it is to give two estimates of growth rate, one based on prices in 1975 and another based on prices in 1979. You work out what the total physical output produced in 1975 would have sold for in terms of 1979 prices and compare that to what the 1979 output actually sold for, and vice versa using 1975 prices.

127. "In general, the abolition of money is inevitable in Communist society, where there is no individual or group accounting of who takes what and how much. Socialism, however (because it is socialism and not communism), does have this accounting, though eventually it is applied only to a section of the products distributed. Moreover, socialism does not completely exclude the market for those branches of the economy, for example, for petty production—which are not yet socialized. True, these branches, and the market with them, gradually wither away under socialism. But they wither away gradually, as socialism gradually turns into communism—being, as it is, merely unfinished, undeveloped communism. Finally, under socialism voluntary, amateur industry and art develop, activities in which the workers under the socialist state engage after they have fulfilled their obligatory spell of work, and the products of which are exchanged for money, as happens now. But of course the role of money in these conditions is not at all the same as under the capitalist or commodity-socialist systems. In these latter, money served as the yardstick of the value of commodities, the means of circulation and the means of payment. It was one of the means whereby the spontaneous regulation of the process of production and exchange took place. When, however, all decisive branches of the economy became subject to planning, and when, consequently, exchange between these branches also became subject to planning, with planned accumulation and planned distribution of consumer goods, then money was transformed into a mere auxiliary instrument of planned distribution. It retained its former status only for the non-socialized part of the economy, and even there not for the whole but only for its market in the narrow sense of the word, that is, for the market in which exchange within the non-socialized part of the economy took place." (Preobrazhenski 1973, Lecture 11.)

"Today there are two basic forms of socialist production in our country: state, or publicly-owned production, and collective-farm production, which cannot be said to be publicly owned. In the state enterprises, the means of production and the product of production are national property. In the collective farm, although the means of production (land, machines) do belong to the state, the product of production is the property of the different collective farms, since the labor, as well as the seed, is their own, while the land, which has been turned over to the collective farms in perpetual tenure, is used by them virtually as their own property, in spite of the fact that they cannot sell, buy, lease or mortgage it.

The effect of this is that the state disposes only of the product of the state enterprises, while the product of the collective farms, being their property, is disposed of only by them. But the collective farms are unwilling to alienate their products except in the form of commodities, in exchange for which they desire to receive the commodities they need. At present the collective farms will not recognize any other economic relation with the town except the commodity relation—exchange through purchase and sale. Because of this, commodity production and trade are as much a necessity with us today as they were, say, thirty years ago, when Lenin spoke of the necessity of developing trade to the utmost." (Stalin 1952, chapter 2.)

128.   "Everyone knows that when supply and demand are evenly balanced, the relative value of any product is accurately determined by the quantity of labor embodied in it, that is to say, that this relative value expresses the proportional relation precisely in the sense we have just attached to it. M. Proudhon inverts the order of things. Begin, he says, by measuring the relative value of a product by the quantity of labor embodied in it, and supply and demand will infallibly balance one another. Production will correspond to consumption, the product will always be exchangeable. Its current price will express exactly its true value. Instead of saying like everyone else: when the weather is fine, a lot of people are to be seen going out for a walk. M. Proudhon makes his people go out for a walk in order to be able to ensure them fine weather.

What M. Proudhon gives as the consequence of marketable value determined a priori by labor time could be justified only by a law couched more or less in the following terms:

Products will in future be exchanged in the exact ratio of the labor time they have cost. Whatever may be the proportion of supply to demand, the exchange of commodities will always be made as if they had been produced proportionately to the demand. Let M. Proudhon take it upon himself to formulate and lay down such a law, and we shall relieve him of the necessity of giving proofs. If, on the other hand, he insists on justifying his theory, not as a legislator, but as an economist, he will have to prove that the time needed to create a commodity indicates exactly the degree of its utility and marks its proportional relation to the demand, and in consequence, to the total amount of wealth. In this case, if a product is sold at a price equal to its cost of production, supply and demand will always be evenly balanced; for the cost of production is supposed to express the true relation between supply and demand." (Marx 1847.)

129.   Marx ridiculed the idea that he proposed any system of socialism in a one-line aside in his notes on Wagner (Marx, 1975).

130.   There is some dispute amongst Marxists about whether the "law of value" only applies to the production of commodities; even those who limit it to commodity production usually see it as related to a more general law of the distribution of labor-time among different production processes (Littlejohn, 1979). If the latter, more general law is also referred to as the law of value, then the concept expresses the proportion of the total labor-time available to a society (within a given time-period, say a year) which is devoted to a particular production process. Each of the products of that production process thus embodies a value which is a fraction of the proportional labor-time devoted to that production process. In other words, if

one thousand products are produced in a year, then each product embodies one-thousandth of the value of that production process. If two thousand products are produced, then the value of each product is halved. Thus the value of each product is inversely proportional to the productivity of the production process associated with it. The value of a product thus refers to the amount of labor time (as a proportion of the total socially available labor-time) which is necessary (Hirst 1977; Hindess 1978). to produce it: the value of a product is the embodiment of the socially necessary labor-time required to produce it, and the socially necessary amount of labor-time depends on the productivity of the particular production process and its economic relation to other production processes. In the case of commodity production, according to Marx, where the fact that commodities are exchanged has an effect on the social distribution of labor-time between different production processes, the absolute amount of labor-time embodied in a product is not measured. Only the relative amount of labor-time is measured, and this occurs in the process of commodity exchange where the relative amount of labor-time is expressed by the ratios in which the commodities exchange for each other. If one pound of sugar regularly exchanges for ten pounds of potatoes, then for Marx this is because these physical quantities of the products each take the same amount of socially necessary labor-time to produce. Whether that labor-time is one hour or five days cannot be directly measured by this exchange ratio of one to ten, which only indicates the relative value of the products. This "exchange value," as Marx calls it, forms the basis for the price of commodities, once money becomes an integral part of commodity exchange. According to Marx, this occurs on the basis of one commodity becoming a socially acceptable measure in terms of which all the other exchange ratios are established (Littlejohn 1981, p. 20).

131. Note that the European Union–mandated VAT is called *mehrwertsteuer* in German, literally "surplus value tax."

132. Along with Allin Cottrell I have written extensively on the policy proposals alluded to briefly here. See in particular Cockshott and Cottrell (1989), Cockshott and Cottrell (1992) or Cottrell and Cockshott (1993).

133. The original paper was Kantorovich (1960); I explained for a modern readership how his technique worked in Cockshott (2006b).

134. You can get a good lay person's introduction to the use of computers in Soviet planning in the novel *Red Plenty* (Spufford, 2010).

135. "The global energy model TIMER looks into long-term trends in the energy system. The model describes the demand and supply of nine final energy carriers and ten primary energy carriers for 26 world regions. The demand sub-model of TIMER determines demand for fuels and electricity in five sectors (industry, transport, residential, services and other) based on structural change, autonomous and price-induced change in energy intensity (energy conservation) and price-based fuel substitution. The demand for electricity is fulfilled by fossil-fuel or bioenergy based thermal power, hydropower, nuclear power and solar or wind." (Van Vuuren et al. 2011.)

136. Radiative forcing is the difference between energy arriving from the Sun and the energy being re-emitted as infrared to space. Any excess causes warming of the oceans, melting of ice, etc.

137. Data from U.S. Energy Information Administration, Annual Energy Outlook Report 2015.

138. Licht et al. (2012) claim that their proposed STEP process would actually be cheaper than the current method of cement production. But their costings depend

on operating the process at a higher temperature at which the outputs would be CO and O_2 rather than elemental carbon and oxygen. They then propose to sell the carbon monoxide as a feedstock for plastic production. But this process would not be carbon neutral, as part of the plastics would eventually end up being burned and entering the air.

139. I recall my grandfather describing to me the sight of one of these ships in the 1920s. At the time I could not understand how it could work.

140. Restrictions on fossil fuel for ships may first come as bans on the use of high sulfur oil. The threat of this has alone been enough to spur the revived experimental work on wind power.

141. This is similar to the model of delivery that existed in the United Kingdom in the period immediately after nationalization of the railways and road transport in 1948: railways for long distances; small trucks for final delivery.

142. For an idea of what was anticipated for transport in the early 1970s, see Ellison and Bahmanyar (1974) and Ross (1973).

143. Close examination of figure 7.6 shows that while Japanese productivity growth fell almost to zero in the late 1990s, it recovered to about 2 percent in 2007.

144. Similar thermodynamic constraints affect other heat engines. Less obviously, thermodynamics also limits the performance of computers, as we showed in Cockshott et al. (2012).

145. "On the one hand information wants to be expensive, because it's so valuable. The right information in the right place just changes your life. On the other hand, information wants to be free, because the cost of getting it out is getting lower and lower all the time. So you have these two fighting against each other." (Brand 1987.)

146. The idea that human labor is now obsolete is particularly pernicious. All the evidence from trends in productivity is that human labor is being dispensed with far more slowly than it was in the mid-twentieth century.

147. One possible protocol for participatory direct democracy is the Handivote system (Cockshott and Renaud 2010; Cockshott and Renaud 2009; Renaud and Cockshott 2010) that we have developed, but there are certainly many others that could be used, for example Liquid Democracy (Paulin 2014).

148. They thus differ from the technology matrices of Morishima (1973), though as we shall see, there is an underlying relationship between the two.

Index